STREET

Competition, Entrepreneurship, and the Future of Roads

SMART

Independent Studies in Political Economy

STREET

Competition, Entrepreneurship, and the Future of Roads

SMART

EDITED BY

GABRIEL ROTH

Foreword by Mary E. Peters

Transaction Publishers
New Brunswick (U.S.A.) and London (U.K.)

Library of Congress Catalog Number: 2005053880
ISBN: 0-7658-0304-6 (cloth); 1-4128-0518-X (paper)
Printed in the United States of America

Library of Congress Cataloging-in-Publication Data

Street smart : competition, entrepreneurship, and the future of roads / Gabriel Roth, editor.
    p. cm.
    Includes bibliographical references and index.
    ISBN 0-7658-0304-6 (cloth : alk. paper)—ISBN 1-4128-0518-X (pbk. : alk. paper)
      1. Roads—Economic aspects. 2. Roads—Finance. 3. Privatization.
  I. Roth, Gabriel Joseph, 1926-

HE336.E3S87   2006
388.1—dc22   2005053880

*Dedicated by the authors to road users
and providers in all countries*

Contents

Acknowledgment

Thanks are due to David Theroux, founder and president of the Independent Institute, for his unwavering support of this volume. And to Tony Gee and Michael Paley for preparing the text, figures, and tables for publication.

I am particularly indebted to Alex Tabarrok, the Institute's director of research, who worked closely with me in editing the book. Dr. Tabarrok reviewed all its draft chapters, and gave invaluable advice on the text and on many other relevant matters.

Gabriel Roth
Chevy Chase, Maryland
September 2005

Foreword

Having served both as a State Director of Transportation and as Administrator of the Federal Highway Administration at the U.S. Department of Transportation, I recognize what a vital role transportation plays in the economy. When roadways allow people and products to move safely and efficiently, goods cost less and choices are more broadly available to consumers. People can make decisions about where to live, work, and send their children to school based on the quality of their lives, not the length of their commute. Unfortunately, in many areas, that is not the case today. One business at a time, one commuter at a time, congestion is robbing our nation, indeed the world, of productivity and quality of life.

I suggest that this is the case because the systems and structures in place today are not able to respond to the significant growth of business and personal travel. This serious mismatch between supply and demand has commuters and businesses stuck in traffic with no relief in sight. Traditional funding, and methods of allocating those funds, simply will not close the gap. This is caused by a number of factors, including lack of investor confidence, project decisions made by political allocation, and the inability of fossil-based fuel taxes to act as proxies for needs.

So, are we indeed stuck in traffic without remedy? No, in fact far from it! The same market forces that took us from Ma Bell's black, boxy, static, rotary dial telephone to today's era of wide consumer choice can relieve congestion, operate roadways more efficiently, and improve the safety of our highways. When given a choice, consumers are willing to pay for quality, convenience, and reliability. When given the option, consumers will pay for faster travel on less congested roadways that will reliably and predictably get them to their destinations on time. This holds true whether the journey involves picking up a child from daycare on time or supplying a business dependent on just-in-time materials delivery.

Services such as electricity, telecommunications, and water supply are provided by market forces in response to demand from consumers, most of whom pay the costs associated with their choices, and expect to get what they pay for. This book demonstrates that those same free market systems can be applied to roadways as well. The private sector has, in fact, already played a significant role in providing roads:

- Two hundred years ago private investors provided over 10,000 miles of toll roads in the young United States;
- One hundred years ago William Vanderbilt provided the first toll express-way—the Long Island Motor Parkway;
- Ten years ago the California Private Transportation Company provided, on California's State Route 91, the first road with variable tolls designed to ensure congestion-free travel at all times.

The pace of privatization has quickened in recent years:

- A private consortium led by CINTRA/Macquarie has paid the city of Chicago $1.83 billion to allow it to receive the Chicago Skyway tolls for ninety-nine years.
- To relieve congestion on the Washington Beltway, the Virginia Depart-ment of Transportation has approved a proposal from Fluor Enterprises to add four HOT (High-Occupancy or Toll) lanes to a fourteen-mile seg-ment of the Beltway at a cost of nearly a billion dollars. These lanes are to be financed by electronically collected tolls, varied to ensure conges-tion-free travel at all times.
- The biggest private road investment proposed to date is $7.2 billion for the first major project of the Trans-Texas Corridor from north of Dallas to south of San Antonio. I was privileged to participate in the signing cer-emony on March 11, 2005.

There are numerous examples outside the United States:

- In Australia, private investors have built a dozen inner-urban express-ways, about half of them in tunnels, with minimal government support beyond initial environmental clearances and permitting.
- Britain's only new motorway in several decades, the M6 Toll, opened in 2003, and was provided by Midland Expressway Ltd. at a cost of £900 million on a fifty-three-year franchise to relieve congestion in the Birm-ingham area.
- In China, a peasant named Yuan Hudang invested the equivalent of US$200,000 in the construction of a twenty-km village road, and man-aged it until his investment was recovered. China is now building a

national highway network based mainly on investor/provincial-government partnerships. These include the $1.2 billion Guangzhou-Shenzhen Superhighway conceived by Gordon Wu when, as an engineering student at Princeton University, he admired the New Jersey Turnpike.

- Italy's first toll motorway, from Milan to Lake Como, was opened in 1924. Half of Italy's toll motorways are now fully investor owned by the publicly traded and internationally active Autostrade SpA.

Market forces do not work without some form of pricing. With roadways, this often takes the form of tolling. Tolling is not only a viable option for financing infrastructure; through variable rate tolling it is an excellent tool for managing congestion and increasing throughput as well. Technology allows these tolls to be collected without requiring vehicles to stop at tollbooths.

The time has come for us to acknowledge that the pricing and investment principles governing the provision of a telecommunications network can also be applied to roadways. The time has come to unleash the power of the private sector to deliver the innovation, cost savings, quality, and choice it has delivered in telecommunications and other industries. Free markets work!

While not necessarily supporting every recommendation in this book, I commend it to all interested in the future of roadways. It represents an important contribution to the ongoing debate on how best road services might be provided, not only in the United States, but also in other countries.

Mary E. Peters
Director, Arizona Department of Transportation, 1998–2001
Administrator, Federal Highway Administration, U.S. Department
of Transportation, 2001–2005

Part I
Introduction

1

Why Involve the Private Sector in the Provision of Public Roads?

Gabriel Roth

Will Rogers is reported to have said that the way to end traffic congestion is to have the government build the cars and private industry the roads.[1] The purpose of this book is to demonstrate that only the latter recommendation is necessary.

Many Americans, especially those living outside congested areas, are probably satisfied with the state of their roads. "Why," they might ask, "should roads be privatized? Why not leave things as they are, and let our elected representatives take care of our needs?" These are good questions, to which at least three answers can be given.

The Present Unsatisfactory Situation of Road Provision

Costs Associated with Political Control

First, as road systems are outside the market economy, and unresponsive to consumer needs, road systems exhibit the usual "command economy" characteristics of congestion, queuing, deterioration, and waste. For example, travel on the US Interstate Highway system increased by 38 percent from 1991 to 2001, but additional lane mileage on the system grew by only 5 percent—one seventh of the rate of traffic growth. One result was that the mileage considered to be severely congested on the urban portions of the Interstate system increased 31 percent from 1996 to 2001—from 2,342 miles to 3,059 miles (TRIP, 2003).

As pointed out by Semmens in chapter 2, a major cause of the inefficiency is the political control of road systems, which enables road users to shift the costs they impose to other road users, and even to other taxpayers. Farmers in

3

Kansas, for example, pay to rebuild the Wilson Bridge over the Potomac to relieve congestion in Washington D.C. Those who underpay are thus encouraged to increase their road usage at the expense of others, illustrating Bastiat's insight that government is seen as a device to enable everybody to live at everybody else's expense.

Another major cause of waste is the low priority accorded to routine road maintenance because new construction is more popular with politicians. Delays in maintenance can double or triple the costs of subsequent road repair and reconstruction. In the United States, federal grants favor new construction over maintenance. In Sub-Saharan Africa, a third of the main road system was eroded as a result of poor maintenance (Heggie 1995).

The excessive costs of the public ownership of roads are not confined to the management of existing roads. There is little reason to believe that governments will build new roads where they are most needed, as road construction responds to political pressures. The U.S. Congress has a 1914 rule[2] prohibiting the funding of specific roads. This must have been waived in 1982, when ten "demonstration projects" (subsequently called "high-priority projects" or "earmarks") were funded, at a cost of $362 million, to enable members of Congress to reward potential voters at public expense. Twenty-three years later, the "Transportation Equity Act: A Legacy for Users," enacted in 2005 to authorize additional highway spending, appropriated $24.215 billion for 6,373 "High Priority Projects" selected by House and Senate members.[3] Few, if any, of these projects were considered to be of "high priority" in the states concerned.[4]

Urban highways in Boston illustrate the waste—particularly federally funded waste—in the political provision of roads. Following the establishment of the Federal Interstate Highway Fund in 1956, Boston's road planners proposed the construction of an elevated "Central Artery" along the waterfront, three stories high, 1.5 miles long, and 100 feet wide. According to MIT Professor Alan Altshuler, who later became state secretary of transportation, this road was conceived as a result of "a highway juggernaut driven by the lure of 90 per cent federal dollars that had nothing to do with the welfare of Greater Boston" (Altshuler 2002). At the time he wrote that,

> An effort to accommodate all potential demand by commuters for high capacity into downtown Boston would be outrageously expensive in terms of highway investment dollars, increased transit deficits, social disruption and environmental degradation.

This elevated highway, for which neither Boston nor the state of Massachusetts would have been prepared to pay, was nevertheless built and, as it aged, carried

200,000 vehicles a day and became one of the most congested highways in America. What to do? Local highway planners decided to use federal funding to demolish the elevated highway after replacing it by a tunnel. An additional tunnel was funded to draw more support, and thus was born the "Central Artery/Tunnel" project (popularly knows as "The Big Dig") initially estimated to cost $3.3 billion. The use of federal funds was led by Speaker of the House of Representatives "Tip" O'Neill (who also represented a Boston district), and was vetoed by President Reagan. The President's veto was narrowly overridden, due in part to the vote of Senator Sanford of North Carolina, in exchange for support for tobacco subsidies. So the project went ahead, with the cost now estimated to exceed $14.6 billion.

Thus, the availability of outside funding discouraged consideration of market solutions, or even of modest non-market solutions, to the urban congestion problem. This illustrates the point, made in chapter 20 by Samuel, that efficient solutions to the problems of scarcity are more likely in times of shortage than in times of plenty.

Costs Associated with Congestion

Second, many road users endure excessive traffic congestion in urban areas. The increase in congestion in US urban areas can be seen in the table below:

Table 1.1
Annual Delays per U.S. Motorized Urban Traveler 1982 to 2002

Very large U.S. Urban Area	ANNUAL HOURS OF DELAY		
	1982	1992	2002
Boston, MA; NH; RI	20	40	54
Chicago, IL; IN	18	43	56
Detroit, MI	17	65	53
Dallas, Fort Worth, Arlington, TX	13	43	61
Houston, TX	39	32	58
Los Angeles, Long Beach, Santa Ana, CA	47	114	93
Miami, FL	11	39	52
New York, NY; Newark, NJ; CT	18	33	50
Philadelphia, PA; NJ; DE; MD	14	31	40
San Francisco, Oakland, CA	30	60	73
Washington, DC; VA; MD	21	48	67
Average for 11 Very Large U.S. Urban Areas	**24**	**55**	**62**
Average for 85 U.S. Urban Areas	**16**	**38**	**46**

Source: Texas Transportation Institute, "The 2004 Urban Mobility Report," Table 4.

Traffic congestion is not a new phenomenon. Residents of ancient Rome were kept awake at night by the noise of carts that were excluded from the city in daytime because of congestion.[5] Traffic speeds in modern cities range from 40 miles/hour in Sacramento (Cox 2000) through 20 miles/hour in Washington D.C.; 9 to 10 miles/hour in London; 8 miles/hour in Bangkok (Cox 2000); to 6 miles/hour in Manila (Roth/Villoria, chapter 8). This congestion is "excessive" in the sense that, if given the opportunity, many road users would be prepared to pay to travel in less congested conditions.

Congestion occurs when vehicles on the same road network slow each other down, and thus impose costs on one another. For example, an additional vehicle might reduce the average road speed so that other vehicles traveling at the same time and in the same vicinity arrive at their destinations with a thirty seconds delay. Thirty seconds doesn't sound like much, but if 180 vehicles are delayed and if people value their time at an average of $10 an hour, each vehicle imposes a total cost on others of $15. Because it is imposed on others, this $15 cost is said to be "external." All vehicles on a road network, not just the latecomers, contribute to congestion. External costs do not enter into a driver's calculations of when and how much to use a road. As a result, roads tend to be over-used because drivers will use a road whenever their own private benefits exceed their perceived private costs, which are, necessarily, lower than the total costs (private costs plus external costs) resulting from their road use.

In 1924, Frank Knight (Knight 1924) pointed out that if roads were provided by private owners they would not be over-used. Although the costs that the driver of an additional vehicle imposes on others are external to the driver, they are internal to a road owner because such costs reduce the price that the other drivers are willing to pay to use the road. A private road owner, therefore, would allow an additional vehicle on to the road only so long as the price that the drivers were willing to pay exceeded not only their private costs but also the costs imposed on other vehicles. In fact, in a competitive market, prices would tend to just cover all private and congestion costs, so that roads would be neither over- nor under-used.

However, it is possible to envisage a level of "optimum" congestion even in the absence of free markets. When the journey benefits to the user of a road exceed the costs imposed on other road users, the road may be considered under-used, in the sense that benefits to additional users could exceed the additional costs due to them. But when the costs imposed on others exceed the benefits to additional users, the road is overcrowded, and the removal of some traffic could increase its usefulness. If road use could be priced to accurately reflect congestion costs, the optimal economic charge would just equal the costs imposed by vehicles on the rest of the traffic, and the resulting congestion could also be regarded as economically "optimal." Mohring (chapter 7) and Roth/Villoria (chapter 8) show how to calculate these charges.

Would it be desirable to eliminate congestion entirely? Free markets may offer congestion-free roads to those willing to pay for them, in the same way that private tutors can be hired as an alternative to sending children to school. This would be an expensive solution, but the Long Island Motor Parkway, financed and opened in 1908 by William K. Vanderbilt, was indeed a congestion-free toll road.[6] However, in modern large cities eliminating congestion entirely would be impossible without eliminating not only the bulk of existing traffic, but also the much more voluminous potential traffic that would be attracted to a free and uncongested road system.[7]

Economists associate traffic congestion with under-priced road space and, in the absence of market pricing, are unable to accurately estimate the costs of congestion. Estimates made by Douglass Lee of the Volpe National Transportation Systems Center (Lee 1982), and updated for this volume, concluded that the delays from traffic congestion in 2000 cost about $108 billion, but that the corresponding economic loss is only about $12 billion, because road users would be prepared to accept much of the delay, rather than pay for its elimination.[8] Economic pricing of roads in urban areas could, of course, have profound effects on urban travel. It could encourage the use of public transport and, by discouraging long trips, have significant effects on city form and size.

Loss of Personal Freedom

Third, personal freedom is involved. People everywhere strive for mobility to enhance the scope and quality of their activities. Mobility in modern times is increased by the use of cars—trips by public transport typically take twice as long as by car. The use of cars requires roads. In most countries people are allowed to purchase vehicles, but in none can they exercise their powers as consumers to improve the roads they use. Users of freeways in Los Angeles are frequently delayed by congestion, but there is no mechanism available to enable them to buy better service. This is a curtailment of personal freedom, as explained by emeritus London School of Economics professor Alan Day:

> If road users are prepared to pay a price for the use of roads that is greater than the cost of providing additional road space (including all the costs, externalities, land costs, a sensible measure of the costs of disturbing any areas with special wildlife and all the other genuine costs which can be identified) then the additional road space should be built. (Day 1998)

In free societies, those in need of goods or services can choose to buy them from appropriate providers. Owners of congested facilities tend to raise their prices, and the resulting potential for increased profits attracts investment to relieve shortages. The application of these principles to roads is illustrated in chapters 7 and 8, which present calculations made for the Twin-Cities (Mohring) and for Manila (Roth/Villoria).

Road congestion and waste may be tolerated without major distress in the wealthy United States, but the poor condition of roads in other countries is a major obstacle to development. In Manila, for example, many people spend four hours each day traveling to and from work. In all countries, with the significant exception of Singapore, congestion and mismanagement coexist with lack of funding for road improvement.

Private Sector Roles in Road Provision

How might the private sector be involved in the provision of roads or road services for ordinary people? Free markets are flexible and can serve in a variety of ways to improve highway services. At least four roles are possible, beyond the well-known one of working under contract on the design, construction, or maintenance of governmentally provided roads:

- Testing and licensing of vehicles and drivers;
- Management of government-owned facilities;
- Franchising; and
- Outright private ownership.

Testing and Licensing of Vehicles and Drivers

Every year more than 1.17 million people die in road crashes around the world. About 70 percent of these deaths occur in developing countries. Sixty-five percent of deaths involve pedestrians, and 35 percent of pedestrian deaths are of children. Over 10 million people are crippled or injured each year (WHO 2004). Poorly maintained vehicles and incompetent drivers contribute substantially to this tragic toll. In the maritime sector, where safety has traditionally been taken very seriously, ships and their crews are tested and licensed by those (e.g. Lloyds of London) who insure them. Road vehicles and their drivers, on the other hand, are inspected and tested by government officials who, while usually conscientious, lack the incentive of a financial interest in safety. Semmens's proposal to enhance road safety by requiring insurers to test and license the drivers and vehicles they insure is set out in chapter 5.

Management of Government-Owned Facilities

After roads are built, they have to be maintained. Most roads are maintained either by government employees, or else by private contractors who perform specified tasks such as cleaning drains, weeding verges, filling pot-holes, painting lines, or re-graveling. In chapter 15, Zietlow describes recent reforms in the management of road maintenance that result in government agencies specifying the required road condition (e.g., a level of roughness) and contracting with private firms to do what they—the private contractors—consider necessary to keep the roads they maintain in the condition specified by the government agencies. Such arrangements encourage private providers to develop ways that are more effective to meet road maintenance standards and, as a result, have brought about substantial cost savings.

Franchising

In this role, a government agency contracts with a private entity to provide, maintain, and operate a road for a limited period. For example, in Britain, the Highways Agency invited bids for the provision of fifteen road improvements for which payment to successful bidders would be by means of "shadow tolls." Under "shadow toll" arrangements, private concessionaires finance and build roads at their own risk, maintain and operate them for an agreed period, and then transfer ownership to the government. The franchise owners are paid by the government on the basis of traffic counts, with no tolls collected from users, hence the name "shadow tolls." Contracts for eight of these schemes were let and are now operational. Under this system—known as DBFO ("Design–Build–Finance–Operate")—road users do not have to pay extra for using roads provided and operated by private firms. These arrangements are described by Roden, who participated in their development in the UK Highways Agency, in chapter 17. Other franchising arrangements (e.g., "Build-Operate-Transfer" [B-O-T]) have also been developed and implemented, for instance, the 123 km Guangzhou-Shenzen "Superhighway" conceived and developed by the Hong Kong entrepreneur Gordon Wu, who modeled it on the New Jersey Turnpike, which he admired while studying at Princeton University.

Outright Private Ownership

In this role the private sector takes full responsibility for the road and all financial risks, and is entitled to its rewards. Private ownership of roads was developed in England and the United States even before the advent of automobiles, as described by Benson in chapter 11, and by Klein and Majewski in chapter 12. It is now comparatively rare, for reasons to be discussed later, but is still significant in certain areas. Modern privately provided road projects include the SR91 Express Lanes in California, Canada's Highway 407 near Toronto, and the UK's M6 motorway and Dartford Crossing. Foldvary describes the private ownership of urban roads in the United States in chapter 13 and, in chapter 14, Malmberg Calvo and Ivarsson describe the ownership of rural roads in Sweden and Finland by associations of property owners. In chapter 19, Poole and Orski describe the recent development in the United States of HOT (High-Occupancy or Toll) Lanes and Express Toll Lanes. Levinson in chapter 4 discusses some of the political issues arising out of private ownership of roads.

Advantages of Privatization

It might, however, be argued that road problems could be solved without such a drastic change as privatization, for example by commercialization, which would require government agencies to price and manage roads in a business-like manner, without giving up public ownership. An example of a commercialized road is the New Jersey Turnpike, operated for profit by a corporation wholly owned by the State of New Jersey, and providing high-quality service to millions in the eastern United States. A more comprehensive example, yet to be fully implemented, is given by the proposals to commercialize the roads in New Zealand, as described in chapter 16 by the former deputy prime minister of New Zealand, the Hon. J. K. McLay.

Commercialization could indeed bring many benefits, and may be a useful first step on the road to privatization, but privatization is likely to have distinct advantages over commercialization, for the following reasons:

- Enhanced performance;
- Less concern with politics;
- Lower costs;
- Better information;
- Speed of response;
- Ability to finance expansion; and
- Competition.

Enhanced Performance

In many situations, private ownership is likely to produce better performance than the public ownership of a commercialized entity, such as the New Jersey Turnpike.

In particular, private ownership would be likely to provide more effective monitoring and commercial incentives for the firm's management than public ownership. Private investors would be placing their own wealth at risk by investing in the firm, and would therefore have more incentive to monitor and take an active interest in the commercial performance of the firm and its management. Furthermore, the management of a private firm would have greater incentive to heed the interests of its shareholders, given that it would face the threat of a hostile takeover otherwise, and would possibly face the threat of redundancies if a takeover occurred. This same constraint does not exist in the case of public ownership of a firm. (Meads and Wilkinson 1993, p. 75)

Less Concern with Politics

Privately provided roads are more likely to be provided in response to users' needs than are government programs, which often respond more to political than to economic priorities. Investment in additional facilities is thus often based on the need to satisfy political constituencies in remote areas, rather than on the willingness of road users to pay for better facilities. For example, California's AB 680 legislation (which permitted the private provision of the roads described by Sullivan in chapter 9) stipulated that at least one of the projects it permitted had to be in the north of the state, and at least one in the south, irrespective of merit. In countries—such as France, Japan, Korea, and Spain—in which toll roads are provided commercially by government, surpluses from profitable toll roads are used to cover the losses sustained on unprofitable ones.

Lower Costs

Peter Samuel (Samuel 2000) points out that, while private investors have incentives to reduce costs so as to increase their profits, governments (and obviously their consultants and contractors) have incentives to increase costs, because costly projects generate more power and influence than inexpensive ones.[9] Samuel illustrates the point by comparing the costs of the privately provided A86 tunnel in Paris, which range from $16.5 million to $27 million per lane-km, with the costs of the governmentally-provided Boston Central Artery Tunnel project (part of the famous "Big Dig"), which is costing $47 million per lane-km. He points out that similar tunnels in Australia, also privately provided, have been costing $14 million to $15 million per lane-km, while governmentally provided tunnels in Japan can cost over $200 million per lane-km.

According to Gómez-Ibáñez and Meyer (1993), the costs per km of roads in France built by COFIROUTE were 23 percent below the comparable figures for the government-controlled Sociétés d'Économie Mixte (SEMs).

Ten percentage points of the difference was reportedly because of more cost-sensitive roadway design, including a slightly narrower median and the use of swale drainage systems where possible. The remaining 13 percentage points were from higher productivity of labor and equipment.

Better Information

Private providers on the lookout for profit are likely to be better and more quickly informed about opportunities for road improvement in their areas than are government agencies concerned with operating existing systems. For example, in Britain, opportunities for the conversion of disused railways to roads would be scrutinized as opportunities for profitable investment, with less regard to political correctness. In addition, potential investors in new roads would have better information about the financial operations of the existing ones:

> Share analysts would have incentives to monitor the commercial performance of the firm on behalf of large groups of private or institutional investors, and to distribute the results of this research. Investors would be able to respond to this information by changing the level of their shareholding in the firm. Any resulting adjustment in the firm's share price would provide information to the firm's management on financial markets' assessment of their commercial performance. (Meads and Wilkinson 1993, p. 75)

Speed of Response

If allowed to by the local planning processes, private providers can get roads financed and built more quickly than public institutions. This is not because the private sector employs better people, but because it is not constrained, as public agencies rightly are, by purchasing rules designed to protect the public interest, for example to avoid even the appearance of favoritism or discrimination. Private operators can strike quick deals when speed is to their advantage, and do not have to offer equal treatment to those with whom they do business. Speed in making deals is particularly important in overcoming the difficulty of getting land—"the right-of-way"—for roads. This is often regarded as a major barrier to private provision but, in chapter 3, Benson shows that it is critical only when government is the would-be purchaser.[10]

Ability to Finance Expansion

Private providers have access to sources of funds seeking profitable investments, and can use them to improve and extend road networks. Publicly owned firms, on the other hand, are often (for good reason) subjected to political constraints on expansion.

Competition

One of the most important advantages associated with private provision is competition. A commercialized city road authority, working to financial targets and responsive to its customers, may offer better urban road systems than those found in most cities today. But it is less likely than private firms to provide innovative road links to meet consumer demand. The pioneering Express Lanes project on California's State Route 91 (described in chapter 9) was conceived, financed, and built by private firms to offer congestion-free travel to those willing to pay for it. After its success was demonstrated, a similar project—with more sophisticated pricing—was implemented by the public sector north of San Diego.

In the case of local roads (in, say, gated communities), there can be no competition in the provision of access to individual premises served by only one road. But (as pointed out by Foldvary in chapter 13) competition exists between communities, who are interested in getting high-quality roads to enhance their attractiveness and property values. Hence, competition can be expected between road providers, as exists between providers of elevators in buildings, to meet customers' needs at the lowest costs.

Overcoming Obstacles to the Private Provision of Roads

In view of the well-known advantages of the private sector in providing goods and services to meet customer needs, why does it not have a greater role in the road sector? Entrepreneurs wanting to provide roads are likely to face at least three major obstacles:

- Getting permission from government;
- Getting paid; and
- Competition from "free" roads.

Getting Permission from Government

In the United States and many other countries it takes years for a private company to get permission to provide a public road. This obstacle is additional to the "normal" obstacles to road provision that are faced even by government road entities. In Virginia, for example, Ralph Stanley had to wait four years to get permission to build what was eventually to become the "Dulles Greenway" and, by the time permission was granted, financial conditions had changed, making it much more difficult for him to raise the required finance. In some countries, such as India, there are constitutional restrictions on rights to provide public roads. Most private entrepreneurs do not have the time to wait upon such delays, and seek opportunities in other sectors. Only resolution at the highest level of government can remove this obstacle. Governments wishing to bring their roads into the market economy have to ensure that, once permission is given for a road improvement scheme, private entities are given the opportunity to provide it on terms as good as those obtainable by governmental agencies.

Getting Paid

The private sector cannot provide facilities without a reasonable expectation of being paid, and customers cannot demand goods or services from private suppliers without mechanisms to pay for them. To put the matter in perspective: People wishing to travel by car are usually allowed to buy vehicles, fuel, and similar necessities but, unless they have access to a toll road, they are not able to buy (or rent) road space. There are two aspects to this problem:

1. Devising simple ways to pay for road use, preferably without vehicles having to stop; and
2. Ensuring that payments for road use get to the road providers.

Paying for road use. The traditional way of paying for privately provided roads is by means of tolls, but conventional tolls require vehicles to stop, and the space required for toll plazas often precludes their use in the congested areas where they are most required. Chapters 6, 9, and 10 show how modern electronic tolling methods can be applied in a variety of circumstances. Menon describes the development of pioneering congestion pricing methods in Singapore, in which he himself played a leading role when serving in the Land Transport Authority; Sullivan reviews electronic tolling for travel in Express Lanes in Southern California; and Button describes their use in Norway and London.

Following earlier problems, Germany's high-tech Toll Collect truck toll system began successful operations early in 2005. Toll Collect uses GPS technology to track distances trucks travel on toll roads and wireless networks to transmit data for billing. With the help of GPS and sensors installed in control bridges to confirm the satellite readings, computerized onboard units installed in trucks locate the position of the vehicles, track their routes, calculate toll fees, and transmit the data at regular intervals to a data center for billing. Another 3,700 roadside terminals at service stations are available to drivers who prefer to pay manually. Trucks weighing more than 12 tons must pay 16 cents per kilometer to use Germany's 12,000-km autobahn network. More than one-third of the trucks using the highway system come from outside the country.[11]

Britain is planning a high-tech system to charge all vehicles for road use. Such systems need not necessarily invade the privacy of road users. In Southern California, for example, users of the Express Lanes on State Route 91 were able to open an account with the California Private Transportation Company without revealing their real name. As long as the account was in credit, no information about the payer needed to enter the computer system.[12]

Other methods for pricing road use are being developed. For example, Oregon is experimenting with an on-vehicle device using GPS technology to determine mileage traveled within state borders. Payment of the mileage fee would be at service stations, while refueling. Operators of vehicles equipped with the device would be charged a fee based on miles traveled since the previous refueling. Information about total miles traveled (but not information about where the miles were traveled) would be transmitted by short-range radio signals to electronic readers within the service station. The assessed mileage fee would be added to the cost of the fuel purchased, and a credit given for the amount of state tax included in the price of the fuel. Operators of vehicles not equipped with the new device would buy taxed fuel, as they do now. The two payment systems—by fuel tax or by mileage fee—would coexist for a lengthy period—possibly twenty years—until all vehicles become properly equipped.

But even electronically-levied tolls cannot always be collected on all roads. In some cases, shadow tolls (described in chapter 17) and dedicated road funds can offer other solutions. Dedicated road funds are established to enable road users to finance road maintenance and/or improvement for their mutual benefit. They are generally funded by surcharges paid for the purchase, ownership, or use of motor vehicles, the surcharge on fuel being the most widely used. Such funds, which are discussed by Heggie in chapter 18, exist in the United States and other countries. Their main drawback (another consequence of the political control of road financing) is the ability of governments to "raid" them for other purposes.[13]

Getting the payments to road providers. By what processes do roads get their funding? Countries vary greatly in the governmental level involved. In Britain and Germany, main roads are funded almost entirely out of national budgets. In Japan, France, and Canada, almost no central government funding goes into roads—in Canada because it is left to provincial governments; and in Japan and France because most major roads are tolled, and financed with bonds sold on the strength of prospective toll revenue streams.

The United States is between these two camps. The federal government, which had a minor role in financing roads before 1956, financed most of the construction of the 46,726-mile Interstate Highway System by means of a 4 cents a gallon surcharge on motor fuel.[14] It required matching grants from the states, which nominally own the roads within their borders. Despite the fact that the Interstate system is largely complete, federal funding has not ceased. It is spent on a huge array of new projects, many having nothing to do with roads. As shown by Semmens in chapter 2, this sort of financing has many disadvantages: For example, it encourages states to plan and build more road facilities than they themselves would be prepared to fund; its federal mandates drive up costs; and it enables the federal government to force states to adopt unpopular regulations, such as 55 miles an hour speed limits on Interstate highways. It also prohibits the tolling of most federally funded roads.

Assuming that standardized payment methods are devised for road users, how can the payments reach private providers? In the United States, for example, the portion of federal taxes paid by road users to finance roads is paid into the Federal Highway Trust Fund (FHTF), from which Congress appropriates funding to the fifty states on the basis of an agreed distribution formula. However, none of this revenue is paid to private providers of roads. Instead, users of privately provided toll roads pay twice: once to the toll road company and, secondly, to the FHTF. Road users also pay user fees into various state funds, over thirty of which are dedicated to improving roads.[15]

Financing through government funds need not be an obstacle to privatization. A government could, in theory, collect fees paid for road use and allocate the proceeds, on the basis of traffic counts, to all road suppliers, private or governmental, without discrimination. This could work if the private providers had convincing assurances that they would be paid.

Competition from "Free" Roads

Private road providers generally have to compete against governmentally provided "free" roads. This is a significant barrier, which can be likened to a private school being required to compete with government-financed "free" school. This obstacle can be overcome by the use of "shadow" tolls,[16] as described above, so that road users would not necessarily have to pay extra for using roads provided or operated by private firms. Such contracts, which are described in chapter 17, are already being implemented in England, Finland, Portugal, and Uruguay.

Politics

It would be naïve to suggest that economics alone can determine the disposition of assets as important as roads, or that the benefits to road users or suppliers would be decisive. In all countries, those who make the decisions are politicians and officials, and they are likely to seek to leave the roads in the command economy, where they remain a source of power and influence. In the United States, for example, the chairman of an important Congressional committee persuaded his colleagues to vote that a toll booth in his district be deactivated, allowing his voters to access the toll road at no charge. In response to protests by the toll company, Congress appropriated to it an amount sufficient to cover the consequent revenue loss.

A singularly difficult political problem is posed by the need to raise the prices for the use of congested roads. The problem (discussed by Mohring in chapter 7), is that the reduction in road congestion, and the benefits to those who value their time highly, are at the expense of those "priced off," who would generally be car users whose time is least valuable and whose income is comparatively low. Politicians find it difficult to advocate change—even beneficial change—that would appear to help the "rich" at the expense of the "poor."[17]

Political establishments in the west have tried to meet this difficulty by proposing to dedicate the expected surpluses from congestion pricing to public transport subsidies. For example, surplus revenues arising from London's congestion pricing scheme (discussed by Button in chapter 10) are dedicated to improving public transport, which is used for 85 percent of motorized trips in the central area but is not suitable for many of the journeys of those priced out of their cars. Except in London, such proposals for congestion pricing have not been implemented, and a scheme proposed for Edinburgh was defeated by a referendum in February 2005.

A better way to resolve this issue may have been found in Bergen, Norway, where (as described by Button in chapter 10) charges for the use of congested roads were introduced in 1986, but the surplus revenues were explicitly dedicated to improving the road system to relieve the congestion. In free markets, prices are used not only to restrain demand, but also to stimulate supply.

> It is quite indefensible to argue, as many do, that road pricing should simply be used to ration existing road space. Road pricing should be used both as an allocative device and as a measure of whether or not to add to or subtract from the existing road space. It can and should be used as an investment criterion . . . (Day 1998).

Thus, if roads were privately supplied, and if their expansion was financially attractive, those "priced off" would benefit by the infusion of private investment to relieve congestion in any manner consistent with user choice and sound finance. If the regulations were appropriately drawn up, such investment could also be consistent with improved environment. In this way, private ownership points to a solution to the road congestion problem, which has evaded the public sector throughout the millennia.

An important factor in this struggle is the quantity of resources available to governments to finance the sector. The more money they have, the longer governments can retain control of assets in their countries. It is when governments "run out of other people's money" that they seek help from the private sector. That is why change is most likely to come either in lean times or in "lean" countries. The recent progress (reported by Heggie in chapter 18) in Ghana, Latvia, Malawi, and Zambia might have been due to the enlightenment of governments there, but their tight budgets and unacceptable road conditions must surely have helped them to see the light.

The Road to Privatization

What, then, can be done to encourage the privatization of existing road facilities, and the private provision of new ones? Perusal of this volume suggests the following courses of action:

Commercialization of Existing Roads

Require all road networks to be self-financing, relying for their incomes on payments from road users and/or affected property owners. Develop improved payment methods for the use of roads, ranging from high-tech electronic road pricing to dedicated road funds and lower-tech "shadow tolls," which enable cost-covering payments to be made by road users to road suppliers. If such arrangements were set up, with no discrimination against private sector suppliers, private firms would be encouraged to supply the additional road facilities users choose to pay for.

Private Sector Management

Encourage the formation of property-owners' associations, in both rural and urban areas, to take over the ownership, financing, and management of local roads, assisted as necessary by competitive professional road management firms. Encourage governmental agencies to contract out road maintenance to private firms, requiring those firms to devise their own methods to maintain roads at standards specified by the agencies.

Private Provision of New Roads

Allow, subject only to regulations applying to publicly provided roads, the private provision of new road links, with payment being made by means of "shadow tolls" supplemented, where there is congestion, with additional charges, levied electronically.

Once roads are commercialized, and privately managed and maintained, the transition to private ownership, subject to public regulation, could become politically feasible.

Conclusions

In his discussion of the "Political Economy of Public Roads" (chapter 4), Levinson classifies roads as being "arterials" (long-distance roads such as inter-city freeways); "local streets" (roads giving access to properties); and "collectors" (roads connecting arterials to local streets). Arterial and collector roads are generally not monopolies, and need not be more difficult than electricity and water utilities for private firms to own and manage. There is a long history of privately owned arterial toll roads operating successfully, even without the use of electronic tolling methods, and even before the advent of the automobile.

As for local roads, Levinson, Foldvary ("Streets as Private-Sector Public Goods," chapter 13), and Malmberg Calvo and Ivarsson ("Private Roads to the Future: The Swedish Private Road Associations," chapter 14) point to examples of local roads being privately provided, thus demolishing the conventional wisdom that the monopolies characterizing these roads pose insuperable barriers to their privatization.

The principles governing the provision of scarce resources in free societies are well known. We apply them to such necessities as energy, food, and water, and even to our cars. Is it not time to apply them to the scarce resource "road space"? The main obstacle to private ownership of roads is likely to remain the reluctance of the political class to give up a lucrative source of power and influence. Those who want the provision of road services to be controlled by the interplay of consumers and suppliers in free markets, rather than by politicians, will have to explain the need for change. This volume was written to shed light on these complex issues.

Notes

1. Thomas Sowell, *Controversial Essays* (Hoover Institution Press, 2002), p. 316.
2. Clause 1(q)(10) of Rule X prohibits "inclusion in a general roads bill provisions addressing specific roads." This rule, which does not seem to have been rescinded, can be waived.
3. Taxpayers for Common Sense, "Database of Earmarks in Conference Agreement to the Transportation Bill," updated August 12, 2005. http://www.taxpayer.net/Transportation/safetealu/states.htm

4. A General Accounting Office review reported that, "Generally, demonstration projects we reviewed were not considered by state and regional transportation officials as critical to their transportation needs. In slightly over half the cases, the projects were not included in regional and state plans (GAO 1991).

5. The law excluding heavy goods vehicles from the streets of Rome in daytime hours, enacted by Julius Caesar, can be found in Dessau's "Inscriptiones Latinae Selectae" No. 6085. It is possible that this regulation was copied from earlier laws enacted in Greek cities.

6. I am indebted to Peter Samuel for drawing my attention to this early toll road, described on http://www.nycroads.com/history/motor/.

7. Writing in 1967, Reuben Smeed (Smeed 1968) calculated that "to meet the potential demand for traffic capacity in Central London with a short peak traffic period might well necessitate an increase of road capacity to at least 20 times its present [1967] value."

8. In contrast, researchers at the Texas Transportation Institute (TTI) estimated the "costs of congestion" in the eighty-five major U.S. urban areas in comparison with a "free-flow" environment, defined as a speed of 60 miles/hour on freeways and 35 miles/hour on arterials. On that basis, the TTI researchers calculated the "costs of congestion" in the year 2002 to have been $63.2 billion (TTI 2004). This total was built up from 3.5 billion hours of delay and 5.7 billion gallons of excess fuel consumed. For the average traveler those costs of wasted time and fuel amounted to $829 in the year 2002, comprising forty-six hours of delay and seventy-four gallons of excess fuel.

9. Adam Smith made the same point over 200 years ago: "The proud minister of an ostentatious court may frequently take pleasure in executing a work of splendour and magnificence, such as a great highway, which is frequently seen by the principal nobility, whose applause not only flatter his vanity, but even contribute to support his interest at court. But to execute a great number of little works, in which nothing that can be done can make any great appearance, or excite the smallest degree of admiration in any traveller, and which, in short, have nothing to recommend them but their extreme utility, is a business which appears in every respect too mean and paultry to merit the attention of so great a magistrate. Under such an administration, therefore, such works are almost always entirely neglected." *The Wealth of Nations*, volume 5, article I of part III of chapter 1.

10. Whether roads are privately or publicly provided, it is often possible to find space for additional road lanes within existing road rights-of-way, with no additional land being required. Such surplus land was recently used for privately provided roads in both Virginia and California. It is sometimes possible to build roads on under-utilized railroad right-of-way, which can readily be found in Bangkok, London, New York, and many other places. The Pennsylvania Turnpike, and the Port-of-Spain "Busway" in Trinidad, were both built on abandoned railroad right-of-way.

11. http://europa.eu.int/idabc/en/document/3754/194.

12. It may be significant that fewer than five Californians sought to protect their privacy in this way.

13. The most famous "raider" was Winston Churchill who, when chancellor of the Exchequer (minister of finance) in 1929, transferred for other purposes the accumulated surplus in the British Road Fund, which was mortally wounded and subsequently eliminated.

14. At the time of writing, the surcharge is 18.3 cents per gallon of gasoline (24.4 cents per gallon of diesel fuel), of which 4.3 cents is allocated to general revenues, and 2 cents to "transit."
15. In some of the other states these payments are added to general revenues; in others they finance "transportation" funds, which are used to cover losses made on, for instance, ports or transit.
16. School "vouchers," which enable parents to direct government funds to the schools of their choice, are the education equivalent.
17. The poor who use public transportation would benefit substantially from better road pricing, but their political clout is generally weak. In less developed countries the poorest, who are often unable to pay for public transportation, could benefit from reductions in its costs.

References

Altshuler, Alan. 2002. Shown on the documentary film *The Big Dig*, produced for South Carolina ETV, Great Projects Film Co. Inc.

Cox, Wendell. 2000. Wendell Cox Consultancy, "Roadway Speed & Population Density: International Urban Areas 1990/1991," *Urban Transport Fact Book*, http://www.publicpurpose.com/ut-intlsp&dens.htm.

Day, Alan. 1998. "The Case for Road Pricing," *Economic Affairs*, vol. 18, no. 4, December London: Institute of Economic Affairs.

GAO. 1991. Report GAO/RCED-91-146, "Highway Demonstration Projects." Washington, D.C.: General Accounting Office, Resources, Community and Economic Development Division, May 28.

Gómez-Ibáñez, Jose A., and John Meyer. 1993. *Going Private: The International Experience with Road Privatization*, p. 142. Washington, D.C.: Brookings Institution.

Heggie, Ian G. 1995. "Management and Financing of Roads: An Agenda for Reform." Sub-Saharan Africa Transport Policy Program, Working Paper No. 8. Washington, D.C.: World Bank.

Knight, Frank H. 1924. "Some Fallacies in the Interpretation of Social Costs," *Quarterly Journal of Economics*, vol. 38, pp. 582–606, August.

Lee, Douglass B. 1982. "Net Benefits from Efficient Highway User Charges," *Transportation Research Record No. 858*. Washington, D.C.: Transportation Research Board.

Meads, Chris, and Bryce Wilkinson. 1993. *Options for the Reform of Roading in New Zealand*, CS First Boston New Zealand Ltd., New Zealand Business Round Table.

Samuel, Peter, 2000. "More on Tunnel-highway Costs," *Toll Roads Newsletter*, no. 47, p. 12, March. Frederick, Maryland, tollroads@aol.com.

Smeed, R. J. 1968. "Traffic Studies and Urban Congestion," *Journal of Transport Economics and Policy*, vol. II, no. 1, January, London.

TRIP, 2003. "The Interstate Highway System," The Road Information Program (TRIP), Washington D.C., January, http://www.tripnet.org/InterstateStudyJan2003.PDF.

TTI. 2004. *2004 Urban Mobility Study*, Texas A&M University System, Texas 77843–3135, http://mobility.tamu.edu/ums/.

WHO. 2004. "World Report on Road Traffic Injury Prevention," World Health Organization, Geneva, April, http://www.who.int/world-health-day/2004/infomaterials/world_report/en/.

Part II

Theory, Arguments, and Ideas

2

De-Socializing the Roads

John Semmens[1]

Introduction

Roads are extremely productive assets. The value they provide for users is large even compared to the excessive costs incurred due to the repeated pattern of binge and bust that characterize public funding of roadways. Roads can and should be treated as profit making assets. Economics provides the motive for doing so and modern technology provides the means for a conversion from a financially ill public ownership to a healthy private ownership. In this chapter, I will endeavor to portray a new way of analyzing roadway finance as a step toward persuading policymakers to make changes that can harness the powerfully stimulating incentives of the marketplace to help us get better value from our roadway investments.

Failures of Traditional Highway Finance

Under public sector ownership, U.S. roads are funded through a complicated mixture of user and nonuser taxes at federal, state, and local levels. While all of the federal taxes are nominally user taxes, there is not necessarily a strong link between the amount of road use and the tax liability incurred. For example, vehicles with poor gas mileage pay more in taxes for the same road use as vehicles with better fuel efficiency.

States garner most of their road revenues from gasoline and registration taxes. Many states also attach *ad valorem* taxes to the vehicle registration levy. Not only do such taxes bear little relationship to road use, but the revenues often are diverted to other state-funded programs having nothing to do with road use, construction, or maintenance. To these nominal user fees many states add nonuser taxes as an additional source of funding. Sometimes the nonuser taxes are earmarked for road construction (for example, the half-cent sales tax dedicated to urban freeway construction in the Phoenix, Arizona metropolitan area). At other times, the state legislature will appropriate general fund monies for road purposes.

Counties and cities typically share in state-levied motor vehicle taxes (that is, fuel, registration, and license taxes) according to legislatively set formulas. These formulas reflect the political bargaining power of the various county and municipal jurisdictions more than they do their actual road usage. To these shares of state-levied taxes, local governments will often add property tax monies.

The funding for any particular road can be a mixture of monies appropriated by each governmental level. The Interstate Highway System involves a 90/10 federal/state matching ratio of funding. Other state highways are eligible, if they are in the federal aid system (a list of roadways designated as qualified for federal funding), for varying rates of federal and state or local matching funds. State or local roads not included in any of the federal aid system categories will not normally receive federal funding. City and county roads (with the exception of the few that are in the federal aid urban or secondary systems) do not normally receive federal funding.

While there has been some effort to make roads a user-funded service, the results are haphazard. The link between use and payment is weak. Consequently, there is considerable incentive for all involved to pursue "free-ride" lobbying strategies, that is, to increase the demand for and consumption of road services, while shifting the costs onto others. States struggle with each other over shares of federal spending. Cities and counties struggle over shares of state taxes. User lobbies push for nonuser taxes. Truckers seek to shift more of the burden to auto drivers. Meanwhile, highway agencies get little credit for keeping roads in their jurisdiction in good shape. On the contrary, efficient maintenance makes an agency a more vulnerable target for cuts in the struggle over allocations. A deteriorated road system can serve the politically potent purpose of demonstrating a need for more money and of creating a constituency that will demand that more funds be allocated to the highway agencies.

The winners of this political game are those who contribute the least while consuming the most. This is hardly a formula conducive to wise asset management. On the one hand, insufficient attention paid to maintenance and preservation of pavement assets has led to excess user costs and vehicle damage that was estimated to amount to $30 billion per year in 1989 (Small et al. 1989, p. 3). The projected costs of simply maintaining the U.S. road system's pavements and bridges from further deterioration exceed anticipated revenues from user taxes resources by about $3 to $5 billion per year.

As a consequence of the difficulty of adequately portraying the financial status of roadways using standard public sector accounting methods, roads tend to be neglected in the short run. Roads are, after all, long-lived assets. It may take decades before wear-and-tear becomes readily perceptible. By then, though, the damage is liable to be severe enough to require expensive repair or reconstruction. At this stage, the repairs or reconstruction will likely be beyond the existing means of the public road agency. A crisis ensues. Legislators faced with growing complaints from road users overcome their fear of raising tax rates in order to combat this crisis. The result is typically a surge of new revenues for roadways that will be followed by a public sector highway spending binge that paves the way for an inevitable future replay of the road funding crisis.

A rough road isn't the only service deficiency of highways. Traffic congestion also degrades the quality of the service provided. The Texas Transportation Institute estimates that congestion imposes an annual cost of around $80 billion in the form of 4.5 billion hours of wasted time and 6.8 billion gallons of wasted fuel (Texas Transportation Institute 2001). If our goal is to maintain current levels of service (i.e., to expand capacity to match rising traffic volume and keep congestion from getting worse) on the U.S. road system, an additional $15 to $20 billion per year would be required (Federal Highway Administration 1999, chapter 8).

Moreover, the prospects for spending available resources wisely are not encouraging because pork-barrel construction projects that will provide high profile, ribbon-cutting publicity for politicians and other government officials usually receive higher priority than routine, but necessary maintenance expenditures. Recognition of this phenomenon occurred as early as 1776 when Adam Smith observed in *The Wealth of Nations* (1981, p. 729) that:

> The proud minister of an ostentatious court may frequently take pleasure in executing a work of splendour and magnificence, such as a great highway, which is frequently seen by the principal nobility, whose applause not only flatter his vanity, but even contribute to support his interest at court. But to execute a great number of little works, in which nothing that can be done can make any great appearance, or excite the smallest degree of admiration in any traveller, and which, in short, have nothing to recommend them but their extreme utility, is a business which appears in every respect too mean and paultry to merit the attention of so great a magistrate. Under such an administration, therefore, such works are almost always entirely neglected.

Conventional public sector financial statements for highways have a difficult time conveying the message that we may be under-investing in some roadways and over-investing in others. Frequently, therefore, we misallocate road resources. While there is some lip service paid to the concept of highways as investments, most of the behavior appears to accept a "welfare" approach to obtaining funds. Under the welfare approach, roadway failures and deficiencies are the usual focus of efforts to persuade legislators to raise taxes or otherwise supply more money to roadway agencies. However, the welfare approach is not well suited to the task. Roadways are long-lived assets. Deferral of repairs or improvements has no immediate consequence. By the time roadways reach a decrepit state, the eventual cost of repairs and improvements will be substantially larger than if more timely action had been taken. Yet, a welfare style strategy relies on crises borne of long-term deterioration to motivate legislative action.

A shift away from a "funding-to-stave-off disaster" approach to a more business-like "invest-for-the-long-term" approach is better suited to the assets that roadways are. The pertinent questions are how much should we invest to maintain highway assets and where, specifically, ought new investments to be made. Although it may be tempting to assert that the ideal amount to be invested is always more than currently exists, valuable as highways are, this proposition is false.

It is clear that the public sector highway agencies cannot be relied upon for an intellectually defensible and financially prudent method of evaluating the worthiness of highway investments. A more realistic appraisal is required that would demonstrate that in some instances we need improved highway capacity or pavement surfaces while in others we do not need what we already have. Investing funds where we need improvements would be a wise use of resources. Investing funds where we don't would be a poor use of resources. Determining which condition pertains to any particular use of funds is the key investment issue facing transportation decision-makers.

When it comes to providing guidance for investment decision-making, the traditional "needs studies" used by most roadway agencies are worthless. In these studies, existing road networks are typically taken as an unalterable given. Virtually every road ever built is projected as a perpetually needed facility, even when subsequent construction has rendered some of these routes redundant. Private sector businesses following a similar protocol would find themselves burdened with the expense of maintaining long-obsolete facilities that generate more costs than benefits. Public sector roads are burdened in this way, but lack of businesslike accounting camouflages the waste. The maintenance and preservation costs of the existing road network provide the baseline of costs for most needs studies. The portions of this network that are failing due to poor roadway conditions or inadequate capacity are assumed to need improvements. The cost of making these improvements is added to the baseline maintenance and preservation costs. Then, on top of these costs are added any prospective new roads that are deemed necessary to accommodate growth in traffic or community development. Funds for obsolete or redundant road segments are rarely eliminated from the roster of claimed "needs."

Inevitably, these traditional needs studies produce an escalating spiral of higher needs with every iteration. Legislators are typically confronted with the purported "need" to impose substantial tax increases just to try to "catch up" with the accumulating needs backlog. Suspecting that the needs figures being reported may be exaggerated, legislators are reluctant to impose the tax increases implied by the studies. Uncomfortable with totally rejecting the pleas of the highway lobby, legislators often compromise by offering a tax increase smaller than the needs studies demand, but larger than many taxpayers would like. The result is a ratcheting up of tax rates that neither solves the highway finance problem nor pleases constituents.

An alternative to the welfare-based "needs study" approach to assessing the merits of highway investment is a more business-like return on investment analysis. Such an analysis would look upon highways as investment assets that generate a return that justifies the expenditure of funds to create, improve, or maintain these assets. Crucial to making the correct investment decision is an accurate estimate of the two sides of the financial ledger: costs and benefits. For private sector businesses, the calculation is made simpler by virtue of the fact that sales revenues serve as the measure of benefits. For public sector highway agencies, the calculation is complicated by the lack of direct sales revenue as a clear measure of benefits.

The lack of sales revenue for public sector highways forces roadway agencies to make their own estimates of what these benefits might be. The "more conservative" of these analyses confine their estimates of benefits to those enjoyed by the highway users. These would typically be comprised of savings in vehicle operating costs (for example, less fuel burned by vehicles because a new roadway surface is smoother than the older surface was), safety gains (for example, if a specific improvement is predicted to lower accident rates), and time savings (the cumulative minutes of shorter travel time due to a predicted faster travel between destinations).[2]

The "less conservative" analysts may add other economic benefits to the calculation. Typically, these might include the employment impact of highway construction, the indirect impacts on other segments of the economy as successive ripples of the initial highway expenditures spread through the community, and the stimulation of the local economy due to improved transportation. For example, the Federal Highway Administration's "Highways and the Economy Initiative" website (http://www.fhwa.dot.gov/policy/12a-hmpg.htm) asserts that the *first* reason for investing in highways is that "highway construction supports immediate on-site and off-site employment." The problem with this seemingly innocuous and obvious fact is that it provides no special justification for highway investment. Every expenditure by any entity can be said to support on-site and off-site employment. Extracting funds from taxpayers in order to construct highways prevents these funds from being spent on some other endeavor that would also support employment. Any investment that includes its cost (i.e., the amount spent on construction) as a benefit (i.e., the jobs supported by the expenditure) cannot fail to show a surplus of benefits over costs. Even the most poorly conceived highway project would appear to generate more benefits than costs. Adding in construction outlays and the employment stimulated by these expenditures wrongfully inflates the apparent advantage of highway investment and would, if given free rein, result in an uncontrolled spiral of increased expenditures on facilities of increasingly weak merit. A state or community relying upon such an analysis technique would embrace an endless sequence of tax increases until economic disaster brought a halt to the process.[3]

Highway stimulation of the local economy is a proverbial "chicken-and-egg" conundrum. Obviously, a highway to nowhere is incapable of sustaining economic development. On the other hand, when a highway is built in conjunction with other elements of economic development it may be a crucial component. However, it is not possible to accurately ascertain how much of any economic growth is due to which component contributing to that growth. Nor can we easily determine whether a different investment choice (i.e., something other than highways) would have resulted in a greater economic stimulation.

The substantial deficiencies of the less conservative cost/benefit analysis technique persuade many that a more conservative approach is warranted. While it is true that confining the cost/benefit calculation to only user benefits is less distorting, it still, nonetheless, biases the analysis in favor of highway expenditures. The key source of bias derives from the fact that gains to consumers of highway services are added into the benefit side of the equation but the excess burden of taxation is typically ignored on the cost side.

In forfeiting money to the government, more is lost than is taken as consumers substitute away from the taxed good. A very high tax on apples, for example, would cause losses to apple consumers yet would not raise much revenue as apple consumers switched to non-taxed consumption of other goods. The same principle holds true with respect to taxation of labor or any other good. In addition, taxpayers must also comply with filing and enforcement requirements. In some instances these compliance costs can be substantial. For example, Payne (1993, p. 150) calculates that because of compliance costs taxpayers must pay 1.65 for every dollar in taxes the federal government receives from the income tax. While no such similar analysis has been done for the highway user highway tax structure, it should be apparent that the burden of these taxes is greater than the amount of the tax collected.

In Payne's analysis, the complexity of the tax code and the record keeping required were major contributors to the excess burden. In this regard, commercial vehicle taxes would appear to merit examination. Significant record keeping burdens attach to the diesel fuel tax. Commercial operators must keep track of their vehicle mileage on each state's roads, multiply them by an appropriate tax rate, and forward payments to state revenue authorities. For its part, states conduct random audits to determine whether these businesses have properly counted, calculated, and reported mileage and tax liability. The potential for error and evasion may be high. A study conducted in Arizona estimated that the discrepancy between commercial vehicle mileage measured by traffic counts and that reported for tax purposes was about 35 percent (Sydec 1993, pp. 2–21). If the non-compliance rate is 35 percent, it is three times the size of the estimated non-compliance rate for the federal income tax. That such a large proportion of commercial vehicle operators might be making so many errors or evading taxes in such large numbers suggests that there may be serious problems with commercial highway user tax policy or procedure.

The Inefficiencies of Road Taxes

Possibly the most critical factor contributing to the worsening fiscal condition of our highways is that they are financed by taxes rather than direct users' fees. Since highway users do not pay taxes in proportion to the cost incurred, perverse incentives are created. On the one hand, demand for expensive facilities is not restrained by a requirement that those who use these facilities pay. Battles rage in state and local governments over how limited resources should be spent. Advocates of each specific use can see little reason to moderate their appetites. Funds not spent on favored projects will simply be spent on some other project. Winning the battle for funding has a significant payoff without cost. After all, winners do not have to pay higher taxes than losers. Thus, the incentive is to make excessive demands on highway resources.

In addition, the payment of a tax does not entitle the payer to any specific benefit in exchange for the payment. Those who drive on neglected roads are not relieved of any tax obligation. On the contrary, users of poorly maintained or crowded roads will likely use more fuel and pay more taxes. The lack of a direct link between payment for U.S. roads and services condemns highways to a persistent imbalance between needs and revenue sources. Public highway agencies cannot help but fall short of delivering everything that people want.

Raising traditional highway user taxes will do nothing to remedy the problem of simultaneous under-pricing of some roads and over-pricing of other roads that currently dooms the nation's road network to hopeless inefficiency. If we raise the overall cost of using the highways, it is true that some roads will be brought closer to an economically efficient price level. However, other roads that are already over-priced will be pushed further from an efficient price level. Consequently, the added cost of higher taxes may well exceed the added benefits we are trying to achieve from these roads. Worse yet, if we turn to non-user sources of revenue we will be further subsidizing inefficient uses of the highway system. When highway users do not have to pay the full cost of what they use they are encouraged to consume more than is economically justified. The most obvious manifestation of this is the increased traffic congestion and the air pollution caused by insufficient pricing of road use.

The Need for Market Pricing

If higher tax rates are not the answer to the highway finance problem, then what is? From both an efficiency and an equity standpoint, an optimal solution to the highway finance problem requires that differential roadway pricing be pursued. Those users who place the most expensive demands on the system must be made to pay for what they wish to use. This would have the salutary effect of both generating revenue to cover the costs of genuinely valued road use and discouraging wasteful demands on the road system. This would promote efficiency by directing resources to their most productive uses. Revenues would be earned by meeting real customer needs as expressed by customer purchases. The feedback from these customers would greatly clarify the investment options. Real needs would be more easily distinguished from unviable wishes and dreams.

Pricing road use would also promote equity by directly linking payment to use. A huge amount of waste of public funds springs from the separation of use and payment. Those who can use without paying are encouraged to try to benefit at someone else's expense. Selecting politically weak potential victims and passing the bill for one's indulgences on to them mimics the ethics of thieves. It degrades both public and private morality. The degradation grows more pronounced with each increase in the tax rate. Shifting to road pricing will help diminish this disgraceful tendency. Nothing is fairer than paying for what one uses. The equity of road pricing cannot be matched by any other means of highway finance.

Ideally, each highway user would pay a fee directly linked to the roadway services consumed. This would enable us to determine whether specific highway assets are or are not profitable. Profitability, or lack thereof, is information critical to proper management of resources. Profitable highway segments are evidence of valued service and efficient use of assets. Unprofitable segments warn that a change in investment or operation is warranted. Sometimes unprofitability can be remedied by improved pricing or greater efficiency of input utilization. At other times, though, unprofitability may be a permanent feature of a given highway segment. In such cases, divestiture may be the best course of action.

It would be useful for us to try to illustrate how we should analyze a road system to ascertain where the profits lie. As it currently stands, though, rather than paying directly for each mile of travel, highway users are typically taxed per gallon of fuel, or are assessed lump sum vehicle registration fees and license taxes. While inferior to actual pricing of road services, we could allocate these fees on the basis of vehicle-miles of travel to the roads according to traffic volume and composition. Such an allocation has been dubbed "shadow tolling" (Federal Highway Administration, *The Selective Use of Shadow Tolls in the United States*). Using recent data from the Federal Highway Administration I estimate that autos generate about two cents of highway user "shadow tolls" per vehicle-mile of travel, while trucks, in the aggregate, generate about 12 cents of highway user "shadow tolls" per vehicle-mile of travel (Federal Highway Administration, *Highway Statistics*, 1999, Tables HF-10, FE-10, SF-1 & VM-1). The earnings for any given roadway then would be estimated by multiplying these "shadow tolls" by the volume of traffic in each category.

The earnings by road segment could then be compared to the costs for the segment (including capital and maintenance costs over some investment horizon or lifecycle). Segments that generated more revenues from "shadow tolls" than costs could be considered the "cash cows" of the highway system. The investment decision here is fairly simple: One should continue to feed the "cash cows." Maintaining and improving these segments helps to ensure a favorable cash flow to the highway agency. On the other hand, segments that generated costs larger than the "shadow tolls" revenues could be considered "money losers." The investment decision here is a little more complex. It may be that the roadway in question is a candidate for divestiture (i.e., removed from the investment portfolio). It may be that the roadway in question should be carried as a "loss leader" (i.e., a product that is itself unprofitable, but contributes to the profitability of another product). It may be that the roadway merits a "price" increase. These are the same types of investment decisions faced by private sector firms.

A step toward the type of segment-by-segment analysis necessary for a more businesslike evaluation of highway investments was recently conducted for the Arizona State Highway System (Matranga and Semmens 2000). This statewide analysis compared highway user "shadow tolls" and construction expenditures on a segment-by-segment basis for the period 1986–1998. This time period and the focus on only construction expenditures was chosen to match the data currently available. A more comprehensive analysis would require a more complete analysis of costs. An example for one county in Arizona is shown below. On some segments more was earned than was spent. On other

Table 2.1
Arizona State Highway Segments in Gila County

Route	VMT (millions)	Revenues (thousand $)	Expenditures (thousand $)	REV/VMT (cents per mile)	VMT/EXP (mile per $)	REV/EXP ($ per $)
S 73	124	$3,274	$5,001	2.64	25	0.65
S 77	296	$10,644	$6,243	3.60	47	1.71
S 87	1,476	$42,000	$53,390	2.84	28	0.79
S 88	436	$10,767	$28,011	2.47	16	0.38
S 170	67	$2,030	$339	3.04	197	5.98
S 188	231	$5,678	$66,501	2.46	3	0.09
S 260	631	$18,439	$54,539	2.92	12	0.34
S 288	77	$1,915	$2,170	2.48	36	0.88
U 60	1,679	$55,057	$28,848	3.28	58	1.91
U 70	296	$9,020	$3,553	3.05	83	2.54
TOTAL	5,313	$158,824	$248,595	2.99	21	0.64

Source: Matranga and Semmens, *Traffic and Expenditures on Arizona State Highways.*

segments the reverse was the case. Armed with this kind of information, we could make more rational decisions on how to maximize the return on highway investments.

Admittedly, the scope for decision-making in the public sector is hampered by the clumsy nature of tax financing. "Shadow tolls" are not prices, *per se*; we cannot adjust them with the same degree of precision employed by private businesses in adjusting their prices. Thus, the public highway agency can be simultaneously confronted with excess demand on an under-priced roadway and excess capacity on an over-priced roadway and no latitude to make the obvious price corrections. As long as this condition persists, we will continue to get far less than optimal performance out of our highway system. Under-priced roads will suffer from periodic traffic congestion that wastes time and pollutes the air. Over-priced roads will continue to consume resources for maintenance and preservation while providing benefits to too few users. The combined result is inefficiency and waste of scarce resources.

In the past, we lacked the technology to employ efficient, widespread road pricing. Such road pricing as exists in most places still employs the cumber-some "stop-pay-toll" methods that give many people nightmares of traffic jams and irate motorists. Fortunately, stopping vehicles to collect payment for use of the roads is no longer necessary. Modern technology has overcome this difficulty. Inexpensive transponders make charging for highway use as simple as charging for long distance telephone use. Using this technology will improve both equity and efficiency. Drivers will pay for what they get. They will also get what they pay for. The current tax-funded system assures neither of these outcomes.

Concerns about Private Roads

While most Americans would prefer the private sector to the government for the supply of most goods and services, roads are one of several services for which Americans tend to look to government. They do so because of myths about the private and public provision of roads. First among these myths is the notion that only the government can operate a dependable road network sensitive to the needs of travelers.

The idea of private companies operating roads may seem strange to many Americans. Admittedly, there is a plausible basis for the premise that government must own and operate the roads. Besides the enormous resources available to government to operate the system, transportation is so vital that any breakdown would threaten the nation's security and economy. Can the United States, say critics of private ownership, entrust this function to private firms, which may go out of business, go bankrupt, or otherwise cease to exist?

Unlike government, of course, private sector firms must rely upon resources voluntarily supplied by customers and investors. Private firms cannot compel payment through taxation. But far from being a disadvantage, this encourages private firms to be more prudent in managing resources, more responsive to complaints, and more sensitive to market demand. Private firms have to make good decisions or they are out of business. The purported advantages of the public sector, however, insulate government agencies from the necessity of making good decisions and much of the information from consumers crucial to making good decisions. This absence of a link between services rendered and payments allows public agencies to ignore consumer wishes—as every motorist knows who has complained about a pothole.

A second myth is that roads are a "public good" and thus can only be supplied by government. It often is assumed that roads are an example of what economists call a public good—a good or service that of necessity must be made available to everyone because it is infeasible to separate payers from nonpayers. However, nonpayers of tolls, vehicle registrations, or other charges for roads, for instance, can be, and are, excluded from using the service. Cameras photograph toll evaders. Police issue citations carrying financial penalties to those caught operating motor vehicles without proof they have paid registration fees. Dyes are added to diesel fuels not intended for on-road use in order to prevent trucks from evading taxes by using fuels marked for off-road use.

A third myth is that roads are a "natural monopoly." A natural monopoly is said to exist if the cost of producing an extra unit of a good consistently declines as the scale of production increases, since the most efficient production then takes place when the producer is as large as possible—that is, a monopoly. Even if, for the sake of argument, it were conceded that roads were a natural monopoly, it would not necessarily follow that public ownership would be better than a regulated private monopoly. The relationship between the regulated private firm and the political system is frequently adversarial in nature, leading to close scrutiny of the firm by the political system and an incentive for managers to pursue cost-cutting measures. In contrast, the relationship between the public sector agency and the political system tends to be extremely cooperative, with bureaucrats and politicians serving each other more than they serve the consumers.

A fourth and related myth is that highways cannot compete with each other. It is an obvious fact that only one road can exist in a specific given alignment. Nevertheless, most roads, particularly those in urban areas, in a very real sense compete with each other for carrying traffic and attracting businesses or residences along their routes. This suggests the use of roads has many market-like aspects that bear out the possibility of a competitive market, managed by private sector roadway operators.

Privatization: A New, Greener Pasture

If public roads are inefficiently managed and financial resources are insufficient to provide the transportation systems we need, then perhaps we should consider employing private resources. Of course, to many the idea of the private sector owning and operating roads is implausible. Yet, historical precedent exists. From 1790 to 1830 more than 10,000 miles of roadways were financed and built by the private sector (Klein 1986). While the tolls earned on these roads did not, for the most part, yield satisfactory returns, the gains from land development abutting the roadways were substantial. Eventually, the advent of the railroad put an end to the private toll-road era.

Perhaps the time for private-sector involvement is here again. Highway privatization statutes exist in at least five states: Arizona, California, Florida, Texas, and Virginia. There are privately owned and operated highways in California and Virginia. There is growing interest in so-called "HOT" or "value" lanes (Poole and Orski 1998 and Fielding and Klein 1993). HOT or value lanes are existing HOV (high-occupancy-vehicle) lanes that are converted into lanes that accept single-occupant vehicles that pay a fee for the privilege. This fee would be collected electronically while the vehicles are traveling at normal freeway speeds. The State of Arizona is currently conducting a value lane study for the Phoenix metropolitan region's freeway system (Parsons, research in progress).

All of these projects are designed to provide new facilities. This approach has the political advantage of not tampering with existing roadways. Only users of privately financed highways would be facing toll charges. Since drivers would not be losing any privileges, opposition from highway users may be muted. A disadvantage of restricting privatization to the construction of new facilities is the high level of financial risk. New highways have no established base of traffic. Forecasts of projected toll-paying customers are subject to error. Financiers demand high rates of return in the face of these uncertainties. To get high returns high toll rates might be required, which would further depress traffic volumes.

A less financially risky approach would entail privatizing or commercializing existing highways. These more mature assets would have an established traffic pattern. While this pattern would be affected by the addition of tolls, the resulting traffic volumes are apt to be more predictable than they are for new routes.

At one time, the sale or conversion of highway assets was hampered by federal regulations. However, this impediment was greatly reduced by President Bush's executive order of April 30, 1992, which revised federal regulations to reduce or eliminate the obligation to reimburse the federal government for aid used in any highway that is sold.

Many are vexed by apparent technical difficulties with privatization. They point to toll roads in New Jersey or Pennsylvania and are persuaded that toll collecting is cumbersome and time consuming. Adding tollbooths to highways would seem to be asking for trouble, especially in urban areas. If freeways are slow-going during the rush hour, how much more would traffic be slowed by stopping to pay tolls? Fortunately, this vision of lines of vehicles waiting to pay tolls is more a glance backward than a preview of the future. Modern technology makes it possible to automate toll collections. Vehicles can be equipped with low-cost transponders that allow tolls to be paid while moving at full speed. The vehicle's transponder would communicate with the toll road's computer to record the transaction. The toll would then be billed to the credit or debit card of the driver. This automated toll collection technology has been demonstrated on numerous highways including facilities located in Atlanta, Dallas, Denver, Houston, Miami, New Orleans, New York, New Jersey, Illinois, and Oklahoma (Pietrzyk and Mierzejewski 1994).

The means to implement individual, per-mile charges are available. And there is potential for substantial improvement in the equity and efficiency of highway-user fees. The specific traffic that imposes costs on the system can be directly assessed for those costs. Another benefit of the system is that it allows government to better deal with peak-hour traffic, which is the most expensive to serve. Roads added to serve this traffic are excessive in the off-peak periods. Inasmuch as traditional highway-user taxes do not vary with the time of day, there is reduced economic incentive for users to modify their travel behavior. Surveys show non-commuters account for more than 50 percent of peak-hour travel (Downs 1992, pp. 15–16).

Automated tolling, with higher charges during peak periods, could encourage drivers to drive at less busy times. Variable time-of-day charges for road use also could help ameliorate the financial problems of public transit. If peak hour highway-user charges were employed, transit could become a more viable travel mode during the rush hour. In addition, the appeal of carpooling also would increase. When the out-of-pocket costs of driving one's car are low, the superior convenience and mobility of the single-occupant auto make it the most popular mode of travel. If the out-of-pocket costs for single-occupant autos were higher during peak periods, some of these travelers would shift from this mode of transportation to public transit, carpooling, telecommuting, or some other means of avoiding the increased expense of driving alone.

While it is possible for the benefits outlined above to be achieved in the public sector, it is unlikely that the public sector could progress as far or as fast as the private sector could. The monopolistic, tax-financed character of the public sector insulates it from competition and creates different incentives for public officials. In the private marketplace, being first or best means bigger profits. This inspires risk taking and innovation—with their potential for failure—in pursuit of profits.

Public sector agencies do not earn profits. There are no stock options or capital gains to be earned by managers who take risky actions. Instead, there are criticisms and censure for taking an unusual course of action and failing. It is safer for public sector decision-makers to trod traditional paths than to blaze new trails. A bureaucrat that stays with the herd is less likely to be hunted down and attacked by a news hungry media or pack of angry taxpayers. While staying with the herd seems the safest option for the bureaucrat, it is not in the best interest of the entire herd. The commonly trod ground has become hard-packed and over-grazed. If someone doesn't lead the way to new pastures, the long-term prognosis looks bleak.

Highway privatization is the new, greener pasture that transportation needs. Highway privatization could overcome the inequity and inefficiency of the tax-funded approach to providing highways by harnessing the private sector and its built-in incentives for efficient delivery of service.

Obstacles to Privatization

Privatized highways would be a radical departure from the traditional mode of highway finance. Fear of change can be expected to generate dire prognostications of disaster from so different a means of providing for roads. Those who feel they can manipulate the existing tax-based finance system can be expected to voice determined opposition. I believe this opposition could be countered by marketing the benefits of the proposed change to the highway users. A key element of this marketing effort would be an emphasis on the fact that privatized roadways would eliminate existing highway-user taxes. A second element of the marketing effort would be to highlight the advantages of being a customer as opposed to merely a taxpayer. After all, in the market-place, a "customer is always right." The government environment extends no equivalent reverence for a taxpayer.

Another potential obstacle is the average person's unfamiliarity with how an electronically priced road system would work. It is commonly believed that making users pay directly for roads would require time-consuming toll collection procedures. Demonstrating modern electronic road pricing technology at work would be a means of overcoming this obstacle.

Conclusion

The evidence seems clear: Public ownership and operation of roads is not the most effective way of managing these very valuable assets. Public ownership is a socialist mode of operation. The history of the twentieth century has convincingly demonstrated that the socialist methods of trying to produce goods and services are inferior to capitalist methods. The collapse of the Soviet Union, the world's leading exemplar of the socialist method of producing goods and services, and the growing trend toward market-oriented economies around the globe, signal that people are actually learning from history. Transportation policymakers should also be learning from history. Rather than continue to constrain the provision of roadways within a failed socialist model, we should be looking to adopt the more effective capitalist methods.

By moving roadways out of the socialist mode we would improve the incentives for wiser use of transportation resources. Modern technology that is revolutionizing the communications industry could then be more easily and quickly spread into the transportation industry. The potential ripple effects cannot be fully anticipated at this time, but given the significance of transportation in our economy they are apt to be large.

This glowing picture of the benefits of privatization should not be taken as a sign that the transition to a new way of operating transportation facilities would be easy. The forces of inertia and entropy always work against change. Nevertheless, the well-traveled road of traditional public sector ownership and control of transportation assets leads to a dead end. Getting off of this dead-end road, difficult as it may be, is necessary if improvement of transportation systems is desired.

Notes

1. The views expressed in this chapter do not necessarily represent those of the Arizona Department of Transportation.
2. A common practice has been to assume that the value of time saved can be estimated by summing up all the minutes saved on the millions of trips made and multiplying this figure by an imputed hourly wage. The validity of this practice is highly suspect. Research indicates that the value of saving a few minutes is only a fraction of the hourly wage rate (American Association of State Highway and Transportation Officials, 1977, p. 16). The same research also showed that the value of time saved depends upon the trip purpose. Since time value estimates are typically calculated without regard to these two elements, the resulting estimate of benefits will grossly overstate the likely real benefits.
3. See Weingast, Shepsle, and Johnsen (1981) for a model of how the political incentives to treat costs as benefits lead to inefficient public-sector investment.

References

American Association of State Highway and Transportation Officials. 1977. *A Manual on User Benefit Analysis of Highway and Bus-Transit Improvements.* Washington, D.C.

Bureau of Labor Statistics. "Consumer Price Index—All Urban Consumers: New and Used Motor Vehicles." Retrieved 12/29/00 from http://stats.bls.gov/.

Bureau of Labor Statistics. "Producer Price Index Revision—Current Series: Motor Freight Transportation and Warehousing." Retrieved 12/29/00 from http://stats.bls.gov/.

Bureau of Transportation Statistics. *National Transportation Statistics 1999.*

Downs, Anthony. 1992. *Stuck in Traffic.* Washington, D.C.: The Brookings Institution.

Dunn, James. 1998. *Driving Forces: The Automobile, Its Enemies, and the Politics of Mobility.* Washington, DC: Brookings Institution.

Federal Highway Administration. 1999. *Conditions and Performance Report.* Washington, D.C.

Federal Highway Administration. Various years. *Highway Statistics.* Washington, D.C.

Federal Highway Administration. 2000. *Our Nation's Highways: Selected Facts and Figures.* Washington, D.C.

Federal Highway Administration. *The Selective Use of Shadow Tolls in the United States,* http://www.fhwa.dot.gov/innovativefinance/shadtoll.htm.

Fielding, Gordon, and Daniel Klein. 1993. *High Occupancy/Toll Lanes: Phasing in Congestion Pricing a Lane at a Time.* Los Angeles, CA: Reason Foundation.

Johnston, James D. 1997. *Driving America: Your Car, Your Government, Your Choice.* La Vergne, TN: American Enterprise Institute Press.

Klein, Daniel. 1986. *Private Turnpike Companies of Early America.* International Conference on the Roles of Private Enterprise and Market Processes in the Financing and Provision of Roads, Transportation Research Board.

Matranga, Eric, and John Semmens. 2000. *Traffic and Expenditures on Arizona State Highways*. Arizona Department of Transportation.

Parsons Transportation Group. Research in progress. *Value Lane Study*. Arizona Department of Transportation.

Payne, James. 1993. *Costly Returns: The Burdens of the U.S. Tax System*. San Francisco, CA: ICS Press.

Pietrzyk, Michael, and Edward Mierzejewski. 1994. "Electronic Toll Collection Systems: The Future Is Now," *TR News* no. 175, pp. 14–19.

Poole, Robert W. Jr., and C. Kenneth Orski. 1998. *Building a Case for Hot Lanes: A New Approach to Reducing Urban Highway Congestion*. Los Angeles, CA: Reason Public Policy Institute.

Rowell, Matt, Rick Buoninconti, and John Semmens. 1999. *Analysis of Bonding vs. Pay-As-You-Go Financing*. Arizona Transportation Research Center.

Small, Kenneth, Clifford Winston, and Carol Evans. 1989. *Road Work*. Washington, D.C.

Smith, Adam. 1981 [1776]. *An Inquiry into the Nature and Causes of the Wealth of Nations*. Indianapolis, Indiana: Liberty Press.

Sydec. 1993. *Highway Cost Allocation Study*. Arizona Department of Transportation.

Texas Transportation Institute. 2001. *2001 Urban Mobility Study*, http://mobility.tamu.edu/2001/study/short_report.stm.

Weingast, B. R., K. A. Shepsle,, and C. Johnsen. 1981. "The Political Economy of Benefits and Costs: A Neoclassical Approach to Distribution Politics." *Journal of Political Economy* 89 (Aug.): 642–664.

3

Do Holdout Problems Justify Compulsory Right-of-Way Purchase and Public Provision of Roads?*

Bruce L. Benson

I. Introduction

One of the alleged "justifications" for government provision of highways and roads is that the power of compulsory purchase is necessary in order to overcome holdout problems and obtain right-of-way properties (Goldstein 1987).[1] After all, this argument continues, only the state has such power, so the private sector would be unable to supply the efficient amount of roads and highways.[2] This market-failure justification for public roads is examined from three different perspectives below to demonstrate that it is not valid.[3] The first, and perhaps most obvious, point regarding the compulsory-purchase justification for government provision of roads is that even if this power is required to obtain a right-of-way, the road itself does not have to be sited, constructed, financed, or operated (e.g., maintained, policed) by the government. Section II briefly summarizes some substantial historical and modern evidence demonstrating that members of the private sector are able, and indeed, quite willing, to site, construct, finance, and operate roads if they are allowed to. The implication is that even if compulsory purchase is required in order to obtain a right-of-way, that right-of-way can be turned over to the private sector, which can then build and operate the road. Section III turns to a direct examination of the alleged market-imperfection justification for the use of compulsory pur-

*I want to thank Alex Tabarrok and Gabriel Roth for their helpful comments and suggestions on an earlier draft of this chapter.

chase to obtain right-of-way properties: transactions costs due to the "holdout" problems that are assumed to prevent private sector acquisitions of multiple contiguous land parcels for a roadway (Fischel 1995, pp. 68–70). It is demonstrated that the holdout problem is not nearly as severe as it is assumed to be when private entities are making the purchase. Therefore, while government entities may face significant holdout problems, the magnitude of any *market failure* that might actually exist with a privatized road system is much less significant than this holdout justification for public roads assumes. Furthermore, the use of compulsory purchase actually is undesirable for a number of *government-failure* reasons, as explained in Section IV. Therefore, even *if* there is a potential market-failure limiting the ability of private road providers to obtain right-of-way properties, Section V concludes, not only that: (1) the "need" for compulsory purchase does not justify public provision of roads (as demonstrated in Section II), but that compulsory purchase through government itself is not even justified for the private provision of roads, because (2) the probability of market failure is low in the absence of this power (as illustrated in Section III), and because (3) there is a substantial degree of government failure accompanying the power that appears to more than offset any benefit from overcoming the holdout problem (described in Section IV).

II. Must the State Own, Build, or Operate Roads?

Putting aside, for a moment, the issue of compulsory purchase, we may ask whether the state must own, build, or operate roads.[4] Many of the other chapters in this volume examine this question and the results of these studies demonstrate that the answer is no. There are numerous examples of privately provided roads from highways to local roads, in the United States and internationally, both at the present time and in the past. In addition to the chapters in this volume on Sweden's extensive private road system (Malmberg Calvo and Ivarsson), recent privately built and run highways in the United States (Sullivan), the many privately built and maintained local roads (Foldvary), the history of privately built roads in Great Britain (Benson) and the United States (Klein and Majewski), and the privatization of road management (Zietlow), see Beito (2002) and Newman (1980) for a discussion of the history and recent past of privately provided roads in St. Louis, and Shearing and Stenning (1987) detail the massive role of private security and the resulting order in Disney World, a huge complex with hundreds of miles of private roads and highways (also see Foldvary [1994]). Furthermore, many developing countries are franchising roads to private firms that construct the roads and then operate them, charging tolls to earn the costs of construction and operation, *and* to cover franchising fees paid to the government (Pereyra 2002). Indeed, providing such roads is so attractive, in part because of their impact on real estate values, that it is becoming increasingly common for governments to auction franchises (Engel et al. 2002). Roth (chapter 1 of this volume, and 1996, pp. 180–197) also documents several private road projects in developing and developed countries such as two recent private highways in Great Britain (the Dartford River Crossing Ltd.'s toll bridge crossing the Thames, and Midland Expressway Ltd.'s M6-Toll Road, a 27 mile expressway to relieve congestion in one of England's busiest urban areas). The United States also has begun to develop and even encourage private-highway projects. In fact, the Intermodal Surface Transportation Efficiency Act (ISTEA) of 1991 attempted to stimulate privately provided toll roads, bridges, and tunnels in the United States (as long as they are not part of the Interstate Highway System) by making them eligible for a 50 percent grant from the Highway Trust Fund, and in an effort to take advantage of these available funds a number of states have passed their own legislation to allow private provision of roads (private providers of roads have been reluctant to accept such funding, however, choosing to seek private financing instead, because of the added costs and delays that arise when the federal government becomes involved).

Clearly, private entities can and do finance, build, and operate roads, and they would do much more of it if they could retain profits. Thus, even if compulsory purchase is necessary in order to obtain right-of-way properties (and for many of the above roads, particularly the local roads, compulsory purchase was not necessary), the state could purchase and then transfer the land to private entities. But are compulsory purchase powers actually necessary to obtaining property for a road right-of-way?

III. Holdouts: Do They Justify Compulsory Purchase?

Resources, such as land for a right-of-way, can be taken through compulsory purchase, but from an efficiency perspective, voluntary exchange is clearly more desirable if it is possible. To see why, suppose one person, individual A, wants to obtain possession of a tract of land that is currently legally controlled by another person, individual B. There are two ways for A to obtain the property. One is through bargaining in an effort to achieve a mutually advantageous exchange. The other is through coercion if the person desiring the land has the power to force a transfer or the ability to call on someone (e.g., the legislature) who has. The bargaining option is considered here while the alternative is discussed below.

Suppose that A values the land at $500,000 and B values it at $300,000. A and B are therefore likely to find mutually advantageous terms to make the exchange. At a price of $420,000, for example, both can conclude the exchange and be pleased with the deal they brokered. A fundamental if commonplace fact is that *voluntary* exchange takes place only when *both parties expect to be better off* as a consequence. Voluntary exchanges occur because both parties trade something they value less for something they value more. Therefore, if a successful voluntary exchange takes place the traded good will be *allocated to a higher valued use*.[5] Of course, the goal of allocating things to their highest valued use according to the subjective value of individuals may not be seen as an attractive normative objective by some readers. But remember that voluntary exchange makes both parties to the exchange better off: that is, *voluntary exchange tends to increase "wealth"* (subjective well-being) and it does so in what economists refer to as a *Pareto efficient* way. Pareto efficiency refers to the idea that an action is desirable if it makes someone better off without making anyone else worse off. In general, voluntary exchange does this.[6] Pareto efficiency is not the end of welfare analysis but it is an important component and one that virtually all people should agree is desirable.

Holdout Problems and Involuntary Transfers

Exchange is not costless, of course, so it will never be the case that all mutually beneficial exchanges take place. If transactions costs do prevent some valuable exchanges from occurring then in theory a substitute for bargaining, such as regulation or compulsory purchase, may increase social welfare. In this context, Calabresi and Melamed (1972) point out that an "entitlement" (the right to use an asset or resource) can be "protected" (i.e., supported by the legal system) in three different ways: by a "property rule," a "liability rule," or by "inalienability." An entitlement is protected by a property rule to the extent that someone who wishes to remove the entitlement from its holder must obtain the current entitlement holder's permission *before* the transfer (e.g., in a voluntary exchange). When an entitlement can be taken without prior permission by someone who pays objectively determined compensation after the fact, the entitlement is protected by a liability rule. The government's power of compulsory purchase is an example of a liability rule.[7] Of course, after the entitlement has been taken, the previous holder has incentives to claim that he would have required a substantial price to induce him to sell and the taker has incentives to claim the opposite, so a court often will have to determine liability based on evidence other than the statements of the parties involved.

From an efficiency perspective, entitlements should be protected by a property rule when bargaining is possible, because only the parties directly involved know their subjective values and those relative values are likely to be revealed only through voluntary bargaining. It is often claimed, however, as Posner (1977, pp. 10–12, 51) and Kraus (2000, p. 788) explain, that when transactions costs are high so bargaining is not likely to arise, a liability rule is preferred (e.g., see Barnes and Stout 1992, p. 56; Fischel 1995, pp. 67–70). Both Kraus (2000, pp. 788–790) and Posner (1977, pp. 39–44) emphasize, however, that there are significant problems with this argument.[8] One reason for questioning this widely held conclusion is the often implicit assumption that while transactions costs are high for private parties, information costs are low for judges or juries who must determine compensation (Polinsky 1980). As Kraus (2000, p. 788) notes, if "both transactions costs and judicial assessment costs are high, there is little reason to believe that protecting an entitlement with a liability rule will be particularly conducive to efficiency." Kraus (2000) goes on to explain that there are many reasons to expect that the assessment of compensation will be incorrect. The under-valuation bias discussed below indicates that his argument often applies for compulsory purchases by government.

The primary source of transactions costs that allegedly justify compulsory purchase for right-of-way properties is the so-called "holdout problem" (Posner 1977, pp. 40–41; Fischel 1995, p. 68; Miceli and Segerson 2000, p. 330). This problem is explained quite succinctly by Posner (1977, pp. 40–41):

> An economic reason for eminent domain [compulsory purchase], although one applicable to its use by railroads and other right-of-way companies rather than by government, is that it is necessary to prevent monopoly. Once the railroad or pipeline [or highway] has begun to build its line, the cost of abandoning it for an alternative route becomes very high. Knowing this, people owning land in the path of the advancing line will be tempted to hold out for a very high price—a price in excess of the actual opportunity cost of the land. The high cost of acquiring land will, by increasing the costs of right-of-way companies, induce them to raise the prices of their services; the higher prices will induce some consumers to shift to substitute services; the companies will therefore have a smaller output; and as a result the companies will need, and will purchase, less land than they would have purchased at prices equal to (or slightly above) the opportunity costs of the land. Furthermore, higher land prices will give the companies an incentive to substitute other inputs for some of the land that they would ordinarily purchase. As a result of these factors land that would have been more valuable to the right-of-way company than to its present owners remain in its existing, less valuable uses, and this is inefficient.

Indeed, a holdout problem can be so severe that it prevents the transfers of any property for a right-of-way. If land must be obtained from a large number of landowners who know about the intended purchase ahead of time, they will all want to be the last individual to sell in order to be in a monopoly position and extract the highest possible price. Such strategic behavior on the part of sellers means that the private buyer may expect the transactions costs to be so high that she gives up the effort and the road is never built. Thus, Fischel (1995, p. 68) suggests that "Preventing time-consuming strategic bargaining is an important justification for eminent domain."

Holdout incentives for sellers actually may be weaker than they are often assumed to be, however, particularly if an individual sells only part of his land for a road right-of-way. After all, the increase in the rental value of his remaining land due to proximity and access to the road easily can be substantially more than the price of the land that is sold for right-of-way (consider the amount of land that a developer often sets aside for roads that they also build, for instance, because good roads dramatically raise the value of the lots in the development). Thus, there clearly are strong incentives for many landowners to sell part of their land that can offset the incentives to hold out (e.g., see Engel et al. [2002]). In fact, history demonstrates that many landowners have voluntarily donated land for private sector highway right-of-ways for precisely this reason (Klein 1990). Private developers also frequently donate land to the state so it can build roads that connect their developments to public highways.

Further, note that Posner's description of the holdout problem explicitly assumes that there is only one right-of-way and that the project is begun before all of the land for the right-of-way is purchased. These two assumptions lead to the potential for a single seller to act like a monopolist because the buyer has no substitute to consider. If this is not the case, then, once again, holdouts may not be a serious concern, as Posner (1977, p. 43) observes. In this regard, for instance, Miceli and Segerson (2000, p. 330) note that the land could, in theory, be acquired prior to construction. They recognize, however, that when projects are publicly funded, plans are not likely to be kept secret until after the land is obtained because of the need to appropriate the funds (and, we might add, the prevalence of corruption as public officials sell information to speculators, etc.). On the other hand, they note that private developers who want to assemble large tracts of land do not have the power of compulsory purchase (except through manipulation of the political process), perhaps because it is "easier for them to acquire the property while disguising their ultimate intent, for example, through the use of 'dummy' buyers" (Miceli and Segerson 2000, p. 330). In other words, while Posner (1977, p. 41) explicitly recognizes that the economic justification for compulsory purchase based on the holdout problem actually is "applicable" to private purchasers of right-of-way "rather than the government," private sector purchasers of right-of-way are actually much more likely to avoid the problem than the government is.

Private buyers of multiple parcels can also make their deals much more quickly than public buyers. They do not have to get budgets approved by legislatures, deal with time-delaying statutory procedures, or operate under rules that limit the amount that they can pay on each piece of land (e.g., rules that constrain bureaucrats to paying assessed values, for instance). Therefore, the likelihood that a private firm's plans are going to be discovered is much lower than the similar plans by a government agency will be. Not surprisingly, private developers frequently consolidate large parcels of land without being held up (Starkie 1990).

A private buyer's secret efforts to obtain a right-of-way may be discovered, of course, and when this happens, holdout incentives can arise. Can such transactions costs be avoided? Landsburg (1993, p. 29) provides an interesting solution to what might appear initially to be an intractable problem analogous to the holdout problem by citing a situation from Joseph Conrad's novel, *Typhoon*. A number of sailors stored their gold coins in personal boxes in the ship's safe, but a severe storm caused the boxes to break open and all of the coins were mixed together. Everyone knew how many coins he had placed in the safe but no one knew how many the others had placed there. Therefore, everyone's incentive was to claim that they had more coins in the safe than they actually had and the problem for the captain was to determine how to divide the coins to give each sailor his actual savings. Landsburg's (1993, p. 29) proposed solution: "Have each sailor write down the number of coins he is entitled to. Collect the papers and distribute the coins. [*But*] Announce in advance that if the numbers on the papers don't add up to the correct total, you will throw all of the coins overboard." This clearly reduces, and perhaps eliminates the incentives to *holdout* for more coins than had actually been contributed.

A similar strategy might be used by the private buyer of a right-of-way, even if it is known that a highway is going to be constructed. Suppose, for instance, that the highway provider chooses more than one potential route. She then informs the landowners along the two routes that she would like to purchase specified parcels from each of them, and that each should submit the price at which they are willing to sell (alternatively she might make initial bids that can be accepted, but indicate that each seller has an opportunity to make one take-it-or-leave-it counter offer). In addition, potential sellers are informed that the buyer will only purchase the right-of-way that has the lowest total cost associated with it (a maximum might also be specified, and/or information provided about the total acreage required on each right-of-way). The precise nature of the strategy may be quite different than this, but the fact is that pipeline builders, for instance, "routinely consider alternative routes, negotiate with different groups of owners, and settle with the first group that comes up with an acceptable arrangement. Where buyers compete with competing groups of sellers, there is extra pressure on the sellers to agree to reasonable deals" (Roth 1996, p. 199). When a private buyer structures the bargain appropriately (e.g., by secretly buying land or by simultaneously considering alternative routes and buying the parcels only after every seller has agreed and before the project starts, by choosing routes where landowners only give up part of their land so they can collect rents on the rest, etc.), holdouts are not likely to prevent right-of-way acquisition. Indeed, as Roth (1996, p. 199) notes, the first two modern privately provided highways in the United States, the Dulles Greenway in Virginia and SR 91 in California, both obtained the land that they required from private landowners without relying on compulsory purchase, choosing instead to bargain (some properties were also in existing public roadway corridors that had to be obtained from governments).

Fischel (1995, p. 70), in criticizing arguments against the use of compulsory purchase, notes that the literature has not indicated how the holdout problem is to be dealt with, and suggests that the theoretical progress made regarding methods to induce people to reveal their preferences involve complicated voting rules. Similarly, Lazzarotti (1999) contends that, "without eminent domain, it would be virtually impossible to fathom an alternative means of establishing such a complex network of transportation as exists in this country." However, these arguments either presume that roads are provided by the government or that private entities will face the same holdout problems that government does. The fact is, however, that one reason for the failure of the literature to indicate how to resolve the holdout problem in right-of-way procurement is that the literature has not given sufficient consideration to the possibility of privatized highway and road systems. The presumption of theorists (as well as observers like Fischel and Lazzarotti) is that the government will provide roads and obtain right-of-way properties through compulsory purchase if the holdout problem prevents voluntary purchase, so there is no problem to resolve. However, if serious consideration is given to private road provision, potential solutions might be forthcoming quite quickly. Consider the growing literature on combinatorial auctions, for instance (see De Vries and Vohra [2001] for a review). Among the issues considered in this literature is the structure of auction methods that are employed to simultaneously buy or sell sets of assets that are complementary (and/or perhaps substitutable, e.g., for other sets of assets). Such auctions allow buyers to submit bids on groups of assets and make the purchase of each asset conditional on the purchase of the other complementary assets (and/or perhaps on the combined price being lower than that offered by a substitute bundle). Clearly, the parcels of land for a road right-of-way are complementary (and other the parcels in another potential right-of-way may be substitutes for a particular right-of-way). Alternatively, sellers of a set of complementary assets might offer a combined bundle of such assets to potential buyers (e.g., if a group of landowners wants to increase the rental value of their land they might offer a right-of-way to toll-road developers). Such auctions are in use in a number of areas, and several logistics consulting firms have produced software to implement complex combinatorial auctions. For example, several large firms (e.g., Sears, Walmart, Kmart, Ford Motor Company) use combinatorial auctions to select transportation carriers in order to construct routes that minimize costs by avoiding empty back hauls and other unnecessary costs. The fact is that actual market participants have discovered many ways to induce people to reveal their relative preferences in situations similar to those that would characterize right-of-way purchase by private firms, and this really is the relevant issue, even if theorists do not fully understand how these processes might be refined to accumulate the parcels needed for highway routes. Indeed, the growing literature on combinatorial auctions is developing as theorists are attempting to understand the actual processes that are already being implemented.

IV. Government Failure through Compulsory Purchase

In light of the preceding discussion, recall individual A introduced earlier who valued a parcel of land at $500,000. In the earlier hypothetical, A tried to obtain control of the land through voluntary bargaining but this is not his only choice. Assume that by spending $50,000 (e.g., on a lobbyist, a bribe, or some other method of influencing the city council) he is quite sure that he can get local government officials to decide that the business he is going to establish on the land is in the "public interest" because it will generate employment in the community and increase the tax base (see the discussion of the actual purposes of compulsory-purchase condemnations below where it becomes clear that this would be an adequate justification for such political action). He negotiates with the local officials who decide to condemn the land and sell it to him for $100,000—that is, below market value, because they are convinced (or claim to be convinced) that the project will benefit the community. The city's land appraiser determines that "fair compensation" for the parcel is $250,000 (after all, the assessor cannot determine B's actual subjective value; furthermore, as explained below, there is an under-valuation bias in such assessment processes), which is paid to B. The land, in this case, is still transferred to a higher valued use, but the transfer is not Pareto efficient because B, and the taxpayers who pay the $150,000 difference between the compensation payment and the sales price, are worse off. A is clearly much better off and we know that he could fully compensate B and the taxpayers for their losses if he wanted to (his decision to choose condemnation rather than bargaining suggests that he is not willing to, however). Thus, the "net" gain in social welfare is as large as it was under voluntary exchange but the gain is now distributed so unequally that the "transaction" now makes some people worse off. In this light, note that some economists suggest that the Pareto criterion is too constraining in the public policy arena and that an alternative, called Kaldor-Hicks efficiency (a transfer is said to be efficient if the gainers gain enough to compensate the losers, even if no compensation is paid), is preferable. Recognize, however, that if full compensation is not required when a "Kaldor-Hicks efficient" transfer is made through the government, then the incentives to bargain in the first place are weakened, as a subsidized political transfer is a more attractive option for the "buyer." Why bargain and pay for a property that can be obtained without full payment through the use of political influence (unless the political influence is more expensive than the property would be)? Furthermore, and importantly, under voluntary exchange we know that both parties are made better off by the exchange but there is no guarantee (not even an expectation) that land under compulsory purchase is actually moved to its highest valued use. The example just given, for instance, would work just as well if B valued the land at $550,000, in which case any forced exchange would fail even the Kaldor-Hicks test, and lower net welfare.

Can inefficient transfers be avoided by constraining the use of compulsory purchase powers to a limited set of circumstances? Suppose such purchases can only be made if the benefits to the "public" are clearly very large, for instance where sufficient compensation is paid to avoid making the individual worse off when her property is condemned (i.e., meeting the Pareto criterion). The United States Constitution's Fifth Amendment states, "nor shall private property be taken for *public use*, without *just compensation*" (emphasis added). Thus, it appears that the U.S. government's takings powers are constrained to "public use" purposes (presumably, uses with substantial benefits for many members of the public at large, as opposed to narrowly focused private uses) and that such takings must involve "just compensation." Since the United States Constitution is one of the most widely emulated constitutions in the world, and perhaps one of the most successful at constraining government action over a substantial period of time, let us consider the effectiveness of these constraints on transfer activity. After all, it would be surprising to find constitutional constraints on compulsory purchase in many other countries that are stronger than those that exist in the United States (indeed, in other parts of the world, weaker constraints on government probably mean that compulsory purchase is not used because arbitrary uncompensated takings are practiced instead). First, consider the way that "public use" has been interpreted by U.S. courts to see if it might prevent compulsory purchase for purposes that produce relatively small concentrated benefits and, after that, the "justness" of compensation will be examined.[9]

The Disappearance of the "Public Use" Constraint[10]

James Madison, who wrote the Fifth Amendment, and those who supported him, clearly hoped to restrict the takings behavior that had been going on in the colonies under British rule. Therefore, along with *just* compensation, the amendment explicitly requires that takings be for "public use" rather than public purpose, interest, benefit, or some other term. "Public use" was recognized at the time as a narrower and more objective requirement that such alternative terms might imply (Jones 2000, p. 290). Indeed, this wording was, at the time, conceived of as a strong constraint, since the Framers did not recognize a non-public authority in government; "an express prohibition on 'private' taking would [therefore] have been superfluous" (Jones 2000, p. 289, note 23).

Before 1875, all compulsory purchases in the United States were performed by state or local governments, and therefore, most early litigation over the constitutional limits implied by "public use" in the United States took place in state courts.[11] Evidence from this litigation illustrates that even though state constitutions had takings clauses similar to the U.S. Constitution's Fifth Amendment, there were two interpretations of public use across the states. The narrow interpretation required that the project for which the condemned property was used had to be open to the public (Jones 2000, p. 293), while the broader interpretation "equated *public use* with more nebulous terms such as *public advantage, public purpose, public benefit*, or *public welfare*" (Paul 1988, p. 93). States adopting this broader interpretation allowed transfers of condemned land to private commercial activities under the assumption that "the public" benefited from economic development (Jones 2000, p. 292). Thus, many states used compulsory purchase powers to transfer property from one private entity to another for a variety of private purposes. In other states, however, public use was interpreted by courts to mean "use by the public" (Paul 1988, p. 93).

When the United States Supreme Court began considering compulsory purchase issues, it adopted the narrow view of public use (Jones 2000, p. 292). In *Kohl v. United States* (91 U.S. 367 (1875)), the Court explicitly stated that this power could be used by "a sovereign to take private property for its own public use, and not for those of another" (at 373–374). Furthermore, in *Missouri Pacific Railway Co. v. Nebraska* (164 U.S. 403 (1896)), ruling on a condemnation of railroad property by the state of Nebraska in order to transfer it to a private grain elevator, the court concluded that the taking was an unconstitutional violation of the Due Process Clause of the Fourteenth Amendment, as well as being "in essence and effect, a taking of private property [for a] private use."[12] Two decades later, however, the court reversed itself. The opinion in *Mount Vernon-Woodberry Cotton Duck C. v. Alabama Interstate Power Co.* (240 U.S. 30 (1916)) explained that the Court would exercise great deference when reviewing a state court's findings regarding public use, and in *Old Dominion Land Co. v. United States* (269 U.S. 55 (1929)) the court began to suggest that it would exercise similar deference with regard to legislative decisions about public use. Indeed, a relatively broad definition was explicitly adopted in *Rindge C. v. Los Angeles County* (262 U.S. 700, 707 (1923)): "It is not essential that the entire community, nor even any considerable portion, should directly enjoy or participate in any improvement in order to constitute a public use."

United States ex re. TVA v. Welch (327 U.S. 546 (1946)) came close to withdrawing the federal court from even considering the question of public use when Justice Black wrote, "We think it is the function of Congress to decide what type of taking is for a public use and that the agency authorized to do the taking may do so to the full extent of its statutory authority" (at 551–552). Whatever limitation might have remained was severely undermined by Justice Douglas's decision in *Berman v. Parker* (348 U.S. 26 (1954)). The case involved a District of Columbia condemnation of land in areas of the city that were apparently dominated by slums, with the land subsequently transferred to private developers. The plaintiff owned a department store in one of the areas, and among other things, he objected to the fact that the seized property could be transferred to another private party who would then redevelop it and sell it for private gain. Douglas wrote, "The concept of the public welfare is broad and inclusive. . . . It is within the power of the legislature to determine that the community should be beautiful as well as healthy, spacious as well as clean, well balanced as well as carefully patrolled . . . there is nothing in the Fifth Amendment that stands in the way" (at 33). Paul (1988, p. 94) describes the implications of *Berman v. Parker* as follows:

> In a decision remarkable for its confusion of the central issues, Douglas and his colleagues concluded that the appellants' "innocuous and unoffending" property could be taken for the larger "public purpose" of remediating urban blight . . . traditionally the limitation on the exercise of the police power, the power of the states to regulate property, has been something called the "public purpose." This broad phase allows quite a wide range of state regulatory behavior . . . so long as they serve some loosely defined notion of the public purpose. . . . What Douglas accomplished by his confusion of the more permissive criterion of the police power's public purpose with eminent domain in *Berman v. Parker* was the application of the more permissive criterion of the police power's public purpose to eminent domain. Public use as a constraint on governmental seizures suffered a crippling blow as the result of Douglas's confusion.
> . . . If the legislature is "well nigh" the final arbiter of "public needs," then what is the purpose of the Bill of Rights or the Constitution? The Court apparently lost sight of the purposes behind the Fifth Amendment's property clauses: to limit congressional seizures of property, to place conditions on those seizures that are necessary for a "public use," and to protect individual property rights.

Similarly, Epstein (1985, p. 161) suggests that the public use constraint was given "a mortal blow in *Berman v. Parker* when [the Court] noted that 'the concept of the public welfare is broad and inclusive' enough to allow the use of the eminent domain power to achieve any end otherwise within the authority of Congress." The decision essentially implies that whatever the legislature says is a public purpose (which now is the meaning of public use) is a public purpose and this "opened a Pandora's Box of state interference with individual property rights" (Jones 2000, p. 294). If this decision did not completely eliminate the public use constraint, then subsequent decisions probably have.

Kulick (2000, p. 654) notes that the Supreme Court's treatment of the public use issue has been closely mirrored by the state courts,[13] and it certainly is clear that many state courts, now unconstrained by the federal Constitution's takings clause, have continued to find new kinds of private transfers that are seen as acceptable public uses.[14] One dramatic case occurred when the entire residential community of Poletown was condemned by the City of Detroit in order to provide land for General Motors Corporation to build a new assembly plant. This condemnation displaced 3,438 residents. The city paid $62 million dollars for the land, and another $138 million for other costs including improvements required by General Motors in order for it to establish the facility, for a total of $200 million in taxpayer outlays, and then the city resold it to General Motors for $8 million. The residents of Poletown sued, arguing that the takings did not constitute a public use. The City countered that massive unemployment was going to occur if the plant was not built (General Motors had announced the closing of its Detroit Cadillac and Fisher plants, with some 6,000 employees, but offered to build a new assembly plant if they could obtain a satisfactory 465-acre site in the city), so that was the alleged public-use justification for the transfer. The Michigan Supreme Court agreed with the City, stating that, "The legislature had determined that governmental action of the type contemplated here meets a public need and serves an essential public purpose. The Court's role after such a determination is made is limited" (*Poletown Neighborhood Council v. City of Detroit* (304 N.W. 2d 455 (1981) at 458). Strongly worded dissenting opinions in *Poletown* suggest some of the consequences: Justice Fitzgerald explained that, "The decision that the prospect of increased employment, tax revenue, and general economic stimulation makes a taking of private property for transfer to another private party sufficiently 'public' to authorize the use of the power of compulsory purchase means that there is virtually no limit to the use of condemnation to aid private businesses" (at 644); and Justice Ryan recognized that the majority had "seriously jeopardized the security of all private property ownership" (at 465). Yet, *Poletown* may actually involve more of a "public use" than some cases.

Jones (2000, pp. 296–297) notes that, "In *Hawaii Housing Authority v. Midkiff*, the United States Supreme Court dealt the public use requirement a final mortal wound." Hawaii passed a Land Reform Act that transferred property from private-land owners to the lessees of that land. While the Ninth Circuit Court of Appeals (*Hawaii Housing Authority v. Midkiff* (702 F.2d. at 798)) declared the Act to be "a naked attempt on the part of the state to take land from

A and give it to B solely for B's private use and benefit," the Supreme Court declared the Act to be Constitutional (*Hawaii Housing Authority v. Midkiff* (476 U.S. 229 (1984)). The Court ruled, once again, that if a legislature has determined that a compulsory purchase takings involves "a conceivable public purpose" then the public use requirement has been met. As Kulick (2000, p. 653) explains, "a legislature, under the Supreme Court's guidance from *Midkiff*, can legitimately effectuate public-private takings by merely making some legislative pronouncement that the taking will serve some public purpose or goal."[15] Clearly, there are no longer any significant constitutional barriers to government condemnation of lands in the United States,[16] if they can take land from landlords simply to transfer it to tenants.[17]

The demise of the public-use constraint is undesirable, and this can be seen from a number of perspectives (efficiency liberty, equity—e.g., Epstein [1985, 2001]; Paul [1988]; Jones [2000]; Kulick [2000]).[18] The focus here is on economic efficiency, however. One efficiency implication is that the lack of a public use constraint increases the chance that the benefits of an involuntary transfer will be less than the losses, implying inefficiency even with the weak Kaldor-Hicks efficiency standard, and clearly from a Pareto perspective, particularly if the individuals who lose their property are under-compensated. It might be contended that while the demise of the public-use constraint is problematic the issue does not really apply for privately provided roadways, since there clearly are significant public benefits from transportation improvements, but even if this is the case, the point is that the existence of a power of compulsory purchase to transfer property from one private enterprise to another has not been constrained to situations where the transfer clearly is efficient. Thus, from an efficiency perspective, the question of whether compulsory purchase to transfer property between private entities should be allowed for right-of-way acquisitions must be considered in the broader context: What is the net social benefit or cost of this power? After consideration of the "just compensation" constraint this question will be addressed.

The Systematic Under-Valuation Bias in Compulsory Purchases

The Fifth Amendment to the U.S. Constitution requires "just" compensation. The federal courts actually did not constrain state or local compensation awards in compulsory purchase situations at all, however, until the Fourteenth Amendment and its due process clause was adopted. Prior to that, the Supreme Court ruled that the Fifth Amendment's takings clause only applied to the federal government (*Baron v. Baltimore*, 7 Pet. 243, 247 (U.S. 1833)).[19] The Fourteenth Amendment states: ". . . nor shall any state deprive any person of life, liberty, or property without due process of law; nor deny any person within its jurisdiction the equal protection of the law." This suggests that at least some legislative actions and bureaucratic applications may not meet constitutional standards. Therefore, in *Chicago Burlington and Quincy Railroad Company v. Chicago* (166 U. S. 266 (1897)) the Supreme Court considered a claim that payment of just compensation for a takings was an essential ownership right, implying that any takings without such compensation was a violation of due process. The fact that the Supreme Court decided to consider this issue could have been important since it implied that state court decisions regarding compensation in compulsory purchase could be appealed to the federal level on due process grounds, suggesting a potential constraint on compensation assessments. However, the potential constraint did not materialize. The court ruled that it was improper for it to review state court rulings on matters of fact (under the Seventh Amendment), and that the Illinois court's conclusion that no significant property had been taken was an issue of fact, not law. The City of Chicago had opened a public street on the railroad's land and compensated it with a payment of one dollar, contending that no significant property had been taken because the land's railroad purposes were not impaired (ignoring the fact that the railroad erected a gateway to make the street crossing safe—the court ruled that "Such expenses must be regarded as incidental to the exercise of the police powers of the state").

The Supreme Court has considered federal, state, and local compulsory purchase compensation cases since *Chicago Burlington and Quincy Railroad Company v. Chicago* in 1897, of course, and shaped the law regarding just compensation, just as it has the public use requirement. First recognize that the concept of property (i.e. what really constitutes a takings) and just compensation are intertwined. Compensation could be generous, for instance, but if the definition of property is very narrow so most government actions that affect property uses and values are not considered to be significant takings (e.g., as in *Chicago Burlington and Quincy Railroad Company v. Chicago*), or are treated as police power actions that do not require compensation rather than compulsory purchase actions that do, then compensation will not be paid very often. In this regard, the U.S. Supreme Court's view of property appears to have broadened since 1897. Indeed, the Court has been quite explicit in some instances, stating that the meaning of property is not interpreted in the "vulgar and untechnical sense of the physical thing with respect to which citizens exercise rights recognized by law . . . [Property refers to] the group of rights inhering in the citizen's relation to the physical thing. . . . The constitutional provision is addressed to every sort of interest the citizen may possess" (*United States v. General Motors* 323 U.S. 373, 377–78 (1945)).[20]

In *Olson v. United States* (292 U.S. 246 (1934)), the Court explained that compensation should put an owner "in as good a position pecuniarily as if his property had not been taken. He must be made whole but is not entitled to more. It is the property and not the cost of it that is safeguarded by the state and federal constitutions." Epstein (1985, p. 182) notes that this is an appropriate standard from an economic perspective, as the Pareto criterion is met. If compensation really comes close to making the loser whole, however, then one must wonder why a voluntary exchange did not occur, either between the state and the property owner, or between two private parties. One obvious conclusion is that the compensation is actually less than what a willing seller would accept, as Epstein (1985) observes, because in reality courts do not follow this standard.[21] Instead, they have chosen to ignore subjective value in most cases. This stems from *Monongahela Navigation Co. v. United States* (148 U.S. 312 (1893), at 325–326) wherein the Supreme Court recognized that one of the important reasons for awarding "just compensation" is that "it prevents the public from loading upon one individual more than his just share of the burdens of government, and says that when he surrenders to the public something more and different from that which is exacted from other members of the public, a full and just equivalent shall be returned to him." Yet, the Court went on to hedge this statement by stressing that "this just compensation, it will be noticed, is for the property, and not the owner" (Id. at 326). This qualification has been interpreted to mean that the compensation is for the property taken, and not for losses to the owner that are a consequence of that taking (Epstein 2001, p. 12). In other words, any losses that are collateral to or a result of the taking of property are born by the landowner. In fact, while the *Monongahela* standard might still imply that the person whose property is taken is entitled to be compensated for losses in subjective value, subsequent interpretation has denied such an interpretation. For instance, in *United States v. 564.54 Acres of Land* (442 U.S. 506, 511 (1979)) the Court stated that "the owner is entitled to receive 'what a willing buyer would pay in cash to a willing seller' at the time of the taking."[22] However, as Epstein (2001, 12–13) explains,

> There is a good reason why "for sale" signs do not sprout from every front lawn in the Untied States. In a well ordered society most individuals are content with their personal living or business situation. They do not put their property up for sale because they do not think that there is any other person out there who is likely to value it for a sum greater than they do. In the normal case, use value is greater than exchange value, so the property is kept off the market. The use of the market value standard therefore results in a situation in which the party who owns the property, even if he shares in the social gain generated by the project, is still left worse off than his peers. He is forced to sacrifice the subjective values associated with his property, values which almost by definition he could not recreate through his next best use for the funds received. . . .

After all, an owner purchases property because she values it at more than the purchase price and/or holds onto the property because she places more value on it than the market price she could get for it. Thus, even an accurate assessment of market value "does not leave the owner indifferent between sale and condemnation" (Epstein 1985, p. 183). Indeed, the Court has explicitly recognized that compensations are lower than the level that would actually restore the landowner. In *Kimball Laundry v. United States* (338 U.S. 1 (1949)) Justice Frankfurter noted that "the value of property springs from subjective needs and attitudes; its value to the owner may therefore differ widely from its value to the taker. . . . In view, however, of the liability of all property to condemnation for the common good, loss to the owner of nontransferable values deriving from his unique need for property or idiosyncratic attachment to it, like loss due to an exercise of the police power, is properly treated as part of the burden of common citizenship." Thus, for instance, the laundry owner in *Kimball* could not recover for the dissipation of the "good will" that he had built up at his location because it was not transferred to the State (it was simply destroyed).

Clearly, "The disregard for non-market values . . . creates a systematic downward bias in the price paid in eminent domain proceedings" (Posner 1977, p. 43). Beyond that, the Supreme Court has frequently stated that the fair-market-value standard is not "absolute." In fact, a number of doctrines have been developed by the courts that allow compensation substantially below market value, and even lower than the owner actually paid for the property, thereby guaranteeing that compensation must be below the value that the owner places on the condemned property (e.g., *United State v. Commodities Trading Corp.*, 339 U.S. 121 (1950), and *United States v. Fuller* 409 U.S. 488 (1973)), creating incentives for under-valuation by condemning agencies.

Consider Vera Coking's situation. She had lived in her oceanfront home in Atlantic City for almost four decades when, in May of 1996, she received notice that her property had been condemned by the Casino Redevelopment Authority. She had ninety days to move so her land could be used by the Trump Plaza Hotel and Casino to build a parking area and put in a lawn. The "fair market value" of her home was appraised to be $251,250. However, she had actually turned down a $1,000,000 offer by another casino operator in 1983, suggesting that the actual market value was much higher than the assessed value, but still lower than Coking's personal subjective evaluation. This appraisal was quite consistent with other condemnation assessments done in the same community, however. For instance, a pawnshop that had recently been purchased by the owners for $500,000 (an obvious indicator of actual market value) was assessed at $174,000, and a neighboring restaurant was assessed at $700,000, a value that would not even cover the legal fees and start up costs for the restaurant owners to relocate. Of course, the victims of an under-compensated takings can sue in an effort to overturn the condemnation or increase the compensation (and the victims of the Atlantic City condemnations just mentioned have done so), but this is clearly a costly and time consuming process, with considerable risks involved. Thus, government authorities making the condemnations and assessments have strong incentives to under-value property, and this is a common practice (Starkman 2001). In fact, "initial compensation offers by the government often pale in comparison to the market value of the land" (Kulick 2000, p. 665, note 159) and compared to the value that the victim might ultimately receive through litigation. The recent Mississippi case mentioned above awarded a land owner $20,000 for his 1.6 acres seized in order to build a subsidized Nissan plant, which was more than double the state's highest offer of $9,200 (*Wall Street Journal: WSJ.com— From the Archives*, January 4, 2002). Of course, this landowner probably had to pay his lawyer around 40 percent of that award, so the actual gain from litigating was small, illustrating the disincentives associating with litigating and the bargaining power that compulsory purchase gives to the state.

Not surprisingly, "Once . . . subjective values are ignored [by the courts in setting rules for compensation in compulsory purchases], then institutionally, government behavior will take advantage of the background legal rules. The eminent domain power thus allows the state to push hard so that the landowner will take a price which is . . . lower than he would have taken in any voluntary exchange" (Epstein 2001, p. 7). Indeed, as a result of the bargaining power that compulsory purchase and the high cost of litigation give to government agencies, "government officials are becoming increasingly brazen in invoking eminent domain" to transfer land to private for-profit organizations (NCPA 2002, p. 1), in part because "many owners cave in to the pressure and settle" (Berliner 2002, p. 1). The fact is that the prospect (and expected costs) of fighting a threatened compulsory purchase through the courts in an effort to get more money than was offered by a government official can be sufficiently frightening for many individuals to induce people to accept substantially lower prices than they would otherwise be willing to take. Thus, there is an under-evaluation bias even for "voluntary" sales of property to the government, at least for individuals who do not have sufficient political influence to counter such a bargaining power advantage.

Inefficient Transfers Through Compulsory Purchase

As the public use constraint on compulsory purchase has disappeared, it has become easier for government to use this power to transfer land to other private entities, thus encouraging the use of the process by those with political power to gain wealth transfers for substantially less than they would have to pay through a voluntary purchase. This political transfer seeking activity, often called "rent seeking" (Kulick 2000, pp. 673–675),[23] can involve government condemnation of property for subsidized transfer to other private entities, after all. Recall the *Poletown* case, where the City of Detroit paid $200 million dollars for the condemned property and improvements to it, and then resold it to General Motors for $8 million. Or consider the more recent use of compulsory purchase to attract a Nissan plant to Mississippi, which included more than $300 million in subsidies and tax breaks along with condemnation of the property in question (*Wall Street Journal: WSJ.com—From the Archives*, January 4, 2002). This clearly creates excess demand for private-benefit condemnations relative to what would be necessary with a strong public use constraint. Subsidies also give the private recipient of the transfer a competitive advantage over others who have not obtained similar subsidies, creating incentives for everyone who may want to obtain property for a new, expanded, or relocated business to look seriously at the political process of condemnation as an alternative to direct bargaining.

Subsidies are often explicit, as in the *Poletown* example, but even if the recipient of a condemned property repays the full amount that the government pays as compensation, there is an implicit subsidy if the victim of the condemnation (or condemnation threat) is not fully compensated for subjective losses. In this regard, what apparently is the only empirical study of the use of compulsory purchase found that low valued parcels (that is, those most likely to belong to individuals with little political influence, in part because litigation costs are likely to limit the chances that such owners will challenge the payment) systematically received less than estimated market prices through compulsory purchase in Chicago's urban renewal program (Munch 1976, p. 473).[24] Clearly, such transfers are not efficient in a Pareto sense, and there is no way of knowing whether they are efficient in a Kaldor-Hicks sense. Indeed, as Epstein (2001, p. 6) notes, the under-compensation bias "has the unfortunate effect of inviting government initiatives that do not even meet the hypothetical compensation [Kaldor-Hicks] requirement." But inefficiencies from such transfers go well beyond those implied by under-compensation (Pareto inefficiency) or possibly a net reduction in "social welfare" (Kaldor-Hicks inefficiency) arising from the specific transfers of resources through compulsory purchase. "The inequitable treatment, of course, leads to profound allocative distortions: the lower prices stipulated by government lead to an excessive level of takings, and thereby alters for the worse the balance between public and private control" (Epstein 2001, p. 15).

Government Failure: The Costs of Involuntary Transfers

Political wealth transfers reduce wealth (i.e., are inefficient) for at least five reasons. First, involuntary transfers (e.g., through regulations under the police powers, through condemnation and reallocation of property, as in *Poletown*) generally produce deadweight losses (e.g., a net reduction in wealth). For instance, when explicit subsidies such as those in Detroit (*Poletown*) or implicit subsidies due to under-valuation are implemented, they "encourage economic markets to operate in an economically inefficient state by lowering the cost for firms to purchase property for corporate activities" (Kulick 2000, p. 662). Standard neoclassical production theory suggests that a subsidy to a producer in obtaining a particular input (e.g., land) leads to inefficient over-use of the subsidized input relative to other inputs (e.g., in the Mississippi-Nissan arrangement mentioned above, the Mississippi Supreme Court actually ruled that the state may have taken more land than it needed to in order to meet the alleged public use), and therefore, to inefficient input combinations. These inefficient methods of production mean that less is produced given the true opportunity cost of production than could be for the same expenditures if the prices paid for resources reflected full opportunity costs—there is a "deadweight loss" to society because resources are allocated inefficiently.

Second, Tullock (1967) explains that the resources consumed in the process of seeking such transfers also have opportunity costs. He emphasizes the striking analogy between monopoly achieved through regulation, tariffs achieved through legislation, and theft. Thieves use resources, particularly their time, in order to steal, and potential victims employ resources (e.g., locks, alarms, private security, public police) in an effort to deter or prevent theft. Tullock then points out that precisely the same analysis applies to the political transfer process, or what has come to be known as "rent seeking" (Krueger 1974). Some individuals and groups expend resources (e.g., time to organize interest groups, lobbyists, investments in political campaigns to exchange support for those who have the discretionary power to create transfers) in an effort to gain wealth in the form of subsidies or artificial rents created by government actions (e.g., monopoly franchises, licenses, quotas, tariffs), and others expend resources in an effort to defend against such transfers. These rent-avoidance costs, arising through investments in political information and influence by potential losers in the political transfer process, can be considered as a third source of costs arising in the involuntary transfer process. Because resources used in both rent seeking and rent avoidance have opportunity costs (they could be used to produce new wealth rather than to transfer existing wealth), they are "wasted" (Tullock 1967, Krueger 1974). Yet, individuals and groups have incentives to invest time and resources in an effort to gain wealth through the political process if the net gains are expected to be greater for them (but not for "society") than they can obtain through investments of the resources they control in actual wealth creation alternatives. Clearly, the use of condemnation powers to provide subsidized transfers of property from one private entity to another is part of this rent-seeking process.

Exit is another option for potential victims, perhaps by moving to an alternative political jurisdiction or by hiding economic activity and wealth (e.g., moving transactions underground into black markets). While immobile resources like land cannot be hidden in a gross sense, many attributes of land can be hidden (or destroyed) in order to make it less attractive for taking. Rapid development or exploitation of land might be attractive, for instance, if an undercompensated transfer (or regulatory taking) is anticipated, perhaps because such development eliminates, or at least raises the cost of achieving, alternative potentially more valuable future uses that make the land attractive for seizure. Essentially, the incentives are to capture whatever benefits from the property can be extracted relatively quickly before the property is taken away (or before police powers are exercised through zoning or some other regulatory process that attenuates use rights). Therefore, a landholder might develop (e.g., create a residential or commercial development) or exploit the property (e.g., plant crops that consume the soil's nutrients, harvest its trees and/or minerals) much more quickly than she otherwise would, even though greater benefits potentially exist from later development or exploitation. In order to reduce such "exit" actions and induce compliance with discriminatory transfer rules, other rules are likely to develop, and furthermore the rule makers will generally have to rely on courts and bureaucracies to implement and enforce the myriad of rules that are produced. For example, governments all over the United States have created or are creating development authorities, zoning commissions, growth-management commissions, environmental authorities, and other agencies in order to implement controls on land use. Furthermore, lawyers representing landowners, developers, and government authorities are involved in millions of hours of negotiation and litigation, experts (e.g., assessors), landowners, and many other parties devote many more hours in control and compliance costs, and so on. These implementation, enforcement, and compliance costs are a fourth source of opportunity costs that accompany an involuntary wealth transfer process.[25]

The fifth source of costs may be the most significant. The takings power (including police powers and the power of compulsory purchase) undermines the security of private property rights (Kulick 2000, p. 663), and importantly, insecure private property rights result in the same kinds of "tragedies" as those that arise in a common pool: rapid use (as suggested above) along with undermaintenance of resources relative to the efficient level of conservation.[26] The more frequent and arbitrary transfers are expected to be, the more significant these costs become. The trends in the use or threatened use of compulsory purchase discussed above suggest that this power is being used increasingly frequently and arbitrarily in the United States, although perhaps these actions might not have a tremendous impact on property rights security in the United

States, at least by themselves. When they are put into the context of overall trends in government takings (e.g., through regulatory actions under the police powers), however, it is clear that property rights to land in the United States are becoming less secure. And importantly, compared to much of the rest of the world where the use of government powers is substantially more arbitrary (i.e., less likely to produce net benefits for citizens) and where under-compensation is even more likely, property rights due to takings powers would appear to be very insecure.[27]

Clearly, government takings powers have substantial costs. Indeed, as Epstein (2001, p. 18) concludes, "The consequences are quite sobering. Whatever the theoretical promise of taking property only with compensation, that gain has been nullified in large measure [if not entirely] by the troubling circumstances of its application." Therefore, any justification for such powers (e.g., the holdout problem that may prevent obtaining a right-of-way) that does not also recognize the potential government failure consequences when such powers exist should be questioned.

V. Conclusions

Epstein (1993, p. 4) contends that "the government *must* establish the legitimacy of its taking in order to legitimate its subsequent transfers of the property taken. Otherwise it is little better than the thief who attempts to convey good title to a third person" (emphasis added). Criticism of uses of compulsory purchase powers are widespread and growing, suggesting that in practice at least, the legitimacy of this power is not being established.[28] Nonetheless, even many of the strongest critics of compulsory purchase practices do not conclude that this power should be withdrawn from the government. Jones (2000, p. 286) writes that, "The power of eminent domain is a fundamental and necessary attribute of government," and Epstein (1985, p. 4) contends that, "The formation and operation of the state, moreover, requires transferring resources from private to public use. Yet the power in the state to take for public use arises because the state will not obtain the resources needed to cooperate by voluntary donation or exchange . . . these exchanges do not occur voluntarily and must therefore be coerced." By accepting the theoretical arguments that (1) the government must be the provider of various goods and services such as roads, and that (2) transactions such as the holdout problem will prevent the government from obtaining the resources (e.g., right-of-way properties required to produce those goods and services), the only option left for such critics is to suggest that the government must somehow be more constrained in its use of compulsory purchase powers. Therefore, Epstein (1985, p. 4) contends that, "It becomes critical to regulate the terms on which the [involuntary] exchanges take place"; sixteen years later he still argues that while he is "sufficiently skeptical about the practical success of the constitutional program of forced exchanges to favor a sharp curtailment of the eminent domain process even when full compensation is paid," because he recognizes that "public virtue is a scarce commodity . . .," he favors "a higher level of judicial scrutiny of legislative action to improve the odds of securing limited government by constitutional means" (Epstein 2001, pp. 6 and 33). Similarly, Paul (1988, p. 266), Jones (2000, pp. 305–314), and Kulick (2000, pp. 679–691) propose much stricter public use interpretations by courts rather than stronger constitutional constraints that eliminate the government's power to force involuntary transfers of property. Posner (1977, p. 44) is much more circumspect, however, explaining that while it is easy to identify ways in which the compulsory purchase process clearly could be improved, even if such reforms are adopted,

> the system would be a poor approximation to market transactions . . . and, as a practical matter, they are perhaps no more likely to be adopted than eminent domain is likely to be limited to *the only case in which it is conceivably warranted* on economic grounds: where the need to assemble contiguous parcels creates a *holdout problem*. Even in that case, the argument for eminent domain is *hardly conclusive*. Shopping-center developers—among many other parcel assemblers who do not enjoy eminent domain powers—manage to overcome holdout problems by devices such as option contracts and dummy purchasers. Experiences with these market alternatives to eminent domain must be studied carefully before compulsory purchase can be adjudged the superior alternative. (Emphasis added)

In light of this suggestion, the preceding presentation has examined "the only case in which [compulsory purchase] is conceivably warranted [but] . . . hardly conclusive." First, it was suggested that members of the private sector are willing and able to provide roads if they are allowed to, particularly if they are allowed to make a profit. Then it was contended that the private sector is much more effective at overcoming the holdout problem than government is, so private provision of roads at least (and the same is probably true of many other purposes to which compulsory purchase has been used) is actually likely to be accomplished relatively efficiently with no compulsory purchase powers whatsoever. Finally, the level of government failure in the United States associated with government takings, including compulsory purchases, was considered. The fact is that what may be the most effectively constrained constitutional government in the world has seen the constraints on takings gradually undermined so that today, the costs of government failure are rising continuously. Therefore, even if some roads are relatively expensive or not built at all due to holdout problems, the consequences are likely to be much less severe than the costs arising from government failure. Granting government the power of compulsory purchase does not appear to be the "superior alternative," at least from an economic perspective.[29] Some readers may counter that even if the arguments made here are valid (e.g., private producers will more efficiently provide roads than the government does, holdout problems will not be severe for private road providers, government failure is enhanced by compulsory purchase powers), they are incomplete, because roads are not the only purpose for such powers. Other vital government purchases in national defense, environmental and historical preservation, or public health may not be accomplished without such powers. While this may be true, Posner suggests that merely claiming it is not enough—"market alternatives to compulsory purchase must be studied carefully before compulsory purchase can be adjudged the superior alternative." Admittedly, this presentation does not do so, but its objectives are actually much more modest: to demonstrate that the holdout problem does not provide a justification for public road provision or even for compulsory purchase powers in order to obtain right-of-way properties for privately provided roads. In making this more modest point, however, serious questions about the presumed legitimacy of compulsory purchase powers in general were raised.

Despite Epstein's (1993, p. 4) contention that legitimization "must" be provided for compulsory purchase, this refutation of the legitimacy of compulsory purchase runs up against the reality that governments need only respond satisfactorily to those with political power. If the "third persons" that must be convinced of the justification of takings and transfers are those with sufficient influence to receive the transfers, then the fact that the government is no better "than the thief who attempts to convey good title to a third person" is both true and of little consequence when it comes to trying to make the system more efficient.

Notes

1. In the United States the power to force a private property holder to sell property to a government entity (federal, state, or local government agency) is called eminent domain, but this term is not widely used or recognized in other parts of the world, so the more general term, compulsory purchase, is used in the following presentation, except where eminent domain appears in quotes from other sources.
2. There are other alleged justifications for public roads as well. Perhaps the primary one, at least from a theoretical perspective, is the public-good/free-rider argument, which implies that coercive taxing is needed to pay for roads, and therefore, that the private sector can not provide an efficient supply of roads. This argument is rejected in my other chapter (11) in this volume as well as in Benson (1994). Indeed, private provision of roads is common, as noted below and elsewhere in this volume. Also see Roth (1996, pp. 196–207) for discussion of fallacies in other objections to privately provided roads (justifications for public roads).

3. While there is a substantial literature on such "takings," most of it does not question the validity of government's power to do so. Instead, the literature focuses on three issues that arise given that the government has such powers: (1) what constitutes a legitimate public purpose (an issue discussed in Section II), (2) what constitutes a property takings (that is, where is the boundary between police powers and the power of compulsory purchase, since compulsory purchase requires compensation while police powers do not), and (3) what factors should be considered in determining "fair" compensation. As Paul (1988, pp. 5–6) suggests, however, these issues are secondary to a more fundamental question: Is the power of compulsory purchase (and police powers in general) justifiable?

4. After all, government failure in transportation policy is quite apparent (Winston 2000). Simply examine the level of traffic congestion in most urban areas of the United States, the United Kingdom, or numerous other parts of the world (e.g., consider Seoul, Korea's congestion problems). Winston (2000, p. 2) points out that while transportation "experts" advocate more "efficient" polices such as congestion charges, it is actually "futile to expect public officials to consider such changes because urban transportation policy is largely shaped by entrenched political forces. The forces that have led to inefficient prices and services, excessive labor costs, bloated bureaucracies, and construction-cost overruns promise more of the same in the future. The only realistic way to improve the system is to shield it from those influences and expose it to market forces by privatizing it. Preliminary evidence for the United Kingdom and elsewhere suggests that although a private urban transportation sector should not be expected to perform flawlessly, it could eliminate most government failures and allow innovation and state-of-the-art technology to flourish free of government interference."

5. Of course, someone else may value the land even more, but if this is the case that person should bid more for it. *Competitive bidding should lead to exchanges that result in assets being allocated to their highest valued use* unless something prevents such an exchange (an issue addressed below). This is clearly one reason to encourage both competition to engage in exchanges, and voluntary exchange.

6. Naturally, fraud can lead to non-Pareto improving exchanges, so trust or recourse (e.g., to a legal system) are required to alleviate this problem when there are significant asymmetries in information (Benson 2001). Problems may also arise if there are significant non-pecuniary externalities to the exchange.

7. An entitlement is inalienable to the extent that its transfer is not permitted at all, even from a willing seller to a willing buyer. In other words, the asset is not truly private property. The holder has use rights but does not have the right to alienate.

8. Also see, for example, Polinsky (1980, p. 1111) and Krier and Schwab (1995, p. 45).

9. Other constitutional constraints also were created. For instance, the clauses in Article 1 of the United States Constitution (one of the sections of the Constitution from which the power of compulsory purchase is inferred, as explained below) appear to limit federal takings by requiring the "Consent of the Legislature of the State" in which the property is located. This constraint probably raised the cost of federal seizures somewhat (the states faced no such constraint, however) and limited its use for several decades until the Supreme Court eliminated the constraint in *Kohl v. United States* (91 U.S. 367 (1875)), wherein the federal government was determined to have the power to directly take property in its own name. Prior to this case (which arose because Congress authorized the secretary of the treasury to acquire land in Cincinnati for a public building and federal officials condemned

the land directly rather than obtaining it through state condemnation or voluntary exchange), the federal government had only condemned land through the intermediary of the state government. But as Paul (1988, p. 73) explains, "Justice Strong deduced a federal power to condemn in its own name both from the very nature of sovereignty and, more concretely, from the Fifth Amendment's taking clause. . . . The latter inference was, undoubtedly, inventive. The requirement that the government must pay compensation when it takes was construed to imply a power to take in the first place. This clause, as virtually all commentators agree, is a restriction on government's powers, not a concession."

Today the compulsory purchase power is generally assumed to be implied by such clauses as 7 and 17 of Article 1, Section 8, which give Congress the authority to establish post offices and post roads, and over property purchased for forts, arsenals, and other such facilities, as well as the takings clause of the Fifth Amendment quoted above (Paul 1988, p. 73). In this context, however, one of the arguments against including the Bill of Rights raised by Alexander Hamilton was that "it would contain various exceptions to power which are not granted" (*The Federalist*, No. 84, as edited by B. F. Wright 1961, p. 404). Indeed, some of the founding fathers actually argued for an explicit recognition of private property rights that could not be taken by the government. For instance, Thomas Jefferson contended that all remnants of feudalism in regard to property should be eliminated. Recognize that the feudal underpinnings of the common law of property, including the law of compulsory purchase, were transplanted into the American colonies from Great Britain. Under feudalism, private individuals might "own" land but they did so at the discretion of the king, essentially acting as stewards of the land as the king (and later parliament) could dispossess them if he chose to do so (Benson 2002), although it was also customary to compensate the landowners for the condemned property. Jefferson vigorously pushed for allodial ownership wherein landowners would hold absolute dominion over their property. In other words, he contended that landholders should not be treated as stewards, with property ultimately allocated of the prerogative of the government (Paul 1988, p. 9). He felt that if the government was considered to be the ultimate owner of land, freedom could not be secure, as the state would be in a position to reduce men to poverty or even serfdom. Others obviously had a different view, of course.

10. This subsection draws heavily from Paul (1988), Jones (2000), and Kulick (2000). For similar analysis and conclusions regarding the public-use issue and police powers, see Epstein (1985, pp. 161–181).

11. See note 9 for an indication of why this was the practice even for compulsory purchases of properties to be used for federal purposes.

12. Such rulings were consistent with earlier Supreme Court views of constitutional constraints. For instance, in *Calder v. Bull* (3 U.S. 386, 388 (1798)) the court stated that there "are acts which the Federal or State Legislature cannot do, without exceeding their authority. There are certain vital principles in our free Republican Governments, which will determine and overrule an apparent and flagrant abuse of legislative power . . . [For example, a] law that punishes a citizen for innocent action . . . a law that destroys, or impairs, the lawful private contracts of citizens . . . *or a law that takes property from A and gives it to B*: it is against all reason and justice, for people to entrust a Legislature with such powers" (emphasis added).

13. Some state courts continued to employ a stricter public use interpretation, however, at least for a while. See for instance, *Baycol. v. Downtown Development Authority* (315 So.2d 451 (Fla. 1975)) and *In re City of Seattle* (638 P.2d 549 (1981)).

14. For example, see *People ex rel. City of Urbana v. Paley* (368 N.E. 2d 915 (1977)) from Illinois recognizing the stimulation of economic growth as a valid public purpose; *Courtesy Sandwich Shop Inc. v. Port of New York Authority* (190 N.E. 2d 402, appeal dismissed, 375 U.S. 78 (1963)) regarding the condemnation of property in order to build the World Trade Center with its public purpose of increasing the flow of commerce; *Sun Co. v. City of Syracuse Indus. Dev. Agency* (209 A.D.2d 34 (N.Y. App. Div. 1995)) approving a condemnation in order to make way for a shopping mall; *NL Indus. v. Eisenman Chem. Co.* (645 P.2d 976 (Nev. 1982)) approving a takings to support an "important" industry for the region; *Prince George's County v. Collington Crossroads Inc.* (339 A.2d 278 (Md. 1975)) where the economic benefits from a particular industrial development project were seen as a sufficient public purpose; and so on. See Berliner (2002) for discussion of some of the condemnations that have occurred during the last few years.

15. Since *Midkiff* the Supreme Court has reconfirmed the same public use standard (or perhaps non-standard would be more appropriate). See *National R..R. Passenger Corp. v. Boston & Maine Corp.* 503 U.S. 407, 422 (1992).

16. Indeed, the supposed freedom of religion constraint on government does not even prevent compulsory purchase. Cypress, California condemned land belonging to the Cottonwood Christian Center on May 28, 2002 in order to provide it to Costco for a retail center (Austin 2002), for example. Similarly, in New Cassel, New York, the North Hempstead Community Development Agency seized land owned by St. Luke's Pentecostal Church, land that was to be used to construct a new church (Berliner 2002). The land was condemned in order to provide it to a private retail developer (the condemnation decision was actually made in 1994, before the church purchased the property, but neither the church nor the previous owner had been informed of the decision to transfer the land).

17. Some have suggested that the public use requirement is now being strengthened, however, citing, for instance, that the New Jersey Superior Court ruled, in 1998, that the Casino Redevelopment Authority's condemnation and transfer of a residence to the Trump Plaza Hotel and Casino was not legal (*Casino Redevelopment Authority v. Banin*, 727 A. 2d 102 (N.J. Sup. 1998)), and this decision has been cited by some at least as a more "rational basis for review with a bite" (Kulick [2000, p. 661]); also see Mansnerus (2001) and Starkman (2001) for popular press reports of change. The alleged purpose of the transfer was to build a parking area and lawn ("green space" according to the documents) for the Trump casino, and this (along with the "alleviation of traffic congestion") was sufficient justification for "a conclusion that the primary purpose . . . is a public one." However, there was no contractual restriction guaranteeing that the land would actually be used for the proposed purpose. The implication of the ruling was that the Authority and Trump had to start over and include restrictions in the transferred deed that would prevent Trump from changing the use of the property, at least for a reasonable amount of time, after it was transferred. This case is discussed further below. A Connecticut state judge struck down the condemnation of eleven homes in New London for a similar reason—the authority that had condemned the property was not explicit enough in stating what it was going to do with the land (Starkman 2002). The U.S.

Supreme Court recently considered this condemnation, however, and approved it (*Susette Kelo et al., Petitioners v. City of New London, Connecticut et al.,* 125 S. Ct. 2655; 162 L. Ed. 2d 439; 2005 U.S. Lexis 5011).

The Mississippi Development Authority's condemnation of 30 acres of residential property for a parking lot to be part of a 1400-acre Nissan plant project has been challenged and the Mississippi Supreme Court issued a stay blocking the condemnation in May of 2001 (Starkman 2001). Again, the Court did not rule against the alleged public purpose, finding instead, the Authority may have taken more land than it needed to in order to meet the public use. This was actually a small part of a large financial deal with Nissan that included more than $300 million in subsidies and tax breaks along with a pledge by the Authority to "quick-take" the property in question so Nissan could build a parking lot near the factory, but the executive director of the Development Authority admitted that it did not actually have to seize the land in order to ensure that the factory would be built (*Wall Street Journal: WSJ.com—From the Archives*, January 4, 2002).

Two recent state court cases also appear to be attempting to reinstate some form of public use constraint. First, in June of 2000, a California Court blocked a compulsory purchase condemnation that had previously been rescinded by the City of Lancaster, California (the plaintiff pursued the case even after the rescind order, fearing that the City might reverse itself again). This case, discussed by Starkman (2001), involved condemnation of space within a shopping center that was occupied by a "99 Cents Only Store" (one of a 110-store discount chain) in order to transfer it to a major competitor, Costco Wholesale Corporation. Costco was the mall's anchor and had been in place about ten years, while 99 Cents Only had moved into the mall in 1998. At that point Costco told the city it needed to expand and it demanded the 99 Cents Only Store's space, threatening to move to a mall in a nearby town if it did not get the space. The City manager informed 99 Cents Only that it would have to move and in June of 2000 its site was condemned. The alleged public purpose was to avoid the "future blight" that would arise if Costco left. The Court characterized the condemnation as "nothing more than the desire to achieve the naked transfer from one private party to another" and concluded that, "Such conduct amounts to an unconstitutional taking purely for private purposes." Of course, that does not matter under the *Midkiff* standard, and the City has announced that it will appeal, with the City attorney pointing out that "99 Cents produces less that $40,000 [per year] in sales taxes, and Costco was producing more than $400,000. You tell me which was more important." That may well be a sufficient argument for a public purpose upon appeal. Similarly, Starkman (2002) explains that the Illinois Supreme Court just struck down the condemnation by the Southwestern Illinois Development Authority (*Southwestern Illinois Dev. Auth. v. National City Environmental* (Ill. 2002)) of property belonging to a metal recycling plant that was to be used to "reduce traffic congestion" by serving as a parking lot for the Gateway International Raceway. The majority ruled that the condemnation's primary purpose was to serve the private interests of the race track owners and that "Using the power of government for purely private purposes to allow Gateway to avoid the open real-estate market and expand its facilities in a more cost-efficient manner, thus maximizing corporate profits, is a misuse of the power entrusted by the public" (Quoted in Starkman 2002, p. 2). There was a lengthy dissent by two justices, however, contending that this was a proper public use, and the Southwestern Illinois Development Authority is seriously considering an appeal to the U.S. Supreme Court. Therefore, it may be a while before this potential rein-statement of a public use constraint can be counted on (and then it probably will only hold in Illinois).

18. This conclusion is far from universally accepted of course. For instance, Fischel (1995, p. 74) contends that the broad interpretation of public use is desirable, in part because he sees two other constraints on the use of compulsory purchase. One is that the transactions costs of using it are high, so the "budget-preserving instincts of gov-ernment agencies may usually be depended upon to limit eminent domain," and the other is that the use of compulsory purchase to transfer property for private uses "are also limited by popular revulsion at the government's action." The Constitution is suppose to protect people even when there is not a "popular revulsion" however (i.e., even when the majority supports some action that harms a minority) so it is presum-ably supposed to be a stronger constraint than popular beliefs. Moreover, the budget preserving tendency is not a relevant constraint when powerful political interests are seeking benefits through the political process, particularly if the "fair compensation" constraint is also relatively weak (in addition, revenues matter—see the discussion in note 16, where a condemnation of one business to help another was motivated, at least in part, by fear of losing sales tax revenues). Finally, some bureaucracies have found ways to actually enhance their budgets through compulsory purchase. Recall the Southwestern Illinois Development Authority's seizure for Gateway International Raceway discussed in note 16. Gateway used the Development Authority's standard "application form" for seeking a condemnation for "private use" and paid the $2,500 application fee. The authority also charged a percentage commission for the land: $56,500, a sum greater than the Authority's appropriated budget (officials from the Authority also got free tickets to Gateway events) (Berliner 2002, p. 3).

19. The only other compulsory purchase case to reach the Supreme Court during the first several decades of the country's existence was *West River Bridge v. Dix* (6 How. 507 (U.S. 1848)), but that case was based on Article 1, Section 10 of the Con-stitution where the states are barred from impairing the obligation of contracts. This case is interesting in the context of the privately provided roads issue because it involved a privately operated bridge. Vermont had granted an exclusive franchise to operate a bridge for 100 years. The private firm was clearly willing to operate the bridge, but the state decided to take it over anyway. West River Bridge sued, con-tending that the franchise charter was a contract, and while the Supreme Court agreed that the charter was a contract, it ruled that the state's breach and seizure of the bridge did not violate Article I, Section 10. Instead, the court stated that the state's compulsory purchase powers were "paramount to all private rights vested under the government, and these last are by necessary implication, held in subor-dination to this power, and must yield in every instance to its proper exercise." In other words, contracts, including contracts entered into by a state legislature, can be taken through compulsory purchase, "a rather odd conclusion, one among many that served to eviscerate the contract clause, while strengthening the states' power to take all kinds of interests in property" (Paul 1988, p. 78).

20. Some relatively recent Supreme Court decisions also appear to be broadening the concept of property rights takings that require at least some compensation (e.g., *Lucas v. South Carolina Coastal Council*), but the overall trend in such require-ments is far from clear, particularly given the decision in *Tahoe-Sierra Preserva-tion Council v. Tahoe Regional Planning Agency Planning Agency* (2002). See Greenhouse (2002) for discussion. Also see Paul (1988, pp. 82–91).

21. Another conclusion addressed above is that transactions costs prevent bargaining, but the answer suggested here clearly is relevant in many cases. After all, "abuses in practice are legion" (Paul 1988, p. 81). Furthermore, many loses are still considered to be "incidental," as in *Chicago Burlington and Quincy Railroad Company v. Chicago*. In *United States v. General Motors* the Court ruled that the loss of business goodwill or other injury to a business is not recoverable. Other losses that the Court considers to be unrecoverable included future loss of profits and the expenses associated with removing fixtures or personal property from the condemned property (even though expenses for moving are supposedly recoverable). As Paul (1988, p. 165) explains, "the Court reasoning is that such losses would be the same as might ensue upon the sale of property to a private buyer . . . because when business persons sell their buildings . . . they have presumably factored in these ancillary costs and found the deals satisfactory despite such costs. No such assumption, of course, can be made where the government forcibly takes property . . . over the owner's objection . . . and, indeed, the opposite assumption is far more likely." The Court actually recognized this, however, when it stated that, "No doubt all those elements would be considered by an owner in determining whether, and at what price, to sell. No doubt, therefore, if the owner is to be made whole for the loss consequent of the sovereigns' seizure of his property, these elements should properly be considered. But the courts have generally held that they are not to be reckoned as part of the compensation for the fee taken by the government" (p. 379). In other words, in the past such property takings have not been compensated for, so compensation is not required. As a result, losses arising in many condemnations are considered to be incidental due to the interpretation of "property," and therefore, not warranting compensation.

22. The opinion quotes an earlier ruling, *United States v. Miller* (317 U.S. 369, 374 (1943)), which stated this market value rule.

23. This rent-seeking process and its consequences are discussed in more detail below.

24. Individuals who have political connections are not likely to suffer such losses, however. In the empirical study of compulsory purchase practices in Chicago's urban renewal program, high valued parcels (e.g., those owned by individuals who probably had political clout, in part at least, because of their financial capacity and incentives to challenge payments through litigation) were systematically paid more than estimated market prices (Munch 1976, p. 473). This problem of discriminatory pricing based on political influence is inevitable given the flexibility of the assessment standards and the ease with which some (but not all) individuals and groups are able to influence political decisions.

25. Rules that facilitate voluntary production and exchange (e.g., private property rights, enforceable contracts) also require some enforcement costs, of course, but the level of these costs (e.g., litigation costs, assessment costs, policing costs that arise when individuals attempt to hide their wealth) increases dramatically when laws are also imposed in order to generate involuntary wealth transfers.

26. When a number of people have free access to a resource (e.g., to a pasture to graze their cattle, a fishery, an urban highway), each individual has an incentive to use up as much of the resource as possible before other users do the same. Therefore, the commons becomes crowded (e.g., with cattle or fishermen or cars) and the resource (grass land, fish stock, highway) deteriorates in quality as the result of over-use (over-grazing, over-fishing, traffic congestion). Each user has an incen-

tive to use the resource because she is not fully liable for the cost of doing so. Part of the cost is born by others. None have incentives to reduce their use (the size of their herds, their fishing catch, their highway trips) or to consider other means of maintaining them (for example, by supplementing the grass with feed grown on their private property, privately farming fish, or car pooling). So all of those with access try to use up the resource before someone else does, and the commons deteriorates, perhaps even being destroyed. Contrast this with private property (a private pasture, a fish farm, a private road). If an individual owner overuses his resource he bears the full costs of that action. His resource deteriorates in quality and loses its long run productive value. Therefore, the private owner has incentives to conserve his property so that it can be used to generate income or other benefits over a long period. Crowding is not the only consequence of free access, however. When a resource is overused, it rapidly deteriorates in quality and is used up inefficiently so that the quality of the output (fatter, healthier cattle, the size of fish, travel time, and convenience) diminishes rapidly over time. This could be offset with appropriate investments in maintenance or improvement (e.g., the grass might be fertilized or replanted, a fishery could be restocked, or people could car pool), but the individuals with common access to the resource do not have incentives to invest in maintenance, because they cannot exclude others from benefiting from such an investment (other people's cattle will consume part of the new grass, other fishermen will catch part of the new fish, and other drivers will add trips on the highway). Therefore, there are two characteristics of common pool resources that prevent a Pareto solution. First, since users do not pay for the use of the resource they tend to overuse it. The costs of this overuse are external to the individual decision-makers as they are shared with (imposed on) others. Second, since others cannot be excluded from benefits of investing in maintenance or improvements that would increase the productivity of the resource, these benefits are external to the decision-maker and there is an under-investment in such activities. In essence, the investment in the maintenance of public, common access property generates external benefits. This has been called the tragedy of the commons, a concept originally attributed to biologist Garrett Hardin (1968). The classic treatment of the subject in economics is by Gordon (1954), but substantial research supports the hypothesis (e.g., see Libecap [1984], Johnson and Libecap [1982]). Also see Benson (1996) for a discussion of the consequences of changes in law that reduce the security of property rights and produce results analogous to those in a commons.

27. When property rights are relatively insecure, bargaining is also less likely (Coase 1960). When the insecurity arises because of governments' power to take, however, there is an additional reason for expecting bargaining to decline. People who can effectively operate in the political arena essentially have potential claims on other people's property. Seeking control of the desired land through political channels is, of course, costly, but if it is expected to be less costly than direct bargaining and voluntary exchange, incentives to seek involuntary transfers are strong. Thus, individuals who are active in and familiar with the political process are likely to choose that arena (i.e., the marginal cost of seeking condemnation is very low once someone has invested in building political connections and influence), while individuals who are not politically connected are relatively likely to choose direct bargaining. Furthermore, as the level of state transfer activity

increases, more people will be forced to learn about the political process, so over time, political takings will tend to replace voluntary exchange. On the other hand, increasing the constraints on the state and reducing the ease of transfers would lead to the substitution of voluntary exchange for political actions. Indeed, the fact that compulsory purchase may appear to be necessary to obtain property rights under the existing property regime does not mean that it would be necessary with very secure allodial rights.

28. For instance, the Castle Coalition has been developed by the Institute for Justice as a nationwide network of property owners and community activists dedicated to the prevention of the use of compulsory purchase powers in the United States for transfers to private parties for private uses. See www.castecoalition.org.

29. Economics need not be the only relevant consideration when it comes to issues about appropriate institutions, of course. In this regard, some natural-law theorists have addressed the issue (Stoebuck 1977, pp. 12–13; Paul 1988, pp. 74–77), but not convincingly. As Paul (1988, p. 77) suggests, "None of these arguments for the putative right of the state to take property—whether it be (1) the inherent attribute of sovereignty claim, or (2) the "public good" contention, or (3) the attempt to extract an implied consent to takings from the initial agreement to join civil society—flow inexorably form the natural law position. Indeed, the power of eminent domain seems to fit better with a feudal conception of property. . . . In a Lockean [or natural law] theory of property rights, in which property flows not from the state but from individual labor, and the state is nothing more than a device for the protection of preexisting, individual property, the power of eminent domain is not self-evident."

References

Austin, P. 2002. "Cypress Invokes Eminent Domain to Seize Church Land." *Orange County Register*. OCRegister.com, May 29.

Barnes, D. B., and L. A. Stout. 1992. *Cases and Materials on Law and Economics*. St. Paul, MN: West Publishing Company.

Beito, D. T. 2002. "The Private Places of St. Louis: Urban Infrastructure through Private Planning," in *The Voluntary City: Choice, Community, and Civil Society*, edited by D. T. Beito, P. Gordon, and A. Tabarrok. Ann Arbor, MI: University of Michigan Press.

Beito, D. T, Gordon, P., and A. Tabarrok (eds). 2002. *The Voluntary City: Choice, Community and Civil Society*. Ann Arbor, MI: University of Michigan Press.

Benson, B. L. 1994. "Are Public Goods Really Common Pools: Considerations of the Evolution of Policing and Highways in England." *Economic Inquiry* 32 (2): 249–271.

Benson, B. L. 1996. "Uncertainty, the Race for Property Rights, and Rent Dissipation due to Judicial Changes in Product Liability Tort Law." *Cultural Dynamics* 8: 333–351.

Benson, B. L. 1998. *To Serve and Protect: Privatization and Community in Criminal Justice*. New York: New York University Press.

Benson. B. L. 2001. "Knowledge, Trust, and Recourse: Imperfect Substitutes as Sources of Assurance in Emerging Economies." *Economic Affairs* 21 (1): 12–17.

Benson, B. L. 2002. "Eminent Domain Powers are not Necessary for the Provision of Roads." *Florida State University Working Paper*, presented at the Association of Private Enterprise Education Meetings, Cancun, Mexico, April 8.

Berliner, D. 2002. "Government Theft: The Top 10 Abuses of Eminent Domain, 1998–2002." Report from the Castle Coalition: Citizens Fighting Eminent Domain Abuse (March), www.CastleCoalition.org.

Berliner, D., and Bullock, S. 2002. "Eminent Domain Abuses Unchecked." *Washington Times* (March 4): www.washtimes.com/commentary/20020304–70598748.htm.

Boaz, D. 1997. *Libertarianism: A Primer*. New York: The Free Press.

Calabresi, G., and A. D. Melamed. 1972. "Property Rules, Liability Rules and Inalienability: One View of the Cathedral." *Harvard Law Review* 85: 1089–1128.

Coase, R. H. 1960. "The Problem of Social Cost." *Journal of Law and Economics* 3: 1–44.

De Vries, S., and Vohra, R. V. 2001. "Combination Auctions: A Survey." *Zentrum Mathematik Working Paper*. October.

Engel, E., R. Fischer, and A. Galetovic. 2002. "Highway Franchising and Real Estate Values." *NBER Working Paper No. 8803*, Cambridge, MA: National Bureau of Economic Research, February.

Epstein, R. A. 1985. *Takings: Private Property and the Power of Eminent Domain*. Cambridge, MA: Harvard University Press.

Epstein, R. A. 1993. *Bargaining with the State*. Princeton, NJ: Princeton University Press.

Epstein, R. A. 2001. "In and Out of Public Solution: The Hidden Perils of Property Transfer." *John M. Olin Law & Economics Working Paper No. 129*. Chicago: The Law School, The University of Chicago.

Fischel, W. A. 1995. *Regulatory Takings: Law, Economics, and Politics*. Cambridge, MA: Harvard University Press.

Foldvary, F. 1994. *Public Goods and Private Communities: The Market Provision of Social Services*. Aldershot, UK: Edward Elgar Publishing.

Gage, T. J. 1981. "Getting Street-Wise in St. Louis." *Reason*. 13: 18–20.

Goldstein, A. 1987. "Private Enterprise and Highways," in *Private Sector Involvement and Toll Road Financing in Provision of Highways, Transportation Research Record No. 1107*. Washington D.C.: Transportation Research Board.

Gordon, H. S. 1954. "The Economic Theory of a Common Property Resource: The Fishery." *Journal of Political Economy* 62: 124–142.

Greenhouse, L. 2002. "Justices Weaken Movement Backing Property Rights." *New York Times*, (April 24). www.nytimes.com.

Gunderson, G. 1989. "Privatization and the 19th-Century Turnpike." *Cato Journal* 9 (1): 191–200.

Hardin, G. 1968. "The Tragedy of the Commons." *Science* 162: 1243–1248.

John Jay College of Criminal Justice/CUNY. 1997. "Gated Enclaves are not just for the Well-Healed." *Law Enforcement News* 23 (May 15): 5.

Johnson, R. N., and Libecap, G. D. 1982. "Contracting Problems and Regulation: The Case of the Fishery." *American Economic Review* 72: 1005–1022.

Jones, S. J. 2000. "Trumping Eminent Domain Law: An Argument for Strict Scrutiny Analysis Under the Public Use Requirement of the Fifth Amendment." *Syracuse Law Review* 50: 285–314.

Klein, D. B. 1990. "The Voluntary Provision of Public Goods? The Turnpike Companies of Early America." *Economic Inquiry* 28: 788–812.

Klein, D. B. and G. J. Fielding. 1992. "Private Toll Roads: Learning from the 19th Century." *Transportation Quarterly* 46 (3): 321–341.

Klein, D. B., and C. Yin. 1996, "Use, Esteem, and Profit in Voluntary Provision: Toll Roads in California, 1850–1902." *Economic Inquiry* 34 (October): 678–692.

Kraus, M. I. 2000. "Property Rules vs. Liability Rules," in the *Encyclopedia of Law and Economics*, Vol. 3, edited by B. Bouckaert and G. De Geest, pp. 782–794. Chelthenham, UK: Edward Elgar.

Krier, J. E., and S. J. Schwab. 1995. "Property Rules and Liability Rules: The Cathedral in Another Light." *New York University Law Review* 70: 440–483.

Krueger, A. O. 1974. "The Political Economy of a Rent-Seeking Society." *American Economic Review* 64: 291–303.

Kulick, P. J. 2000. "Rolling the Dice: Determining Public Use in Order to Effectuate a 'Public-Private Taking'—A Proposal to Redefine 'Public Use.'" *Law Review of Michigan State University-Detroit College of Law* 3: 639–691.

Landsburg, S. E. 1993. *The Armchair Economist: Economics and Everyday Life.* New York: The Free Press.

Lazzarotti, J. J. 1999. "Public Use or Public Abuse." *University of Missouri at Kansas City Law Review* 68: 49–75.

Libecap, Gary D. 1984. "The Political Allocation of Mineral Rights: A Reevaluation of Teapot Dome." *Journal of Economic History* 44: 381–391.

Mansnerus, L. 2001. "Refusing to Let Go, Property Owners Test Eminent Domain's Limits." *New York Times: NYTimes.com*, July 25.

Miceli, T. J., and K. Segerson. 2000. In the *Encyclopedia of Law and Economics*, Vol. 3, edited by B. Bouckaert and G. De Geest, pp. 328–357. Chelthenham, UK: Edward Elgar.

Munch, P. 1976. "An Economic Analysis of Eminent Domain." *Journal of Political Economy.* 84: 473–497.

NCPA (National Center for Policy Analysis). 2002. "State and Local Issues: Eminent Domain Used for Economic Development." *National Center for Policy Analysis: Idea House* (March 5): www.ncpa.org/pd/state/pd12298b.html.

Newman, O. 1980. *Community of Interest.* Garden City, NY: Anchor Press.

Parks, R. B., and R. J. Oakerson. 1988. *Metropolitan Organization: The St. Louis Case.* Washington, D.C.: Advisory Commission on Intergovernmental Relations.

Paul, E. F. 1988. *Property Rights and Eminent Domain.* New Brunswick, NJ: Transaction Publishers.

Pereyra, A. 2002. "Auction Theory and Road Franchising." *Departamento de Economia, Universidad de la Republica de Uruguay Working Paper*, February.

Polinsky, M. A. 1980. "Resolving Nuisance Disputes: The Simple Economics of Injunctive and Damage Remedies." *Stanford Law Review* 32: 1075–1112.

Posner, R. A. 1977. *Economic Analysis of Law*, 2nd Edition. Boston: Little, Brown and Company.

Roth, G. 1996. *Roads in a Market Economy.* Aldershot, UK: Avebury Technical.

Shearing, C. D., and P. C. Stenning. 1987. "Say Cheese! The Disney Order that is Not so Mickey Mouse," in *Private Policing*, edited by C. D. Shearing and P. C. Stenning. Newbury Park, CA: Sage Publishing Co.

Starkie, D.N.M. 1990. "The Private Financing of Road Infrastructure." *Transportation and Society Discussion Paper No. 11.* Oxford University.

Starkman, D. 2001. "In the Clash of Eminent Domain and Private Property, Courts are Sending Cities a Message: Enough." *Wall Street Journal: WSJ.com—From the Archives* (July 23).

Starkman, D. 2002. "Most Important Case in Years to Curb Local Government Use of Eminent Domain Powers." *Wall Street Journal: WSJ.com—Law* (April 5).

Stoebuck, W. B. 1977. *Nontrespassory Takings in Eminent Domain.* Charlottesville, VA: The Michie Company.

Tullock, G. 1967. "The Welfare Costs of Tariffs, Monopolies and Theft." *Western Economic Journal* 5: 224–232.

Winston, C. 2000. "Government Failure in Urban Transportation." *AEI-Brookings Joint Center for Regulatory Studies Working Paper 00-8.* Washington, D.C.: American Enterprise Institute & Brookings Institute.

4

The Political Economy of Private Roads

David Levinson

CosaNostra Pizza #3569 is on Vista Road just down from Kings Park Mall. Vista Road used to belong to the State of California and now is called Fairlanes, Inc. Rte. CSV-5. Its main competition used to be a U.S. Highway and is now called Cruiseways, Inc. Rte. Cal-12. Farther up the Valley, the two competing highways actually cross. Once there had been bitter disputes, the intersection closed by sporadic sniper fire. Finally, a big developer bought the entire intersection and turned it into a drivethrough mall. Now the roads feed into a parking system—not a lot, not a ramp, but a system—and lose their identity. Getting through the intersection involves tracing paths through the parking system, many braided filaments of direction like the Ho Chi Minh trail. CSV-5 has better throughput, but Cal-12 has better pavement. That is typical—Fairlanes roads emphasize getting you there, for Type A drivers, and Cruiseways emphasize the enjoyment, for Type B drivers. (Stephenson 1992)

Introduction

This book reflects the increasing interest in the United States and elsewhere in road privatization and alternative financing, not just by science fiction writers, anarchists, and libertarians, but also by economists and policy analysts (de Palma and Lindsey 1998, Viton 1995, Gómez-Ibáñez, and Meyer 1993, Walton and Euritt 1990). With the widened attention to privatization in its many forms, one may think that private roads are just around the bend, that travelers will soon drive on commercialized streets and highways and eschew public sector arteries. While the archetypal private road may include no public involvement, most recent private efforts in the highway sector to date have either been government contracts or required government assistance. They certainly require government permission and have been subject to extensive government oversight.

Many elements of the highway transportation system are already private. Drivers and passengers expend their own time in producing highway trips. Drivers generally own their vehicles, so those too are private. Roadside services (gas, food, lodging) are almost always private, and are necessary elements for many kinds of trips. While in some cases these may be on government owned land (rest stops on turnpikes), on most highways they are on private land. The origin and destination of the trip are also generally in the private sector; these trip generators (generation facilities) may be analogous to the generating plants in the electricity sector. What are not private, of course, are the roads themselves. These network components are at issue in the discussion of private roads. The perceived incentives for the public and the politicians they elect differ from those of economists and free marketeers. The recent (partial) deregulation fiasco in California's electricity sector will serve as cold water (an electric shock) on efforts to quickly and radically restructure the road sector. The burden of proof falls on those trying to change the status quo. Private roads must offer a significant and apparent advantage over public control. The case must be compelling, and for most places to try it, it must have been done somewhere else first. Churchill is attributed the quote, "Indeed, it has been said that democracy is the 'worst' form of Government except all those others that have been tried from time to time." Substitute "government control of roads" for "democracy" and you have the general perception that proponents of private control must challenge.

Much discussion about private roads focuses on the flexibility and choices provided to travelers (who would have the alternative of taking an expensive fast road or an inexpensive slow one). A network with largely or entirely private elements would be very different than the one we face on a daily basis. Just as deregulation of communications created radically new products and services that were unimagined at the time, divestiture of highways may do similar things. However, unlike the American telecommunications sector, streets and highways are government owned. Furthermore, highways are presently financed through gas taxes and general revenue, rather than priced according to use or a contract between service provider and consumer.

There is clearly reluctance to privatize—otherwise we would already be living in a world with private streets and highways. This chapter explores the mechanisms of privatization and the political issues that underlie our current state of affairs and a shift to a new one. While an economist would argue that *if* the total welfare gained exceeds the cost of privatization, it is a good thing and everyone wins, the more politically astute will recognize those gains will be distributed among winners and losers. The losers in particular are a difficulty, as unless they are compensated, they have no reason to lend political support to a privatization proposal, and much reason to act as a roadblock.

This chapter first briefly reviews the history of private roads. Then the functional and economic classification of roadways is presented. This section notes the three different classes of roads will need to be treated in very different ways. The ideology of private roads is then presented. The political factors constraining this ideology from taking root are then discussed. Distributional effects associated with privatization are described, and means for using the proceeds from the sale of roads to compensate losers are shown. Prospects for the future of private roads are discussed in the conclusions.

History

Two private roads garnering much publicity are SR91 in Orange County, California (discussed elsewhere in this volume) and the Dulles Greenway in Loudoun County, Virginia. Though the Dulles Greenway had some early financial difficulties, it has recently added a lane and has seen traffic levels rise significantly in the past few years. These roads may be blips in a state-owned roads sector or a harbinger of a new transportation property rights paradigm. Although building significant new private roads is clearly difficult, as illustrated by their small numbers in the United States, and new private roads are more difficult than new public ones, there are many possible models for private involvement in new roads. Building new private roads is relatively simple compared with the privatization of existing roads. Given that roads in developed countries have largely saturated the market given current technologies, it is the privatization of existing roads that promises the greatest challenges and rewards in terms of serious highway reform. However, private roads are far scarcer in the United States in the early twenty-first century than they are elsewhere in the world, and even in the United States of the early nineteenth century.

Private and public toll roads have a long history, from Greek myth (paying Charon the ferryman to cross the River Styx), to historical evidence in the ancient world. Aristotle's *Oeconomicus* notes tolls in Asian kingdoms (Pritchett 1980). *The Arthasastra*, an Indian text that presents the ideas of Kautilya, India's earliest known political philosopher, mentions tolls prior to the fourth century BC (Lay 1992). At the time of Augustus, Strabo's *Geographies* reports tolls on the Little St. Bernard's Pass maintained by the Salassi Tribe. More recently, in 1364, tolling rights were established on the Great North Road from London. In the 1650s tolls began to be established more systematically in Britain as roads in the non-toll system began to decay (Figure 4.1). This quasi-private financing system peaked in the 1840s and began to decline to almost no toll roads by 1900. The financial system evolved into a quite intricate system, with toll farmers who paid a lump sum to the turnpike trust for the right to collect

Figure 4.1
Turnpikes in Great Britain: 1650–1900

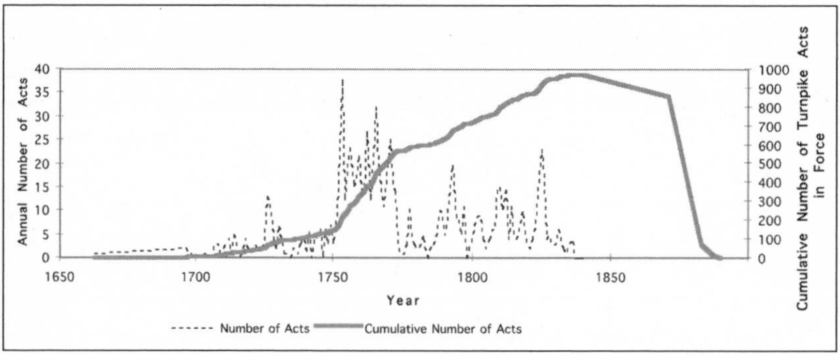

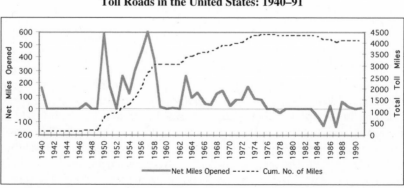

tolls on a turnpike. In the United States, turnpikes began in the late eighteenth century and lasted through the nineteenth century, but were all but eliminated by the early twentieth century. A second turnpike boom, this time entirely public sector, lasted from 1940, with the advent of the limited access highway, to 1956, when the Interstate Act was passed (Figure 4.2).

Several Western European countries (e.g., Spain, France, and Italy) established private concession to operate toll roads in the post-World War II era, though many of these were either consolidated or taken over by the national government. Eastern European Countries have followed in the post-Cold War era. Many developing countries in Asia and Latin America have also experimented with private toll roads (Gómez-Ibáñez and Meyer 1993).

Figure 4.2
Toll Roads in the United States: 1940–91

Not all private roads are limited access highways. The oldest private street in the United States is Benton Place in St. Louis, named for Thomas Hart Benton (Lafayette Square Marquis 1998). This road was laid out across private lots, and was designed intentionally to permit property owners to control traffic and to use the road space for public activity such as children's play. Every property owner is required to belong to an association (Benton Place Association) that regulates annual assessments for maintenance of the street. This objective of local control of streets and limiting their traffic is very much in keeping with modern urban design, the Dutch Woonerf or slow street concept, and traffic calming retrofits that many neighborhoods petition their government for. The difference of course is that in this St. Louis neighborhood, the residents can choose how to use the roads themselves, rather than depend on the proclivities of a remote government. Many other private "places" exist in St. Louis, including Westmoreland and Portland Places (Hunter 1988). Though this arrangement can be thought of in two ways, either as a private road or as a very local form of government (the homeowner's association), the effects are the same: local control by only the abutting property owners. However, another viewpoint holds that these private "places" are simply an attempt to barricade residents from less desirable elements (St. Louis 2001).

The Functional and Economic Classification of Roads

Roads serve two purposes: allowing individuals to access their property, and allowing them to move between places. Engineers and planners describe a hierarchy that separates the access and movement functions of a road, illustrated in Figure 4.3. At the top of the hierarchy are major roads (called arterials) that connect and cross cities, serving only the movement function. At the bottom of the hierarchy are local streets that allow residential neighborhoods to access other areas, functioning as little more than driveways. Of course, the actual network does not adhere strictly to the idealized hierarchy, but new roads, built to formalized engineering standards, do so much more than old. Developing a hierarchy of roads is not unlike other networks (airlines, electricity, natural gas, water, telecommunications) or systems of places that are built hierarchically. A hierarchy of roads has a number of advantages, including cost savings by enabling economies of scale in construction, operations, and maintenance, the aggregation of traffic (enabling economies of consumption by spreading their total cost over more travelers), reducing the number of vehicle conflicts, and contributing to the desired quiet character of residential neighborhoods.

Figure 4.3

Functional Highway Classification and Type of Service Provided

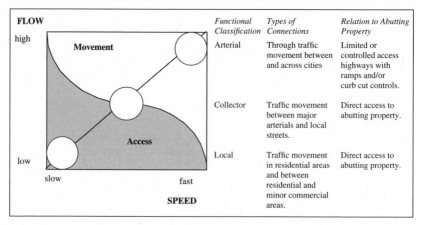

	Functional Classification	Types of Connections	Relation to Abutting Property
	Arterial	Through traffic movement between and across cities	Limited or controlled access highways with ramps and/or curb cut controls.
	Collector	Traffic movement between major arterials and local streets.	Direct access to abutting property.
	Local	Traffic movement in residential areas and between residential and minor commercial areas.	Direct access to abutting property.

Two criteria can help classify a good as public or private: excludability and rivalry. Excludability implies that the provider of a good or service can prevent a user from obtaining it without charge. Rivalry implies that one person's consumption of a particular good prevents another individual from consuming it. Table 4.1 summarizes the goods by type.

The properties of the hierarchy of roads are such that a road's suitability for privatization depends very much on its position on the hierarchy. There are three different models that are appropriate to examine further: private, "congesting," and club. Roads should be considered public goods only if they are neither excludable (either technologically or legally), nor rivalrous. It is clear roads do not continuously constitute such "pure" public goods. While roads may be public for short time periods, when they are non-rivalrous, these same roads exhibit rivalry at other times. Unfortunately, we can't generalize: Roads at different places on the hierarchy at different times exhibit different characteristics.

Table 4.1

Defining Public, Private, Club and "Congesting" Goods

		Excludability	
		Yes	No
Rivalry	Yes	Private	"Congesting"
	No	Club	Public

At the top of the hierarchy, arterials, such as intercity freeways, can potentially be competitively provided by private firms. Intercity roads can be excludable, because they do not serve land access; they serve only the movement function of roads. As they are limited access, tracking entry and exit is not financially or technically difficult. They are also rivalrous. When there is congestion, my consumption of scarce space at a bottleneck at a given time prevents you from doing so: Only one car can occupy a particular piece of the roadway at a particular time. Economists consider goods that are both rivalrous and excludable to be private goods.

On long distance trips, there are often multiple routes an individual can take. Thus the spatial monopoly aspects of these roads are limited by competition. Further ensuring that there is no price discrimination based on origin or destination (e.g. only allowing prices to vary by distance traveled on the roadway, vehicle type, congestion level, time of day, day of week, or month of year) will help further eradicate monopoly powers. Many countries have private intercity roads, and in the United States, many states have turnpikes, which while publicly owned, are more readily privatized than other roads. This layer of the road hierarchy is analogous to the long distance telephone providers, national airlines, Internet backbone, and natural gas pipeline companies, all of which competitively provide network services.

In the middle of the hierarchy, the collectors, usually controlled by local governments, and still serving a land access function for commercial and some residential properties, are the trickiest problem. These roads are not easily excludable, as there are frequent intersections and access points. On the other hand, they are rivalrous, as they are subject to congestion; hence the need for traffic lights. They can thus be considered "congesting" goods. Because of economies of scale, it is not likely that each road segment (each block) could be separately franchised, or even that the full length of a collector road could easily be franchised given the amount of overlap with other cross-streets it would face. However, a community could divest itself of all collector roads as a franchise. Thus, a utility model may be appropriate to consider here. Under this scheme, collector class roads could be converted to publicly or privately owned utilities subject to significant government regulation or oversight (Kahn 1988, Train 1991).

At the bottom of the hierarchy are local streets, the equivalent in scope and distance to the "last mile" discussions often facing local telephony and cable TV companies. Local streets are excludable—witness the gated community—but are seldom rivalrous, as there is little congestion. Thus they may be subject to privatization as a club (Cornes and Sandler 1996, Buchanan 2001). The example presented earlier of the private streets in St. Louis may serve as a model. Many multi-family and townhouse complexes already manage local streets, though they are called driveways. The implications of a club model are extensive, but in particular control would be localized and use of those roads would be limited to trips beginning or ending with the club's domain. Thus some non-local traffic would need to switch to collector roads.

These three models are instances of a broad spectrum of possible private involvement. The degree of private versus public involvement is described in detail in Table 4.2. The level of private responsibility in roadways ranges from private sector contracting to provide specific services (design, operations, and maintenance) for a publicly owned roadway to full private ownership of the road.

The Ideology of Privatization

The full gamut of public and private involvement in roads suggests broad legal flexibility. Early U.S. federal involvement in transportation was based on the idea of *post roads* to improve domestic communication, and later involvement, particularly the interstate highway system, was justified on national defense grounds (its official name is the National System of Inter-

Table 4.2
Realms of Public and Private Involvement

Public ↑		Government	Federal Government	
			State Government	Arterial Roads
				Collector Roads
			Local Government	Collector Roads
				Local Roads
			Homeowners Association	*Local Roads*
		Utility	Transfer to Quasi-Public Authority	*Collector Roads*
	Outsourcing	Service Contract	Operations and Maintenance	*All Publicly Owned Roads*
		Management Contract	Design, Build	*New Arterial Roads*
			Design, Build, Major Maintenance	*(in areas unwilling to give up full control)*
			Design, Build, Operate	
	Franchise	Project Franchise	Lease, Develop, Operate	*New Arterial Roads*
			Build, Lease, Operate, Transfer	
			Build, Transfer, Operate	
			Build, Operate, Transfer	
			Build, Own, Operate, Transfer	
			Build, Own, Operate	
Private ↓	Divestiture	Private Entrepreneurship	Buy, Build, Operate	*Existing Arterial Roads*
			Buy, Operate	

Note: *Italics* indicates suggested ownership/management structure.

state and Defense Highways). Article 1, Section 8 of the Constitution gives the federal government an explicit role in highway transportation:

> The Congress shall have power to lay and collect taxes, duties, imposts and excises, to pay the debts and provide for the common defense and general welfare of the United States; but all duties, imposts and excises shall be uniform throughout the United States; . . . To establish post offices and post roads; . . .

Of course, just because the federal government has the constitutional power to do something does not require it to do so. Madison, Monroe, and Jackson all vetoed road bills. From a legal-constitutional perspective, one can argue that at a minimum, there exists no constitutional prohibition on private roads, and perhaps there should be some government reticence to be involved in this sector. The Ninth and Tenth Amendments support this view:

Amendment IX

The enumeration in the Constitution, of certain rights, shall not be construed to deny or disparage others retained by the people.

Amendment X

The powers not delegated to the United States by the Constitution, nor prohibited by it to the states, are reserved to the states respectively, or to the people.

The Libertarian Party platform (2000), for instance, states: "Government interference in transportation is characterized by monopolistic restriction, corruption and gross inefficiency. We therefore call for the dissolution of all government agencies concerned with transportation. . . . We call for the privatization of . . . public roads, and the national highway system. . . ." This assertion of monopolistic restriction, corruption, and gross inefficiency is a thesis that requires empirical corroboration or refutation. It also begs the question of whether private sector control would also be similarly characterized by monopoly, corruption, and/or inefficiency. Because the advocacy of the dissolution of government involvement in transportation is not a widely held belief, significant work will be required before the libertarian position, or even a more moderate privatization argument, becomes mainstream.

The first claim is that government interference in transportation is characterized by *monopolistic restriction*. Certainly, just as there used to be one phone company there is only one state road agency. Different layers of government may be responsible for different layers of the hierarchy of roads, but there is an almost seamless transition between those layers, and no incentive for competition between roads or layers of government to attract traffic or revenue.

Local governments are rather keen, for good reason, to minimize traffic on their local streets and push it to roads that are under the management of a different layer of government. While traffic on commercial streets is not viewed as a problem (it aids local merchants), traffic on residential streets is undesired.

The viewpoint government agencies hold is that of managing the flows on the network centrally as much as possible to even out traffic and mitigate congestion. Traffic signals and other control devices on collector roads are common, and are often centrally managed to the benefit of most travelers. The case demonstrating the success of freeway management is still open. Nevertheless this evidence of central management further corroborates the claim that roads are monopolies. That only two private roads of significance have been built in the United States in the last century supports this claim. Given that roads are monopolies, we must then ask if this is a problem or a requirement.

Is road transportation a "natural monopoly" at some level? On local streets, only one road provides access to a particular origin or destination. Roads have a physical and undeniable monopoly. The issue becomes who can best own and manage that monopoly. On collectors, there may be some alternative routes, but the tight integration of streets, the difficulty of excluding traffic, and economies of scale probably suggest that those streets too are a natural monopoly. But again, it may not require government ownership—simply oversight. Arterials have the most potential for independent competition, and the framework for privatizing these highways has already been established internationally.

The second libertarian claim is that government interference is characterized by *corruption*. While, as with any sector, there are the occasional illegal activities, the question is whether transportation is exceptional. Perhaps the place it is most exceptional is in terms of what are called "pork barrel" projects. The earmarking and special projects in the federal surface transportation bill, a transportation reauthorization bill, are well documented. But TEA-21 constitutes only a small portion of total earmarks, which are further made by the Transportation Appropriations Subcommittees (Utt 1999). The ethics controversy surrounding the recently retired chairman of the House Transportation and Infrastructure Committee, Bud Shuster, have also been well documented, and led to a rebuke by a House Ethics panel (Washington Post 2001). Whether, as Lord Acton (1887) says, "Power tends to corrupt and absolute power corrupts absolutely" will be left to the reader's judgment and understanding of human behavior.

The third claim is that government involvement leads to *gross inefficiency*. The strongest case for gross inefficiency in the highway sector is the daily congestion seen on limited access roads in large cities, and its rise over time. Because people's individual private cost of traveling on unpriced roads is less than the cost they impose on others, people don't bear the full cost of their trip, and rather make decisions based on the subsidized price. Travel in the peak hours is over-consumed, as is the case with many subsidized goods. The solution advocated by most transportation economists is road pricing. Road pricing may be a necessary prerequisite for full privatization, but it may be that privatization is also a prerequisite for widespread pricing on existing roads. The degree of inefficiency varies from place to place; perceptions are relative. Intolerable congestion levels in one city may be a pleasant drive to the park in another.

However, for the case to change from public to private control to be compelling, the argument must be made that private control would not be characterized by Monopoly, Corruption, or Inefficiency. Starting with inefficiency, a private firm has the incentive to maximize profits. So while public control may be characterized by under-pricing and over-consumption (congestion), the fear is that private control would be subject to over-pricing (and under-consumption), particularly if there is imperfect competition. We can call over- or under-pricing a short run inefficiency, in that it is an inefficiency in price, given the size of the network. Short run inefficiency does not depend on whether the network is optimally sized or not. The opportunity for firms to price discriminate (much as airlines do) is an important element here. The related issue is thus monopoly power. If local and collector roads are natural monopolies, the same complaint against the public sector holds on the private sector. Competition must be safeguarded through antitrust and other pro-competitive laws and regulations. Adam Smith (1776) wrote, "People of the same trade seldom meet together, even for merriment and diversion, but the conversation ends in a conspiracy against the public, or in some contrivance to raise prices." Whether such collusion is explicit, or implicit and never spoken, clearly there is some cause for concern. Markets function best when no producer or consumer is sufficiently sized, or can collude, to affect the price.

The corruption argument, or long run inefficiency in the construction of pork-barrel projects, is probably the easiest case to make in favor of private control. While government may be over-building in some places (due to pork) and under-building elsewhere due to a lack of a price signal or market incentives, firms have the incentive to add capacity so long as their marginal benefit exceeds marginal cost. This incentive is further enforced by the discipline of financial markets. However, monopolies will not necessarily result in an appropriately sized road network. So the long run efficiency benefits associated with private control depend on there being competition, or at least potential competition.

Private, unregulated toll roads will charge profit maximizing prices (otherwise what is the incentive for private investors?). In the absence of strong competition, those prices will be higher than optimal "welfare maximizing" prices. This is shown in Figure 4.4, adapted from Levinson (2001). There are two

Figure 4.4
Welfare, Profit, and Tolls

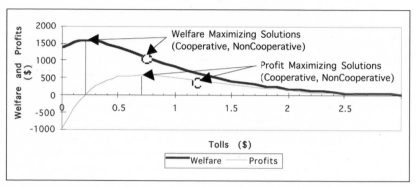

curves, one that shows the welfare resulting from various tolls posted at a frontier between two jurisdictions (for instance a bridge at the state line), the other showing the profits from those tolls. The profit maximizing toll is higher than the welfare maximizing toll. However both welfare and profits depend not only on the decisions that the toll agency or private road make, but also on the decisions made by the adjacent toll road. If the adjacent road charges more, demand, and thus welfare and profits decline. However with cooperation between the two agencies or between the firms (or between an agency and a firm), everyone can benefit. This problem is the classic case of the serial monopolists discussed by Chamberlin (1933).

The issue of profit maximization and monopoly has another aspect as well. A firm building a new private road, or buying a road from the government, will want to maintain a monopoly position and discourage competition. They may try to insert non-compete clauses into their contracts with government agencies, ensuring the government won't build a competing road or allow other firms to do similarly. The absence of a clause may mean the new road is not built (or an existing road can't be privatized), but the presence of the clause diminishes the benefits to the public of private involvement, the creative dynamism and price and service competition, in the roads sector. In fact, this has become an issue with SR91 in Southern California, where the public sector prohibition from expanding the congested parallel road led to a public takeover of the private toll road. Patents may be a useful analog here: Some monopoly profits are awarded to inventors to encourage high-risk ventures; a non-compete clause of a finite duration may have a similar effect. But similar controversies may arise: For instance, people in poor countries cannot afford needed medicines still under patent protection. Some mechanism for buying out the non-compete clause or compensating the private firm for lost revenue if the clause is canceled may be necessary so that the government does not resort to eminent domain and reverse the privatization cycle.

However, such pricing is not necessarily the sole province of private roads. Publicly held toll roads with monopoly power may also charge more than welfare maximizing prices. Public toll authorities have an obligation to maximize the benefits for their owners—the taxpayers in their home jurisdiction—much as private toll roads must satisfy shareholders. While there are principal agent problems all around (do bureaucrats or managers really serve their organization's mission or their own?), the nominal motivations are the same. However, the implications are that to maximize the welfare for its own residents, a jurisdiction must, in a sense, exploit the residents of other states. The more revenue that can be garnered from non-residents, the higher the welfare of residents (a real instance of Monty Python's ideal policy of "taxing foreigners living abroad")[1] This suggests that jurisdictions are not much different from private firms. Empirical evidence supports this hypothesis of jurisdictions playing "beggar thy neighbor" games. Levinson (2001) finds that the more workers a state imports daily, the more revenue it collects from tolls as opposed to taxes.

Unless and until the arguments in favor of private roads are convincing to a large majority, government interference in and ownership of major highway facilities is unlikely to change. It will not simply be sufficient to argue that private control would be more efficient than public control. Politically significant distributional issues must be addressed.

Identifying and Managing the Distribution of Gains and Losses

A number of actors fill the stage when considering the privatization of roads. Three or more layers of government have a say in the matter, depending on the rank of the road in the hierarchy. The federal government will definitely have opinions on the privatization (or even the tolling) of any interstate highway built with federally collected gas taxes. In spite of the 1992 Executive Order 12803, a future federal government may argue that states selling such roads should compensate it for prior federal contributions. The valuation of those contributions will inevitably be a political decision. Smaller jurisdictions might also be concerned that the access prized by their residents would be reduced if the cost of using a facility were to rise, or if a private firm could delete (or add) interchanges affecting local travel patterns. Similarly, states would have a say should a locality decide to privatize collector roads that received any assistance from state based revenue sources. The group with the most at stake however is the traveling public. And the impact on travelers depends very much on the kind of road privatization that is undertaken.

As noted earlier, there are different stages of privatization. Contracting out highway services, while maintaining government ownership and a no-toll status, has little apparent impact on travelers, although will certainly be resisted by the government agency whose services are no longer required. However there are three more significant stages of privatization of limited access arterial class highways that need to be addressed.

The first case is *building a new private road*. The implications for this type of private involvement depend in large part on the alternatives. Would the road have been provided by the public if not by the private sector, or is the road above and beyond what the public sector would have produced? If the public sector were not going to produce the road, there are few grounds for complaints by either the public sector agencies or by travelers, who can now save time, and it would appear that all travelers are winners. Environmental groups may still have differences with the road, especially if the road does not fully internalize its environmental impacts or increases pollution, and neighbors may be annoyed with the noise from the new road. Landowners may support the road if they voluntarily enter an agreement to sell their land, or are given access to the road, but not if the land was taken by the government and then resold to the private sector.

Case 2, *privatizing (and tolling) an existing (congested) free road*, has the most pronounced effects. Because the road had been under-priced, there was congestion, thus privatization that imposes tolls and thus congestion relief should benefit travelers with a high value of time, even if there is over-tolling

Table 4.3
Distributional Effects of Three Privatization Schemes
for Limited Access Arterials

Value of Time	Case 1: Construction of New Private Road	Case 2: Privatization of Existing (Congested) Free Road (Tolls from 0 to Profit Max.)	Case 3: Privatization of Existing (Uncongested) Toll Road (Tolls from Welfare Max. to Profit Max.)
High	Winner	Winner	Loser
Medium	Winner	?	Loser
Low	Winner	Loser	Loser

and under-consumption after the price imposition. This case also leads to the argument of "double taxation." Travelers will feel that they paid for roads with gas taxes and now they are being asked to pay again with tolls. Properly informing travelers of the benefits, for instance by distributing shares in the private toll companies, is likely to be important in overcoming this perception.

Oddly, the easiest case to implement, Case 3, the *privatization of an existing toll road*, has primarily negative effects on travelers. Assuming tolls were previously set at or near welfare maximizing levels, the road would be relatively uncongested. Privatization would result in the objective switching to profit maximizing, and thus higher toll levels, as shown in Figure 4.4. Because there is little if any congestion reduction for the additional toll, most travelers are worse off (except those with a very high value of time). The state, or the public, would gain revenue from the sale of the road, which could be redistributed.

If losers can be identified, a community has two choices: compensate them or not. Many economists oppose compensation because it provides incentives for inefficient behavior (rather than avoid or prevent an externality, a compensated individual may choose to embrace the externality and the associated compensation). Politically it may be necessary to create a working consensus. Compensation may be achieved in a number of ways. First, the remedy may occur on an everyday basis, through subsidies for other transportation modes, or by discounts, or some other daily mechanism. Alternatively, the compensation may be undertaken as a one-off expense, by ensuring that the classes of losers on a daily basis from privatization are compensated by being given a greater share of the private road concern, or by being given a larger share of the proceeds from such a privatization.

Suppose the political will has been gathered in favor of privatization. There remains a complex decision tree regarding the means for this program. The public can choose to (A) sell shares in the company to investors, or (B) distribute shares in the company to residents. If it decides to sell shares there are several choices concerning the proceeds. The public may (1) keep the proceeds to pay off debt, (2) keep the proceeds to provide some other public services, or (3) return the proceeds to taxpayers. If proceeds are returned to taxpayers, then the question is how? Proceeds can be redistributed in accordance with payment for the roads (try to rebate the gas tax somehow), or in accordance with income, or as a lump sum to current residents.

Similarly, if it chooses (B), to distribute shares, rules must be established that are not necessarily going to be universally agreed upon. Because interstate roads were paid for with gas taxes, it can be argued that those who paid those taxes have the greatest claim on the share in the road, while a transit user, who paid no gas taxes, has little claim. Alternatively, it may be fairer just to give

1 share per person, or 1 share per household, or 1 share per taxpayer, or 1 share per year in the state, or some other formula only a politician can imagine.

The point is not that there is some right formula, but rather that there is no formula that will be universally agreed to. Any formula will have to address a number of political issues, including compensation of the clear losers from road privatization. This may not prove a fatal flaw in privatization efforts; certainly privatization has occurred in other countries and other sectors. However, it is a political hurdle that must be thought through before any successful privatization effort will take place.

Conclusions

Private roads will be more popular for expansion of the existing highway network than as privatization of public roads. This is because of the distributional issues involved, and who perceives themselves as winners and who as losers. Though revolutionary shocks have been known to happen in history, privatization is unlikely to be wholesale or rapid. There are many vested interests in the way between the current state ownership and privatization. Privatization will probably occur in steps: continued devolution of powers from higher to lower levels of government (ultimately down to the homeowner's association), competitive contracting out for services previously provided by government agencies, allowing new roads to be built with private money, and converting existing toll roads to electronic toll collection. While tolling is often considered a congestion reduction mechanism, many people who still see or recall excessive placement of manually operated toll plazas view tolling as a cause of congestion. This old image, needlessly fostered by agencies slow to change to electronic toll collection, will need to be eradicated before there is even lukewarm support for the idea. With a new view of how tolls operate, selling shares in existing toll road agencies, rather than removing those tolls, becomes a realistic possibility.

Once all of these preliminary steps are undertaken, we are still left with the vast network of roads under state control. An important stage in the commercialization of roads will be the replacement of the gas tax with tolls or similar user fees. Why would states or the federal government do this? Several scenarios jump to mind, relating to environment, technology, financing, and congestion. Environmentalists and economists have long advocated internalizing the social costs of the automobile (in particular, the costs of air pollution). Environmentalists have also advocated replacing the internal combustion engine with low or "zero" emission vehicles, that is, replacing the vehicle powerplant from one that is fueled by gasoline to one fueled by other sources (or fueled on much less gasoline than conventional engines), which would greatly crimp the revenue available from the gas tax. Finally, congestion does not appear to be getting any better in the absence of tolling. These all argue in favor of usage fees such as place and time specific electronic tolls. By the time this tolling framework is in place, privatization is not such a large leap.

Note

1. The reference was suggested by Brian Taylor of UCLA.

References

Acton, Lord. 1887. "Power tends to corrupt . . ." in a letter to Bishop Mandell Creighton, April 3.

Beito, David T., with Bruce Smith. 1990. "The Formation of Urban Infrastructure Through Non-Governmental Planning: The Private Places of St. Louis." *Journal of Urban History* 16 (May): 263–303.

Buchanan, James M. *The Demand and Supply of Public Goods.* Library of Economics and Liberty. Retrieved September 3, 2001 from http://www.econlib.org/library/ Buchanan/buchCv5c9.html.

Chamberlin, E. 1933. *The Theory of Monopolistic Competition: A Re-orientation of the Theory of Value.* Cambridge, MA: Harvard University Press.

Cobin, John. 1999. "Market Provision of Highways: Lessons from Costanera Norte." Planning and Markets 2:1 article 3, http://www.pam.usc.edu/volume2/v2i1a3print .html.

Constitution (U.S.). 1789.

Cornes, R., and T. Sandler. 1996. *The Theory of Externalities, Public Goods and Club Goods*, 2nd Edition. New York: Cambridge University Press.

de Palma, A., and R. Lindsey. 1998. "Private Toll Roads: A Dynamic Equilibrium Analysis." Presented at Western Regional Science Association Meeting, February, Monterey, CA.

Dupuit, J. 1849. "On Tolls and Transport Charges." Reprinted in *International Economic Papers* 11 (1962): 7–31

Fielding, Gordon J., and Daniel B. Klein. 1993. "How to Franchise Highways." *Journal of Transport Economics and Policy"* (May): 113–130.

Gómez-Ibáñez, Jose A. 1992. "The Political Economy of Highway Tolls and Congestion Pricing." *Transportation Quarterly* 46 (3): 343–360.

Gómez-Ibáñez, Jose, and John Meyer. 1993. *Going Private: The International Experience with Transport Privatization.* Washington, D.C.: Brookings Institute.

Hambros SG. 1999. "Public-Private Partnerships for Highways: Experience, Structure, Financing, Applicability and Comparative Assessment." Objective One Final Report for Council of Deputy Ministers Responsible for Transportation and Highway Safety, March.

Hunter, Julius K. 1988. *Westmoreland and Portland Places: The History and Architecture of America's Premier Private Streets, 1888–1988.* Columbia, MO: University of Missouri Press.

Kahn, Alfred. 1988. *The Economics of Regulation.* Cambridge, MA: MIT Press.

Klein, Daniel B. 1990. "The Voluntary Provision of Public Goods? The Turnpike Companies of Early America." *Economic Inquiry* (March).

Lafayette Square Marquis. 1998. "Benton Place: The Nation's Oldest Private Street," http://www.lafayettesquare.org/marquis/december98/benton.html, 20:7 December.

Lay, M. G. 1992. *Ways of the World: A History of the World's Roads and of the Vehicles That Used Them.* New Brunswick, NJ: Rutgers University Press.

Levinson, David. 2001. *Financing Transportation Networks.* Cheltenham, UK: Edward Elgar Publishers.

Libertarian Party of the United States. 2000. Libertarian Party Platform.

McCormack, John, and Robert Rauch. 1997. "Initial Thoughts on the Mexican Toll Road Restructuring." BradyNet Inc. www.bradynet.com/n036.html.

Pawson, Eric. 1977. *Transport and Economy: The Turnpike Roads of Eighteenth Century Britain.* New York: Academic Press.

Payne, Peter L. 1956. "The Bermondsey, Rothermithe and Deptford Turnpike Trust: 1776–1810." *Journal of Transport History* 1:2:3: 132–143 (May).

Pritchett, William Kendrick. 1980. *Studies in Ancient Greek Topography Part III (Roads).* University of California Publications in Classical Studies, Vol. 22, p. 183. Berkeley, CA: University of California Press.

Smith, Adam. 1776. *An Inquiry into the Nature and Causes of the Wealth of Nations*, p. 128.

St. Louis. 2001. "Community Planning," http://stlouis.missouri.org/government/heritage/history/planning.htm.

Stephenson, Neal. 1992. *Snow Crash.* New York: Bantam Spectra Books, p. 7.

Tarr, Joel A., and Charles D. Jacobson. 1996. "No Single Path: Ownership and Financing of Infrastructure in the 19th and 20th Centuries." In *Infrastructure Delivery: Private Initiative and the Public Good*, edited by Ashoka Mody. Washington, D.C.: The World Bank, pp. 1–35.

Train, Kenneth. 1991. *Optimal Regulation.* Cambridge, MA: MIT Press.

Utt, Ronald D. 1999. "How Congressional Earmarks and Pork-Barrel Spending Undermine State and Local Decision-making." Heritage Foundation Backgrounder #1266, April 2, http://www.heritage.org/library/backgrounder/bg1266.html.

Viton, Philip A. 1995. "Private Roads." *Journal of Urban Economics* 37: 260–289.

Walton, C. Michael, and Mark Euritt. 1990. "Highway Finance and the Private Sector: Issues and Alternatives." *Transportation Research A* 24A(4): 265–276.

Washington Post. 2001. "Shuster Investigation." http://www.washingtonpost.com/wp-srv/politics/special/highway/shuster.htm.

Webb, Sidney, and Beatrice Webb. 1913. *English Local Government: The Story of the King's Highway.* London: Longmans, Green and Co.

5

Improving Road Safety by Privatizing Vehicle and Driver Testing and Licensing

John Semmens[1]

The Problem

In forty-four states plus the District of Columbia, the law requires owners of vehicles to carry liability insurance in order to register their vehicles (Insurance Research Council 1999, pp. 28–29). The idea is that vehicle owners should be held accountable for any damage they may cause while operating their vehicles. Yet, a considerable portion of the vehicles on the roads is without this legally mandated insurance. The Insurance Research Council's report—*Uninsured Motorists, 2000 Edition*—estimated that about 14 percent of motorists in the nation are operating uninsured vehicles (Insurance Research Council 2001). Among the states that require auto liability insurance, the failure to procure insurance ranged from a low of 4 percent of motorists in Maine to a high of 32 percent in Colorado. Among the six states that don't require auto liability insurance, the uninsured motorists ranged from a low of 9 percent for New Hampshire to a high of 25 percent for Alabama and Mississippi. These estimates, though, relied upon a survey of the self-reported assertions of individuals. Since almost all states require liability coverage, many individuals may have been reluctant to admit breaking the law. The actual percentage of uninsured vehicles could be considerably higher.

The reasons given by survey respondents for not having insurance are heavily tilted toward self-justifying rationales. About 41 percent claim that they can't afford to buy insurance or that the premium is too high. Another 41 percent assert that the uninsured vehicles are not in operating condition or are not currently in use (Insurance Research Council 1999, p. 12). This latter reason, if true, should be reflected in the statistics for accident claims. That is, if unin-

Figure 5.1
Reasons for Not Having Insurance

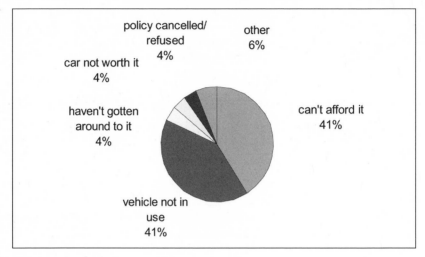

sured vehicles are not being driven, they shouldn't be involved in crashes. However, the data on accidents do not substantiate a contention that uninsured vehicles are not in the traffic stream. Uninsured motorists account for about 14 percent of the crashes resulting in bodily injury claims paid by insurance companies (Insurance Research Council 1999, pp. 20–21). Since this matches the percentage of motorists who admit to owning uninsured vehicles it probably means that the survey respondents were less than fully honest about the inoperability or non-use of the uninsured vehicles they own. Either the admittedly uninsured vehicles are being driven at rates approximating those of insured vehicles or, if a substantial portion of the uninsured vehicles is not in use, the percentage of uninsured vehicles must be far higher than 14 percent. If the respondents are being honest about their uninsured vehicles and a large portion of them are not being used, an alternative explanation for the uninsured vehicles' 14 percent representation in bodily injury claims must be that drivers of these vehicles are worse than average and get involved in a disproportionate number of crashes. Whichever explanation holds—that uninsured drivers are less honest or more dangerous—it is clear that there is a serious problem.

The magnitude of the problem can be illustrated by a couple of additional statistics. If we look at the admitted percentage of uninsured vehicles (14 percent) and the 2.7 trillion vehicle miles of travel in the United States in 1999 (Federal Highway Administration 2000, Table VM-3), we come up with an estimate that there may be nearly 400 billion vehicle miles of travel by unin-sured vehicles. In 1997, insurers paid out nearly $32 billion for bodily injury losses. Approximately $2.4 billion of this amount was paid for injuries under the uninsured motorist coverage bought by drivers who purchased such cover-age (Insurance Research Council 1999, p. 1). There are several reasons why the payments made by insurers understate the actual damages caused by unin-sured motorists. First, the "uninsured" and "underinsured" coverage offered by insurers reimburses only bodily injury medical expenses. It does not cover damage to property. The insured motorist is supposed to purchase collision coverage to compensate for property damage to his vehicle. Neither does unin-sured/underinsured coverage make up for lost wages. Nor does it award com-pensation for pain and suffering or other tort-related damages.

Second, not everyone who is insured purchases these coverages. Many expect their medical insurance rather than their auto insurance to cover their bodily injury expenses. So some of the damage caused by uninsured or under-insured motorists will not show up in the insurance industry's figures for pay-ments made under "uninsured" or "underinsured" coverage.

Finally, the uninsured losses borne by individuals are also not captured by the insurance industry's uninsured/underinsured damage figures. For example, one uninsured driver may cause damages to another uninsured driver. So, in terms of the order of magnitude of the problem, we are probably talking about a figure far in excess of $2.4 billion per year in costs imposed on the victims of accidents or their insurers.

There are over six million motor vehicle crashes a year (National Highway Traffic Safety Administration 2000). In two-thirds of these crashes there are no bodily injuries reported. There is only property damage. An estimate of the total cost of motor vehicle crashes for 1998 can be found in *Injury Facts 1999* (National Safety Council 2000). This cost estimate of $192 billion is nearly six times as high as the $32 billion in insurance claims paid for bodily injuries. If uninsured motorists represent 14 percent of the vehicles and are involved in 14 percent of the bodily injury crashes, it is not unreasonable to project that they may account for 14 percent of the total damages. This puts the total annual cost of uninsured vehicle crashes at around $27 billion.

Uninsured vehicles, of course, are only half the problem. Other vehicles are grossly underinsured. Most states that require auto liability insurance allow absurdly low minimum amounts of coverage. Arizona, for example, permits vehicles to be operated with liability coverage as low as $15,000/$30,000/$10,000. What this means is that the insurer will cover bodily injury damages up to $15,000 for a single victim, up to a $30,000 total for multiple victims, and up to a $10,000 total for property damage. It doesn't take much of a wreck to "total" a car. Replacing one "totaled" car could easily cost more than $10,000.

Table 5.1
Uninsured Vehicle Statistics

State	Percent Uninsured Motorists	Mandatory Insurance	Uninsured % of Injury Claims	Vehicle Miles of Travel (millions)	Uninsured Vehicle Miles of Travel (millions)
Alabama	25%	no	28%	56,165	14,041
Alaska	16%	yes	22%	4,545	727
Arizona	16%	yes	16%	46,829	7,493
Arkansas	11%	yes	12%	29,247	3,217
California	22%	yes	26%	300,066	66,015
Colorado	32%	yes	34%	40,732	13,034
Connecticut	9%	yes	11%	29,926	2,693
Delaware	11%	yes	15%	8,542	940
District of Columbia	21%	yes	22%	3,462	727
Florida	20%	yes	20%	141,903	28,381
Georgia	13%	yes	15%	98,859	12,852
Hawaii	10%	yes	16%	8,116	812
Idaho	8%	yes	9%	13,976	1,118
Illinois	13%	yes	12%	102,394	13,311
Indiana	12%	yes	15%	70,041	8,405
Iowa	10%	yes	10%	29,138	2,914
Kansas	9%	yes	8%	27,699	2,493
Kentucky	10%	yes	12%	47,816	4,782
Louisiana	8%	yes	12%	41,205	3,296
Maine	4%	yes	5%	14,143	566
Maryland	16%	yes	17%	49,126	7,860
Massachusetts	7%	yes	7%	51,820	3,627
Michigan	13%	yes	14%	95,644	12,434
Minnesota	12%	yes	14%	51,410	6,169
Mississippi	25%	no	29%	34,880	8,720
Missouri	13%	yes	13%	66,735	8,676
Montana	9%	yes	10%	9,835	885
Nebraska	7%	yes	7%	18,011	1,261
Nevada	15%	yes	16%	17,391	2,609
New Hampshire	9%	no	9%	11,894	1,070
New Jersey	15%	yes	12%	65,540	9,831
New Mexico	30%	yes	27%	22,362	6,709
New York	7%	yes	8%	126,491	8,854
North Carolina	6%	yes	5%	87,759	5,266
North Dakota	7%	yes	8%	7,262	508
Ohio	13%	yes	14%	105,487	13,713
Oklahoma	17%	yes	19%	42,569	7,237
Oregon	12%	yes	15%	34,680	4,162
Pennsylvania	9%	yes	13%	102,014	9,181
Rhode Island	11%	yes	20%	8,283	911
South Carolina	28%	yes	22%	44,146	12,361
South Dakota	6%	yes	6%	8,244	495
Tennessee	18%	no	20%	64,755	11,656
Texas	18%	yes	21%	210,874	37,957
Utah	9%	yes	9%	22,044	1,984
Vermont	9%	yes	10%	6,867	618
Virginia	12%	no	15%	73,904	8,868
Washington	15%	yes	17%	52,714	7,907
West Virginia	8%	yes	9%	19,033	1,523
Wisconsin	11%	no	11%	56,960	6,266
Wyoming	7%	yes	8%	7,797	546
Nationwide	14%	88%	14%	2,691,335	397,679

Sources: Insurance Research Council, *Uninsured Motorists*; Federal Highway Administration, *Highway Statistics*.

Considering that about 85 percent of the traffic accidents in the United States involve more than one vehicle (National Highway Traffic Safety Administration 1999, p. 72), it should be readily apparent that many crashes will produce property damage in excess of the minimum mandated liability coverage. As it is, the *average* cost of a "property damage only" accident is in the thousands of dollars. Estimates for the state of Arizona place this figure at around $6,400 (Williams 1999, p. 5). Minor injury accidents result in costs *averaging* nearly $15,000 per accident. Major injury accidents generate an *average* cost of $44,000. Fatal accidents produce damages in the million-dollar range. Next to this, the typical $15,000 to $30,000 coverage for injuring or killing someone is hopelessly inadequate. When the damage caused by a driver is not covered by his liability insurance (either because he has none or is underinsured) it is borne by the uninsured driver or the victim.

Modeling a Solution

There are two models useful in analyzing this situation. On the one hand, we could view roads as falling into the "ballpark" model. In the ballpark, customers are warned that the management assumes no responsibility for any injuries or damages suffered by their customers in the event that they are harmed by baseballs, bats, or players in the normal course of the game. If this model were applied to the roads, anyone who paid the price of admission to the roadways (i.e., purchased the necessary licenses and vehicle registrations) would have access. Road users would be forewarned that the government assumes no direct or indirect responsibility for any injuries or damages. Anyone venturing onto the roads would do so at his or her own risk and with the explicit warning that they might be harmed by others who would not be able to compensate them for any damage they suffer. Road users, then, would determine whether to buy insurance or not.

The chief advantage of the "ballpark" model is that it would remove the ambiguity regarding who should bear the responsibility of insurance. No one could venture onto the roadways under the impression that the state has guaranteed him or her that the other drivers are insured. The knowledge that there are no insurance requirements would inspire those who desire to be indemnified against damages that may be caused by other drivers to purchase their own adequate levels of insurance coverage. Those willing to bear the risks of going without insurance would be permitted to do so. Since the accident rate in the United States is about one per 400,000 vehicle miles of travel each year (National Highway Traffic Safety Administration 2000), the odds of any one driver being in a crash are very small. Given a typical annual 12,000 miles of travel for each automobile, there is a 97 percent chance that the vehicle won't be involved in any kind of accident and a 99 percent chance that the vehicle won't be involved in a bodily injury accident in any one year. When we factor in the possibility that one can significantly reduce the chances of accident involvement by adopting safer driving habits (e.g., obeying traffic rules, keeping the vehicle in good running order, and not consuming alcohol), the decision to go without insurance may not be entirely unreasonable. There are over 200 million registered vehicles in the United States (Federal Highway Administration 2000, Table MV-1). Dividing the number of vehicles into the $192 billion in crash damages gives us an estimated annual cost of around $900 per vehicle. If the cost to obtain insurance for a vehicle is greater than this amount, going without insurance could be a logical economic decision for a person who is not risk averse.

The chief disadvantage of the "ballpark" model is that driving might become more financially risky. Even though the reduction of the impact of "moral hazard" (i.e., the tendency for humans to exert less care in preventing events that are covered by insurance) on driving behavior in the "ballpark" model would tend to reduce the frequency of traffic accidents, the financial impact on those unfortunate enough to experience them could be substantial. Those without insurance could easily sustain losses that could bankrupt them. Those who do purchase insurance might well have to buy substantially larger amounts of coverage since there would likely be larger numbers of uninsured drivers. So, even though the total number of vehicle crashes and the social cost of traffic accidents would likely be lower if the "ballpark" model were implemented, the increased incidence of bankruptcy among the uninsured and the subsequent redistribution of financial burdens to those risk-averse enough to purchase insurance might be viewed as undesirable by many.

An alternative to the "ballpark" model is the "Disneyland" model. In Disneyland, customers are covered by the business' liability insurance. Consequently, the management sets its own risk reducing restrictions on who may use various facilities. Customers may be barred from some rides or attractions for being too small, too big, too frail, too pregnant, etc. Since the business is held strictly liable for any damages suffered by those entering the park, management will undertake a substantial effort to enforce its rules in order to avoid having to compensate injured parties for any harm done to them while in the park.

Like the "ballpark" model, the "Disneyland" model would also reduce the ambiguity concerning who will be responsible for damages. In this case, obtaining insurance would be a prerequisite of venturing out onto the roadways. Enforcement of the insurance requirement would be best achieved by having the insurers issue the licenses and vehicle registrations. This differs from the current system wherein the mandatory insurance is sold by private vendors, but is enforced by the public sector. The current system of public sector enforcement has serious flaws that undermine its effectiveness. The government charged with enforcing mandatory insurance laws does not assume liability for damages done by drivers that fail to comply with the insurance requirement. There is no significant financial consequence to the government for failure to enforce the mandatory insurance requirement. Hence, we must rely solely upon the government bureaucracy's devotion to duty as the main motivation for enforcement of the mandatory auto insurance law. As dedicated to duty as many individual bureaucrats may be, bureaucracy itself is not noted for efficiency or effectiveness.

Meanwhile, private insurance companies have very weak incentives to guard against persons buying inadequate insurance or canceling coverage once their vehicle obtains the desired registration tags from the state's motor vehicle authority. Inasmuch as insurance premiums are directly related to amount of coverage and the risk of having to pay, rates will vary. Some of the worst drivers—those most likely to inflict substantial damages on others and consequently facing higher insurance premium costs per dollar of coverage—buy only the minimum amount of coverage required by law. These drivers fall into the pool of "underinsured" risks on our roadways. The insurance industry knowingly sells these inadequate policies because the insurer's liability is capped by the low amounts of coverage provided. So, while the premiums paid by these high-risk drivers are sufficient to cover the losses of the insurers, they are not sufficient to cover the full actuarial cost of the damage that is the likely result of their risky driving behavior. These uncovered costs are shifted to the victims of these drivers.

In addition to buying an inadequate amount of coverage, another way of flouting the intent of the mandatory auto insurance law is to buy a policy in order to obtain the vehicle registration tags or plates, but cancel the coverage after the tags or plates are received. When the policy is cancelled, the insurance company is typically required to notify the government's motor vehicle authority. In Arizona, on average, there is about two weeks elapsed time between the termination of a policy and the insurance company's notification of the state's Motor Vehicle Division. Once notified, Arizona's Motor Vehicle Division sends a letter to the vehicle owner to let him know that the state is now aware that he has cancelled his insurance. If there is no response from the vehicle owner, this failure to carry insurance will be entered into a computerized database accessible by law enforcement officers. Then, if these officers have occasion to call for information on the vehicle, the lack of insurance will be one of the pieces of information they will be given. Obviously, given this largely "paper enforcement," an individual could drive around for a considerable period with no insurance. If, during this period, there is an accident, the victim or victims will have no assurance that they will be compensated for any damages caused by this uninsured individual.

If the current, weakly enforced mandatory auto insurance laws were to be replaced by a fully privatized system based on the "Disneyland" model there would be a much stronger incentive to ensure that all vehicles had adequate insurance coverage. This would also help to keep the worst drivers off the roads. If insurance companies had to accept full liability for whomever they issued a driver license and vehicle registration the problem of "underinsureds" would vanish. By definition, there would be no limit to the liability assumed by the insurer. The insurer would, in fact, be insuring that whatever damage was caused by one of its policyholders would be covered. Bad drivers would not have the option of buying a woefully inadequate policy. They would be forced to pay the full cost of their actuarial risk in order to obtain a driver license and vehicle registration. The insurance company would see to this as a matter of business survival.

The chief advantage of the "Disneyland" model is also, in many people's view, its chief disadvantage. Many high-risk drivers would not be able to purchase insurance. Either the price to cover the likely damages they might cause would be higher than they would be willing or able to pay, or they may be unable to find an insurer willing to sell them coverage at any price. This would effectively deny them the legal right to drive on the roads. Keeping these high-risk drivers off the roads, then, could create some hardship for them by greatly reducing their mobility.

As we can see, both the "ballpark" and "Disneyland" models have their advantages and disadvantages. Either could work because the responsibility is clearly assigned. The current mandatory auto insurance laws fit into neither model. The idea behind mandatory auto insurance laws—that users of the roads should be responsible for the damages they may cause—is not a bad one. However, the enforcement of the current mandatory auto insurance laws has proven troublesome. The fines for failure to carry liability insurance are typically low. In Arizona, the fine is only $250 for a first offense. The amount of this fine is less than the typical six-month insurance premium on most vehicles. Even then, the law says the fine may be waived if the cited individual purchases insurance prior to his court appearance (Arizona Revised Statutes Title 28, Section 1251). Many financially irresponsible drivers may choose to go without insurance when facing these cost trade-offs. So, even though the state nominally requires users to be insured, since the state is not held liable for allowing uninsured vehicles onto the roads the incentives to enforce the mandatory insurance law are weak. As a result, victims of high-risk under-insured or uninsured drivers must suffer billions of dollars per year in uncompensated costs.

A Privatization Solution

Given the problem of a significant annual burden due to uncompensated costs that are being inflicted on victims of underinsured and uninsured drivers, a coherent solution is needed. The contrasting "ballpark" and "Disneyland" models each offer a coherent solution. However, it is my opinion that the "Disneyland" model provides a solution that most people would find more satisfactory. While each model is likely to make the roads safer, the "ballpark" model does this by imposing more of the burden on the cautious drivers. The "Disneyland" model, in contrast, would make the roads safer by removing more of the high-risk drivers.

Assuming that we would like to explore the "Disneyland" model in more detail before deciding whether to implement it, let's take a look at how it might work. Conceivably, one might assert that the same entity that issues the licenses and registrations ought to supply the insurance. This would entail the state government getting into the auto insurance business. While plausible on paper, government insurance schemes have not fared well in practice. The Old Age, Survivors' and Disability Insurance (i.e., Social Security) program has had repeated financial problems and may be unable to fulfill its financial obligations to future retirees. Government medical insurance (i.e., Medicare and Medicaid) has seen expenses soar beyond the government's planned outlays on a regular basis. Government insured student loans have an extraordinarily high non-repayment percentage. It seems improbable that a government-run auto insurance program could avoid these kinds of problems. So, if having the state run an auto insurance program is a bad means of consolidating the insurance and licensing/registration functions, the alternative of having the insurers issue the licenses and registrations merits examination.

Having insurers issue licenses and registrations amounts to a "privatization" of this activity. Nominally, a privatization law would state that vehicle registrations and driver licenses would be issued by those willing and able to assume full responsibility for any damage caused by the vehicle and its driver. Normally, we would expect that this would mean that insurance companies would issue the registrations and driver licenses. If insurers issued licenses and registrations it would be absolutely clear who was legally responsible for a particular vehicle being on the road. Insurers would have a very strong incentive to make sure that every vehicle and driver insured by them has adequate coverage. Insurers would also have a strong incentive to make sure that uninsured vehicles and drivers did not use the roadways.

To clarify financial responsibility for potential damages done on the roadways, the privatization law would state that as long as a vehicle bore the license plate of an insurer, that insurer would be held liable for any damages caused by that vehicle. With this kind of provision in the law, it is likely that insurers would only issue plates after thoroughly testing the skills and investigating the driving records of those they are insuring. We could also expect that insurers would insist on receiving an adequate premium from the insured individual before issuing him plates. Insurers should not be allowed to escape liability (as they now often are) by later showing that the insured lied on his application to purchase the insurance. This may seem hard on the insurers, but consider the alternative. When an insurer can bail out of a policy, this means that the victims of the erstwhile insured party are apt to be left without any recourse for ameliorating the damages they have suffered. Future potential victims have no reasonable means of investigating all potential high-risk drivers that might be on the roads. On the other hand, insurers do have a reasonable means of conducting such an investigation of their prospective customers prior to issuing a policy. If an insurer is not satisfied that a prospective customer is truthful or a good risk, it can refuse to issue a policy. Under the proposed vehicle registration privatization scheme, suspect applicants will not be able to legally use the roads until they can find an insurer willing to issue them a policy and its verifying license plates.

Since issuing an auto insurance policy and issuing license plates would be simultaneous events, those without insurance would be easier to spot on the roads. They would be operating vehicles without plates. This would be a more obvious sign of lack of insurance than is currently the case. Indeed, given the greater degree of responsibility placed on each insurer, it seems likely that steps to improve the "visibility" of license plates would be undertaken. For example, the much-tested, but little deployed "electronic license plate" would likely be a widespread innovation under a privatized licensing system. Under an electronic license plate regime, plateless vehicles could be detected via automated means and would be even more conspicuous to enforcement personnel.

The dodge of buying insurance just to obtain a vehicle registration tag and then canceling the insurance once the tags are received would become much more difficult. Since the insurer would be responsible for damages done by vehicles bearing the insurer's plates, there is a very strong incentive to require a substantial insurance payment or deposit that will only be refunded when the plates are turned back to the issuer. While this return-for-refund process may be less convenient than canceling one's insurance by phone, it should virtually eliminate the problem of uninsured vehicles resulting from canceled policies. It would essentially implement the revocation of driving privileges that a survey of state motor vehicle departments indicated would be the most effective measure for enforcing mandatory insurance requirements (Insurance Research Council 1999, p. 35). Given the many insurance sales locations and the interconnection of these offices via computer networks, obtaining or returning plates ought to be a lot more convenient than it is to deal with the government's motor vehicle authorities on these issues in the current environment.

Individuals would be free to shop for the best license, registration, and insurance deal they could find. Each insurer would be free to establish its own criteria for issuing policies and license plates. Some insurers may opt to cover only low-risk drivers. Other insurers may opt to cover high-risk drivers at correspondingly higher premiums. Some insurers may wish to give written and/or road tests to prospective customers. Some insurers may want to conduct regular safety inspections of their customers' vehicles. Some insurers may wish to encourage or require some or all of the vehicles they insure to be equipped with safety-enhancing devices (for example, an ignition that can only be activated after the driver passes an automated, on-board breathalyzer test). Customers may choose to accept some limitations on their driving in exchange for reductions in premiums (for example, driving only during daylight hours). Other may prefer to pay more in order to escape driving restrictions. In short, there is likely to be a wide variety of payment/license/registration options available. Nevertheless, those who could not meet the minimum requirements of *any* insurer would not be issued vehicle plates. Insurers would have no incentive to assist individuals in "beating" the government's mandatory insurance requirement. The streets would be safer because vehicles without insurance would also be without license plates and would be easier for police to spot and remove from the roads.

Privatizing the issuance of licenses and registrations in this fashion would also do away with underinsured vehicles. Since the issuer of the vehicle plates would be responsible for whatever damage is caused by one of its policyholders, there would be no motive for selling low-dollar-coverage liability insurance. The current policy of allowing "judgment proof" drivers (i.e., those who do not fear the financial consequences of the damage they may do because they are unable to pay) to buy insurance that may fall far short of compensating victims for any harm they suffer at the hands of these "judgment proof" drivers is irresponsible and, in many instances, inhumane.

Estimating the Benefits

The potential benefits would occur in two areas. We have already estimated that the current system causes the victims of uninsured drivers to be burdened by $27 billion per year in uncompensated costs. Adopting the proposed reform of privatizing vehicle registrations would shift these costs off the innocent victims of bad driving and back onto those who cause the accidents. As the perpetrators of damage were forced to bear a larger share of the consequences of their actions we could expect some modifications in their behavior. Insurers, in order to make a profit and stay in business, would have to do a good job of matching premiums to risk. This would motivate them to take actions that would reduce risk. A price structure that accurately reflected risk would push drivers toward safer behavior. A refusal to insure the worst risks would take many of the really dangerous drivers off the roads entirely. So, over the long run, not only would the $27 billion of uncompensated losses be shifted back to those at fault, it is also likely that losses would be reduced as driving behavior improves and the worst risks are taken off the roads.

The other source of potential benefits would come from eliminating functions of the state Departments of Transportation. Currently, the Motor Vehicle Division of the Arizona Department of Transportation is budgeted for an annual expenditure of around $80 million. While the costs of specific activities are not published, I estimate that about half of this outlay is the result of vehicle registration activity. Of the remaining activities (issuing driver licenses, recording vehicle titles, collecting highway user taxes, and manning the ports-of-entry) issuing driver licenses is probably the most expensive. So, if we privatize the registration and driver license functions we could probably reduce public sector spending by about $50 million per year in this one state. Extrapolating this to encompass a nationwide privatization, public expenditures could probably be reduced by around $2.7 billion.

Some may argue that the $2.7 billion per year saving of public expenditure will be offset by an increase of private sector spending as insurers undertake the effort to issue registrations and driver licenses. This apparent offsetting expense, though, may be exaggerated. As it now stands, auto dealers must compile all the data necessary to register newly sold vehicles. This data is then forwarded to the state motor vehicle agencies for entry on the state's vehicle registration database. Selling insurance and issuing registrations on the spot might actually be easier than the current process. The perception that this might be the case inspired an Arizona auto dealership to volunteer to pilot test a program wherein the dealership would issue the vehicle registrations. The Arizona Department of Transportation estimated that this "third party" registration procedure could save up to $1 million a year if adopted statewide. One third of the projected savings would be in postage alone (Scarp 1993, p. A-1). Arizona law now permits the director of Arizona's Motor Vehicle Division to authorize "third parties" to issue vehicle registrations (Arizona Revised Statutes, Title 28, Section 1471). While Arizona's "third party" vehicle registration program has gone part of the way toward privatization and demonstrated that it is feasible for the official government tasks of vehicle registration to be handled by private businesses, it has stopped short of full privatization. This has kept the savings small and does nothing to mitigate the uninsured/underinsured vehicle problems.

The potential for a "one-stop-shopping" convenience under full privatization would appear to be substantial. One could buy a car, get it registered, and insure it all at one location. The insurers and auto dealers would have an incentive to make the process as expeditious as possible. In fact, competition among insurers and dealers would help promote efficiency and convenience.

Consider a typical transaction with the current state motor vehicle agency. It's your lunch hour. You have chosen this opportunity to take care of some business down at the Department of Motor Vehicles' nearest branch office. Maybe you need to renew a driver license, register a vehicle, or obtain a title. Your first task is to find the local Department of Motor Vehicles' nearest branch office. They're not always conveniently located. They're certainly scarcer than any other auto related business location you might have need of. As your search for the Department of Motor Vehicles' nearest branch office drags on, you pass numerous gasoline stations, a half-dozen auto parts stores, several auto insurance sales offices, and a few auto dealerships.

Finally, you locate the Department of Motor Vehicles' nearest branch office. You walk in and join the line of people waiting for service. Your advance to the head of the line is not hastened by the fact that a goodly percentage of Department of Motor Vehicles personnel have also chosen this time to take their lunch break. When your turn finally arrives you are greeted by an employee whose occupation was ranked last in a survey of civility published by the *Wall Street Journal*. That is, on a scale of zero to ten (with zero being the worst and ten being the best), Department of Motor Vehicles employees have been rated 0.2. This is below ratings received for comparable customer contact employees like sales clerks (7.5), grocery check-out cashiers (7.0), gas station attendants (6.2), bank tellers (6.0), stadium ticket sellers (3.5), city bus drivers (1.6), and utility company employees (0.8) (Smith 1986).

You think the service could be more convenient, expeditious, and courteous, but it isn't and won't be likely to get that way. The monopoly position of the state agency authorized to handle matters relating to the operation of vehicles on public roads pretty much assures that it won't. After all, it is not as if you could take your "business" elsewhere. Reducing the incidence of the above-mentioned type of transactions would be another benefit of privatizing the vehicle registration and driver license functions of the Motor Vehicle Division.

Achieving Reform

Shifting the issuance of vehicle registrations and driver licenses to the private sector would require legislation. Any prospective legislation must overcome the normal obstacles of the legislative process. A bill privatizing registrations and driver licenses would have to clear committees in both houses of the legislature, get a majority vote in each house, and be signed by the governor. This is an arduous process that trips up many a bill.

This proposal will likely be resisted by the state motor vehicle agency bureaucracy. After all, if the agency is no longer needed to register motor vehicles or issue driver licenses we may well question whether it is needed at all. At the very least, we may be talking about a 50 percent cutback in its budget. Hundreds of people would see their public sector jobs eliminated. These prospective impacts will inspire those likely to be affected to object to the proposed privatization reform.

We may also expect some initial opposition from the auto insurance industry. At the outset, the increased responsibility thrust upon the insurance industry will provoke uncertainty. Businesses generally do not like uncertainty. Uncertainty increases risk. New means of coping with this risk and making a profit would have to be learned. However, once the insurers understand that they will be compensated by their customers for the costs of issuing registrations and licenses, that privatization will not saddle them with requirements to provide subsidies to high-risk drivers, they should be more receptive to the idea. The opportunity to play a more direct role in controlling the risk of the roadway environment should be perceived as a means of reducing underwriting losses over the long term. As the environment becomes safer, insurers' losses will fall (ultimately, premium rates would be expected to fall as well, but not as rapidly as underwriting losses). This should improve insurer profitability. In addition, many of those currently evading the mandatory insurance law will become the reluctant customers of the insurance industry. This also should increase insurer profitability. Lastly, many of those currently underinsuring their vehicles would be required by insurers to buy adequate coverage. This will also increase insurer profitability.

The general public may be apprehensive about letting the private sector insurers decide who gets onto the roads. The idea that this would be less desirable than allowing a government bureaucracy that bears no responsibility for the consequences of bad decisions or weak enforcement of traffic and mandatory insurance laws to determine who gets onto the roads is not a foregone conclusion. We have grown accustomed to allowing private sector businesses to decide who can and cannot obtain credit. Obtaining a loan to buy a house or a car must pass private sector scrutiny. Obtaining a more general access to credit is achieved by getting a credit card issued by a private sector financial institution. We have learned to live with this system. We expect the decisions to be made on rational criteria. And they are. Reflection upon how the private sector has handled this vital segment of contemporary life combined with the greater convenience of the hours kept by insurers and the assurance that responsible drivers would not have to pay high premiums to cover damage done by uninsured or underinsured drivers should help to alleviate some of the general public's apprehension.

Of course, that segment of the population that is currently flouting the mandatory insurance law or exploiting it by underinsuring their vehicles would be expected to raise quite a fuss over this privatization reform proposal. While we should not be persuaded by the objections of those who wish to continue passing the burdens of their own risky driving behaviors on to others, we can envision some means of addressing their legitimate concerns.

The case most deserving of sympathy is that of the individual whose past driving behavior has taught him a lesson. It is unfortunate for such individuals that many more proclaim to have learned lessons than actually have. Consequently, individuals with bad driving records would undoubtedly have trouble obtaining insurance and permission to use the roads. I would expect insurers to establish methods of serving this market niche. One method would be to require the vehicle of such a person to be equipped with devices that enhance the safe operation of the vehicle. We already mentioned the possibility of a "breathalyzer-ignition" link. Other options could include vehicles that could only run during daylight hours (perhaps having a solar collector connection to the engine or transmission) or vehicles whose maximum speed could not exceed a low setting (perhaps having "speed governors" placed on the engine). Insurers might want to require periodic safety inspections of the vehicle as a condition of issuing a registration. Insurers might see fit to require regular driving tests for individuals whose driving behavior has been demonstrated to be more hazardous than average.

It may then be feasible for some high-risk, but repentant drivers to work toward a full reinstatement of driving privileges by demonstrating meritorious performance under limited driving privileges. For others, though, the outlook will be less sanguine. There are some people who should not be behind the wheel of a car. Stopping them from driving not only helps to preserve the health and lives of others, but also may save the driving-deprived individual from injuring or killing himself. Incompetent drivers must find other means of meeting their transportation needs. Carpooling is one obvious option. Living or working closer to the places where one needs to travel is another option. Riding the bus is another option. Even if these options are less convenient, the rest of society should not be obliged to bear the risk of allowing persons who cannot cover the costs of any damage they are likely to cause to drive vehicles on the roadways.

It may be preferable to try this reform in a pilot project in a localized region prior to full-scale statewide or nationwide implementation. This would enable insurers to gain some experience with the process before having to rely on it for the more than 200 million vehicles registered in the United States. The selection of a specific localized region should be made jointly by the insurance industry and government officials. This use of a localized experiment would enable us to better anticipate any transitional difficulties and prevent them from becoming a crisis.

Conclusion

Making our roads safer by holding drivers responsible for any damages they might cause is a legitimate role for government to play. Requiring autos to be insured as a prerequisite to obtaining a registration is intended to fulfill this role. After more than a decade of state mandatory auto insurance laws, though, it is clear that the current system is falling short of its intended effect. Too many vehicles are being operated without insurance. Others are being operated with inadequate amounts of insurance coverage. This inflicts uncompensated damage on innocent victims.

The current mandatory insurance laws provide insufficient incentives for safe and responsible behavior. The laws themselves typically impose mild sanctions on the uninsured while explicitly allowing underinsured drivers to impose uncompensated costs on others. Irresponsible drivers have the means and opportunity for evading the intent of the mandatory insurance laws. The government motor vehicle agencies bear no significant consequence for inadvertently or negligently allowing irresponsible drivers to escape the burdens of their actions. Insurers are currently mere intermediaries with no effective methods for promoting a safer traffic environment. These defects can and should be remedied by having insurers issue the vehicle registrations and driver licenses.

It is not everyday that we have an opportunity to improve public safety and reduce the costs of transportation. Privatizing the issuance of vehicle registrations and driver licenses would appear to be an instance of the much-coveted "win-win" situation. All that is required is the will to act and the patience to work out the details of this innovative solution to a chronic problem.

Note

1. The views expressed in this chapter do not necessarily represent those of the Arizona Department of Transportation.

References

Federal Highway Administration. 2000. *Highway Statistics 1999*. Washington, D.C.
Insurance Research Council. 1999. *Uninsured Motorists*. Malvern, Pennsylvania.
Insurance Research Council. 2001. Press release, February 1. Malvern, Pennsylvania.

National Highway Traffic Safety Administration. 1999. *Traffic Safety Facts 1998.* Washington, D.C.

National Highway Traffic Safety Administration. 2000. *Traffic Safety Facts 1999.* Washington, D.C.

National Safety Council. 2000. *Injury Facts 1999.* Itasca, Illinois.

Scarp, Mark J. 1993. "Brock Auto Mall Tests License Plate Program," *Scottsdale Progress/Tribune*, October 15, p. A-1.

Smith, Donald G. 1986. "Rating Occupations on a Civility Scale," *Wall Street Journal.*

Williams, Jim, et al. 1999. *Motor Vehicle Crash Facts 1998*. Phoenix, Arizona: Arizona Department of Transportation.

Part III

Improving the Pricing of Roads

6

Congestion Pricing:
The Singapore Experience

Gopinath Menon[1]

Background

Whether roads are publicly or privately owned, the efficient use of congested facilities requires the imposition of extra charges during periods of extra demand. This is known as congestion pricing. Such views about congestion pricing have been around for a long time and came into fashion again in the 1960s. There was the realization that road building could not be the sole answer to solving traffic problems. New roads occupy space, are costly, and take considerable time to be completed. Road building programs cannot keep pace with the increase in vehicle population. To keep traffic problems within manageable levels, there has to be a lid on the amount of vehicle usage on the roads. When a motorist uses the road, he is only aware of the cost incurred to him for his immediate needs, such as paying for gasoline. When there is no traffic congestion, these costs may approximate total costs. But as traffic increases and there is congestion, the motorist imposes cost on the community that rise above private costs. Congestion pricing works on the principle that the motorist should pay for all the costs of his trip, including congestion costs. When a motorist pays all the costs of his trip, he will be more selective and discriminating in making his trips resulting in a more efficient distributing of trip time and places.

Some privately owned roads do exercise a loose sort of control of use of the road via road tolls. However, unless most roads are privately owned, only a public authority will be in a position to implement congestion pricing on an area-wide basis.

This chapter describes the experience of Singapore in implementing and managing congestion pricing.

Background on Singapore

Singapore is an island city-state located at the tip of the Malayan Peninsula in South-East Asia. The vital transport statistics in 2004 are:

Area	700 sq. km
Length of roads	3200 km (approximately 12 percent of land area)
Population	4.24 million
Vehicle population	727,000 (of which 417,000 are private automobiles)
Auto:person ratio	1:10
Main public transport	train, bus, taxi
Modal split (all trips)	public:private (60 percent:40 percent)

Transportation Strategy

When Singapore gained independence in 1965 from Britain, the country was beset by transportation problems caused by rapid development. After studying the issue, the transportation authorities concluded that building more roads was not going to solve the problem. For a small country with limited land space, sheer building of roads meant taking up land that could be put to more productive use. It also meant massive destruction of built-up areas for road building and widening and in the process destroying the living environment. Two transportation studies carried out in the early 1970s came to the conclusion that some sort of restraints on auto ownership and usage would be necessary in the future. This implied that radical changes would have to be made on policies and attitudes on auto usage. There would also have to be a large shift to the widespread use of public transport. To achieve this, public transport had to be improved and given priority over private transport.

A balanced transportation strategy evolved from these considerations:

The components of this transportation strategy for the past thirty years were

a. integrated land-use and transportation planning policy to improve accessibility to all developing areas;

b. provision of a good and modest road network complemented by good traffic management, including harnessing technology for intelligent transport systems (ITS) to maximize road capacity;

c. continuous improvements to public transport (bus and rail) to make them the predominant mode of travel;

d. travel demand management to curtail excessive demand for private auto travel.

The first three components of this strategy fall under what is known as the provision of supply: the provision of more road capacity and passenger capacity for traveling. Many city authorities in the world have adopted these three components in managing their transport situation. But most of them have found that they have not been able to meet the transport demand by the mere use of supply measures. Demand for transport soon outstripped the supply. The fourth component is a demand management measure. A judicious choice of demand management measures can keep a lid on the demand for making trips. Singapore introduced *two* demand management measures: a vehicle quota system to keep vehicle ownership to manageable levels (called the vehicle quota system) and congestion pricing, that is, vehicles pay for the congestion they are causing when using the roads. Restraints on vehicle ownership may not be desirable or feasible in other countries. So the vehicle quota system is discussed only briefly with the main discussion focusing on congestion pricing, which has desirable aspects wherever traffic congestion is a serious problem.

Restraint on Vehicle Ownership

In Singapore, the vehicle quota system complements congestion pricing. Members of the public wishing to purchase new vehicles have to obtain a certificate of entitlement (COE) during a fortnightly bidding exercise. The number of COEs that are available for bidding is announced prior to each exercise. The bidding process is similar to that of an open auction. Would-be buyers of new vehicles bid electronically by specifying the maximum amount that they are willing to pay for the COE (also known as the reserve price). The system will bid on their behalf. Bidders can check the current COE price at any time during the bidding exercise and revise their reserve price. At the close of the auction, successful bidders pay the Quota Premium (QP), which is the highest unsuccessful reserve price plus S$1 (US$0.57) (minimum bid amount) to get the COE. For example, if the quota for a particular vehicle category is 1,000 and there are 2,500 bidders in that vehicle category, then all successful bidders (1st to 1000th ranked in price from the highest reserve price) for COEs in that category will pay the QP that is equivalent to the 1001st reserve price plus $1. New vehicles can only be bought with a valid COE. The current price of a COE (in 2005) for autos is about S$20,000. The vehicles that do not need COEs are public buses, school buses, emergency vehicles such as fire engines, ambulances, and police cars, vehicles belonging to the diplomatic corps and engineering plants, and vehicles registered under disabled persons and charitable voluntary organizations.

The COE is valid for ten years and is tied to the vehicle. If the owner wishes to retain the vehicle after ten years, he can renew the COE for another ten years by paying the prevailing quota premium, which is the average of the past three months' average QPs of the fortnightly exercise for that vehicle category.

The total number of annual COEs is set based on Singapore's long-term road building, public transport, and traffic management program and aimed at limiting vehicle population increases to about 3 percent per annum.

Motorist's View of Congestion Pricing

Congestion pricing is difficult to sell to the motorists. While most would not argue against paying for the use of water and electricity, the concept of paying for the use of road space is alien to them. The use of roads has always been free in most cities. So any attempt to charge for its use is seen as a means to raise revenue for the public authorities. Some cities have managed to persuade the motorists that tolls can be charged to pay for recovering the cost of building new roads. This cost recovery is seen to be logical and is more acceptable to many.

Congestion pricing has to be sold to motorists as part of an overall transportation package of supply and demand management measures. It must be stressed that the supply measures by themselves cannot take care of the transportation problems and that demand management measures are needed to attain a balance. A mixture of supply and demand measures working together is the best way to keep transportation problems within manageable levels, as has been experienced in Singapore.

Toll Roads vs. Congestion Pricing

Although both collect fees for the use of the road, there is a subtle difference between toll roads and congestion pricing.

The tolls collected are meant to cover the capital costs for building of the road, its maintenance, operation, and a reasonable profit for the operator. It is understandable that the private sector has an interest in toll roads and there are several instances in many countries where public authorities let out build-operate-transfer projects on major toll roads. The generation of sufficient revenue is the major factor in determining the toll fee. The toll road operator welcomes a greater use of the road by motorists.

In a congestion pricing scheme, fees are meant to regulate the use of the road. They are set to obtain the desired traffic conditions along the road and the generation of revenue is not a consideration. The operator is indifferent to whether more or less motorists use the road, as long as the desired traffic conditions are met. Where there is no profit motive, congestion pricing is likely to be a public sector initiative. It is possible that the fees collected could go towards making other transport improvements.

Area Licensing Scheme (ALS):
The Manual Congestion Pricing Scheme 1975–98

In 1975, Singapore introduced a *manual* congestion pricing scheme called the Area Licensing Scheme for the city. The aim of the scheme was to charge vehicles for the use of the road at times and at places when and where they caused congestion. Under the ALS, an imaginary cordon was drawn around the most congested parts of the city, and the enclosed area was called the Restricted Zone (RZ) with an area of 720 hectares. Each of the thirty-three entry points to the RZ was demarcated by an overhead gantry sign. To enter this area, restricted vehicles had to pay a fee. Since there was no experience in setting such a congestion fee, it was decided to set it such that the total cost of driving into the city doubled. To most motorists, the cost that they incurred in those days was the cost of the daily parking fee, which was S$3 (US $1.70) Therefore, the initial daily congestion fee (area license fee) was set at the prevailing cost of daily parking of S$3. This meant that the total monthly cost of entering and parking in the city would be about S$120 (for twenty days) compared with about S$30 if he opted to park and ride at fringe car parks just outside the RZ. The objective was to reduce the number of vehicles entering the RZ during the rush hours to the levels that were experienced during the off-rush hours, when traffic conditions were satisfactory. This required a reduction of about 30 percent in total traffic volumes entering the RZ. Each daily entry for an auto or taxi into the RZ between 7:30 A.M.–10:15 A.M. cost S$3. Motorists could make unlimited number of entries with the area license. With the initial S$3 charge, there was a drop of 44 percent in traffic volumes during the rush hours and there were some comments about the "overkill" situation, with the roads in the RZ being underutilized and forcing traffic to use roads outside the RZ and causing congestion. No attempt was made to bring down the rates to encourage more vehicles to enter the RZ because it was accepted that more vehicles would do so naturally as they got used to the system. As expected, there was a gradual creep in the number of entering vehicles and, by 1988, when the scheme was first revised, the percentage reduction was about 31 percent, which was what had been expected when ALS was first introduced in 1975. The ALS lasted for a period of twenty-three years until 1998, when it was automated by an electronic road pricing (ERP) system. During this period the ALS underwent many changes, which were necessitated by the natural growth in the city, growth in vehicle population, and the traffic conditions along the city roads.

The three important milestones were:

   a. In 1975, the restricted vehicles were private autos and taxis during the morning peak hours (rush hours) of 7:30 A.M. to 10:15 A.M. on weekdays and Saturdays. All other vehicles and carpools (four occupants in a car including driver) were exempted.

b. In 1989, the restricted vehicles were revised to include all vehicles during the morning peak hours of 7:30 A.M. to 10:15 A.M. on weekdays and Saturdays and the evening peak hours of 4:30 P.M. to 6:30 P.M. on weekdays. Public buses and emergency vehicles were exempted. The carpool exemptions were withdrawn. It can be asked why the carpool exemption was withdrawn. The initial reason for giving exemptions for carpools (and taxi pools) was to counter the criticism that the ALS favored the rich who could easily afford to pay the area license fee. Carpools did indeed find favor among the motorists and at one time more than half the cars entering the RZ in the morning were by way of carpools. A genuine carpool system is one in which four auto owners get together to use one auto for the journey. A closer examination showed that what was happening was not carpooling, but hitchhiking. Many motorists stopped at bus stops to pick up three passengers to form the carpool and offer free rides to bus commuters. The carpool system had been reduced to a system of getting around the ALS. In the earlier years of the ALS, such carpools helped reduce demand on an overstretched bus system, but by the late 1980s the public transport system had improved considerably. The carpooling exemptions had outlived their usefulness and hence they were removed.

c. In 1994 the ALS was extended for the whole working day of 7:30 A.M. to 7 P.M. on weekdays and 7:30 A.M. to 2 P.M. on Saturdays, with higher morning and evening peak hour area licensing fees and lower off-peak hour fees. Public buses and emergency vehicles were exempted.

Until 1998 (just before the conversion to ERP), to enter the Restricted Zone during the period of 7:30 P.M. to 7 P.M. on weekdays and 7:30 A.M. to 2 P.M. on Saturdays, restricted vehicles had to buy and display an area license. License fees varied for different classes of vehicles. These paper licenses came in daily and monthly types and had to be displayed prominently on the vehicle windscreens, or on special holders on the motorcycle handlebars. The area licenses, which cost between 70 cents and S$3 for daily use (depending on the classification of the vehicle and the time of entry), and between S$20 and S$120 for monthly use, were distinguishable from each other by their shape and color. This permitted easier identification by police officers at the entry points. The area licenses were sold at post offices, convenience stores, gasoline stations, and at special area license sales booths set up along the approach roads to the RZ. Licenses could not be purchased at the entry points. Police officers stationed in sentry huts at all the entry points (under the overhead gantry signs) enforced by observing whether the entering vehicles had the correct valid area licenses as they passed. The penalty for a violation was set at S$70. Escape routes were designated at the main entry points to ensure that motorists were not forced unwittingly to enter the RZ. There was no policing within the RZ. Vehicles were free to move around and leave the RZ. Whole-day licenses were valid for entry during the whole of the restricted period between 7:30 A.M. and 7 P.M. on weekdays and 7.30 A.M. and 2 P.M. on Saturdays. Part-day licenses (which cost about 2/3 of the whole-day licenses) were valid for entry only during the off-peak hours, namely between 9:30 A.M. and 4:30 P.M. on weekdays and 9.30 A.M. and 2 P.M. on Saturdays.

What Did the Manual Congestion Pricing Scheme (ALS) Achieve?

Over the twenty-three years (1975–98) that the ALS was in operation, the city had grown by about 30 percent in terms of area with increases in employment and commercial activity. The vehicle population had increased threefold over the same period. Yet traffic conditions on the city roads within the Restricted Zone were better than what they had been in 1975. The average traffic speeds in the city during the working day varied from 26 kph to 32 kph, as compared with 15 kph to 20 kph, prior to implementation of ALS. The increase in speeds came about because of the reduction in vehicles entering the RZ. This reduction was partly caused by some motorists changing their behavior by changing times of travel or using public transport. Some motorists who had their origins and destinations outside the RZ, but used the RZ roads as a through route, also stopped doing so. Speeds on roads in the range of 26–32 kph were considered good for a city of Singapore's size.

A substantial shift took place in modal split with the introduction of ALS. In 1975, the bus share of the work trips to the RZ in the morning was 46 percent. Private transport trips were 46 percent by car, 6 percent by motorcycles, and 2 percent by other modes. In 1983, the bus share had gone up to 69 percent and the car share decreased to 23 percent, the other two remaining constant. In 1987, a mass rapid transit (MRT) urban rail system was introduced and has since been expanded. A survey carried out in the mid-1980s before the carpool exemptions were withdrawn showed that the average auto occupancy went up from 1.4 to 2.2 during the morning hours for the autos entering the RZ. As mentioned before, this was a case of some bus commuters getting free rides from drivers. In 1998, the bus and the MRT share (public transport share) of the work trips during the morning rush hours was 67 percent (estimated at about 180,000 trips). No comparisons had been made for trips made for other purposes. Congestion pricing had persuaded some motorists to change to public transport. This reinforced the point that "pull and push" factors are needed to shift travel to public transport. The "pull" factors are improvements in the quality of service for public transport passengers and the "push " factor is getting motorists to consider the public transport option. ALS had achieved the latter to some extent. With the gradually increasing patronage, public transport operators had been able to improve the quality of their services.

A World Bank Report of 1984 estimated that additional investments of new roads in the order of S$1.5 billion would have been necessary to cope with the increased demand without the ALS of 1975. However, ALS was never considered as a substitute for road building.

Extension of the Manual Congestion Pricing System to Expressways

On the heels of the success of the ALS for the Restricted Zone in the city, the same concept of charging a congestion fee was extended to three congested expressways (high-speed access-controlled roads) during the mid-1990s. Motorists had to pay a fee to pass through the most heavily used sections of the expressways during the morning peak hours of 7:30 A.M.–9:30 A.M. on weekdays. This scheme required separate licenses than those used for the ALS. It was still not a toll road system because the aim was to curb congestion and not to generate revenue from the use of the expressways. This scheme also had a degree of success in curbing excessive use of the expressways during the rush hours.

Issues Related to the Introduction of ALS in 1975

There has been the nagging suspicion that the scheme was meant to raise funds for the government. The use of roads has always been free and there was some difficulty in motorists understanding why they should suddenly be charged for their use. Besides, motorists paid other taxes such as an annual road tax and gasoline tax.

a. There was much debate on the advantages and disadvantages of congestion pricing. No city had ever tried out such a system. There were calls from motorists and motoring associations to exhaust all other alternatives before embarking on congestion pricing. Many of them saw more road building as the solution. Many claimed that they had no alternative to driving because the public transport was not good enough.

b. There was a fear that the city would lose its vibrancy and that many firms would move out of the Restricted Zone. This did not happen because the city was still the most attractive place to do business and the accessibility for the labor force improved with better traffic conditions and improved public transport services after the ALS was introduced.

c. There was a fear that the cost of doing business in the city would go up.

d. There was some unhappiness from residents who lived within the RZ. If they drove out of the RZ and returned home, they had to purchase an area license to get home. As opposed to this, there were advantages for such residents whose offices were in the RZ. They did not need to pay a fee to get into the RZ.

e. There was a call to give exemptions to those who needed to use their vehicle to go to the city. This was not possible because it would have been difficult to come to an agreement on who these motorists would be.

f. There was a claim that the ALS would merely shift congestion to other roads. This did happen on the ring road skirting the RZ.

g. There was a claim that ALS would result in under-utilization of the roads that were built at a great cost, resulting in wastage of resources.

h. This initial resistance was largely overcome when congestion pricing was sold as a part of an overall package of transport measures that also included new roads, traffic management, and improved public transport. Although skeptical at first, the motorists noticed that the words were followed up by deeds over the next two decades. The road building and traffic management programs have continued unabated, new urban rail systems have been built, and the bus services have been upgraded. The congestion pricing has indeed been only one of the measures and not the only measure to contain the transportation problem.

The Need for a Change from a Manual to an Automatic Congestion Pricing System

The manual congestion pricing systems were labor-intensive and required 150 persons to operate them. Staff was needed at the license sale booths and at the entry points. The ALS started in 1975 in a simple way with restrictions on autos and taxis during the morning peak hours. Over a period of twenty-three years, it went through many transformations and the complexity increased. Many new types of paper licenses were introduced to allow entry during different periods, at different places, and for different vehicles. In 1998, there were twenty-four daily area licenses for the motorist to choose from. The regular motorists were familiar with the licenses that they required, but the occasional user of the schemes faced confusion. The police manning the control points had to be extra alert for long periods to observe whether the vehicles had valid licenses. During unusually wet weather and heavily overcast days when the ambient light was poor, they had some difficulty in spotting the licenses.

The main drawback was that with the area license, motorists could make unlimited number of trips to the restricted zone or along the priced expressways. This works against the concept of congestion pricing, which is meant to make the motorist pay for the costs he imposes. A fairer way would have been to make the motorist pay each time he used the road, when there was congestion.

A search for an automatic system started in 1989 when technologies for automatic vehicle identification and debiting started appearing on the market. This resulted in the conversion to the electronic road pricing (ERP) system in 1998 for the RZ and other priced expressways and roads.

Issues Considered in the Change from a Manual
to an Electronic Road Pricing System

Over a twenty-three-year period, motorists had come to accept congestion pricing, albeit reluctantly. In making a change to an electronic road pricing system, the main considerations were

From the motorists' point of view:

a. they should find it convenient to use;

b. they should find all gadgets user-friendly;

c. they should not be unfairly penalized by system errors.

From the authorities' point of view:

d. the system should be extremely reliable;

e. the system should be easy to administer and operate.

Unlike a toll system, where booths are provided for payment, the system had to operate on an open road with no tollbooths. The technical requirements were:

a. it shall be a multi-lane system with no booths;

b. vehicles in each lane shall be charged even if several vehicles pass the entry point simultaneously;

c. there shall be no manual payments at all;

d. vehicles shall not need to slow down;

e. speeding vehicles or vehicles straddling lanes shall not escape payment;

f. clear photographs shall be taken of the rear license plates of violating vehicles

Selection of a System

When Singapore opted for an electronic road pricing system in 1992, there were no such comparable systems operating anywhere. There were some electronic toll collection systems, but they fell short of the requirement of multi-lane pricing without the need to slow down or stop. Three international consortia were pre-qualified and paid S$1.5 million each to tailor-make a mini system to demonstrate a working system at a selected site. All three systems used dedicated short-range radio communication systems to detect passing vehicles with transponders, which then deducted a congestion pricing charge from a pre-paid stored-value "smart card." Since the ERP system was to be in an open multi-lane environment where vehicles did not have to slow down or stop and could travel abreast, the main challenge was on how to spot each individual vehicle and charge accordingly. The automatic vehicle identification and detection software had also to tie up with the enforcement system to ensure that violators' images were captured. In addition, a host of traffic conditions found along the roads was simulated to check that the system recognized and deducted a charge in each case. Over a period of six months, each consortium chalked up a large number of ERP transactions, which were used to determine reliability. The results of these tests featured prominently in the selection of the successful contractor.

After the award of the ERP contract, the successful contractor was required to carry out a System Qualification Test (SQT) to prove the reliability of his final system. On a test track, he set up the system and ran test vehicles to chalk up 5 million transactions over a period of six months. A simulated control center recorded the transactions, violations, and faults. Situations such as stop-start, speeding, changing lanes, and riding abreast were all checked to ensure correct operations. The system had to pass the SQT before the ERP system was finally implemented. Such quality control was necessary to ensure that motorists would not be inconvenienced by technical errors.

In 1998, the manual systems were replaced by an electronic road pricing system. ERP gantries replaced the overhead gantries at each entry point.

Electronic Road Pricing System:
The Automated Congestion Pricing Scheme

The ERP system is a dedicated short-range radio communication system (DSRC) using a 2.40 GHz band. The main components are:

- The In-vehicle Unit (IU) to be used with a contact smart card (with integrated circuit chip)

This is a pocket-dictionary-sized device getting its electric power from the vehicle battery and fixed permanently at the lower right hand corner of the windscreen of vehicles (the driver's seat is on the right). On motorcycles and scooters, the IU is on the handlebar. The IU has a slot for receiving a prepaid stored value smart card called the CashCard (see Figure 6.1).

- CashCard

A consortium of local banks manages the sale and distribution of CashCard, which is a prepaid contact integrated circuit chip plastic card. It can be topped up with money at automatic teller machines and at gasoline stations. The CashCard can also be used for buying gasoline, groceries, and paying car parking charges.

- ERP overhead gantries (or outstations) located at the control points

There are two sets of overhead gantries at each entry point, set apart at 15m. They carry radio antennae for communicating with the IU of vehicles, optical sensors to detect passing vehicles, and enforcement cameras to take photographs of the rear license plates of violating vehicles. There is a local con-

Figure 6.1
How does ERP Work?

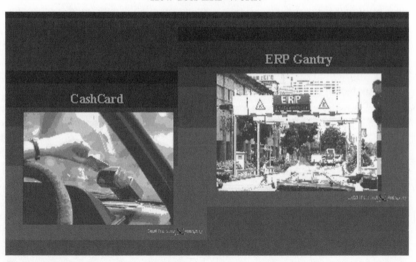

Photographs courtesy of LTA Singapore.

troller at each outstation that houses the logic for controlling all the ERP gantry equipment and for communicating with the central computer system at the control center via telephone lines (see Figure 6.2).

- Control Center

The control center receives the records of all ERP transactions, records of any faults in the ERP equipment, and digital photographs of violating vehicles from all the outstations. The control center does the daily cash settlement with the CashCard operator, sends out summons demanding fines from violating drivers, and invites drivers of vehicles experiencing errors to send their vehicles for free inspection. The consortium of local banks manages the money float from the sale of CashCards and reimburses the authorities daily, based on the total number of ERP transactions.

Figure 6.2
System Operation

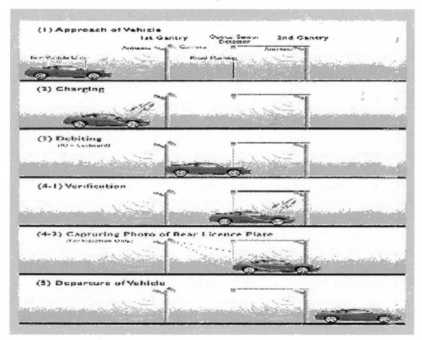

Photographs courtesy of LTA Singapore.

How Does ERP Work?

The ERP system only charges a fee when a vehicle goes under the entry point during the hours of operation. When the vehicle approaches the first of the two ERP gantries at the entry point (outstation), the gantry's radio antenna interrogates the IU, determines its validity and its vehicle classification, and instructs it to deduct the appropriate ERP fee. When the vehicle is traveling between the two gantries, the IU deducts the appropriate ERP fee from the stored value of the CashCard and confirms that it has done so to the radio antenna at the second ERP gantry. If there is no valid ERP deduction for some reason, the enforcement camera takes a digital photograph of the rear license plate of the vehicle, recording the reason for the violation or the error. The local controller at the outstation sends back the ERP fee deduction data and digital photographs to the control center at regular intervals.

User-Friendliness of ERP

All that the motorist has to remember is to insert a CashCard with sufficient cash balance into the IU before he drives under any ERP gantry. The deduction of the ERP fee will be made automatically. To make it easy for him, the back-lit liquid crystal display on the IU shows the cash balance in his card when he first inserts it. The IU does self-diagnostics (health checks) on itself and on the CashCard when the card is first inserted. Different icons appear on the display to show errors. Various long beeping sounds accompany these error displays. When the vehicle goes under the ERP gantry, the IU display shows the new balance in the CashCard after the ERP fee deduction. To ensure that motorists are not forced into a situation with insufficient money in the Cash-Card for subsequent trips, there is a low balance indicator icon on the display, which appears whenever an IU with a CashCard with a low balance (less than S$5) goes under the ERP gantry.

The fitting of IUs is not compulsory, but about 98 percent of the vehicle population have them in the vehicles. As in the case of the manual system, there are different ERP charges for different classes of vehicles. Therefore, IUs are color-coded for different classes of vehicles to prevent swapping. Only emergency vehicles such as fire engines, ambulances, and police cars are exempt from the ERP fees. They are fitted with special IUs that do not need CashCards. Without IUs, they would be photographed each time they pass an ERP outstation.

Treatment of Foreign Vehicles

Foreign vehicles can enter Singapore by two road routes from peninsular Malaysia. Those who frequently use Singapore roads could install permanent

IUs. The occasional visitor who wants to enter the Restricted Zone or use the priced expressways could rent a temporary IU at some gasoline stations and IU commissioning stations near the border. Foreign vehicles can also drive on any ERP-priced roads during ERP operational hours without installing an IU. They will be charged an ERP fee of S$5 for each day they drive on ERP-priced roads. This fee is payable when the vehicle departs the country.

ERP Violations and Errors

The violation and error categories are shown in the table.

Violation	Error
No in-vehicle unit	No battery power to in-vehicle unit
No CashCard	Faulty in-vehicle unit
Insufficient cash balance in CashCard	Faulty CashCard
	Communication error

Daily violations are about 3 per 1,000 ERP transactions, showing that the compliance rate is high. The majority of the violations (4 out of 5) result from having no CashCards in the IU. Since many motorists protested that this error occurred because of their forgetfulness, those with CashCard violations only pay a small additional administrative charge on top of their ERP fee, as compared with the normal heavier fine for having no IU on the vehicle. Daily errors are about 3 per 10,000 ERP transactions, showing that the ERP system is very reliable. To identify violators, the rear license plate of the violating car is photographed as the violator proceeds under the gantry. The cash-card system does not photograph or otherwise identify non-violators, thus the system does not conflict with the privacy of travelers.

Fixing of ERP Fees

The ERP operates only on weekdays from 7:30 A.M.–7 P.M. for the Restricted Zone and from 7:30 A.M. –9:30 A.M. on some selected expressways (including 6:00 P.M.–8:00 P.M. on one expressway) and major arterial roads. There are no restrictions on Saturdays, as was the case under the manual system.

As a first cut, the fees used for the manual road pricing system were used to determine the ERP fees. Since ERP gave the flexibility of charging for many different time periods, it was decided to use half-hour periods as the minimum time for fixing fees. Since then, the ERP fees have been reviewed and adjusted at three monthly intervals based on prevailing traffic speeds. Such frequent changes of fees would have been nightmarish under the manual scheme.

The aim of ERP or any congestion pricing scheme is to have neither excessive congestion nor under-utilization of the roads. This is achieved if roads operate within a range of acceptable speeds. Based on research conducted in Singapore, the optimum speed range is 45–65 kph for expressways and 20–30 kph for the arterial roads. When the monitored speeds for half-hour intervals on the expressway or arterial road in the RZ fall below 45 kph or 20 kph respectively, the ERP fees are raised for that half-hour. Similarly, when speeds exceed the higher value of 65 kph or 30 kph, ERP fees are lowered.[2] This means that the motorists' behavior decides the ERP fee.

The passenger car unit equivalents (pcu) are used to determine the ERP fees for different vehicle classes. The pcu is a proxy measure of the dynamic road space occupied by a vehicle when it is traveling. Automobile, taxi, and light goods vehicle are 1 pcu each, motorcycle 0.5 pcu, heavy goods vehicle 1.5 pcu, and large bus 2 pcu. Therefore, a motorcycle will pay half the ERP fee that an auto pays during the same half-hour period.

Effectiveness of ERP

The success of ERP in combating congestion can be measured by the speeds experienced along the major roads within the RZ during the ERP operations. These are all within the desired optimal speed range of 20–30 kph for arterial roads in the city. The traffic speeds do not drop during the half-hour period of 7:00 A.M.–7:30 A.M., just prior to start of the ERP period. But, travel speeds drop marginally after 7 P.M. for a period of 45 minutes after the ERP is lifted, when many vehicles rush in.

On the ERP priced expressways and major arterials, there are the pre-ERP and a post-ERP rush with good traffic conditions during the ERP hours with speeds in the desirable range of 45–65 kph for expressways and 20–30 kph for major roads.

The ALS was already a congestion pricing scheme for the Restricted Zone. After switching from the ALS to ERP, there were further reductions in the number of vehicles entering the RZ during the morning peak hours and for the whole day. Results of interviews with motorists showed that this reduction in traffic volumes occurred as a result of a reduction in the number of multiple trips into the RZ, which used to occur with ALS. Under the ALS, an area license gave motorists unlimited number of entries into the RZ. Now, motorists plan the routes of their journeys into the RZ more carefully, so as to pass the ERP gantry only once. Once they are in the RZ, they also choose their routes more carefully, so that they do not leave the RZ and reenter again if they are proceeding to another part of the RZ. This demonstrates the superiority of ERP over ALS. Motorists are now better aware of the true costs of using congested roads and thus are more responsive to road conditions.

There is an undesirable practice of vehicles loitering and slowing down along approach roads to ERP gantry points to wait for ERP to end or to avoid a higher priced half-hour period. During the initial period, a few motorists caused some minor rear end accidents in front of ERP gantry points. They did so by suddenly slowing down to insert CashCards into the IUs or by trying to change lanes to get to an escape route to avoid the ERP gantry. This is despite the fact that the presence of the ERP gantry has always been well announced by information signs put up in advance of the location. To discourage motorists from speeding up or slowing down to avoid paying higher ERP charges, ERP changes have been made more gradual.

An ERP system or any congestion pricing system using cordon pricing improves traffic conditions within the cordoned area and on the approach roads to it. However, the effects of such pricing extend beyond the borders of the cordon. One option that drivers always have is to avoid the roads in the Restricted Zone by using the ring road that skirts the city. When expressways and major roads are priced, motorists have the option to use the nearest parallel unpriced major roads. There is some congestion for short periods on these alternative roads.

Flexibility of the ERP System Over a Manual System

The ERP system is superior to a manual system (ALS) because almost everything is done by software.

a. It is simple to assign different fees since different classes of vehicles have different types of IUs;
b. It is simple to change fees and different fees can be assigned for each half-hour period without the need for multiple types of paper area licenses;
c. It is simple to change the hours of operation by switching on/off the ERP gantries;
d. It is relatively simple to include/remove areas under congestion pricing just by installing/removing ERP gantries.

Choices Offered to Motorists by the ERP

ERP offers the motorist many choices because he is made aware of the cost of the congestion he is contributing to.

a. He can choose to pay the ERP fee and enjoy smooth traffic conditions. There is some benefit to the community because he is paying for the use of congested roads.

b. He can choose to shift his time of travel and pay a lower ERP fee or not pay at all. There is benefit to the community because the spreading of the rush hours reduces congestion.

c. He can choose to use another route that has no ERP. In doing so, he causes congestion on other roads and makes circuitous journeys. There is a cost to the community because congestion is transferred to other roads.

d. He can choose to switch to public transport. This is a benefit to the community because more efficient passenger-carrying vehicles are using the roads and reducing congestion.

e. He can choose to change destination and avoid the ERP areas.

Issues Related to Electronic Road Pricing

a. By the time that ERP was implemented in 1998, congestion pricing had been accepted, albeit reluctantly by most motorists. The major concern of the motorists on the change was the reliability of the technology. They had to be assured that the system would not penalize them unfairly if there were faults.

b. Some motorists wanted the ERP to give them unlimited entries once they paid the initial charge as was practiced under the ALS. They wanted to cap their fees to a daily maximum. Some motorcycle dispatch riders delivering mail and parcels would make multiple trips to RZ in a day in the course of their work and thus were afraid of chalking up high fees. Unlimited entry, however, would violate the principle that road users should pay for the congestion costs that they impose upon others.

c. Motorcyclists have always felt that they should not be made to pay the ERP fees because they do not contribute to traffic congestion. They could not be exempted because they constitute about 15 percent of the total vehicle population. Recognizing that they contribute less to congestion, their ERP charges are only half of what autos pay.

d. Demand price elasticity values calculated from the regular three monthly changes in ERP fees do not yield any definite patterns. Nevertheless, the price elasticity values for motorcyclists are higher than for others showing that they are more likely to change their traveling behavior with price changes.

e. Some still claim that the government should adjust ERP fees and extend it to other areas to extract more revenue from motorists. As for extending to other areas, government has always made it clear that ERP is one tool among many that have been used to keep traffic problems within manageable levels. If there are other areas experiencing undue congestion, ERP may be extended to such places. The raising and lowering of the ERP fees have been pegged to prevailing traffic speeds, as mentioned earlier.

f. This ERP system is an active system, which works on the principle of making instantaneous payment from the CashCard as the motorist passes the ERP gantry point. In this way, the motorist feels the "pinch" of the congestion pricing scheme. There were some who asked for a central billing system whereby they did not need to insert a CashCard in the IU, but would pay a monthly bill at the end of the month for the number of times that they used the ERP roads. Some motorists felt that the insertion of a CashCard was burdensome and they could end up with fines for forgetting to do so. Some fleet operators issued their drivers with CashCards, but did not want these CashCards to be used for personal purchases by the drivers. They also preferred a central billing system. The central billing system used by some toll road agencies was ruled out during the initial planning of ERP. A central billing system would involve the setting up of a large bureaucracy. Under the active system, it is an offense involving a fine if a motorist fails to pay; with a central billing system, it would be a bad debt if the motorist fails to pay. It is much easier to collect a fine for an offense than a bad debt.

g. The insertion of CashCards into the IU continued to be a topic for debate. Failing to insert CashCards tops the list of violations. Many claimed that CashCard violations occurred as a result of forgetfulness and that they had no intention of cheating the system. While motorists (other than motorcyclists) had been advised to keep the CashCard in the IU, some removed them for fear of having the CashCards stolen and then forgot to insert them again when they started their journey.

h. Taxi commuters have to pay the ERP fee that their trip incurs. This fee is shown on the taxi's IU. However, if a taxi enters the RZ empty, the taxi driver has to pay the fee. There was a concern that this would mean a shortage of taxis in the city, but this did not materialize, although commuter waiting times at taxi stands in the RZ did increase. Recently, taxi fares have been deregulated and taxi companies can set their own fares to suit market conditions.

i. Non-motorized vehicles such as cycles and three-wheeled trishaws (which are mainly used by tourists for sightseeing) do not have IUs fitted to them because they are not covered under ERP. Without an IU, they will be photographed if they pass under the ERP gantries. The numbers of such photos are not large enough to be of concern.

j. There have been neither reported cases of fraud nor switching of IUs between vehicles. However, there is always a need for constant vigilance.

Publicity and Public Relations for ERP

A massive publicity program was mounted for a year before the ERP was launched. Motorists were educated on how to use their IU and CashCards. The ERP gantries were switched on in a "test mode" for three months with zero charging before the actual start date—for motorists to drive under, become familiar with the system, and to check that their equipment worked.

Is Congestion Pricing a Fair Way to Go?

In Singapore's case, it was considered as a fair method to complement the other methods to keep transportation problems within manageable levels. Simply relying on other methods such as road building and traffic management would not have been tenable. The one important prerequisite for an ERP is that there should be convenient alternatives for those who would be disadvantaged by congestion pricing. In Singapore's case, no effort is being spared to provide this alternative by an efficient public transport system of buses and trains. Although building of new roads will continue at a modest rate, roads are not the alternative to ERP. Neither is ERP an alternative to road building.

On the other hand, congestion pricing on its own is not the panacea to solving traffic problems and each city authority must decide whether it can be implemented in its jurisdiction.

Use of Revenues Collected from Congestion Pricing

The annual revenues from congestion pricing account for 0.3 percent of total government revenue. It is only about 8 percent of the annual expenditure on building, maintaining, and operating of the land transport (road and rail) infrastructure. The congestion pricing revenues go into a general pool. Congestion revenues are not earmarked for transport related projects. All transport projects need separate economic justification for financial allocation from a central pool of development funds.

Road Building and ERP

An island with a land area of 700 sq km cannot go on a large road building spree and the additional tool of ERP ensures that only a modest road construction program is needed to keep the traffic moving. Road building still continues at a modest pace. The main thrusts are to provide access to new areas of development, to provide logical missing links in the road network, and to address congestion. To address congestion, roads are widened along the problem spots and road junctions improved by construction of flyovers and underpasses.

Traffic Management and ERP

Traffic management has always featured prominently in combating traffic problems. Traffic management cannot create road capacity, but maximizes the use of available capacity of the road network. The traffic management schemes range from simple turn restrictions at signalized junctions to sophisticated measurement and dissemination of journey times to motorists via the Internet.

The first application of intelligent transport systems (ITS) was the linking and coordination of traffic lights within the city area where the random operation of closely-spaced intersections caused unnecessary delay to vehicles. The initial system in the early 1980s was a simple computerized fixed time coordination system using pre-timed plans worked out by the traffic signal software TRANSYT. The current computerized system, known as GLIDE, uses the Australian SCATS system to control and coordinate all traffic lights on the island. GLIDE uses loop detectors at the stop lines at signalized junctions to sense traffic flow. This traffic adaptive system uses data from the detectors to adjust green times and coordinate closely-spaced traffic lights so that vehicles on the main road can catch the "green wave" as they travel from junction to junction.

Closed circuit cameras, called "junction eyes," are being installed at some critical junctions so that operators at the control center can detect abnormal traffic conditions, such as vehicle breakdowns, illegal parking, and roadworks, and take corrective action.

Much of the delay along expressways (freeways) is caused by non-recurrent causes such as breakdowns and accidents, commonly referred to as incidents. Such incidents also add to the danger of secondary accidents on expressways. The method of dealing with such incidents is to quickly detect them as they occur, render quick assistance to the motorists in distress, and forewarn approaching motorists of danger of traffic congestion. Our 150 km of expressways have been installed with image processing cameras with virtual loops at regular intervals. Special algorithms process the image and sense congestion, after which surveillance cameras (closed circuit television cameras) are automatically turned on at a central control center to observe the incident. The operators send out a roving recovery crew to render assistance and to remove the vehicles from the expressway. They also put out variable message signs on display boards located at vantage points to forewarn approaching motorists of impending danger or congestion. Since the regularly placed cameras are able to measure speeds of passing vehicles, variable message signs at the entrances to the expressways also announce the expected travel time between major destinations and expected congestion (if any) to the drivers.

About 18,000 of the taxi fleet of 20,000 use a GPS-based taxi location system to enable taxi companies to respond to taxi bookings and allocate the taxis. They are also effective as vehicle probes and they provide some useful speed data along the major expressways and roads.

Each of these systems provides a vast amount of information. Much of it is used for long-term and short-term planning of road development and traffic management. Such information is also processed and brought together under an Internet website called traffic.smart. Anyone can access this website, which provides real-time information on factors that affect traffic flow, including incidents and scheduled road works. Real-time data on prevailing expressway speeds and selected pictures from CCTV cameras installed on the expressways and junctions are also available.

In the longer term, service providers are expected to make such information even more available to the public through mobile phones, pagers, and wireless computer terminals.

ITS will facilitate traffic flow and will manage expectations of motorists and give forewarning, so that motorists can make informed choices on the routes to take, time to travel at, and the mode to use.

Public Transport and ERP

An important factor for the success of any traffic restraint measure such as ERP is the need for an accompanying improvement to the alternative modes of transport. The two elements of vehicle restraint and public transport improvement must go hand in hand, each supporting and reinforcing each other. In the 1970s, for example, the Malaysian capital Kuala Lumpur considered but eventually rejected the proposals for auto restraint because they felt that the public transport alternatives were not good enough yet. In Singapore, the restraint measures have been accompanied by significant spending on public transport infrastructure.

The high cost of auto usage is a consideration for many to use public transport if it is of good quality and affordable.

The government recognized that the cornerstone of the transportation strategy was the improvement of public transport and encouraging its usage. Only heavy rail systems could meet the demands of heavily-used corridors and provide a reliable form of public transport. Although the government continues to own the infrastructure for the rail systems, two private companies signed a long-term licensing and operations agreement to operate the train services and do so without any government subsidy for operations and maintenance. It is anticipated that the current rail length (partly underground and partly elevated) would increase to about 500 km by 2030.

The bus fleet provides more degrees of freedom than a rail system, but buses, which do not have their own right-of-way, are subject to delays on the road network. Nevertheless, buses, which are operated by the same two private companies, are helped by bus priority measures such as bus lanes and special bus signals and continue to be the backbone of the public transport system for the time being, providing a wide coverage of services, also without any government subsidy for operations and maintenance.

Much effort has also gone into physical and fare integration. Transport terminals are within easy reach of each other to make transfers between modes convenient. Common tickets are used on both trains and buses of both companies.

Future Possibilities

It is fair to say that Singapore has more experience with congestion pricing and currently has the most advanced pricing system in the world. Deteriorating traffic conditions in other cities around the world, however, have generated increased interest in congestion pricing. In the twenty-first century, it is likely that many more cities will create pricing systems using advanced technologies. The current Singapore ERP system, for example, is only capable of charging vehicles as they enter an area or pass a controlled point. But global positioning satellite (GPS) technologies could charge for the distance that vehicles travel along a congested road or the time that they spend in a congested area. Toll roads that charge vehicles for kilometers traveled are quite common and GPS technology could broaden this approach to all roads or all roads within a congested area. These more flexible pricing technologies are likely to be combined with dynamic road maps, per-kilometer car insurance, emergency response beacons, and other conveniences for passengers, making road travel later in the twenty-first century more convenient, quicker, and safer than at present.

Notes

1. The author thanks the Land Transport Authority of Singapore for giving permission to write this chapter. The views expressed are personal.
2. The fees for each half-hour are reviewed at three monthly intervals and fixed for a three-month period. The fees are then announced via newspaper advertisements.

Bibliography

Articles and Reports

Barter, Paul, Jeff Kensworthy, Chamloong Poboon, and Peter Newman. 1994. *The Challenges of Southeast Asia's Rapid Motorisation: Kuala Lumpur, Jakarta, Surabaya and Manila in an International Perspective*. Perth: Asia Studies Association of Australia Biennial Conference.

Behbehani, Redha, V. S. Pendakur, and Alan T-Armstrong Wright. 1984. *Singapore Area Licensing Scheme: A Review of Impact*. The World Bank, July.

Lim Leong Geok. 1975. *Case Study of Singapore*. Paris: OECD Conference on Better Towns with Less Traffic.

Lew, Yii Der, Jacqueline Lee, and A.P.G. Menon. 1994. *Electronic Road Pricing in Singapore: Demonstration Project. Proceedings of the International Conference on Advanced Technologies in Transportation and Traffic Management*. Singapore, pp. 105–112

Menon, A.P.G. 1997. *Two Decades of Congestion Pricing*. Proceedings of the 9th Conference of the Road Engineering Association of Asia and Australasia, Wellington, New Zealand, pp. 83–89.

Menon, A.P.G. 2000. *ERP in Singapore: A Perspective One Year On*. Traffic Engineering & Control, February. London, UK: Hemming Group, pp. 40–45.

Menon, A.P.G., and Chin Kian Keong. 1998. *The Making of Singapore's Electronic Road Pricing System*. Proceedings of the International Conference of Transportation into the Next Millennium, Singapore, pp. 179–190.

Research Report NTU/CTS/95-01. 1995. *Speed-flow Relationships for Expressways and Arterial Roads*. Singapore: Centre for Transportation Studies, Nanyang Technological University.

"Singapore Mass Transit Industry." 2002. *Mass Transit Today*, Jan.–Mar., pp. 33–41.

World Bank Staff Working Paper No. 281. 1978. *Relieving Traffic Congestion: The Singapore Area Licensing Scheme*. Washington, D.C., June.

7

Congested Roads: An Economic Analysis with Twin Cities' Illustrations

Herbert Mohring

Producing the typical commodity of economics texts involves physically transforming things from one form to another by people and machines located at one point in space. Transportation entails moving people and things through space without (except accidentally) physically altering them. The state has played a much more pervasive role in providing transportation than in providing typical textbook commodities. It provides highways and air control facilities, it dredges and dams waterways, by invoking its powers of eminent domain, it directly or indirectly provides rights-of-way for most forms of transportation. The state regulates these activities, once in minute detail albeit much less so now.

Transportation technology is such that virtually all service providers must supply multiple products. Heavy trucks and light automobiles use urban expressways. A road optimally designed just for trucks would differ substantially from one designed just for autos. One hundred-or-so times as many people use urban highways at 5pm on a weekday as at 5am on a Sunday. A bus has empty seats on some portions of its route; on others, it is so full that it has no room for additional passengers.

Perhaps because of these institutional peculiarities, it was once thought that problems arise in the economic analysis of transportation activities that are qualitatively different from those with which other branches of economics deal. Cost allocation is particularly prominent in this regard. In cost allocation studies, after assigning to each customer class those carrier costs that can be directly attributed to it, a substantial residual of unassignable "common costs" is almost invariably left. Transportation economists devoted much debate and many reams of paper to devising principles for allocating these common costs to individual users groups.

Standard economic analysis pays little attention to cost allocation. It some-times mentions certain "adding-up" propositions that apply in markets where production involves constant returns to scale (i.e., doubling inputs, for exam-ple, precisely doubles output). *If* a firm's output is sold at a price equal to the additional or marginal cost incurred in producing it, and *if* each input used in its production process earns a wage equal to the decline in the value of the firm's output had that unit of input been employed elsewhere in the economy, *then*, the firm's revenues exactly cover its total costs. Similarly with multi-product firms. Again, given constant returns to scale, *if* the price of each of a firm's products equals the long-run marginal cost of producing it, *then* the firm's total revenues exactly cover its total costs.

During the last fifty-or-so years, research has brought transportation into the mainstream of microeconomic analysis. This research has made it clear that the special tools of analysis once thought to be essential in studying trans-portation really are not. Economists' basic theories of price and value—the tools they use to determine the optimal input combinations and output levels for a dam, a steel mill, or an orange grove, or to place a value on any of them— can, without fundamental alteration, provide the same services for transporta-tion activities.

This theoretical revolution in transportation economics raises the possibil-ity that a parallel revolution in transport practice might be both feasible and desirable. If the standard tools of microeconomics can be used to understand the supply and demand for transport, then might it not be possible to rely on market processes—the method on which we rely to provide most commodi-ties—to provide transport services? Substantial deregulation of trucking and airlines has already occurred. Some countries, notably Great Britain, have deregulated buses. Economists have developed innovative plans to use markets to deregulate buses, taxis, and other inter-city transport services such as jit-neys.[1] Road pricing has changed from an esoteric subject even within eco-nomics to a much-discussed and occasionally employed tool of road planning throughout the world. Notable road-pricing projects have been implemented in the United States, Canada, Singapore, Western Europe, and elsewhere. Pri-vately operated toll highways have come into being. Further travel along this road seems inevitable.

This chapter's first section describes the parallel between the economics of roads and of the "widget" industry of standard texts. Section II deals with research that estimates the benefits and costs of shifting from present-day pric-ing to cost-based pricing of the Twin Cities Metropolitan Area's road network. The concluding section provides a summary and discusses the short- and long-run problems that must be faced in developing the road-network equivalent of competitive widget markets.

I. Competitive Markets and Competitive Roads

Widespread adoption of a simple conceptual trick played a particularly important role in bringing transportation into mainstream economic analysis. We once thought of transport markets as involving the purchase and sale of such products as seat miles and ton miles. The conceptual innovation was to think of trips and shipments as the commodities demanded and of buyers as combining self-supplied inputs (their own time or that of commodities they own) with seller-supplied inputs (e.g., airplane, train, road, or bus capacity) to produce finished products. Thinking of a traveler or shipper not as a buyer of finished carrier services but, rather, as both demanding finished products and supplying inputs vital to their production makes it much easier to see the relationship between equilibrium in transport and widget markets.

Congestion, a key ingredient of transport economics, arises when (1) buyers supply some of the variable inputs needed to produce a final good—most commonly their own time or that of goods they own—and (2) the quantity of these inputs per unit of output, the quality of the product, or both depend on the rate at which purchases are made. With this definition, congestion occurs in many economic activities. The wait for service in a department store is typically substantially longer during the week before Christmas than in late January. As for quality-of- product, as the number of people attending a movie performance increases, the odds of finding a seat with an unencumbered view of the screen diminishes. And, of course, in driving on urban roads, more congestion means more time consuming and, for most, less pleasant trips.

In heavy but free-flowing expressway traffic, something—for instance, an accident, unusually heavy entry at some interchange—forces a few drivers to slam on their brakes. Their abrupt slowdowns force those who follow to slam on *their* brakes. The resulting chain reaction abruptly changes a traffic stream averaging 50 mph into one in which all vehicles travel in lock step at 5–20 mph. This phenomenon can be modeled by exploiting a variant of the commonly cited safety rule that drivers should stay 2–3 seconds behind the vehicles they follow. Suppose that all drivers stay 1.8 seconds behind the vehicles in front of them.[2] As roads become more crowded, the distance between vehicles must diminish. The speed required to stay 1.8 seconds behind must, therefore, also diminish. By reducing the average distance between the vehicles it contains, each traveler in a traffic stream imposes a cost on all others in the stream by slowing them down.

If *all* travelers follow the stay-1.8-seconds-behind rule, the average and marginal costs of travel time per mile at alternative traffic volumes would follow the relationship suggested by the *AVC* (average variable cost) and *SRMC* (short-run marginal cost) curves in Figure 7.1 (where, for convenience, traffic

Figure 7.1
Urban Road Equilibria with and without Congestion Pricing

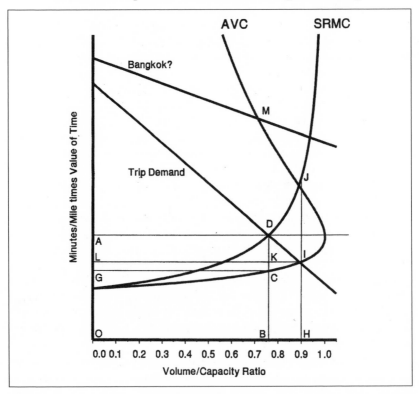

volume has been divided by road capacity). *AVC* depicts the cost of travel time per mile that the occupants of the average vehicle would incur, and *SRMC* includes this cost plus the cost of the congestion each vehicle's occupants impose on all other others in the traffic stream. The *AVC* curve illustrates a commonly observed phenomenon of urban-expressway travel. At speeds above about 30 mph, *reduced* speeds are associated with *increased* traffic flows. In the top, backward-bending portion of *AVC*, however, *reduced* speeds accompany *lower* traffic flows.

The parallels with widget production are, in most respects, straightforward. For both trips and widgets, *AVC* and *SRMC* reflect the economist's "law of diminishing marginal productivity." Each additional widget or trip requires successively larger doses of variable inputs (typically labor time and materials, for example, with widgets and travel time with roads) as fixed capital (factories and machinery for widgets and rights-of-way, pavement, bridges, and the like for roads) is used more intensively.

In one very important respect, the widget case differs from that of roads in interpreting Figure 7.1. Neither widget buyers nor widget sellers ever see the backward-bending part of the *AVC* curve. There, more variable inputs are applied to a fixed stock of capital than are necessary to produce the level of output achieved. No business firm would voluntarily operate in such a fashion. However, rare is the urban freeway user who has not participated in this sort of inefficiency during peak periods. Indeed, some of the world's most congested cities—Bangkok, Athens, Rome, Jakarta—seem to be in this unpleasant state most of the time.

The buyers of competitively priced widgets never see the backward-bending part of *AVC* because the difference between *SRMC* and *AVC* is built into the price they pay. Not so for road users: In deciding whether and when to make trips, most travelers take into account the costs congestion imposes on them. Few worry about the costs their trips impose on others by slowing *them* down. *This unrecognized external cost or "externality" of travel sometimes forces road users into the backward-bending part of AVC. This externality, even when less severe, underlies economists' espousal of pricing congestion.*

With widgets, if the competitive-market price is *OA*, a manufacturer would produce *OB* units a week, the rate at which its short-run marginal cost equals the market price. This output rate would generate total weekly revenues of *OADB*. These revenues would cover the firm's total variable costs, *OGCB*, leaving *ADCG* as a reward to the firm's bond and stock holders for supplying its fixed capital. If *ADCG* exceeds the costs of financing and maintaining the firm's fixed capital, it and other firms would profit in the short run by expanding capacity. If they do, both the market price and weekly returns per unit of output will fall until, in long-run equilibrium, the weekly counterpart of *ADCG* just covers weekly capital costs.

To introduce the customer side of the urban trip market, suppose that a household gets utility from consuming a general-purpose commodity, stuff (*S*), conveniently priced at $1 a unit, and from what happens at the ends of the *T* round trips a week that its members take downtown. Each round trip costs $*F* (for "Fare") and requires *t* (for "travel time") minutes. Travel itself is unpleasant, however. Each household allots its income to stuff and trips so as to maximize its utility, a function $U = U(S, T, tT)$ where *tT* is total travel time. It turns out (see the appendix) that such households act as if the price of a trip is the dollar outlay, *F*, it requires plus *Vt*, the cost it attaches to the time the trip requires. *V* (with dimension $/hour) is the rate at which the household would be willing to sacrifice stuff to save travel time—its "value of travel time"—for short $F + Vt$ is commonly termed the "full price" of a trip to distinguish it from the money component, F, of its price.

Accepting the notion that it is the full price of a trip that affects travel decisions and ignoring vehicle-operating and accident costs, Figure 7.1 can be used to discuss the short- and long-run optimizing behavior of a benevolent highway authority that strives to maximize the social contribution of its roads. With no tolls, consumers would continue to consume trips until the personal cost of the marginal trip given by the AVC curve just equals their willingness to pay given by the demand schedule. This equality occurs at a volume to capacity ratio of OH. At this equilibrium, each traveler imposes a cost of IJ on all other travelers by adding to the level of congestion. The discussion of section II refers to IJ as the "gap" between the full cost to society of a trip and the cost each individual traveler bears directly.

Associated with gap IJ is a "dead-weight loss"[3] of area DIJ for trips that are valued at less than their aggregate social costs. Imposing a toll of DC per trip would induce travelers to reduce their travel by the BH trips that account for this loss. On the good side, the toll would not only eliminate the dead-weight loss, DIJ, but would also generate revenues of $ADCG$. On the bad side, however, the BH eliminated trips had an aggregate net value of DKI to those who formerly took them. In addition, tolling would increase by DK the *full* price of a trip for the average remaining traveler,[4] a total of $LKDA$ for all who continue to travel despite increased costs. That tolls would eliminate the dead-weight losses from unpriced congestion and lower the time costs of still-made trips guarantees that the increased toll revenues would exceed consumer losses. Hence, in principal, a compensation system exists that would not only make better off those whose travel costs increase but also leave funds for the highway authority to do Good Works. Sadly to say, the data required to construct such a system could rarely be found. Still, toll revenues could be used in a way that would make a majority of an urban area's households better off with congestion tolls than without them—see section III.

The similarities that result from using figure 7.1 to compare the behavior of a profit-maximizing business firm and an optimizing road authority extend to the relationship between capital costs and quasi-rents[5] in long-run equilibrium. Suppose the road-services production function exhibits constant-returns to scale—i.e., that a doubling or halving of each input respectively doubles or halves total output. Suppose also that road authorities do not influence the prices they pay for inputs. Then, the appendix shows, an optimally designed and priced road's revenues would equal its capital costs just as in a competive market in long-run equilibrim. But are roads subject to constant returns? Probably not: Revenues would probably fall short of costs for an optimally sized network with marginal-cost tolls. Section III presents evidence on the subject.

II. What Could Congestion Pricing Do for Us?
Some Evidence from the Twin Cities

The assumptions underlying the section I discussion of a competitive road market lack reality. Real-world travelers differ greatly in what they would willingly pay to save travel time. The characteristics of roads in urban areas differ greatly, ranging, as they do, from two-lane residential streets with frequent stop signs to eight-lane expressways on which 80 mph speeds are possible if not legal. Roads must be wide enough for vehicles to pass each other. They usually contain an integral number of 10- to 12-foot lanes. Expressways are so large and have so much capacity that, in selling their services, private owners would not be subject to the sorts of market pressures that firms experience in the competitive markets of economic texts. Assembling rights-of-way for their roads would be prohibitively expensive unless the state could be induced to use its powers of eminent domain on their behalf.

Section III discusses the difficulties of coping with these problems. For present purposes, suppose that a Philosopher King and Queen assume control of an urban area's road network. They desire to optimize its characteristics and to use the price system to finance it and to control its use. Optimization requires, first, establishing marginal-cost congestion tolls for the network that presently exists. It requires, second, expanding or contracting the network until the last dollar spent on capacity yields future user benefits with the present value of a dollar. These requirements for optimization are not independent. In particular, the second requirement is appropriate only if the first is met. To describe this capacity-optimization problem in the simplest possible way, consider just one road that is used at the same rate all of the time and, again, suppose that time is the only cost of travel. The hourly cost of providing *and* traveling on this road is

$$C = V N \, t(N/K) + P_K K \qquad (1)$$

where V is the average value of user travel time, N is the hourly travel rate, K is the road's hourly capacity, and P_K is the hourly cost of providing a unit of capacity.[6] Assuming P_K to be independent of the capacity provided is equivalent to assuming constant returns to scale in the roads operation. To repeat, if the value of K that minimizes this expression is established, the appendix shows that the marginal-cost congestion tolls collected each hour exactly suffice to cover that hour's road-capacity costs.

To emphasize: In long-run equilibrium, the difference between the daily revenues that marginal-cost prices generate for a widget manufacturer and the daily costs of variable inputs just suffice to cover the daily cost of its capital equipment. So, too, with roads. With constant returns to scale, daily revenues that marginal-cost tolls would provide the owner of a long-run optimal road would just suffice to cover the daily cost of providing the road's capacity.

In addition to providing financial support, using congestion pricing on a road network would have two sorts of benefits: First, marginal-cost tolls would discourage inefficient trips—trips with total costs that exceed their benefits to those who take them. Second, tolls would induce a more efficient allocation of trips to the network's roads.

Regarding this second benefit, in an urban area, there is usually more than one way to travel between a trip's origin and destination. Transportation planners commonly assume that travelers seek the route that minimizes some measure of the "impedance" to travel. In the absence of tolls, the impedance measure usually adopted is time; travelers are assumed to choose the routes that minimize travel time. If so, in equilibrium, travelers would use more than one route between any origin/destination pair only if travel times on all of them are equal. Such an equilibrium is usually inefficient. To see why, suppose that both an expressway and arterial streets connect points X and Y. In Figure 7.2, OZ people an hour (each, for simplicity, having the same travel-time value) desire to make round trips between these points. Figure 7.2 shows the short-run-marginal and average-variable trip costs on each route. Expressway travel is measured from left to right and arterial travel from right to left. If travelers really do strive to minimize their travel time when no tolls are charged, in equilibrium, they would take OB and BZ hourly trips respectively on the expressway and the arterials, that being the travel-time equalizing distribution of trips. At those traffic levels, the marginal cost of an expressway trip is BE while that on the arterials is appreciably less, BD. Why the difference? To equalize travel time on the two routes, congestion must be much smaller on the arterials than on the expressway. With less congestion comes a smaller gap between average-variable and short- run marginal costs. This being the case, were one vehicle to shift from the expressway to the arterials, it would impose costs of CD on other arterial users but reduce by substantially more, CE, the costs incurred by those who remain on the expressway.

The optimal allocation of trips between the two routes is that which minimizes the resource costs (i.e., the time costs in the case at hand) of all X to Y travelers—OA and AZ of them respectively on the expressway and the arterials. In going from the equal-travel-time to the equal marginal-cost equilibrium, the first traveler to shift from the expressway to the arterial would save ED in aggregate travel-time costs. Successive additional shifts would yield successively smaller aggregate benefits. When all XY travelers have shifted, aggregate hourly travel-time costs would have fallen by area DEF.

The resource-cost-minimizing distribution of trips could be achieved by charging tolls of FH and GH respectively on the expressway and arterials.

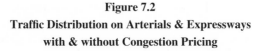

Figure 7.2
Traffic Distribution on Arterials & Expressways
with & without Congestion Pricing

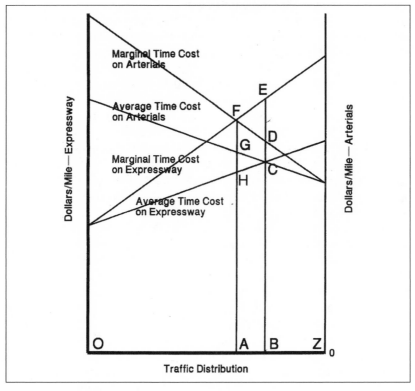

Traffic Distribution

Alternatively, because of the completely inelastic demand for *OZ* trips implicit in Figure 7.2, a toll of *FG* just on the expressway would also do the trick.

To illustrate the importance of the "Figure 7.2 effect," call it, the empirical research about to be described looked at the effects of shifting from no tolls to tolling all congested roads. Suppose that the full-price elasticity of demand is −1.0, that is, that a 1 percent increase in the fill price leads to a 1 percent reduction in the rate at which at which trips are taken. Tolling would reduce traffic on both arterials and expressways, but the decline would be substantially greater on expressways (19 percent) than on arterials (8 percent). If, alternatively, trip demand is completely inelastic, the toll-induced rearrangement of travel routes would cut aggregate travel costs by about 5 percent.

David Anderson and I have used two urban transportation-planning computer programs, Tranplan and Emme 2, to analyze data from the 1990 Travel Behavior Inventory (henceforth, TBI) for the Twin Cities Metropolitan Area (henceforth, TCMA) to estimate the benefits, costs, and income-distributional consequences of shifting from the present road financing system—one primarily based on fuel taxes—to a system that relies entirely on congestion tolls. The results reported here deal mainly with trips on the road network during the morning peak hour.

Each of the approximately 50,000 trips studied originated in one of the 1,200 "traffic-analysis zones" into which planners have divided the metropolitan area. Each trip terminated in one of the remaining 1,999 zones; congestion on intrazonal trips is generally ignored. The network studied consists of the 20,336 road links on which more than 1,000 trips were taken on an average 1990 weekday. These "coded" links connected 7,363 "nodes," that is, intersections. Examples of links include several-block stretches of an arterial or collector street and, on expressways, an access ramp, high-occupancy vehicle (HOV) lane, or one-way segment between two interchanges.

TBI surveys obtain origin and destination addresses for each trip but not the route taken. The parts of the traffic-analysis programs on which we rely most intensively rest on the assumption that each traveler selects those links for each trip that minimizes the trip's "impedance." Again, average travel time is the usual measure of impedance. The programs use iterative techniques to "load" trips onto the network. Equilibrium is reached when no traveler can lower impedance by changing route.

To predict equilibrium travel patterns with congestion tolls when we ignore differences in the travel behaviors of different income groups, we suppose that users directly incur costs equal to the marginal travel times associated with their trips. We use the average value of travel time for each income group—see Table 7.2 below—when we recognize that travel behavior does differ among income groups.

Peak-period travel does not take place at a constant rate but, rather, gradually increases, then decreases. The computer packages cannot handle continuously changing traffic flows. We are, therefore, forced to suppose trips to be distributed uniformly through the periods under analysis. Also, the computer packages cannot handle backward-bending average-variable-cost curves of the sort depicted in Figure 7.1. The programs' usual default measure of travel time for some link, call it link I, is what the manual for one program terms "the historic standard Bureau of Public Roads capacity restraint formula." Using it, the time required to traverse link I, t_i, is

$$t_i = t_{i0} \left(1 + 0.15 \left(N_i/K_i\right)^4\right) \qquad (2)$$

where N_i is the rate at which vehicles travel on link I, K_i is a measure of the link's capacity, and t_{i0} is the time required to traverse it when no other travelers use it.

Figure 7.3 compares equation (2) with the backward-bending curve depicted in Figure 7.1. The Figure 7.1 curve has a "capacity" in the sense of the absolute maximum output that could be produced by using a fixed capital stock. Equation (2) does not; with it, any output can be produced from any capital stock albeit with very high marginal costs for very large output/capacity ratios. As Figure 7.3 suggests, at low outputs, average and marginal costs rise more slowly with the backward-bending curve than with equation (2) but more rapidly as output approaches capacity. Indeed, with the backward-bending curve, marginal cost is infinite at capacity output. If, as I believe to be the case,

Figure 7.3

Relationships between Volume/Capacity Ratios and Travel Time

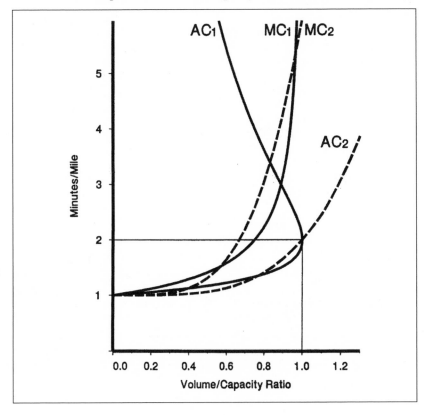

the backward-bending curve more accurately reflects actual road conditions, the peak-period tolls and costs that I report here understate true marginal costs and marginal-cost tolls during peak travel periods but overstate them during the off-peak.

We assume travel time to be the only cost of trips that travelers bear directly; sensitivity analyses indicate that incorporating vehicle-operating costs would not appreciably affect our results. Ignoring the effects of income differences on travel behavior for the moment, we multiply the average value of travel time for all travelers (we assume $12.50 per vehicle-hour) by the difference between the marginal and average travel times on link *I* implied by equation (2) to estimate the cost an additional traveler imposes on all other link-*I* travelers by increasing its congestion level.

Table 7.1 and Figure 7.4 summarize the results of that part of our work that ignores income-group differences in travel behavior. With an average travel-time value of $12.50 a vehicle hour, the time cost travelers directly incurred

Table 7.1
Present and Toll Equilibria for 1990 Morning Peak Hour*

| | All Roads Tolled | | |
Price Elasticity of Demand	0.0	−0.5	−1.0
Trips (1,000s) (518.1 with no tolls)	518.1	478.1	400.0
Travel Time Cost ($1,000) ($1,900 without tolls)	1,833.8	1,600.0	1,498.8
Toll Revenue ($1,000s)	672.8	406.8	323.5
Efficiency Gains ($1,000s)	52.4	93.6	104.9
Revenue *plus* Efficiency Gains ($1,000s)	725.2	500.4	428.4
(*less*) Lost Surplus ($1,000s)	620.3	313.1	218.6
Net Gain ($1,000s)	104.9	187.3	209.8
Tolls on expressways only**			
Trips (1,000s)	518.1	513.4	510.5
Travel Time Cost ($1,000)	1,882.5	1,846.3	1,825.0
Toll Revenue ($1,000s)	69.8	66.1	63.7
Efficiency Gains ($1,000s)	14.3	26.7	32.0
Revenue plus Efficiency Gains ($1,000s)	84.1	92.8	95.7
(less) Lost Surplus ($1,000s)	55.5	39.4	31.7
Net Gain ($1,000s)	28.6	53.4	64.0

*All travel time valued at $12.50 an hour.
**Link tolls equal 25 percent of the difference between average and marginal trip costs.

Figure 7.4

Morning Peak-Hour Congestion Costs, Tolls, & Traffic Reductions:
Full-price elasticity $= -1$, All congested roads tolled

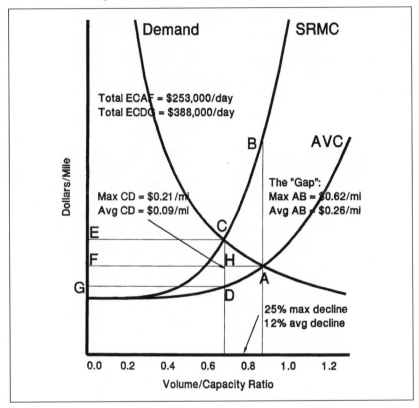

averaged 37 cents a vehicle mile during the morning peak hour in 1990. The costs this average trip imposed on all other travelers averaged 26 cents a vehicle mile. Once more, we call this difference "the gap" in what follows. On average, drivers' directly-experienced time costs accounted for a bit less than 60 percent of the full costs to society of their morning peak-hour trips. On the most congested ten-mile stretch of freeway, the gap was 62 cents a vehicle mile. On a few scattered road links, it exceeded $5 a mile.

Suppose that the full-price elasticity of demand was -1.0 in 1990 and that advanced electronics could collect tolls from vehicle operators without delays or, for the moment, capital or operating costs. It would then be efficient to impose marginal-cost tolls on *all* congested roads whether they be freeways, arterials, or collectors. With a "congested" road defined as one which experiences delays that cost more than the 2.5 cents a mile or so that fuel taxes impose on auto trips, about 2,000 of about 9,700 miles of road were "congested" during the morning peak hour.[7] Tolling all of these roads by the difference between their marginal and average travel costs would have reduced traffic volumes by about 12 percent on average and by about 25 percent on the most heavily congested stretches of freeway. On these heavily congested stretches, tolls would have averaged about 21 cents a vehicle mile; on the average road, about 9 cents a mile.

As Figure 7.1 suggests, the direct effect of congestion tolls would have made the average road user worse off. Almost all would have paid more for the trips they continued to take and would no longer have taken some trips that formerly yielded net benefits. While all travelers would have benefited from faster trips, toll payments would have exceeded the value of these time savings for most. Only two small groups would have reaped net benefits from congestion pricing regardless of the uses to which revenues were put. These were then-current mass-transit users and very high-income auto travelers. Tolling would have induced some travelers to divert from auto to bus. Those who already used transit would have benefited from the more frequent service generated by these additional patrons. They would also have benefited from faster travel times at least on freeways. On the most congested roads, for auto users with incomes greater than about $80,000 a year, travel-time savings would have exceeded their toll costs. On less congested roads, only travelers with incomes well into the six-figure range would have had net benefits from congestion pricing.

For the morning peak hour, total toll collections (area *ECDG* in Figure 7.4) would have been about $390,000 per weekday. Day-as-a-whole collections would have been about $1.5 million. Morning peak-hour tolling would have imposed costs (area *ECAF*) of about $250,000 from foregone trips by tolled-off travelers (area *CHA*) and the difference between their tolls and their travel-time savings on trips the remaining travelers continued to make (area *ECHF*). Thus, during the morning peak hour, congestion pricing would generate about $390,000/250,000 = $1.54 of revenue for each dollar of traveler costs. Informal reports from California's State Route 91 tollway indicate collection costs on its very simple system to be less than 10 percent of its revenues. Electronic toll-collection costs are higher on more complicated systems, but still only a modest fraction of toll revenues. In principle, anyway, a scheme for redistributing this loot that would make everyone better off is possible.

One of the computer packages we used, Emme/2, enables analyzing differences in the travel behavior of different income groups that is attributable to any given menu of tolls. The iterative process required to find an equilibrium distribution of trips is time consuming. Although the 1990 Travel Behavior

Inventory distinguished eight income classes, we have thus far collapsed them into four groups. Even then, finding an equilibrium takes about two days on a reasonably fast Pentium computer. Table 7.2 gives some details on these income groups and on their travel patterns.

Table 7.3 summarizes the effects of tolls on travel rates and costs, on revenue and efficiency gains, and on consumer-surplus losses for different income groups. Note that, for the reasons suggested by Figure 7.2, tolling would produce efficiency gains even if demand is completely inelastic. Note also that the adverse effects of tolling diminish with increased income. With totally inelastic peak-hour travel, low-income travelers would have the worst of all worlds. Seeking uncongested routes to avoid tolls would result in their trips becoming so circuitous that they would be burdened not only by tolls, but also by spending more time on the road than in the absence of tolls; their time plus money costs of travel would almost double. In the inelastic-demand case, congestion pricing would increase their travel costs by 96 percent as opposed to 24 percent and 42 percent, respectively, for the high-income group and all travelers. With a -1.0 full-price elasticity of demand, their surplus loss would equal 34 percent of the pre-toll total costs of their trips. The corresponding fractions are 5 percent for the high-income group and 13 percent for all travelers.

That electronic toll collection is costly implies that tolling lightly congested roads would be inefficient. Indeed, at 1990 and perhaps even present congestion levels, transactions costs may be so great that tolling only limited access roads might be optimal. For them, tolling requires monitoring only exit and access ramps. Also, since the capital costs of monitoring are largely independent of traffic levels, the more heavily traveled a road, the greater would be its gross returns per dollar of monitoring costs. Limited access roads are much more heavily traveled than most other roads; in the Twin Cities in 1990, they

Table 7.2
Data on the Four Morning Peak Hour Travel Groups in 1990

Household Income Bracket	Average Annual Household Income	Fraction of All Households	Travel-Time Value ($/hour)[8]	Number of Trips (1,000s)	Time Cost ($1,000)
<$35,000	$25,900	36.8%	5.40	104.9	161.8
$35–55,000	$44,900	28.8%	11.25	213.4	724.5
$55–75,000	$65,000	16.2%	6.25	117.4	584.7
>$75,000	$87,520	18.2%	21.88	82.3	563.7
Sums/Averages		100.0%	12.88	518.0	2,034.7

Table 7.3
1990 Peak Hour Travel of Four Income Groups on
Twin Cities Roads and Their Responses to Tolls

Time-Value Group	Trips Taken	Time Cost	Tolls Paid	Total Time + Toll Costs
With No Tolls				
Low	104,994	$161,819		
Med.-Low	213,391	$724,475		
Med.-High	117,429	$584,690		
High	82,262	$563,737		
All	518,076	$2,034,721		
All Roads Tolled—Inelastic Demand				
Low	104,994	$178,351	$138,395	$316,746
Med.-Low	213,391	$703,560	$384,710	$1,088,270
Med.-High	117,429	$545,124	$241,240	$786,364
High	82,262	$521,735	$175,551	$697,286
All	518,076	$1,944,770	$939,896	$884,666
All Roads Tolled— −1 Full-Price Elasticity of Demand				
Low	80,375	$117,227	$44,956	$162,183
Med.-Low	185,544	$554,982	$171,162	$726,144
Med.-High	107,720	$463,613	$121,520	$585,133
High	78,511	$467,996	$96,203	$564,199
All	452,150	$1,603,818	$433,841	$2,037,659

accounted for less than 7 percent of total roadway mileage but 42 percent of peak-hour vehicle miles.

Suppose that highway authorities price only expressways but set tolls on them equal to the full difference between the marginal and average-variable costs of trips. Such a policy would divert many trips from expressways to arterials thereby increasing congestion on them. Indeed, we found that, with this pricing policy, arterial congestion costs would increase by so much that the benefits derived from the road network would be smaller with congestion pricing than without it. For this reason, if tolls are not charged on all roads, constrained efficiency dictates that prices less than full marginal costs should be imposed on tolled roads. The optimal difference between actual and full marginal-cost prices increases with increases in the fraction of road capacity that goes untolled. This being the case, with costly pricing, efficiency requires tolls to be imposed on some lightly congested roads even if revenues fall short of collection costs on them. Subsidizing collection on these roads would increase the optimal toll on other tolled roads thereby yielding prices closer to the marginal cost prices on them. These price increases, in turn, would increase aggregate net benefits.

There is an extensive economic literature dealing with problems similar to constructing constrained-optimal tolls for a subset of a network's congested roads. Incorporating this literature into our analysis has been difficult. Thus far, we have worked only with setting charges on each tolled link equal to the same fraction of the difference between that link's marginal and average congestion costs (again, "the gap" for short). In the Twin Cities, with elastic demands, aggregate benefits do not vary greatly for fractions in the 20–40 percent range. With inelastic demand, tolling each expressway link at one-fourth of the gap turns out to be optimal for the morning peak hour and nearly optimal for the afternoon peak period.

The bottom half of Table 7.4 summarizes the results for expressway-only tolling. They suggest that tolling only these roads would be appreciably more acceptable politically than tolling all congested roads. A toll equal to 25 percent of the gap yielded consumer losses and toll revenues that are respectively only 10–15 percent and about 30 percent of those with all roads tolled. The average toll would be only 3.5 cents per freeway mile driven. Toll revenue would be insensitive to the elasticity of demand; for elasticities in the 0 to -1 range, weekly revenue would range between \$60,000–\$70,000 and \$55,000–\$62,000 for the morning and afternoon peak periods respectively.

III. A Summary and Some Problems

What have we found? The economics of optimally built and priced roads has much in common with the economics of the competitive industries that populate economics textbooks. Recognizing that travelers not only experience road congestion but also cause it forms the basis of "competitive" road pricing. The increasing congestion that accompanies increasing travel on a given road is the transportation counterpart to the increasing short-run marginal cost of widgets that accompanies increasing output from a given widget factory. Both increases result from more intensive use of durable capital equipment—the law of diminishing returns at work.

In deciding whether, when, and how to travel, travelers usually take into account the congestion they will encounter but not the congestion they will cause. Just as charging marginal-cost prices rewards widget manufacturers for the capital they provide, charging travelers marginal-cost tolls for the congestion they cause rewards road providers for capital services as well, of course, as

Table 7.4
Tolling All Roads and Expressways Only

Income Group	ELASTICITY: 0		ELASTICITY: −1			
	Time	Toll	Lost Time	Toll	Lost Cost	Surplus Cost
Aggregate Effects (in $1,000s) with All Roads Tolled						
Low	178.4	138.4	150.9	117.2	45.0	54.5
Medium-Low	703.6	384.7	363.8	555.0	171.2	124.0
Medium-High	545.1	241.2	201.7	463.6	121.5	58.4
High	521.7	175.6	133.5	468.0	96.2	27.2
Per Trip Effects (in $s) with All Roads Tolled						
Low		1.32	1.44	0.56	0.52	
Medium-Low		1.80	1.70	0.92	0.58	
Medium-High		2.05	1.72	1.13	0.50	
High		2.13	1.62	1.23	0.33	
Aggregate Effects (in $1,000s) with Only Expressways Tolled at 25 Percent of "Gap"						
Low	168.5	8.1	14.7	156.7	7.3	9.3
Medium-Low	718.7	45.8	40.0	694.3	40.0	18.2
Medium-High	571.6	36.0	23.0	559.3	33.5	5.8
High	548.6	27.2	12.1	542.0	25.8	0.0
Per Trip Effects (in $s) with Only Expressways Tolled at 25 Percent of "Gap"						
Low	0.08	0.14		0.07	0.09	
Medium-Low		0.21	0.19		0.19	0.09
Medium-High		0.31	0.20		0.29	0.05
High	0.33	0.15		0.31	0.00	

discouraging trips that would cost society more than their values to those who would otherwise take them.

In the markets that populate economics texts, Adam Smith's invisible hand maximizes social benefits without government intervention. Would the many virtues of emulating textbook-competitive markets in pricing and developing roads make it desirable to turn over the duties of the Federal Highway Administration and state departments of transportation to free enterprise? Sadly to say, before such a step becomes optimal, problems must be solved that result from differences between the technology of roads and that which justifies laissez faire in dealing with the firms that populate textbook-competitive markets.

Indivisibilities and Economies of Scale in Providing Road Services

Textbook competition exists when minimum-cost production of a commodity can be achieved by enterprises that are so small relative to the demand for it that their actions do not appreciably affect its price. Road-service markets are not of this type. Roads must be wide enough to allow vehicles to pass. A road with one 12-foot lane in each direction is commonly regarded as having a capacity of about 2,000 vehicles an hour regardless of their directional division; on such roads, a traveler in one direction must wait for both an adequate view of the other direction and a gap in its traffic. With four-lane roads, restrictions on passing are much less severe. Expanding the road from two to four lanes therefore increases its hourly capacity to 2,000 vehicles *per lane*; doubling lanes quadruples capacity.

A standard rural expressway has, in each direction, two 12-foot lanes with wide paved shoulders on each side. The driving lanes themselves account for less than half of such a road's right of way and of the costs of the earth moving required to create it. An additional lane in each direction would add 50 percent to its capacity but considerably less than 50 percent to its capital cost.

Urban expressways have many more interchanges and overpasses per mile than do their rural counterparts. Doubling the span of a bridge more than doubles its costs. For this reason, scale economies are considerably smaller for urban than for rural roads. Even in urban areas, however, studies of the subject have generally found modest expressway scale economies.[9] Because of the lumpiness and scale economies inherent in constructing roads, few if any markets exist in which sellers of road services would be price takers. Unregulated road entrepreneurs could not generally be relied on to set marginal-cost prices.

But wholesale conversion of road-service provision to private enterprise is unlikely in the near future. Those entrepreneurs who enter the road-service business will continue to face serious competition from publicly provided "free" roads.[10] Is this competition so severe that it would come close to forcing private road operators to behave in a fashion close to that of textbook competition?

In answering this question, we can usefully supplement section II's discussion of the inefficient distribution of trips on a road network to which unpriced access gives rise. Figure 7.2 was central to that discussion; Figure 7.5 adds some necessary complexity to it. The earlier discussion of this figure argued that free access to an expressway and arterial surface streets would lead to "too much" expressway travel; from the equilibrium to which unpriced access would give rise, aggregate resource costs could be reduced by shifting trips

Figure 7.5
Traffic Flows and Tolls on "Free"
Arterials & Entrepreneurial Expressways

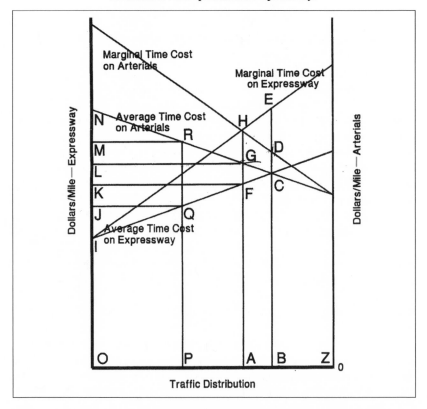

from the expressway to the arterials. Specifically, in Figure 7.5, congestion tolls of *FH* and *GH* on the expressway and arterials respectively would shift *AB* travelers to the arterials and would provide an hourly resource saving of *DEH*.

Suppose that our Philosopher King and Queen take charge of the expressway. Suppose also that they are asked to allocate trips between arterials and the expressway so as to minimize aggregate road-user costs given that access to arterials is untolled. Suppose finally that they have no budget constraint; the expressway's capacity costs are covered from revenues other than road tolls. Setting an expressway toll of *FG* would optimize the traffic distribution and would generate hourly toll revenues of *FGLK* . If the roads are of roughly the size needed to minimize aggregate travel *and* road-provision costs, congestion tolls of *FH* and *GH* respectively on expressway and arterials would roughly cover all road costs. Revenues from these tolls far exceed those generated by the toll that minimizes hourly travel-time costs with untolled arterials.

Suppose, alternatively, that private entrepreneurs have built the expressway, that they have free-road competition, and that they desire to maximize their profits. Clearly, a toll of *FG* would not do the trick. Given the geometry of Figure 7.5, it turns out that a toll of *QR would* do so.[11] It would generate hourly revenues of area *JQRM*. Nothing general can be said about the relation between the equivalent of *JQRM* toll collections and the revenues necessary to finance any particular toll road. In the case at hand, though, the expressway would be a big loser: The profit-maximizing toll, *QR*, is slightly smaller than *FH*, the approximate toll that, by assumption, would make the expressway self-supporting if paid by *OA* hourly travelers. *OA* is almost double the *OP* hourly travelers who would use the road with profit-maximizing pricing.

If four lanes would be the optimal expressway for travel between *X* and *Y* with marginal-cost pricing on both roads, private entrepreneurs with free-road competition would not build it. If a six- or eight-lane expressway would be optimal, private entrepreneurs might find it profitable to build a narrower expressway providing that the local road authority guaranteed that it would not build a competing free expressway or additional arterial capacity.

To summarize, if our Philosopher King and Queen had no budget constraint and were given control of a toll expressway that has free-road competition, they would set freeway tolls to minimize the user costs of serving the equilibrium level of system traffic. In doing so, they would effectively consider as a system cost the additional free-road congestion a traveler shifted away from the toll road would cause. Not so with profit-maximizing road entrepreneurs. On each of their roads, marginal revenue would equal marginal cost.[12] In ignoring the costs their price increases would indirectly impose on free-road users, their toll rates would exceed those the no-budget-constraint Philosopher King and Queen would charge even if the entrepreneurs had discovered a way to provide costless road capacity. Given costly road capacity, entrepreneurs with free-road competition would build smaller than optimal roads and, even then, only if free-road providers guarantee that they will not increase free-road capacity.

Question: How serious a failing of private roads is the likelihood of less-than-optimal pricing? Answer: If all we are concerned about is monopoly profits for toll-road providers, at least in urban areas, "Not very," given competition from free roads. The subsidies that untolled publicly provided roads give peak-period users seriously limit the monopolistic powers of entrepreneurs who have free-road competition. But with free-road competition, the requirement that their revenues must cover their capital costs implies that what roads they build will be substantially smaller and have higher prices than would be optimal.

Just one example of the effect of free-road competition on toll-road entrepreneurs: The California Private Transportation Company (CPTC) built an expressway in the median strip of heavily traveled State Route 91 (SR 91), which connects Orange and Riverside Counties in Southern California. Fearing monopolistic excesses, the California Department of Transportation (CalTrans) attached strings to the right to build SR 91. It required lower—initially zero—tolls for vehicles with more than two passengers and limited the rate of return that CPTC may earn.

Peak-period travel on SR 91 is predominantly toward Orange County in the morning and away from it in the afternoon. SR 91 itself is heavily congested in the peak direction during those periods. Those who use its private toll road in the peak direction save considerable time and, of course, pay substantial tolls for doing so. Time savings are not great during off-peak periods and on the lower-flow side of the tollway during peak periods. Traffic on the CPTC road is modest during these periods. It does not release financial results. A signal that they are not robust was given by its invocation of a right to cancel free travel by three-plus-person carpools when financially necessary; these carpools now pay half the regular tolls.

CPTC's contract with CalTrans had a "non-compete" clause: Unless it paid appropriate compensation, it could not build additional capacity for its system, which would reduce the demand for CPTC's services. CalTrans paid appreciable sums under that provision. The Orange County Transit Authority, the organization that runs Orange County's mass transit system, is now buying CPTC's investment. It has announced that it will be changing the road's toll structure—could it possibly be to obtain a more nearly optimal allocation of traffic between the toll roads and free roads?

Acquiring Rights-of-Way for Private Roads

Like railroads before them, roads must provide continuous paths between the points they connect. Therefore, if road entrepreneurs are to obtain rights-of-way at less than overwhelming costs, action by the state is essential. In the nineteenth century, railroad robber barons were granted eminent domain powers that are still in effect. Should road entrepreneurs be given similar or, perhaps, less sweeping rights? Or should our Philosopher King and Queen play a more active role in their land-acquisition activities by, for example, exercising some or even total control of right-of-way selection? Right-of-way problems are discussed by Bruce Benson in chapter 3 of this volume. I defer to him on this issue.

*How Can We Tell whether Toll Revenues Would be Great Enough
to Justify Publicly or Privately Financed Road Expansion?*

On the surface, the rule seems simple: Add to road capacity as long as the last dollar spent on it generates user benefits with a present value greater than $1. The problems: How can we learn how much capacity a dollar would buy? How can we learn the value to users of the benefits that would result?

Although they tend toward low-ball estimates, civil engineers can provide us with tolerably good information for a given project of the costs of pushing earth around, laying reinforcing rods, building bridges, and pouring cement. The really difficult data problem is valuing the right-of-way on which this work would be done. Determining the cost of buying and demolishing the property needed for a major expansion of an urban expressway is a time consuming and expensive activity. The following procedure might work as a way to get a preliminary estimate of whether potential benefits stand a good chance of justifying this expense: By estimating marginal-cost congestion tolls for the route to be improved, we also have found the marginal cost of present travel on it. From this, we can infer the cost reductions that more capacity would provide. We can then find the present value of these cost reductions. Deducting estimated construction costs from this present value leaves an estimate of the right-of-way cost above which expansion would not be justified.

Here is a sketch of this procedure using Twin Cities data that could be followed to estimate the user value of new capacity: David Anderson and I calculated that, in 1990, a stretch of Interstate 35W just south of Minneapolis was the most heavily congested part of the Twin Cities freeway network. Using $12.50 a vehicle hour as a population average travel-time value, Figure 7.4 indicates that the average "gap" in that stretch of road was 26 cents a vehicle mile while directly-experienced travel costs were 43 cents a mile. This direct cost implies a travel speed of about 30 mph. Assuming a full-price elasticity of demand of -1, imposing marginal-cost tolls on all congested roads would have resulted in reducing traffic on this link by about 25 percent, a 21 cent per mile toll, and an average speed of about 48 mph. That the trip costs directly borne by a vehicle's passengers would be 31 cents a mile implies that they are traveling at 1.4880 minutes per mile, which, in turn, implies that the road would operate at an volume/capacity (N/K) ratio of 83.54 percent. Expressway capacity is commonly regarded as being 2,000 vehicles per lane-hour. An 83.54 percent N/K ratio implies that the four-lane expressway would be carrying 3,342 autos toward the Minneapolis central business district on its two inbound lanes during the morning peak hour.

Suppose that hourly capacity of each lane is expanded by ten vehicles each. Doing so would reduce their N/K ratios to 83.16 percent—a ratio that implies traveling at 1.4783 minutes per mile, a saving of 0.0097 minutes per vehicle mile or 32.42 minutes for all 3,342 inbound travelers. Multiplying this saving by $12.50 per vehicle hour and dividing by the twenty units of capacity analyzed yields $0.3377 as the value per morning peak hour of the marginal product of a unit of capacity.

The same procedure could be followed for additional increments to Interstate 35W during the morning peak hour, for the remaining twenty-three hours of a day and, given projections of future traffic and travel-time values, for the life of the improvement.

What about the Effects of Congestion-Priced Roads
on the Income Distribution?

Those who build roads for a living largely oppose congestion pricing. They generally justify their opposition as resulting from concern for those low-income folks who would be forced off roads by congestion pricing; they rarely mention the effect pricing might have on the demand for their services. Finding ways to overcome these widely held objections is essential if congestion pricing—on publicly or privately supplied roads—is to become a widespread reality.

Excepting one group, congestion pricing would, indeed, be regressive. The exception: Congestion pricing would induce some travelers to shift from auto to mass-transit travel. The resulting increase in mass-transit demand would increase service frequency thereby diminishing the waiting delays experienced by those who already use mass transit. With that exception, the higher the incomes of those charged, the lower their toll burdens would be. Should our Philosopher King and Queen take steps to reduce the burden of congestion pricing on the poor?

In the Twin Cities, congestion pricing would generate roughly $1.50 for every dollar in travel costs it imposes on users. Gains of this sort from efficient pricing are always to be expected; moving from an inefficient to an efficient pricing system for anything would invariably produce revenues and benefits greater than buyer costs. Contemporary American citizens dislike taxes and distrust governments. Congestion-pricing packages will continue to be a very hard sell unless we can (a) find a way to use toll revenues to reimburse losers in a fashion that does not distort their travel behavior appreciably away from the with-toll optimum or (b) discover a detailed expenditure program for toll revenues that, a substantial majority agree, justifies paying tolls or (c) find a way to use toll revenues to create enough winners to offset the objections of losers.

Unless those tolled are very stupid, even with a substantial lag, returning just to them the tolls they pay would destroy the incentive effects of pricing. Giving toll revenues to each member of a group to which all toll payers belong regardless of their actual travel behavior would be better, but finding such a group is not easy. Item: In 1990, less than 20 percent of Twin Cities households had one or more members who traveled during the morning peak hour. Returning average toll collections per toll-paying household to *all* households would require much more cash than congestion tolls would provide. Sadly to say, it seems a financial impossibility to compensate losers fully in a way that maintains the incentive effects of pricing.

The transportation- and city-planning communities like congestion pricing for the revenue it will produce for such—to them—wonderful things as light-rail transit systems built to induce higher residential density thereby combating that great evil of the automobile age, sprawl. Unfortunately for the planning community, the market behavior of urban citizens suggests that, even with congestion pricing, the fraction of them who favor sprawl is considerably greater than the fraction who oppose it. The likelihood that planners will produce an expenditure program for toll-revenue of which a majority will approve seems small.

Creating a substantial number of winners seems fiscally possible. Using some congestion-toll revenues to pay a dividend to *all* Twin Cities households would have made winners of the 80 percent of them who do not contain peak-period travelers and, hence, are potential supporters of congestion pricing. Devoting a substantial fraction of toll collections to lump-sum grants to *all* households in an urban area would not compensate the big losers from congestion pricing. But, at least in the Twin Cities, lump-sum household grants would make congestion-toll winners of 80 percent of them—a powerful potential support group in a campaign to institute congestion pricing.

Again, those who build roads for a living tend to oppose congestion pricing. They generally justify their opposition out of concern for those low-income folks who would be tolled off roads by congestion pricing. Their solution for this problem of the poor is to give all of us—poor and rich alike—a free ride.

This is a really bad solution. After all, the problems of the poor are not really that they are ill-housed, ill-fed, ill-transported, or ill-lawyered. It is, rather, that they are poor. I have long supported marketable peak-period road scholarships for the poor. I want these scholarships to be marketable so that the poor can get cash for them if they prefer it to peak-period auto travel. After all, the least cost way per unit of satisfaction conferred is to give the poor cash, not subsidies of commodities they purchase and certainly not subsidies of commodities that all of us buy just because the poor also buy them.

Appendix: Proofs of Propositions about Traveler Behavior
and the Optimal Design and Pricing of Roads

Traveler Behavior and the "Full Price" of Travel

Suppose that a household derives utility from consuming S units per week of a general purpose commodity, stuff, conveniently priced at $1 a unit. It also derives utility from what happens There during each of the B trips per week it takes from Here to There and back. However, it incurs disutility from the time, $t\,T$, it spends traveling where t is the number of hours required for a trip.

The household's problem, then, is to maximize its utility, $U(S, T, t\,T)$, subject to its budget constraint, $I = S + FT$, where F is the round-trip fare. Setting up the LaGrangian expression

$$Z = U(S, T, Tt) + \lambda(I - S - FT)$$

and differentiating with respect to S and T yields

$$Z_S = U_S - \lambda = 0 \tag{A1}$$
$$Z_T = U_T + \lambda(t\,U_{tT} - F) = 0 \tag{A2}$$

as first order conditions for utility maximization where subscripts refer to partial derivatives. Dividing (A2) by (A1) gives

$$U_T/U_S = t\,U_{tT}/U_S - F \tag{A3}$$

In equation (A3), U_{tT}/U_S, the ratio of the marginal disutility of travel time to the marginal utility of dollars—the rate at which the household would be willing to sacrifice S to reduce travel time—has the dimension dollars per hour. It seems reasonable to call this ratio $-V$, the money cost the household attaches to its travel time, its "value of travel time," for short. Doing so changes equation (A2) to

$$U_T/U_S = F + Vt \tag{A3'}$$

This relationship says that the household will equate the ratio of the marginal utility of bus trips to that of dollars with the fare plus the time cost of a trip, an expression that is commonly referred to in the transportation-economics literature as the "full price" of a trip.

The Optimal Relationship between Congestion Tolls and Capacity Costs

If producing trips on a highway involves constant returns to scale, travel time per trip can be written as a function of the volume-capacity ratio, N/K. The hourly cost of capacity can be written as $P_K K$ where P_K is the hourly price of a unit of capacity—depreciation, maintenance, and the interest that the funds invested in capacity could have earned if invested elsewhere. Ignoring vehicle operating costs for simplicity and denoting the average value to vehicle occupants of an hour's travel time by V, the total variable costs of the trips taken during an hour can be written

$$\text{Variable Costs} = V N T = V N \, t(N/K) \tag{A4}$$

Differentiating with respect to N yields the short-run marginal cost of a trip as

$$Vt(N/K) + V N \, t'/K \tag{A5}$$

The first term on the right of equation (A5) is the average time cost per trip; the second is the difference between the trip's average and marginal time costs—the cost each vehicle in the traffic stream imposes on the occupants of all other vehicles in the stream by slowing their trips. To set the price of a trip equal to its marginal cost, a toll equal to this latter amount must be charged each of the N travelers. If this were done, total toll collections would be $V t' N^2/K$.

A plausible highway-authority objective is to select that capacity level for a highway that would minimize the total costs of travel on it—the time and other costs that users incur directly *plus* the cost to the authority of providing the highway's services, $P_K K$. More capacity means faster trips, but greater highway capital costs. The total cost of N trips an hour on a highway is

$$\textit{Total Costs} = V N \, t(N/K) + P_K K \tag{A6}$$

Differentiating with respect to K, setting the result equal to zero, and rearranging terms yields

$$-t' N^2/K^2 + P_K = 0 \tag{A7}$$

as the condition that must be satisfied by the cost-minimizing capacity level. In words, this equation says that the last dollar per hour spent to expand capacity should yield hourly user-cost savings of a dollar.

Multiplying equation (A7) through by K and rearranging terms yields

$$V\,t'\,N^2/K = P_K K \qquad \text{(A8)}$$

The right-hand side of (A8) is the hourly cost of the road's capacity. Again, from equation (A5), total toll collections would be $V\,t'\,N^2/K$. But this is the left-hand side of (A8), which equals the total hourly cost of the highway. Thus, given constant returns to scale, an optimally priced road that has been designed to minimize the sum of user and provider costs would generate toll revenues just sufficient to cover its provider's costs. Given constant returns to scale, optimally designed and priced roads would be exactly self-supporting.

How the Rule "Stay X Seconds Behind the Vehicle You Follow"
Leads to the Backward Bending Relationship in Figure 7.1

Sweeping under the rug worries about how to take into account the preferences of drivers to travel at different speeds, a relationship commonly used by civil engineers is

Flow (in vehicles/hour) = Speed (in miles per hour) ·
Density (in vehicles per mile)

Driving-instruction manuals say that, for safety, the relationship between speed and density should be linear: "Stay two seconds behind the car in front of you" for young people; stay three seconds behind for slow-reacting elderly.

Suppose that the speed-density relationship *is* linear and that S^* and D^* are respectively the speed at which vehicles would travel—60 mph, say—if there is no one else on the road and the density at which the road becomes a parking lot. We can then write:

$$S = a + bD$$

Using $S = S^*$ when $D = 0$ and $D = D^*$ when $S = 0$ to solve for a and b gives

$$S = S^* - D\,S^*/D^* \ \text{ or } \ S/S^* = 1 - D/D^* \qquad \text{(A9)}$$

Flow on this road is maximized when $S = S^*/2$ and $D = D^*/2$. Hence, maximum flow is $F_{max} = D^* S^*/4$. From (A9),

$$F = SD^*(1 - S/S^*) = N$$

and

$$F/F_{max} = 4SD^*(1 - S/S^*)/(S^*D^*) = 4S(1 - S/S^*)/S^* = F/K \qquad (A10)$$

The traveler input for trips is time = 1/speed, not speed itself. Therefore, (A10) can be written as

$$F/F_{max} = N/K = 4t^*(1 - t^*/t)/t$$

where $t^* = 1/S^*$. Solving for the roots of this quadratic that involves the lower travel time yields

$$t = 2t^*(1 + (1 - N/K)-)/(N/K) \qquad (A11)$$

Differentiating (A11) with respect to N gives

$$dtN /dN = t^*/(1 - N/K)-$$

The capacity of each road lane is:

(60 sec/min) · (60 min/hr)]/(1.8 sec/veh) = 2,000 veh/hr.

At 30 mph, a vehicle travels 44 feet in a second or 79.2 feet in 1.8 seconds. If all vehicles in a traffic stream that pass a given point during some hour are evenly spaced and travel at 30 mph, they will be spread over a 30-mile stretch of road.

[(30 mi) · (5,280 ft/mi)]/(79.2 ft/veh) = 2,000 veh/hr.

So, if each vehicle stays 1.8 seconds behind the front of the vehicle in front of it, at capacity, they travel at 30 mph.

Notes

1. See Daniel B. Klein, Adrian Moore, and Binyam Reja, *Curb Rights: A Foundation for Free Enterprise in Urban Transit* (Washington, D.C.: Brookings Institution Press, 1997).
2. Gabriel Roth pointed out to me that 2,000 vehicles per lane hour as "capacity" is probably an hourly flow that U.S. traffic engineers once selected as a level that isn't nice to exceed. I chose a 1.8-seconds-behind rule to give an hourly capacity of 2,000. Many flows greater than 2,000 have been observed on heavily traveled expressways.

3. The amount by which the cost of producing a group of commodities (*BH* trips in the case at hand) exceeds the value their consumers attach to them.

4. The sum of the money outlay a trip requires *plus* the amount a traveler would be willing to pay to avoid the travel time the trip requires.

5. "Rent" in the sense of being a payment to an input that is not required to evoke its services; "quasi" in the sense that, if it earned no compensation, the services of fixed capital would be provided only until it depreciated or could in some way be transferred to another use.

6. To emphasize, throughout this chapter, "cost of a unit of capital" refers to the cost per time period of using its services, and not to the purchase price of that unit.

7. If tolls were to be imposed on all roads with any level of congestion, such presently employed dedicated user charges as fuel taxes and vehicle licensing fees that exceed registration costs would involve double charging at least in urban areas. Our analysis implicitly assumes these taxes to be part of congestion charges in urban areas and to remain in place for, e.g., uncongested rural expressways. By ignoring the potential disappearance of fuel taxes and the like, we underestimate the benefits of urban congestion pricing. We have not estimated the size of this underestimate.

8. In his 1967 University of Chicago doctoral dissertation, Thomas Lisco found that, in choosing between rail and auto commutes between the Chicago central business district and a Chicago suburb, Skokie, travelers' implied average time values increased linearly from zero for someone with no income to 50 percent of income for those with incomes of $40,000 a year in present day prices. Travel-time values averaged 50 percent of income for travelers with incomes greater than $40,000 a year. We used the Lisco relationship to value the travel time of our sample of Twin Cities travelers. See Thomas Edward Lisco, *The Value of Commuters' Travel Time: A Study in Urban Transportation* (Chicago, IL, 1967).

9. See Theodore E. Keeler and Kenneth A. Small, "Optimal Peak Load Pricing, Investment, and Service Levels on Urban Expressways," *Journal of Political Economy* 85 (1977): 1–26 and Marvin Kraus, "Scale Economies Analysis for Urban Highway Networks," *Journal of Urban Economics* 9 (1981): 1–22.

10. In this context, by "'free' roads" I mean roads funded by the same taxes—fuel, in particular—that are paid by those who use toll roads.

11. The left axis and the lines showing average travel-time costs at alternative traffic volumes form a triangle, *ICN*. A toll such as *QR* times the hourly expressway traffic volume it would induce, *OP*, gives the hourly revenue generated by that toll, area *JQRM*. The rectangle with maximum area that can be inscribed in triangle *ICN* is formed by a vertical line half way between the triangle's base and apex. *QR* is that line. Note that it generates a traffic volume equal to *OP*, half that which would be generated if both the expressway and arterials have no tolls.

12. The marginal *full* cost—the costs they *and* their customers incur—is what profit-maximizing entrepreneurs would consider in setting tolls. Indeed, if all travelers have the same full-price elasticity of demand, such entrepreneurs would set tolls and capacity levels that would minimize their and their customers' full costs of travel. With different full-price elasticities, entrepreneurs would weight the preferences of high-elasticity customers more heavily than their low-elasticity counterparts. See my 1985 paper, "Profit Maximization, Cost Minimization, and Pricing for Congestion-Prone Facilities," *The Logistics and Transportation Review*, 21 (1): 27–36.

8

Estimating Congestion Prices, Revenues, and Surpluses: An Example from Manila

Gabriel Roth and Olegario G. Villoria, Jr.

Introduction

Traffic congestion is often experienced, but rarely understood. It is not some inevitable "disease of civilization" but a predictable result of charging too little for use of the scarce resource "road space." It can be compared to over-fishing in public waters and over-grazing on public land. But the root cause of traffic congestion is the absence of property rights in roads. As Frank Knight (1924) pointed out, if roads were privately owned by entities competing against one another, the owners would strive to charge competitive prices. If, Knight argued, this were technically possible, the imposition of such charges would result in a socially optimal degree of congestion. Knight's assertion was challenged by James Buchanan (1956) and David Mills (1981). Both argued that Knight was right only if roads were provided competitively; if roads were owned by a monopolist, prices could be raised to maximize profits rather than to the level required to optimize social benefits.

The following calculations, based on observed traffic conditions in Manila, show how to calculate "optimal" prices for the use of congested roads. Then, on the assumption that a road-owning Manila Commercial Highway Organization (MaCHO) would be required to charge these "optimal" prices, the potential profitability of Manila's roads are calculated.

What are Congestion Costs?

Congestion costs arise out of the tendency of vehicles on the same road network to slow one another down. The sole user of a road network may travel safely on it at high speed, but congested conditions can bring all traffic to a stop. Although speeds drop as more vehicles join the traffic, it has to be recognized that all vehicles, not just the latecomers, contribute to congestion.

However, not all vehicles contribute equally, as some types of vehicle slow traffic down more than others. Traffic engineers use the term "passenger car unit" (*pcu*) to indicate the effect of a vehicle on the rest of the traffic. *pcu* values in the Metro Manila area are shown in Table 8.1. The *pcu* values were determined on the basis of previous traffic studies undertaken by the Philippine Department of Transportation and Communications (DOTC) and on assumptions generally accepted by professional traffic engineers.

Table 8.1
Passenger Car Unit (*pcu*) Equivalents

Vehicle Class	
Cars/Jeeps/Utility Vehicles	1.00
Jeepneys	1.50
Buses	2.25
Trucks/Trailers	2.50
Tricycle/Motorcycle	0.50

Source: Department of Transportation & Communications, Government of the Philippines.

The Magnitude of Congestion Delays in Metro Manila

The most recent comprehensive study of travel in Metro Manila has been the Metropolitan Manila Urban Transport Integration Study (MMUTIS) (1999), which was financed by the Japan International Cooperation Agency and carried out under the auspices of the Department of Transportation and Communications, the Metropolitan Manila Development Authority, the Department of Public Works and Highways, the National Economic Development Authority, Philippine National Police, Housing and Urban Development Coordinating Council, Environmental Management Board, and the University of the Philippines' National Center for Transportation Studies. The data used in the MMUTIS were collected in 1996. ·

From unpublished studies carried out by the DOTC on relationships between traffic volumes and speeds on Manila's roads, it is possible to calculate how average traffic speeds fall as more vehicles enter the Metro Manila road network. The relationship shown below was estimated using regression analysis on a set of data points extracted from linear speed-volume relationships developed by the DOTC. The relationships found between traffic volumes and traffic speeds enable the delays due to one additional *pcu* to be calculated for different traffic volumes, as is shown in Table 8.2 below. The effect of additional vehicles in slowing down traffic was modeled by the following linear mathematical relationship:

$$V = 49 - 0.02345q$$

where,

V = Average traffic speed, in km/hour
q = traffic volume, in *pcu*/hour
49 = Traffic speed when there is no congestion, in km/hour
0.02345 = Constant

Traffic speeds would be limited to 49 km/hour even in the absence of congestion, due to traffic lights and other obstacles that would impede even a single vehicle traversing the road network. A linear relationship is found to provide adequate approximation to actual traffic volumes in the range of speeds covered by our investigation. However, at very low speeds, such as can bring traffic to a halt, a parabolic relationship may give better representation of traffic conditions.

This relationship between traffic volumes and traffic speeds enables us to calculate the delays, in minutes/kilometer, imposed by a *pcu* on other vehicles in Metro Manila's congested traffic under the conditions prevailing in 1995. Table 8.2, below, shows speeds and delays at different traffic volumes. The delaying effect of an additional *pcu* is calculated by applying the speed/volume relationship to the reduction in speed due to one additional vehicle, and multiplying the consequent delay by the total number of *pcu*s in the traffic stream.

Estimating the Costs of Using Motor Vehicles in Metro Manila's Traffic

The costs of using vehicles are made up of two elements:

(a) The value of the time of the occupants, and
(b) The vehicle operating costs, the principal ones being the costs of fuel, oil, tires, maintenance, and depreciation arising from vehicle use.

Table 8.2
Delays to Traffic Imposed by an Additional *pcu* in Metro-Manila

Traffic Volume (*pcu*/hour) (1)	Travel Speed (km/hour) (2)	Time to travel one kilometer at given volume (minutes) (3)	Time to travel one kilometer at one less *pcu*/hour (minutes) (4)	Delay imposed on traffic stream by an additional *pcu* (minutes) (5)
200	44.8	1.3398	1.3391	0.1395
300	42.0	1.4138	1.4131	0.2334
400	40.1	1.4965	1.4957	0.3490
500	37.7	1.5895	1.5885	0.4923
600	35.4	1.6947	1.6936	0.6719
700	33.1	1.8149	1.8137	0.8991
800	30.7	1.9535	1.9520	1.1906
900	28.4	2.1149	2.1132	1.5701
1000	26.0	2.3055	2.3034	2.0731
1100	23.7	2.5337	2.5312	2.7543
1200	21.3	2.8122	2.8091	3.7013
1300	19.0	3.1594	3.1555	5.0606
1400	16.6	3.6044	3.5993	7.0923
1500	14.3	4.1953	4.1884	10.2928
1600	12.0	5.0179	5.0081	15.7025
1700	9.6	6.2418	6.2267	25.8040
1800	7.0	8.2555	8.2289	47.7575

Source: AGILE computations based on MMUTIS data.

Explanatory Notes:
Col. 1   Volume
Col. 2   Speed = 49.4714207 − 0.0234464 × Col. 1
Col. 3   Time, in minutes, to travel 1 km
Col. 4   Time, in minutes, to travel 1 km at 1 fewer *pcu*/hour than the volume in Col. 1
Col. 5   Col 1. × (Col. 3 − Col. 4)

Both elements can be expressed by the formula

$$C = \text{Time Cost} + \text{Vehicle Operating Cost}$$

where,

Time Cost = travel time × value of travel time, different for each vehicle class,
Vehicle Operating Cost = a + b/V, "a" and "b" are constants, different for each vehicle class,
V = average speed in km/hour, the same for all vehicle classes.

From these formulae, and from the speed-volume formula described earlier, the costs borne by the average vehicle can be calculated for any level of output, in vehicle-km, "produced" by the street network.

Estimating the Value of Time Lost or Saved in Metro Manila's Traffic

Estimates of the relevant time values, in Philippine pesos (Php) per hour, for each vehicle class, were made on the basis of MMUTIS data and are presented in Table 8.3 below. The value of time per person is based on income data obtained by surveys; the value of time "per vehicle" equals the time per person multiplied by the vehicle occupancy; and the value of time "per *pcu*" equals the value of time per vehicle divided by its *pcu* value, from Table 8.1.

Table 8.3
Value of Time By Vehicle Class

Vehicle Class	*pcu*	Vehicle Occupancy	VALUE OF TIME IN PHP/HR		
			Person	Vehicle	*pcu*
Car	.00	1.8	29.35	51.36	51.36
Utility Vehicle	.00	3.1	11.71	36.53	36.53
Jeepney	.50	15.0	3.90	58.36	38.91
Bus	2.25	50.6	4.32	218.45	97.09
Trucks	2.50	2.1	24.81	51.36	20.54
Motorcycle/Tricycle	0.50	1.1	11.82	13.24	26.48

Source: Authors' calculations based on MMUTIS data.

Note: During 1998/1999, the exchange rate ranged from Php36 to 40 per US$1.

Deriving Total Vehicle Costs for the Different Vehicle Classes

The total of the time and vehicle operating costs, in Php/*pcu*-km, for each vehicle class, are shown in Table 8.4 below, for the initial condition of traffic speed equaling 9.61 km/hour. Similar calculations can be made for costs at other speeds.

Calculating Benefit-Maximizing Congestion Charges

Congestion costs on roads are excessive because those who use congested roads are not confronted with prices that take account of the delays they impose on other road users. For example, Table 8.2 shows that, when traffic volumes average 1,700 *pcu*/hour, traffic speeds average 9.6 km/hour and the delays imposed by one extra *pcu* on the rest of the traffic average 25.8 minutes/km. Assume for illustration that the monetary value of the delay is Php20/km. If it were technically possible to charge users of congested roads for the delays they

Table 8.4
Derivation of Time and Operating Costs for Different Vehicle Classes
(at initial condition of 1700 *pcu*/hour)

Vehicle Class	Speed km/hr	Vehicle Operating Cost, Php/km	Time Cost Php/km	Total Cost Php/km
Cars	9.61	5.08	5.34	10.42
Utility Vehicles	9.61	4.98	3.80	8.78
Jeepneys	9.61	6.43	4.05	10.48
Buses	9.61	13.39	10.10	23.49
Trucks/Trailers	9.61	16.48	2.14	18.62
Tricycle/Motorcycle	9.61	0.04	2.75	2.79

Source: Authors' calculations based on MMUTIS data.

impose, careful road owners, whether in the private or the public sector, would attempt to keep off their roads any vehicle whose journey was of less benefit than the cost of the Php20/km imposed on the rest of the traffic by each *pcu*. The simplest way to achieve this is to charge every vehicle Php20/km per *pcu*, if there were a way to do so. The effect of such a charge would be to reduce average traffic volumes, because not all road users would pay it. The new flow might be 700 *pcu*/hour, at which, as can be seen from Table 8.2, the speed would rise to 33.1 km/hour, and the congestion cost imposed on others would fall to below the imposed fee of Php20/km per *pcu*.

Under these new circumstances, the Php20/km per *pcu* fee would be too high, and intelligent road owners would lower it, trying to price the charge at a level that would just equal the costs imposed on the rest of the traffic in the conditions prevailing after the charge was imposed. This price would be the best from society's point of view, because a higher one would deter too many vehicles, including some vehicle users imposing costs that were lower than the fee they were charged, while a lower price would allow road use to too many vehicles, including some vehicle users imposing on the rest of the traffic costs in excess of the benefits they themselves received.

How can this benefit-maximizing charge be calculated? To arrive at a certain answer, it is necessary to know the extent to which traffic would diminish in response to a fee, assuming one could be charged. Economists use the term "elasticity" to describe a percentage change in usage in response to a percentage change in price. A negative elasticity indicates that an increase in price is associated with a reduction in the amount demanded. The reaction of traffic to a congestion charge cannot be known for certain without actually imposing it, but a range of elasticities can be assumed and the resulting charges calculated.

On a congested road network, each vehicle imposes costs on the rest of the traffic and, in its turn, bears costs because of the presence of all the other vehicles. On the basis of the vehicle costs at different traffic volumes, and the effect on speed due to the introduction of one other vehicle (more precisely, one other *pcu*), we calculated the costs imposed by an additional *pcu* on the rest of the traffic at different speeds.

The optimum congestion charge, per *pcu*, is the amount that will just equal the congestion cost per *pcu* under the conditions prevailing after its imposition. By trial and error, it is possible to find out, for each assumed elasticity, the traffic volume at which the congestion charge would equal the congestion cost at that volume. The necessary iterations were carried out using the Excel spreadsheet shown in Table 8.5 for an assumed elasticity of −1.0. The process is illustrated in Figure 8.1, "Derivation of optimal congestion charge at Elasticity −1.0."

Similar calculations were made for other elasticities, namely: −0.10, −0.25, and −0.50, and the results are summarized in Table 8.6.

Available evidence (such as assembled by Oum, Waters, and Yong 1992) suggests that changes in road use as a result of increased costs are consistent with elasticities of −0.5 or less. However, as most of the published data on demand elasticities for road space are based on experience in Western countries, we thought it prudent to increase the range to −1.0, to allow for the possibility that elasticities would be greater in less-developed countries, due to the wider availability of public transportation options.

The results indicate that, over a wide range of elasticities ranging from −0.1 to −1.0, the optimal congestion charge would vary from Php 6.08 to Php 13.76/*pcu*/km. Imposition of such a charge would be likely to result in average traffic volumes falling by 11 percent to 24 percent, and traffic speeds increasing by 44 percent to 101 percent, the greater fall in volume being associated with the higher elasticity and with the higher increase in speed.

Under conditions of high elasticity road users are likely to have readily available alternatives (such as carpooling, public transport, or traveling elsewhere or at different times), so a comparatively low price change would encourage many to leave the congested road, and increases in efficiency are obtained at comparatively low cost. The reverse is the case under conditions of low elasticity, which implies the absence of readily available substitutes. Under those conditions higher charges would be needed to shift traffic and more travelers stay in the congested traffic despite having to pay higher charges. These effects are demonstrated in Table 8.6.

Table 8.6 also shows that the proportional changes in speed are some four times as high as changes in traffic volumes. This is a characteristic of Manila's

Table 8.5
Estimation of Benefit-Maximizing Congestion Charge
(Elasticity Scenario of −1.0)

(No.) Description	Units	Car	V	Jeepney	Bus	Truck	MC	Fleet
(1) Initial volume	pcu/hr							700
(2) Initial proportion of traffic	percent	38.8%	2.6%	6.5%	.7%	4.9%	.5%	100%
(3) Traffic volume per vehicle class	pcu/hr	660	54	111	28	254	93	1700
(4) Initial speed	km/hr	9.61	9.61	9.61	9.61	9.61	9.61	
(5) Cost to travel 1 km	Php/km	10.42	8.78	10.48	23.49	18.62	2.79	
(6) Congestion charge	Php/pcu-km							2.2
(7) New cost to travel 1 km	Php/km	12.7	11.0	12.7	25.7	20.9	5.0	
(8) Elasticity		−1.0	−1.0	−1.0	−1.0	−1.0	−1.0	
(9) Percentage change in cost		22%	26%	21%	10%	12%	80%	
(10) Percentage change in volume		−22%	−26%	−21%	−10%	−12%	−80%	
(11) Change in volume		−142	−142	−24	−3	−31	−75	
(12) New Volume		518	412	87	26	223	18	1284
(13) New proportion of traffic	percent	40.3%	32.1%	6.8%	2.09%	17.4%	1.4%	100%
(14) New speed	km/hr	19.36	19.36	19.36	19.36	19.36	19.36	
(15) Fleet Volume	pcu/hr							1284
(16) Vehicle Speed	km/hr							19.36
(17) Vehicle Speed at one pcu/hr less	km/hr							19.38
(18) Average cost/vehicle	Php/pcu-km	6.369	5.316	6.380	16.200	14.173	1.403	7.513
(19) Average cost/vehicle at one pcu/km less	Php/pcu-km	6.364	5.312	6.375	16.191	14.167	1.402	7.508
(20) Costs imposed on rest of traffic by one extra pcu	Php/pcu-km							6.074
(21) Total costs due to one extra pcu	Php/pcu-km							13.59
(22) Percent change in cost	percent							24.5
(23) Elasticity								−1.00
(24) Resulting Speed	km/hr							19.36
(25) Resulting volume	pcu/hr							1284
(26) Equilibrium demand price	Php/pcu-km							13.59

Explanatory Note: This Excel spreadsheet utilizes the SOLVER function to find the "Congestion charge" (Line 6), which equates the "Total cost due to one extra pcu" (Line 21) and the "Equilibrium demand price" (Line 26). The "Total costs due to one extra pcu" varies with "Congestion charge" and the consequent changes in traffic volumes and speeds, taking into account changes in traffic composition by vehicle class. The "Equilibrium demand price" varies in accordance with the assumed elasticity, with the change in traffic conditions from the initial to the final condition determined by the Excel model.

road network, which appears to be functioning at close to its physical capacity. Under those conditions, the addition of even a small amount of traffic can cause substantial slowdown and its removal can bring substantial relief.

Optimal congestion charges by elasticity and vehicle class are shown in Table 8.7. These were calculated by multiplying the optimal congestion

Figure 8.1
Derivation of optimal congestion charge
Elasticity −1.0

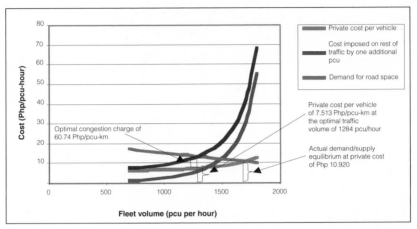

charges in Table 8.6 below with the appropriate *pcu* values for each vehicle class.

The calculations and iterations carried out in Table 8.5 take account of the assumed time values of the different vehicle classes. The different time values associated with the various vehicle classes make no difference to the congestion costs they impose—an empty bus can cause as much congestion as a full one.

Table 8.6
Optimal Congestion Charges/*pcu* for Different Assumed Elasticities

INITIAL CONDITION:			COST VOLUME SPEED	10.91 PHP/KM 1,700 *PCU*/HR 9.61 KM/HR			
Elasticity Scenario	Volume *pcu*/hr	Speed km/hr	Optimal Payments at Relevant Speeds Php/km	Costs already incurred Php/km	Optimal Congestion Charge PhP/km	Overall Change in Volume	Overall Change in Speed
−0.10	1520	13.84	22.52	8.76	13.76	−11%	44%
−0.25	1429	15.98	17.93	8.14	9.79	−16%	66%
−0.50	1355	17.71	15.38	7.78	7.60	−20%	84%
−1.00	1284	19.36	13.59	7.51	6.08	−24%	101%

Source: Authors' calculations based on MMUTIS data.

Table 8.7
Optimum Congestion Charges for Different Vehicle Classes

Php/*pcu*-km

Vehicle Class	*pcu*	DEMAND ELASTICITY SCENARIO			
		−0.10	−0.25	−0.50	−1.00
Cars	1.00	13.76	9.79	7.60	6.08
Utility Vehicles	1.00	13.76	9.79	7.60	6.08
Jeepneys	1.50	20.65	14.68	11.40	9.12
Buses	2.25	30.97	22.02	17.10	13.68
Trucks/Trailers	2.50	34.41	24.46	19.00	15.20
Tricycle/Motorcycle	0.50	6.88	4.89	3.80	3.04

Source: Authors' calculations based on MMUTIS data.

But the difference in time values has a significant effect on the response to the rise in traffic speed resulting from the imposition of a congestion charge. Those who place a high value on their time would benefit more from the increase in speed than those with a lower value of time; they would suffer less from the monetary charge, and would be less likely to reduce their travel. Therefore a uniform congestion charge/*pcu* would result in a change in the composition of traffic. The proportion of traffic associated with high time values would increase, and the proportion of traffic associated with low time values would decline. These changes can be seen in Table 8.8 below, which shows the initial and final traffic compositions by vehicle class, for each of the elasticities considered.

Table 8.8
Effect of Congestion Charges on the Composition of Traffic in Metro Manila

Vehicle Class:	PERCENTAGE						
	Cars	Utility Vehicles	Jeepneys	Buses	Trucks	Motorcycle	Total
Initial Composition:	38.8	32.6	6.5	1.7	14.9	5.5	100
Final Composition:							
Elasticity of −0.10	39.4	32.4	6.6	1.8	15.8	4.0	100
Elasticity of −0.25	39.7	32.3	6.7	1.9	16.4	3.1	100
Elasticity of −0.50	40.0	32.2	6.7	1.9	16.8	2.3	100
Elasticity of −1.00	40.3	32.1	6.8	2.0	17.4	1.4	100

Source: Authors' calculations

Implications for the Philippines

To be efficient and effective, charges for the use of congested roads should be applied selectively, with the prices reflecting congestion levels at different places and at different times of the day, as is done with telephone charges. For this reason alone, collection at conventional tollbooths would be impracticable. Conventional tollbooths would also impose unacceptable delays to traffic.

However, electronic charging systems, which are now used in Canada, France, Norway, Singapore, and the United States, can enable fees to be collected without vehicles having to stop, or even to slow down. Fees can be varied from one place to another, with different rates for peak and off-peak travel times, without the use of conventional tollbooths. Further information on these can be found in Johansson and Mattsson (editors 1994); Hubert H. Humphrey Institute (1996); Roth (1996); and Button and Verhoef (editors 1998).

It is too early to say whether such systems would, or would not, be either desirable or acceptable in the Philippines. They should certainly not be introduced without the support of the people directly concerned. Enforcement and equity issues would have to be discussed and settled. We do not recommend introducing electronic road pricing in the whole of the Metro Manila area unless preceded by successful small pilot projects in the area or elsewhere. We are not aware that any government agency, or international lender, is considering the introduction of congestion charges in Manila, or elsewhere in the Philippines.

Would it be Equitable to Impose Congestion Charges?

Discussions on congestion charges are bedeviled by the natural objection to any suggestion that road users already suffering from congestion should be required to pay extra. Requiring those who are already getting a bad deal to become worse off, so as to enable some to become better off, seems to fly in the face of what is fair. Egalitarians may consider it fairer that all should get equal but poor service, rather than that some would become worse off and some better off.

Four points can be made about this:

- Because congestion pricing would likely speed up travel by buses and jeepneys substantially, public transportation users, many of whom have low incomes, would certainly benefit from time savings, and possibly even from fare reductions.

- Similarly, the speed-up of trucks could increase their productivity to the extent that the costs of many goods might not rise significantly, and some prices might even fall.

- While the immediate losers could be low-income car users, they too would benefit by being able to travel more speedily on the occasions they have to. Under present conditions, the travel of all in Manila is constrained, irrespective of urgency.

- To the extent that revenues from congestion pricing are used to expand travel facilities, the benefits of an improved infrastructure would flow to all road users.

Financial Implications of Levying Benefit-Maximizing Congestion Charges in Metro Manila

Congestion costs are not ordinary costs, but reflect the failure to collect the opportunity costs (in economic jargon, the "economic rent") that can be earned by the scarce resource "road space." We do not often hear about congestion costs posing problems in the hotel and theater businesses, nor even with respect to telephone and electricity supply. If there were congestion in those commercial sectors—manifested, for example, by long queues of customers waiting to be served—prices would be raised to expand supply and dampen demand. In the Philippines, for example, prices for long-distance telephone calls and commercial electricity supply are raised in peak periods.

What would be the implications of treating roads in a commercial manner, like electricity or telecommunications? To explore this question, we make the hypothetical assumption that technical and political problems have been overcome so that a Manila commercial highway organization (MaCHO) is established that would:

- Collect the benefit-maximizing charges calculated above;
- Pay all the costs—including rents and taxes—payable by other commercial organizations in Metro Manila; and
- Use its profits to expand congested facilities for the benefit of Manila's travelers.

For simplicity, we shall assume that the costs of maintaining and operating the existing road system would be exactly covered by charges (such as surcharges on fuel, annual license fees, and import duties) that are levied on all road users in the Philippines to maintain the roads, even those that are not congested.

If MaCHO were a monopoly supplier of roads, it would have a financial incentive to charge not "benefit-maximizing charges" but profits-maximizing charges, which would be higher than the ones we derived. This could result in lower traffic volumes traveling at higher speeds compared to the estimates shown in Table 8.6 above. We assume this option would be prohibited by regulation.

Plausible Revenues

Tables 8.6 and 8.7 above show the congestion charges that could plausibly be appropriate in Metro Manila. But how much would be collected as revenues? Table 8.9 below shows, for each type of vehicle (except tricycles and motorcycles), the daily distance covered, the charge payable per kilometer, and the revenues collected, subject to the following assumptions:

- Congestion charges would apply in the fourteen heaviest hours of travel;
- Charges would be imposed only on streets south and west of the Epifanio De Los Santos Avenue (EDSA).

Table 8.9
Estimates of Revenues from Optimal
Congestion Charges in Metro Manila[a]

PHP THOUSANDS

		DEMAND ELASTICITY SCENARIO			
Vehicle Class	1996 Vehicle Trips/Day[b] Thousands	−0.10	−0.25	−0.50	−1.00
Cars	955	23.6	16.8	13.0	10.4
Utility Vehicles	801	19.8	14.1	10.9	8.7
Jeepneys	460	17.0	12.1	9.4	7.5
Buses	77	4.3	3.0	2.4	1.9
Trucks/Trailers	201	12.4	8.8	6.9	5.5
Tricycles/Motorcycles[c]	1,062	—	—	—	—
Total Vehicle Trips/Day	3,556				
Revenue/Day		77.1	54.8	42.6	34.0
Revenue/300-Day Year		23,140.6	16,452.1	12,778.3	10,2219.0

Explanatory Notes:
[a]Authors assumed that only 16 percent of vehicle trips are subject to congestion charges and average vehicle trip is 11 km.
[b]Authors' estimate based on MMUTIS survey data on person-trips, mode share, and vehicle occupancy.
[c]Authors assumed that Tricycles/Motorcycles are excluded from congestion pricing.

On the basis of readily available information, we can make only rough estimates of the funds that could be collected from congestion charges. These would depend on the operational hours (which would have to be a substantial proportion of the working day), on the treatment of weekend traffic, and on collection costs. Assuming that penalty charges would cover collection and enforcement costs, net revenues in the range of Php12.8 to Php23.1 billion a year from congestion charges seem plausible. Note that the higher revenues are associated with lower elasticities; because, at low elasticities, road use is less sensitive to price, higher prices would be needed to achieve optimum conditions and higher revenues would result.

MaCHO, being a commercial organization, would also collect payments from cars parked on its streets. MMUTIS estimates that there is a demand for over 200,000 commercial parking spaces in Metro Manila. Assuming daily average earnings of 40 Php/day for each of 300 days each year, collected from 200,000 spaces, and assuming that penalty charges would cover collection and enforcement costs, the net total collected per year in parking charges could be in the order of Php 2.4 billion. Thus, MaCHO revenues totaling Php 15.2 billion to Php 25.5 billion/year can be envisaged.

Plausible Expenses of a Manila Commercial Highway Organization

Because of the assumption made earlier that the costs of operating and maintaining the road system of Metro Manila would be met out of revenues from license fees and surcharges on fuel, these costs and revenues balance each other and can be ignored. There is also no need to depreciate the value of investment in roads, since roads can be expected to last indefinitely, provided they are well maintained, and maintenance costs are fully allowed for. Thus, the main expenditures of MaCHO would be:

- Rent for the land used for roads;
- Interest on recent investments in roads;
- Real estate taxes on the value of its properties; and
- Taxes on its profits, paid at the rates currently prevailing.

To determine the rent payable for the land to be used by MaCHO for its roads, it is necessary to know the area occupied by roads within EDSA. This has been calculated to be about 17 million square meters. Land values vary greatly within Metro Manila, with pockets of high-value land coexisting with large areas where values are much lower. In the absence of professional surveys to determine land values, the figure of Php100/square meter/year is assumed and this gives a rental value of Php1.7 billion a year.

The interest payable on investments can be calculated as the commercial borrowing rate for investments made over the previous twenty years. In the case of Metro Manila, the total interest payable per year is unlikely to exceed Php 2 billion. Real estate taxes have been estimated from the value of the land to be used by MaCHO and other taxes from the profits of its operations.

*Plausible Surpluses or Deficits to a Manila
Commercial Highway Organization*

The results obtained in the earlier sections are summarized in Table 8.10.

Although the figures in Table 8.10 have to be treated as gross approximations, they do suggest that a regulated commercial highway organization in Manila, charging no more than "optimal" congestion charges, could earn substantial revenues, which could plausibly produce an after-tax surplus in the range of 6 to 14 billion Php a year for the benefit of the road users and local authorities concerned.

Conclusions

Several conclusions may be drawn from this study, which could be replicated in other cities.

The most important is that substantial revenues could be raised from congestion charges, and that these could exceed the costs of road provision. There-

Table 8.10
Income and Expenditure of a Manila Commercial Highway Organization

Elasticity Scenario		-1.0	-0.10
Income	Parking Charges	2.4	2.4
	Congestion Charges	10.2	23.1
Total income		12.6	25.5
Expenditures	Rent for land	1.7	1.7
	Interest on investments	2.0	2.0
	Administration	0.2	0.2
	Real estate taxes	0.5	0.5
Total Expenditures		4.4	4.4
Gross Profit		8.2	21.1
Less tax on profit		2.6	6.8
Net profit after tax		5.6	14.3

Source: Authors' estimate based on AGILE study.

fore the provision of urban roads, even when priced at a socially "optimal" level, could be a profitable operation. In other sectors of the market economy, profitability tends to attract investment to expand the congested facility. The same could be true of congested roads, if they, also, were in the market economy. This suggests that at least some urban road networks could be privately financed and operated without subsidy.

The second major finding is that the optimal congestion charge in an urban road network does not seem to be sensitive to the elasticity of demand for road space. Although the elasticities selected for our estimates varied by a factor of ten, the optimal congestion charges varied only by a factor smaller than three.

Admittedly, our study ignored the practical difficulties of implementing congestion pricing. However, as electronic road pricing has been shown to work in Canada, France, Norway, Singapore, and the United States, we believe that the main obstacle to its implementation is political, not technical, and that it is therefore appropriate to explore the consequences of implementation on the basis that practical difficulties can be overcome.

Acknowledgments

The results described above are partly based on the findings of a road user charges study carried out in 1998/1999 for the Department of Finance of the Government of the Philippines, as part of the Accelerating Growth, Investment and Liberalization with Equity (AGILE) project that was financed by the United States Agency for International Development (USAID). The AGILE consultants were Development Alternatives Inc; the Harvard Institute for International Development; Cesar Virata & Associates, Inc.; and Pricewaterhouse-Coopers. Gabriel Roth was the team leader for the road user charges study, and Olegario G. Villoria, Jr. the road transport specialist.

The authors thank the Government of the Philippines, USAID, and the AGILE consultants for permission to use study data in this chapter, and their team members Ma. Theresa J. Villareal and Teresa Taningco for their roles in assembling the data.

Thanks are also due to Rodrigo Archondo-Callao, currently serving in the World Bank's Transport and Urban Development Department, for developing the Microsoft Excel model used in our calculations, and for comments by Elizabeth Pinkston of the Congressional Budget Office.

References

Buchanan, J. M. 1956. "Private Ownership and Common Usage: The Road Case Reexamined." *Southern Economic Journal* 22 (January): 305–316.

Button, Kenneth J., and Erik T. Verhoef, editors. 1998. *Road Pricing, Traffic Congestion and the Environment*. Cheltenham, UK: Edward Elgar Publishing Limited.

Hubert H. Humphrey Institute of Public Affairs. 1996. "Buying Time." University of Minnesota, State and Local Policy Program.

Johansson, Börge, and Mattsson, Lars-Göran. 1994. *Road Pricing: Theory, Empirical Assessment & Policy*. Norwell, MA: Kluwer Academic Publishers.

Knight, Frank H. 1924. "Some Fallacies in the Interpretation of Social Cost." *Quarterly Journal of Economics* 38 (August): 582–606.

Metro-Manila Urban Transport Integration Study (MMUTIS). 1999. Draft Final Report. Unpublished report prepared by the Japan International Cooperation Agency (JICA) Study Team for the Government of the Republic of the Philippines. [Data in Manila obtainable from: The National Center for Transportation Studies, Computer and Information Systems Division, 28 Apacible Street, University of the Philippines, Diliman, Quezon City, Metro-Manila.]

Mills, David E. 1981. "Ownership Arrangements and Congestion-Prone Facilities." *American Economic Review* 71, 3 (June): 492–502.

Oum, Tae Hoon, W.G. Waters II, and Jong-Say Yong. 1992. "Concepts of Price Elasticities of Transport Demand and Recent Empirical Estimates: An Interpretative Survey." *Journal of Transport Economics and Policy* XXVI, 2 (May): 139–154, and 164–169.

Roth, Gabriel. 1996. *Roads in a Market Economy*. Aldershot, UK and Brookfield, VT: Ashgate Publishing Ltd. See http://home.earthlink.net/~roths/.

9

HOT Lanes in Southern California

Edward C. Sullivan

Introduction

In Southern California, important experiments in demand-based tolls have been providing new information about travelers' responses to innovative road pricing. Southern California, famous as the birthplace of freeways and for its alleged love affair with automobiles, has been the setting for two groundbreaking developments in the provision and pricing of road capacity: the State Route 91 Express Lanes and the San Diego Interstate 15 HOT lanes. Of the two, the State Route 91 project is especially noteworthy as California's first modern example of private investment to create new urban highway capacity. Of further interest is the fact that both projects rely exclusively on electronic toll collection technology, using equipment compatible with other conventional toll facilities throughout the state.

The two Southern California projects are applications of "value pricing," described in a U.S. DOT report to Congress as "a market-based approach to traffic management which involves charging higher prices for travel on roadways during periods of peak demand. Also known as congestion pricing or road pricing, value pricing is designed to make better use of existing highway capacity by encouraging some travelers to shift to alternative times, routes, or modes of transportation" (U.S. Federal Highway Administration 2000). The Interstate 15 project uses dynamic value pricing where the toll can change in real time to adapt to unusual changes in demand. However, a schedule of typical daily tolls is also published. The State Route 91 project sticks to a published toll schedule, based on established patterns of daily demand.

These projects have enjoyed substantial public acceptance, in part because they have been marketed as a kinder and gentler form of congestion pricing, in which innovative pricing is used to create a new product—a congestion-free travel option in an otherwise congested commute corridor. Travelers are free to use or avoid the value priced facilities as they see fit, since the original congested travel options remain available. This approach stands in sharp contrast to mandatory pricing of all private vehicle trips at targeted locations and times, which some regard as ideal congestion pricing. Value pricing, as implemented in California and other U.S. locations, may be the first important step toward gaining widespread public acceptance of market-based road pricing, making feasible more extensive future applications of these principles.[1]

Both the State Route 91 (SR 91) and the Interstate 15 (I-15) projects serve busy suburban commute corridors and share rights-of-way with major non-toll highways. Both travelers who pay and travelers who avoid the tolls can see the traffic conditions on the option not chosen. This has created two valuable laboratories for observing travel behavior in the presence of innovative pricing. Experience has revealed complex responses in which many commuters show a great deal of selectivity in deciding whether or not it is worthwhile to pay the tolls on any given trip.

The history and motivation for these two projects are different, although both facilities now operate in a similar manner. The SR 91 project began as the result of the California Legislature's interest in trying to attract private capital to highway capacity expansion. The I-15 project came from a confluence of interests among local political leaders and the federal Value Pricing Program for conducting a pricing experiment that would improve corridor travel and enhance bus services.

Both projects have experienced major changes in their fairly brief lifetimes, and both will probably change further, leading to additional insights and lessons in years ahead. Important changes seen to date include both physical and operational adjustments as well as significant changes in traveler behavior and some shifts in public opinions concerning the projects.

This chapter describes in detail the operating characteristics and observed results to date from these two groundbreaking experiments in road pricing. By examining their similarities and differences, lessons can be drawn that may be applicable to other settings considering projects of this nature.

Table 9.1 summarizes the major features of the two projects. The next section presents detailed descriptions of the projects and information about usage trends and overall operating characteristics. Subsequent sections address selected findings from travel behavior research conducted in the two corridors, including observations about time-of-day shifts related to delays and tolls, changes in use of ride sharing and public transportation, and differences related to traveler demographics such as income and gender. Attention is then given to public perceptions about the projects, with particular focus on conflicts sur-

Table 9.1
Comparison of Project Features (as of 2003)

	State Route 91	Interstate 15
Location	East of Anaheim	North of San Diego
Length	10 miles	8 miles
# of Lanes	4 lanes (2 each way)	2 reversible lanes
Hours of Operation	24 hours, 7 days per week	5:45–9:15 A.M. southbound; 3:00–7:00 P.M. northbound; weekdays only
Pricing	Fixed toll schedule with range $1.00–$5.50	Dynamic toll schedule with typical range $0.75–$4.00, and ceiling of $8.00
Toll Categories	One toll, HOV3+ go free except in heaviest periods, when a 50% discount applies for 3+ occupant vehicles	One toll for single occupant vehicles; all HOV free
Capital Outlay	$134 million	$8 million
Source of Capital	Private investment and commercial debt	Federal grants and local in-kind match for transit
Annual Revenue	$29 million	$2 million
Toll-Paying Traffic	10 million/year	1.3 million (Single-Occupant Vehicles)

rounding the SR 91 private toll lane project, and its eventual conversion to public ownership. The chapter concludes by reviewing the major lessons learned.

Project Characteristics

The State Route 91 Express Lanes

The California SR 91 Express Lanes extend 10 miles (16 kilometers) in the freeway median from the State Route 91/State Route 55 junction in Anaheim to the Orange/Riverside County Line (Exhibit 9A and Exhibit 9B). The toll facility provides two lanes in each direction, separated from the adjacent freeway by a "soft" barrier consisting of a painted buffer with pylons (Exhibit 9C). The lanes are an express facility; that is, there are no intermediate exits or entrances along its 10-mile length. Except for motor homes and buses, heavy vehicles are prohibited.

The toll lanes were built in what had been one of the most heavily congested freeway corridors of California. Before the lanes opened in December

Exhibit 9A
Location of SR 91 Project in Orange County, California

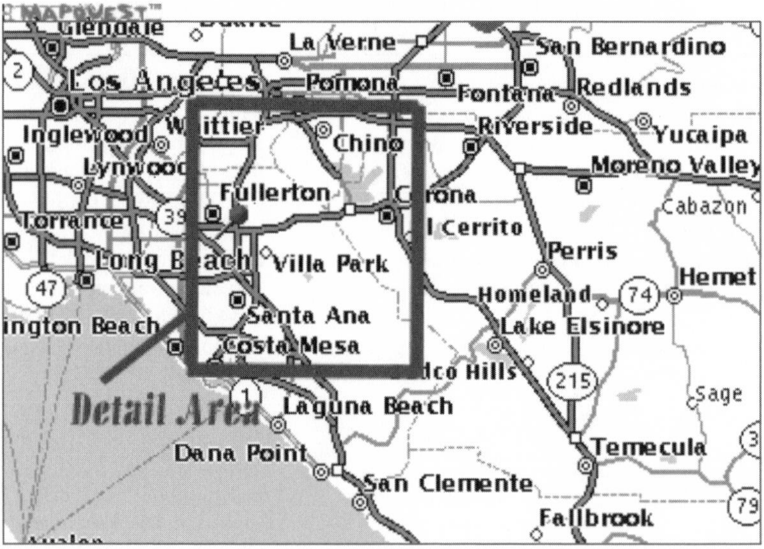

Map provided by www.mapquest.com (©2000 MapQuest.com, Inc., ©2000 GDT, Inc.)

1995, peak period delays of 20–40 minutes were typical. The increased capacity from adding two new lanes in each direction initially cut peak period delays in the parallel free lanes to less than 10 minutes. Congestion has since returned, and delays in the free lanes are approximately at the level experienced before the toll lanes opened.

The four-lane toll facility was constructed for a total project cost of approximately $134 million as a private for-profit investment, one of four such ventures authorized by the California Legislature under the AB 680 legislation enacted in 1989. To date, it is the only AB 680 project operating; however, an additional project, SR 125 in San Diego County, is under construction and scheduled to open in 2006.

Following legislative requirements, the SR 91 project was selected based on a proposal submitted to the State by an industry consortium. This project was attractive to the State in part because it would have taken five or more extra years for similar improvements to be funded through normal State highway financing methods. The corridor presented an attractive investment prospect because of high current demand and growth potential, a partly graded existing right-of-way and in-place environmental approvals, as well as practically nonexistent competition from parallel facilities.

Exhibit 9B
Site Map Showing Locations of 91 Toll Lanes and the ETR

Map provided by www.mapquest.com (©2000 MapQuest.com, Inc., ©2000 GDT, Inc.)

Under Caltrans supervision, the express lanes were designed, built, and originally operated, to early 2003, by the California Private Transportation Company (CPTC), a company created for the project, whose general partners were Level 3 Communications Inc. (formerly Kiewit Diversified Group), Granite Construction Company, and Cofiroute, the French toll road company. The toll lanes were constructed on land leased from the State. The franchise agreement with the State gave CPTC thirty-five years to operate the toll lanes, after which the facility would return to the control of Caltrans, the State Department of Transportation. The franchise holder performs traffic management and motorist assistance, while contracting with Caltrans for regular road maintenance and with the California Highway Patrol for enforcement.

In early 2003, CTPC sold the SR 91 Express Lanes franchise to the Orange County Transportation Authority (OCTA) for $207.5 million. The sale to this public agency was motivated by a combination of factors including the

Exhibit 9C
The SR 91 Toll Lanes in the PM Peak Period

reported wish of some general partners to move on to other ventures once the project was fully operational, strong public outcry against CPTC exercising its rights under the non-compete clause of the franchise agreement, and a taint of scandal surrounding CPTC's earlier efforts to sell the franchise, perceived by some as a sweetheart deal that would result in windfall profits. These controversies are discussed further below.

The franchise holder can set toll levels as it chooses, subject to a maximum rate-of-return limit specified in the franchise agreement. The franchise agreement also requires offering incentives to high occupancy vehicles with three or more persons (HOV3+). Initially, HOV3+ users traveled toll-free, although they were required to carry transponders like all other users. Beginning January 1998, the HOV3+ toll was set to 50 percent of the published toll. After OCTA took over in early 2003, HOV3+ vehicles again traveled free, except during the heaviest afternoon peak periods, when they pay 50 percent of the published toll.

Tolls on the SR 91 facility vary hour by hour to control demand and keep traffic in the express lanes at free flow. The tolls also reflect the value of the time saved by toll lane users compared to travelers on the adjacent non-tolled freeway. From opening day, there has been roughly an average of one general toll increase per year.

The tolls in effect in late 2003 are shown in Exhibit 9D. Tolls vary from $1.00, during periods of lowest demand, to $5.50 at the height of the Thursday and Friday afternoon peaks. At a given time, all vehicles pay the same, except for the discounted 50 percent tolls for HOV3+ users and some other special incentive toll categories.[2] The complexity of the toll schedule shown in the exhibit contrasts dramatically with the initial toll schedule implemented immediately after the express lanes opened in December 1995. Then, there were only six toll levels ($0.25, $0.50, $1.00, $1.50, $2.50, and $2.75) and the maximum $2.75 toll applied during the entire four-hour afternoon peak period (six hours on Friday). With experience, the more complex toll structure gradually evolved, with hour-by-hour variations for fine-tuning demand first introduced in September 1997.

Exhibit 9D
SR 91 Toll Schedule Effective August 1, 2003

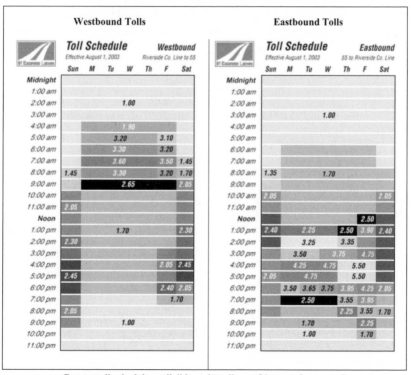

Current toll schedule availaible at: http://www.91expresslanes.com/.

The "91 Express Club," first established in January 1997, now lets frequent users pay a flat $20 monthly fee and receive a $1.00 discount on every trip, at any hour of the day. Belonging to the Express Club saves money for persons who use the express lanes more than twenty times per month. Express Club membership has the effect of entirely eliminating the marginal toll for the lowest toll periods. Generally the Express Club has not attracted many members, about 12 percent of transponder holders according to a past survey.

In part due to width limitations in the original SR 91 freeway median, all tolls are collected by Automatic Vehicle Identification (AVI). Only registered customers equipped with suitable transponders may utilize the toll lanes. The AVI requirement also applied to HOV3+ users from opening day, even though that group traveled toll-free.

Through FY 2002/03, the SR 91 had issued about 143,500 "FasTrak" transponders.[3] Through the same period, 406,500 additional FasTrak transponders were issued by other regional authorities, primarily the Transportation Corridor Agencies (TCA), which operate the 67-mile network of public toll roads under development in Orange County (see Exhibit 9E). 24,700 transponders were issued by SANDAG, operator of the San Diego HOT lanes project about 80 miles (130 km) to the south.[4] The transponders, which use a read-write RF tag technology,[5] are manufactured by SIRIT[6] (formerly Texas Instruments). All transponders are compatible with California's "Title 21" open stan-

Exhibit 9E
SR 91 and the Orange County Public Toll Road System

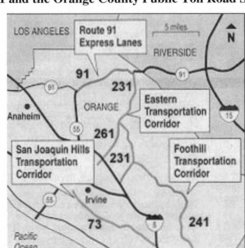

Transportation Corridor Agencies web site at http://www.tcagencies.com/.

dard and may be used on any toll facility throughout California, including the Golden Gate Bridge and other State-owned toll bridges. Customer service and electronic toll collection systems for the 91 Express Lanes were supplied by MFS Network Technologies.[7]

Deposits are not explicitly required on AVI transponders in California; however, a positive account balance is required. A credit card customer pays $30 to replenish an account whenever the balance falls below $10. Cash customers pay $50 to replenish an account whenever the balance falls below $25. In 1997, CPTC began to assess service charges on low activity accounts. Currently, "Standard Plan" customers pay a $6 per month minimum charge. "Convenience Plan" customers may avoid the monthly minimum by paying a one-time non-refundable $50 fee.[8] On the whole, OCTA has so far continued CPTC's pricing policies.

From the beginning, CPTC elected to operate the SR 91 Express Lanes using a published toll schedule rather than with dynamic tolling, as on the San Diego I-15 project. While dynamic tolling is within the technical capability of the SR 91 electronic toll system, CPTC's marketing showed that potential customers were uncomfortable with the unpredictability of dynamic tolls.

Table 9.2 summarizes operating results based on data from the first four CPTC annual reports, updated with revenue data from OCTA's annual report for fiscal year 2003. In addition to the operating expenses shown, revenues must serve accumulated debt and, during the CPTC period, provide a rate of return on capital investment.

CPTC's first annual report stated that, after three months of operation, revenues reached a level sufficient to cover operating expenses, but not to cover debt service and return on investment. In August 1998, the company reported that revenues had reached the overall "breakeven" level, sufficient to cover both operating expenses and debt service.

Table 9.2
CPTC Reported Annual Revenues and Expenses (CPTC 1999)

Year	Total Revenue	Total Operating Expenses
1996	$7.1 million	$6.3 million
1997	$13.9 million	$9.1 million
1998	$20.1 million	$8.7 million
1999	$19.5 million	$9.1 million
FY 00/01	$22.3 million	—
FY 01/02	$27.2 million	—
FY 02/03	$28.9 million	—

CPTC's reports consistently asserted that the 91 Express Lane project shows acceptable financial performance. An independent appraisal done in conjunction with the OCTA buyout reached the same conclusion. Indeed, the trend in revenues compares favorably to expenses, and the project seems poised to yield a favorable rate of return over its thirty-five-year lifetime. It should be noted, however, that it is rare for new urban highway construction to have this project's unusual combination of relatively low capital costs (less than $3.5 million per lane-mile), large immediate demand, and favorable conditions for quick implementation, since Caltrans had already obtained the necessary environmental clearances for highway expansion in this corridor.

The long-term financial performance of the 91 Express Lanes is significantly affected by competing highway capacity. The nearest major freeway providing independent parallel capacity, State Route 60, runs east-west approximately ten miles (16 km.) north of SR 91 (see Exhibit 99B). In the SR 91 corridor itself, the Eastern Toll Road (ETR) (Eastern Transportation Corridor) competes with SR 91 for trips to Irvine and vicinity (see Exhibit 9E). As seen in the weekday traffic trend of Figure 9.1, opening the Eastern Toll Road in October 1998 resulted in a significant, although temporary, setback in the SR 91 project's traffic and revenue growth.[9]

There is no direct connection between the 91 Express Lanes and the ETR. Therefore, ETR users must use the congested SR 91 free lanes to cross the Orange/Riverside County Line, while 91 Express Lane users largely bypass

Figure 9.1

**Trends in Eastbound (EB), Westbound (WB), and
Total Average Daily Traffic (ADT) on the SR 91 Toll Lanes**

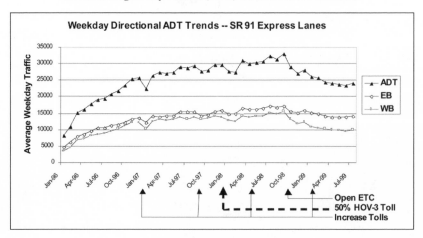

this congestion. Tolls on the ETR vary with trip length but remain the same through the day. For example, the one-way toll between SR 91 and the ETR terminus in Irvine is $3.25.[10] Unlike 91 Express Lane users, ETR users may use cash. Through summer 1999, a consistent 35–40 percent of weekday ETR users chose to pay cash.

Figure 9.1 shows that the 91 Express Lanes experienced steady traffic growth from opening day through the opening of the ETR. The first general toll increase, which occurred in January 1997, was followed by a significant and permanent reduction in the rate of toll traffic growth. Subsequent toll increases, which were less substantial and emphasized fine-tuning of the hour-by-hour toll schedule, were not accompanied by visible changes in the overall trend in average daily traffic (ADT).

After the 91 Express Lanes opened in December 1995, congestion on the SR 91 freeway declined dramatically, as would be expected with the addition of two new lanes in each direction. As seen in Figure 9.2, in 1995, before the express lanes opened, during the 4:00–6:00 P.M. period, it took 45–60 minutes to travel the 11.3-mile section between the La Palma overcrossing and Coal Canyon Road, near the county line. In 1996, that travel time fell to 15–20 minutes, a decrease in per trip delay of 30–40 minutes. This immediate benefit realized by non-toll-paying corridor users was clearly an important factor in the early public acceptance of the new project.

With time, congestion increased gradually due both to regional development and an increase in discretionary peak period travel in light of the dramatically

Figure 9.2

Trends in Estimated SR 91 Freeway Travel Times (PM Eastbound)

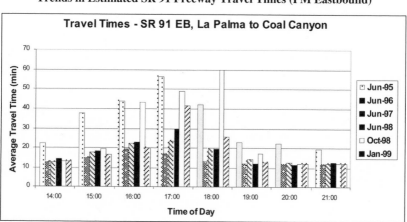

improved travel conditions. In fall 1998, peak period delays suddenly became much higher following opening of the new Eastern Toll Road, which added two more lanes of traffic directly upstream of the bottleneck at the Orange-Riverside County line. While the severity of peak congestion after October 1998 returned to close to pre-1995 levels, the duration of the congestion was less, and the overall number of trips being accommodated in the corridor was substantially greater than pre-1995. Through all these changes and traffic adjustments, the SR 91 Express Lanes continued to operate under free flow conditions, providing the option of a congestion-free ride to those for whom the benefits exceed the tolls.

During the eight months after the ETR opened, the midweek average daily traffic (ADT) on the 91 Express Lanes declined about 30 percent. Over the same period, the ETR midweek ADT reached over 33,000 vehicles per day, of which about 30 percent are attributed to trips diverted from the SR 91 toll lanes.[11]

The franchise agreement between CPTC and Caltrans included a "non-compete" provision in which Caltrans agreed not to make freeway improvements that undermine CPTC's business, unless necessary for highway safety. This non-compete provision became a source of conflict between CPTC, the State, and other parties, as Caltrans sought to mitigate traffic problems in the SR 91 bottleneck between the ETR and State Route 71. This conflict is discussed in more detail later in the chapter. As part of the OCTA acquisition of the operating franchise, the non-compete provision was eliminated.

In addition to the controversy over the non-compete provision of the franchise agreement, conflicts arose surrounding CPTC's early efforts to sell its business to a new non-profit corporation. CPTC contacts cite two principal reasons for selling the business: (1) An original general partner regards continued participation as incompatible with their core corporate strategy, and (2) tax laws make operating the toll lanes by a non-profit more attractive than continued operation as a for-profit business. CPTC's efforts to assist a prospective non-profit buyer were publicly characterized as marred by conflict of interest, and the expected sale fell through under a cloud of investigation. This issue is also discussed further later in the chapter.

The San Diego Interstate 15 Project

The Interstate 15 (I-15) HOT lane project is an 8-mile (13-kilometer) express facility located north of San Diego in the median of the I-15 freeway, just north of its junction with State Route 163 (Exhibits 9F and 9G). The facility provides two extra lanes in a reversible configuration separated from the adjacent freeway by concrete barriers (Exhibit 9H). The lanes operate southbound during the morning commute period (5:45–9:15 A.M.) and northbound

Exhibit 9F
Location of I-15 Project in San Diego County, California

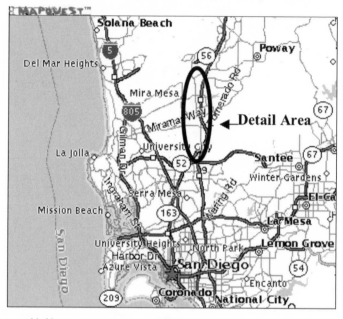

Map provided by www.mapquest.com (©2000 MapQuest.com, Inc., ©2000 GDT, Inc.)

during the afternoon (3:00–7:00 P.M.).[12] During other hours, as well as weekends and holidays, the freeway is generally free flowing and the reversible express lanes are closed to both directions by raised ramp barriers.[13] There are no intermediate entrances or exits and, except for buses, three or more axle vehicles are prohibited.

The I-15 lanes serve a busy commute corridor connecting San Diego with rapidly growing bedroom communities to the north. The facility was originally constructed by Caltrans and first opened in 1988 as a high occupancy vehicle (HOV) facility for rideshare groups of two or more persons. The fairly low utilization of the reversible HOV lanes adjacent to the severely congested freeway was of concern and, in 1991, the San Diego Association of Governments (SANDAG) passed a resolution calling for a demonstration of selling excess capacity to single occupant vehicles (SOVs) with the revenues used to support improved corridor bus service. Jan Goldsmith, mayor of Poway and SANDAG board member, is credited for his leadership in making this initiative successful. Subsequently, funding for the demonstration project was secured through the FWHA Value Pricing Program, and enabling legislation (AB 713)

Exhibit 9G
Site Map Showing Location of I-15 FasTrak Lanes

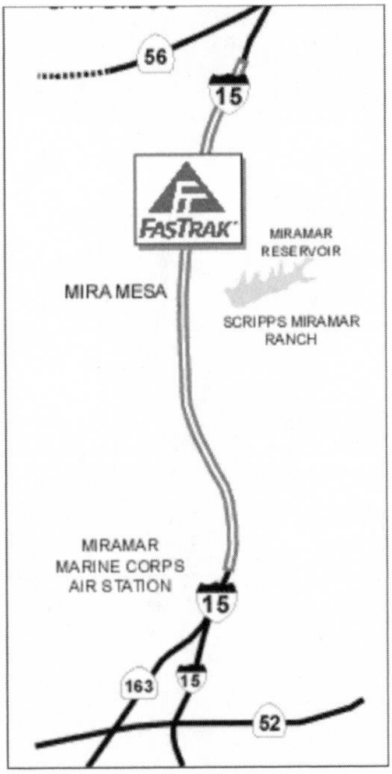

Retrieved in February, 2001, from http://www.sandag.cog.ca.us/data_services/fastrak/info.html.

was introduced by then-Assemblyman Goldsmith and passed by the California Legislature. The original 1994 law contained a sunset provision for the HOT lanes to operate only through 1998. The ending date was later extended to 2000 by additional legislation and more recently extended indefinitely. A project is currently underway to widen and lengthen the I-15 HOT lane facility to an overall length of 20 miles (33 km.).[14]

Modification of the original HOV facility to create HOT lanes was funded by approximately $8 million in federal grants, supplemented by local in-kind match of about $2 million for new corridor transit services. The HOT lane service was implemented in two phases.

Phase I, from December 2, 1996 to March 30, 1998, utilized a permit system that let SOVs use the lanes for a flat monthly fee. Subscribers initially paid $50/month, increased to $70/month in March 1997. To ensure that traffic would flow at level of service C or better, as required by the enabling legislation, the number of permits was cautiously increased, starting with 500 and gradually increasing in steps to 1,000 permits by the end of Phase I. Initially,

Exhibit 9H
The I-15 HOT Lanes

SANDAG photo

subscribers received colored-coded monthly permits to display in their wind-shields. After six months, the color-coded permits were replaced by transponders; however, the monthly fee remained in effect.

In Phase II, the monthly fee was replaced by a toll per trip, and access to the HOT lanes opened to any SOV with a California-standard FasTrak transponder. Like the Orange County SR 91 toll lanes, cash is not accepted. Unlike the SR 91 lanes, high occupancy vehicles on the I-15 project are not required to carry transponders.[15] By December 1999, SANDAG had issued over 11,000 FasTrak transponders in 7,635 separate accounts (an average of 1.45 transponders per account).

Unlike the SR 91 project, the toll level on the I-15 project is set dynamically. Every six minutes, the HOT lane traffic count for the previous 12 minutes is examined, and an appropriate toll is set to maintain free flow of traffic. That toll is displayed on electronic signs at the entrances. The pricing procedure has a "damping" feature to avoid changing the toll more than $0.50 during any six-minute period, and is constrained by maximum tolls established for different times of the day. The toll-traffic count relationship used on I-15 appears in Table 9.3.

The dynamic tolling procedure is designed to keep traffic in the facility operating above a specified level of service (LOS) threshold. Level of service is a

Table 9.3
I-15 Tolls and Volume Thresholds
AM Peak Period Southbound (effective 8/2/99)
(SANDAG 1999b, Figure 3)

12-Minute Volume Lower Threshold	Level of Service	Toll Rate	Time Period When Maximum Rate
<200	A	$0.50	
200	A	$0.75	5:30–6:00 A.M. and 9:00–9:30 A.M.
300	B	$1.00	6:00–6:30 A.M. and 8:30–9:00 A.M.
320	B	$1.25	
340	B	$1.50	
360	B	$1.75	
380	B	$2.00	6:30–7:00 A.M. and 8:00–8:30 A.M.
400	C	$2.25	
420	C	$2.50	
440	C	$2.75	
450	C	$3.00	
460	C	$3.25	
470	C	$3.50	
480	C	$3.75	
490	C	$4.00	7:00–8:00 A.M.
520	C	$4.50	
540	C	$5.00	
560	C	$5.50	
580	C	$6.00	
600	C	$6.50	
620	D	$7.00	
640	D	$7.50	
660	D	$8.00	

widely accepted standard for measuring crowding and congestion in traffic. Initially, I-15 tolls were set to achieve level of service B, which was the traffic condition in the HOV facility measured prior to implementing the HOT lane project. LOS B corresponds to unusually low density traffic for urban conditions, and this criterion was soon recognized as unnecessarily strict. Subsequent legislation changed the target LOS threshold to C, still a very favorable operating condition for urban peak period traffic.[16] The purpose of tying toll levels to LOS B/C operating conditions was to avoid degrading the travel conditions of the HOV commuters for whom the facility was originally constructed.

Probably this LOS-based toll-setting criterion proved helpful in achieving public acceptance of the project. However, the resulting tolls probably lead to travel behavior somewhat different from the behavior that would maximize overall user benefits.

On a typical day, tolls vary from $0.75 to $4.00. However, if an unusual condition causes traffic to approach the upper range of LOS C, tolls can increase to $8.00. This extreme toll level has rarely occurred during the project's history. SANDAG publishes a typical toll schedule, shown in Exhibit 9I, informing customers what they can expect to pay under normal traffic conditions.

The I-15 and SR 91 projects are similar operationally and with respect to customer service. As with SR 91, most I-15 customers tie their prepaid transponder accounts to credit cards. Account policies are similar.[17]

The I-15 project also contracts with the California Highway Patrol (CHP) for enforcement. An interesting observation is that, prior to 1996, the I-15 HOV lanes had a violation rate of 15 percent. The violation rate fell to 3–4 percent after the HOT lanes were implemented. The change is attributed both to

Exhibit 9I
Schedule of Typical Tolls on I-15 HOT Lanes (Effective 6-30-00)

Maximum Toll	Morning Period (Southbound)							
$4.00				■	■			
$3.00				■	■			
$2.50				■	■			
$2.00			■	■	■	■		
$1.50			■	■	■	■		
$1.00		■	■	■	■	■	■	
$.75	■	■	■	■	■	■	■	■
$.50	■	■	■	■	■	■	■	■
	5:45-6:00	6:00-6:30	6:30-7:00	7:00-7:30	7:30-8:00	8:00-8:30	8:30-9:00	9:00-11:00

Maximum Toll	Evening Period (Northbound)							
$4.00					■			
$3.00					■			
$2.50				■	■			
$2.00			■	■	■	■		
$1.50			■	■	■	■		
$1.00		■	■	■	■	■		
$.75	■	■	■	■	■	■	■	■
$.50	■	■	■	■	■	■	■	■
	12:00-1:00	1:00-3:30	3:30-4:00	4:00-4:30	4:30-5:00	5:00-5:30	5:30-6:00	6:00-6:30	6:30-7:00

Retrieved February 1, 2001 from http://www.sandag.cog.ca.us/data_services/fastrak/. Typical Friday afternoon tolls also appear, where the peak $4.00 toll starts a half hour ealier than other weekdays.

increased CHP presence because of the enforcement contract and the possibility that previous violators in SOVs became legitimate HOT lane customers.

The I-15 web site reports that, in early 2001, the project was self-supporting with $1.2 million in annual toll revenues.[18] Revenues exceeding the $430,000 annual operating costs plus the $60,000 enforcement contract with the CHP are allocated to an express bus service known as the "Inland Breeze." However, it should be emphasized that, unlike the privately financed SR 91 project, the publicly developed I-15 HOT lanes carry no debt service because the highway infrastructure already existed and other start-up costs were fully covered by $8 million in federal grants.

The traffic trends on the I-15 facility are illustrated in Figure 9.3, which shows the average weekday counts for the selected month of October (Supernak et al. 2000a, Figure 10).[19] Although the effect of implementing the HOT lanes was confounded by increasing the hours of operation in November 1997, the data clearly show that significant traffic growth accompanied the start of the permit HOT lane operation in December 1996, and of the FasTrak operation in March 1998.

The dynamic toll scheme has proven successful in preventing congestion in the I-15 HOT lanes, and satisfying the level of service C operational constraint. Results are mixed regarding the hoped-for traffic congestion mitigation effects in the parallel freeway lanes. The impact study measured travel times in the southern 5.9-mile section of the corridor and found that traffic and traffic delay in the free lanes decreased initially during 1997, as expected, due to the oppor-

Figure 9.3
Trends in Weekday Directional Traffic on the I-15 HOT Lanes

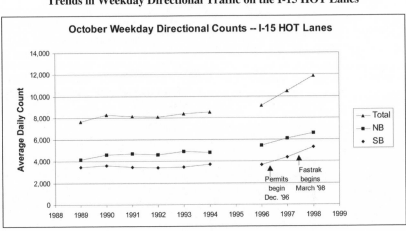

tunity for some freeway traffic to divert to the HOT lanes. However, freeway traffic and delays unexpectedly increased again in 1998. In all cases, the worst delays observed in the section were 4–5 minutes per vehicle and the changes observed were mostly under 3 minutes. These mixed results may be attributed to development along the corridor and a construction project on the parallel Interstate 5, which may have caused significant amounts of traffic to divert to the I-15 corridor. In any case, the measurable traffic consequences on the parallel freeway due to the I-15 HOT lane operation are minor, compared to the SR 91 project.

Travel Behavior Responses to Innovative Road Pricing

Southern California commuters appear to be discriminating and savvy consumers in adjusting their behavior to the innovative pricing implemented in the SR 91 and I-15 corridors. Some observations about travel behavior changes follow. Most of these observations are somewhat dated since they are all based on evaluation studies that concluded about the year 2000.

Observations Concerning Selection of Toll Facility v. Time and Cost

A strong correlation was seen between commuters' use of the SR 91 Express Lanes and time-of-day-dependent travel time savings.[20] During the period of observation, the percentage of SR 91 commuters using the express lanes ranged from about 7 percent in the midday off-peak, when time savings were minimal, to about 35 percent at the height of the PM peak hour, when freeway delays were greatest. The relationship for the seven-hour afternoon period (14:00 to 21:00) in June 1997 is shown in Figure 9.4. The hourly counts and percentages using the toll lanes follow the same general trend, which is illustrated by a regression line fit to the data. The shape of this relationship remained stable over the period of observation.

A similar relationship appears in the data collected for the AM peak period on I-15[21] (Supernak et al. 2000a, Table 22 and Figure 55). Figure 9.5 shows how the I-15 HOT lane counts of toll-paying traffic for 15-minute time periods varies in relation to the estimated trip time saved by using the toll facility. The relationships are shown for October 1997 and October 1998, for the three-hour AM peak. HOT lane counts in 1998 are considerably higher than in 1997 because Fastrak and dynamic tolling began in March 1998, removing the limitation on SOV access that existed under the previous Phase I permit system. The data for both SR 91 and I-15 show clearly that commuters generally understand how travel conditions compare over time in the toll lanes and free lanes, and adjust their purchasing behavior accordingly.

Figure 9.4

Comparison of Toll-Paying Traffic and Trip Time Saved on SR 91

(June 1997)

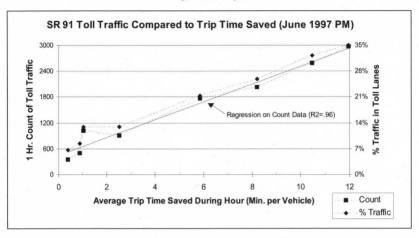

Although the data in the two graphs suggest that travelers quite accurately perceive the relative magnitudes of their time savings, survey findings show that commuters typically overestimate their absolute time savings. In the case of SR 91 commuters, it was estimated from survey data that trip time savings

Figure 9.5

Comparison of Toll-Paying Traffic and Time Saved on I-15

(Oct. 1997 & 1998)

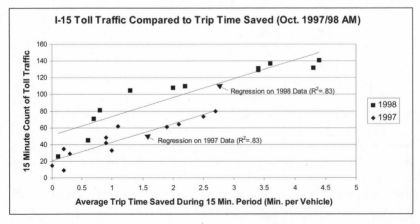

are typically overestimated by amounts between 5 and 30 minutes. This conclusion was drawn from comparing travelers' reported time savings to the corresponding measured travel times through the highway network.

Despite the strong correlation between travel time savings and the amount of traffic using the toll lanes, some travelers choose to use the toll lanes under conditions where the value of their expected time savings is clearly less than the tolls paid. In both 1996 and 1999, driving comfort and the perception of greater safety were cited by SR 91 travelers as principal motivations for this behavior. Another consideration is that some transponder holders (about 10 percent on I-15 and over 15 percent on SR 91) do not pay their own tolls.

With regard to safety, the number of SR 91 commuters who think the toll lanes are safer than the adjacent freeway outnumber 4:1 those who think the lanes are less safe. Similarly, surveys with I-15 HOT lanes users found that 50–70 percent regard the HOT lanes as "much safer" than the adjacent freeway, with 5–10 percent more SOV toll-paying users holding that view than HOV commuters (Supernak et al. 2000b). I-15 commuters expressed satisfaction with the improved reliability of travel time, although SR 91 commuters ranked reliability a distant third in importance, following reduced travel time and better safety.

Observations Concerning Time-of-Day Shifts and the Effect of Tolls

Time of day distributions for SR 91 traffic show that, during 1996, soon after the express lanes opened and highway capacity no longer severely constrained demand, the PM peak traffic distribution gradually became much sharper than prior to and shortly after the opening. This effect is illustrated in Figure 9.6. The reemergence by 1997 of a sharp afternoon peak around 5:00 P.M. occurred in the presence of a toll schedule that charged the same amount, $2.75, for the entire peak period between 3:00 and 7:00 P.M.

The introduction of a more differentiated toll structure for SR 91 in September 1997, with tolls varying by the hour, had little effect on the shape of the afternoon time-of-day distribution in the overall corridor, or for toll lane traffic in particular. However, there did occur some peak-flattening in the morning, accompanying the more substantial hourly differences in tolls implemented for that time period.

In an effort to quantify the possible influence on travel behavior of the time-dependent tolls, a group of logit-type travel choice models were calibrated using 1999 survey data from the SR 91 corridor.[22] These models relate travelers' demographic characteristics, tolls, travel times, and other trip attributes to various aspects of travel behavior, including choice of route, time-of-day of travel, whether to rideshare, and whether to acquire a transponder (required to

Figure 9.6
Shifts in the Time of Day Distribution of PM Traffic on SR 91
(Toll and Free)

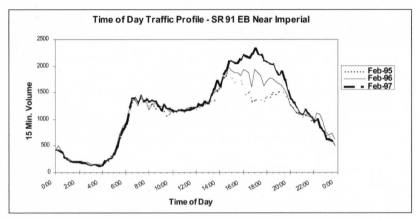

use the SR 91 toll lanes but optional on the competing Eastern Toll Road route). These models give estimates for implied values of travel time of $13–16 per hour. Corresponding price elasticities for using the SR 91 Express Lanes during the 6-hour period of heaviest demand (morning westbound and afternoon eastbound) were estimated as 0.7 to 0.8. The estimated elasticities for the one-hour "peak of the peak" are consistently 0.9 to 1.0. These results indicate that there exists scope for adjusting toll schedules, even in as small as one-hour increments, in order to regulate demand.

In the case of the I-15 HOT lanes, an ideal experimental condition occurred in August 1998, when in an effort to spread peak traffic, the difference between the usual peak hour toll ($4) and the toll in the adjacent time periods was increased from $1 to $2, while tolls farther from the peak hour were reduced even further. Using a method of time-series modeling called intervention analysis, an assessment of traveler time-of-day shifts was performed (SANDAG 1999a). Similar to the SR 91 findings, the I-15 researchers concluded that the toll changes were accompanied by a statistically significant impact on time-of-day choices in the AM peak period, especially shifts to later travel times, but changes during the PM peak were minimal.

Observations Concerning Use of Ride Sharing and Public Transportation

Within three months after the SR 91 toll lanes opened, PM peak traffic observations on all lanes of the highway showed a greater than 40 percent jump in high occupancy vehicles carrying three or more people (HOV3+). This increase in HOV3+ traffic could be expected since, at the time, HOV3+ vehicles paid no toll, even though they had to carry transponders.

When HOV3+ users began to pay 50 percent tolls in January 1998, about a third of the HOV3+ traffic (around 2,000 vehicles per day) left the express lanes; however, HOV3+ traffic in the parallel freeway lanes increased by the same amount. These shifts occurred mostly in shoulder hours, although much less on Friday afternoon. It was surprising that, after the HOV3+ commuters were required to pay tolls, the total PM peak HOV3+ traffic in the corridor remained at the same high level. Also surprising is that counts of dual occupant (HOV2) vehicles remained essentially constant throughout the observation period, even though the per capita toll for these HOVs is half that of drive-alones. Also, despite the 50 percent toll discount for HOV3+ commuters, the difference in the proportions of HOV2 and HOV3+ groups using the express lanes is not statistically significant.

The I-15 HOT lanes opened in 1988 as HOV-only lanes (2+ occupants) and, in subsequent years, almost all traffic growth in the corridor occurred in the form of HOV traffic and public transit. After the conversion to HOT lanes in December 1996, HOV traffic in the I-15 corridor changed as summarized in Table 9.4.

Most of the change in I-15 HOV traffic between fall 1996 and fall 1998 can be explained by diversion from the freeway to the HOT lanes. Why this happened is not clear, since there was no change in the incentives for this group to use these special lanes. However, there may be some tie to the publicity during the period about the advantages of using the HOT lanes. Clearly there was an overall decrease in peak period HOV ridership, about 4 percent of the approximately 15,000 HOV trips per day using the corridor in 1996. This HOV decrease is only partly explained by increased transit use, as a surprisingly high portion of the corridor growth in bus use occurred in the off-peak direction. It appears, therefore, that some decrease in HOV use occurred due to the new opportunity to travel as a drive-alone in the I-15 HOT lane.

Table 9.4
Changes in HOV Traffic on I-15 from 1996 to 1998
(Supernak et al. 2000b)

	CHANGES IN OBSERVED HOV TRAFFIC ON I-15		
	HOT Lanes	**I-15 Free Lanes**	**I-15 Overall**
AM Peak Period	+846	−1262	−416
PM Peak Period	+272	−449	−177

Overall, the two HOT lane projects had mixed but generally positive results for ridesharing. 1995 and 1996 surveys of SR 91 users found that more SR 91 commuters shifted from single occupant vehicles (SOV) to high occupancy vehicles (HOV) than vice versa in the first year of express lane operation. Surveys on SR 91 in 1999 showed no further mode shifts since 1996. Even though HOV use on I-15 declined about 4 percent in the two years after the HOT lanes opened, this amount seems small in light of the attractive new option made available to SOV commuters, which had previously been available only to HOV commuters. Only 5 percent of SOV drivers using the I-15 HOT lanes reported they were in carpools before becoming toll-paying HOT lane customers.

There is no evidence that opening the 91 Express Lanes adversely affected public transportation in that corridor. In particular, the commuter rail line that runs parallel to the facility continued to develop ridership throughout the observation period. Since I-15 revenues are earmarked for corridor transit improvements, the San Diego project was accompanied by a significant increase in bus ridership.

Observations on Toll Facility Use and Commuter Demographics

Over time, the proportions of corridor commuters who used the toll facilities increased. For example, the proportion of commuters who used the 91 Express Lanes at least some of the time increased from 28 percent in 1996 to 42 percent in 1999.

As is true for other discretionary goods, the proportion of commuters who use the toll facilities increases with income. The income relationship for SR 91 appears in Figure 9.7. A noteworthy change observed from 1996 to 1999 is a decrease in the percentage of trips in the toll lanes for the $40–60K income category, from 40 percent in 1996 to 25 percent in 1999. This suggests that middle-income commuters may have been especially sensitive to the toll increases during this period.

SR 91 commuters have a median income of approximately $70,000, and the median income for I-15 commuters is over $100,000. About half of the I-15 HOT lane users who pay tolls have incomes over $100,000, which appears to match the commute population generally (Supernak et al. 2000b, p. 32). Both corridors serve mostly affluent commuter populations where the possibility of tolls disadvantaging low-income workers is minimal.

Female commuters are more likely to use the toll facilities than males. For example, on SR 91 in 1999, 45 percent of females compared to 32 percent of males reported using the toll lanes. Only among HOV3+ commuters on SR 91 is the proportion higher for males than females. These observed gender dif-

Figure 9.7

Income Related to SR 91 Toll Facility Use for Peak Period Trips in 1999

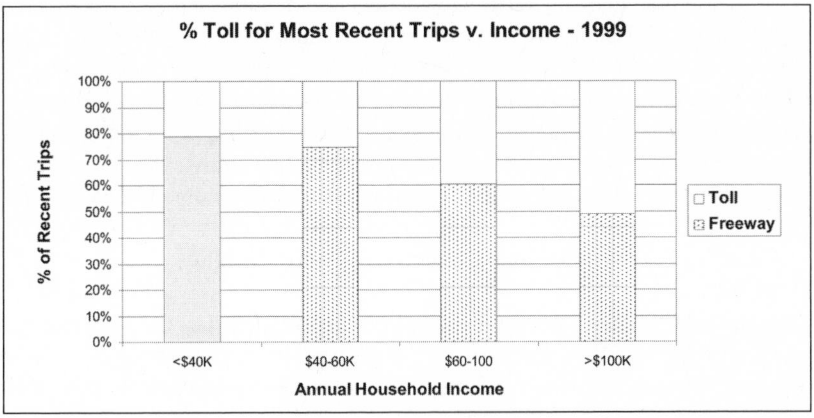

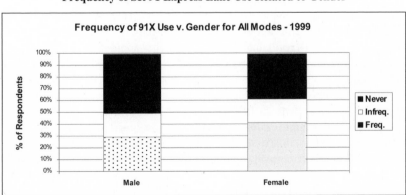

ferences on SR 91 have remained stable over time. The I-15 study also saw high growth in HOT lane use among females, especially females of middle age.

The data also suggest that the youngest and oldest travelers are less likely to be frequent toll lane users than travelers in intermediate age categories. Education level is also positively related to the amount of use of both the toll facilities.

These conclusions regarding the influence of demographic variables are based on direct analysis of survey data and also emerged from multivariate analysis where the survey data from SR 91 were used to calibrate choice mod-

Figure 9.8

Frequency of SR 91 Express Lane Use Related to Gender

els, as discussed previously. An interesting observation made during the work on multivariate modeling is that women aged thirty to fifty are more likely to choose a toll road than any other age/gender classification, and the effect seems to hold across different levels of time savings and tolls.

In all, the impact studies have shown that the value-priced toll facilities, where travelers can bypass congestion for a price, are associated with significant and systematic responses in travel behavior. This suggests that demand-dependent pricing can be a powerful tool for managing highway traffic and providing more choices to the traveling public in similar corridors elsewhere.

Observations Concerning Public Opinion

Public opinion about these innovative pricing projects has varied over time, especially for the SR 91 Express Lanes. Both project operators have worked diligently to keep the public and the media informed, and to present their projects in a positive manner. On the whole, these efforts have proven successful, although controversy and unfavorable media coverage has occurred in connection with the SR 91 project. Controversies and the return of severe congestion following the opening of the Eastern Toll Road in fall 1998 appear to have adversely affected public opinion concerning many aspects of this project.

However, the basic idea of providing new toll facilities to bypass congestion (with no mention of variable tolls) has been consistently popular among commuters. For example, in a series of travel surveys conducted on SR 91 from 1995 to 1999, approval for new toll facilities consistently scored in the 70–80 percent approval range for persons recently using toll facilities and, after 1996, in the 60–70 percent range for persons not recently using toll facilities. These approval levels subsequently declined by 5–10 percent, although ratings consistently remained above 50 percent, as seen in Figure 9.9. The figure shows differences over time related to both toll lane use and rideshare categories, since opinions vary significantly with these factors. These approval levels are fairly insensitive to commuters' incomes, with only the very highest income group (>$100,000) expressing significantly higher approval.

Public approval of demand-based variable tolls on SR 91 has consistently lagged approval of toll facilities in general. Approval of variable tolls has also varied considerably over time. Figure 9.10 shows that approval of variable tolls increased significantly from 1995 (pre-project) to 1996, a year after opening; however, by 1999, approval had returned to pre-opening levels or below, especially among non-users. These effects are also largely insensitive to income. The 1999 decline in approval of variable tolls among SR 91 commuters probably reflects unhappiness with increased freeway congestion and negative media coverage concerning congestion and other issues (see below).

Figure 9.9

**Approval of SR 91 Commuters for Providing Toll Lanes
to Bypass Congestion**

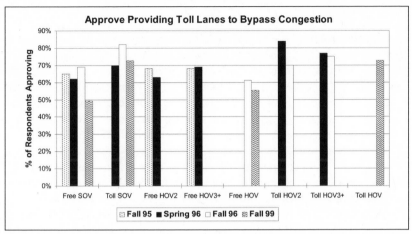

A very similar pattern appears regarding approval for having private enterprise operate the toll lanes for a profit.

Surveys in the San Diego region show that nearly 90 percent of SOV I-15 HOT lane users regarded their project as a "success," although the definition of

Figure 9.10

Approval of Congestion-Based Tolls among SR 91 Commuters

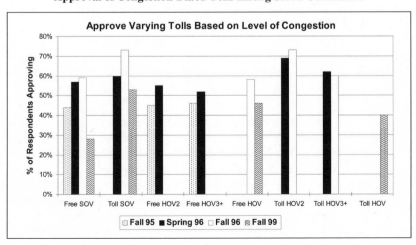

"success" was left up to the respondents. HOV users were more skeptical at first but increasingly regarded the project as successful over time (33 percent regarded the project as successful in fall 1997, increasing to 56 percent in fall 1998) (Supernak et al. 2000b, 35–36; SANDAG 1999b, 16). A smaller proportion of non-participants viewed the project as successful, although that also increased over time (24 percent in fall 1997, increasing to 30 percent in fall 1998). The majority (75–85 percent) of all commuters said that they regarded the I-15 project as fair to both users and non-users.

Surveys with I-15 project participants revealed strong agreement with the concept of allowing SOVs to use the HOT lanes for a fee. The majority in other commute groups also strongly agreed or somewhat agreed with the concept. Approval remained stable over time among participants and increased over time for the other commute groups.

Surveys of SR 91 commuters conducted in 1999 also revealed high levels of support for the HOT lane concept in general, despite lower approval for certain aspects of the SR 91 project in particular. 60–75 percent of SOV commuters and 45–50 percent of HOV commuters said they approved of permitting SOVs to buy excess HOV lane capacity as long as the lanes do not become congested. Approval of the HOT lane concept was found to be fairly insensitive to commuters' incomes.

Controversy Surrounding SR 91[23]

In 1998 and 1999, local media coverage portrayed the SR 91 project as a clash between competing interests—public v. private, safety v. profit, Riverside County v. California Private Transportation Company and Caltrans, taxation v. private ownership, non-profit v. for-profit enterprise. The controversies can be traced to the unique institutional features of the SR 91 project, and weaknesses in the agreements among the principal parties. It was one of the precipitating factors that ultimately led to a local public agency, OCTA, purchasing the SR 91 franchise in 2003. No such controversies affected the publicly operated I-15 project.

Media coverage of SR 91 questioned the private role in toll roads and how well the enabling AB 680 legislation was written. Coverage noted that CPTC had a thirty-five-year "monopoly" over the 91 freeway (Bowles 1999). This "monopoly" comes from a provision of the AB 680 law called the "absolute protection zone." The absolute protection zone, commonly called the "non-compete provision," prohibited the State from improving alternate public highways in order to protect the company's investment and revenue stream (Bowles and Garrett 2000; Kelleher and McKim 2000). Although the absolute protection zone was created in good faith to encourage private investment in toll facilities, it was not depicted this way. It was characterized as giving private companies power to prevent the State and other agencies from making any road improvements, even for safety reasons. Highway privatization by the State was termed an "incredible breach of public trust" (Berkman and Bowles 1999) and "failing in its duty to protect the traveling public" (Bowles and Garrett 2000). Caltrans was said to have "overstepped its authority agreeing to not build road improvements that would compete with the toll lanes" (Steele 2000).

Coverage reported a "significant increase in accident rates" on State Route 91 and, in one area, "accident rates jumped by as much as 183% since the toll lanes opened in late 1995" (James 2000a) and "accident rates along the freeway are as much as 72 percent higher than on comparable stretches of freeway throughout California" (Bishop 2000). Indeed, the data show that the peak period, peak direction accident rate in Riverside County, just east of the SR 91 Express Lanes, increased significantly about the time the express lanes opened; however, the accident rate in the Orange County section containing the express lanes decreased temporarily.[24] At both locations, effects appear closely correlated with changes in congestion and, overall, the SR 91 Express Lane facility operates at an acceptable level of safety (Sullivan 2000, chapter 6).

Lawsuits and investigations that have surrounded the project since its early history also probably influenced public opinion. In 1994, prior to the project opening, Riverside County officials filed suit against CPTC stating that they were "never consulted on the legislation or tollway deal" (Berkman and Bowles 1999). Riverside County reportedly felt short-changed that a highway in Orange County upon which its citizens heavy rely could only be upgraded through toll financing. This lawsuit ended in a settlement. Later, the Riverside County Transportation Commission sued CPTC and the State of California, stating that "Caltrans has allowed the private toll-road company to illegally use public carpool lanes in Riverside County that are adjacent to the toll lanes," contending that "Caltrans breached an agreement it had with the County in an effort to assist the private operator of the toll lanes" (James 2000b) by allowing express lane customers to use contiguous carpool lanes on entering and exiting the facility. The chairman of the Riverside County Transportation Commission stated that he was "deeply concerned over the close cooperation between CPTC and Caltrans against the public in Riverside County" (James 2000b).

In 1997, the idea of a non-profit corporation buying the SR 91 Express Lanes was introduced to the public and received considerable media attention. The Riverside County Transportation Commission prepared a proposal to "encourage a nonprofit corporation to buy the 91 Express Lanes from the toll lanes' for-profit owner." A non-profit would "better serve those who commute," stated Jack Reagan, executive director of the Commission, and non-profit owners would be more concerned with "maintaining traffic flow" than producing revenue (Scott 1997a).

In 1998, it seemed likely that the toll lane franchise would soon be sold. A non-profit organization called NewTrac entered negotiations to purchase the business. The public was told that if the acquisition went through, "carpools would again ride for free and money that would otherwise have gone to profit would instead go back to the public" (Pund 1998). However, a 1999 article charged that CPTC "structured the sale [to NewTrac] to reap a substantial profit from their struggling investment" (Bowles 1999). The Riverside County Transportation Commission threatened to sue NewTrac, which led to an investigation by the State Attorney General's office to determine whether or not CPTC and NewTrac had a conflict of interest (Bowles 1999). This occurred at the same time that Caltrans was threatened by a lawsuit from CPTC after that agency proposed to improve the parallel State Route 91 free lanes in response to congestion and safety concerns from opening the Eastern Toll Road. Caltrans eventually shelved the improvement plan (Garvey 1999).

While some conflict existed since the beginning of the project, by the late 1990s relationships among key participants had become increasingly adversarial, adding to the difficulty of compromising on critical unresolved issues. Probably the most critical unresolved issue was the need to devise suitable guidelines permitting improvements of parallel highways without unduly undermining the financial performance of the toll lanes. If a positive solution to this issue could have been found, it might have led to other accommodations such as permitting the sale or reorganization of the business to improve its organizational and tax status. Hindsight suggests that future private projects within urban networks should place high priority on reaching clear prior agreements with public authorities on criteria for improving competing facilities, probably based on measures of level of service and accident experience, in order to protect the public interest and provide fair protection to investors. In the case of the SR 91 Express Lanes, this was not accomplished and the operating franchise returned to the public sector.

Closure—Some Lessons Learned

In the author's view, the following are the key lessons learned to date from these two innovative projects:

- Experience in Southern California demonstrates that increasing numbers of commuters will voluntarily pay tolls to enjoy the benefits of reduced travel time, improved driving comfort, and the perception of improved safety. Although many commuters do not find it worthwhile to pay tolls on every commute trip, with experience and increasing congestion, the percentages of toll-paying users on both facilities has increased over time. While toll lane use varies significantly with income, gender, age, and other characteristics, people from all demographic backgrounds use the facilities. Analysis shows that being female is the factor most strongly associated with toll lane use, while high income, age, education, and traveling to work are all important influences on travelers' likelihood of being toll lane customers.

- Initial concerns that the HOT lane facilities might result in serious erosion to ridesharing and public transit use did not materialize in these corridors.

- Value pricing is associated with highly selective travel behavior. Travelers' decisions to use the toll lanes is strongly related to hour-by-hour variations in traffic conditions, as well as to price levels, but less strongly. The existence of moderately price-sensitive demand, with estimated elasticities (for SR 91) in the range of 0.7–1.0 provides substantial scope for fine-tuning hourly demand through the use of time-variable tolls.

- Although controversy linked to the "non-compete" provision of the SR 91 project reversed an initial positive approval trend among SR 91 commuters, approval levels in the San Diego region remained high, and survey respondents in both locations remained positive about innovative pricing to expand travel opportunities through high occupancy toll (HOT) lanes.

- The evidence from both Southern California facilities proved that value-priced facilities can be financially successful in selected applications. However, both Southern California projects enjoyed the advantages of unusually low capital requirements, because of preexisting infrastructure, and favorable institutional environments for rapid implementation. While opportunities clearly exist for new private highways in or near urban areas (for example, Toronto's Route 407), the enormous construction costs found in many built-up areas suggest the need for new models of private-public sharing of investments, and new ways of thinking about highway finance and system improvement priorities when private investments are involved.

- The final verdict has not yet been reached regarding the acceptability of public-private partnerships for accelerating needed highway projects in California. The non-compete provision of the SR 91 project produced an impasse in this public-private relationship. While it seems reasonable that private investors would need some assurance that government will not arbitrarily build competing capacity to undercut its business, it is also essential that government be able to improve nearby highways to provide equitable levels of service and traffic safety compared to other sections of the regional highway system. In California, suitable criteria to balance these legitimate interests have not yet emerged.

- Both California projects will undergo additional changes in years to come. How these changes play out will continue to provide useful lessons for innovative road pricing in other locations.

Notes

1. An overview of these and other value pricing projects in the United States appears in Berg et al. 1999.
2. Discounts also apply to motorcycles, zero-emission vehicles, and disabled person accounts.
3. Source: Orange County Transportation Authority. 91 Express Lanes Fiscal Year 2003 Annual Report. Online at http://www.91expresslanes.com/generalinfo/91annualreport.pdf.
4. Source: San Diego Council of Governments. Fact Sheet—Interstate 15 Fastrak. October 2003. On-line at http://www.sandag.cog.ca.us/uploads/publicationid/publicationid_831_3823.pdf.
5. For additional technical details concerning transponders in general, see http://www.ettm.com/avi.html.
6. See http://www.sirit.com/body_main.html for more specific information about SIRIT transponders.
7. See http://www.mfsdatanet.com/mfs-network-technologies/for information about MFS Network Technologies.
8. CPTC charges, promotions, and related business procedures can be seen at http://www.91expresslanes.com/.
9. Figure 9.1 and the other detailed charts that follow are from the SR 91 impact study that monitored project implementation through 1999 (Sullivan 2000). More recent data are unavailable.
10. With assistance from the federal Value Pricing Program, the TCA is studying the possibility of instituting time-varying tolls on portions of its network. However, no decision to do so has yet been made as of the time of writing.
11. Considerable additional detail about traffic trends appears in the SR 91 impact study final report (Sullivan 2000).
12. Prior to November 1997, the operating hours were 6–9 A.M. southbound and 3–6:30 P.M. northbound.
13. Closure during the off-peak facilitates the changeover between southbound and northbound operations. Also, on occasion, the express lanes are used during off hours as a test track for special projects, such as demonstrations of automated highway technologies.
14. Source: San Diego Council of Governments. Fact Sheet—Interstate 15 Managed Lanes, August 2004. On-line at http://www.sandag.cog.ca.us/uploads/publicationid/publicationid_6_1065.pdf.
15. Initially, the I-15 HOT lane section was widened to three lanes in the "toll zone," and SOV customers were required to use the extra lane where their transponders

were charged electronically. Staff in an observation booth ensured that vehicles not in the transponder lane contained two or more people. This layout is similar to the toll zone which continues to be used on SR 91. However, on I-15, in response to complaints about the difficulty of merging, the third lane was removed and transponder readers placed above all lanes. SANDAG transponders come with a silver static bag so customers in carpools can shield their transponders while passing through the toll zone.

16. There are six LOS categories, A through F, loosely analogous to grades given in school. On urban freeways, traffic sometimes slows down slightly under LOS C operation; however, slowing only becomes noticeable under LOS D operation or worse. Bumper to bumper congestion corresponds to LOS F.

17. I-15 credit card accounts are replenished by $40 when the positive balance falls below $10. Cash customers are asked to replenish their accounts by $50 when the balance falls below $20. A $40 transponder deposit is charged, although credit card customers do not actually pay unless they fail to return the transponder at account termination. This information retrieved February 1, 2001, from http://www.sandag.cog.ca.us/data_services/fastrak/. The I-15 electronic toll system is operated by Transcore (http://www.transcore.com/).

18. Source: On-line at http://www.sandag.cog.ca.us/data_services/fastrak/info.html.

19. Data are from the cited I-15 impact study, which monitored project implementation through 1999. No more recent data are available. The study selected October and April for reporting data. Counts consistently cover 6–9 A.M. and 3–7 P.M. In November 1997, operating hours were extended from 6–9 A.M. and 3–6:30 P.M. to 5:45–9:15 A.M. and 3–7 P.M.

20. The trip time savings shown in the graphs are from network travel times based on field measurements.

21. The PM data are more erratic, probably because a particular highway section having substantial delays in the northbound direction is omitted from the reported travel time data.

22. The models were calibrated by researchers at the University of California, Irvine, led by Professor Kenneth Small, using data collected by Cal Poly. Details appear in the report by Professor Small and graduate student Jia Yan (Sullivan 2000, chapter 5).

23. This section is adapted from material originally written by Cal Poly student Dina Cadenazzi.

24. In the Orange County section, the lower accident rate may also be related to the cessation of construction activities.

References

Berg, J., et al. 1999. "Value Pricing Pilot Program." *TR* (*Transportation Research*) *News*, No. 204, Sept.-Oct. Washington, D.C.: Transportation Research Board.

Berkman, L., and J. Bowles. 1999. "Analyst Assails Tollway Takeover: Plan for 91 Lanes Called Wasteful." *The Press Enterprise*, December 15, p. A-1.

Bishop, D. 2000. "Tough Toll Road Questions: Has the Public Been Endangered or

Defrauded?" *The Sacramento Bee*, January 11.

Bowles, J. 1999. "Sale of Toll Lanes Halted: As Officials Meet to Quash Bond Sales for the Highway 91 Lanes, the Deal is Pulled." *Press Enterprise*, December 14, p. A-1.

Bowles, J., and R. Garrett. 2000. "How California Sold the Future of a Highway: Tax Shortage Led to Private Toll-Lane Deal." *Press Enterprise*, January 2, p. A-1.

CPTC—California Private Transportation Company. 1999. *1999 Annual Report*. Anaheim, CA.

Garvey, M, and M. James. 1999. "Controversy Stops Sale of Toll Road in Orange County." *LA Times*, December 14, p. B-1.

James, M. 2000a. "Legislators Vow Quick Action for Commuters." *LA Times*, February 3.

James, M. 2000b. "Caltrans' Link to 91 Toll Lanes Decried." *LA Times*, March 17, p. B-4.

Kelleher, J., and J. McKim. 2000. "Difficult Path for Toll Roads Transportation: The Idea of Creating a Network of Public-Private Roads Hasn't Worked as Planned." *Orange County Register*, January 5, p. C-1.

McKim, J., 2000. "Initiative Brushed Aside in 91 Deal? Transportation: Sales Tax Approved in 1990 Could Have Paid for Car-Pool Lanes and Prevented Toll Lanes, Critics Say." *Orange County Register*, February 5, p. B-1.

Pund, E. 1998. "New Toll Lane Will Make Cars Breathe Easier." *Press Enterprise*, October 10, p. F-1.

SANDAG—San Diego Association of Governments. 1999a. *FasTrak Users Response to Toll Pricing Change: A Time Series Analysis of Time of Travel*. July. Retrieved January 2001, from http://www.sandag.cog.ca.us/data_services/fastrak/library.html.

SANDAG—San Diego Council of Governments. 1999b. *Report to the California Legislature: San Diego's Interstate 15 Congestion Pricing & Transit Development Demonstration Program as Required By Section 149.1(G) of the Street & Highways Code*. December. Retrieved January 2001, from http://www.sandag.cog.ca.us/data_services/fastrak/library.html.

Scott, G. 1997a. "Officials Want Toll Lanes Sold." *Business Press/California*, September 29, p. 3.

Scott, G. 1997b. "Inland Empire Focus Driving the Economy: Roads to Aid Commerce." *Business Press/California*, October 13, p. 1.

Steele, J. 2000. "Panel Urges Purchase of 91 Toll Lanes." *Press Enterprise*, April 13, p. B-1.

Sullivan, Edward. 2000. *Continuation Study to Evaluate the Impacts of the SR 91 Value-Priced Express Lanes—Final Report*. San Luis Obispo, CA: Applied Research and Development Facility, Cal Poly State University. December. Available February 2001, from http://ceenve.calpoly.edu/sullivan/sr91/sr91.htm.

Supernak, Janusz, et al. 2000a. *I-15 Congestion Pricing Project Monitoring and Evaluation Services—Phase II Year Two Traffic Study*. Report to San Diego Council of Governments. Department of Civil and Environmental Engineering. San Diego State University. April 3. Retrieved January 2001, from http://www.sandag.cog.ca.us/data_services/fastrak/library.html.

Supernak, Janusz, et al. 2000b. *I-15 Congestion Pricing Project Monitoring and Evaluation Services—Phase II Year Two Overall Report*. Report to San Diego Council of Governments. Department of Civil and Environmental Engineering. San Diego State University. May 16. Retrieved January 2001, from http://www.sandag.

cog.ca.us/data_services/fastrak/library.html.

TCA—Transportation Corridor Agencies. *1999 Annual Report.* Retrieved October 2000, from http://www.tcagencies.com/.

U.S. Federal Highway Administration. 2000. *Report On The Value Pricing Pilot Program.* U.S. Department of Transportation. July. Retrieved on February 9, 2001, from http://www.fhwa.dot.gov/policy/final.htm.

10

How Should the Revenues from Congestion Pricing Be Spent?*

Kenneth J. Button

Introduction

Urban traffic congestion is a major and growing problem. Using prices to control the problem is now a central theme of political agendas in many countries. The evidence shows that road pricing can be an efficient mechanism for controlling congestion. Road pricing would also provide the road authorities with a significant fiscal dividend. The issue examined here is how the dividend should be spent.

Advocates of road pricing have long argued that pricing can improve the use of existing urban road networks and inter-urban systems. Mathematical models of bottleneck pricing, system wide pricing, second best principles, and so on abound (Button and Verhoef 1998; Lindsey and Verhoef 2001; Verhoef 1996). Technological advances have also made road pricing more relevant as tolls can now be collected electronically with no reduction in traffic flow. Electronic tolls also allow real-time price adjustments to reflect variations in traffic flow. Simpler systems, such as ring tolls, whereby road users pay every time they cross a cordon, or area licenses still have some advantages, however, such as letting users know in advance of travel what the exact road price will be. Ring systems may also be cheaper although that advantage is fast diminishing as electronic toll technology improves. Simpler regimes may provide important measures along the way to electronic pricing as they illustrate the power of prices to influence travel behavior and create political support for more efficient

*I would like to thank Kimberly Vachel for her help in preparing this chapter.

methods of pricing (Behbehani et al., 1984). The fact that there is no ideal method of charging for road congestion does not mean that there are no significant social benefits from deploying imperfect systems.

Much less attention has been given to the issue of how to spend road pricing revenues than to calculating optimal toll prices.[1] The expenditure issue is not one that has been entirely ignored although the relevant material is rather fragmented.

If roads were provided privately and competitively then the inefficient congestion problem would not exist. Road owners would price to maximize profits and in so doing would take into account the costs of congestion each driver imposes on other drivers.[2] In addition the issue of net investment would also be taken care of as prices would accurately convey information about where and when to build new roads.[3]

Prices administratively set by the authorities, however, will rarely mimic those that would be set by the forces of supply and demand. The authorities, for example, must rely on estimates of the underlying market parameters in setting charges and these are inevitably not totally accurate and in any case bureaucratic incentives are unlikely to be coincident with the profit and loss incentives of entrepreneurs. Administrative charges, however, are generically a more efficient mechanism than devices such as queuing and congestion to allocate scarce publicly owned resources (Baumol and Oates 1975).

The problem of the surpluses can be seen from another, welfare economics-based, perspective. What congestion charges do in theoretical terms is to produce a Hicks-Kaldor-Scitovsky improvement in welfare. This means that there would be an aggregate social gain from such charges. What they do not do is produce a Pareto improvement that would require that no one is made worse off by the charges. This is, to reiterate the situation, because the main immediate direct beneficiaries of road pricing are the pricing authorities that take the windfall net revenues of pricing. It is a Hicks-Kaldor-Scitovsky improvement because these authorities could compensate those road users who lose out, pay for the administration of the system, and still have surplus revenue. Whether this compensation is actually given is a crucial matter when looking at the implications of the distribution gains from road pricing. It also determines the degree of opposition to it.

Pricing in a market context serves as an indicator of when more of a commodity should be provided and as a mechanism for generating the revenues necessary to expand supply. Hence in the longer term even those initially priced out of the market may have greater opportunities to consume if they are willing to wait and then pay the price that emerges after long-run output is optimized. But with the adoption of the Hicks-Kaldor-Scitovsky criteria in the road pricing context, there is no mechanism that automatically offers a stimulus for such an expansion of road capacity. The way net revenues could be spent is divorced from where they are collected and from the demands of previous and remaining road users.

The Problems of Spending

Efficiency Considerations

It's often suggested that road revenues be used to offset license, car, or fuel taxes. Sharp (1966), however, pointed out this complicates the issue of pricing since it would cause road users to "buy back" some of the road space. Reducing fuel taxes, for example, would increase the incentive to drive. If the money is instead dispensed to non-related areas, say to the elderly, then this buy-back would likely be negligible. Given modern information systems and charging technologies it is still not a trivial matter to determine feedback effects, but total perfection in setting any price is a utopian notion.

Distribution Considerations

When looking at distribution issues there is sometimes confusion between the positive aspects of describing changes from the status quo with normative consideration of whether the effects of road pricing are in some way "inequitable." Robbins' (1932) view, that economics should be purged of value judgments, has merit in this respect. Whilst analysis of the implications of road pricing for different groups in society is unquestionably important in understanding why it is not widely used, whether the distribution of these impacts is fair or not is a matter for others.

Sharp touches upon distribution issues. He argues that those potential motorists "excluded" from the road would only be as well off after the initiation of road pricing if public transport were so improved by the decreased congestion that it provided service that the "excluded" motorists regarded as being as good as (and no more costly than) the road space that they formerly consumed. The matter of distribution effects is not, however, dealt with in any detail.

The problem of spending road pricing revenue was resurrected in a little more detail by Richardson (1974). He argued that road pricing has important distribution implications in terms of who is affected. It benefits the wealthy, who would gain from the combination of them having a high value of time and the ability to make faster trips. It benefits existing, largely low-income, urban bus users because their services would be faster and more reliable. It has adverse effects for middle-income groups priced off the road and having to transfer to what they consider inferior public transport. Use of revenue from road pricing is seen by Richardson as a mechanism for, at least partly, compensating this group if it is expended on public transport improvements, especially if they improve service quality.

Gómez-Ibáñez (1992) goes to a further level of disaggregation and looks at eight groups who either directly gain or lose from road pricing. While his findings are not seen as reflecting any judgment about whether the distribution outcome meets any criteria of equity, the wide-ranging impacts are seen as reflecting the difficulties of obtaining political acceptance for road pricing. The degree of disaggregation can be taken further. For example, Giuliano (1994) considers implications according to gender, opportunities to work flextime, availability of transit, etc. rather than income classes. But whichever way it is looked at, there are inevitable winners and losers and who they are is influenced by the way road pricing revenues are spent.

What these studies tend to neglect is that a full network-based system of road pricing would not only increase the price of using congested facilities but would logically reduce the costs of using many uncongested sections (notably inter-urban roads). This was an implicit point made by Newbery (1988) in the context of the UK road network. The overall implications for distribution of impact across the motoring public would then depend on the relative use of different elements of the network as would the total net revenues collected. There is an argument, that in some countries the outcome could be revenue neutral and the distributional issue be reduced to the impacts on various groups of road user (Roy 1998).

Political Acceptability Considerations

Since road pricing does not meet strict Pareto criteria and, because it is unlikely that revenues will be used to fully compensate those adversely affected, there is a pragmatic need to ensure that net revenue is spent in ways that make road pricing attractive to a winning coalition of people. Winning coalitions are not simply coalitions of road users but may include a variety of other interests with "voting rights." Since comprehensive road pricing would involve charging for both existing infrastructure and for new infrastructure the issue is not even a static one amongst road users. Successful efforts at initiating quasi-road pricing measures have often involved concessions for certain road user groups (car pools in Singapore), improvements to alternative modes (subsidies to transit in Oslo), increased choice for car users (HOT lanes in California), or additional road capacity (toll rings in Norway).

Arguing for the need to form dominant coalitions of advocacy to gain acceptance for road pricing a number of academic studies have sought to look at ways of in which distributing the proceeds of road pricing may assist in this process. Goodwin (1989) came up with the idea of a "Rule of Three." This, rather arbitrary, rule would involve distributing the proceeds, although not in equal part, to improve the road system, to improve public transport, and to reduce taxation, or to be spent as part of general expenditure. The improved road network would appease those forced to pay the road price and in the longer term reduce the number priced from the system. Improved public transport would partly placate those forced from the road as well as gaining the support of existing users. Lower taxes or increased general public expenditure would appeal more generally.

This theme of triple dispensation has been taken up by Small (1992), who looks at ways of using the net revenues from road pricing to improve transportation and make the package more attractive. He argues that regional-wide pricing in the Los Angeles region would generate about $3 million annually that could be used to offset regressive taxes and especially those such as fuel and sales taxes that are used to finance public transportation. And in particular, to gain the support of those in a small number of relatively concentrated geographical areas, the revenue could be used to subsidize local transport.

The economic difficulty with putting large sums into public transport, however, is that it may be wasteful and result in much of the benefits of the system being lost. In the past subsidies have been captured by the suppliers of public transportation services and by the labor operating those services. Studies of the UK bus industry prior to regulatory reform in the 1985 Transport Act indicated that a large proportion of subsidies, up to 50 percent, was absorbed in lower productivity and higher wages (Bly et al. 1980). There are ways of containing but not eliminating this problem. The regulatory changes that introduced network tendering in London in 1985, whilst not eliminating the problem, would seem to have reduced the seepage. Kennedy (1995) estimates the cost saving emanating from the London regime was about 20 percent over the previous regime of subsidies.

Broader Issues of Earmarking or "Ring-fencing"

Many economists dislike the earmarking of revenues,[4] their tying to particular expenditure items, in the ways that Goodwin, Small, and others have discussed. Beside the fact that they are arbitrary, the argument is that any rational company in the private sector does not limit itself in the ways in which it spends its revenue flow. It seeks out those activities that generate the highest potential profits. Indeed, if this were not the case then there would be little innovation in the economy as investments would exclusively be channeled back into existing activities. The Wright bothers, for example, could not have financed flight development without the profits earned in their cycle business. The parallel argument for a public sector undertaking is that government should use any revenue that it gets to finance activities that produce the highest social rate of return.

The analogy of a government budget to the revenues of private firm, however, is flawed. A private firm faces a direct market test: If consumers do not regard its products as good value at the prices that it charges the firm will go bankrupt. Revenues are thus tied to consumer benefits. Taxes, however, are not prices and we have no direct way of assessing whether taxes paid are more than matched by benefits received. Voting is an indirect method of testing whether government is performing at par but voting is at best only a coarse test. Votes are typically registered only every four or more years and they are made over large bundles of goods that the voter cannot untie (a voter, for example, cannot vote for one party's position on the military and another party's position on the environment).

To begin the analysis of earmarking with the argument that it would be inefficient to constrain a private firm to spend its revenues in prescribed fields is to miss the point. The problem that earmarking attempts to address is one that private firms do not face. Earmarking tries to ensure that citizens can see how taxes paid are matched by benefits received.

For these sorts of reasons, Buchanan (1963) and others have advocated the use of earmarking. Earmarking is seen by advocates as more transparent than general taxation and provides the populace with a clearer picture of the options confronting them and allows subsequent monitoring of actions. Accountability is stronger. Earmarking does not necessarily imply putting the revenues from the revenue back into the same activity from which it is raised but rather into some pre-specified expenditure package. From a public policy perspective, it provides "voters" with choices of policy packages.

Earmarking, however, need not work in this way. Lottery funds "earmarked for education," for example, rarely result in more being spent on education; there is just a reshuffling of fungible revenues (Borg and Mason 1990). In these cases earmarking is a form of fiscal illusion (Lee 1997).

Earmarking may also be necessary to create a dominant political coalition.[5] In some cases such coalitions may have some economic logic as when road revenues are earmarked for road building—thus ensuring that road users are not inefficiently subsidizing non-users and non-users are not subsidizing users. In other cases, however, especially when the revenue and expenditures sides are not closely related, the coalition may be purely political.

The FasTrak HOT lanes on an eight-mile section of I-15 north of San Diego are priced on a real time basis and run parallel to free lanes. Stretches of private road in Orange County California are priced in accordance with a pre-established timetable. Opposition from road users to the charge was placated in part by the fact that the revenue from the charges is put into maintaining and improving the road. This benefits not only the user of the FasTrak facility but also users of the free parallel road that is now also less congested.

The evidence from numerous surveys also generally indicates road users favor the earmarking of net revenues from road pricing. For example, a National Economic Development Office (1991) study in London found that 43 percent of adults questioned supported road pricing as a stand-alone measure but this figure rose to 63 percent when hypothecation of revenues for purposes favored by respondents was part of the package. In particular, 38 percent wanted it spent on public transportation, 25 percent on road improvements, and 14 percent on non-transportation services such as the National Health Service. Jones (1991) surveyed studies of attitudes towards road pricing in the UK and found that public acceptance required that revenues be dedicated to local transport and environmental projects. More recent generic findings are contained in the UK Department of Environment, Transport and the Regions (2000) consultation document, *Breaking the Logjam*. Forty-four percent of respondents said that road pricing revenues should be earmarked for better public transportation.[6]

The experience of FasTrak, small as the sample is, indicates that private sector road suppliers find putting surplus revenue back into road infrastructure a commercial proposition, at least with current capacity and demand parameters. It also reflects the fact that prices do not simply ration out scarce resources but also act to stimulate an expansion in those resources. The difficulty with the public sector is that while earmarking to a portfolio of outlays may obtain a political coalition in favor of road pricing, this portfolio may well reduce the efficiency of the regime and be highly wasteful of resources. Earmark systems, even when seen as efficient in curbing government failures to spend wisely in the short-term, are notoriously rigid in the face of changing circumstances.

Bergen and Other Norwegian Schemes

Despite all the difficulties with introducing road pricing, a number of systems with some of the characteristics of road pricing are in place. The Norwegians have introduced from the late 1980s a series of cordon-pricing regimes, "toll rings," around a number of their cities (Trondheim, Bergen, and Oslo). These essentially involve payment for entry to the city. The geography of Norway, with its mountainous terrain and small cities with limited access points makes this a relatively straightforward way of charging road users. The monies are collected through both electronic and manual systems. Over time, as practical experience has been gained and as technology has developed, so the systems have become more technically sophisticated. In all cases, the initial technology was not state-of-the-art but well tested to ensure that minimal operational problems would arise. Details of the various to toll ring schemes, together with some data on the cities themselves, are provided in Table 10.1.

The schemes are not strictly road pricing in the Pigouvian sense. They are more in the tradition of tolls. They do not directly relate to levels of congestion and, indeed, in some cases there are discounts offered to frequent users of the systems. As can be seen from Table 10.1 the charges are also relatively low. The positioning of the toll rings was also not designed to optimize traffic flows. They were located largely to capture revenue in what was seen as a politically equitable fashion. Nevertheless, since a charge is levied in the cordon schemes,

Table 10.1
The Norwegian Toll Rings (data for 1992)

	Bergen	Oslo	Trondheim[a]
Population of urban area (thousands)	300	700	136
Percent inside toll ring	10	28	40
Starting date of toll ring	January 1986	February 1990	October 1991
Number of stations	7	19	11
Entry fee for cars (NOK)[b]			
Single trip (manual or coin)[c]	5	11	10
Per trip (subscription)[d]			
With prepayment[e]	4.50	7.43	7
Off-peak discount (after 10pm)	NA	NA	2
Monthly pass[f]	100	250	NA
Time charges are in effect			
Days	Monday-Friday	All days	Monday-Friday
Hours	6 A.M.–10 P.M.	All hours	6 A.M.–5 P.M.
Average daily crossing during toll hours (thousands)	40.5	68	204.4
Percent by subscribers	59	63	85
1992 gross revenue (million NOK)	63	628	70.7

Notes:
[a]Figures exclude the preexisting Ranheim toll station, which has higher rates applicable in both directions and at all times.

[b]For 1992 the exchange rate was NOK1 = $0.16.

[c]Bergen: all stations manned. Oslo: all stations manned, eight have coin lanes. Trondheim: one station manned, others coin or magnetic card only.

[d]In Trondheim subscribers are charged for no more than one trip per hour and no more than seventy-five per month. Trondheim subscription rates rose in 1994 for people making ten or fewer crossing per month.

[e]Charges shown are for the following prepayment quantities. Bergen: booklets of twenty. Oslo: 350 trips. Trondheim: NOK 1500 prepayment. A post-payment option is also available in Trondheim.

[f]Six- and twelve-month passes are available at lower rates.

Source: Small and Gómez-Ibáñez (1998).

it is almost inevitable that there will be some impact on travel behavior and, *ipso facto* they have implications for congestion. In all cases there is a large element of earmarking in the ways revenues are used and this has also been seen as having longer-term implications for traffic congestion. In the case of Oslo where a ring system was initiated in 1990, for example, an argument has been advanced that since the revenue collected is used largely to construct ring road facilities this will ultimately contribute to reducing congestion in the central area of the city. A further 10 percent of revenue is earmarked for public transportation, which, it is argued, has an additional positive substitution effect (Solheim 1990).

The Bergen system of cordon tolling was initiated in 1986 (Larsen 1988) and is perhaps the most studied of the Norwegian rings. The city is small and the initial toll ring had six stations with another added after the completion of a new road link. The evidence from the outset was that, whilst the tolls were not specifically designed to impact on congestion, they did lead to some limited spreading of peaks. The initial system covered the period 6 A.M. to 10 P.M. each weekday and hence did not differentiate peak flows. The result was a very rapid reduction of traffic in the urban area by some 6 percent to 7 percent. Small reductions were initially recorded in Oslo, but within nine months traffic had built up again in the urban core. The Trondheim system has the least impact on congestion because about a third of the region's drivers live within the toll ring (Ramjerdi 1994).[7]

Whilst there are technical issues of toll collection technologies and the like that are of interest in the Norwegian case, of more importance is perhaps the political mechanisms by which the authorities gained acceptance for their policies. In all cases there was earmarking of revenues. In the case of Oslo, the introduction of a toll ring was coincidental with the opening of an express bypass that would be financed from toll revenues. Despite this, surveys indicate that only 29 percent of those questioned in Oslo before the toll rings were introduced had a positive view of the scheme, with 7 percent in Trondheim. The figures rose to 39 percent and 20 percent respectively after a short period of operation. While clearly still not a majority, this does indicate a rapid change of opinion for a large number of people. Similar feelings were expressed in Bergen.

The crucial point about the Norwegian toll rings is rather less the impact they have had on traffic congestion in the short term, and the support that some of the schemes have given to the technology possibilities, than how one can gain increased political acceptance for what were at the outset unpopular measures. The ideas outlined earlier for earmarking road pricing revenues for road improvements, public transportation subsidies, and for reduction in other (possibly partly car-related) taxes largely fall into this coalition forming framework.

Road Pricing in London

Congestion Charging in London

Over the years a number of proposals have come forward for the introduction of road pricing in London. Much of the debate in the *Smeed Report* of the early 1960s was about London. While attracting public and political attention, the idea was abandoned in favor of institutional and urban planning reforms with a focus on improving public transport.

Road pricing was reconsidered in detail in the 1970s and major studies of the implications of a system of "supplementary licensing" were undertaken. A number of variants were considered but an option involving a daily fee of £2.00 (1973 prices) per vehicle driving on inner London roads between 8 A.M. and 6 P.M. on weekdays was subjected to considerable scrutiny. The simulations indicated that this would reduce peak traffic in the 3.4 square miles of Central London and raise speeds by up to 40 percent (May 1975).

The 1980s saw a restructuring of the local government in London and another resurgence of interest in road pricing (May et al. 1990). This also coincided with a shift in national transportation priorities with more emphasis on traffic management and making better use of existing networks. Cordon pricing was examined in detail with London divided into six zones with all-day charges for crossing screenlines between the inner zones and peak charges only for crossing the boundaries of outer zones. Estimates of the most favored toll structure found that peak traffic in London would decline by 15 percent with a 25 percent fall in Central London.

Another set of studies were completed in the early 1990s, looking mainly at cordon pricing around Central London deploying somewhat higher fees than previous work had assumed (ranging up to £14.00 for a peak inward crossing). The cordon charges were explored in combinations with changes in parking and public transportation policies. The models indicated that traffic speeds would rise in Central London by up to 32 percent with traffic volume falling by up to 22 percent. Additional traffic reductions could be attained by adopting more cordons but only at the cost of more complex and expensive structures (Bates et al. 1996).

A further restructuring of London's government has brought about a much less academic approach to road pricing. UK transportation policy shifted in 1998 to explicitly facilitate local government to initiate road pricing within their jurisdictions allowing them, at least at the outset of any scheme, to retain all revenue generated. More germane here, the Greater London Authority Act 1999 conferred road user charging powers in Greater London on the Authority. Subsequently, the mayor of London, Ken Livingstone, developed plans to introduce a simple form of road pricing within the capital largely based on the report of the Government Office for London (2000). The report concluded that a daily charge between 7 A.M. and 7 P.M. for cars of £5.00 per day (£15.00 for trucks) with very few exemptions and enforced by digital cameras would reduce traffic by about 12 percent. The study also found that a daily charge of this magnitude would generate about £200 million annually.

Following a period of consultation between July 2000 and January 2001, the proposals were fine-tuned and in February 2003 Transport for London initiated a congestion-charging scheme for central London. This requires vehicles that are not exempt or enjoy a 100 percent discount to pay £5.00 for each day they enter the charging zone between 7 A.M. and 6:30 P.M. Residents pay only 10 percent of the charge, and buses, taxis, disabled people, emergency vehicles, and some vehicles with cleaner emissions are exempt.[8] Within the charging zone, traffic has fallen by 16 percent (some 50,000 fewer cars being driven in the charging zone daily), congestion as measured by the difference between night- and day-time speeds has fallen by 30 percent, and traffic emissions of nitrogen oxide and particulates both by about 12 percent. Bus service quality has improved with service irregularities falling by 30 percent and disruptions due to traffic delays by 60 percent, while overall bus speeds in the charging zone have risen by 6 percent. There has been little impact on traffic in zones adjacent to where the charge is levied and a survey of businesses at the end of 2003 found that about 80 percent supported the scheme.[9]

Spending the Revenues

Here we are not much concerned with whether £5.00 (now £8.00) is a reasonable figure in terms of its impact on congestion, whether the enforcement technology is appropriate, or whether the temporal and spatial boundaries are optimal. Rather, attention is with the implications of the funds suddenly becoming available to London's public authorities and with the distribution of impacts and the ways it is spent. These latter considerations are important because the desktop studies supporting the daily charge indicated that reduced traffic congestion would, despite any financial payments, generate benefits for bus users and freight transportation and for medium- and lower-income car users. This, however, runs counter to the general arguments of Richardson cited above and seems somewhat counterintuitive. In fact the evidence to date on these sorts of matter is still relatively scant.

To begin with the net revenues from the London congestion-charging scheme are considerably less than initially projected. Forecasts indicated first-year revenues of about £138 million in fees and £22 million in penalties giving net receipts of about £130 million for investments in transport. In fact, net revenues were only $68 million in the first year of operation and are now forecast to be in the order of £80 million to £100 million in future years.[10] Enforcement, and particularly legal costs of court cases involving disputes have been more expensive than anticipated but also the higher than estimated elasticity of demand for car use meant fewer vehicles are paying the charge.[11]

The UK legislation only guarantees that a local authority may maintain the rights to this for ten years. This is clear, if limited, earmarking in the sense that the ring fencing implicitly means the revenues must be spent locally. The Government Office for London study indicated that the traffic benefits from road pricing would be greater if the scheme were complemented by improved public transportation. Its modeling efforts, however, involved only a limited number of scenarios that directly looked at taking monies from road users to fund public transportation.[12] But, equally, the models, largely because of the complexity of London's transportation system, did not consider potential traffic gains from investing revenues into improved road infrastructure—either in terms of civil engineering schemes or improved telematics (other than for public transport) and control systems. Nevertheless, the vast majority of monies raised have gone to public transportation.

The issue ultimately comes down to whether a fairly crude form of road pricing that reduces congestion in Central London and enhances public transport service quality is justified if its political acceptance depends upon revenues collected being earmarked for public transportation. The successful adoption of the Norwegian schemes was largely predicated on the basis that the majority of revenues would go to clearly defined road projects. In some cases public transportation would receive some limited resources. While it may be true that public transportation in London is in need of additional investment, it is also true that the road network is in need of improvements.

Perhaps more important is the potential resource loss that could stem from road pricing revenues crowding out other sources of funding for London's public transportation. The reduced car traffic flows of over 15 percent inevitably produce an outward shift in the demand for public transportation that would make private investment in that mode more attractive. The subsidization of additional investment or the provision of operating subsidies effectively competes with this commercially-driven finance. Unless it is clearly demonstrable that the subsidized activities generate more social welfare than those favored by the market then resources that could be utilized with benefit elsewhere are wasted.[13]

The reduction in car traffic in London since 2003 has certainly partly been the result of the congestion charging but it is also a reflection of a series of measures to enhance public transport, some of which have been funded from the road user charge. Since 2000 about £500 million has been used to enhance the bus network, and has included doubling traffic lanes exclusively for bus use. This not only amounts to a subsidy of at least £0.61 per passenger compared to £0.24 in

2000, but also has reduced effective capacity for cars. The lack of a genuine market means that there is no way of knowing if this money, including that taken from the congestion charge, is being spent efficiently, and even if public transport is a good investment, fixed track systems may be more economically efficient.

Finally, the focus on public transport as an alternative to car use may neglect other consumer choices. There is the potential substitution of resources to other activities that may be socially preferable to offering publicly financed transportation. Indeed, the record of Singapore, which introduced area licensing a quarter of a century or so ago, is that it is extremely difficult to foresee what happens after charges are initiated. In this case the expectation that there would be a substantial mode switch to local buses proved wrong: People carpooled or switched travel times, and many of the new bus depots were very rapidly abandoned. The London case may be different and the situation is certainly more complex. Nevertheless, public transportation expansion may not be the optimal approach. As an example, the ability of many of those in the service sector to telework at least part of the week now allows them to avoid many higher priced car trips. Offering public transportation at artificially low costs would not encourage this natural form of substitution.

The Differential Charges

Although the differential charges that the exemptions and reduced charges in London imply do not constitute a revenue-expenditure issue in the very strictest sense, they have the same *de facto* implications. Those paying the lower charges or are exempt from the charges may be viewed as having a refund given to them equal to the differential between the full charge and what they pay. This has efficiency implications in that many of these road users may well have high values of time and can now use a much more efficient road network for a trivial or zero congestion charge. They are, as a result, likely to use the network more—Sharp's notion of the buy-back effect comes into play.

There are also equity and distributional considerations. The road infrastructure in London is not financed entirely from local sources; considerable funding comes from the general taxpayer and from non-transport-related local taxes. Even within London there seems little reason that some groups of road users, such as local car-using residents, should enjoy lower charges on any form of efficiency grounds.[14] There would also seem to be a limited aggregate case for giving discounts in terms of equity; London has a relatively high per capita income compared to the rest of the UK, and lower-income groups tend not to own or use cars anyway. Rather, the exemptions and reduced charges have largely been granted to gain local political acceptance.

The need to develop viable coalitions to initiate the London scheme was inevitable, and bringing in the support of local car owners would equally seem to be part of this. What it does do, however, is to build in the potential for rigidity that can lead to longer-term problems of modifying the regime. Residents of London have essentially enjoyed a windfall from having faster traffic flows and enhanced public transportation at a minimal cost to themselves. The majority of revenues come from those outside of the area but those within the charging area gain most. The evidence from history is that hysteresis is the norm when it comes to giving groups concessions. The longer-term need to remove the exemptions and differential charges may prove as challenging as introducing the simple congestion regime that has been initiated.

Conclusions

The idea that urban traffic flows would be considerably more efficient if road users were made to make more rational payments for their use of the system has been around for a long time. Road pricing does not meet the theoretical ideal of eliminating excessive congestion costs of trips but it is an efficient way of achieving many public policy objectives.

Efforts to introduce it, however, have seldom met with success despite numerous studies of various forms of charging showing how society would benefit. For technical reasons there is certainly no ideal way of charging road users but there are many road pricing options that are tractable and would certainly generate significant societal gains if initiated. One of the obstacles to action is that the main immediate beneficiaries of road pricing are the revenue-gathering authorities. There are thus important redistribution implications involved. To gain wider acceptance there would appear from both desktop studies and the experiences of where quasi-road pricing has been implemented in Norway, the need to develop a coalition of interests favoring congestion charges.

The difficulty is that while, by definition, there should be sufficient revenues to "buy off" all adversely affected parties after introducing road pricing, how this is done can affect overall societal welfare. This is aside from any normative questions concerning the extent that it is desirable to do so.[15] To use it most effectively would not involve earmarking but this seems to be a necessity in most cases for gaining the minimum public acceptance. Its use as a source of funds for road improvements would seem a logical initial application given that the need for congestion pricing *per se* indicates a high social return from capacity expansion.

The crucial policy question for London is whether a sub-optimal, at least from an efficiency perspective, road pricing system with earmarking of significant revenues to public transportation is justified. In a sense, the political constraint that revenues will revert to general taxation after ten years may reduce any longer-term distortion effects. Certainly, from what has occurred in Norway, where pure revenue collecting approaches are gradually evolving into congestion charges, it does seem that reforms can take place once a regime is in place. There would seem from the experiences of Norway and from some of the admittedly limited survey analysis conducted of road users in the UK, that if ring-fencing of revenues is done then there is at least a better case for ensuring that monies are devoted to road improvements where there is demonstrable demand, than to public transportation. Indeed, since public transportation often uses a common track there are potential synergies.

Notes

1. Indeed, the *Smeed Report* (UK Department of Transport, 1964), which is often cited as one of the key pioneering of road pricing, twice explicitly states that that consideration of the use of the congestion tax was outside of its terms of reference.
2. Knight (1924) stated this point clearly in his critique of certain sections of Pigou's *Economics of Welfare*.
3. Strictly this assumes that there are no economies or diseconomies of scale in road provision and that the provider optimizes investment decisions (Mohring and Harwitz 1962). If there are increasing returns to scale for road provision then there is in theory an efficiency case for subsidizing roads beyond the revenue collected from the optimal road price (unless some optimal form of price discrimination is possible) even if capacity is optimal. Only if roads suffer from decreasing returns to scale at the optimal charge is there a reason for revenue from an optimal road price to exceed the costs of road provision and maintenance.
4. The term "ring-fencing" has often been used in a variety of contexts by UK authorities to denote limitations on ways particular revenue sources may be used. It circumvents the use of the term "earmarking," which, for historic reasons, is anathema to the Treasury. For example, in the specific case of congestion charges, the 1998 UK legislation discussed later in the paper explicitly "ring-fences" road pricing revenue for local authority improvements in roads and public transport in the area where road pricing is introduced.
5. See Keeler (1984) for analysis of the coalitions involved in U.S. domestic aviation policy and Button (1989) for UK bus deregulation.
6. Care should be taken with interpreting survey findings in this context. How the question is posed can seriously bias the responses forthcoming. Car users, for example, may favor funding public transportation on the basis that it will attract others from using their cars. Equally, studies such as that reported in *Breaking the Logjam* do not represent systematic sampling but rather responses to an open invitation to comment.
7. In 1997 three new "inner" screenlines were proposed to capture revenue from those inside the original ring.
8. This means that only about 45 percent of vehicles pay the full charge, 29 percent enjoy discounts, and 26 percent are exempt. In a sense the granting of exemptions and discounts may be seen as inducing a "buy-back" effect of the type described

earlier. Those living within Central London now pay a relatively small amount to use roads but gain from faster traffic speed, which for many reduces the generalized cost of driving and will stimulate these people to use their cars more.

9. Transport for London (2004). Transport for London also maintains a website with up-to-date information on its five-year monitoring of the system and details of proposed future modifications to the scheme. See http://www.tfl.gov.uk/tfl/cclondon/cc_monitoring.shtml.

10. This should be put in the context of an overall annual budget of £4.5 billion for Transport for London.

11. A common feature of the London and Singapore schemes is that the reaction to congestion charges was larger than expected, indicating that traditional transport forecasting models may be inherently biased against the positive traffic implications of adopting fiscal policy measures.

12. This included the provision of ten high-quality bus routes between Inner and Central London costing £100 million and reduced bus fares involving a £100 million per annum subsidy.

13. There are theoretical arguments concerning asymmetry of risk bearing that could justify transfers to public investment, but these need to be empirically demonstrated on a case-by-case basis.

14. Stretching things a little, temporary differential charges could be justified on efficiency grounds as a transitional mechanism that minimizes stranded costs as the population adjusts its long-term consumption patterns to the new pricing regime. There may also be generally accepted social grounds for exempting emergency vehicles.

15. If only a limited number of individuals and groups are needed to create a dominant coalition in favor of road pricing then use of revenue to compensate others effectively becomes a redistribution rather than an efficiency concern.

References

Bates, J., I. Williams, D. Coombe, and J. Leather. 1996. "The London Congestion Charging Programme: 4. The Transport Models." *Traffic Engineering and Control* 37: 334–339.

Baumol, W. J., and W. E. Oates. 1975. *The Theory of Environmental Policy: Externalities, Public Outlays and the Quality of Life.* New York: Prentice-Hall.

Behbehani, R., V. S. Pendakur, and A. T. Armstrong Wright. 1984. *Singapore Area Licensing Scheme: A Review of the Impact.* Washington, D.C.: World Bank Water Supply and Urban Development Department.

Bly, P. H., F. V. Webster, and S. Pounds. 1980. "Effects of Subsidies on Urban Transport." *Transportation* 9: 311–331.

Borg, M. O., and P. M. Mason. 1990. "Earmarked Lottery Revenue: Positive Windfall or Concealed Redistribution Mechanism?" *Journal of Education Finance* 15 (Winter): 289–301.

Buchanan, J. M. 1963. "The Economics of Earmarking." *Journal of Political Economy* 71 (5): 457–469.

Button, K. J. 1989. "Economic Theories of Regulation and the Regulation of the UK Bus Industry." *Antitrust Bulletin* 33: 489–515.

Button, K. J., and W. Rothengatter. 1997. "Motor Transport, Greenhouse Gases and Economic Instruments." *International Journal of Environment and Pollution* 7: 327–342.

Button, K. J. and E. Verhoef, editors. 1998. *Road Pricing, Traffic Congestion and the Environment.* Cheltenham, UK: Edward Elgar.

Giuliano, G. 1994. "Equity and Fairness Considerations of Congestion Pricing, in Transportation Research Board." *Curbing Gridlock: Peak-Period Fees to Relieve Traffic Congestion*, TRB Special Report 242. Washington.

Gómez-Ibáñez, J. A. 1992. "The Political Economy of Highway Tolls and Congestion Charges, in Federal Highway Administration," in *Exploring the Role of Pricing as a Congestion Management Tool.* Washington, D.C.: FHA.

Goodwin, P. B. 1989. "The Rule of Three: A Possible Solution to the Political Problem of Competing Objectives for Road Pricing." *Traffic Engineering and Control* 29: 495–7.

Government Office for London. 2000. *Road Charging Options for London.* London, UK: HMSO.

Jones, P. M. (1991) Gaining public support for road pricing through a package approach, *Traffic Engineering and Control*, 32: 194–196.

Keeler, T. E. 1984. "Theories of Regulation and the Deregulation Movement." *Public Choice* 44: 103–45.

Kennedy, D. 1995. "London Bus Tendering: The Impact on Costs." *International Review of Applied Economics* 9: 305–317.

Knight, Frank H. 1924. "Some Fallacies in the Interpretation of Social Cost." *Quarterly Journal of Economics* XXXVIII: 582–606.

Larsen, O. I. 1988. "The Toll Ring in Bergen Norway: The First Year of Operation." *Traffic Engineering and Control* 22: 216–22.

Lee, D. R. 1997. "Overcoming Taxpayer Resistance by Taxing Choice and Earmarking Revenues," in *Taxing Choice*, edited by W. Shughart. Oakland, CA: Independent Institute, pp. 105–116.

Lindsey, R., and E. Verhoef. 2001. "Traffic Congestion and Congestion Pricing," in *Handbook of Transport Systems and Traffic Control*, edited by K. J. Button and D. Hensher. Oxford, UK: Pergamon.

May, A. T. 1975. "Supplementary Licensing: An Evaluation." *Traffic Engineering and Control* 16: 162–167.

May, A. T., P. W. Guest, and K. Gardner. 1990. "Can Rail-Based Policies Relieve Urban Traffic Congestion?" *Traffic Engineering and Control* 31: 406–407.

Minard, J. 1850. "Notions élémentaires d'économie politique appliquée aux travaux publics." *Annales des Ponts et Chaussés: Mémoires et Documents*, 2d ser. 19 (1): 1–125.

Morrison, S. A. 1986. "A Survey of Road Pricing." *Transportation Research* 20A: 87–97.

National Economic Development Office. 1995. *A Road User's Charge—Londoners Views.* London, UK: NEDO.

Newbery, D. M. G. 1988. "Road User Charges in Britain." *Economic Journal Supplement* 98: 161–76.

Pigou, A. 1920. *The Economics of Welfare.* London, UK: Macmillan.

Ramjerdi, F. 1994. "The Norwegian Experience with Electronic Toll Rings," in *Proceedings of the International Conference on Advanced Technologies in Transportation and Traffic Management.* Singapore: Nanyang Technological University.

Richardson, H. W. 1974. "A Note on the Distributional Effects of Road Pricing." *Journal of Transport Economics and Policy* 8: 82–5.

Robbins, L. 1932. *Essay on the Nature and Significance of Economic Science*. London, UK: Macmillan.

Roy, R. 1998. "Infrastructure Cost Recovery under Allocatively Efficient Pricing." UIC/CER Economic Expert Report.

Sharp, C. H. 1966. "Congestion and Welfare: An Examination of the Case for a Congestion Tax." *Economic Journal* 76: 806–17.

Small, K. A. 1992. "Using the Revenue from Congestion Pricing." *Transportation* 19: 359-381.

Small, K. A., and J. A. Gómez-Ibáñez. 1998. "Road Pricing for Congestion Management: The Transition from Theory to Policy," in *Road Pricing, Traffic Congestion and the Environment*, edited by K. J. Button and E. Verhoef. Cheltenham, UK: Edward Elgar.

Solheim, T. 1990. "The Toll-Ring in Oslo." Paper presented to the Ecology and Transport Conference, Gothenburg.

Transport for London. 2004. *Congestion Charging Central London: Impacts Monitoring Second Annual Report*. London, UK: Transport for London.

UK Department of Environment, 2000. Transport and the Regions. *Breaking the Logjam: The Government's Response to the Consultation*. London, UK: HMSO.

UK Ministry of Transport. 1964. *Road Pricing: The Economic and Technical Possibilities*. London, UK: HMSO.

Verhoef, E. 1996. *The Economics of Road Pricing*. Cheltenham, UK: Edward Elgar.

Walters, A. A. 1968. *The Economics of Road User Charges*. Baltimore, MD: Johns Hopkins Press.

Part IV

History of Privately Provided Roads

11

The Rise and Fall of Non-Government Roads in the United Kingdom[*]

Bruce L. Benson

I. Introduction

Highways and roads are frequently cited as "important examples of production of public goods," and it is often contended that "private provision of these public goods will not occur," as in Samuelson and Nordhaus (1985, pp. 48–49, 713). Most people probably think that a "public good" is "a good produced by the public sector (i.e., the government)," but this is not the case, at least as the term is used by policy analysts concerned with the question of whether a good or service *should* be produced by the public sector. Perhaps the most widely accepted definition of a public good in this context originates with Samuelson's now-classic analysis (1954, 1955, 1969) and involves two elements: non-excludability and indivisibility or non-rivalrous consumption (Cowen 1988, p. 3). Non-rivalrous consumption means that even though one person consumes the benefits of the good, everyone else can consume the same undiminished benefits. Thus, for instance, if roads are public goods, then the fact that one person benefits from the ability to drive on an interstate highway or an urban street would not prevent another person or another million persons from consuming the *same* level of benefits (i.e., time costs would not rise due to congestion). Non-excludability means that, not only unlimited numbers of people consume the benefits, but no one can be prevented from consuming

[*]This chapter freely draws from but also expands on Benson (1994). I want to thank Gabriel Roth, as well as Alex Tabarrok, for their helpful comments and suggestions on an earlier draft.

245

them either, even if they do not pay their share of the costs. Such free access creates "free-rider" incentives: Individuals recognize that they can consume the benefits without paying, so they will not voluntarily pay for the good. This in turn means that private producers will not produce the good because they cannot collect revenues to cover costs (or, at least, that they will not produce enough of the good because, while everyone can free ride, some may not), and provides the basis for arguments such as those in Samuelson and Nordhaus (1985, pp. 48–49, 713), which contend that the private sector will not provide roads and highways. Indeed, given free riding and the market's failure to produce enough of the good, such analysis provides a justification for coercive taxation to collect from free riders.[1]

Despite the widespread characterization of roads as public goods, the fact is that privately provided roads were common in the area now constituting the United Kingdom. Public highways evolved, not because of the absence of privately produced roads, but because of government-mandated changes in and limitations on property rights that undermined incentives to produce and maintain the private alternatives.[2] Thus, the contention here is that roads and highways are not natural "public goods" that are *necessarily* characterized by non-excludability and non-rivalrous consumption. Instead, given the current property-rights framework, roads are better understood as "common pools," goods that can become congested and likely will become congested when free access, that is, non-excludability, is mandated by government. By adjusting the property rights framework to allow excludability, roads can become either private goods or club goods. A private road is one owned by an individual or an economic organization (e.g., a firm) with a right to exclude everyone else (e.g., a road on a privately owned farm with a locked gate). The owner's use (consumption) decision prevents others from consuming the good, although the owner may choose to allow selective access, of course, perhaps by charging a toll. A club good is one for which access is limited to those who are members of the club (e.g., residents of a private development or homeowners association that owns the roads in the community), so it too can be non-rivalrous and likely will be non-rivalrous if the owners and managers of the good are able to (allowed to) exclude non-paying customers (e.g., with gates, tolls, etc.). Note that if a good is subject to congestion at realistic levels of consumption and if it can be made excludable, either as a private good or a club good, at reasonable cost then the argument that government provision is either necessary or desirable is quite weak, certainly much weaker than if the good were a pure public good.

The institution of property (the network of rules regarding ownership, access, and transfer procedures) determines how the resources of society will be brought into use. For the most part, scarce resources will be used no matter what the property rights system is, however; the nature of the rights structure influences the way they will be used, and therefore, the potential for enhancing well-being or wealth.[3] When people have free or "common" access to a scarce resource (e.g., an urban highway) the "common pool" becomes crowded (e.g., with cars) and the resource (the highway) deteriorates in quality as the result of over use (traffic congestion). This has been called the "tragedy of the commons,"[4] and it arises largely because no user is fully liable for the cost of his or her use. Part of the costs is shifted onto other users (other drivers who are delayed, suffer accidents, and so on) and potential users (e.g., people who would use it but for the rapid deterioration, which "crowds them out," inducing them to choose some alternative), so users have relatively weak incentives to reduce use (highway trips). Therefore, the commons deteriorates rapidly (e.g., congestion and delay is common, potholes and other damage occur), perhaps even being destroyed.

Crowding and rapid deterioration are not the only consequences of common access. The deterioration in quality could be offset with appropriate investments in maintenance or improvement, but the individuals with common access to the resource do not have incentives to make such investments because they cannot charge others who consume the benefits or prevent them from doing so (other drivers will add trips on the highway). While this looks like a free rider problem it is actually a common pool under-investment problem. Indeed, while some may contend that "non-excludable public goods" and "free-access common pools" are simply two terms for the same concept because the under-investment implications are the same, this inference is inappropriate.[5] As Minasian (1964, p. 77) explains, for instance, the public goods terminology often is "asserted" to imply that non-excludability is an intrinsic problem that cannot be resolved without coercing free riders into paying for the good. In contrast, the common pool terminology emphasizes that incentives arise because of the definition of property rights, and therefore, that another property rights assignment may alter such incentives. That is, while the common-pool under-investment problem looks like a public good free-rider problem, the incentives motivating such behavior are quite different and so are the solutions. The implication of free riding is that taxes should be charged because non-payers cannot be excluded, but the implication of common pool resources is that access should be limited (i.e., property rights should be assigned), perhaps by charging a price (toll) for use and excluding non-payers, or by erection of gates at the entrance to a private community to exclude people who are not residents or guests (other limits on access to roads are often practiced by governments, of course, thus undermining the non-excludability claim: These include licensing requirements, laws against drunk driving, fuel taxes, and even public tolls in some cases, although some of these limits are very costly to enforce and all of them are likely to be subject to polit-

ical manipulation that benefit some groups at the expense of others). Beyond
that, a property rights approach actually explains both the historical evolution and modern production of highways, in the United Kingdom at least; public goods analysis does not.

The United Kingdom actually had an extensive system of voluntarily created
and maintained roads, but actions taken by various kings and then by parlia-
ments changed the effective property rights arrangement and undermined the
incentives to maintain the system. The state was then forced to step in, creating a system of "public" (i.e., common-pool) highways. The voluntary non-
governmental provision of early roads and highways in the United Kingdom
is described in Section II. The actions taken by the state that undermined this
arrangement, consisting of a mix of club goods and private goods, are also considered in Section II. Section III considers the rise and fall of an alternative private arrangement that developed as a consequence of the breakdown in the voluntary system: the turnpike trusts and their toll roads. Despite initial success
and widespread use, the political manipulation of trusts and their tolls (e.g.,
mandating that trusts could not earn profits, preventing competition, granting
exemptions to tolls for some groups, setting excessive tolls for others) led to
significant inefficiencies within this system and its ultimate demise, as demonstrated in Section III. Thus, it was government failure that undermined private
provision of roads, not market failure. Section IV concludes.

II. Roads in Medieval Great Britain

There is evidence of a network of roads in Britain prior to the Roman conquest, although much of it is indirect (Jackman, 1966, p. 3; Gregory, 1932,
pp. 45–55). The Romans, who arrived in 43 AD, built some "great military
highways" in Britain as they did elsewhere in their empire, in order to move
their legions into the remote regions of the Island where the Briton's resistance was strongest (Jackman, 1966, p. 1). These roads also facilitated trade
and other types of long-distant travel, of course. There is little doubt that the
Roman roads, largely constructed with "public" funding, were important transportation arteries for centuries, but the Roman road system "was by no means
so good nor so complete" that a much larger system of other roads was not
needed (Jackman, 1966, p. 4; also see Gregory, 1932, p. 94), and these other
roads were not funded or maintained by government.[6]

Roads in the Early Medieval Period

With the fall of Rome, Europe moved into a period dominated by very
localized and largely self-sufficient agricultural communities, and this was

accompanied by a dramatic decline in the amount of long-distant travel. Direct knowledge of the process of development and maintenance of roads in Britain during the early medieval period between the Roman occupation and the twelfth or thirteenth century is almost non-existent, but a good deal of understanding can be inferred by considering evidence of the kinds of travel that still did occur, and by examining the system of roads and customary arrangements for road maintenance that existed shortly thereafter. For instance, the fact that at least some roads were in good condition (some of them probably being Roman in origin) is evidenced by the records of military marches, some averaging as much as fifty miles per day (Gregory 1932, p. 94). Similarly, Anglo-Saxon and early Norman kings (after 1066) and their courts "also moved incessantly around the kingdom, occasionally with the army" (Hindle 1982, p. 193), traveling from estate to estate throughout the year, thus requiring passable roads to carry a "very sizable company" (Stenton 1936, p. 6). Royal income for Anglo-Saxon kings was mostly in the form of the agricultural output of the royal estates, and the king had to travel from estate to estate in order to consume this output and maintain his court (Benson 1992). Records also indicate that representatives of the king traveled extensively, and the level of such travel increased dramatically after the Norman Conquest. The Normans established one of the most centralized governments in Great Britain that existed in all of Europe at the time, and this required a substantial amount of travel by government officials such as tax collectors and judges (who often were the same individuals [Benson 1992]), as well as politically connected citizens (e.g., barons, representatives of the major Church institutions such as abbeys and monasteries) who had to visit the court. Furthermore, Britain had reasonably steady advances in population and in culture during this period, and trade also was clearly expanding throughout Europe during eleventh and twelfth centuries (Benson 1989): Within Britain (and elsewhere), this required increasingly extensive internal communications (Gregory, 1932, p. 95; Willan 1976, p. 13). Most commercial retailing activities took place at fairs during this period, and merchants traveled from fair to fair in order to sell their wares and buy others (Benson 1989). Finally, representatives of the Church with its widespread holdings also traveled extensively, as explained below. Clearly, as Stenton (1936, p. 21) notes, the road system in medieval Britain was adequate for "the requirements of an age of notable economic activity, and it made possible a centralization of national government to which there was no parallel in Western Europe." However, the system of roads was not being created nor maintained by that centralized national government.

While an increasing amount of long-distant travel occurred in the early medieval period in Britain, the fact is that the vast majority of travel by road still involved local people traveling short distances (Beresford and St. Joseph 1979, p. 273):

> Journeys to markets, churches and courts are the principal exceptions to the generalization that most medieval roads were entirely local in purpose with an ambition no higher that to serve the villagers' immediate wants. There was need for lanes to provide access to holdings in the fields; to take loaded wagons to the windmill or to the watermill in the meadows; to reach the woodland with its timber, its fruit and its pannage for swine; to take the flock to the common pastures and heaths. The course of the roads with a purpose so narrow would be determined only by local needs.

Thus, most of the benefits of roads were internal to the members of local close-knit communities, and local institutions and customs determined how those roads were created and maintained, because for all intents and purposes, these roads were club goods. Outsiders (representatives of the king and the Church, merchants) could not necessarily be excluded, but their use of any particular road was actually extremely limited, so virtually all of the benefits of road provision and maintenance were captured by the individuals who lived in the local area.

By the tenth century, there was a clearly recognized institutional arrangement in Anglo-Saxon England called the "hundred." Blair (1956, p. 232) points out that two of the primary purposes of these organizations were to facilitate cooperation in rounding up stray cattle and in pursuing justice. When a theft occurred, for example, the several "tithings" that made up the hundred were informed: They had a reciprocal duty to cooperate in pursuit and prosecution. A tithing was apparently a group of neighbors, many of whom probably were kin. The tithing and hundred performed many other functions, however, including dispute resolution, and road maintenance. A primary reason for recognizing reciprocal duties, such as duties to pursue stray cattle and thieves, and to maintain local roads, that went along with membership in the tithings and hundreds was that these organizations produced a number of private benefits, such as the return of stray cattle, restitution to a victims, rights of passage and clear routes for members in order to travel in the local area, and so on. Fulfilling one's duties to his neighbors was expected to result in reciprocal benefits in the future when the individual might need the support of his neighbors.[7] This was a system of "bottom-up" (customary) club good provision based on reciprocity arising through voluntary repeated exchange, rather than a system of top-down command from the royal court.

While there is no actual documentation of local road maintenance and production before manorial records began to be produced in the twelfth and thirteenth centuries (Webb and Webb 1913, p. 5), several inferences can be drawn regarding what was done. First, road construction and maintenance did not involve anything like modern highway construction with special road surfaces (Rome used surfacing materials but in early medieval Britain such technology was either unavailable or too costly, given the benefits and the lack of congestion costs and overuse). Indeed, the word road apparently comes from the Anglo-Saxon word "ridan" (to ride), which may derive from the verb "rid," meaning to free or clear away any obstruction. This is suggested by the fact that those with customary obligations to other members of a hundred to maintain roads within the area were primarily responsible for removing any impediments to travel such as overhanging trees, hedges, logs, and perhaps water, through a drainage ditch (Webb and Webb 1913, pp. 6–7). Second, some of the customary property rights to the land over which a road passed actually "belonged" to the owner of the land on either side of the road: if a road was abandoned (e.g., because travelers began beating a different path), it would revert to that landowner (Pawson 1977, pp. 65–66). However, under Anglo-Saxon custom, one of the rights to that property was assigned to the community: "[T]he right of passage was a communal right" (Pawson 1977, p. 66). Indeed, the concept of the highway referred to this customary right of passage rather than to the roadway or path itself (Jackman 1966, p. 5). Third, manorial records indicate that all landowners had a customary obligation to the rest of the local community to watch over the roads that were on their land and keep them clear of obstructions (Jackman 1966, p. 4). And it also became the common custom that the members of the hundred (and later the parish) were responsible for seeing that all members maintained the roadways over their lands (Jackman 1966, p. 33). The actual need for enforcement was rare (Bodey 1971, p. 14) due to the reciprocities that existed within these communities. Individuals cleared the roads out of recognition of the benefits of cooperation with their neighbors.

As inter-community trade developed and other long-distance travel increased, particularly by members of the Church and by government officials, some local roads that connected with neighboring local roads into a web of potential long-distance travel came under increasing pressure. As the demand for good connections between different communities' road networks increased, the customary right of passage that had evolved, primarily as a right for members of local communities, was being extended to community outsiders (e.g., traveling merchants, representatives of the Church and of the crown) and apparently, for some of those communities, creating a common pool problem of over use. There also was a growing problem of under-maintenance for these long-distance connections as most members' local communities had relatively little interest in maintaining connecting arteries and bridges to benefit the long distance travelers who would use them.[8] Of the three groups demanding a means for long-distance travel, and who were therefore most responsible for the increasing costs of road maintenance, however, it was the Church and the merchant community that took up the task, not the royal government. As Albert (1972, p. 3) explains: "In England the various transport sectors developed gradually and were controlled almost entirely by private enterprise."

Merchants and Monasteries: Connecting Roads in the Late Middle Ages

Numerous examples of individual merchants and merchant organizations contributing to the construction and/or maintenance of roads, and especially bridges, can be found (Jackman 1966, pp. 15–16, 30–32; Gregory 1932, pp. 97–98). Some guilds were particularly active in this regard, especially up to and including the fifteenth century, when most of the business of the country was conducted at local fairs to which merchants traveled. After the fifteenth century the importance of fairs declined, in part because of the establishment of more permanent markets (Benson 1989).[9] However, some guilds and wealthy merchant benefactors continued supporting bridges and roads well into eighteenth century, as Pawson (1977, p. 73) explains:

> Many private improvements were, of course, carried out purely in self interest. New roads were built to promote the exploitation of mineral wealth within estates, and to enable landowners to divert existing highways . . . Sometimes an economic interest led to improvements in the surrounding area, benefiting everyone. . . . However, when there was little direct return to those involved in private schemes, there efforts were primarily for the social good. It was illegal for a toll to be charged on a public highway without the consent of parliament so it was not possible to charge those who benefited from such works except by voluntary means.

Nonetheless, there were actually some very important rewards for such local benefactors in the form of local prestige and respect. After all, roads played a very significant role in determining the success of a town and its established markets (Hindle 1982, p. 207), so other members of the community would tend to be very grateful to someone who aided the community in this way. Building and maintaining roads and bridges was an investment in reputation, not unlike advertisers who pay for television programming to be broadcast free of charge (see Minasian 1964).[10] Thus, the roads and bridges created by merchants were either private (e.g., a road on private land leading to a mine or some other economically important location) or club goods, where the club was functionally based (a guild, the merchant community that traveled over particular routes) and not necessarily geographically based (e.g., a local community), although it could be (the merchant community of a market town). And for Christians even more significant personal benefits were anticipated from participation in the provision of roads as a club good.

The medieval Church probably had greater demands for long-distant travel than the medieval royal court. The Church encouraged pilgrimages (e.g., the road from Winchester to the shrine of Thomas Beckett in Canterbury became known as the Pilgrims Way and was immortalized by Chaucer). The Church also maintained frequent tours by peripatetic preachers and friars. Perhaps the most significant source of Church travel was the monasteries, however: Their scattered estates required constant visits (Gregory 1932, p. 95; Jackman 1966, p. 8). Thus, the Church promulgated the belief that care of the roads was "a work of Christian beneficence, well pleasing to God" (Jackman 1966, p. 8). This created incentives for private citizens who held strong Christian beliefs to aid in the maintenance of roads and bridges, and the bishops' registers throughout the United Kingdom provide ample evidence of such activity (Jackman 1966, p. 16). Indeed, it was not uncommon for bequests to be left for the construction or maintenance of a road or bridge (Jackman 1966, p. 15; La Mar 1960, p. 13). More importantly, the monks were assigned, by custom, the responsibility of maintaining the roads and they willing took on the task because it "was a pious work highly to be commended" (Jackman 1966, pp. 30–31). Such religious beliefs also probably explain the longstanding customary obligation that local parishes had for road maintenance (Jackman 1966, p. 30; Pawson 1977, p. 68) after the decline of the hundreds. By promulgating such beliefs, the Church hierarchy could create incentives for local parishioners to maintain roads throughout the country. Indeed, with the breakdown of the Anglo-Saxon hundreds under the Normans, the parishes apparently took on the major obligations of road maintenance, with the aid, encouragement, and where necessary, supervision of the monasteries and bishops of the Church.[11]

The various groups and individuals who maintained roads in the United Kingdom prior to 1500 were apparently quite effective, given the technology available. Indeed, the "essence of a modern road pattern existed in the early fourteenth century" and transportation of goods and passengers "could be easily and efficiently undertaken by road" at least throughout southern England and the Midlands (Darby 1973, pp. 174, 287). The system of voluntary road maintenance, based on the cooperation of the monasteries and parishes, was ultimately undermined, however, by the almost continuous struggle for power between the English kings and the Church. Henry VIII finally dissolved the monasteries in 1536–39, divided their properties, and transferred them to "a class of rapacious landlords who would be slow to recognize any claim upon their rents for the maintenance of roads. . . . The inevitable result would be a rapid decadence of many highways which had hitherto been in common use" (Jackman 1966, p. 29; also see Gregory 1932, p. 96; and Parkes 1925, p. 7). While various individuals and guilds continued to provide support for some roads and bridges, the elimination of the monasteries and the undermining of the incentives of the Church to encourage its parishioners to maintain roads in general was apparently quite significant, at least in some areas. Parishes continued to maintain roads that were primarily used for local travel and therefore not subject to heavy use and damage (probably 80 to 85 percent of the actual roads in Great Britain, as explained below), but those routes that were heavily used by long-distance travelers (possibly 15 to 20 percent of the roads), and that had been maintained by the monasteries, began to deteriorate. Indeed, Jackman (1966, pp. 30–31) contends that this was the primary reason for passage of the "Statute for Mending of Highways" in 1555, which mandated that parishes establish a very specific institutional arrangement for maintenance of *all* roads in each parish.

The Parish System

Parish members had long recognized a customary reciprocal obligation to one another to keep the roads within a parish clear of obstacles, but the incentives to do so were being undermined where substantial use by non-parish members existed. Therefore, under the 1555 statute, the parishes were mandated to perform certain obligations for all travelers. Two surveyors of highways were to be chosen by the local justices-of-the-peace (JPs) from a list provided by each parish.[12] The surveyors were ordered to travel the parish at least three times a year to inspect the roads and bridges, see to it that the owners of the land over which roads passed were keeping the roads and ditches clear of impediments, watch for and stop any wagons that were drawn by more than an allowed number of horses or oxen, and announce before the church meeting any violators of the statute. They were also required to collect and account for the fines, compositions, and commutations that arose in conjunction with highway maintenance or lack thereof. The JPs were to audit the surveyors' accounts, hear pleas of excuse for non-fulfillment of the statute's labor requirements (discussed below), levy fines and order seizures for violations, and when necessary, collect a tax from the parish residents to cover an extraordinary expense. Furthermore, both the JPs and the surveyors were to perform their tasks without compensation. All of the manual labor, tools, horses, and carts needed for repairing the roads were to be provided by the parishioners, also without any compensation: "Every person for every plough-land in tillage or pasture" and "every person keeping a draught (of horses) or plough in the Parish" had to provide a cart with oxen or horses, the necessary tools and two men annually to work four eight-hour days (raised to six days in 1563) in road maintenance on the days chosen by the surveyors. Those households that did not own farm land, horses, or a plough were also required to provide labor, either in person or hired, for the same period.[13]

For most of the roads where travel remained largely local, the mandated obligations of the highway statute of 1555 were largely unnecessary, and for roads that were heavily used by travelers who did not live in the local community, they were unsuccessful. In most rural areas where through traffic was minimal so that the benefits and costs of road maintenance were largely internal to the parish, it appears that roads were not deteriorating significantly. On the other hand, the mandated obligations were not sufficient for the maintenance of many of the major arteries of long-distance travel—those roads over which government officials and merchants traveled, and where traffic by heavy wagons, long pack trains, and herds of cattle "kept the roads in a perpetual slough" (Parkes 1925, pp. 6–7)—particularly in the area of London. As Parkes (1925, p. 8) notes, "Though an elaborate system, it neither sought to introduce any effective method of repair nor took heed of the frailty of human nature." Parishioners were unwilling to bear the high costs of maintenance (Albert 1972, p. 8; Darby 1973, pp. 290, 372) when the road was a free-access common pool whose benefits were being consumed by outsiders (Pawson 1977, pp. 68–69). Indeed, these costs were often made even higher because the best time of the year for road repairs was also the busiest time of the year for most parishioners since they were engaged in agricultural production (Parkes 1925, p. 9). Furthermore, the burdens placed on the parishioners seemed to them to be very inequitably distributed (Webb and Webb 1913, p. 29). Thus, many did not show up for the mandated work, others sent their children or some other substitute instead, and as Parkes (1925, p. 9) reports, those who did present themselves for work, "often poor men who could ill afford wageless days—would spend most of their time in standing still and prating, or asking for largesse of the passers-by . . . so that they became known as The King's Loiterers, in derision of their earlier title, the King's Highwaymen." This meant that JPs were obliged to collect large numbers of fines from those who were unwilling to work (Willan 1976, p. 3). Indeed, a long series of statutes followed that attempted to create sufficient negative incentives for the parishioners and surveyors to do their mandated duties. Ultimately none worked and the system of fines developed into commutations to be collected from individual parishioners that relieved their obligations to perform the statutorily mandated duties and allowed the JPs to hire laborers to work under the supervision of the surveyors (Pawson 1977, p. 71; Webb and Webb 1913, pp. 20–21). This source of funds proved inadequate for the heavily traveled arteries, however: "Indeed, what with the lack of any definite valuation roll or fixed assessment, the complications and uncertainty of the law, and the unwillingness of both Surveyors and Justices to be at the trouble of legal proceedings against their neighbors, it is plain that under the commutation system the greatest inequality and laxness prevailed" (Webb and Webb 1913, p. 36). Thus, commutations were supplemented with a general highway tax from the mid-seventeenth century onward. However, an even more important source of funds was generated through the criminal law by fines levied through presentment or indictment of the parish as a whole for the non-repair of its highways (Webb and Webb 1913, pp. 51–61). Some parishes were perpetually under indictment, and "At varying dates in the different Counties, but eventually . . . nearly all over England, it became the regular thing for a parish periodically to find itself indicted at the Sessions for neglecting to keep its highways in repair" and to pay a substantial fine rather than repair the roads (Webb and Webb 1913, pp. 53–54). Despite these sources of revenues, however, the quality of road and bridge construction and repair on the major arteries did not compare to what had been done under the supervision and encouragement of the monks in the previous centuries (Parkes 1925, p. 30; and see Jackman 1966, pp. 48–49). Part of the problem was that surveyors, typically farmers who served for a single year, had no expertise in organizing road repairs and no incentives to see that it was done well (after all, some other farmer would be responsible for taking care of the problems next year if they were not completed), in contrast to the monks who had specialized in such activities and considered them to be long-term obligations to God. In addition, the mandated repair procedure (e.g., periodic large-scale efforts rather than ongoing repairs as damage began to appear) was itself not the most efficient way to carry out the task (LaMar 1960, pp. 8–10).

III. An Alternative Solution: Turnpike Trusts and Toll Roads

Roads obviously do not have to be treated as common pool resources. Tolls can be charged and non-payers can be excluded, given appropriate property rights and enforcement. However, in the United Kingdom, the right to charge a toll was severely restricted by kings and then by Parliament. Landowners could charge for the right to pass through private grounds as long as a customary right of passage had not been established, and there is considerable evidence that enterprising landowners began to establish and charge tolls on new "private roads" that allowed travelers to avoid the "ill-repaired public highways" (Pawson 1977, pp. 73–74). Furthermore, the king, and later Parliament, could grant the power to collect tolls to private individuals or organizations, and there is evidence that the burgesses (merchants who formed local governments) of several market communities had petitioned for and been granted the right to collect tolls as early as 1154 (Jackman 1966, pp. 9–11).

Tolls were, in fact, an important source of royal revenues (e.g., see Jackman 1966, p. 11), however, although the officials and communities that collected them could retain some portion for their own purposes, including for road and bridge maintenance (but these revenues were rarely directed at this function). Therefore, those in government were reluctant to grant the power to collect tolls to others. The dissolution of the monasteries and the failure of the parish system to maintain the major long-distance arteries of the country left the government with few options, however. One that was tried was the passage of a long series of regulations defining "unreasonable" uses of the roads by establishing weight limits, limits on the number of horses, and so on (see Pawson 1977, pp. 74–75). That is, there was an attempt to ration the commons through various restrictions on how it could be used. The local officials expected to enforce these laws were reluctant to do so, though (except on the turnpikes discussed below), because they were expected to carry out their enforcement duties without compensation. The second and more important approach was to loosen the central government's control over and claim to tolls so that charges for actual road users could be made by local organizations.

A long series of Acts were passed beginning in 1663 that enabled the establishment of local ad hoc bodies known as "Turnpike Trusts." It must be emphasized that these turnpike trusts were not government innovations. The initiative was at the local level (Albert 1972, p. 12). Members of local parishes who were burdened by the high costs of road maintenance under the parish system began to petition Parliament for the right to charge a tax on heavy loads. Indeed, the earliest Trusts were run by local JPs, although later Trusts had independent bodies of trustees.[14]

After about 1700 the process became increasingly standardized. A group of local landowners and/or merchants would accumulate the money necessary to fund a Turnpike Act in Parliament and to carry the cost of the trust through its start-up period (Moyes 1978, p. 406). Most Turnpike Acts gave legal standing to a Turnpike Trust made up of a number of local landowners, and/or other important parishioners. The Trustees were, by law, unpaid and forbidden to make personal profit from the trust. They were responsible for erecting gates to collect tolls, and for appointing collectors, a surveyor to supervise repairs, and a clerk and treasurer to administer the affairs of the trust. The funds collected could only be applied to the road named in the Act. These roads were usually existing highways, although new roads were also built, particularly after 1740, and the extent of roads that were "usable" for heavy traffic expanded significantly once the trusts began to innovate and improve the roads they controlled (Webb and Webb 1913, p. 144), as noted below. The Trusts were granted a monopoly power over the road (generally for a period of twenty-one years), so that the customary right of passage was fundamentally altered: The roads were no longer common pool resources. Most trusts used the money collected to repair and improve roads, but if the tolls were insufficient to cover the upfront costs, the trusts were allowed to borrow money at a rate of interest fixed by the Act.

The early turnpikes were not an advance from a technological point of view. The turnpikes were maintained using the same techniques that the monasteries and parishes had employed before (Darby 1973, p. 374). Indeed, only about one fifth of the nation's roads became turnpikes (Darby 1973, p. 502) and in general the turnpikes were not in any better condition than the parish roads (Darby 1973, p. 454). This does not mean that the same expense and effort was required to maintain the parish and turnpike roads, of course. Turnpikes developed in the parishes where the commons problems of overuse and under-investment by long-distance travelers were the greatest, while the roads in the remaining parishes were primarily used by members of the community for local travel who willingly kept their roads in repair. Trusts were needed where roads were not kept up by the parishes so considerable additional effort was required to bring these roads up to the quality of those maintained by parishes for their own internal use. At least initially, the turnpikes used conventional methods of repair, but did so far more intensively (Pawson 1977, p. 107). However, Trusts did hire paid surveyors who, thorough specialization, developed expertise in road maintenance, and after 1750 there is considerable evidence of experimentation and innovation in maintenance by some of these specialists. Webb and Webb (1913, p. 144) note, for instance, that,

> Between 1750 and 1770, when the number of Turnpike Trusts was actually trebled, the contemporary self-complacency over the new roads rises to dithyrambic heights. "There never was a more astonishing revolution accomplished in the internal system of any country," declares an able and quite trustworthy writer in 1767, "than has been with the compass of a few years in that of England. The carriage of grain, coals, merchandize, etc., is in general conducted with little more than half the number of horses with which it formerly was. Journeys of business are performed, with more than double expedition. . . . *Everything wears the face of dispatch* . . . and the hinge which has guided all these movements and upon which they turn is the reformation which has been made in our public roads [the turnpikes]."

Innovations in surfacing, road widening, and banking (Webb and Webb 1913, pp. 133–134), and later, improvements in administration (primarily through the combination of small turnpike trusts into larger administrative units supervised by professional road managers/surveyors, thereby reducing the numbers of toll booths and stops that travelers had to make, as discussed below) all made travel in the United Kingdom faster and less expensive, while simultaneously expanding the system of roads that could be used for heavy traffic. As the preceding quote suggests, Turnpike formation really accelerated during the 1750s (and actually, during the 1740s as well), and by 1770 Trusts controlled almost 16,000 miles of turnpikes (Moyes 1978, p. 407). Private control of turnpikes peaked in 1837 when there were 1,116 Turnpike Trusts operating 22,000 miles of roads (Jeffreys 1949, p. 4).

The correspondence between the timing of the turnpike era in the United Kingdom and the beginnings of the industrial revolution is more than accidental. As Webb and Webb (1913, pp. 143–144) explain,

> With the coming the Industrial Revolution, with a rapidly increasing population, with manufactures ready to leap from the ground, with unprecedented opportunities for home and foreign trade, improvement of communication between different parts of the kingdom became, from the standpoint of material property, the most urgent requirement. Today, the railway and the tramway, the telegraph and the telephone, have largely superseded roads as the arteries of national circulation. But, barring a few lengths of canal in the making, and a few miles of navigable river estuaries, it was, throughout the eighteenth century, on the King's Highway alone that depended the manufacturer and the wholesale dealer, the hawker and the shopkeeper, the farmer, the postal contractor, the lawyer, the government official, the traveler, the miner, the craftsman and the farm servant, for the transport of themselves, and the distribution of their products and their purchases, their services and their ideas. . . . And all contemporary evidence indicates that, what with the surface-making and embanking, widening and straightening, leveling and bridging, the mileage of usable roads was, by the eighteenth-century Turnpike trusts, very greatly extended.

The industrial revolution created much stronger demands for transportation services, including expansions in highway networks and increased maintenance of heavily traveled arteries. Indeed, the tremendous increase in economic activity that began during the mid-to-late 1700s could not have occurred without the simultaneous improvements in transportation. The government did not respond by producing highways, so it was left to the private sector to find a way to respond, given the legal constraints imposed by the central government. Thus, it is not surprising that the boom period of the turnpike movement (about 1750 to 1830) corresponds to this period of rapid industrialization, and that the majority of the new trusts were in industrialized areas (Pawson 1977, p. 122). The growth in transportation demands to haul heavy industrial inputs and outputs (along with the increased need to transport agricultural products into the industrial areas to support the manufacturing workforce) also was a major source of road damage, and therefore, it was in these areas that the turnpike option was most attractive due to the more intensive maintenance that they tended to engage in relative to the less used parish roads, as well as to the innovations and improvements in roadways that began to be made, particularly by the larger and more successful (revenue generating) trusts. The early period of the industrial revolution was supported by turnpike road (and to a degree, by water) transport, then, rather than by the railroad system that often seems to get credit for supplying the transportation needs of the revolution. And as Pawson (1977, p. 338) explains,

> The turnpike road system . . . played a fundamental role in repairing and improving the existing road network for the needs of an industrialized nation. It helped to

ensure that transport and communication became quicker, cheaper and more reliable. It fostered the extension of the market and the growth of the information services. In doing so, it played an important and necessary part in the development of agriculture, industry and settlement patterns, in structural change, specialization and expansion . . . many of the changes which have been traditionally ascribed to the railways . . . were already in the eighteenth century, encouraged by the modernization of road transport services and public highways [toll roads].

In fact, the railroads in Britain did not lead economic growth, but tended to respond to it (Pawson 1977, p. 7). More importantly, in this context, the development of the British railroad system did not really begin until the 1820s as the turnpike system was nearing its peak (Pawson 1977, Fig. 3, p. 8), and well after the beginnings of the industrial revolution.[15] And as the railroads spread, providing competition for the turnpike trusts, the trusts responded with even more improvements in roads (Webb and Webb 1913, p. 179) (innovations in road transportation also arose to compete with the railroads, as explained below). Yet, aspects of the industrial revolution also helped lead to the demise of the turnpike system as competing modes of transportation, including the newly developing railroads, and shippers, including manufacturers who wanted reduced their own transport costs (part of which was the tolls they had to pay), manipulated the political process in order to influence the tolls that trusts could charge.

Reasons for the End of the Turnpike System

The Turnpike era came to an end due to a combination of at least three political economy factors. First, the structure and characteristics of the trusts created significant principal-agent problems. The trustees were not allowed to earn a profit. Therefore, even though the trustees had sufficient incentives to invest in the formation of a trust, they generally were not interested in the day-to-day operation of the road. The toll gates were farmed out, and while trustees were supposed to monitor the gate-keepers and surveyors, their incentives to do so were very weak. After all, their primary income generating activities were elsewhere (their farms or businesses) and these enterprises commanded most of their attention. Indeed, they probably got involved in a Turnpike Trust in order to relieve themselves of their parish obligations or fines so they could focus more fully on their potentially profitable enterprises (perhaps along with a desire to improve the roads in their area, particularly if their business required good roads to attract customers or transport inputs and/or products). Their incentives to focus time and effort in monitoring the operations of the toll road were, therefore, very weak. Had these trusts been allowed to earn and retain profits, profit-seeking entrepreneurs would have specialized in the turnpike business, producing very different monitoring and maintenance incentives.

Furthermore, the trusts had monopoly rights and there was no threat of takeover (although a consolidation movement did begin toward the end of the turnpike era, as indicated below), so the market regulator (e.g., the competition for corporate control that regulates managerial behavior in modern corporations) was not at work. With little monitoring and no competition, corruption was rampant "and only a small part of the money collected for the upkeep of the road was in fact used for that purpose" (Hindley 1971, p. 63). Many small trusts fell into financial difficulty, borrowed excessively to build, maintain and/or improve roads because they had to make up for their inefficient management systems, and ended up being unable to meet their debt payments.

Second, the political limitations on trusts also led to significant complaints by shippers and travelers. While they did not want to pay tolls at all, that may not have been the most significant cost imposed by the turnpike system. A serious complaint about the turnpike system as it evolved was that there were too many toll booths, requiring too many stops, thereby slowing transportation services unnecessarily. Gregory (1932, p. 193) suggests, in fact, that this was the most important complaint against the turnpikes: "Road users declared that they would rather pay twice the amount if they could be saved the annoyance of the delay." This problem resulted from the fact that most of the turnpike trusts controlled only short sections of roadway within a parish, so travelers had to pay new tolls each time they left one trust's road and entered another (Webb and Webb 1913, p. 177). While consolidation of small trusts was desirable in order to avoid the problems with excessive stopping and delays (as well as in order to capture various scale economies in management and maintenance), the trusts operated at the prerogative of Parliament, and any formal consolidation required parliamentary approval. Political resistance to consolidation (e.g., by local trustees who did not want to lose control of their roads, and probably by competitive modes that did not want competition from more efficient turnpikes, as explained below) was strong, so even though efforts were made to obtain parliamentary approval to combine small trusts into larger organizations (particular after the reason for doing so was articulated by John Loudon Macadam, beginning around 1810), Parliament did not respond with necessary enabling legislation that might have led to widespread consolidation, choosing instead to deal with such proposals individually and quite slowly (Webb and Webb 1913, pp. 177–180). Some limited consolidations were allowed where advocates had sufficient political influence (Gregory 1932: 194), but the vast majority of the small trusts remained independent until their demise.

Third, there was significant political opposition to the trusts themselves. Opposition came from those involved in competitive transportation modes such as the river and canal barges and railroads (see the discussion below, for instance, regarding the railroads' influence over tolls set on steam carriages), from the trade centers that already had effective transportation connections and feared competition from other centers if their road connections were improved, from some landowners and farmers who feared that better roads would make it easier for their low-wage laborers to be attracted away, from farmers who supplied local markets and feared that improved roads would bring in competition from distant suppliers, from heavy road users who did not want to pay tolls for access even though they wanted the roads to be maintained, and so on. Therefore, in order to gain sufficient support for passage, Turnpike Acts always had to reflect significant political compromise, including long lists of toll-exemptions for some of the powerful individuals and groups who opposed each Act (Albert 1972, pp. 12, 24–29). Agricultural interests and, in some areas, industrial groups, were particularly effective at obtaining exemptions (Jackman 1966, pp. 260–261). Often those who obtained exemptions were some of the worst abusers of what to them remained a common pool resource. Exemptions grew over time (all individual Trust Acts were periodically renewed, with revisions possible) and seriously reduced the revenues of the trusts (Jackman 1966, p. 261).[16] Politics determined the tolls that could be set, not economic considerations. Thus, for instance, "There was no invariable relation, and no necessary connection, between the amount that it cost to keep a particular mile of road in repair, and the amount that could be collected in tolls" (Webb and Webb 1913, p. 216). Indeed, as some road users who did considerable damage to roads were exempted, prohibitively high tolls were established for some types of transportation that did little damage, if it threatened the market for other modes such as railroads.

Politics and the Inefficiency of Transportation Systems: An Example

The political manipulation of turnpike trust legislation by interest groups did more than undermine the development of effective private toll roads. As suggested above, representatives of various transportation industries (e.g., railroads and barges) opposed the establishment of turnpikes that competed with them. However, an extensive turnpike system was actually in place before the railroad system began to develop, so the railroads also attempted to manipulate the tolls that existing turnpikes could charge for various kinds of road use that were particularly competitive. Thus, even when they could not prevent turnpike establishment (because so many turnpikes were in place before the railroads became economically and politically important), they could undermine their competitive impact to a degree by influencing the level of tolls mandated by Parliament. The resulting inefficient allocation of transport services and slowing of innovations for road transportation can be illustrated by examining the way these statutes treated the development of steam-powered carriages, which began to appear on the roads of the United Kingdom in the 1820s, just as the railroads were also being established. Indeed, while it is widely believed that the general use of mechanically propelled road vehicles began in the late nineteenth century, the fact is that sophisticated steam powered vehicles had both commercial and technical success sixty years earlier (Gurney 1831, p. 12; Dance 1831, p. 45; Dalgleish 1980, p. 117). These vehicles could maintain high speeds relative to horse-drawn carriages (24 miles per hour over four miles, and an average of 12 miles per hour over longer distances) and carry more passengers (up to fourteen in 1831). Estimates of the relative costs of operation suggested that steam carriages could run at about a half to a third of the cost of horse-drawn stagecoaches (Gurney 1831, p. 18; Dalgleish 1980, p. 122), and in the absence of discriminatory tolls, per passenger fares were apparently about one half those of stagecoaches (Gurney 1831, p. 12; Dance 1831, p. 45). They were also much safer as they were much less likely to overturn, and steam engines did not "run away with" passengers the way horses could (Gurney 1831, p. 20). While steam carriages were clearly a competitive threat to horse powered transport, they also threatened railroads. These carriages were not limited in the places that they could travel to by the need for rail lines as steam-powered trains were. In addition, railroad passenger service over particular routes was generally monopolized (Dalgleish 1980, p. 117), allowing the railroads to charge relatively high prices. The steam carriages also were a significant competitive threat as compared to horse-drawn carriages because of their speed and carrying capacity. The threat was not allowed to develop, however, as their development was stopped by the extremely high tolls or outright prohibitions imposed by parliamentary mandate (Gurney 1831, p. 17), due to political pressure from railway and horse-carriage interests.

As steam carriages were introduced parliamentary imposed tolls were set at least six times higher than those on horse-drawn stagecoaches (Gurney 1831, p. 22; Dalgleish 1980, p. 117). Furthermore, Parliament imposed outright prohibition of steam carriages in a large number of Turnpike Acts (Dance 1831, p. 48). These very high tolls and prohibitions were imposed despite the fact that "highway engineers were unanimous that injury to the road surface from the action of horses' feet exceeded that caused by the wheels of traffic by a factor of three" (Dalgleish 1980, p. 119). Furthermore, the wheels on horse-drawn vehicles were necessarily made narrow to reduce the effort required of the horses, and these narrow wheels caused considerable rutting. Steam carriages, on the other hand, had very wide tires in order to give them greater traction, and these wide tires did virtually no damage to road surfaces, according to engineers such as Thomas Telford (a leading engineer and road builder who co-founded the Institution of Civil Engineers and was its first president) who testified before a Parliamentary Select Committee that was convened in 1831 to consider the exorbitant tolls on steam carriages and to consider the potential future use of mechanical (steam and gas powered) vehicles (Dalgleish 1980, pp. 118–119). The steam carriages also had innovative braking systems that did not lock and drag like horse-drawn transport, and therefore did less damage to roads, as well as one driving wheel with the potential of engaging a second to prevent slippage.

In light of their safety, cost advantages, speed, capacity, and reduced road damage, the 1831 select committee recommended that the tolls on steam carriage be dramatically reduced (Select Committee on Steam Carriages 1831; Gurney 1831), and if this had occurred, there is "little doubt that a network of good toll roads would have soon been built to take the new vehicles" and that a substantial part of the United Kingdom's railway system would not have been built (Dalgleish 1980, p. 128). However, as Dalgleish (1980, p. 125) notes,

> the prejudices which always beset new inventions proved too powerful. From today's experience of the lobbies which always arise to oppose new developments, we can well imagine what happened. The many interests—corn merchants, harness makers, horse-copers, railway promoters, iron masters hoping to make rails, and those who were simply against change—would unite against steam carriages. It was only necessary for parliament to do nothing for them to be killed off, and nothing is what it did.

Dance (1831, p. 46) also notes that coach proprietors, coachmen, and postboys were in the opposition. As a result of such widespread political resistance to competition, the use of mechanical vehicles on Britain's roads was delayed for some sixty years.[17] But the political barriers to efficient tolls, whether too high as was the case for steam carriages, or too low, as often was the case for agricultural and industrial shippers, did much more than protect the railroads and horse-drawn carriage industries and their suppliers. It undermined the incentives of voluntary organizations to provide and maintain toll roads.

The success of the railroads and their carriage industry allies in undermining the innovations in steam carriages was probably an important reason for the demise of the turnpike trusts. Webb and Webb (1913, pp. 215–216) describe the "calamity of the railways" (terminology they adopted from Sir James Macadam) that befell the turnpike trusts. With the development of the short lines between Stockton and Darlington in 1825 and then between Liverpool and Manchester in 1830, passenger traffic by turnpike (stagecoaches, postchaises, and private horse-drawn carriages) between these points declined dramatically. The turnpikes had come to depend on such passenger traffic for revenues, in part because so many other forms of traffic had toll exemptions or limitations. Ironically, for the horse-drawn passenger service industry and its supporters who joined the railroads to undermine the development of the steam carriage industry, the advantage going to the railroads quickly led to the end of horse-powered passenger transportation as well. Without the steam carriage as a more effective competitor for the railroads, "The transfer of this business was instantaneous and complete. Every coach had to be taken off the road the moment the railway was open to the towns along its route" (Webb and Webb 1913, p. 215). The railroads under-priced the stagecoaches and traveled much faster. As the railroads spread road traffic declined. The last stagecoach between London and Birmingham went out of business in 1839, for instance, with other routes from London ending their runs over the next few years (to Bristol in 1843, Plymouth in 1847, Bedford in 1848). Turnpike toll revenues fell by one third between 1837 and 1850 as railroads spread through the country. As a result, more and more Trusts were unable to maintain their financial solvency, defaulting on debt payments, let alone generating sufficient revenues to maintain their roads (for many, creditors took immediate possession of tolls and all revenues were used to cover interest on bonds).

Public Takeover of Roads

The combination of the lack of a profit motive and competition, which created serious principal-agent problems and corruption, political exemptions of many heavy road users, and mandated high tolls on some road transport services (e.g., steam carriages) that were seen as competitive (i.e., low cost) threats to other transport modes with political connections (e.g., railways, horse-drawn carriages), meant that many trusts were unable to fully finance road maintenance. Rather than solving the underlying incentive problems, however, by allowing trusts to charge market determined tolls and perhaps even earn profits, and by allowing competition to develop, the government began to empower the trusts to draw on "statute labor" (the labor that the parishioners were mandated to provide under the 1555 highway statute). Initially the trusts were required to pay wages fixed by Parliament, but later a portion of the labor was required without payment (Hindley 1971, p. 62). Some trusts were even given parliamentary authority to appropriate materials without payment. Finally, the parishes could still be held responsible for the conditions of a turnpike. Indeed, under the law, the parishes had never lost this liability although it had not been enforced on the turnpikes, and while they were supposedly able to recover any money they spent from the turnpikes' revenues, the trusts that failed in their road maintenance were generally so far in debt that parishes had little chance of repayment. As chronic insolvency spread with the spreading "calamity of the railways," the burden of maintenance for more and more turnpikes was shifted, once again, onto the parishes. The same incentives were at work in the parishes that existed at the beginning of the turnpike era, of course, so this reversion to common pools simply led to resentment that actually flared into a "conclusive popular rebellion known as the Rebecca Riots" in South Wales during 1842–43 (Webb and Webb 1913, p. 217). This led to a royal Commission to inquire about the grievances in South Wales, and finally to the dismissal of all Turnpike Trustees throughout the area and the merger of all trusts into "County Road Boards," which took over the roads, their debts, and the tolls of the former trusts. A "General Superintendent of County Roads in South Wales" was also appointed by the central government, putting the roads in the area "Under what was virtually Government control," which also advanced 218,000 pounds to pay off creditors and consolidated debts, county by county, at lower interest rates (Webb and Webb 1913, pp. 219–220). These county organizations substantially reduced the number of toll gates as well as the level of tolls that had led to the revolts. The consolidated Trusts actually were able to operate efficiently enough to pay off their debts over the next thirty years, suggesting that if Parliament had responded earlier to the need for consolidation the riots and subsequent government control might have been avoided. Furthermore, if consolidation of a similar "sort could have been done with the English Turnpike Trusts in 1844, they might have been spared the long-drawn-out agony of the ensuing half-century. But every attempt at legislation was defeated" (Webb and Webb 1913, p. 220). Efforts that involved central government control was opposed by Justices of the Peace and other local groups,[18] and consolidation efforts in general were resisted by the self-interested employees of the local trusts (treasures, attorneys, clerks, toll collectors). Efforts to consolidate the debt of the more than 1,100 local trusts in England also proved to be a serious impediment (the central government would have had to put up substantial amounts of funds and the creditors would have had to give up their high interest rates). As Webb and Webb (1913, p. 220) explain, "So far as the government was concerned, under the timid and unresourceful advice of the Home Office, and the refusal of successive Cabinets to trouble themselves about the subject, the Turnpike Trusts were allowed to go on just as before, annually getting their expiring terms renewed by Parliament, as a matter of course, falling, most of them, progressively further and further behind their task, and many of them, deeper and deeper into insolvency."

Finally, in the early 1860s, political sentiment shifted enough so that Parliament was ready to begin getting rid of tolls and therefore Trusts. The political manipulation of tolls meant that powerful groups were getting exemptions. Others felt that they should too. Opposition to the turnpikes grew, from farmers, miners, and non-exempt carriers who also wanted free access to carry large loads over the turnpikes (Albert 1972, p. 26). These groups also wanted the free access roads to be maintained, of course, but they did not want to contribute either mandated labor services or toll payments to that maintenance. The Highway Act of 1862 started the process of creating Highway Boards throughout the rest of the United Kingdom to which the turnpikes would be entrusted. A Select Commission of the House of Commons was formed in 1864 to consider the question of how to end all tolls. The Commission's report concluded that the tolls were "unequal in pressure, costly in collection, inconvenient to the public, injurious as causing a serious impediment to intercourse and traffic" (all of which arose because of the politically created constraints on the trusts, of course), that the trusts should be abolished, and that the best course of action would be turn the roads over to a government authority, as in South Wales (Quoted in Webb and Webb 1913, p. 221). Nevertheless, Parliament did not respond to these recommendations by establishing a general policy. Instead, a gradual abolition of more and more tolls began. Most Trusts, and especially those that were financially sound, were renewed each year, although from 1864 onward, twenty to thirty trusts were dissolved each year, with the roads turned over to a local parish or a highway district. Dissolution began to accelerate, however, and in 1871 all tolls were ended in the London area. The number of trusts was down to 854 in 1871, 588 in 1875, 184 in 1881, seventy-one in 1883, fifteen in 1887, and two in 1890. The last trust ended its operations in November of 1895, at almost the exact time that the parish obligation to maintain highways came to an end.

The increasing rate of dissolution of the trusts rapidly placed thousands of miles of roads back into the care of the parishes, leading to increased local resentment. In order to mitigate some of the local resentment the central government began giving Grants in Aid in 1876 to help cover the cost of maintenance. Then in 1878 the Highway and Locomotive Act ordered the counties to contribute half of the annual cost of maintaining the former turnpike roads. The Local Government Act of 1888 granted more aid from the central treasury to counties for road maintenance but required the county governments to take over full maintenance obligations for all of the "main" roads in their counties. Thus, county governments were becoming the local road authority, and as noted above, the parishes were finally formally dissolved of their road maintenance liability in 1895. "Thus at length the British road system was placed under control of elected public authorities each representing larger areas" (Gregory 1932, p. 196). Funding shifted from tolls to county (or in places, borough or other local government[19]) taxes along with some subsidies from the national government, and government expenditures on roads increased rapidly. The average government expenditure per mile of county roads rose from 43 pounds in 1890 to 69 pounds in 1902, for instance while expenditures on urban roads increased from 49 to 207 pounds over the same period (Gregory 1932, p. 196).

Free access to roads led to new types of road users, as first bicycles and tricycles began to appear. By the end of the nineteenth century many highways had more bicycle traffic than horse drawn traffic, and virtually every country home had a bicycle. As Webb and Webb (1913, pp. 240–241) report, "What the bicyclist did for the roads, between 1888 and 1900, was to rehabilitate through traffic, and accustom us all to the idea of our highways being used by other than local residents. It was the bicyclist who brought the road once more into popular use for pleasure riding." This was followed by the automobile (excessive tolls had kept the steam carriage off the roads, but the end of tolls and the advent of light internal combustion engines in 1885 led to the introduction of the first petroleum driven motor cars in England in about 1894).

The commons problem was becoming evident as bicycles and especially automobiles alarmed horses and pedestrians, and raised dust due to their speed (roads were largely still surfaced with gravel at this time): "[T]he turning loose on our roads of tens of thousands of heavy vehicles, often travelling at speed of an express train, amounted to a real aggression on the safety and comfort of all the other users of the roads" (Webb and Webb 1913, p. 214). Accidents increased dramatically, generally at the cost of those who did not enjoy the benefits of the new transportation methods (pedestrians, users of horses), and road damage (ruts created during rainy weather, the pounding of the road surfaces when dry which created an unanticipated problem of "waviness" [Gregory 1932, p. 257], and the use of "armoured tires" with iron studs to prevent side slipping significantly increased maintenance costs). Those who wanted to use the roads for traditional horse drawn traffic protested loudly, but with no tolls to manipulate, raising barriers to bicycle and automobile use of the roads proved to be difficult. For instance, as motorcars began to appear a requirement that each such vehicle be preceded by a man carrying a red flag was created. This obviously reduced their attractiveness by slowing their speed, but the requirement was abolished in 1896 (this was celebrated in November of that year by an organized "run"—not a race since racing on the public roads was not allowed—from London to Brighton, an event that apparently is still celebrated each November by people driving antique cars). Indeed, efforts to prevent or severely limit the use of motorized vehicles were generally resisted by the growing power of motor vehicle owners, although several actions were taken that limited road access to a degree and/or raised the cost of using such vehicles. The Motor Car Act of 1903 required new vehicles to be registered and licenses and to carry "conspicuous identification numbers back and front," for instance, and drivers were also required to be licensed. The costs of automobiles were increased due to requirements of lights and alarms that could be sounded, and speed limits were established. These limitations were clearly not sufficient, of course, and the ownership and use of motorcars expanded. The cost of road maintenance and improvement due to these "new users" rose rapidly during the first decade of the twentieth century and the central government was continually pressed to provide relief to the local taxpayers. It was felt that the users of motor vehicles should share in the costs of maintenance but the local road authorities (counties, boroughs, etc.) were not able to charge most of them who traveled through their areas because they could not charge tolls. Finally, a national tax on petrol was established in 1909 along with increased licensing fees paid to the central government. These new road revenues were administered by a new Road Board with the power to subsidize local road authorities—not for general maintenance, but for specific types of road improvements and new roads. The new road users demanded a very different type of road than horse-drawn transport required, after all, and as the political power of the owners of motor vehicles increased, more pressure was brought to bear on Parliament to provide roads suitable to such traffic.

The Road Transport Board was created in 1918 (during the First World War[20]) to coordinate all work on roads, and it continued to function as a Department of the Ministry of Transport. Its role was one of centralized supervision of road development, but it also was given the power to allocate grants from the central government's Road Fund (Gregory 1932, p. 248). British roads were divided into three classifications for the distribution of grants. Up to 50 percent of the cost of maintenance and improvement of first class roads was to come from the national government, while the second class roads were to get up to 25 percent and third class roads were to receive no aid. At the time, 26,000 miles of Britain's 179,000 total miles was classified as first class, and 15,800 miles fell into the second class. As Gregory (1932, p. 248) notes, however, "It is a natural desire of local road authorities to transfer roads from the grant-less third class," and since the division between road classes was based on their width (60 feet for first class and 50 for second), local authorities began finding ways to widen roads. This did not mean that roads actually had to be widened, however: "Each class must have a minimum carriage way of 20 feet, with one footpath. Therefore a third class road which has a footpath and a grass verge on each side, can be promoted to the second class and made eligible for a grant, by the simple process of absorbing a footpath and part of the verge into the carriage way, to the detriment of the safety of the pedestrian and the appearance of the road" (Gregory 1932, pp. 248–249). Grants could then be obtained to surface formerly graveled third class roads with tar, making them more suitable for motor vehicles. Thus, the funding of roads was being shifted more and more to the central government, as local authorities found ways to move their roads into higher classifications, and political pressure from effectively-organized motor-vehicle owners and local road authorities to increase the share of funding from the central government. This centralization process for funding is not surprising, given the inability of local road providers, whether private or public, to charge tolls that reflected the costs the new road users were imposing.[21]

IV. Conclusions

Hindley (1971, p. 63) sums up the mistaken view of many who took part in or look back at the events described above, concluding that, "What was needed, of course, was some mechanism of national road policy." Indeed, Hindley (1971, p. 73) goes on to state that, "Whatever other thoughts may be provoked by a study of the history of English roads during the eighteenth century at least we may be led to doubt whether the Englishman's much-vaunted love for personal liberty is not quite simply a dislike of efficiency and a scarcely secret love of violence. The refusal to countenance the expenditure of public money on road-building, or on a central and effective police force, guaranteed him a road system that was among the least serviceable and most dangerous in Europe." Obviously, such arguments were persuasive, as the Turnpike Trusts and parish system gave way to tax-supported free access public roads and highways. But the analysis presented here suggests a *very* different conclusion: Government action undermined the incentives and means to provide and maintain the turnpikes, and created the incentives to oppose them. A series of property rights alterations and limitations made by the government of the United Kingdom undermined the incentives of individuals to cooperate in the production of roads and road maintenance. The taking of the monasteries' land holdings, and the limitations on the rights of turnpike trusts to consolidate into efficiently sized organizations and to charge market determined tolls in a for-profit competitive market for roads created significant problems that government production has not been able to overcome. Suggesting that roads are now public goods, even up to the point where crowding sets in, is analytically empty because, as Minasian (1964, pp. 79–80) explains, "the theory generates economic analysis which is not based on the opportunity cost notion." Scarcity and common access mean that crowding is the inevitable reality. Rationing of scarce resources cannot be avoided by declaring common property rights so that no one can be excluded; that simply means that first come first served and its accompanying congestion costs determine who gets what, or that regulations on use must be passed. Recognition of the fact that public roads are really common pools reinforces Minasian's (1964, p. 79) point that the outcomes observed are a result of the property-rights/institutional arrangements that exist and that "alternative exclusion and incentives systems" would produce very different results. The road system in Great Britain became unserviceable and dangerous because of government failure in the form of constraints on the private provision and pricing of road services that created a common pool, not because of market failure in the form of a public good problem. The solution to this massive government failure is not more government spending through coercive taxes, but privatization of roads so that, where appropriate,[22] road-providing firms can set tolls reflecting the demand for access to road transportation and the costs of supplying this service.

Notes

1. It does not follow that a public bureau must produce the good, however, so the public good argument is not a justification for public production. Instead, it implies that the government must serve as a collection agent, but this could be done by taxing in order to pay private providers under contract. Actual public provision requires consideration of other factors (e.g., relative efficiency and quality, potentials for abuse, and so on).
2. Private provision of roads was also common in U.S. history (Gunderson 1989; Klein 1990; Klein and Fielding 1992; Klein and Yin 1996; Roth 1996).
3. Non-use is possible if the cost of enforcing a "non-use" requirement (i.e., where no one is given a right to use a resource) is low enough, of course, and that may be the case in some situations, particularly where use is very visible. Thus, for instance, the U.S. government prevents oil drilling in some of its coastal waters (e.g., off the coast of Florida), and because drilling would be so easy to observe, the known reserves in the area are not being extracted (in this case, current non-use is a "use" of course, involving such things as: conservation for future consumption; use of the complementary resource, the surrounding sea, for recreation, fishing, etc.). However, in most cases, the cost of enforcing a non-use rule is too high to actually prevent use. For instance, hunting and fishing prohibitions (e.g., of endangered species), as well as seasons and limits on such activities, are generally quite costly to enforce, and poaching is common. Similarly, no one is supposed to use resources to grow narcotics or marijuana in much of the world and consumption is also prohibited, but both production and use are widespread.
4. This concept of the tragedy of the commons is originally attributed to biologist Hardin (1968), and the classic treatment of the subject in economics is by Gordon (1954). Substantial research supports the hypothesis.
5. The terms are, of course, related in a number of ways. Before crowding sets in, for instance, a common pool good or resource will have the characteristics of a public good, but given the inevitable congestion that arises with free access, it quickly takes on the characteristics of a common pool proper.
6. The term "government" is used here in the modern conventional sense, to mean the rules and processes associated with the institutions of nations and their internal geographically identified sub-jurisdictions (e.g., states or cantons, counties, municipalities). If every system of governance (e.g., the rules and processes of clubs, associations, unions, religions) is labeled as a government then this statement is not true since various community organizations (tithings, hundreds, parishes, all of which are discussed below) provided roads within their communities.
7. See Benson (1992, 1994) for a more detailed discussion of these organizations and the incentives that members had to cooperate with one another.
8. It appears that some bridges were built and maintained by hundreds, however, since the term "Hundred Bridges" actually continued in use into the eighteenth century (Webb and Webb 1913, p. 107).
9. The decline of fairs also reflected the increasing problems of crime on the roadways (Gregory 1932, p. 100), due to the failure of the local voluntary policing systems.

See Benson (1992, 1994) for detailed discussion of the fact that this occurred, in large part, because kings took away victims' rights to restitution and substituted royal fines and confiscations, undermining the incentives for victims and their supporters in the hundreds to pursue criminals.

10. See Klein (1990) for an excellent discussion of the interplay between self-interests and social pressures in the private development of highways in the early history of the United States.

11. See Benson (1992, 1994) for a discussion of the reasons for the declining roll of the tithings and hundreds in policing, as well as in other activities such as road maintenance.

12. The office of Justice of the Peace was created in 1326. Stephen (1883, p. 190) notes that at that time, JPs were simply "assigned to keep the peace," but in 1360 they were empowered "to take and arrest all those they may find by indictment or suspicion and put them in prison." JPs were appointed by royal commission for each county, and Langbein (1974, p. 5) observes that as with much of the local apparatus of justice, these men were expected to perform their functions without monetary compensation. The same was true with the local apparatus of road maintenance, as explained here, and over thirty statutes were issued from the late fourteenth to the middle of the sixteenth centuries, establishing various additional functions for JPs, including those having to do with the road maintenance process.

13. See Webb and Webb (1913, pp. 14–26) for more details on this statute and some of the others that followed.

14. For extensive discussions of the Turnpike Trusts, see Pawson (1977), Webb and Webb (1913), and Albert (1972).

15. The beginning of the industrial revolution in England cannot really be pinned to a particular date, of course (in fact, the precise origins is still an issue of considerable debate), but the general consensus appears to be that it occurred in the last half of the eighteenth century (Kreis 2001), after the seventeenth- and early eighteenth-century agricultural revolution that allowed for increased specialization in labor. Whatever the date, it was well before railroads were available to transport the inputs and outputs of the new factories that were evolving, and England was an "industrial giant" long before the miles of railways in the country approached the miles of turnpikes.

16. Shifting from politically determined tolls to fuel taxes does not alleviate the potential for favoring some transport services relative to others. Some observers allege that the trucking industry in the United States benefits from substantial subsidization because the taxes they pay for roads are lower than the cost of providing them with roads (Massa 2000/2001), for instance, although this claim remains controversial. Clearly, any such subsidies (or the opposite—taxes that actually exceed the costs of providing roads) can give one mode of transportation a competitive advantage over another for some services. Similarly, differential regulatory treatment can also give one mode an advantage over another. In this regard, see Benson (2002) for detailed historical analysis of the impact of Interstate Commerce Commission regulations that influenced the relative competitiveness of railroads and trucking in the United States.

17. The steam carriage industry did not give up with this defeat. For instance, at least one group including Thomas Telford initiated an effort to run steam-carriage services on their own improved road between London and Birmingham, with intentions of extending the services beyond this route (Dalgleish 1980, pp. 125–128). This group organized the "Steam Company," surveyed the route, and gained sup-

port from innkeepers and canal operators (who hoped to compete with railroads by connecting with the steam carriages). The railway serving the route objected strongly, of course. The group apparently was relying on Telford's prestige to carry them through parliamentary approval, however, and when he died in September 1834, the project was abandoned. Yet another initiative by the advocates of steam-powered road travel was the formation of the "Institute of Locomotion for Steam Transport and Agriculture" for the purpose of pursuing the application of steam power to transportation, agriculture, and other economic purposes through both economic *and* political means (Gordon 1833, p. 1). Political efforts to alleviate the restrictions on steam carriages clearly continued after the 1831 Select Committee report (see for instance, the report of the Select Committee on Mr. Goldsworthy Gurney's Case [1834]; Gurney was an active advocate and promoter of steam carriage transportation [Gurney 1831]).

18. Local resistance to centralization of power in the hands of the national government was the norm during this period. See Benson (1992) for discussion of the resistance to the creation of government policing and prosecution, for instance.

19. There was a legislative loophole in the consolidation effort due to the Local Government Act of 1858, which authorized any parish to become an "Urban Sanitary District," and these districts could not be included in any larger Highway District (Gregory 1932, p. 195). Parishes whose local officials wanted to maintain control of their roads used this process to do so, and as a consequence, a number of small districts avoided political consolidation.

20. War often serves as a basis for government growth (Higgs 1987).

21. Indeed, efforts by local spending authorities to shift revenue collections to larger taxing authorities is to be expected, as is the inevitable competition between these local authorities seeking to increase their share of the intergovernmental transfers that follow (Benson 2000).

22. This does not imply that tolls will be charged for all privately provided roads, of course. Private roads in many residential and commercial developments today do not charge tolls, for instance, although access is often limited in other ways (e.g., gates, security guards).

References

Albert, W. 1972. *The Turnpike Road System in England, 1663–1840*. Cambridge: Cambridge University Press.

Anderson, T., and P. J. Hill. 1975. "The Evolution of Property Rights: A Study of the American West." *Journal of Law and Economics* 18: 163–179.

Benson, B. L. 1989. "The Spontaneous Evolution of Commercial Law." *Southern Economic Journal* 55 (3): 644–661.

Benson, B. L. 1992. "The Development of Criminal Law and Its Enforcement: Public Interest or Political Transfers." *Journal des Economistes et des Etudes Humaines* 3: 79–108.

Benson, B. L. 1994. "Are Public Goods Really Common Pools: Considerations of the Evolution of Policing and Highways in England." *Economic Inquiry* 32 (2): 249–271.

Benson, B. L. 2000. "Fiscal Competition in a Federal System," in *Federalist Government in Principle and Practice*, edited by D. P. Racheter and R. E. Wagner. Boston: Kluwer Academic Press.

Benson, B. L. 2002. "Regulatory Disequilibrium and Inefficiency: The Case of Interstate Trucking." *Review of Austrian Economics* 15 (2–3): 229–255.

Beresford, M. W. and J. K. S. St. Joseph. 1979. *Medieval England: An Aerial Survey.* Cambridge: Cambridge University Press.

Blair, P. H. 1956. *An Introduction to Anglo-Saxon England.* Cambridge, England: Cambridge University Press.

Bodey, H. 1971. *Roads.* London: B. T. Batsford, Ltd.

Coase, R. H. 1974. "The Lighthouse in Economics." *The Journal of Law and Economics* 17: 357–376.

Cowen, T. 1988. "Introduction. Public Goods and Externalities: Old and New Perspectives," in *The Theory of Market Failure*, edited by T. Cowen. Fairfax, VA: George Mason University.

Dalgleish, A. 1980. "Telford and Steam Carriages," in *Thomas Telford: Engineer*, edited by A. Penfold. London: Thomas Telford Ltd.

Dance, Sir C. 1831. *Postscript to Steam Carriages on Common Roads.* A pamphlet possibly prepared as evidence to the Parliamentary Select Committee on Tolls.

Darby, H. C., editor. 1973. *A New Historical Geography of England.* Cambridge: Cambridge University Press.

Jeffreys, R. 1949. *The King's Highway.* London: The Batchworth Press.

Gordon, A. 1833. *Institute of Locomotion for Steam Transport and Agriculture.* Report regarding this organization.

Gordon, H. S. 1954. "The Economic Theory of a Common Property Resource: The Fishery." *Journal of Political Economy* 62: 124–142.

Gregory, J. W. 1932. *The Story of the Road: From the Beginning Down to A.D. 1931.* New York: Macmillan Co.

Gunderson, G. 1989. "Privatization and the 19th-Century Turnpike." *Cato Journal* 9 (1): 191–200.

Gurney, G. 1831. *Steam Carriages on Common Roads.* A pamphlet possibly prepared as evidence for presentation to a Select Committee of the House of Commons.

Hardin, G. 1968. "The Tragedy of the Commons." *Science* 162: 1243–1248.

Higgs, R. 1987. *Crisis and Leviathan: Critical Episodes in the Growth of American Government.* New York: Oxford University Press.

Hindle, P. B. 1982. "Roads and Tracks," in *The English Medieval Landscape*, edited by L. Cantor. Philadelphia: University of Pennsylvania Press.

Hindley, G. 1971. *A History of Roads.* London: Peter Davies.

Jackman, W. T. 1966. *The Development of Transportation in Modern England.* New York: Augustus M. Kelley, Publishers.

Klein, D. B. 1990. "The Voluntary Provision of Public Goods? The Turnpike Companies of Early America." *Economic Inquiry* 28: 788–812.

Klein, D. B. and G. J. Fielding. 1992. "Private Toll Roads: Learning from the 19th Century." *Transportation Quarterly* 46 (3): 321–341.

Klein, D. B. and C. Yin. 1996. "Use, Esteem, and Profit in Voluntary Provision: Toll Roads in California, 1850–1902." *Economic Inquiry* 34 (October): 678–692.

Kreis, S. 2001."The Origins of the Industrial Revolution in England." *The History Guide: Lectures in Modern European Intellectual History* 17 (http://www.historyguide.org/intellect/lecture17a.html).

LaMar, V. A. 1960. *Travel and Roads in England.* Washington: The Folger Shakespeare Library, Folger Booklets on Tutor and Stuart Civilization.

Langbein, J. H. 1974. *Prosecuting Crime in the Renaissance: England, Germany and France*. Cambridge, MA: Harvard University Press.

Massa, S. 2000/2001. "Surface Freight Transportation: Accounting for Subsidies in a Free Market." *New York University School of Law Journal of Legislation and Public Policy* 4: 285–342.

Minasian, J. R. 1964. "Television Pricing and the Theory of Public Goods." *The Journal of Law and Economics* 7: 71–80.

Moyes, A. 1978. "Transport 1730–1900," in *An Historical Geography of England and Whales*, edited by R. A. Dodgshon and R. A. Butlin. London: Academic Press.

Parkes, J. 1925. *Travel in England in the Seventeenth Century*. London: Oxford University Press.

Pawson, E. 1977. *Transport and Economy: The Turnpike Roads of Eighteenth Century Britain*. London: Academic Press.

Roth, G. 1996. *Roads in a Market Economy*. Aldershot, UK: Avebury Technical.

Samuelson, P. A. 1954. "The Pure Theory of Public Expenditure." *Review of Economics and Statistics* 36: 387–389.

Samuelson, P. A. 1955. "Diagrammatic Exposition of a Theory of Public Expenditure." *Review of Economics and Statistics* 37: 350–356.

Samuelson, P. A. 1969. "Pure Theory of Public Expenditures and Taxation," in *Public Economics: An Analysis of Public Production and Consumption and Their Relations to the Private Sectors*, edited by J. Margolis and H. Guitton. London: Macmillan.

Samuelson, P. A. and W. D. Nordhaus. 1985. *Economics*. New York: McGraw Hill.

Select Committee on Mr. Goldsworthy Gurney's Case. 1834. *Report from Select Committee on Mr. Goldsworthy Gurney's Case; with the Minutes of Evidence*. London: House of Commons, 17 July.

Select Committee on Steam Carriages. 1831. *Report from Select Committee on Steam Carriages; with Minutes of Evidence and Appendix*. London: House of Commons, 12 October.

Stephen, Sir J. 1883 [1963]. *A History of the Criminal Law of England*. New York: Burt Franklin.

Stenton, Sir F. 1936. "The Road System of Medieval England." *Economic History Review* 7: 1–21.

Webb, S. and B. Webb. 1913 [1963]. *The Story of the King's Highway: English Local Government Volume 5*. Hamden, Conn.: Archon Books.

Willan, T. S. 1976. *The Inland Trade: Studies in English Internal Trade in the Sixteenth and Seventeenth Centuries*. Manchester: Manchester University Press.

12

America's Toll Road Heritage:
The Achievements of Private Initiative
in the Nineteenth Century

*Daniel Klein and John Majewski**

Before Americans built the Erie Canal or hammered the first railroad spike, private toll roads shaped and accommodated trade and migration routes, leaving social and political imprints on the communities that debated and supported them. Private road building came and went in waves throughout the nineteenth century and across the country. All told, between 2,500 and 3,200 companies successfully financed, built, and operated their toll road. Although most of these roads operated for only a fraction of the 100+ period, the combined mileage of private toll roads that operated at any point in time would be in range of 30,000 to 52,000 miles.

America's 100+ year experience with private toll roads offers valuable lessons for policymakers and citizens today. American toll road history is pretty well covered by considering three episodes: the turnpike era of the eastern states 1792 to 1845; the plank road boom 1847 to 1853; and the toll roads of the Far West 1850 to 1902.

The Failure of Local Government Road Service

Prior to the 1790s Americans had no direct experience with private turnpikes; roads were built, financed, and managed mainly by town governments.

*The authors are grateful to Gabriel Roth, Alex Tabarrok, and Christopher Baer for many helpful comments, and to Bill Sundstrom and Alex Field for useful suggestions. The authors also acknowledge Christopher T. Baer, Chi Yin, and Gordon J. Fielding for their contributions to this chapter by way of coauthoring works upon which it is partly based.

Typically, townships compelled a road labor tax. The State of New York assessed eligible males (often farmers) a minimum of three days of roadwork under penalty of fine of one dollar. The labor requirement could be avoided if the worker paid a fee of 62.5 cents a day. As with public works of any kind, incentives were weak because the chain of activity could *not* be traced to a *residual claimant*—that is, private owners who claim the "residuals," profit or loss. The laborers were brought together in a transitory, disconnected manner, preventing them from developing the appropriate skills and pride in the job. Since overseers and laborers were commonly farmers, too often the crop schedule, rather than road deterioration, dictated the repairs schedule. Except in cases of special appropriations, financing came in dribbles deriving mostly from the fines and commutations of the assessed inhabitants. Commissioners could hardly lay plans for decisive improvements. When a needed connection passed through unsettled lands, it was difficult to mobilize labor because assessments could be worked out only in the district in which the laborer resided. Because work areas were divided into districts, as well as into towns, problems arose because the various pieces were not working together. Thus road conditions remained inadequate, as New York's governors often acknowledged publicly (Klein and Majewski 1992, pp. 472–75).

The Race is On!

To American fortune seekers, the ratification of the U.S. Constitution was like the "bang" of a starting gun. The Constitution resolved what Robert Higgs (1997) has called "regime uncertainty," by building an interstate framework for financial, legal, and political affairs (Hurst 1956, p. 10; North 1966, pp. 50–51). The race was afoot—to capture the trade of the interior, to develop western lands, to expand population, to build the leading entrepot. In 1790, the steamboat was still in its infancy, canal construction was hard to finance and limited in scope, and the first American railroad would not be completed for another forty years. Better transportation meant, above all, better highways.

Alexis de Tocqueville remarked on the impulse of Americans to push onward. He describes an attitude about the environment very different than today:

> The wonders of inanimate nature leave [Americans] cold, and, one may almost say, they do not see the marvelous forests surrounding them until they begin to fall beneath the ax. What they see is something different. The American people see themselves marching through wildernesses, drying up marshes, diverting rivers, peopling the wilds, and subduing nature. (Tocqueville, p. 485 of Lawrence/Mayer ed.)

America's very limited and lackluster experience with the publicly operated toll roads of the 1780s hardly portended a future boom in private toll roads, but the success of private toll bridges may have inspired some future turnpike companies. From 1786 to 1798, fifty-nine private toll bridge companies were chartered in the northeast, beginning with Boston's Charles River Bridge, which brought investors an average annual return of 10.5 percent in its first six years (Davis 1917, II, p. 188). Private toll bridges operated without many of the regulations that would hamper the private toll roads that soon followed, such as mandatory toll exemptions and conflicts over the location of tollgates. Also, toll bridges, by their very nature, faced little toll evasion, which was a serious problem for toll roads.

The more significant predecessor to America's private toll road movement was Britain's success with private toll roads. Beginning in 1663 and peaking from 1750 to 1772, Britain experienced a private turnpike movement large enough to acquire the nickname "turnpike mania" (Pawson 1977, p. 151; Benson this volume). The term "turnpike," in fact, comes from Britain, referring to a long staff (or pike) that acted as a swinging barrier or tollgate. In nineteenth-century America, "turnpike" specifically means a toll road with a surface of gravel and earth, as opposed to "plank roads," which refer to toll roads surfaced by wooden planks. Later in the century, all such roads were typically just "toll roads."

Although the British movement inspired the future American turnpike movement, the institutional differences between the two were substantial. Most important, perhaps, was the difference in their organizational forms. British turnpikes were incorporated as trusts—non-profit organizations financed by bonds—while American turnpikes were stock-financed corporations seemingly organized to pay dividends, though acting within narrow limits determined by the charter. Contrary to modern sensibilities, this difference made the British trusts, which operated under the firm expectation of fulfilling bond obligations, *more* intent and more successful in garnering residuals. In contrast, for the American turnpikes the hope of dividends was merely a hope, usually a faint hope, and never a legal obligation. Odd as it sounds, the stock-financed "business" corporation was better suited to operating the project as a civic enterprise, paying out returns in use and esteem rather than cash.

The Turnpike Era, 1792–1845

"[T]he states admitted that they were unequal to the task and enlisted the aid of private enterprise" (Durrenberger 1931, p. 37). The first private turnpike in the United States was chartered by Pennsylvania in 1792 and opened two years later. Spanning 62 miles between Philadelphia and Lancaster, it quickly attracted the attention of merchants in other states, who recognized its potential to direct commerce away from their regions. Soon lawmakers from those states began chartering turnpikes—and the race was on.

By 1800, sixty-nine turnpike companies had been chartered throughout the country, especially in Connecticut (23) and New York (13). Over the next decade nearly six times as many turnpikes were incorporated (398). Table 12.1 shows that in the mid-Atlantic and New England states between 1800 and 1830, turnpike companies accounted for 27 percent of all business incorporations.

As shown in Table 12.2, a wider set of states had incorporated 1,562 turnpikes by the end of 1845. Somewhere between 50 to 70 percent of these succeeded in building and operating toll roads.

Although the states of Pennsylvania, Virginia, and Ohio subsidized privately operated turnpike companies, most turnpikes were financed solely by private stock subscription and structured to pay dividends. This was a significant achievement, considering the large construction costs (averaging around $1,500 to $2,000 per mile) and the typical length (15 to 40 miles). But the achievement was most striking because, as New England historian Edward Kirkland (1948, p. 45) put it, "the turnpikes did not make money. As a whole this was true; as a rule it was clear from the beginning."

Generally speaking, turnpikes eked out enough toll revenue to pay for maintenance, and not more. Organizers and "investors" generally regarded the ini-

Table 12.1
Turnpikes as a Percentage of All Business Incorporations, by Special and General Acts, 1800–1830

State	All Incorporations	Turnpike Incorporations	% Turnpikes of All Incorporations
New York	993	339	34
Pennsylvania	425	199	46
New Jersey	190	47	25
Maryland	194	54	28
Connecticut	234	77	33
Rhode Island	127	34	27
Massachusetts & Maine	880	104	12
New Hampshire	304	51	17
Vermont	177	41	23
Total	3,527	946	27

Source: For all states through 1800, Davis 1948: vol. 2, 22–27, 216; for New Hampshire, Vermont, Massachusetts, and Rhode Island, Taylor 1934:339–44, 346; for Connecticut, ibid., pp. 338–39, and Reed 1964:75; for New York, New Jersey, and Maryland, Evans 1948:12–17; for Pennsylvania, Miller 1940:158–59.

Table 12.2
Turnpike Incorporation, 1792–1845

State	1792–1800	1801–10	1811–20	1821–30	1831–40	1841–45	Total
NH	4	45	5	1	4	0	59
VT	9	19	15	7	4	3	57
MA	9	80	8	16	1	1	115
RI	3	13	8	13	3	1	41
CT	23	37	16	24	13	0	113
NY	13	126	133	75	83	27	457
PA	5	39	101	59	101	37	342
NJ	0	22	22	3	3	0	50
VA	0	6	7	8	25	0	46
MD	3	9	33	12	14	7	78
OH	0	2	14	12	114	62	204
Total	69	398	362	230	365	138	1562

Sources: For all states through 1800, Joseph Stancliffe Davis, *Essays in the Earlier History of American Corporations* (Cambridge, Massachusetts, 1948), II, pp. 22–27, 216; for NH, VT, MA, and RI, 1801–1845, Philip E. Taylor, "The Turnpike Era in New England," (Ph.D. thesis, Yale University, 1934), pp. 339–344, 346; for CT, 1801–1821, Nathaniel Reed, "The Role of the Connecticut State Government in the Development and Operation of the Inland Transportation Facilities from 1784 to 1821," (Ph.D. diss., Yale University, 1964), p. 75; for CT, 1822–1845, Taylor, pp. 338–339; for NY, NJ, MD, and OH, 1801–1845, George Herberton Evans, Jr., *Business Incorporation in the United States, 1800–1943* (New York, 1948), pp. 12–17; for PA, 1801–1845, William Miller, "A Note on the History of Business Incorporation in Pennsylvania, 1800–1860," *Quarterly Journal of Economics* 55 (November, 1940), pp. 158–159; for Virginia, Robert F. Hunter, "The Turnpike Movement in Virginia, 1816–1860," (Ph.D. thesis, Columbia University, 1957), pp. 313–315.

tial proceeds from sale of stock as a fund from which to build the facility, which would then earn enough in toll receipts to cover operating expenses. One might hope for dividend payments as well, but "it seems to have been generally known long before the rush of construction subsided that turnpike stock was worthless" (Wood 1919, p. 63).[1]

Because turnpikes held the promise of facilitating movement and trade, the region's merchants, farmers, landowners, and ordinary residents would benefit from a turnpike. Gazetteer Thomas F. Gordon aptly summarized the relationship between these "indirect benefits" and investment in turnpikes: "None have yielded profitable returns to the stockholders, but everyone feels that he has been repaid for his expenditures in the improved value of his lands, and the economy of business" (quoted in Majewski 2000, p. 49). Gordon's statement raises an important question. If one could not be excluded from benefiting from a turnpike, and if dividends were not in the offing, what incentive would anyone have to help finance turnpike construction? The turnpike communities faced a serious free-rider problem.

Tocqueville's America

Nevertheless, hundreds of communities overcame the free-rider problem. Alexis de Tocqueville observed that, excepting those of the South, Americans were infused with a spirit of public-mindedness. Their strong sense of community spirit resulted in the funding of schools, libraries, hospitals, churches, canals, dredging companies, wharves, and water companies, as well as turnpikes (Goodrich 1948). Vibrant community and cooperation sprung, according to Tocqueville, from the fertile ground of liberty:

> If it is a question of taking a road past his property, [a man] sees at once that this small public matter has a bearing on his greatest private interests, and there is no need to point out to him the close connection between his private profit and the general interest. . . . Local liberties, then, which induce a great number of citizens to value the affection of their kindred and neighbors, bring men constantly into contact, despite the instincts which separate them, and force them to help one another. . . . The free institutions of the United States and the political rights enjoyed there provide a thousand continual reminders to every citizen that he lives in society. . . . Having no particular reason to hate others, since he is neither their slave nor their master, the American's heart easily inclines toward benevolence. At first it is of necessity that men attend to the public interest, afterward by choice. What had been calculation becomes instinct. By dint of working for the good of his fellow citizens, he in the end acquires a habit and taste for serving them. . . . I maintain that there is only one effective remedy against the evils which equality may cause, and that is political liberty. (Alexis de Tocqueville, pp. 511–13, Lawrence/Mayer edition)

Tocqueville's testimonial is broad and general, but its accuracy is seen in the archival records and local histories of the turnpike communities. Here we find countless episodes, often charming and amusing, in which early Americans employed shrewd social tactics, as well as practiced solidarity and spontaneous generosity. Tocqueville's America was a web of neighbors, kin, and locally prominent figures interacting voluntarily, often by means of intentional associations. Tocqueville's America spoke in turnpike appeals made in newspapers, local speeches, town meetings, door-to-door solicitations, correspondence, and negotiations in assembling the route.[2] Purchasers of stock were often explicitly moved to think of a turnpike's potential, not for dividends, but for community improvement. Furthermore, many toll road projects involved the effort to build a monument and symbol of the community. Participating in a company by donating cash or giving moral support was a relatively rewarding way of establishing public services; it was pursued at least in part for the sake of community romance and adventure as ends in themselves (Brown 1973, p. 68). Consequently, "investors" tended to be not outside speculators, but locals positioned to enjoy the turnpikes' indirect benefits. "But with a few exceptions, the vast majority of the stockholders in turnpike were farmers, land speculators, merchants or individuals and firms interested in commerce" (Durrenberger 1931, p. 104).

Champions of government enterprise in the nineteenth century persistently complained of a "shortage of capital" necessitating government investment, but the turnpike movement showed how local projects could tap into savings of numerous individuals. A large number of ordinary households held turnpike stock. Pennsylvania compiled the most complete set of investment records, which show that more than 24,000 individuals purchased turnpike or toll bridge stock between 1800 and 1821. The average holding was $250 worth of stock, and the median was less than $150 (Majewski 2001). Such sums indicate that most turnpike investors were wealthier than the average citizen, but hardly part of the urban elite that dominated larger corporations such as the Bank of the United States. County-level studies indicate that most turnpike investment came from farmers and artisans, as opposed to the merchants and professionals more usually associated with early corporations (Majewski 2000, pp. 49–53). Widespread participation by relatively modest investors underscores the extent to which Americans practiced boosterism and chipping in for the common good.

Government Regulations Hampered Turnpikes

Government regulation made profitability even more remote than it would have been in a more laissez-faire environment. Legislators wrote numerous restrictions into the charters, as conciliation towards objectors to both the specific project and to turnpike companies in general. At this time, in many fields, the corporate form had a public-service ethos, aimed not primarily at paying dividends, but at serving the community (Handlin and Handlin 1945, p. 22; Goodrich 1948, p. 306; Hurst 1970, p. 15). This, however, does not mean that such corporations had a governmental flavor, just that they did not have a strongly commercial or market flavor.

Turnpike opposition was of two kinds: ideological and opportunistic. Some opponents claimed that turnpikes were tools of aristocrats, corporate monopolists, and oppressors of the poor. Most opposition, however, came from those who used protest as a means of gaining what they no doubt saw as just concessions (Klein and Majewski 1992 pp. 486–98). A significant portion of turnpikes were built partly over paths, trails, or ill-maintained roads that the public had been accustomed to using without charge. Petitions yielded several restrictions on turnpike operators, including "progressive" restrictions on stockholder voting and specification of road quality, toll rates, tollgate locations, and toll exemptions. Tollgates, for example, often could be spaced no closer than every five or even ten miles. This regulation enabled some users to travel without encountering a tollgate, and eased the practice of steering horses and the high-mounted vehicles of the day off the main road so as to evade the toll gate, a practice known as "shunpiking."

The charters or general laws granted numerous exemptions from toll payment. In New York, the exempt included people traveling on family business, those attending or returning from church services and funerals, town meetings, blacksmith's shops, those on military duty, and those who lived within one mile of a tollgate. In Massachusetts some of the same trips were exempt and also anyone residing in the town where the gate was placed and anyone "on the common and ordinary business of family concerns" (Laws of Massachusetts 1805, chapter 79, p. 649). Needless to say, this last was the subject of some controversy. In the face of exemptions and shunpiking, turnpike operators sometimes petitioned authorities for a toll hike, stiffer penalties against shunpikers, or the relocating of the tollgate. The record indicates that petitioning the legislature for such relief was a costly and uncertain affair (Klein and Majewski 1992, pp. 496–98).

Turnpikes were also encouraged by government, sometimes by the granting of existing trails or public roadbeds to turnpikes, sometimes guarantees against new parallel routes, and typically the granting of eminent domain powers. Were these governmentally granted aids important? After surveying the historical sources and digging into many primary materials, we really cannot say. We suspect that, by and large, landowners, sensible to the prospects of improved transportation and higher land values, sold or even gave land to turnpike routes in the same neighborly spirit that Tocqueville described[3]—and that they would have readily done so even if companies had not had eminent domain powers. Playing "holdout" games surely would have seemed unneighborly; cooperating would be a genuine and highly visible act of generosity and public spirit. In the 1990s, toll road projects in Virginia and southern California benefited from just such willing participation from large landowners.

A few state governments (in Pennsylvania, Virginia, and Ohio) even encouraged turnpikes by purchasing stock. Yet, despite these advantages, all but a few turnpikes lost money. In New York, under state law, tolls could be collected only after turnpikes passed inspections, which were typically conducted after 10 miles of roadway had been built. Only 35 to 40 percent of New York turnpike projects—or about 165 companies—reached operational status. In Connecticut, by contrast, where settlement covered the state and turnpikes more often took over existing roadbeds, construction costs were much lower and about 87 percent of the companies reached operation (Taylor 1934, p. 210). We guess that up to 1845 nationwide at least one-third of the chartered companies never constructed enough roadway to justify a tollgate.

Ye Olde Privatization Debate

Although it was mainly practical ambitions that led Americans to privatize the roads, ideological concerns occasionally appeared in the arguments of both turnpike supporters and opponents. In an article in the Albany (NY) *Register* of June 13, 1796, Elkanah Watson, a leading turnpike advocate, argued for highway user fees by appealing to moral sentiments similar to what we might hear articulated by a contemporary privatization advocate: "[N]o tax can operate so fair and so easy, as that of paying a turnpike toll, since every person is taxed in proportion to the benefit he derives from a good road, and all strangers and travellers are made equally tributary to its support—What can be more just?" (quoted in Klein and Majewski 1992, p. 481)

Strongly committed to the cause of turnpikes, Watson even kept track of his opponents' arguments in his scrapbook. His chief opponent, "Civis," claimed that turnpiking is "hostile to sound republican maxims," that it "evinces a transition...from freedom toward despotism," that turnpikes "encourage unfair speculation," that they "tend to make the rich richer and the poor poorer [and] divide the community into two orders of opposite interests, payers and receivers." Civis raised the specter of corporate privilege: "[I]t is not turnpike corporations only that excite my apprehension. [W]e are continually incorporating companies of various description, of a combined interest, distinct from the general interest of the people" (Klein and Majewski 1992, p. 488). Such arguments are, of course, alive and well today.

According to Watson, "[s]trong prejudices have been excited against Turnpikes . . . by a few leatherheads." In America's first era of road privatization, people realized very quickly that turnpikes were not rapacious monopolies but rather locally initiated improvement projects looking to the legislature mainly for the permission to go forward as a legally recognized undertaking. In 1802, Watson scribbled into his notebook:

> [T]his Civis was a member of the Legislature[,] a Doct[or] M[oses] Younglove from Columbia County—a man seeking popularity—he found means to prejudice 2/3's of an ignorant Legislature who were opposing Turnpike incorporations . . .—at length t'wards the Close of the Session . . . they gave way to Reason & conviction & several turnpikes were incorporated.

The Success of Private Initiative

All told, and in view of the apparent free-rider problem, the success was striking. The movement built new roads at rates previously unheard of in America. Table 12.3 gives ballpark estimates of the cumulative investment in constructing turnpikes up to 1830 in New England and the Middle Atlantic. Repair and maintenance costs are excluded. These construction investment figures are probably too low—they generally exclude, for example, toll revenue that might have been used to finish construction—but they nevertheless indicate the ability of private initiatives to raise money in an economy in which capital was in short supply. Turnpike companies in these states raised more than $24 million by 1830, an amount equaling 6.15 percent of those states' 1830 GDP. To put this into comparative perspective, between 1956 and 1995 all levels of government spent $330 billion (in 1996 dollars) in building the Interstate Highway System, a cumulative total equaling only 4.30 percent of 1996 GDP. Table 12.3 shows the comparison. This calculation confirms Gerald Gunderson's claim that the relative investment in early American turnpikes exceeded investment in the post-World War II Interstate Highway System (Gunderson 1989: 192). In real per capita terms the amount that was raised voluntarily in Tocqueville's America significantly exceeded the amount raised in post-World War II America for the government's feted highway system.

The organizational advantages of turnpike companies relative to government road care did indeed translate into roads of better quality (Taylor 1934, p. 334; Parks 1967, pp. 23, 27). New York state gazetteer Horatio Spafford (1824, p. 125) wrote that turnpikes have been "an excellent school, in every road district, and people now work the highways to much better advantage than formerly." In case law, judges said that turnpikes were "valuable and meritorious enterprises" and that they further "the advancement and prosperity of the commercial, agricultural and social interests of the community" (quoted in Klein and Majewski 1992, p. 502).

Spontaneous Network Integration

Transportation researchers, theorists, and engineers exhibit their own versions of the timeless division between central planning and decentralized (or "spontaneous") order. Speaking for "The Systems Approach to Transport Planning," David T. Kresge and Paul O. Roberts (1971, p. 1) wrote in a book published by The Brookings Institution, "any comprehensive, long-run transport plan will need to take into account the interdependency between the transport system and the general economy as well as the systems or interaction effects within the transport network itself." Only a centralized agency would have the respon-

Table 12.3
Cumulative Turnpike Investment (1800–1830) as Percentage of 1830 GDP

State	Cumulative Turnpike Investment, 1800–1830 ($)	As Percent of the state's 1830 GDP	The Cumulative Investment divided by 1830 total population ($)
Maine	35,000	0.16	0.09
New Hampshire	575,100	2.11	2.14
Vermont	484,000	3.37	1.72
Massachusetts	4,200,000	7.41	6.88
Rhode Island	140,000	1.54	1.44
Connecticut	1,036,160	4.68	3.48
New York	9,000,000	7.06	4.69
New Jersey	1,100,000	4.79	3.43
Pennsylvania	6,400,000	6.67	4.75
Maryland	1,500,000	3.85	3.36
TOTAL:			
31 years (1800–1830) of private expenditure on construction of turnpikes	24,470,260	6.15% of 1830 GDP of those 10 states	$4.49 per person
40 years (1956–1995) of government expenditure (all levels) on construction of the Interstate Highway System	330 Billion (in 1996 $s)	4.30% of 1995 GDP (in 1996 $s)	

Sources: Pennsylvania turnpike investment: Durrenberger 1931, p. 61; New England turnpike investment: Taylor 1934, pp. 210–11; New York, New Jersey, and Maryland turnpike investment: Fishlow 2000, p. 549. Only private investment is included. State GDP data come from Bodenhorn 2000, p. 237. Figures for the cost of the Interstate Highway System can be found at http://www.publicpurpose.com/hwy-is$.htm, created by Wendell Cox and calculated from Federal Highway Administration data. Please note that our investment figures generally do not include investment to finish roads by loans or the use of toll revenue. The table therefore underestimates investment in turnpikes.

sibility to survey the whole system, and only such an agency could have the authority to integrate its parts and coordinate its functions. Such integration and coordination could never be achieved by piecemeal or decentralized efforts (Christopher Nash 1988 propounds this view in urban transit research).

Albert Gallatin, secretary of treasury under Jefferson, was America's first national transportation planner. He submitted a plan for an interlocking national system of roads and canals, to be financed chiefly by the federal government (once the Constitution was suitably amended). One rationale was to bind the Union politically. But also he wrote in the central planning spirit: "The National Legislature alone, embracing every local interest, and superior to every local consideration, is competent to the selection of such national objects" (p. 741). Furthermore, Gallatin argued that private capital was too scarce to undertake large, risky improvement projects. Gallatin's plan was never enacted, but it did help to win support for federal funding of certain internal improvement projects.

Despite such doubts about private action, the turnpike experience suggests that a company would intelligently develop roadway to achieve connective communication. The corporate form traversed town and county boundaries, so a single company could bring what would otherwise be separate segments together into a single organization. "Merchants and traders in New York sponsored pikes leading across northern New Jersey in order to tap the Delaware Valley trade which would otherwise have gone to Philadelphia" (Lane 1939, p. 156). Or road organizers would develop new connecting pieces in a system of roads.

Decades before the Erie Canal, private individuals realized the natural opening through the Appalachians and planned a system of turnpikes connecting Albany to Syracuse and beyond. Figure 12.1 shows the principal routes westward from Albany. The upper route begins with the Albany & Schenectady Turnpike, connects to the Mohawk Turnpike, and then the Seneca Turnpike. The lower route begins with the First Great Western Turnpike and then branches at Cherry Valley into the Second and Third Great Western Turnpikes. Corporate papers of these companies reveal that organizers of different companies talked to each other; they were quite capable of coordinating their intentions and planning mutually beneficial activities by voluntary means (see inset letter). When the Erie Canal was completed in 1825 it roughly followed the alignment of the upper route and greatly reduced travel on the competing turnpikes (Baer, Klein, and Majewski 1992).

Another excellent example of network integration achieved by voluntary planning is the Pittsburgh Pike. The Pennsylvania route consisted of a combination of five turnpike companies, each of which built a road segment connecting Pittsburgh and Harrisburg, where travelers could take another series of turnpikes to Philadelphia. Completed in 1820, the Pittsburgh Pike greatly

Figure 12.1
Turnpike Network in Central New York, 1845

Central New York Turnpikes, 1845

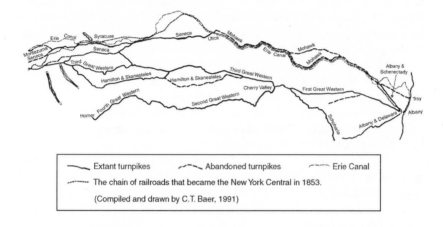

Extant turnpikes   Abandoned turnpikes   Erie Canal

The chain of railroads that became the New York Central in 1853.

(Compiled and drawn by C.T. Baer, 1991)

January 29, 1803

Dear Sir [Charles R. Webster],

This will be handed to you by Dr. Moore whom I take the liberty of introducing to your acquaintance—Dr. Moore is sent by a number of inhabitants in this neighborhood as an agent for the purpose of obtaining a grant for a Turnpike road. . . [T]his road is nothing more than a continuation of the [First] Great Western Turnpike of which I observe that you are a Director, and as such I request the favor of you to consult with Dr. Moore upon the subject and to lend him all the assistance in your power, which I am persuaded you will readily grant, not only for my sake, but from a full persuasion that the road which we have in view will be highly beneficial to your Turnpike, as well as to the community at large—

With sincere friendship and regard I remain

Dear Sir your friend and humble servant

J. Lincklaen

[John Lincklaen's project took the name Third Great Western Turnpike and was chartered later that year 1803; Lincklaen was president and a major stockholder. The turnpike operated until 1859. See map above for its place in the network of private roads.]

Note: We have corrected spelling and written out abbreviations.
Source: Fairchild Collection, New York Public Library, NYC, Box 5.

improved freighting over the rugged Allegheny Mountains. Freight rates between Philadelphia and Pittsburgh were cut in half because wagons increased their capacity, speed, and certainty (Reiser 1951, pp. 76–77). Although the state government invested in the companies that formed the Pittsburgh Pike, records of the two companies for which we have complete investment information shows that private interests contributed 62 percent of the capital (calculated from Majewski 2000, pp. 47–51; Reiser 1951, p. 76). Residents in numerous communities contributed to individual projects out of their own self-interest. Their provincialism nevertheless helped create a coherent and logical system.

In the far West, there were even road systems developed by a single entrepreneur. In southwestern Colorado, Otto Mears built a system that "comprised some 300 or 400 route miles" (Ridgway 1932, p. 169; Kaplan 1975). In Shasta and Trinity counties, California, William S. Lowden had a large interest in several toll road and bridge companies (Cage 1984).

Many have claimed that we need master planning by government to achieve coordinated, integrated transportation networks. But history would seem to refute that claim.

The National Road: America's First Great and Glorious Federal Boondoggle

The Pittsburgh Pike fared far better than centrally planned routes such as the National Road. Financed by the federal government, the National Road was built between Cumberland, Maryland, and Wheeling, West Virginia, where it was then extended through the Midwest with the hopes of reaching the Mississippi River. Although it never reached the Mississippi, the federal government nevertheless spent $6.8 million on the project (Goodrich 1960, pp. 54, 65). The trans-Appalachian section of the National Road competed directly against the Pittsburgh Pike. As noted above, the state of Pennsylvania invested in the Pittsburgh Pike, but the state government tended to be a passive investor. The Pittsburgh Pike was thus far more private in character than the National Road. From the records of two of the five companies that formed the Pittsburgh Pike, we estimate it cost $4,805 per mile to build (Majewski 2000, pp. 47–51; Reiser 1951, p. 76). The federal government, on the other hand, spent $13,455 per mile to complete the first 200 miles of the National Road (Fishlow 2000, p. 549). Besides costing much less, the condition of the privately controlled Pennsylvania route was much better. The tollgates along the Pittsburgh Pike provided a steady stream of revenue for maintenance and repairs. The tollgates also provided a way of regulating road use, such as discouraging the use of narrow-wheeled wagons that could damaged the road's surface.

Lacking private owners, the National Road was often in poor condition. The project relied on intermittent outlays by the federal government for repairs. Even when the money was available the results were poor because supervision of contractors was lax. Since there was no means of regulating road use, travelers often abused the road by dragging heavy logs or locking narrow-wheeled wagons when descending steep slopes. One army engineer in 1832 found "the road in a shocking condition, and every rod of it will require great repair; some of it now is almost impassable" (quoted in Searight, p. 60). Another traveler sardonically noted that, "the ruts are worn so broad and deep by heavy travel, that an army of pigmies might march into the bosom of the country under the cover they could afford" (quoted in Peyton, p. 149). No wonder that historians have found that travelers generally preferred to take the Pittsburgh Pike rather than the National Road. Reuben Gold Thwaites, who edited thirty-two volumes of travelers' accounts dating from 1746 to 1846, concluded that, "Much ado was made over the opening of the Cumberland Road across the Alleghenies [the National Road], but . . . the central Pennsylvania route [the Pittsburgh Pike] seems to have been the popular one from Washington and Philadelphia to Pittsburgh" (Thwaites, vol. 9, 1907, pp. 64–65).

The Plank Road Boom, 1847–1853

By the 1840s the major turnpikes were increasingly eclipsed by the (often state-subsidized) canals and railroads. Many toll roads reverted to free public use and quickly degenerated into miles of dust, mud, and wheel-carved ruts. To link to the new and more powerful modes of communication, well-maintained, short-distance highways were still needed, but because governments became overextended in poor investments in canals, taxpayers were increasingly reluctant to fund internal improvements. Private entrepreneurs found the cost of the technologically most attractive road surfacing material (macadam, a compacted covering of crushed stones) prohibitively expensive at $3,500 per mile. Thus the ongoing need for new feeder roads spurred the search for innovation, and plank roads—toll roads surfaced with wooden planks—seemed to fit the need.

The plank road technique appears to have been introduced into Canada from Russia in 1840. It reached New York a few years later, after the village Salina, near Syracuse, sent civil engineer George Geddes to Toronto to investigate. After two trips Geddes (whose father, James, was an engineer for the Erie and Champlain Canals, and an enthusiastic canal advocate) was convinced of the plank roads' feasibility and became their great booster. Plank roads, he wrote in *Scientific American* (Geddes 1850a), could be built at an average cost of $1,500—although $1,900 would have been more accurate (Majewski, Baer and Klein 1994, p. 109, fn15). Geddes also published a pamphlet containing an influential, if overly optimistic, estimate that Toronto's road planks had lasted eight years (Geddes 1850b).

No less important than plank road economics and technology were the public policy changes that accompanied plank roads. Policymakers, perhaps aware that overly restrictive charters had hamstrung the first turnpike movement, were more permissive in the plank road era. Adjusting for *deflation*, toll rates were higher, tollgates were separated by shorter distances, and fewer local travelers were exempted from payment of tolls.

Although few today have heard of them, for a short time it seemed that plank roads might be one of the great innovations of the day. In just a few years, more than 1,000 companies built more than 10,000 miles of plank roads nationwide, including more than 3,500 miles in New York (Klein and Majewski 1994; Majewski, Baer, and Klein 1993). According to one observer, plank roads, along with canals and railroads, were "the three great inscriptions graven on the earth by the hand of modern science, never to be obliterated, but to grow deeper and deeper" (Bogart, 1851).

Except for most of New England, plank roads were chartered throughout the United States, especially in the top lumber-producing states of the Midwest and Mid-Atlantic states, as shown in Table 12.4.

New York, the leading lumber state, had both the greatest number of plank road charters (350) and the largest value of lumber production ($13,126,000 in 1849 dollars). Plank roads were especially popular in rural dairy counties, where farmers needed quick and dependable transportation to urban markets (Majewski, Baer, and Klein 1993).

The plank road and eastern turnpike episodes shared several features in common. As in the early eastern turnpike movement, investment in plank road companies came from local landowners, farmers, merchants, and professionals. Stock purchases were motivated less by the prospect of earning dividends than by the convenience and increased trade and development that the roads would bring. To many communities, plank roads held the hope of revitalization and the reversal (or slowing) of relative decline. But attaining these benefits, again, faced a free-rider problem. Thus, investors in plank roads, like the investors of the earlier turnpikes, also were motivated often by esteem mechanisms— community allegiance and appreciation, reputational incentives, and their own conscience.

Table 12.5 shows the residences of plank road stockholders in five New York counties that each had a large city and an agricultural hinterland. Only 26 percent of the funding came from the five big cities, even though the five cities had 36 percent of the population and 50 percent of the assessed real estate in the five counties. If people bought plank road stock primarily for anticipated dividends, wouldn't the big city folk have taken a larger portion of it?

Table 12.4
Plank Road Incorporation by State

State	Number
New York	335
Pennsylvania	315
Ohio	205
Wisconsin	130
Michigan	122
Illinois	88
North Carolina	54
Missouri	49
New Jersey	25
Georgia	16
Iowa	14
Vermont	14
Maryland	13
Connecticut	7
Massachusetts	1
Rhode Island, Maine	0
Total	**1388**

Notes: The figure for Ohio is through 1851; Pennsylvania, New Jersey, and Maryland are through 1857. Few plank roads were incorporated after 1857. In western states, some roads were incorporated and built as plank roads, so the 1388 total is not to be taken as a total for the nation. For a complete description of the sources for this table, see Majewski, Baer, and Klein 1993, p. 110.

Table 12.5
Capital Stock Owned by Big City Investors
in Counties with a Big City

County (Big City)	Total Capital Stock ($)	Investment from Big City ($)	Percentage from Big City
Albany (Albany)	66,800	37,625	56
Erie (Buffalo)	63,675	10,200	16
Monroe (Rochester)	111,175	26,825	24
Oneida (Utica)	264,275	42,950	16
Onondaga (Syracuse)	100,165	40,325	40
Totals	606,090	157,925	26

Note: "Total Capital Stock" refers to the total amount of stock purchased by residents of the county.

Source: Articles of association of plank road companies (Majewski, Baer, and Klein 1993, p. 115).

Rather, this evidence supports the view that stock was purchased by towns-people seeking to link up with the big cities and the major rail and canal con-nections. Use and esteem, not dividends, motivated much of the participation.

Although plank roads were smooth and sturdy, faring better in rain and snow than did dirt and gravel roads, they lasted only four or five years—not the eight to twelve that promoters had claimed. Thus, the rush of construction ended sud-denly by 1853, and by 1865 most companies had either switched to dirt and gravel surfaces or abandoned their road altogether.

Toll Roads in the Far West, 1850 to 1902

Unlike the areas served by the earlier turnpikes and plank roads, Colorado, Nevada, and California in the 1850s and 1860s were the frontier. These areas lacked the settled communities and social networks that induce fellows to par-ticipate in community enterprise and improvement. Miners and the merchants who served them knew that the mining boom would not continue indefinitely and therefore seldom planted deep roots in their communities. Nor were the large farms that later populated California ripe for civic engagement in any-where near the degree of the small farm communities of the east. Society in the early years of the West was not one where town meetings, door-to-door solicitations, and newspaper campaigns were likely to rally broad support for a road project.

The lack of strong communities also meant that there would be few oppo-nents to pressure the government for toll exemptions and otherwise hamper toll road operations. These conditions ensured that toll roads would tend to be more profit-oriented than the eastern turnpikes and plank road companies. Still, it is not clear whether on the whole the toll roads of the Far West were profitable.

The California toll road era began in 1850 after passage of general laws of incorporation. In 1853 new laws were passed reducing stock subscription requirements from $2,000 per mile to $300 per mile. The 1853 laws also dele-gated regulatory authority to the county governments. Counties were allowed "to set tolls at rates not to prevent a return of 20 percent," but they did not inter-fere with the location of toll roads and usually looked favorably on the toll road companies. After passage of the 1853 laws, the number of toll road incorpora-tions increased dramatically, peaking to nearly forty new incorporations in 1866 alone. Companies were also created by special acts of the legislature. And some-times they seemed to have operated without formal incorporation at all. David and Linda Beito (1998, pp. 75, 84) show that in Nevada many entrepreneurs had built and operated toll roads—or basic social infrastructure—before there was a State of Nevada, and some operated for years without any government author-ity at all. It wasn't by the grace of government "preconditions" that they acted and succeeded. Freedom to act and security from government encroachment is all society needs to move forward.

All told, in the Golden State, approximately 414 toll road companies were initiated,[4] resulting in at least 159 companies that successfully built and operated toll roads. Table 12.6 provides some rough numbers for toll roads in western states. The numbers presented there are minimums. For California and Nevada, the numbers probably only slightly underestimate the true totals; for the other states the figures are quite sketchy and might significantly underestimate true totals. Again, an abundance of testimony indicates that the private road companies were the serious road builders, in terms of quantity and quality (see the ten quotations at Klein and Yin 1996, pp. 689–90).

A Rough Tally

Table 12.7 makes an attempt to justify guesses about total number of toll road companies and total toll road miles. The first three numbers in the "Incorporations" column come from Tables 12.2, 12.4, and 12.6. The estimates of success rates and average road length (in the third and fourth columns) are extrapolations from components that have been studied with more care. We have made these estimates conservative, in the sense of avoiding any overstatement of the extent of private road building. The ~ symbol has been used to keep the reader mindful of the fact that many of these numbers are guesstimates. The numbers in the right hand column have been rounded to the nearest 1,000, so as to avoid any impression of accuracy. The "Other" row throws in a line to suggest a minimum to cover all the regions, periods, and road types not covered in Tables 12.2, 12.4, and 12.6. For example, the "Other" row

Table 12.6
Rough Minimums on Toll Roads in the West

	Toll Road Incorporations	Toll Roads Actually Built
California	414	159
Colorado	350	n.a.
Nevada	n.a.	117
Texas	50	n.a.
Wyoming	11	n.a.
Oregon	10	n.a.

Sources: For California, Klein and Yin 1996, pp. 681–82; for Nevada, Beito and Beito 1998, p. 74; for the other states, notes and correspondence in D. Klein's files.

Table 12.7
A Rough Tally of the Private Toll Roads

Toll Road Movements	Incorporations	% Successful in Building Road	Roads Built and Operated	Average Road Length	Toll Road Miles Operated
Turnpikes incorporated from 1792 to 1845	1562	~55 %	~859	~18	~15,000
Plank Roads incorporated from 1845 to roughly 1860	1388	~65 %	~902	~10	~9,000
Toll Roads in the West incorporated from 1850 to roughly 1902	~1127	~40 %	~450	~15	~7,000
Other	~<1000> [a rough guess]	~50 %	~500	~16	~8,000
Ranges for TOTALS	5,000–5,600 incorporations	48–60 percent	2,500–3,200 roads	12–16 miles	30,000– 52,000 miles

Source: Those of Tables 12.2, 12.4, and 12.6, plus the research files of the authors.

would cover turnpikes in the East, South, and Midwest after 1845 (Virginia's turnpike boom came in the late 1840s and 1850s), and all turnpikes and plank roads in Indiana, whose county-based incorporation, it seems, has never been systematically researched. Ideally, not only would the numbers be more definite and complete, but there would be a weighting by years of operation. The "30,000–52,000 miles" should be read as a range for the sum of all the miles operated by any company at any time during the 100+ year period.

Governmental Preconditions for Economic Development?

The success of American toll roads calls into question the prevailing assumptions among many historians and developmental economists regarding the need for government action. In nineteenth-century-America historiography, the larger "Commonwealth school," and to a great extent the mainstream of historians, have sought historical precedence and justification for twentieth-century levels of government activism (see Lively 1955). Books such as George Rogers Taylor's *The Transportation Revolution, 1815–1860* (1951) affirmed the centrality of government in establishing order and basic services, the "preconditions" or "framework" of American life. In his *State Government and Economic Development: A History of Administrative Policies in California, 1849–1933*, Gerald D. Nash repeatedly suggests that the state government was the precondition of enterprise and the source of progress.

In economics, for ages it has been conventional wisdom that "markets fail" when it comes to certain public utilities and public goods, and that government intervention and tax dollars are required to build roads. In the more specialized field of development economics, many researchers and officials believe that government must provide basic infrastructure to lift a developing society through the early stages of economic growth. These ideas have helped to justify government projects in the developing world, as well as foreign aid. Referring to the early 1960s, a page at the Website of the U.S. Agency for International Development (US AID) says: "The economic development theory of W.W. Rostow, which posited 'stages of economic development,' most notably a 'takeoff into growth' stage, provided the premise for much of the development planning in the newly-formed U.S. Agency for International Development" (US AID 2002). Although the theories of W.W. Rostow may be *passé* in academic circles, the notion that government needs to build (or rebuild) a society's infrastructure remains dominant.

America's vibrant nineteenth-century toll road movement suggests that what is really important is freedom to act and security from government encroachment. It's true that the moral sensibilities of Americans in the nineteenth century were especially favorable to their lifting themselves up by their own bootstraps. And it's true that throughout the country and the century toll road companies were typically granted eminent domain powers and often preexisting paths or roadbeds. But, again, it is by no means clear that these forms of privilege and subsidy were crucial (see Bruce Benson's chapter on eminent domain in this volume). Moreover, these forms are minor in comparison to common practice today, namely, funding by taxpayers and planning and operation by government. The massive toll road experience in America, spilling over 100+ years, ought to lead one to reconsider any presumption about government dominating the field of road provision, as well as any presumption about government dominating or leading the process of economic development.

The Toll Road Company versus Progressivism

In 1880 many toll road companies nationwide continued to operate—probably in the range of 400 to 600 companies.[5] But by 1920 the private toll road was almost entirely stamped out. From Maine to California, the laws and political attitudes from around 1880 onward moved against the handling of social affairs in ways that seemed informal, inexpert, and unsystematic. Although there was never an age of laissez-faire, during the late nineteenth century the social and political mindset was becoming something more directly at odds with spontaneous order. Important social affairs would be administered free of peculiar economic or political interests by professional experts. They would centrally plan and optimize systems for the overall benefit of society. The independent private toll road did not fit the program.

Progressivism was a burgeoning of collectivist ideology and policy reform. Many progressive intellectuals took inspiration from European socialist doctrines. Although the politics of restraining corporate evils had a democratic and populist aspect, the bureaucratic spirit was highly managerial and hierarchical, intending to replicate the efficiency of large corporations in the new professional and scientific administration of government (Higgs 1987, pp. 113–116; Ekirch 1967, pp. 171–94).

How this translated into public policy was captured by H. L. Mencken in 1926: "The Progressive is one who is in favor of more taxes instead of less, more bureaus and jobholders, more paternalism and meddling, more regulation of private affairs and less liberty."[6] Progressivism in the United States was the first big wave of a sea change—the onset of the kind of social democracy (big, democratic government that readily taxes, spends, and intervenes in the name of serving "the general welfare")—that now blankets the so-called free world.

One might point to the rise of the bicycle and later the automobile, which needed a harder and smoother surface. But that is a demand-side change that does not speak to the issues of road ownership and tolling. Automobiles achieved higher speeds, which made stopping to pay a toll more inconvenient, and that may have reinforced the anti-toll-road company movement that was underway prior to the automobile. Such developments figured into the history of road policy, but they really did not provide a good reason for the policy movement against the toll roads. The end of the toll roads, then, did not come principally from developments in road management or technology, or particular failings of the road companies still in operation.

The following words of a county board of supervisors in New York in 1906 indicate the methods and ideas used against the toll road companies:

[T]he ownership and operation of this road by a private corporation is contrary to public sentiment in this county, and [the] cause of good roads, which has received so much attention in this state in recent years, requires that this antiquated system should be abolished. . . . That public opinion throughout the state is strongly in favor of the abolition of toll roads is indicated by the fact that since the passage of the act of 1899, which permits counties to acquire these roads, the boards of supervisors of most of the counties where such roads have existed have availed themselves of its provisions and practically abolished the toll road.

In other words, county governments are justified in shutting down the companies because governments are shutting down the companies.

Inside the U.S. Department of Agriculture, the new Office of Road Inquiry began in 1893 to gather information, conduct research, and "educate" for better roads. They opposed toll roads and the Federal Highway Act of 1916 barred the use of tolls on highways receiving federal money (Seely 1987, pp. 15, 79). Anti-toll-road sentiment became state and national policy. Since then, highways in the United States have been run mainly along socialist lines, although state governments later reintroduced toll financing, and in the 1990s federal resistance to tolling declined and several stretches of highway were built and managed by private companies (see Sullivan this volume, Samuel this volume).

Lessons for Highway Policy Today

Toll road history offers perspectives on many sweeping subjects such as the potency and forms of voluntary association, the relationship between commerce and community, and the changes that have taken place in America's character and ideology.

But here we confine ourselves to some highway-policy lessons that apply today not only in America but in other countries as well:

- Private toll roads brought advantages in terms of quantity, quality, and efficiency. These benefits were apparent in comparison to local government road care or the federal government's National Road. The virtues of private ownership—decisive authority over the resources, private ownership that tastes profit and loss, incentives to reduce costs and improve efficiency, dependence on the payments of customers, and lack of access to government largesse—still recommend private enterprise over government as the way of efficiently matching highway supply to demand.

- Private companies spontaneously developed extensive networks and systems of highway. The notion that highway integration must be centrally planned should bear the burden of proof.

- Over-regulation hampered the old toll roads. Regulatory demands for better service and user concessions often resulted in worse road conditions or no road at all. Policymakers today must understand the deleterious long-run consequences of restricting private road companies.

- The old toll roads faced significant regulations, but until the end of the century they were pretty confident in the rules of the game. In modern times the rules are prone to change harshly and without much warning.

To give private investors the confidence to undertake massive projects that will pay off over the course of decades, the government must ensure the integrity of the rules.

- Unlike the olds, the modern highways are often plagued by traffic jams. Today, electronic tolling enables automatic charging without vehicles having to stop and without the provision of large toll plazas and toll collectors. Under conditions of congestion the road officials can increase throughput simply by setting higher charges. It is worth noting that congestion constraints induce the private highway-owner to vary the toll charge roughly in keeping with social-welfare maximization. Furthermore, such charges not only reduce congestion on existing roads; they can help investors identify profitable ways to provide new ones.

- The old toll roads were plagued by toll evasion. The feasibility of private roads today is enhanced by electronic technologies that ease toll collection and prevent toll evasion.

- The old toll roads assembled and cleared their route swiftly and easily. Today the process of environmental clearance involves tremendous delays, outlays, and uncertainties. If new road facilities are going to be built, whether by private enterprise or by government, the clearance and entitlement process must somehow be simplified.

Looking back, one might say that the American people ran an experiment: 100 years with extensive privately managed toll roads, and then another 100 years primarily of government managed "freeways." The historical record suggests that road provision is another case where the advantages of private ownership, relative to government ownership, and of user-fees, relative to tax financing, apply. Learning from the mistakes of both epochs, Americans and people in other countries should embark on a new century of road provision.

Notes

1. For a discussion of returns and expectations, see Klein 1990, pp. 791–95.
2. See Klein 1990, pp. 803–808; Klein and Majewski 1994, pp. 56–61.
3. Illustrative tidbits are found at Klein 1990, p. 807.
4. The 414 figure consists of 222 companies organized under the general law, 102 charted by the legislature, and ninety that we learned of by county records, local histories, and various other sources.
5. Durrenberger (1931, p. 164) notes that in 1911 there were 108 turnpikes operating in Pennsylvania alone.
6. From an article by Mencken in the Baltimore *Evening Sun*, January 19, 1926; the passage also appears in DuBasky 1990, p. 385.

References

Baer, Christoper T., Daniel B. Klein, and John Majewski. 1993. "From Trunk to Branch: Toll Roads in New York, 1800–1860." *Essays in Economic and Business History* (Selected papers from the Economic and Business Historical Society 1992) XI: 191–192.

Beito, David T., and Linda Royster Beito. 1998. "Rival Road Builders: Private Toll Roads in Nevada, 1852–1880." *Nevada Historical Society Quarterly* 41 (Summer): 71–91.

Benson, Bruce. 1994. "Are Public Goods Really Common Pools? Consideration of the Evolution of Policing and Highways in England." *Economic Inquiry* 32: 2.

Bodenhorn, Howard. 2000. *A History of Banking in Antebellum America.* New York: Cambridge University Press.

Bogart, W. H. 1851. "First Plank Road." *Hunt's Merchant Magazine.*

Brown, Richard D. 1973. "The Emergence of Voluntary Associations in Massachusetts, 1760–1830." *Journal of Voluntary Action Research* Spring: 64–73.

Cage, R. A. 1984. "The Lowden Empire: A Case Study of Wagon Roads in Northern California." *The Pacific Historian* 28 (Summer): 33–48.

Davis, Joseph S. 1917. *Essays in the Earlier History of American Corporations.* Cambridge: Harvard University Press.

DuBasky, Mayo. 1990. *The Gist of Mencken: Quotations from America's Critic.* Metuchen, NJ: The Scarecrow Press.

Durrenberger, J. A. 1981. *Turnpikes: A Study of the Toll Road Movement in the Middle Atlantic States and Maryland.* Valdosta, Ga.: Southern Stationery and Printing Co.

Ekirch, Arthur A., Jr. 1967. *The Decline of American Liberalism.* New York: Atheneum.

Fishlow, Albert. 2000. "Internal Transportation in the Nineteenth and Early Twentieth Centuries" in *The Cambridge Economic History of the United States, Vol. II: The Long Nineteenth Century*, edited by Stanley L. Engerman and Robert E. Gallman. New York: Cambridge.

Gallatin, Albert. 1808. "Report on Roads and Canals." Published in *American State Papers*, Miscellaneous Vol. I. Washington D.C.: Gales and Seaton, 1834: 724–741.

Geddes, George. 1850a. *Scientific American* 5 (April 27).

Geddes, George. 1850b. *Observations Upon Plank Roads.* Syracuse: L.W. Hall.

Goodrich, Carter. 1948. "Public Spirit and American Improvements." *Proceedings of the American Philosophical Society* 92 (October): 305–309.

Goodrich, Carter. 1960. *Government Promotion of American Canals and Railroads, 1800–1890.* New York: Columbia University Press.

Gunderson, Gerald. 1989. "Privatization and the 19th-Century Turnpike." *Cato Journal* 9 (1), Spring/Summer: 191–200.

Handlin, Oscar and Mary F. Handlin. 1945. "Origins of the American Business Corporation." *Journal of Economic History* 5 (May): 1–23.

Higgs, Robert. 1987. *Crises and Leviathan: Critical Episodes in the Growth of American Government.* New York: Oxford University Press.

Higgs, Robert. 1997. "Regime Uncertainty: Why the Great Depression Lasted So Long and Why Prosperity Resumed after the War." *The Independent Review: A Journal of Political Economy* 1(4), Spring: 561–600.

Hurst, James Willard. 1956. *Law and the Conditions of Freedom in the Nineteenth-Century United States.* Madison: University of Wisconsin Press.

Hurst, James Willard. 1970. *The Legitimacy of the Business Corporation in the Law of the United States, 1780–1970*. Charlottesville: University Press of Virginia.

Kaplan, Michael D. 1975. "The Toll Road Building Career of Otto Mears, 1881–1887." *Colorado Magazine* 52 (Spring): 153–170.

Kirkland, Edward C. 1948. *Men, Cities and Transportation: A Study in New England History, 1820–1900*. Cambridge, Mass.: Harvard University Press.

Klein, Daniel. 1990. "The Voluntary Provision of Public Goods? The Turnpike Companies of Early America." *Economic Inquiry* October: 788–812. Reprinted as chapter 4 in *The Voluntary City*, edited by D. Beito and P. Gordon. Ann Arbor, Michigan: University of Michigan Press for The Independent Institute, 2002.

Klein, Daniel B., and Gordon J. Fielding. 1992. "Private Toll Roads: Learning from the 19th Century." *Transportation Quarterly* 46, 3 (July): 321–341.

Klein, Daniel B., and John Majewski. 1992. "Economy, Community and Law: The Turnpike Movement in New York, 1797–1845." *Law & Society Review* 26 (3): 469–512.

Klein, Daniel B., and John Majewski. 1994. "Plank Road Fever in Antebellum America: New York State Origins." *New York History* 39–65.

Klein, Daniel B., and Chi Yin. 1996. "Use, Esteem, and Profit in Voluntary Provision: Toll Roads in California, 1850–1902." *Economic Inquiry* October: 678–92.

Kresge, David T., and Paul O. Roberts. 1971. *Techniques of Transport Planning, Volume Two: Systems Analysis and Simulation Models*. Washington D.C.: Brookings Institution.

Lane, Wheaton J. 1939. *From Indian Trail to Iron Horse: Travel and Transportation in New Jersey, 1620–1860*. Princeton: Princeton University Press.

Lively, Robert A. 1955. "The American System: A Review Article." *Business History Review* 29 (March): 81–96.

Majewski, John. 2000. *A House Dividing: Economic Development in Pennsylvania and Virginia before the Civil War*. New York: Cambridge University Press.

Majewski, John. 2001. "The Booster Spirit and 'Mid-Atlantic' Distinctiveness: Shareholding in Pennsylvania Banking and Transportation Corporations, 1800 to 1840." Manuscript, Department of History, UC Santa Barbara.

Majewski, John, Christopher Baer, and Daniel B. Klein. 1993. "Responding to Relative Decline: The Plank Road Boom of Antebellum New York." *Journal of Economic History* 53, 1 (March): 106–122.

Nash, Christopher A. 1988. "Integration of Public Transport: An Economic Assessment," in *Bus Deregulation and Privatisation: An International Perspective*, edited by J. S. Dodgson and N. Topham. Brookfield, Massachusetts: Avebury, pp. 97–223.

Nash, Gerald D. 1964. *State Government and Economic Development: A History of Administrative Policies in California, 1849–1933*. Berkeley: University of California Press (Institute of Governmental Studies).

North, Douglass C. 1966. *Growth and Welfare in the American Past*. Englewood Cliffs, NJ: Prentice-Hall.

Parks, Roger N. 1967. *Roads and Travel in New England, 1790-1840*. Sturbridge, MA: Old Sturbridge Inco.

Pawson, Eric C. 1977. *Transport and Economy: The Turnpike Roads of Eighteenth Century Britain*. London: Academic Press.

Peyton, Billy Joe. 1996. "Survey and Building the [National] Road" in *The National Road*, edited by Karl Raitz. Baltimore: Johns Hopkins.

Poole, Robert W. 1996. "Private Toll Roads," in *Privatizing Transportation Systems*, edited by Simon Hakim, Paul Seidenstate, and Gary W. Bowman. Westport, CT: Praeger.

Reiser, Catherine Elizabeth. 1951. *Pittsburgh's Commercial Development, 1800–1850*. Harrisburg: Pennsylvania Historical and Museum Commission.

Ridgway, Arthur. 1932. "The Mission of Colorado Toll Roads." *Colorado Magazine* 9 (September): 161–169.

Roth, Gabriel. 1996. *Roads in a Market Economy*. Aldershot, UK: Avebury Technical.

Searight, Thomas B. 1894. *The Old Pike: A History of the National Road*. Uniontown, PA: Thomas Searight.

Seely, Bruce E. 1987. *Building the American Highway System: Engineers as Policy Makers*. Philadelphia: Temple University Press.

Spafford, Horatio Gates. 1824. *A Gazetteer of the State of New York*. Reprinted 1981, Interlaken, N.Y.: Heart of the Lakes Publishing.

Sullivan, Edward C. 2006. "HOT Lanes in Southern California." Chapter 9 in this volume.

Taylor, George R. 1951. *The Transportation Revolution, 1815–1860*. New York: Rinehart and Co.

Taylor, Philip E. 1934. "The Turnpike Era in New England," Ph.D. thesis, Yale University.

Thwaites, Reuben Gold. 1907. *Early Western Travels, 1746–1846*. Cleveland, Ohio: A. H. Clark.

U.S. Agency for International Development. 2002. "A History of Foreign Assistance." On the US AID website. Posted April 3, 2002. Accessed January 20, 2003.

Wood, Frederick J. 1919. *The Turnpikes of New England and Evolution of the Same through England, Virginia, and Maryland*. Boston: Marshall Jones Co.

13

Streets as Private-Sector Public Goods

Fred E. Foldvary

Many private communities own their streets, often with higher-quality service than governmental provision provides. Broadly regarded, including corridors and alleyways for vehicular or pedestrian traffic, private streets are ubiquitous in malls, apartment houses, hotels, and other real estate.

Nevertheless, streets have conventionally been regarded as public goods that are natural monopolies. As public goods, the market-failure argument has been that once provided, it is not feasible to exclude people, so many will be free riders, using the streets without paying, because there is no way a private firm can efficiently charge the users. Streets have also been regarded as monopolies, since a typical residence or business faces one street, and a private owner could exploit the residents with excessively high charges, as there is no competitive alternative to that street.

Both these arguments are unwarranted both in theory and in practice. Private streets are economically feasible when a firm or association controls the space and the common elements of a community, and can therefore collect the associated rentals from the members or the public. Charges for parking, congestion, transit curb rights, pollution, as well as fines, can complement the rental financing of streets and the associated lights, signs, sidewalks, and drainage.

The monopoly nature of streets is overcome by offering the street as part of a whole package of civic services. A guest at a hotel is not exploited by the hotel's monopoly of the corridor. The guest has a gratis use of the hallway, along with other facilities, when he pays for a room. A member of a residential association likewise pays an assessment for the private street, along with other services such as bus transit, parking, community buildings, and security. There is competition among hotels or associations, and one does not find separately owned hotel hallways or community streets. A typical customer or member would not enter into such an exploitative contract.

Examples of Private Streets

The Private Places of St. Louis

Since the middle 1800s there have been "private places" in St. Louis and neighboring towns in which the streets are owned by a private association. The association maintains the street, some of them closing one end with a gate for passage control. With greater surveillance complementing the reduced access, there has been less crime in the private places, resulting in higher property values.

While private streets are provided by many private communities and some firms run private toll roads, major avenues are typically operated at the city level, but in St. Louis, some boulevards have been privately owned. An advantage of such ownership is the ability to control the utilities along the route (Beito and Smith 1990, p. 288).

The St. Louis "private places" are a prime example of single-family housing in private associations in the midst of a city. These are integrated within the city of St. Louis and the towns of St. Louis County. In St. Louis, "street ownership [has] represented the means to control the 'commanding heights' of the local economy" (Beito 1989, p. 35). Despite the expense, some streets that were not private have become so since World War II (Savage, 1987, p. xi). Among these is Waterman Place, an integrated lower-class neighborhood that was experiencing crime and physical deterioration. In 1974, the residents formed a residential association and partially closed the street, spending $40,000 to erect a gate. A block watch was started, and crime decreased. The association was able to borrow funds to improve the street and housing. Property values doubled (Fitzgerald 1988, p. 47; Frazier 1989, p. 64).

Since the city does not reduce the property tax by what it saves in not having to maintain the street, there is an imposed cost on the private places. The fact that they flourish in the face of the extra cost demonstrates the value of having a private street.

Rossmoor, California

Rossmoor is an adult residential association in Contra Costa County, California, within the City of Walnut Creek, in the eastern part of the San Francisco Bay Area. The builder, Ross W. Cortese, began development in 1963. Terra California purchased the development from the Rossmoor Corporation in 1968, and in 1984, Terra California was purchased by the Universal Development Corporation.

Terra paid $12 million for 1,300 acres, 600 developable, or $20,000 per buildable acre. After grading the land and paving the streets, the improvement costs of $19,000 brought the cost of the sites to about $40,000 per acre of buildable area (Henry 1984, p. 32, citing a 1971 letter from the president of Terra California).

Rossmoor now has 2,200 acres, about 65 percent of which is open space, and over 9,000 residents living in 6,400 "manors" or residential units. Rossmoor was patterned after a previous Cortese development at Seal Beach, California, built in 1961 (Henry 1984, p. 2). There are other Cortese adult communities in Laguna Hills, California, and in New Jersey and Maryland. The community streets, street lighting, and other facilities were conveyed from the developer to the community association.

Currently there are 6,500 dwelling units, with an expected build-out of 7,000. Of these, 40 percent are garden-style condominiums, the remaining being mid-rise condominiums and cooperatives. A few single-unit houses have also been built.

The minimum age requirement is fifty-five years for one spouse, but the community is not exclusively for retirement, since some members work (but residents may not be employed for wages by Rossmoor or its local neighborhood "Mutuals"). Most residents are retired and elderly; the average age of female residents is seventy-seven, and that of male residents is seventy-eight. Among the amenities offered are two golf courses, clubhouses, swimming pools, tennis courts, a library, and a computer center.

The streets are owned by the community, and there are controls at its single entry gate. Some 9,500 vehicles enter per day. There are 12 miles of streets, with 314 streetlights, as well as 10 acres of parking.

Residents have a vehicle identification decal for expedient entry, and guests obtain a pass to display in the car. Residents may obtain a limited number of passes for visitors and must telephone in advance to allow one-day clearance for guests, but family and friends may also obtain a one-year pass. The twenty-four-hour safety system operated by the Rossmoor Public Safety Department operates the entrance and patrols the community, responding to emergencies and requests. Due to these security measures, Rossmoor is almost crime free.

In exchange for the right of exclusion, Rossmoor owns, maintains, and finances its streets and street lighting. The street maintenance is contracted to private firms (Schrantz, 2001).

The funding for Rossmoor's public works comes from their reserve fund, and the street maintenance constitutes more than half of the total $595,676 budgeted for trust reserve works, not including the medical center, and the largest budget item within the public works is street repair and maintenance (Schrantz, 2000).

As a community of older people, sidewalk maintenance is vital, since the residents are vulnerable to falling if the sidewalks have cracks and holes. The sidewalks as well as the streets are maintained to quality standards superior to those in a typical city (Schrantz, 2001).

Besides providing access to the residences, the streets are also adjacent to several pet exercise areas. The speed limit in Rossmoor is 25 miles per hour. Being within the city limits of Walnut Creek, all city ordinances are in force at Rossmoor, as is the Vehicle Code of California. Speed limit and other signs and regulatory markings are under the responsibility of the City of Walnut Creek Traffic Engineer. All law enforcement agencies have unrestricted access to the community (Grant 1999, p. 1).

Rossmoor is divided into neighborhood associations called "Mutuals." Each Mutual is governed by a board of directors and has authority over its "entries" or internal streets. A resident is thus a member of both the Golden Rain Foundation, which manages the whole community, and the local Mutual Benefit Housing Corporation.

Exhibit 13.1

Rossmoor operates its own private bus system, which operates nine buses on five routes seven days per week at a cost of about $1 per mile. The buses also travel to nearby shopping centers and the Rossmoor Medical Center located just outside the community. A paratransit bus service with a wheelchair lift serves handicapped residents. Feedback from the residents is an important criterion for judging how much bus service to provide (Hansen 2001). Such resident feedback demonstrates demand, which also affects the price of properties, thus indirectly the spending for the bus service is tied to the value of the manors, particularly their land value.

The residents pay association dues (called "coupon" payments) ranging from $340 to $600, which includes the basic fee for the Golden Rain Foundation, the trustee and managing agent for Rossmoor, and the local Mutuals. There is a one-time membership fee of $5,000 that finances the trust reserve fund, from which the street maintenance is financed. Owners of recreational vehicles pay a yearly fee for parking. There are also fees for using the golf courses.

Unlike a city government, Rossmoor must pay the county property tax on its community-owned property. Thus Rossmoor as a private community subsidizes government-owned city space, which takes rather than pays taxes.

Exhibit 13.2

Other Private Streets

Some examples of private streets are provided here to demonstrate their use in many areas of the world.

Florida. Walt Disney World has what may be the world's most famous private street: Main Street. The Reedy Creek Improvement District was created to facilitate the private development of WDW within a largely autonomous governmental structure. An objective of the District is "to provide streets, roads, bridges and street lighting facilities" (Berliner 1978).

Opened in Orlando, Florida, in 1971, "Main Street" in WDW, as in Disneyland in California, is one of the key attractions. On Main Street, the sidewalks are paved with resilient asphalt, which keeps legs from aching, and there are places to sit (Zehnder 1975, p. 259). Main Street is lined with Victorian shops, an evocation of "Main Street America." One of Disneyland's planners stated that its Main Street is "what the real Main Street should have been like" (Zukin 1991, p. 222). This utopian street is actually an image of what one would wish it were like rather than a realistic reconstruction. The buildings are built to from 5/8 to 7/8 of full size, a movie-set technique that renders them friendly to children while creating the illusion to adults that everything is smaller than they remembered. The street recreates Disney's hometown, Marceline, Missouri. Main Street is the heart of WDW, the "key to the secret of the Disney vision," recalling a time when America was simpler and more coherent (Stern 1986, p. 211).

Celebration, a town (legally, the Celebration Community Development District) owned by the Disney Corporation, was conceived by Walt Disney during the 1960s, but not inaugurated until 1996. The concept, in the spirit of the "New Urbanism," was to create a traditional American small town, one with clean, palm-lined streets, modern amenities, and rules that to some may seem restrictive and to others offer protection from blight and visual pollution. For example, no cars are allowed to park on the streets in residential areas. There has been no crime (Marjorie 2000).

The community is located on 4,900 acres in northwest Osceola County, south of Walt Disney World. On completion, Celebration will have some 8,000 houses and apartments, a small commercial district, a K-12 school, a teaching academy, a "wellness center," an eighteen-hole golf course, a 109-acre office park, and a recreational park with a swimming pool, tennis courts, basketball and volleyball courts, picnic areas, and eight miles of trails (Oliande and Brady 1997).

In the attempt to include a street life, the downtown area is connected by small, pedestrian-friendly streets accessible by car but designed to encourage walking. Commercial properties and public spaces, including the streets, are owned by the Celebration Company, while residential properties are owned by the homeowners who form the Celebration Residential Owner's Association. Through an arrangement with Osceola County, the association fees are charged as part of a resident's annual tax bill to the county ("Celebration, USA" 2001).

Philippines. Several communities in the Philippines have private streets. Among these are Camp John Hay in Baguio, Borocay, and the Ayala and Fort Bonifacio Development between Makati and Pasig (Taningco 2000).

Texas. The "Streets of Laredo" is a traditional western song; today, one could compose a song of the "private streets of Laredo," which during 1982–1985 sold 150 blocks to private enterprises and organizations. Until then, many of the city streets were still unpaved or needed repaving. The city officials decided to put the streets up for sale. Streets were purchased by motel owners, lumberyards, a railroad, a supermarket, a trailer park, and ordinary residents (Fitzgerald 1988 pp. 163–4).

Virginia. Located near Williamsburg, Virginia, Ford's Colony is a 2,500-acre residential community with single-family houses, townhouses, and condominiums, which opened in 1985. The main attraction is the golf course, which has its own membership. The "Ford's Colony at Williamsburg Homeowners Association" owns the streets and roads within the development. According to Mel Overman (1990), a salesman for the developer, the Ford's Colony road is maintained at a higher standard than those maintained by the public sector. Entrance to the property is through one secured gate with twenty-four-hour guards ("Ford's Colony Fact Sheet" 1990).

The Economics of Private Streets

Streets as Capital Goods Attached to Land

A "street" is an urban pathway other than a limited-access thoroughfare, the paths forming a grid over which traffic flows. The typical city street includes lanes for motor vehicles, sidewalks for pedestrians, traffic signs and possibly lights, lighting during nighttime, poles for telephone and other wires, and possibly sculptures, fountains, and plants along the sidewalk or a strip along the middle. Associated with the street and its traffic is an array of civic services such as policing and cleaning, possibly space for outdoor furniture (chairs and tables for cafes), and utility conveyance media such as water pipes and lines for telephones, cable television, and electricity. The urban street is thus a complex of goods and services requiring substantial maintenance along with the initial building.

The function of streets is to provide a transit medium for transportation and communications, lighting for safety and visibility, and a public space for urban social life. A street is thus not merely an urban circulatory system, but provides the fundamental infrastructure for urban life.

The three classical factors of production are land, labor, and capital goods. Land consists of all natural resources, including the three-dimensional space around the earth. Capital goods are produced goods that in turn are used to produce other goods. Labor includes all human exertion in the production of wealth.

Streets and associated utilities are thus in the category of capital goods. Streets, like parks and other public works, are "civic capital goods," community products that make urban life and commerce more productive or enjoyable. Like houses, streets are attached to land, taking up space and having a location. The provision of street service therefore includes the natural space, the produced capital goods, and the labor used in building and maintaining the goods. Capital goods depreciate both in wearing out and becoming obsolete, and much of the servicing of streets consists of the labor and capital goods applied to make up for the capital consumption of the street.

Because streets are long-lasting and retain much of the initial value added (including preparing the ground and blueprinting a development), much of the economic return from street provision consists of an implicit interest return on the capital invested. The same amount of funds would earn interest if it were in bonds, so the street is worth producing if it yields benefits of at least as much. Even though this interest is implicit, not paid in cash, it should be taken into account, whether by a private community or a government.

The Generation of Rent and Site Value

The privatization of streets also privatizes the relevant public finance. Governmental financing is usually based on the "ability to pay," which in practice is government's ability to extract revenue from sources offering the least political resistance, such as sales and general income. These sources are usually explicit flows, "anything that moves," unrelated to specific benefits. Because government funding is imposed by force, it does not need to link costs to benefits.

In contrast, the private financing of streets is based on voluntary contract, and competition leads to payments based on benefit. Civic associations or proprietary communities typically tap sources such as the value of membership, or the rental value generated by the service. The private-sector financing is more efficient in both having a lower economic burden and in being more directly related to the benefit provided.

The return on land, what tenants would bid to use it, is "rent." Strictly, pure rent is only the return on the natural qualities of land, such as its location and features such as the climate. The presence of civic capital goods such as streets, parks, and utilities increases the demand for residents and enterprises to be located in the territory. This demand increases the bids to rent and buy real estate, and these increases are a return to the civic capital goods rather than pure "land" rent.

Streets along with other civic goods thus become capitalized into site values. The price of an asset with a perpetual yield, such as a land, equals its annual return divided by the rate of interest, since the return is the interest rate times the price. A tax rate gets added to the rate of interest, since the yield or rent must pay the normal market return to the owner (price times interest rate) plus the tax (price times tax rate). Therefore, the price of a site, or plot of land, exclusive of the improvements on the site, is basically determined by the equation

$$p = r/(i + t) \tag{1}$$

where p is the purchase price of the site, r is the annual rental, i is the real interest rate, and t is the tax or assessment rate based on p. For example, if the price is \$100,000 and $t = .06$, the annual tax or assessment is \$6,000. If, say, the interest rate is 6 percent and the tax rate is 4 percent, then an improved street that raises the site rent from \$100 to \$120 will raise the price of the land from \$1000 to \$1200.

The existence of this rental implies that the local users of the civic goods are not generally free riders. They must pay the rental, whether explicitly to a landlord or implicitly as a mortgage and in the purchase price of the site, in order to access the territory's civic goods.

The economic reason why beneficiaries should pay for civic services is that this efficiently allocates goods to uses most highly valued by consumers. If beneficiaries do not pay for the cost of what they receive, then they are subsidized. Voluntary subsidies do not impose a burden on the economy, since the donors are just spending their resources where it gives them the most value. But when subsidies are imposed by government, it creates price distortions that skew resources away from where the marginal social value just equals the social marginal cost. Morally, subsidies imply a tax on those who are forced to provide the subsidy to the privileged recipients, taking wealth without any compensating benefit, violating the moral principle of equality before the law.

Income and sales taxes are not linked to any specific benefits. These taxes are arbitrary takings of explicit flows of revenue, allegedly based on "ability to pay." Aside from the personal and business burdens of paying the taxes, such taxes impose an excess burden on the economy by raising costs above true economic costs, reducing production and growth. In contrast, benefit-based public finance does not impose a burden, because the cost is offset by the benefit, which can often be greater than the tax-cost—there can be a beneficiary surplus just as there is a consumer surplus when a good is worth more to a consumer than what he pays.

As Friedman and Boorstin (1951, p. 230) pointed out, persons living by a road or street may be willing to pay much more for the road than a non-resident. They also noted that we "should try more than we have in the past to find ways of measuring the economic advantage which private individuals (other than travelers) receive from particular roads, to make them pay fairly for these advantages." These positive externalities or "neighborhood effects," they said, "are likely to be particularly important in cities."

There is a way in principle to measure the advantages from the neighborhood effects or external effects: by the site rent generated by the street. This is the extra rental due to the presence of a street and all its facilities and qualities. The neighborhood improvements can also make the local wages and capital values higher as well, if they are not very mobile.

This rental generated by territorial goods such as streets provides the means by which private enterprise can finance them. A company or civic association can collect a periodic rental or assessment, which the residents willingly pay in order to have the civic goods. In actual practice, private communities do in effect finance their civic goods by the generated rents rather than with charges based on sales or the incomes of the residents (Foldvary 1994). As Roth (1996, p. 98) states, providers in a market must cover their costs either from users "or beneficiaries, such as land-owners."

In some cases, such as Arden, Delaware, where the village land is owned by a trust, the payment is explicitly a site rental paid by a leaseholder. In most cases, the payment is an equal charge on all members or, as with condominiums, based on a "percentage interest" based on some initially determined relative market value for the unit. The economic effect in either case is similar to paying a rental independent of the value of the property value that is owned by the unit owner.

Governments could use the site rentals to finance their public goods, and some cities such as Sidney, Australia, do tax only the site value of real estate and not the improvements. Hong Kong has used leasehold rents for half its governmental revenue. Exempting the buildings and other improvements from taxation avoids inflicting a penalty on new construction, while the tax on the land rent or land value does not hamper investments, because the land is there anyway, and the tax is not passed on to tenants if the landlords were already charging what the market could bear.

The site rent can be collected in various methods. Aside from the explicit taxation of rent, localities obtain some of the rent when they tax real estate property. Private residential associations implicitly collect site rent in their monthly assessments. Entry fees and displayed licenses or permits also collect rent implicitly. Singapore created a central "Auto Restricted Zone" and "Area License Scheme" in 1975, requiring cars to display permits on their windscreens (Roth 1996, pp. xviii, 118). Such a cover charge for the use of space in effect charges rent. Technological advances can now shift the payment method to electronic signals, which then also enable time-of-day pricing.

If the civic goods and services are provided by government and financed by taxes that fall mostly on labor and business profits, including real-estate improvements, then in effect the users pay twice for the streets, once when paying the rental and again when paying taxes. In that case, the free rider is not a tenant user but the landowner, who benefits from both the civic goods and the increase in his explicit or implicit rental income.

Income and sales taxes on labor and enterprise as well as real-estate improvements (buildings) may actually fall partly on landowners when labor and capital are mobile and effectively placed lower bids on rents that equalize their returns relative to places with lower taxes relative to wanted government services. But such capitalization is incomplete, since the taxes impose an excess burden both in the compliance costs and because of the costs of moving, and because most jurisdictions also impose similar taxes.

Political pressures have induced most city and higher-level governments to base public financing on total real-estate value (including buildings and other improvements) as well as sales and income taxes, permit fees, business taxes, and other sources not related to site values. In contrast, private communities, not able to forcibly extract payments based on sales and income, have used rentals as their primary financing basis, the market tending to indeed use the more efficient methods of financing civic goods. Also, voting by tenants will induce higher expenditures than voting by owners, the latter tending to favor spending mainly when there is a rent-enhancing benefit.

The use of taxes on wages, profits, and sales to finance the streets and other civic infrastructure has an excess burden, a social welfare cost more than the transactions costs and loss of social efficiency, as it artificially raises prices on the items taxed, shifting resources away from uses where they are most wanted. Moreover, if streets are financed from taxes on non-rent sources, then improvements such as the reduction of congestion and commuting times with more and larger freeways have a perverse result: They increase the demand for such locations, hence land rent and prices. Tenants as well as new buyers may end up with little net benefit as the savings in commuting time is offset by both higher taxes and the higher cost of using the land. As Stern and Ayres

(1973, pp. 146–7) put it, "Residual consumer surpluses will be passed on to users but this will, in turn, result in increased land rents. . . . The value of time saved is captured *at the margin* by the landowner" at the time the improvement is made.

With private streets, this problem is largely alleviated. Without the power of the state to extract the cost from workers and consumers, developers and ultimately the site owners pay for the streets, so the value added by the improvements is in turn used to finance them. The use of the rental to finance the works is then capitalized into a lower land price. This eliminates the subsidy windfall to landowners and the double payment faced by workers and consumers; there is only one payment, namely the rental.

On the cost side, in a study by Robert Deacon of twenty-three associations and forty-one comparable towns, associations are reported as paying 58 percent of what governments would spend for similar police services, and 70 percent of similar sovereign expenditures for street maintenance (Frazier 1980, p. 100). One factor accounting for the less efficient government service is the independent civil service, which is less responsive to the residents.

Fees for Parking, Parades, and Other Uses

Private communities can generate other revenues from streets besides rentals or assessments. Parking meters collect a rental for the use of street space. The primary normative purpose of meters, however, should be the efficient allocation of parking space, rather than revenue. The ideal fee is just high enough to remove congestion, so that one may usually find a parking space within one or two blocks. (The parker pays the marginal cost of imposing a congestion cost on others.) Modern metering technology enables cars to park for indefinite periods of time without having to enter coins, and with charges that can vary during the day (Shoup 2003).

Marginal-cost pricing could also be used to prevent the congestion of the street itself. Electronic methods, with devices in cars, would enable charges that vary during the day, payments being just high enough per hour to avoid congestion. David Friedman (1989 [1970], p. 15) reported a marginal congestion cost at about $5 per trip at rush hour in 1970, which at the present day would probably be $10. Many non-commuters would avoid the highest charge by driving during less costly times, and the charges would induce many commuters to take public transit and carpools, and some firms to have more flexible work times.

Pilot projects on "variable pricing" are already underway; Maryland, for example, has three demonstration projects. They are starting with "eye-ballable hang-tags" and are expected to progress to electronic tolling (Samuel 2000, p. 5).

In dense cities, congestion charges would induce people to use public transit, which the private community could also provide. Private communities could sensibly reverse the tendency of governments and provide gratis public transit while charging cars for the use of the streets during the most crowded times.

William Vickrey (1969) distinguished several categories of congested situations. Single interaction involves two cars that are close enough so that one must be delayed to avoid collision, typical of light traffic. Multiple interaction involves higher levels of traffic density; the delay experienced by the marginal car inflicts a multiple of that delay on others. Besides delay, a cost of congestion is increased vehicle accidents.

Roth (1996, p. 76) points out that the optimal road density may not be an absence of congestion, but that amount whereby "those who find it least worthwhile to use the network receive benefits from using it equal to the costs imposed by them on the rest of the traffic." Some amount of crowding may be tolerated if it is of value to have more cars on the street, even if they move more slowly. This is something that could be adjusted by trial and error. Normally, the streets should be decongested enough so that a car may keep moving, even if not at top speed.

Street Furniture, Utilities, and Security

The proprietor or developer of a community can provide an enhanced urban environment with appropriate street furniture such as sculptures and fountains, especially in the downtown centers. The sidewalks can have benches and shelters, especially at bus stops. Having plenty of trash collection containers enhances the beauty and health of the environment. The lighting fixtures can also be a type of art, such as having nostalgic historical designs. All these types of street furniture add to the attractiveness of the community and enhance site values.

Urban utilities such as water, sewerage, lighting, and drainage can be provided privately and financed by the rentals. A private community would then be able to charge more rationally than is typically done by city governments. For example, water is usually charged by volume rather than also by location. Given some central source of city water (after being transported into the city), it is more costly per unit of volume to service the fringes of the city than the center. The delivery of water to the fringe requires pipe capacity all the way to the center (Gaffney 1964). Longer distances are thus more costly, and if the user does not pay this cost, he is implicitly subsidized. Gaffney (1964, p. 18) notes that with a unitary real-estate tax, "by taxing buildings we are taxing vertical transportation" including stairs and elevators, while subsidizing horizontal streets and transportation. Such a subsidy increases the site value at the fringe relative to the center, which is effectively taxed to subsidize the fringe dwellers. A new buyer of fringe land does not even benefit, since the subsidy is reflected in the higher price for the site; the gain goes to the owner at the time the construction was made. A profit-seeking private provider would maximize returns by efficient pricing, unlike governments, which are subject to political pressures.

Private commercial communities such as hotels and shopping centers employ security services, and civic associations may also have private security. Usually the policing services of private communities are directed at safety rather than also policing for more cultural concerns, such as preventing gambling. Residential associations also enforce covenants regarding the appearance and architecture of the dwellings.

Restricting Access to Streets

Security devices in private communities can include the entrances of "gated" communities through which one must enter and submit identification or ask permission for entrance. Many private communities are not gated, as there is a cost to gating, and when access is restricted, it is to protect the community from harm. In St. Louis, some of the private neighborhoods have closed off one end of the street (see Figure 13.1). The residents also provide for surveillance, and they have had less crime as a result (Newman 1980).

Figure 13.1
Aerial view of a typical set of private closed streets in St. Louis, Missouri. Street closures by residents have reduced crime and stabilized communities.

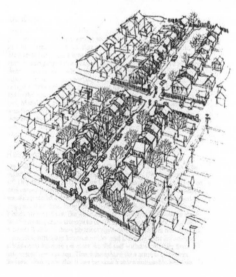

Access can also be restricted by making passage slower and more difficult, such as with narrow, winding, and one-way streets. In Atlanta, Georgia, and Richmond, Virginia, neighborhoods with such streets were found to have less crime.

Singapore has financially restricted access by requiring permits to use a central "Auto Restricted Zone," but anyone may buy a permit, something that could be done by private communities. Many private streets have no restricted access. Congestion is better handled with timed fees rather than restricting access for whole days or months. Signs at the entrances can also warn visitors about special restrictions or even an unusual absence of restrictions, such as, in Cap d'Agde, France, the absence of clothing requirements.

Access to the streets is also effectively limited by residency requirements. A retirement community may require some minimum age for residency. Visitors can still be of all ages, but the main users would be residents who meet the age limitation.

Many cities have laws requiring dogs to be leashed, but the laws are often ignored. Private contractual communities can be more restrictive, such as banning dogs completely, or less restrictive, allowing animals to run loose, according to the wishes of the founders and residents.

Heath and MacCallum on Hotels and Other "Entrecoms"

The concept of the hotel as a community analogous to a municipality originated with Spencer Heath in his main work, *Citadel, Market and Altar* (1957). Heath had developed his concepts earlier in a manuscript entitled *Politics versus Proprietorship* (1936), subtitled "A Fragmentary Study of Social and Economic Phenomena with Particular Reference to the Public Administrative Functions Belonging to Proprietorship in Land—Proprietorship as a Creative Social Agency."

In one paper, "Creative Association," Heath wrote that the value of public services is manifested as the rent "which attaches to exclusive locations in proportion to benefits received by or at these locations" (p. 2). This central idea he obtained from Henry George (1879), and the major essay in the 1936 collection is entitled "Henry George: A Further Application of his General Principles." Whereas George theorized about rent as an efficient source for governmental public finance, Heath applied the economic concept to proprietary communities where private enterprise creates site values with civic improvements, for which rentals can be charged.

Although there is no present-day example of nation-wide proprietary administration, "In a modern hotel community, however, the pattern is plain. It is an organized community with such services in common as policing, water, drainage, heat, light and power, communications and transportation, even educational and recreational facilities such as libraries, musical and literary entertainment, swimming pools, gardens and golf courses, with courteous services by the community officers and employees" (Heath 1957, p. 82).

Spencer Heath MacCallum has pursued the concepts pioneered by his grandfather. In "The Social Nature of Ownership" (1965), MacCallum considers the relationship between property and society. He notes that, "in the United States and Canada there has been a major development since World War II of a distinctive form of association based on the organized ownership and unified administration of land" (p. 57). Examples include "shopping centers, industrial parks, professional and research centers, marinas, mobile home parks, medical centers, and scores of multifunctional building complexes, such as Prudential Center, Century City, Gateway Center and so forth of which Rockefeller Center was the prototype" (pp. 57–8). These have been evolving to include complementary land uses, such as occurs in shopping centers with many different enterprises (banks, theaters) besides retail stores. Such clusters have on a smaller scale "all of the functional requirements of municipalities" (p. 58).

In *The Art of Community* (1970), MacCallum examines the proprietary community as a vehicle that resolves the twin public-goods dilemma, free riding and transfer seeking, combining governance with market. He observes that, "an empirical art of community has developed within Western society since mid-century. . .in the real-estate field, outside the cognizance of the social sciences" (p. 1). By "proprietary" MacCallum means property under a "single ownership" (p. 55) as opposed to fractionated titles, such as occurs both in sovereign governance and with civic associations. A proprietary owner has a contractual relationship with his tenants or customers.

MacCallum (2001) also calls such entrepreneurial communities "entrecoms" or "multiple-tenant income properties." He emphasizes that with MTIP properties, there can be an integration of infrastructure of "community roots" such as streets, water, communications, electricity, and security. The key proposition by MacCallum is that with unified ownership, the street grid can be redeveloped when facilities become obsolete, something that subdivided titles would inhibit.

As pointed out by Heath and MacCallum, corridors, stairways, and other passageways in hotels, office buildings, shopping centers, and other real estate are branches of the private street family operating under similar financial and organizational structures. Including these types, private streets are ubiquitous worldwide. In almost all such passageways, there is no user charge, the cost being financed from the rentals to tenants and guests.

Transition to Private Streets and Neighborhoods

A partial privatization of streets can contract out the maintenance rather than have it as a governmental monopoly. Under Mayor Goldsmith, Indianapolis implemented competitive bids for street maintenance. The city workers actually bid below their private competitors and won the job. A breakthrough occurred when the city invited bids for street repairs, previously done by unionized city workers. When the workers discovered that high middle-management costs would make their bid uncompetitive, Goldsmith agreed, cutting eighteen expensive slots. The workers revised their proposal to dispatch one truck rather than two on most jobs, and to reduce work crews from eight to five workers. And with that, they won the contract (Peirce 1995).

Many new housing developments include residential associations that own and manage local amenities such as recreation, parking, grounds, and security. The developer also designs and builds the streets, and in some cases the streets are retained as private by the association, and in others, the streets are turned over to the local city or county government. If the residents could get a tax rebate or reduction for their association assessments, there would be a great incentive to have more private streets.

A problem that large developments may have is obtaining the rights-of-way from previous owners when there are holdouts. Governments solve this by brute force, condemning the land by eminent domain. For private communities, the land problem has not been insurmountable. Several large private developments, including Walt Disney World (Foldvary 1994), have assembled the land without invoking government power.

Still, when a street or road must traverse private property, there is a potential acquisition problem. When the titleholder retains the site rent, the street might just not be built. But if the property context is one in which the land rent is being assessed and collected by higher-level associations, then the holdout problem becomes more tractable. The land desired for the street becomes more valuable as the bids for it are elevated. The holdout must then pay a higher rent assessment, and with this substantial carrying cost, the owner would let the property go.

The main policy that would facilitate private streets is to legally enable the landowners of a neighborhood to create a private district, shifting ownership of the street, lighting, and other services such as garbage collection to the association or proprietor. Robert Nelson (1999) suggests a majority of 60 percent having the power to set up an association, but another, and more voluntary, possibility is to let any number of landowners withdraw from various city jurisdictions and shift the operation to a civic association. Such service substitution would include tax substitution, a reduction in taxes (or equivalent rebates) equal to the reduced expenses of the city or county.

If some residents object to such partial withdrawal from the jurisdiction of the city government, they could stay in the city, so that the private district would not be contiguous or have city enclaves. In that case, there would be a higher-level joint council made up of representatives from the private sector and the government sector. The street maintenance and other services would then either be provided by the joint council, or else one party would contract for it from the other.

The private streets of a community could be available for the transit services of other private communities or of governments. The owners would lease property rights in curb zones, bus turnouts, and bus stops, creating a system of "curb rights" (Klein et al. 1997, p. 3). Transit services such as taxis, jitneys, and buses would have specified places where they can park and pick up passengers.

The fully private provider would have its own traffic rules and policing, with fines for violations. It could require all users of the local streets to be equipped with electrical identifiers, and may charge high rates for traffic shown by the equipment as moving quickly through the area. Such a fee could be zero or low for people who live, visit, or work in the area, and high for those who use the private streets as a short cut to get to somewhere else.

A street provider could also collect revenue for special uses, such as parades and street fairs. A private community could also collect charges from vehicles that pollute the air. Recent technology, such as the Stedman remote sensing device (Roth 1996, p. 92; Klein 2003) has made this feasible with devices placed at intersections. These measure various pollutants in the exhaust when cars pass by, and then photograph the license plates of polluters above some threshold.

Technological progress has increased the ability of streets to handle multiple utilities and other infrastructure. It is less costly now to provide underground lines, and to monitor car exhaust and traffic. It is becoming ever more feasible to charge for street usage electronically. These technologies all enhance the profitability of private streets, and private ownership presents fewer obstacles, such as permitting and public hearings.

A purely private street would not only have private financing and maintenance, but also private traffic rules and even private law enforcement. To provide the most effective service, the community governance could use modern (or future) monitoring technology to provide efficient rules, such as citing offenders only when warranted by the traffic, penalizing drivers only when they have actually imposed a danger rather than merely a technical violation. A little-recognized cost of governmental streets is that the policing can include possible negative effects. Some towns might have speed traps with hidden signs to extract revenue from passersby. Even when such explicit fraud is not committed, speed limits are often set higher than necessary for safety, and zealous zero-tolerant traffic enforcement with high fines can act as a revenue rather than safety device. Moreover, the police in some cases can use traffic stops to search vehicles and seize them using civil asset forfeiture if some offense is suspected.

Private law enforcement by competitive private communities would have an incentive be more user- and member-friendly, with rules and enforcement geared to preventing unsafe driving rather than extracting revenue or imposing arbitrary restrictions.

In conclusion, private streets would provide the incentives to more efficiently allocate parking and vehicles, reduce pollution, and provide better protection from crime. The public finances for streets would be based on benefits, and would also promote an efficient use of urban space for buildings, reducing both wasteful sprawl and urban decay. "Sprawl" can be considered a use of land greater than would occur in a pure free market, since without maximum-density zoning and without subsidies to the suburbs and tax-driven costs in the central cities, urban land would most likely be used more compactly.

The implication of this analysis and evidence is that private streets are not merely economically feasible, but superior in efficiency and service in the financial and organizational context of the decentralized, competitive, and responsive private communities in which they would be provided. From a purely economic and ethical perspective, it is not private streets but governmental streets financed by forceful means that require justification and explanation.

References

Beito, David T. 1989. "Owning the 'Commanding Heights:' Historical Perspectives on Private Streets." *Essays in Public Works History* 16 (December): 1–47.

Beito, David T., and Smith, Bruce. 1990. "The Formation of Urban Infrastructure Through Nongovernmental Planning: The Private Places of St. Louis, 1869–1920." *Journal of Urban History* 16, 3 (May): 263–303.

Berliner, Harold A. 1978. *The Real Magic in the Magic Kingdom: Disney World's own Local Government.* n.p.

"Celebration, USA." 2001. http://www.xone.net/celebration/

Cisneros, Henry G. 1996. "Defensible Space: Deterring Crime and Building Community." *Cityscape* (December). U.S. Department of Housing and Urban Development, Office of Policy Development: 15–34.

Fitzgerald, Randall. 1988. *When Government Goes Private.* New York: Universe Books.

Foldvary, Fred. 1994. *Public Goods and Private Communities.* Aldershot, UK: Edward Elgar Publishing.

"Ford's Colony Fact Sheet." 1990. Ford's Colony, VA: Realtec, Inc.

Frazier, Mark. 1980. "Privatizing the City." *Policy Review* 12 (Spring): 91–108.

Frazier, Mark. 1989 [1988]. "Seeding Grass Roots Recovery: New Catalysts for Community Associations," in *Residential Community Associations: Private Governments in the Intergovernmental System?* Washington, DC: ACIR (Advisory Commission on Intergovernmental Relations), pp. 63–74.

Friedman, David. 1989. *The Machinery of Freedom.* 2nd ed. La Salle: Open Court.

Friedman, Milton, and Daniel Boorstin. 1951 [1996]. "How to Plan and Pay for the Safe and Adequate Highways We Need," epilogue in *Roads in a Market Economy.* Aldershot: Avebury Technical, pp. 223–245.

Gaffney, Mason. 1964. *Containment Policies for Urban Sprawl.* Lawrence, KS: University of Kansas Publications.

George, Henry. 1975 [1879]. *Progress and Poverty.* Rpt. NY: Robert Schalkenbach Foundation.

Grant, Margaret E. 1999. "Rossmoor Present," in *Rossmoor Walnut Creek: 35 Years of History.* Walnut Creek, Calif.: Community Club of Rossmoor, pp. 1–54.

Hansen, Gretchen. 2001. (Head of the Rossmoor bus service.) Interview, January 22, at Rossmoor.

Heath, Spencer. 1936. *Politics Versus Proprietorship.* Manuscript.

Heath, Spencer. 1957. *Citadel, Market and Altar.* Baltimore: Science of Society Foundation.

Henry, Gerald C. 1984 (1999). "Rossmoor Past," in *Rossmoor Walnut Creek: 35 Years of History.* Walnut Creek, Calif.: Community Club of Rossmoor, pp. 1–84.

Klein, Daniel. 2003. "Fencing the Airshed: Using Remote Sensing to Police Auto Emissions," in *The Half-life of Policy Rationales: How Technology Affects Old Policy Issues,* edited by Fred E. Foldvary and Daniel B. Klein. New York: New York University Press.

Klein, Daniel, Adrian Moore, and Binyam Reja. 1997. *Curb Rights.* Washington D.C.: Brookings Institution Press.

MacCallum, Spencer. 1965. "The Social Nature of Ownership." *Modern Age* 9, 1 (Winter 1964/5): 49–61.

MacCallum, Spencer. 1970. *The Art of Community.* Menlo Park: Institute for Humane Studies.

MacCallum, Spencer. 2003. "Community Technology," in *The Half-life of Policy Rationales: How technology Affects Old Policy Issues,* edited by Fred E. Foldvary and Daniel B. Klein. New York: New York University Press.

Nelson, Robert. 1999. "Privatizing the Neighborhood: A Proposal to Replace Zoning with Private Collective Property Rights to Existing Neighborhoods." *George Mason Law Review* 7, 4 (Summer): 827–880.

Newman, Oscar. 1980. *Community of Interest.* Garden City, NY: Anchor Press/ Doubleday.

Oliande, Sylvia, and David Brady. 1997. "A Visit to Celebration." http://www.primenet .com/~dbrady/oliande/celebration.html, 2001

Overman, Mel. 1990. Conversation at Ford's Colony.

Peirce, Neil. R. 1995. "Competition: Now OK with Public Unions?" Alliance for Redesigning Government. (Washington Post Writers Group). http://www.alliance .napawash.org/ALLIANCE/Picases.nsf/e24ffc586e80044a852564ed006eb5be/8105 0f1b26e69c82852564740076ff75?OpenDocument

Roth, Gabriel. 1996. *Roads in a Market Economy.* Aldershot, UK: Avebury Technical.

Samuel, Peter. 2000. "Maryland's Variable Pricing Program." *Toll Roads Newsletter* 51 (Sept./Oct.).

Savage, Charles C. 1987. *Architecture of the Private Streets of St. Louis.* Columbia: University of Missouri Press.

Schrantz, Dan. 2000. "Memo, YR2001 Reserve Work Program." Rossmoor Walnut Creek.

Schrantz, Dan. 2001. (Head of the Rossmoor public works.) Interview, January 22, at Rossmoor.

Shoup, Donald. 2003. "Buying Time at the Curb," in *The Half-life of Policy Rationales: How Technology Affects Old Policy Issues*, edited by Fred E. Foldvary and Daniel B. Klein. New York: New York University Press.

Stern, Martin O., and Robert U. Ayres. 1973. "Transportation Outlays: Who Pays and Who Benefits?" in *Government Spending and Land Values*, edited by C. Lowell Harriss. Madison: University of Wisconsin Press, pp. 117–54.

Stern, Robert A. M. 1986. *Pride of Place*. New York: Houghton Mifflin Co.

Taningco, Teresa. 2000. Email message, December 8.

Underwood, Marjorie. 2000. "New Urbanism: A New Name for Segregation." http://northonline.sccd.ctc.edu/jwu/pathfinders/sum2000/underwoo.htm

Vickrey, William. 1969 [1994]. "Congestion Theory and Transport Investment." *American Economic Review* 59: 251–60. Rpt. *Public Economics*, edited by Richard Arnott et al. Cambridge, UK: Cambridge University Press, pp. 320–332.

Zehnder, Leonard E. 1975. *Florida's Disney World: Promises and Problems*. Tallahassee, FL: The Peninsula Publishing Co.

Zukin, Sharon. 1991. *Landscapes of Power: From Detroit to Disney World*. Berkeley: University of California Press.

14

Private Roads to the Future:
The Swedish Private Road Associations[*]

Christina Malmberg Calvo and Sven Ivarsson

Private road associations (PRAs) manage two thirds of the road network in Sweden. They manage the roads at less cost and with better results than the government road agencies. In fact, the PRAs perform so well that some urban municipalities request the associations to manage the municipal roads that connect to the private roads. There are also PRAs that are responsible for ferry services, for example in the Stockholm archipelago.

The Low Volume Road Challenge

Unit costs for low volume road construction and maintenance are low compared to those for higher level roads. The problem is that in many countries this network is vast, and the total cost requirements to ensure minimum access, particularly for rural residents, are enormous. In addition, it is difficult to ensure that the "right" amount of roads is provided if roads are locally used but provided by higher level governments. The result can be, as in the United States, substantial waste in the provision of local roads, as shown by John Semmens in chapter 2 ("De-Socializing the Roads") of this volume. This waste is partly due to "pork barrel" legislation—when taxes are raised nationally but spent locally, there is incentive at the local level to spend well in excess of benefits since local

---

[*]Review of and advice for this chapter were provided by Professor Ian Heggie (University of Birmingham), Daniel Klein, Gabriel Roth, and Alexander Tabarrok, and Stephen Brushett and Antti Talvitie of the World Bank.

constituents face only a small proportion of the costs. Alternatively, when roads are locally used but provided by higher level government, local roads are undersupplied and under-financed. This is often the case in developing countries, particularly in rural areas.

Another challenge in the construction and maintenance of low volume roads comes when locals are not the predominant users of the roads. One alternative (adopted in eighteenth-century United Kingdom and often tried and subsequently abandoned by rural communities to date in developing countries) is toll collection. It has obvious problems: When traffic is low, cost of collection may render tolling unprofitable. In addition, it is difficult to ensure that the collector does not pocket part of the revenues. Another alternative has been employed in Sweden, where government has opted to not use tolls but instead to provide incentives for private road ownership (and squeeze the most they can get out of the local user pays principle). The result is a private-public partnership where government subsidizes road costs with grants from the budget.

This partnership for low volume roads is highly efficient—a 2001 government commissioned evaluation confirmed that the cost of operating and maintaining private roads of equal standards and use as local government roads is lower even when the opportunity cost of in-kind voluntary contributions of goods and labor are costed (SOU: 2001:67 2001). In fact, the evaluation confirmed that the cost is often less than half the cost of publicly managed roads.[1] The reason for this, as explained by Swedish road administration officials, is mainly "a stitch in time," that is, prompt intervention and preventive actions in response to road deterioration, coupled with an uncontestable aspect of private ownership—it is the same owners who will face the financial and physical consequences of any delayed intervention. The evaluation concluded that the private-public partnership for low volume roads is economically desirable and recommended continued public funding to PRAs.[2]

The Swedish model for managing low volume roads is simple and efficient and can easily be adapted to a variety of circumstances in both rich and poor countries. It provides legal and financial incentives for local property owners to associate and assume responsibility for their roads. It is remarkable that only a few countries have adopted similar institutional arrangements for the very lowest but most extensive part of the road network. Could it be because they do not have a tradition of community involvement in roads? Or is it lacking political will? Another possibility is that the Swedish experience based on a well-tested partnership between the private and public sector simply is not internationally known. The challenge involved in managing and financing low volume roads is examined below, primarily in the Swedish context but also by drawing on experience from elsewhere.

Sweden's Roads

The Swedish road network measures 419,000 kilometers (see Table 14.1). The Swedish National Road Administration (SNRA) manages one quarter of the network (98,000 kilometers), and the municipalities 10 percent (38,000 kilometers). The remaining two-thirds (283,000 kilometers) are privately owned and managed roads. The SNRA roads carry 70 percent of the traffic, the municipal roads 26 percent of the traffic, and the private roads the remaining 4 percent of the traffic. While the private roads arguably constitute a low volume network, some serve vacation home areas and about 50 percent are forest roads mainly opened for commercial purposes,[3] about one sixth (more than 40,000 kilometers) of the private road network carries more than 100 vehicles per day, including some up to a 1,000 vehicles per day throughout the year. This chapter focuses principally on the 50 percent of the private road network that is owned and managed by communities, half of which receive state subsidies.

A Legal Tradition of Community Road Management

The Swedish road legislation is based on a concept of justice with roots in the Iron Ages—perhaps as early as the fifth century. During the introduction of Christianity in Sweden in the eleventh century, the laws governing the various provinces started to converge, and as the Church became more powerful, it demanded roads to the places where the tithe should be paid. All farmers had to pay a tenth of their harvest ("income") in kind. Roads and transport to the collection points were essential to deliver this payment.[4]

King Magnus Eriksson's Law from the middle of the fourteenth century was the first road act governing all roads in Sweden. It states in its first chap-

Table 14.1
Lengths of Road in the Swedish Road Network

	Length (km)
National roads	98,000
Municipal roads and streets	38,000
Private roads with state subsidies	73,000
Private roads without state subsidies	210,000
Total	419,000

ter that, "There shall be one public road to each village and another one from the village." In the second chapter it reads: "Everybody shall be responsible for roads and bridges as far as his property ranges."

Already here we find that the responsibility for the roads rests with those living along the network. This concept has carried through into modern times, and it was not until 1944 when traffic development and transport needs prompted state management of the first national road network.[5] At that time, the City Councils had been responsible for their streets for more than a hundred years. But city roads were only a very small part of the network as Sweden up until this time was primarily a rural society.

After World War Two, with the increased use of heavy vehicles and cars, the owners of the private road network started to complain about the increased road damage caused by the growing traffic from the mechanization of farming and forestry, and from small and medium industries. Around the same time, demand increased for the construction of more and better roads in previously undeveloped areas. (The steady improvements in living standards enabled more households to purchase summer and weekend homes and cars.) Many of these areas were of interest also to people who did not own properties there.[6] As a result, private road owners increasingly demanded compensation from government for the additional maintenance burden. A road network administration became necessary and in the beginning of the 1950s, Parliament instructed SNRA to design a system whereby the state would compensate private road owners for the public use of private roads.

Private Road Associations

Today, approximately 60,000 PRAs own about 140,000 kilometers of road in Sweden.[7] They are responsible for the operation and maintenance of the roads. The associations and their members may choose to carry out the road works by themselves or employ a contractor.

The Swedish government strongly supports the establishment of PRAs because they contribute to a number of political goals including:

- encouraging and making it easier to live and settle in remote and sparsely populated areas;
- facilitating quality road transport in areas where the cost for providing such services is high but promotes trade and industrial development;
- providing access to areas of public recreation and leisure;
- securing the road capital investment; and
- ensuring general traffic safety and environmental interests.

SNRA determines whether a road should be government owned or private. The private roads have a well-articulated legal framework, described in the next section, but what constitutes a private road is not defined precisely in law but according to regulations, which change from time to time. There are thus some gray areas with regard to road designation that are subject to interpretation. If the owners of a private road disagree with SNRA's decision on the status of a road, they can make a court appeal. Past verdicts indicate that a road is considered the responsibility of government when:

- the through-traffic exceeds 100 vehicles per day;
- the locally generated traffic exceeds 130 vehicles per day;
- more than 200 people live along the road; and
- the road is used for traffic between a number of places and alternatives are detours of more than 20 kilometers or a twenty-minute drive.

Conversely, a road is considered private when:

- a new road has been built to replace it but the old road is still serving people living along it;
- a public service institution served by the road is closed down;
- vehicular through-traffic is less than fifty vehicles per day;
- locally generated traffic is less than seventy vehicles per day; and
- the number of residents along the road is less than forty people.

The Private Roads Act governing the PRAs provides the framework for private roads. This framework has three main components: i) legal ownership and survey, ii) the PRA Board and by-laws, and iii) cost-sharing arrangements. A very important actor in representing the interest of PRAs at the national level and in political discussion is the National Federation of PRAs (NFPRA). Each framework component and the NFPRA are described below.

Legal Ownership and Survey

In Sweden, the legal framework, the Private Roads Act, is the most important part of the institutional framework for private roads. Strictly speaking, no one can be held legally responsible for a specific road unless that person or entity has been granted or has established legal ownership. When a road is designated, this act is usually published as a notice in the government gazette (or other official publication) used to record official acts of the government (Malmberg Calvo 1998).

In Sweden, most private roads are cited under the Private Roads Act. The first modern private roads act dates from 1939. Since then it has been revised on numerous occasions, most recently in 1998. In 1998 the acts governing private roads in both urban and rural areas were joined together in a common framework.[8] The Private Roads Act outlines how property owners can form themselves into PRAs and how these organizations should be organized and run.[9] It sets out how the PRA should be proclaimed and how the costs of the road should be assigned among the different property owners, principally according to road use and benefit. It also specifies how a property owner can challenge her/his allocation. A government officer who carries out a survey of the road's usage determines the allocation.

A PRA is usually established by means of a legal survey.[10] The initiative for the survey can come from one or several of the private property owners along the road by means of application to the County Cadastral Authority. Certain authorities, such as SNRA, can also take the initiative for the survey. The Cadastral or Land Survey Office appoints an impartial government or municipal officer to carry out the survey.

The objective of the survey is to establish the members of the association (property owners along the road), and their individual "shares" in the road. The determination of individual "shares" serves to allot the maintenance and other road costs to the members according to the size of their property and the traffic they generate (benefit and use). Key determinants include length of road from the property to the state road, and extent of any commercial activities or public services such as a milk-producing farm, local shop, or post office. A fee will be imposed on each member according to the shares determined by the survey.

The proposed size of individual PRA member shares is presented at a meeting organized by the surveyor and to which all association members are invited. At this meeting property owners will be asked to elect a board for the association. Membership in the PRA is mandatory; the survey is legally binding and if a member fails to pay his/her share, the association can ask the local tax authority to collect the payment. Swedish Law gives priority to the collection of the unpaid fee of a PRA member before the collection of other types of debt, and in case payment is not forthcoming, the tax authorities can impose sale of the property.

The PRA Board and By-Laws

Most community managed private roads are administered by PRAs. An elected board administers each PRA and is governed by a set of by-laws. Board members are not necessarily technical persons but good organizers and well-trusted members of the community. The legal surveyor will help to set up the PRA, including the registration and election of the board officers. The size of the association will vary depending on the number of member property owners. Some associations pay the board members; others do not.

The board is responsible for ratifying the association's rules and drawing up a plan of operations. This plan is used to estimate the association's annual budget and anticipated expenditures. A board member may be in charge of the day-to-day operations of the association or the association may hire someone to manage the account and other issues on its behalf.

The board has to call all PRA members to a general meeting at least once a year. This meeting usually tables four main items: i) the board's administration for the year is scrutinized (audit of the accounts and the "management letter"), ii) election of officers takes place, iii) it is decided which investment and improvements are to be undertaken for the coming year, and iv) the board has to respond to the sometimes critical observations of the members.

Cost-Sharing Arrangements

The financial responsibility for the construction, upgrading, operation, and maintenance of private roads rests with the PRA members, that is, the concerned property owners. This includes responsibility for any bridges on the roads as well as the drainage, any road furniture, and traffic lights.[11] In the case of construction of large bridges, SNRA provides technical assistance to the PRAs in the preparation of tender documents, bid evaluation, and works supervision. SNRA recognizes that it is not reasonable that a handful or two of property owners would assume responsibility for the construction of bridges worth more than half a million dollars.

All costs are shared among the members according to road use and benefit. The PRA can request grants to offset some of these costs from three main sources: the central government, the local government/municipality, and close-by property owners who use and benefit from the road but who are not directly located on the road (there is no tolling of roads in Sweden[12]). The latter two are in most cases insignificant. Many municipalities opt not to issue grants to PRAs because these grants would have to be financed by the taxes collected from the same local inhabitants.

The Swedish central government subsidizes private roads because it recognizes that significant use of these roads by outsiders can substantially increase the costs of road operation. Private roads frequently supplement the government owned roads by serving as connectors or short cuts for people who are not members of the specific PRA. In fact, in Sweden every fourth trip starts or ends on a private road. Against this background, the Swedish government subsidizes private roads that satisfy the following conditions stipulated by the SNRA:

- have a minimum length of 1 kilometer;
- are technically and functionally sound;
- have reasonable operation and maintenance costs;[13]
- have formed a PRA to manage and operate the road; and
- are open for public use.

The SNRA provides a grant of between 40 to 80 percent of road maintenance costs depending on the type of settlements along the road (permanent or temporary), the road type (for example, a road that connects two higher level roads usually receives the highest subsidy[14]), and the availability of public services. The application of these criteria can be gleaned from Table 14.2, which gives a breakdown of the type of roads that receive grants. The highest priority is assigned to through roads, which in 1999 received the maximum grant of 80 percent; the second priority (grants covering 70 percent of costs) was given

Table 14.2
Statistics Relating to the Private Road Network
which Receives Grant (1999)

	Length of road in each category (km)	Size of grant received (percentage of cost)	Annual costs of upkeep (SEK million)
Through roads	7,000	80	55
Roads giving access to permanent residences in rural areas	53,000	70	375
Roads giving access for commercial activities	5,000	70	37
Recreational roads	3,000	50	11
Roads giving access to permanent residences in urban areas	2,000	40	7
Roads giving access to recreational properties	3,000	40	15

to roads that provide access to permanent residences in rural areas and roads that had commercial activities.[15]

Road maintenance costs are based on an estimation of "reasonable local costs." Cost estimates include the road surface, the traffic type and volume, and local costs for inputs such as gravel. This means that a PRA that is located next to a gravel pit receives a smaller grant than a PRA that is further from the gravel pit, all other things equal.[16]

Most private roads are narrow—about 3 to 4 meters wide and of simple construction.

Winter management features strongly in most PRA budgets because of frequent snow plowing and spring repairs of ground frost-related surface damage—often 25 percent of the budget. All road markings, signs, and standards for visibility have to conform to those of government owned roads. Design plans for new construction or large rehabilitation works are reviewed by SNRA.

In addition to the mandatory annual financial audit that each PRA that receives government grants has to commission, SNRA carries out its own periodic financial and physical audit. Every five years, an SNRA official meets with the PRA board members, visits the road(s), and assesses the association's performance and financial needs, including whether the road(s) qualify for additional financial assistance, for example in case of larger repairs or changes in the traffic level. The audit determines the grant amount for the following year. This amount is then adjusted annually at the rate of inflation for the following four years.

The amount the central government expends on grants is large and has been constantly growing—about US$70 million per annum in 1999. The lion's share of the grants is for operation and maintenance—about 10 percent is dedicated to upgrading and 8 percent for new construction. Few households in any PRA contribute more than US$100 per year. Local contractors generally undertake the upkeep and maintenance works. Rural PRA members often have tractors, scrapers, and other tools, and accept to do work at a very low cost. Many association members are also willing to clean verges and culverts, and clear brushwood to keep down membership fees.

About 25 percent of all private roads receive grants (about 74,000 kilometers; see Table 14.2 for the characteristics of these roads). Most roads receive the same per kilometer cost (about US$800). The remainder of the private road network either does not qualify or property owners do not request grants, likely because they do not wish to abide by the rules set out in the private roads acts for roads that receive grants, for example, that the roads have to be open to the public. The financial support to the PRAs is seen as critical to government policy to assure and reduce the cost of access in remote areas, and preserve existing road assets.

The National Federation of Private Road Associations

PRAs are non-governmental organizations. They can be thought of as cooperatives of people who live or have a property in an area with a road or several roads of common interest. Most PRAs are rather small and would on their own not be able to effectively represent or defend their interests at the national level. With the steadily increasing level of motorization in the 1950s and 1960s, many PRAs found that they needed to join together to lobby for compensation for the public traffic on their roads. Their management and technical skills, however, were often limited, and they lacked legal competence. As a result, in the 1960s, board members of a number of PRAs came together and established the National Federation of Private Road Associations (NFPRA).

In 2000, more than 6,000 PRAs had joined the NFPRA, that is, about 10 percent of all PRAs. Together they account for 25,000 kilometers of private roads and represent 350,000 properties all over Sweden. Most PRAs that join NFPRA are large—the average NFPRA member has 4.2 kilometers of road and fifty-eight properties, which is substantially larger than most PRAs.

An important task for the NFPRA is to meet regularly with national politicians including members of Parliament and the Cabinet, and also to frequently brief the Ministry of Transport and Communications of the views and concerns of its members. The NFPRA board has four officials: a politician who serves as chairman, a solicitor, a road engineer, and a cadastral surveyor. The affiliation of the politician does not matter—only the keen interest in private roads is considered. The appointment to the NFPRA board is considered an honor and is unpaid. Up to 2001, the NFPRA employed only one part-time clerk responsible for the registers and day-to-day correspondence. Given the increased importance of ensuring continued political support at the highest levels, the NFPRA, since 2002, is engaging the services of its vice chairman, a retired official of the SNRA, on a part-time basis.

The NFPRA annual membership fee per PRA is about US$50 plus US$5 per kilometer. The fee includes a comprehensive package of insurance covering liability, fidelity, property damage, bodily injury, and legal expenses. NPFRA has purchased the insurance for more than thirty years from one of the largest Swedish insurance companies. The coverage has broadened over the years. The annual premium for about 6,400 associations is about SEK 1 million (US$110,000). During the 1990s, when NFPRA grew rapidly, claims increased proportionately as well. The insurance company found that it breaks even at about 4,500 PRAs. Claims have amounted to about 80 percent of premiums over the last few years.

Most claims stem from liability and legal expenses. For example, provided it can be proven that the PRA was aware of an existing pothole but did not take appropriate action, a bicyclist who is injured when s/he falls off the bike due to a pothole in the road can sue for reimbursement of expenses not covered by her/his own accident insurance and loss of income. The insurance will cover the award the court assigns to the claimant.[17] Another example includes damage to the road by a contractor working on one of the properties. If the contractor refuses to pay, the PRA can sue and the insurance will cover the legal expenses. In the opinion of the NFPRA, it is unlikely that PRAs would have sued had they not had insurance.

NFPRA, together with SNRA and the Country Cadastral Survey Offices, also organizes a wide range of training courses for PRA boards and interested members such as traffic safety, environmental issues, surface options, winter maintenance, and so on.

Three Different Private Road Associations

The sizes of PRAs vary widely. Most have just a few kilometers of road and have three to four single-family homes as members. But some have 70 kilometers of road and include up to 3,500 properties. Most PRAs manage just one small road; others manage a whole development and roads on behalf of the local government. The three PRAs of Broby, Saltaro, and Akersberga, all within the greater Stockholm area, illustrate the range of PRAs—from the small to the large (see Boxes 14.1, 14.2 and 14.3).

International Experience

Apart from Sweden and Finland, few countries have explicit legal arrangement for the management of low volume private roads. Some provinces in Canada, for instance Ontario, share costs with local residents when they have organized themselves into local road boards. In apartheid South Africa, commercial farmers received grants to share in the cost of maintaining their rural access roads. This system is now under review as there are many rural areas that have no roads at all. In urban areas in South Africa, there is a 1998 experiment to transfer ownership of streets to the residents of the streets—"Street Bodies Corporate" (Clifford 1998). It is based on similar principles to those applied to the administration of housing, that is, residents will manage not only their own buildings but also their streets. Each Street Body Corporate or PRA elects representatives who meet periodically with each other and the city management. The concept aims to empower individuals "to be responsible for their own local affairs through participatory democracy," and engender "respect for shared property and resources." Street expenditures are shared between the PRA and the municipality.

Box 14.1
Broby PRA—Small, Beautiful, and Cost-Efficient

Broby PRA is a very small association. It has 1.2 kilometers of road and consists of the seven properties of Broby village, situated in Vallentuna municipality (about 40 km from Stockholm center). The village has two farms and five additional homes whose owners commute to work.

The most interesting aspect of Broby PRA is that its members do a lot of labor-based activities on their road. In this way, they minimize the need for cash fees. The members gather on a Saturday in September to carry out routine maintenance works including regravelling of the carriageway, clearing of drainage ditches, vegetation control, and other activities they can perform by hand.

SNRA estimates the reasonable local cost of road operation and maintenance to Broby PRA to be US$1,700. The government grant to Broby PRA is US$1,000, that is, 60 percent of the estimated cost. The labor cost is included as a costed item in the association's annual budget and therefore forms part of the estimate for the government grant. The annual state grant and savings arising from the use of their own labor are used to purchase materials and for paying contractors for the work the members cannot perform themselves, such as snow plowing. In fact, given the significant labor contribution of the property owners and their constant vigil, Broby PRA has not had to charge members any cash fees for several years.

Broby PRA has divided the road into seven sections to conform to the number of properties. During winter, each property is responsible for the basic maintenance of their respective section. To facilitate snow plowing, even in a snowstorm with limited visibility, poles painted orange (the stems of six- to–eight-year-old trees that have been stripped of branches except on top) are used to guide the snowplow.[18] The poles are placed about 50 meters apart and checked every time a household member travels on the road—the wife, husband, and even the children on their way home from school. All household members are well aware that the road is their mutual responsibility and that they have to ensure it is operational, safe, and maintained.

Similarly, along the lines of the Swedish model, some of the Baltic States and countries in Eastern Europe, like Estonia and Romania, which are struggling with the deterioration of the rural road network, are exploring the option of establishing a network of private roads.

Box 14.2
Saltaro PRA—Growing and Needing Investment

Up until the 1960s, Saltaro was one single farm on an island in the Stockholm archipelago. In the 1970s, the owner cut up a few plots and sold them for summer homes. Shortly afterwards, the original owner found he had no less than 400 neighbors, with a peak during the month of July. Over the years, the new homeowners began to spend more and more time on the island and the original summer homes became all year round leisure homes. Eventually some property owners relocated permanently to the island, and a public bus line was established between Stockholm and Saltaro, facilitating a daily commute.

The road quickly became a common concern among the property owners. In the 1970s, as the first summer home owners came to the island, there was only one single-lane road—between the farmer's barn and home—used by the tractor and the cows. As the resident population on the island grew to about 400 properties, something had to be done. SNRA was consulted and it was recommended to build a new road justified on the basis of accessibility, road safety, and environmental concerns. The new road was 4 kilometers and cost more than SEK half a million (US$60,000). A government grant covered 70 percent of the costs. An additional 10 percent was received from the local bus company because the new road made it possible to operate standard buses. The remainder was shared between the property owners (about US$250 each). With the assistance of SNRA, designs were drawn up and approved, a bank loan was granted (with the 400 properties as security), and a contractor was engaged to carry out the construction. The new road is 6 meters wide and meets the environmental requirements.

Today, Saltaro PRA is responsible for a total of 30 kilometers of road of which 14 kilometers qualify for government grant support (10 kilometers are gravel and 4 kilometers are paved). It receives a grant that covers 40 percent (about US$7,200) of the required annual expenditures. The PRA was instrumental in bringing the property owners together and in harnessing the required capacity for collective action.

In Zambia, as part of an effort to sustainably improve the condition of the road network, and increasingly involve the private sector in infrastructure management, the setting up of community rural road associations is being experimented with. By the end of 2001, a substantial amount of spot improvement

---

Box 14.3
Akersberga PRAs Manage the Council's Roads

Akersberga has grown from a village of 150 people in 1950 to a community with 6,000 inhabitants in 2001. During the 1960s people working in Stockholm began to settle in Akersberga, which is only a half-hour travel from the city. As a result, demands for a modern road network increased. A PRA has always managed the community's roads, as was the norm in Swedish villages in the 1950s. As Akersberga grew, a number of PRAs were established to manage the roads. The total road network is 69 kilometers, most of it is paved, serving 3,200 properties.

Road needs in Akersberga were large and funds were scarce. The roads required paving, sidewalks, upgrading, and street crossings. At one point it was proposed the municipality take over the responsibility for the roads in the community as was common in other Swedish cities. The options were to either have the City council run the roads and finance expenses out of the tax base, or to let the PRAs continue to own and manage the roads. A large majority of the Akersberga residents opted to keep the PRAs and let them manage the road network.

The typical PRA board in Akersberga has seven members and employs a retired person by the hour to take care of the day-to-day administration. The annual cost of the roads is around US$130 per property owner. Akersberga PRAs receive no government grant because central government considers the roads the responsibility of the urban municipality. Akersberga is an example of where the PRA model has been applied beyond its conventional application to manage all the roads in a municipality. This is a clear testament to the high appreciation in Sweden of the efficiency of private ownership and management of low volume roads. The Akersberga residents are quite pleased with both their PRAs and the quality of their roads.

---

had taken place, including repair of bridges, culverts, and fords, and more than twenty road associations had been formed. These associations receive cost-sharing grants for maintenance from the National Roads Board (NRB), which manages the road fund to help cover the expenses of technical supervision and materials that are not locally available, such as cement for the repair of culverts. A high-level delegation from Zambia visited Sweden in 2000 for the purpose of assessing the usefulness of the private roads system. The Zambian government is now considering including a provision for the establishment of private roads in their Roads and Road Traffic Act, which is currently under revision. The NRB believes there is scope for establishing PRAs also in urban areas. The board has been approached by residents of high- to middle-income neighborhoods in Lusaka who request assistance in improving their roads. These are areas that often are given priority in road rehabilitation in developing countries. Establishing PRAs would mean that these roads would become less of a drain on public resources. The PRAs could thus potentially serve as models for organizing management of low volume roads in both urban and rural areas of developing countries.

Notwithstanding the examples from Canada, South Africa, and Zambia, only Finland, which "inherited" the Swedish legal system, has fully adopted and adapted the Swedish concept and model of private roads.[19] Three quarters of the Finnish road network are designated as private roads (280,000 kilometers). A total of 700,000 of Finland's 5 million inhabitants live along these roads, and another half million people rely on them to reach their vacation homes. Finland's Private Roads Act was modernized in 1962. It governs the use and management of roads that have more than one owner. These roads are managed by road cooperatives. The legal framework requires compulsory participation of all property owners who live along a private road and the main transporters (Isotalo 1995). The road cooperatives operate much the same as the Swedish PRAs (see Box 14.4).

In Finland, about one third of the private network has been legally established as road cooperatives. About 87,000 kilometers of cooperative roads (17,400 cooperatives) receive financial support from the central government, a municipality, or from both. Similar to Sweden, the cost of operation and maintenance is low. Cooperative members rarely complain about the condition of the road because they know the trade-offs. This can be contrasted with cases where the management of previously private roads has been transferred to the national road administration. In such cases demands for upgrading, surface dressing, or an asphalt pavement have been made almost as soon as the users no longer have to directly pay for the cost (Isotalo 1995).

Conclusions

A strong argument can be made in favor of property owner associations managing and maintaining low volume roads—private ownership can reduce the cost of maintaining roads to less than half the cost of government provided roads and significantly increase the kilometers that receive regular maintenance. Increasing efficiency and effectiveness of public expenditures and working in partnership with the private sector are highly relevant for both developed

---

Box 14.4
Sakkola Road Cooperative

Sakkola road cooperative in the southern Finland municipality of Kar-
jalohja owns a four and half kilometer road. The cooperative has thirty-
five members. Only five families are permanent residents. The rest own
holiday homes, or forest or farm properties along the road. Because most
of the permanent residents are old, the cooperative—its account and maintenance works—is managed by a trustee from a neighboring village. The
annual maintenance costs, including regravelling and snow plowing, is
about US$3,000. The government grant covers about 45 percent of the
cost. The municipality provides another 15 percent and the rest is split
among the thirty-five members, depending on property size and road use.
The trustee bills about US$200 per year. A supervisor from the National
Road Administration inspects the road every two years.

Source: Isotalo 1995

---

and developing countries. The Swedish private roads model is a true win-win
in the sense that communities and road users get the roads they are willing to
pay for while the government gets a better road network at lower cost.

The Swedish model shows that a well-structured institutional framework
for private ownership of low volume roads can bring impressive results. Such
a framework should include a law on private roads, and financial and technical incentives. The Swedish and Finnish experiences both point to the pivotal
importance of political will and skill. Without support at the highest level, the
Private Roads Acts would not have been updated and financial support would
likely have waned. The Swedish NFPRA performs a critical role in leading
the national dialogue on private road issues and defending the interests of its
member road owners. As representative for almost 400,000 properties corresponding to at least half a million votes (in a country with 9 million inhabitants), politicians are willing to listen.

But most developing countries do not have anything close to an institutional
or legal framework for low volume or community roads. Grant support to road
improvements is in many countries offered through various donor supported
community funds. After the roads have been improved, the financial and technical support ends, because it is assumed that the communities will maintain
the roads that serve them. This has, in many cases, been disappointing. There is

no reason why more developed and developing countries could not adapt to local circumstances the Swedish model of private or community ownership of roads as an integral part of their efforts to improve road access in a constrained budget environment and in partnership with the private sector. Indeed, private-public partnerships for road management and financing are particularly relevant for countries whose most numerous private sector group are small-scale farmers. The interest of this group in good roads and value for money remains an untapped significant source of development potential.

In summary, in order to bring low volume roads under efficient and effective maintenance, there is a need to go below the level of local governments and tap community initiative and dedication. The PRA concept is very simple and can be replicated easily. But to work it requires an enabling legal framework and strong political commitment. Money for cost-sharing grants is helpful but it is not the most critical component of the model.

Notes

1. The evaluation estimated the annual average cost of operation and maintenance of a private road to be about US$1.20 per meter compared to US$2.40 per meter for the upkeep of an equivalent public road.
2. The evaluation also recommended an assessment of the rules for changing the ownership of roads from public to private and vice versa. Some public officials in Sweden would like to further increase the proportion of the network managed by PRAs due to the associations' ability to operate and maintain roads at relatively low cost, and, at the same time, reduce the level of subsidies. There are, however, risks involved in increasing this network—as the roads get larger and the through-traffic increases, the close connection between the use of the road and the property/road owners declines. In addition, if the subsidies fall below a certain level, PRAs may opt to close their roads to the public. In other words, it is critical to ensure there is a balance between the public subsidies and the demands placed on the PRAs.
3. Forest roads are classified as private roads because there are legally only three classes of roads in Sweden—state, municipal, and private. Forest roads are generally referred to separately from the community managed private roads as "roads in the forest."
4. The Church has played a major role in road provision in many countries throughout history, for example the English monasteries, the Archbishop of the Democratic Republic of Congo (then Zaire), and many faith-based non-governmental organizations in developing countries.
5. Before 1944, a regional engineer was charged with the responsibility of checking on the road network condition (and reporting to the king), however, there was no state road agency.
6. In Sweden there is a customary right of public access (so called "everyman's right") for berry picking, swimming, and camping for a night or two as long as there is no interference with the property owners.

7. The remainder of the private road network are "roads in the forest" that are cleared periodically principally for logging purposes.
8. The 1939 Private Roads Act stipulated that rural PRAs divide road costs among the property owners according to road usage/benefit, and urban PRAs allot costs according to the property taxation value. In 1973, the act governing rural PRAs was replaced by an act that governs a variety of common properties such as recreation areas and playgrounds. In 1998, the 1939 act governing urban PRAs was incorporated in a revised version of the 1973 act, that is, the rules governing both the rural and urban PRAs are now joined and costs are shared among the members according to road usage/benefit.
9. The PRAS are also recognized under the "Land Code" of 1970, the "Real Property Formation Act" of 1970, the "Joint Facilities Act" of 1973, and the "Joint Property Units (Management) Act" of 1973.
10. A couple of thousand PRAs are not legally constituted. These PRAs depend on 100 percent unanimity in all decisions. In cases where there is disagreement, they will have to proceed to carry out a legal survey. This was the case in 2002 in one PRA in Roslagen, just north of Stockholm. This PRA had operated with thirty-five members for more than thirty years without being legally constituted. As a new property owner moved into the community, there was disagreement, and the PRA proceeded by requesting assistance from the NFPRA and a legal survey.
11. The National Federation of PRAs, however, would like SNRA to take over the responsibility for the upkeep of the bridges on those roads that receive public grants. It estimates that there is a maintenance backlog of about US$37 million on the bridges and actively lobbies the SNRA and government decision-making bodies on this issue. But the SNRA is reluctant to accept any additional responsibility being hard stretched to meet its existing commitments. This is a key argument of the Federation in its pressure to avoid cuts in funding levels.
12. The recently (July 2000) constructed bridge between Malmo and Copenhagen is an exception to this rule—all traffic pays toll on the bridge.
13. Some PRAs receive state grants even though they are not legally constituted, provided their roads qualify and they have a board, an annual meeting, a budget, and carry out independent audits.
14. In 2001, however, only ferries received the maximum grant of 80 percent.
15. Funding levels fell even further in 2002, which meant that roads that had received 70 percent grant support in 2001 only received 60 percent, and so forth.
16. The estimates of the required grants in each local office of the SNRA are then aggregated nationwide to arrive at the requested budget support from central government.
17. The SNRA can also be sued if it has not kept "public roads in a satisfactory condition for the users." While this is so far a rare occurrence, it may become more frequent. One recent case that went to the supreme court awarded the plaintiff compensation for a traffic accident on an icy road even though there had not been much time for the SNRA to remove the ice.
18. Many PRAs use similar poles and they are usually replaced every year, The poles are virtually at zero cost as the property owners get them from their own forests—all PRAs work hard at keeping down costs, thus membership fees.
19. The similar legal, institutional, and financial framework for private roads in Sweden and Finland stems from their common legal heritage, which derives from the fact that Finland was part of Sweden until 1809.

References

Clifford, J. 1998. *Engineering and Urban Revolution.* Cape Technikon, Cape Town, South Africa: School of Civil Engineering.

Heggie, I. 1995. "Management and Financing of Roads: An Agenda for Reform." World Bank Technical Paper 275. Washington, D.C.: World Bank. http://www.worldbank.org/afr/ssatp/rmipubs.htm

Heggie I., and P. Vickers 1998. "Commercial Management and Financing of Roads." World Bank Technical Paper No. 409. Washington D.C.: World Bank. http://www.worldbank.org/afr/ssatp/rmipubs.htm

Isotalo J. 1992. "Community Experience in Rural Road Maintenance: Finnish Experience and Lessons for Sub-Saharan Africa Transport Policy Program." Infrastructure Note. Infrastructure and Urban Development Department. Washington, D.C.: World Bank. http://www.worldbank.org/transport/publicat/tdinflst.htm#roads

Isotalo, J. 1995. "Development of Good Governance in the Road Sector in Finland." Sub-Saharan Africa Transport Policy Program Working Paper No. 21. http://www.worldbank.org/afr/ssatp/rmipubs.htm

Ivarsson, S., and B. Nydahl. 1995. "Private Roads In Sweden." Mimeo.

Malmberg Calvo, C. 1998. "Options for Managing and Financing Rural Transport Infrastructure." World Bank Technical Paper 411. Washington, D.C.: World Bank. http://www.worldbank.org/afr/ssatp/rttppubs.htm

National Federation for Private Road Associations. http://www.revriks.se/

SOU: 2001:67. Statens Offentliga Utredningar. 2001. "Utredningen on Bidrag och Regler for Enskilda Vagar—BREV." http://www.sou.gov.se/brev/

World Bank. n.d. Brief write-up of the institutional arrangements for community roads in Zambia. http://www.worldbank.org/html/fpd/transport/rural_tr/goodprac.htm#zambia

15

Role of the Private Sector in Managing and Maintaining Roads

Gunter J. Zietlow

Introduction

Roads are the most valuable public assets worldwide, representing between 15 and 50 percent of countries' annual Gross National Product. In addition, road transport forms the backbone of any modern transport system with more than 85 percent of all transport going by road. But, despite its enormous importance, roads are often under-financed, poorly managed, and badly maintained. Developing countries, especially, spend on average only between 20 and 50 percent of the amounts necessary to preserve their roads in good condition. Therefore only between 10 and 50 percent of roads in developing countries are in good condition, resulting in huge losses to the economy. Poor road conditions are responsible for higher vehicle operating costs and additional road rehabilitation works, draining the economies annually between 1 and 3 percent of their Gross National Product. But developing countries are not the only ones having road maintenance problems. In the United States, for example, the road maintenance backlog amounts to more than US$200 billion.

Insufficient budget allocations and inefficient public road administrations are the root of the problem. Road maintenance always has to compete with supposedly more urgent political priorities. Since politicians tend to prefer glamorous transport investments, road maintenance is being neglected. A new public-private partnership is needed to get things back on track.

Fortunately, the private sector is playing an ever-increasing role in improving road maintenance. Traditionally, this has been the domain of public road administrations. But it is changing. With the global trend of redefining the role of government, which started in the early 1980s and accelerated during the

1990s, an increasing number of road administrations around the world have started a restructuring process, revising their role from being an operational organization to that of being an enabling body, for operations performed by the private sector. Shortage of government funds and the necessity to reduce staff often played a crucial role in jumpstarting this process. The road reform in New Zealand can be cited as an excellent example (see Dunlop 1996).

In North America, the province of British Columbia in Canada was first to start privatizing all highway maintenance in 1988 and other provinces followed suit. In the United States, outsourcing of road maintenance has developed rather slowly. While maintenance contracts of limited scope have become fairly common, outsourcing the maintenance of road networks, such as in the States of Florida, Virginia (VDOT 2000), Texas, and in the District of Columbia (Federal Highway Administration1999) has started only recently. In Europe the United Kingdom was the first country to embrace the idea of privatizing road maintenance on a large scale. Since then a number of highway authorities in the UK have transferred their direct labor organizations to the private sector. More recently the Nordic countries in Europe have begun resorting more and more to road maintenance by contract as well. Finland for example wants to have its state–owned highways maintained by private companies by 2005.

But not only countries in the developed world have engaged in restructuring their road administrations and have called upon private contractors to maintain their roads. Many countries in the developing world have followed suit. The road maintenance crisis in the 1980s, especially in Africa and Latin America, has stimulated this restructuring process, supported by development agencies, such as the World Bank. The donor driven Road Maintenance Initiative in Africa as well as the PROVIAL in Latin America have played an important role, not only to foster the contracting out of road maintenance to the private sector and to assist in helping road administrations to assume their new role as managers of the road networks, but also to secure the crucial funding for road maintenance. The establishment of road funds in many countries of Africa and Latin America is owed to these initiatives (Heggie and Vickers 1998; Zietlow 2005).

The spectrum of contracting out road maintenance ranges from undertaking specific works, like repairing potholes, cleaning drainage systems, or trimming vegetation, to actually managing and maintaining road networks on a long-term basis. The scope of these contracts is not only restricted to managing the actual maintenance works but to managing the operation of roads as well. As such they cover, for example, the asset inventory and condition assessment, snow and ice control, safety management, traffic control, and emergency response.

Such Performance-Based Road Asset Management and Maintenance Contracts are opening a completely new promising line of business to the private sector and most likely will become standard practice in the future.

The consulting industry in particular is likely to benefit most since this new kind of contract requires planning and management knowledge and skills normally not found in the traditional construction industry, such as the use of pavement management systems or the application of the highway design and maintenance models.

Nature of Performance-Based Road Asset Management and Maintenance Contracts (PAMMC)

What is a Performance-Based Road Asset Management and Maintenance Contract or a Performance Specified Road Maintenance Contract (PSMC) as referred to in Australia, New Zealand, and Latin America? The traditional way of contracting road maintenance is based on the amount of work being measured and paid for on agreed rates for different work items. By contrast, Performance-Based Road Asset Management and Maintenance Contracts define the minimum conditions of road, bridge, and traffic assets that have to be met by the contractor, as well as other services such as the collection and management of asset inventory data, call-out and attendance to emergencies, and response to public request, complaints, and feedback. Payments are based on how well the contractor manages to comply with the performance standards defined in the contract, and not on the amount of works or services executed. The nature of the contract allocates responsibility for work selection, design, and delivery solely to the contractor. Hence, the choice and application of technology and the pursuit of innovation in materials, processes, and management are all up to the contractor. This allocates higher risk to the contractor compared to the traditional contract arrangement (see Figure 15.1), but at the same

Figure 15.1
Distribution of Risks to Road Agencies and Contractors with Different Forms of Performing Road Maintenance Services

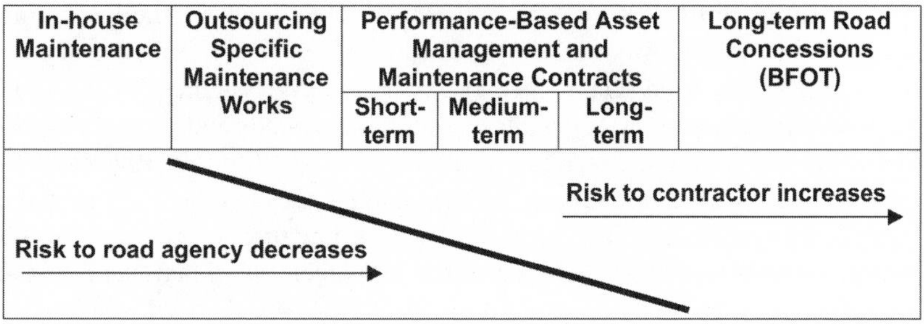

In-house Maintenance	Outsourcing Specific Maintenance Works	Performance-Based Asset Management and Maintenance Contracts			Long-term Road Concessions (BFOT)
		Short-term	Medium-term	Long-term	

Risk to contractor increases

Risk to road agency decreases

time opens up opportunities to increase his margins where improved efficiency and effectiveness of design, process, technology, or management are able to reduce the cost of achieving the specified performance standards.

A special risk with long-term Performance-Based Road Asset Management and Maintenance Contracts might be the overloading of vehicles, a problem often faced by developing countries. Since the deterioration of pavements exponentially rises with the increase of axle loads, maintenance costs increase as well. There are two ways to deal with this problem: either to take this risk into consideration when calculating expected maintenance cost or to enforce axle load limits. To keep costs down, Argentina, for example, decided to include the building and operation of axle weigh stations into their road concession contracts. Since the contractors do not have the legal power to enforce axle load limits they have contracted the police force to do so.

The Evolution of Performance-Based Road Asset Management and Maintenance Contracts

The development of Performance-Based Road Asset Management and Maintenance Contracts (PAMMC) for roads goes back to the late 1980s and early 1990s when the Province of British Columbia started to contract out the maintenance of all its roads to the private sector. Contractors had to meet certain performance standards and had to rectify deficiencies within defined response times. Performance standards were still more oriented towards work procedures or materials to be used rather than result oriented, very much limiting the contractor in the application of new technologies or new work procedures (Ministry of Transport and Highways 1994).

In 1991 Argentina started to concession approximately 10,000 kilometers of its national road network applying genuine maintenance performance standards and introducing a penalty system for not meeting response times. In the mid 1990s Argentina applied a similar scheme to its rehabilitation and maintenance contracts for most of the remaining national road network.

Also, in the mid 1990s the International Road Federation, the Economic Commission for Latin America and the Caribbean, and the German Agency for Technical Cooperation (GTZ) further developed Performance-Based Road Asset Management and Maintenance Contracts for roads and promoted pilot projects in several Latin American countries (Zietlow 2005). In 1996 the first pilot contracts started in Uruguay for the national highways and a part of the arterial urban roads of Montevideo. This new contracting scheme was so successful that only five years later, more than 50 percent of all national roads in Uruguay were managed and maintained by Performance-Based Road Asset Management and Maintenance Contracts.

Other countries in Latin America followed suit, and by now such contracts can be found in Argentina, Brazil, Chile, Colombia, Guatemala, and Honduras. Basically, two different schemes are being applied. One, where a single contractor is managing and maintaining between 300 and 500 kilometers of roads, and the other one where management services are separated from service delivery. In general, countries with a fairly well developed road construction industry, such as Brazil, Chile, and Colombia, are favoring the first system, while the other countries prefer to take the second route in order to build up their road maintenance industry first. Bolivia, Ecuador, Honduras, and Guatemala are among those countries using small-scale enterprises, each of them taking care of the maintenance services of 30 to 50 kilometers of roads, while the road management activities and supervision are carried out by small road management companies. In both countries extensive training programs have helped to qualify these firms for the new tasks. A positive side effect is that this system helps to create much needed employment, especially in rural areas.

In 1990 the Road and Transport Authority (RTA) of New South Wales initiated the development of a pilot road maintenance contract in its Sydney region (see Box 15.1). Prior to 1990 road maintenance in New South Wales was mainly a government monopoly, the private sector having little involvement other than as an activity, or job creator. The objectives of the pilot were to establish the feasibility of contracting road maintenance and to measure differences in cost, quality, and responsiveness between a contractor and the RTA workforce. The RTA pilot comprised two networks of approximately 100 kilometers of roads each. The maintenance services of one network were contracted to a private contractor and the other network was to be maintained by the RTA workforce. The management of the maintenance services for both networks was contracted to a private firm. This contract included network inspection, defect prioritization, work definition, budget development and control, quality assurance of works, treatment design, and reporting. After the initial two-year contract, the services were re-tendered for a further two-year term.

"The result of the pilot left little doubt as to the feasibility and effectiveness of road maintenance contracting, and led to the RTA restructuring its entire Sydney organization to take advantage of the gains in efficiency and effectiveness which resulted from the adoption of this new maintenance management philosophy, and to commence planning for a new generation of contract based on performance specification" (Frost and Lithgow 1996, p. 5).

As a result the RTA let the first full-fledged Performance-Based Road Asset Management and Maintenance Contract for portions of the urban roads in Sydney in 1995 (see Box 15.2). Since then more contracts have been implemented in New South Wales, Tasmania, and Southern and Western Australia. But not all of them are pure Performance-Based Road Asset Management

---

Box 15.1
New South Wales Initiates Pilot Road Maintenance
Contract Project in Australia

In 1990 the Roads and Traffic Authority of New South Wales (RTA) initiated the development of a pilot road maintenance contract in its Sydney
region. The objective was to establish the feasibility of contracting road
maintenance and to measure differences in cost, quality, and responsiveness between a contractor and the RTA workforce. Prior to the time
when the pilot contract was let, road maintenance was essentially a government monopoly. The private sector had little involvement other than
as an activity, or job, contractor; see Frost and Lithgow 1996, p. 4.

"The RTA pilot comprised two contracts with the private sector
and, for the purposes of comparison, a 'contract agreement' with the
RTA workforce entity responsible for the network prior to the pilot.
    The 2 private sector contracts were:

(a) Maintenance management contract
    A contract for the provision of maintenance management services,
including network inspection, defect prioritisation, work definition
and direction, budget development and control, quality assurance of
works, treatment design, and reporting.
    This contract included a specifically designed 'Code of Practice'
as its technical specification, which defined the level of performance,
in terms of intervention standards, expected from the maintenance
manager.
    The initial contract was awarded for a 2-year term, and included 2
networks of approximately 100 kilometres of roads in western Sydney. The works delivery on one network was a private sector contractor (see (b) below) and on the other network was the RTA workforce. Identical documentation and management procedures were
used on both networks.

(b) Maintenance delivery contract
    A comprehensive Schedule of Rates contract for the provision of
maintenance services, which involved the delivery of works as
directed by the contracted maintenance manager in accordance with
the time, cost and quality requirements specified in the direction.
    The contract utilised standard construction contract conditions
and specifications, which were heavily modified to make them

appropriate to a maintenance contract. The contract was a Quality Assurance contract.

After tender, the initial contract was awarded for a 2-year term, and included a network of approximately 100 kilometres of roads in western Sydney."

"Together, the 2 contracts constituted a form of 'performance contract' where the product was identified by the performance parameters defined in the maintenance manager's Code of Practice. However, the RTA's retention of budgetary control limited the latitude of the contractor in this instance.

The style of maintenance services contract allowed for a detailed evaluation of the comparative costs and productivity of the contractor with the RTA. Such an evaluation is difficult with a performance specified style of contract."

"The results of the pilot over its initial twelve months were impressive and beyond initial expectations.

The contractor demonstrated an ability to respond to all emergency situations, which arose, including accidents and a prolonged flood and storm emergency. The contractor's emergency response capability completely satisfied the requirements of the police and other emergency services agencies.

There was no identified or demonstrated difference in the quality of the work undertaken by the contractor and the RTA.

The maintenance manager quickly adopted network management processes, and procedures, that were equal to, or in some cases superior to, those traditionally used by the RTA.

At the commencement of the contract term the contractor's average costs were measured at 16% less than those of the RTA's workforce operating under similar operating conditions.

Over the first twelve months of the contract term the RTA's workforce achieved measured improvements in average productivity of 22%. This improvement was a direct result of the introduction of competition into the workplace.

Over the term of the contract the condition of the assets and the level of service provided was maintained.

As contractual work is initiated in response to road need, without consideration of resource utilisation constraints, the effectiveness of the distribution of the routine maintenance budget improved by an average 10%. This means that 10% more of the budget was able to be diverted to activities supporting the safety and structural outcomes of road maintenance than was possible in non-contract areas, where the need to utilise available resources led to the scheduling of a greater proportion of labour intensive environmental works than required by the needs of the network." See Frost and Lithgow 1996, pp. 4 and 5.

Re-tendering of these maintenance services has produced even more spectacular savings. The second tender in 1993 brought down the private sector contractor's average rates of maintenance services by 37 percent in relation to RTA's rates in 1991 (Frost and Lithgow 1996, p. 6), while the third round of tenders in 1996 produced average rates that were even 52 percent lower than the 1991 reference rates of the RTA. During this time the competing workforce of the RTA managed to reduce their rates by approximately 40 pecent overall (Frost and Lithgow 1996, p. 20).

and Maintenance Contracts; some contain work elements, which are paid based on unit prices and quantities of work executed. This cautious approach is being chosen to limit the risks involved and to gain experience with this new type of contract.

In 1998 New Zealand let its first Performance-Based Road Asset Management and Maintenance Contract of 406 kilometers of national roads to a private contractor and is now maintaining more than 14 percent of its national road network under the new contracting scheme.

In the United States the Virginia Department of Transportation was first to implement a Performance-Based Road Asset Management and Maintenance Contract for approximately 250 miles of Interstate Highways in 1996 (see Box 15.3). In the year 2000 the District of Columbia followed suit, signing a contract for the management and maintenance of 74 miles of federal roads in its jurisdiction (Federal Highway Administration 1999). Both contracts are being considered pilots and are being monitored carefully to establish the feasibility of such contracts for widespread use in the United States. Nevertheless, several other U.S. states have already either started to implement such contracts themselves or are considering to do so.

Performance Standards

The primary objective of road maintenance is to preserve the road asset on a long-term basis, taking into consideration road user costs as well as safety and

Box 15.2
Sydney has Pioneered Full-Fledged Performance-Based Road Asset
Management and Maintenance Contracts in Australia

On October 24, 1995 the Roads and Traffic Authority of New South Wales (RTA) let what they called a Performance Specified Road Maintenance Contract (PSMC) to a large Australian construction contractor, Transfield Maintenance (Transfield) for a large portion of the arterial road network in Sydney.

Services to be Undertaken by the Contractor

Under the contract Transfield has to achieve specific condition standards for a period of ten years in return for a fixed payment stream. Transfield's obligations are to inspect, prioritize, finance, design, and execute works, including routine, periodic, rehabilitation, and replacement works. Hence, the contract effectively transfers the management of the network and all its assets, in terms of condition, from RTA to Transfield.

The target performance standards to be achieved by the contractor are specified in a Code of Maintenance Standards and payments are based on a Commercial Schedule that covers twelve items, such as Base Fees, Rates for Provisional Services, Rates for Inventory Adjustments, and other cost adjustments. The Schedule also includes deductions applied to payments for failure to respond to intervention demands within specified times or to deliver key management activities in accordance with the Maintenance Service Specifications defined in the contract. The amount of the deductions increases with the number of occurrences. If the number of incidents surpasses a specific maximum number, the noncompliance of the contractor becomes a material breach of contract. Hence, the contract makes provisions to ensure that RTA gets the services it pays for and provides sufficient incentives to Transfield to achieve the targeted road condition standards.

Quality Regime

The Performance Specified Road Maintenance Contract is a quality assurance contract and is managed in accordance with the international quality standard ISO 9001.

Under the contract Transfield has to prepare and follow procedures that include:

- Quality Plan
- Contract Management Plan
- Environmental Management Plan
- Incident Response Plan
- Community Relations Plan
- Asset Management System
- Occupational Health Safety and Rehabilitation Plan
- Technical Specifications

Transfield is required to monitor its own performance and compliance with these procedures. Hence the need for close surveillance and audit of work quality by RTA is avoided to a large extent. However, RTA regularly audits the compliance of the contractor with contract procedures based on samples of each asset.

Technology and Innovation

The contract requires Transfield to undertake reviews of, and update where necessary, its maintenance methods with regard to world best practice, developing standards, technological developments, and changes to work practices affecting the general road industry. This is clearly in the interest of the contractor, since it helps to reduce costs, which will result in a commensurate increase in the contractor's margin under this fixed price contract.

Cost Comparison

RTA estimated that this contract is saving 60 percent compared to its own cost in 1991 or prior to the pilot maintenance contract. In addition to this financial saving RTA has also discharged a large portion of its road maintenance risks to Transfield. The value of other improvements that might arise from the contract, in the areas of responsiveness, technical innovation, and environmental management, has not been estimated and is therefore not taken into account in the above-mentioned cost savings (Frost and Lithgow 1996).

Box 15.3
State of Virginia is the First to Let a Performance-Based Road Asset Management and Maintenance Contract in the United States

In December 1996 the Virginia Department of Transportation (VDOT) awarded VMS, Inc. (VMS) a contract for asset management and maintenance of 1,250 lane miles or approximately 250 miles of Interstate Highways. The contract was developed on the basis of performance criteria with clearly defined outcomes. This contract is the first road asset management and performance-based contract in the United States and an innovative approach to provide a high and well-defined quality of service to the user at lower cost. Interestingly, VMS is an independent company with two consulting firms as prime investors that made an unsolicited offer to VDOT for this contract, sensing that this line of business is especially apt for consulting firms and is going to have a great future in the United States.

Cost Savings

VDOT estimated to save with this contract approximately 16 percent over the five and one-half year contract period maintaining the highway in its existing conditions.

A report issued by VDOT in December 2000 showed that actual conditions indicate significant improvements resulting in further savings. In addition, VMS has implemented a number of pavement material innovations, including Roadflex, Novachip, and a crack seal program that has improved the service life of the Interstate Highways.

With a "just-in-time" delivery of maintenance services the contractor engages resources—labor, materials, and equipment—on an as needed basis. This lowers total cost by avoiding excess inventory and underutilization of resources.

Asset Management Services

Under the contract VMS is responsible for managing and maintaining the following features to pre-established outcomes:

• Pavement
• Roadside Assets

- Drainage System
- Bridges
- Vegetation and Aesthetics
- Traffic Services
- Emergency Response Services
- Snow and Ice Control

Within each feature there is a series of functional activities. For example, the pavement group includes activities such as pothole patching, base repair, pressure grouting, and asphalt resurfacing. Each asset has been assigned a tolerance level of acceptance, which VMS is expected to meet or exceed. For example, potholes are not acceptable if bigger than 75 mm $\times$ 100 mm (3" $\times$ 4') and more than 25 mm (1') deep. VMS guarantees services to meet agreed upon standards and performance measures and backs this guarantee with performance bonds. These outcomes were developed jointly between VDOT and VMS during contract negotiations and provide measurable standards that are monitored on a quarterly basis.

Under the contract VMS is also responsible for traffic control and assistance to the Virginia State Police and to local police and fire authorities. VMS' response time is 20 minutes during normal working hours and 40 minutes during non-working hours. After major incidents a critique of how well VMS responds and manages traffic control is performed. In addition, VDOT submits questionnaires to all nine Virginia State Police units along the interstate corridors managed by VMS. Past results have indicated that VMS' performance was highly appreciated.

Subcontractors

In-house staff is providing only approximately 15 percent of VMS' services. The remaining services are being subcontracted. In order to raise the quality of services of subcontractors and improve competition among them, VMS engaged in an extensive training program for small contractors. This way better quality could be provided at lower cost. (Lande 1999; VDOT 2000) environmental aspects. The task is to develop performance standards that will ensure that the objective is being met as effectively as possible. This is a rather complex and challenging task. Normally, several performance standards have to be defined for each asset to be preserved. To avoid ambiguity, performance standards have to be clearly defined and objectively measurable.

Typical examples of performance standards for the maintenance of road assets are:

- The International Roughness Index (IRI) to measure the roughness of the road surface, which affects vehicle operating cost;
- The absence of potholes and the control of cracks and rutting, which effects safety and pavement performance;
- The minimum amount of friction between tires and the road surface for safety reasons;
- The maximum amount of siltation or other obstruction of the drainage system to avoid destruction of the road structure; and
- The retro reflexivity of road signs and markings for safety purposes.

For each performance standard there is a response time in which the contractor has to rectify any deficiencies. For example, in the case of the Sydney contract (see Box 15.2) the contractor has to repair surface defects deeper than 50 millimeters within four hours and traffic signals between two hours and seven days, depending on the importance of the signal. The contract in New Zealand, on the other hand, allows up to four potholes with a diameter of 70 millimeters on any 10 kilometers of highway sections with more than 10,000 vehicles per day (see Table 15.1).

But what is the "right" maximum roughness of the road surface, the maximum allowable width of a crack in the pavement, or the minimum amount of friction between tires and road surface? How much time shall be allowed to repair a pothole or a traffic light? Defining these standards is a rather complex and challenging task, since there are numerous factors influencing the "right" choice, such as traffic volume, climate conditions, and cost to maintain the standard, to name only a few. The decision is always based on a trade-off between what is desirable and what is financially and technically feasible. Mathematic models such as the Highway Design and Maintenance Model or standards that have developed over time, based on long-time experiences, are being used in the decision process. Nevertheless, the determination of appropriate performance standards is still evolving and continues to be a subject of further debate (Frost and Lithgow 1998). The World Bank has developed a

Table 15.1
Examples of Performance Standards Applied in the Contract of New Zealand (Transit New Zealand 2005)

Feature	Contract Standard	Response Time
Potholes on highways with > 10,000 vpd	Not more than 3 potholes with a diameter greater than 70 mm on any 10 km section	48 hours
Potholes on all highways	No potholes greater than 150 mm in diameter	48 hours
Depressions and Rutting	No ponding greater than 30 mm in depth at any location	6 months
Edge Break	No more than 2 m of edge break within any continuous kilometer greater than 0.5 m	1 month
Lined Channels	No lined channels with more than 10% of the cross-sectional area obstructed, and free of vegetation	1 week

"Sample Bidding Document" that might contribute to a more unified approach (World Bank 2005).

Performance Monitoring and Payments

How can one make sure that the contractor complies with the performance standards specified in the contract? Crucial to the success of this new way of contracting road maintenance is to have appropriate control procedures, as well as penalties for non-compliance, well defined in the contract documents. Control procedures and incentive systems to guarantee compliance vary from country to country.

Contracts in Australia, New Zealand, and the United States have comprehensive management programs and plans in place and contractors are responsible for quality control, which includes quality plans, manuals, and procedures (see "Quality Regime" in Box 15.2). Daily activity logs have to be maintained where defects that have been detected as well as actions taken by the contractor are being recorded. In the case of the contract in Sydney, Australia, the contractor has to submit to the client a monthly non-conformance report. In addition, the client has the right to request such reports on an ad hoc basis.

Normally, the contracts call for an independent annual audit of the performance of the contractor and allow for random audits by the client as well. This makes the monitoring and evaluation of the work of the contractor much easier for the road administrations in relation to traditional work based contracts. On the other hand, Performance-Based Road Asset Management and Maintenance Contracts require more qualified and responsible contractors.

In Latin America Performance-Based Road Asset Management and Maintenance Contracts are normally less complex and require self-monitoring by the contractors (see Box 15.4 and 15.5). In these cases road agencies are getting much more involved in controlling the conformance of the performance standards on a regular basis. The contracts in Chile, for example, foresee four kinds of inspections:

1. monthly inspections covering 10 percent of the roads under contract. Stretches of 1 kilometer each are selected on a random basis defined in the contract;
2. weekly inspections looking at 5 percent of the roads randomly selected;
3. non-programmed inspections to respond to complaints by road users; and
4. follow-up inspections to verify that appropriate action has been undertaken by the contractor to rectify non-compliance.

In this case payments to the contractor are based on the results of the monthly inspections. A percentage of compliance is calculated based on a formula using the results of each individual performance standard as input data. Full payment of the monthly fixed fees is only made if the compliance is 100 percent. During the first two years of the contract, compliance has been around 95 percent. In addition, penalties are applied if the contractor does not rectify established deficiencies within a certain time limit.

In the case of the Performance-Based Road Asset Management and Maintenance Contracts of Australia, New Zealand, and the United States, contractors receive monthly installments of the fixed fee agreed upon in the contract. If audits reveal that the contractor failed to comply with his obligations under the contract a certain portion of the fee can be retained. In addition, the client may make deductions from the monthly installments if response times were not met. But certainly the most important "incentive" for contractors to meet their contractual obligations is the possibility that the client might terminate the contract if contractual obligations are not being met. Very strict in this respect is the Performance-Based Road Asset Management and Maintenance Contracts of New Zealand (Transit New Zealand 2005).

Box 15.4
Uruguay was Quick to Adopt Performance-Based Road Asset Management and Maintenance Contracts

National Road Network

In 1996 the Ministry of Public Works started a program to introduce performance-based contracts for the maintenance of the national road network of Uruguay. Basically, there were two types of contracts: One covered routine maintenance only and the other one included initial rehabilitation and periodic and routine maintenance.

The first type of contract was developed to give employees of the Ministry of Public Works an opportunity to form their own private enterprises and to reduce the Ministry's staff at the same time. To provide additional incentive the staff was given the opportunity to return to the Ministry during the first year of the contract in case the system failed. None of the contracts failed and more people wanted to join the new system than new contracts could absorb.

The second type was introduced as a pilot project and rapidly went beyond this stage as the system was producing excellent results in a fairly short time-period. By January 2000 42 percent of the national road network was being maintained by performance-based road maintenance contracts. Key to the success was careful planning and implementation of contracts. Due to legal restrictions contract duration is limited to five years.

City of Montevideo

Montevideo started the first performance-based contract for 138km of its city roads in 1996 as well. Due to deficiencies parts of the road network required initial spot rehabilitation, which was paid for on a unit price basis. The three-year contract allows for a three-year extension, whereby the monthly fixed payments will be reduced by 40 percent during this extension period.

Performance standards, response times, and penalties for non-compliance are defined for

- Pavements
- Shoulders
- Drainage systems

Since actual road conditions were substantially below the performance standards defined in the contract, the contractor was given between three and twelve months to upgrade the different assets to the required standards.

Box 15.5
Asset Management Contracts to the Rescue:
The Experience of the Municipality of Popayán in Colombia

Until June 1999, the Municipality of Popayán executed all routine road maintenance activities with in-house staff. Periodic maintenance, as well as road rehabilitation and improvements, have been contracted with the private sector. The municipality decided what to do, when, and how. Interventions by the municipality were rather reactive than proactive, waiting for roads to deteriorate or for citizens to complain. This system turned out to be ineffective and very costly. Therefore, the municipality decided to introduce a new road management and maintenance system making maximum use of the private sector.

Objectives

Under the new system the road maintenance services have been contracted to small-scale enterprises (private road maintenance cooperatives) and the management to private road administration firms. The new system was designed to satisfy the following objectives:

• Secure effective and efficient road maintenance
• Create additional employment, giving special opportunities to women
• Reduce the vehicle operating cost
• Increase road safety
• Raise public awareness of the importance of road maintenance and actively engage citizens in road issues

It is planned to contract fifteen road maintenance cooperatives that will be responsible for maintaining the 580 kilometers of municipal roads in Popayán. Each cooperative will have between nine and twelve members and will take care of approximately 39 kilometers of roads. Six road administration firms will undertake the management of these roads, each supervising between two and three road maintenance cooperatives.

Services to be Provided

The road cooperatives will perform routine maintenance activities, such as patching of potholes, cleaning of the pavement and removal of litter, cleaning of the drainage system, maintenance of road signs, control of vegetation, control of erosion, and emergency response. The road administration firms will take care of the road inventory, traffic counts, inspection of roadways and bridges, training and supervision of the road cooperatives, design and supervision of minor works to be contracted to other contractors, road user surveys, emergency response, and environmental protection. The road cooperatives, as well as the road administration firms, have to comply with performance standards. Total road maintenance cost per kilometer based on the first contracts is equivalent to approximately US$1,700.

Progress

As of December 2000, six cooperatives and three road administration firms have been contracted. One of the cooperatives has been formed to take care of a nursery to provide trees, bushes, and plants to be planted alongside the roads. The nursery has already outgrown its original purpose and is now selling plants to the general public as well.

With their bright yellow overalls the workers are highly visible in the municipality. The citizens of Popayán have learned to appreciate not only their excellent road maintenance services but also their commitment to the environment.

Cost Savings

As has been mentioned earlier, budget reductions and political pressure were the main drivers of change. But reducing cost and maintaining or even improving quality at the same time are the actual objectives of outsourcing the management and maintenance of roads to the private sector. The RTA through its pilot maintenance contracts mentioned above has demonstrated how such a challenging task can be accomplished.

While there was no identified or demonstrated difference in the quality of the work undertaken by the contractor and the RTA, costs were driven down in a spectacular way. Due to the competition between the highly motivated team of RTA and the contractor, the average rates for maintenance services of the private contractor were down by 52 percent after the third round of tenders in 1996. At the same time, the RTA's workforce, who competed with the private contractor, managed to reduce their rates by approximately 40 percent overall, compared to the RTA's rates in 1990 (see Box 15.1).

These tremendous cost savings were achieved mainly due to the element of competition both between the contractors during the bidding process and between the RTA's workforce and the successful contractor. This also clearly demonstrates that public sector workforces are able to substantially improve their efficiency when exposed to competition. But generally, public sector rules and regulations put its public workforce at a slight disadvantage compared to the private sector, with regard to possible efficiency gains.

When most of the Latin American countries introduced road maintenance contracts in the late 1980s and early 1990s, they were experiencing average savings between 20 and 50 percent for comparable road maintenance works.[1] New Zealand reported savings of 30 percent using consultants for management and 17 percent using contractors when compulsory tendering was introduced in 1991 (Dunlop 1996). British Columbia, on the other hand, did not report any significant cost savings although an increase in quality had been noted (Madar 1993).

While actual cost savings very much depend on the specific circumstances in each country, it remains clear that competition can substantially improve the efficiency of providing road maintenance services.

But introducing performance-based road asset management and maintenance contracts, which combine road management and maintenance for whole road networks on a long-term basis, can achieve even further efficiency gains. For example, when the RTA let its first full-fledged Performance-Based Road Asset Management and Maintenance Contract in Sydney, cost comparisons revealed overall savings of approximately 60 percent in comparison with RTA's costs in 1990 (see Box 15.1). In addition, some assets were upgraded to a higher standard, resulting in further savings.

When the State of Virginia let a similar type of contract to manage and maintain 1,250 lane miles on three Interstate Highways in 1998, the Virginia Department of Transportation (VDOT) estimated the savings at 16 percent compared to their costs. Here too, assets were upgraded to a higher standard (see Box 15.3). New Zealand had similar experiences when they started their first Performance-Based Asset Management and Maintenance Contract in 1998. Contract costs turned out to be 15 percent below comparable costs of traditional contracts. With contractors becoming more and more experienced and more competitive, it can be expected that maintenance costs will drop even further.

Although substantial cost savings that can be achieved by outsourcing road maintenance very much depend on the specific circumstances in each individual country, it seems that typically between 20 and 50 percent can be saved with traditional unit price contracts versus 40 to 70 percent with Performance-Based Road Asset Management and Maintenance Contracts (see Figure 15.2).

Figure 15.2

**Cost Comparison of Contracting Road Maintenance Services
in Percentages with Relation to Work Done by In-House Staff
of Road Agencies, which Does Not Face Competition**

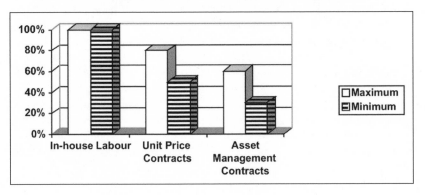

On the other hand substantial cost savings can be achieved in the public sector as well if exposed to private sector competition.

Nevertheless, the public sector is falling short of what the private sector can achieve in reducing road maintenance costs due to a completely different goal and incentive system. The private sector has a clear-cut goal to maximize profits. As long as there is strong competition this translates into delivering good services at the lowest cost possible, putting a constant pressure on providers to improve management and work procedures, to improve the efficiency of staff through incentives and training, to get the best prices from subcontractors, etc. This kind of pressure or incentive is missing in the public administration. Hardly anybody in a public administration will get more pay if he or she is working more efficiently nor will somebody be fired for doing things the "old way." A good example that highlights the difference between the private and public sector approach is compiled in Box 15.6.

Road administrations are trying to overcome this disadvantage by introducing benchmarking. There are certainly examples where road administrations have been able to improve efficiencies this way. Transit New Zealand is one of them. With a small staff of 125 persons it is managing a road network of approximately 10,000 kilometers of asphalted roads. All planning, design, execution, and supervision of road construction, improvement, and maintenance works are undertaken by the private sector.

But Performance-Based Road Asset Management and Maintenance Contracts may also result in higher initial costs due, for example, to the lack of competi-

Box 15.6
Cutting Cost through Mobile Pothole Patching

Prior to contracting the road asset management and maintenance to VMS Inc. in Washington D.C. the Public Works Department was paying to the contractor an average of US$120 per patch. Patching was done the conventional way, using hand tools and simple machinery. It was always done this way and it would have probably continued this way for a long time to come. Everybody was happy. The contractor had his work and the potholes got fixed eventually. And if the same pothole had to be fixed the following year it was normally blamed on the strong winter and not on poor workmanship. Potholes are subjects of frequent complaint by D.C. citizens.

Photo: Courtesy of VMS Inc.

All this has changed with the new National Highways System Preservation Contract, at least for those D.C. roads that form part of the National Highway System. VMS Inc., who won this five-year contract, is using a completely different approach. Since the contractor is being paid a fixed monthly fee and not per patch, there is a strong incentive to use the most efficient work method and materials. They came up with a mobile patcher (see picture above) using compressed air, emulsified asphalt, and graded stone. Average unit cost per patch is now only US$22 per patch. On top of reducing the unit cost per patch the number of patches will be reduced in the future due to the new longer lasting material being used. Traffic will benefit due to reduced lane closures times and last but not least D.C. citizens will have less to complain about, as potholes will have to be fixed almost instantly. Potholes that are a safety hazard have to be repaired within four hours of the noted deficiency and others within forty-eight hours. One of VMS' first tasks was to repair 2,000 potholes drastically reducing the complaint rate by D.C citizens (VMS Inc. 2001).

tion, poor qualifications of the contractor, or because the contractor had to assume too much risk. Recently, the National Highway Department of Brazil had to cancel tenders for the rehabilitation and maintenance of parts of its national road network based on performance standards, because prices turned out to be much higher than anticipated. This was mainly due to the contractors' calculated risk that the government might not honor their payment commitments.

Lessons Learned

Almost all Performance-Based Road Asset Management and Maintenance Contracts have been highly successful. Road administrations as well as contractors have expressed satisfaction with the new contracting scheme and results have often surpassed initial expectations. Although these contracts are still in an early stage of development, some lessons can be learned from the experiences gained so far.

- *Pilot schemes for contracting out road maintenance based on performance standards should be carefully planned and implemented.* The complexity of the contracts, especially with regard to performance standards, road surfaces, and contract duration should be based on past experience in contracting out road maintenance, the ability of the road administration to prepare and monitor such contracts, and the qualifications of local contractors to manage these new road maintenance contracts. Wherever there is little experience with contracting out road maintenance, a gradual approach is recommended, starting with short-term contracts and simple performance standards with regard to the control of potholes and cracks and the cleaning of the drainage system. Whenever roads are not in maintainable conditions, prior rehabilitation is necessary, either based on unit prices or included in the fixed monthly payments the contractor receives over the contract period. It has been proved highly beneficial to resort to the experience of other countries when implementing this new contracting scheme.

- *Close cooperation between road administrations and contractors during the development as well as the execution of the pilot contracts has turned out to be crucial for success.* Both sides have to be comfortable with their new role, understand the opportunities and risks involved, and work closely together to solve the problems that inevitably will arrive during the implementation of these pilots. In almost all pilot contracts at hand, contractors have been provided valuable input for the definition of performance standards, response times, and control procedures. During contract execution close cooperation between the two contracting parties has helped to solve problems in a timely and orderly manner and to avoid major confrontations or even premature termination of contracts.

- *Outsourcing road maintenance to the private sector, especially through long-term Performance-Based Road Asset Management and Maintenance Contracts, can substantially reduce road maintenance costs.* Strong competition, the introduction of private sector management, and the application of new technologies have played a key role in reducing road maintenance costs. Whenever competition among contractors is lacking, as has been the case in some of the developing countries, the development of the road maintenance industry needs to be encouraged. In some cases, initial costs might turn out to be higher than expected due to improper allocation of risks or because the contractor overestimates the risks involved. Proper risk allocation between the road administration and the contractor, as well as full information on the possible risks involved, can help to reduce this problem.

- *Asset management contracts may encourage technology transfer from contractors to road administrations.* As has been the case of VDOT and in several of the Australian contracts, new management procedures as well as the application of new technologies have been adopted by the road administrations for their in-house operations. VDOT, for example, is now using the same methods and materials for crack sealing as have been introduced by VMS.

- *With less experienced contractors, especially newly-formed small-scale road maintenance enterprises, training in management, financial, and technical skills is essential for the success of the pilot projects.* In Honduras, Guatemala, and Colombia extensive training programs for small-scale road maintenance enterprises, as well as road management firms, have produced excellent results. But even in developed countries small contractors might require training as has been demonstrated in the case of the Virginia contract where it has helped to decrease prices through better quality of works and increased competition (Lande 1999).

- *Proper control and application of sanctions for non-compliance with performance standards is equally vital for the new scheme to be successful.* In principle, these contracts are far easier to control than traditional contracts. Supervision of the pilot projects might be contracted out, applying stiff penalties if controls are not enforced properly. In addition, as long as performance standards are made public, road users will become the best "inspectors" and will complain if standards are not being met. Unfortunately, some of the pilot projects in Latin America have not been supervised properly in their initial phase, reinforcing the rather poor performance of the contractor. In contrast, whenever proper controls have been enforced and the appropriate penalties have been applied in the case of non-compliance with the performance standards, contractor performance has improved significantly.

Performance-Based Road Asset Management and Maintenance Contracts are still in their infancy and will require further development to unfold their full potential. Nevertheless, the new contracting scheme has already demonstrated that it is capable of reducing road maintenance costs and can improve road conditions at the same time. Competition among contractors and close cooperation between the public road administration and the private contractors seem to be most crucial for success. Especially in developing countries funding problems often need to be solved before the new scheme can be applied on a large scale. As for the developed world, it can be expected that Performance-Based Road Asset Management and Maintenance Contracts will receive worldwide acceptance, eventually replacing the "traditional" way of contracting out road maintenance based on unit prices.

Note

1. Brazil experienced approximately 25 percent and Colombia 50 percent in savings when switching to contracting out road maintenance compared to work done by the public sector work force.

References

Dunlop, R. J. 1996. "Roading Agency of the Future." Paper prepared for the International Road Federation Asia-Pacific Regional Meeting, Taipei, R.O.C., November 17–22. Paper can be downloaded from http://www.zietlow.com/docs/Srdnz.htm.

Federal Highway Administration. 1999. "Asset Preservation Plan for the District of Columbia National Highway System." Federal Highway Administration, U.S. Department of Transportation and District of Columbia Department of Public Works, November. Document can be downloaded from http://www.zietlow.com/docs/washdcap.pdf.

Frost, M., and C. Lithgow. 1996. "Improving Quality and Cutting Cost through Performance Contracts—Australian Experience." Paper prepared for Road Management Training Seminar of the World Bank, December 17–18. Can be downloaded from http://www.zietlow.com/docs/frost.htm.

Heggie, I. G., and P. Vickers. 1998. "Commercial Management and Financing of Roads." World Bank Technical Paper No. 409. Washington, D.C.: The International Bank of Reconstruction and Development.

Hughson, S., M. Frost, and C. Lithgow. 1999. "Long Term Road Maintenance Contracts: Having the Right Performance Criteria are Key Ingredient to a Successful Outcome." Technical Paper. Maintenance Management Australia.

Lande, K. 1999. "Privatized Highway Asset Management—Management of Subcontract Maintenance." Paper prepared for the Symposium on Innovative Financing of Transport Projects, Hanoi, September 29–October 1. Paper can be downloaded from http://www.zietlow.com/docs/vms1_00a.htm.

Madar, A. F. 1993. "La Experiencia Canadiense en Privatización del Mantenimiento Vial." Paper presented to the First Regional PROVIAL for the Andean Region, Colombia.

Ministry of Transport and Highways. 1994. "Maintenance of Provincial Roads and Bridges—Highway Maintenance Services." The Province of British Columbia.

Transit New Zealand. 2005. "State Highway Maintenance Contract Proforma Manual SM032." New Zealand, March. The document can be downloaded from http://www.transit.govt.nz/technical_information/view_manual.jsp?content_type=manual&=edit&primary_key=28&action=edit.

VDOT. 2000. "Report on VDOT's Comprehensive Agreement for Interstate Asset Management Services." Richmond, Virginia, December.

VMS Inc. 2001. "Privatized Highway Asset Management." Presentation given at the 80th Annual Meeting of the Transport Research Board, Washington D.C., January 8.

World Bank. 2005. "Procurement of Works and Services under Output- and Performance-based Road Contracts." Sample Bidding Document. Washington, D.C.: World Bank, September. The paper can be downloaded from http://web.worldbank.org/WBSITE/EXTERNAL/PROJECTS/PROCUREMENT/0,,contentMDK:20646773~menuPK:84284~pagePK:84269~piPK:60001558~theSitePK:84266,00.html.

Zietlow, G. 2005. "Cutting Costs and Improving Quality through Performance-Based Road Management and Maintenance Contracts—The Latin American and OECD Experiences." Paper prepared for the Senior Road Executives Programme on Restructuring Road Management, University of Birmingham, April 24–29. The paper can be retrieved from http://www.zietlow.com/docs/PBRMC-05.pdf.

Note: More documents on Road Funds and Performance-Based Road Asset Management and Maintenance Contracts can be found at: http://www.zietlow.com.

Part V

Roads to Privatization:
Getting from Here to There

16

New Zealand's Path to a Good Road

The Hon. J. K. McLay

What happens when a country two thirds the size of California, but with a taxpayer base barely half that of the Bay Area, realizes it can no longer meet the costs of its road system?—with vehicle use increasing 4 percent annually (a much larger 8 percent in the largest city)?

That was the challenge given to New Zealand's Roading Advisory Group, known by the inelegant acronym RAG. The proposals in RAG's November 1997 report[1] were described as "a revolution in roading," and prompting the suggestion that, at least at that time, New Zealand was "a world leader in its thinking about roading."

The Group's immediate task was to address the issue of road pricing. However, as work progressed, it found it also had to deal with other social, economic, managerial, and political issues relating to the provision of roads.

Although this chapter is a contribution to the quest for a better road, it does not offer a prescription for whatever ails roads in other countries. The folly of suggesting that "one size fits all" is clearly understood. However, in any public policy debate there are many universal truths. These confirm that there are better ways of doing things, and we should share thoughts on these. And there is definitely a better way of delivering infrastructure outcomes; a new route is just waiting to be followed.

Something about New Zealand

For readers unfamiliar with New Zealand, a brief description is required. It is 1,200 miles from its nearest neighbor, half a world from many of its largest markets. Its land area is greater than Japan or Britain, but its population is just over 4 million.[2] It exports about 27 percent of its Gross Domestic Product compared to about 17 percent for Australia, 12 percent for Japan, and 8 percent for the United States. Therefore, exports are significantly more important to its economy than to many others, and reducing transport costs has been vital to improving international competitiveness. After the United States—and equally with Canada and Australia—it has more cars *per capita* than any other country. By world standards Auckland,[3] the largest city, suffers serious traffic congestion, which a business leader has described as "a national disgrace."

New Zealand is governed at just two levels, central government (not unlike U.S. federal government) and local government; there are seventy-four elected local councils and twelve regional councils (the latter with largely regulatory functions). Councils get most of their revenue from property rates (value-related taxes that, to assist a wider audience, are referred to here as "property taxes").[4]

During the 1980s and 1990s, New Zealand undertook a series of radical economic reforms, moving "from what had probably been the most protected, regulated and state-dominated system of any capitalist democracy to an extreme position at the open, competitive, free market end of the spectrum . . . New Zealand accomplished a more extreme change than any other democracy."[5] The *Wall Street Journal* editorialized that "this tiny faraway democracy began its break from limp socialism. It was the most ambitious assault of any Western nation on the system of entrenched privileges that made an elite rich and resulted in reduced opportunities for everyone else."[6]

Among the changes, all government trading activity was transferred from government departments to companies called State-Owned Enterprises that were required to operate commercially, a process known as "corporatization." Many were later privatized.

New Zealand Transport Sector

As part of this process, much of the transport policy framework was successfully reformed. Road freight was deregulated, allowing it to compete directly with rail. Ports were deregulated and corporatized; some were privatized. State-owned railways were corporatized and privatized.[7] Air New Zealand was privatized[8] and air traffic control[9] was corporatized. Coastal shipping (made uncompetitive by a notorious, union-inspired monopoly) was deregulated. Air, marine, and rail transport now operate in fully commercial structures, all providing innovative, flexible, and cost-efficient services. Internal transport costs have halved. All this has improved international competitiveness.

Despite this deregulation, the management and funding of roads remains one of the few areas where governments (local and central) still control pricing and investment. Road managers have no commercial focus and are not required to earn a return on capital. There is, therefore, little discipline in the use of capital.

Transport costs have been described as "a key issue for a small, remote economy . . . [that] can only prosper through specialisation and trade. . . . We have made much progress with domestic transport services such as air travel, rail, trucking, taxis and coastal shipping. The standout exception is roading."[10]

New Zealand's Roads

About 10 percent of New Zealand's roads by length (50 percent by traffic volume) comprise a State Highway network. These major arterial routes are owned and operated by Transit New Zealand, a government entity, independent of political control, run on corporate (but not yet commercial) lines. Transit is funded by Land Transport New Zealand ("LTNZ"), previously called Transfund, another stand-alone agency that makes project funding decisions independent of political direction.[11] This "funder-provider split" was the basis of many of New Zealand's public sector reforms.

LTNZ is Transit's only funding source,[12] through its National Land Transport Fund (NLTF), which also finances road safety, and partly funds local roads (as well as public transport walking and cycling). Transit currently receives capital for new roads if a project achieves a benefit-cost (BC) ratio of BC 4; a project's benefit must exceed the cost by at least 4 times.[13] NLTF income comes from three principal sources:

1. A petrol excise (in this chapter called "fuel tax"), 50 percent of which goes to roads, the rest to general revenue,[14] currently accounting for 39 percent of total NLTF income;

2. Road User Charges—mileage- and weight-related charges paid by heavy trucks[15]—43 percent; and

3. Part of all vehicle registration and annual licensing fees, 14 percent.[16]

The remaining 90 percent of public roads are owned and operated by the seventy-four local councils. Half the operating costs for existing roads and half the capital for new roads[17] comes from local property taxes, the rest from LTNZ. Again, these capital requirements must meet the BC 4 test.

Debt is rarely used to fund new roads. There is, effectively, a government prohibition on Transit raising loans,[18] and councils are reluctant to do so because they can only pledge their general revenues, not present or future road income, as security. Therefore, this year's revenues (raised from current users and taxpayers) pay for this year's roads, even though they have a long economic life that benefits future users.

These structural and funding relationships are complex and are best illustrated in diagrammatic form:

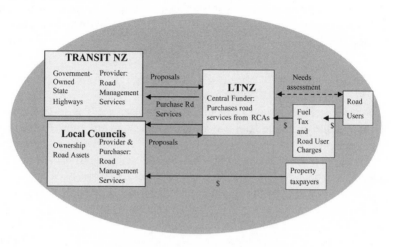

Deficiencies of the Present System

The present structure—particularly the independence of LTNZ and Transit—is an improvement over past, politically managed systems, but still has serious defects. Among many criticisms, the country's Automobile Association has pointed out that New Zealand has "one of the lowest levels of road funding per vehicle fleet in the OECD."[19] Another critic summarized the shortcomings thus:

> Roading is determined by central and local government planning—it is not driven by consumer demands. Resources are allocated . . . by political and bureaucratic processes rather than commercial criteria. Rationing in the form of congestion, rather than pricing, is the norm in key parts of the system. Capital funds are allocated by an arbitrary benefit/cost limit that tells us that something is seriously wrong with either the level of funding or the calculations, or both.[20]

In the week RAG's report was published, an *Economist* cover story on roads endorsed, conceptually, many of the ideas favored by the Group saying:

> If roads continue to be operated as one of the last relics of a Soviet-style command economy the consequence will be worsening traffic jams and eventual Bangkok-style gridlock . . . roads should be priced like any other scarce commodity. . . . In 20 years time, when payment for road space will be regarded as the norm, people will look back and wonder why they were ever prepared to put up with the pollution, noise and paralysis of today's cities.[21]

As if to prove a Soviet mentality that ignores consumer needs, one regional council proposed that "the capacity of [regional roads] should only be extended to meet the needs of commercial road users and off-peak, rural and recreational travellers, rather than the needs of peak period car commuters." Of a similar British mindset, Martin Wolf, *Financial Times* economics editor, wrote:

> Imagine that customers were deterred from visiting a supermarket by the length of its checkout queues. It would be astounding if the company's board refused to expand capacity on the grounds that this, too, would ultimately become crowded. Yet the same people assert that additional road space should not be provided because it will become congested. . . . The rational approach is to manage congestion through prices, rather than queues, and to invest in additional space, provided users are prepared to cover marginal costs, including the social and environmental costs.[22]

Against a background of entrenched attitudes, vested interests, and hardwired politics, it is hardly surprising that, in many countries, road funding and management (and the related policy area of public transport) has been one of the last bastions to succumb to liberal economic reform.

Fuel Tax

Worldwide, the days of using fuel taxes to fund roads must be numbered. They are an increasingly unreliable way of measuring road use. In New Zealand, improved vehicle efficiency has kept this income at constant levels (reducing in real dollars) since 1992.[23] Newer cars burn less fuel but wear down roads just as much as old ones. If fuel tax is a charge for road use, why should older cars pay more than new cars? That may be good for the environment, but fuel tax is not imposed to address environmental externalities.

If these were the only problems, they might possibly be addressed by regular increases in the tax rate (although that could have political and equity implications). However, new technology is also undermining the system.[24] Within the next decade, any significant step-change in vehicle efficiency (possibly from wider use of hybrid technology) could make reform urgent. If nothing is done, fuel tax revenue will continue to decline.

Furthermore, fuel taxes offer no rewards for putting less pressure on roads, and no sanctions for imposing more. Vehicle weight is irrelevant. Fuel tax is also an average price, which implies all roads cost the same regardless of location and time of use. Users pay the same for driving on a country road at 2 A.M. as for a busy freeway in rush hours, and that doesn't make sense. If we tell motorists that all road usage is priced the same, they will often use roads inefficiently. Motorists don't cause traffic congestion out of perversity. They react logically to prices they are charged. These charges were:

Road User Charges

Road User Charges are imposed on heavy vehicles and relate to vehicle weight and distance traveled. These charges, which also apply to all small diesel vehicles, are clearly better than a fuel tax on diesel because charges relate directly to weight and distance. However, the system still ignores the road used and time of use and doesn't reward trucks with modern suspensions that impose less pressure on roads. The transport industry regularly complains that it funds an unfair share of road costs. Consumers and exporters pay for this inefficiency.

Vehicle Registration and Licensing Fees

Vehicle registration and licensing fees relate to vehicle ownership, not their use (and similarly with property taxes). Those who pay these high fixed charges then face lower charges on additional road use, making greater use economically more attractive.

Property Taxes

Use of property taxes to fund roads varies greatly between town and country. In cities, about 15 percent goes to roads, but in rural areas it ranges from 50 to 70 percent, resulting in significant regional variations in household contributions to road costs. Agricultural road users earn two thirds of New Zealand's export income. Again, these distortions reduce their international competitiveness. Farmers and plantation foresters criticize their property tax burden as a fixed charge imposed regardless of road usage; unsurprisingly, they are among the most vocal advocates of road reform.

Property taxes are also unfair on low-income earners and elderly taxpayers who use roads less but pay the same taxes. An elderly couple with one small car, traveling largely between home, doctor, pharmacy, supermarket, and grandchildren, pays the same property taxes as a neighbor with three teenagers, a front yard that looks like a used car lot, with numerous trips to sports, school, college, work, or friends.

Shortcomings

The system therefore has many shortcomings. With seventy-five managers, it is highly fragmented. Users do not pay the actual costs of their road use.

There are no rewards for putting less pressure on roads and no sanctions for imposing more. Most charges do not reflect actual use, resulting in inefficient and unfair cost allocation and distorting public transport choices. The system makes no distinction between the roads used or times of use; users should pay for roads when they use them, not otherwise.

Management is inefficient and unresponsive to users' needs (could there be a better example than a council suggesting that future roads should not meet the "needs of peak period car commuters"?). It lacks direct accountability for the way revenue is spent. Management is not dynamic and cannot easily adapt to change or emerging congestion problems.

Investment and maintenance decisions are essentially administrative. Investment is largely unrelated to actual users' demands and has a short-term focus with poor accountability to users.

Today's users fund tomorrow's roads, whereas costs should be apportioned between present and future users. Property taxpayers subsidize other road users and fund roads they don't use. Further road investment is required, but revenue is reducing.

Rail, air, and sea transport modes complain about unfair competition from inappropriately priced roads.

Problems such as congestion aren't addressed. In larger urban areas, pricing encourages private car use at the expense of public transport, creating serious congestion. Charging the same price for all road use regardless of conditions creates a vicious cycle. Average pricing penalizes those who underutilize roads and advantages those who overutilize them. It also encourages more traffic: We build more roads; average pricing then generates even more traffic; and so on. We can hardly expect road users to change behavior when prices they pay tell them that there is nothing wrong with—indeed, appear to support—their existing usage patterns.

Inefficient road pricing distorts usage patterns. Off-peak users—who contribute nothing to congestion—pay the same as peak-users. Long ago, telephone utilities realized the advantages of off-peak pricing; it's amazing that road managers have taken so long to acknowledge the same reality.

Unless we are prepared to build new road capacity *ad infinitum* (a proposition so unreal it need not be explored), we must acknowledge that roads are a scarce resource. The economic theory that follows from that obvious acknowledgment is not rocket science: As with every other scarce commodity, proper pricing is the best way of communicating scarcity to road users.

Because of inefficient pricing, New Zealand faces increased congestion, worsening environmental outcomes, and increased accidents. New Zealand is not, of course, alone in these concerns. Similar complaints echo in many other countries.

An optimal road system should achieve two key goals. First, it must be *fair*: Users should pay only the actual costs of their road use. Secondly, it must be *efficient*: It must maximize national efficiency and economic benefit. Investment decisions should be made only when the present value of benefits exceeds the present value of costs. Road pricing should incorporate the opportunity cost of capital. Consumer decisions (particularly in relation to public transport) should not be distorted. There should be comparability between transport modes. Road managers should be responsive to user demands and accountable for their decisions. Safety and environmental requirements should be met. Management should have incentives to manage and optimize risk, and the inbuilt dynamism and flexibility to manage change.

Moves to Reform

Against this background, the New Zealand government initiated a *Land Transport Pricing Study* that identified five possible future models, ranging from the status quo (regarded as non-viable) to a fully corporatized, commercial structure.[25] RAG was then established to advise which model might be adopted.

The Group worked within two government-imposed constraints: The existing road network must remain publicly owned and not be privatized (although that did not preclude private sector, capital market participation in future projects). And it was required to have regard to the 1840 Treaty of Waitangi, under which indigenous Maori have certain rights.[26] The "no privatization" edict was based on political realities; but in any event the Group concluded that there were constitutional, legal, and practical reasons why privatization was unachievable.[27]

The Group looked at systems in many countries, as well as numerous studies produced elsewhere. It found that the costs and benefits of road provision and use had never been properly quantified, and confirmed two fundamental problems (already discussed):

1. Charges do not reflect road use costs.[28]

2. There is no direct link between providers and users; investment decisions are not directly linked with prices or users' demands.

In effect the Group reached four basic conclusions:

1. The present system of funding and managing roads is unfair, inefficient, and delivers sub-optimal outcomes.

2. These shortcomings could best be addressed by fairer and more efficient road pricing.

There was little disagreement here. These conclusions were similar to those of studies in other countries. It was the third and fourth findings that provoked debate:

3. The best way of delivering fair and efficient road pricing was through a commercial—or, at the very least, more business-like—structure, with vehicles charged only for their actual road use. Previously, this had not been possible because, while available, the required technology was not yet cost-effective for private cars.
4. However, the timing of RAG's study meant that, for the first time, it was possible to say that, within a reasonable planning period (ten years), the technology would be cost-effective.

Detailed Proposals

The Group then recommended a new, competitive, commercial structure broadly modeled on the operation of a regulated public utility. In each region, all State Highways and local roads would be combined, owned, and managed by a small number of road companies (replacing the seventy-five local council road agencies) jointly owned by central and local government, with stock allocated in accordance with the value of the assets each contributed. They would operate commercially, pay tax, earn financial returns, and pay dividends. They would price, maintain, and invest in roads, and set charges based on their capital, operational, and maintenance costs. Pricing should also reflect other factors such as congestion, time-of-use, and vehicle weight.

The companies would be subject to new safety and environmental requirements and to a commercial regulatory regime. They must take into account community concerns about road provision and must disclose their investment and maintenance policies. Existing common law road access rights would be retained and made part of statute law. Pedestrians and cyclists were not forgotten: Their access rights could also be translated into statute, and would be better protected by the new safety regime.

After a transition period, all roads would be funded only from direct charges for actual road use, together with some access and congestion charges. All existing road-related charges (fuel tax, Road User Charges, licensing fees, and property taxes) would be phased out. Even without privatization, capital market funding of roads would also be possible. The Group proposed electronic charging, probably using GPS (global positioning satellite) technology.

Implementation would take ten years, possibly less. Reform would proceed as the charging technology became cost-effective (it already is for trucks).

Likely Outcomes

The Group concluded that these reforms would result in a system more responsive to user demands, with a more direct linkage between managers and users; deliver maximum economic benefit at least possible cost; and achieve required safety and environmental goals. Road users would pay only the direct cost of their road use and would no longer subsidize other users. Clear price signals would encourage transport choices based on actual cost. Road managers would manage and optimize risk and would have the right incentives for investment and accountability.

The Group commissioned independent studies to assess the impact of these reforms on the economy, investment patterns, maintenance, road use, regions (particularly lower socioeconomic regions), households, and administrative structures. These showed that there would be identifiable national economic gains through more rational investment, cost-effective maintenance standards, reduced administrative costs, efficient road charges, and use of congestion pricing. Even on conservative projections, net economic benefits would be considerable, particularly for industrial and agricultural users, the more so once investment decisions became better aligned to users' requirements. Regional effects would vary, particularly if cross-subsidies were removed, but adverse impacts could be controlled by regulation. As with other commercially operated networks, road companies would probably continue some internal, commercially appropriate cross-subsidies.

Impact on households would vary. Elimination of cross-subsidies would be most advantageous to major city households, and least to those in distant, low-populated areas. Maintenance costs would decline in rural areas with lightly used roads. Congestion pricing would impact on household expenditure, but households would also be the major beneficiaries of reduced congestion, with those in outer—generally less affluent—suburbs being the biggest winners. And the replacement of property taxes with direct user charges would have different impacts on households depending on their present tax levels as against their road usage.

Overall, the benefits of reform would include fairer, more transparent charges and less peak-time congestion. Users would be directly exposed to the consequences of their road use. A more responsive system would deliver better management and investment. All this should lead to less road construction and improved environmental outcomes. There would be fairer competition with other transport modes and improved international competitiveness.

RAG's proposals would reallocate the sources of road revenue. Obviously, some users would pay more, others less (particularly with the reduction in property taxes). Peak-time users, diesel cars, and local road users would probably pay more. Property taxpayers with low vehicle use (for example, the elderly) would pay less. Clearly, if more money for roads is required, then overall charges will increase. That is, however, inevitable under any system; at least under a reformed structure charges would be more fairly allocated. Road use has never been free. Even now, New Zealanders pay directly for roads through various "user payments" and property taxes. Under a reformed system people won't suddenly *start* paying for roads; but they won't *stop* paying either.

Access to Roads

There was concern that commercial imperatives, unfair pricing, or other restrictions—even closing "uneconomic roads"—might restrict road access rights. It would not, however, be commercially sensible to restrict access. Furthermore, common law road access rights date back to the Middle Ages, and RAG proposed that these be retained and—to provide even greater assurance—be made part of statute law.

So-called "uneconomic roads" are often lightly used rural roads requiring less maintenance. They only become "uneconomic" when requiring major capital expenditure (for example, replacing a damaged bridge). Local councils face this problem now. Commercially run networks (of whatever type) are maintained and operated, even the "uneconomic" parts. However, as an added assurance, the Group proposed that existing statutory processes applying to road closures be retained.

Natural Monopolies

Road companies would, of course, be substantial natural monopolies. But the present system also has significant monopoly characteristics. Provided there is an appropriate regulatory regime, commercial structures are the best way of managing a monopoly network. This is confirmed by New Zealand's experience of corporatizing other monopolies including Airways Corporation (air traffic control) and Transpower (national electricity grid). Both remain publicly owned, but operate much more effectively than their government department predecessors, including earning profits and paying both taxes and dividends to the government.

Under New Zealand legislation there is usually no formal recognition of monopoly status, nor is it general practice to accord any entity—government or privately owned—a statutory monopoly. Monopolies exist nonetheless and cannot, of course, misuse their dominant market position[29]; but, beyond that, unless Parliament passes specific legislation imposing some form of regulation, they are not regulated. Even where regulation is introduced (for example, electricity lines and aspects of telecommunication networks), it is usually "light handed" (and therefore low-cost). The proposed road companies would be subject to such a regime.

Under RAG's model, a private sector operator could (at its own risk) build, own, and operate a road and make charges similar to those imposed by competing public road corporations. However, a private owner would not have access to legal rights such as eminent domain that allow public entities to take land for public works. Accumulating land for a significant road link (particularly in an urban area, the most likely location) would be difficult if not impossible. Therefore, while such competition is theoretically possible under the model, it is unlikely.

What about Tolls?

Traditionally, tolls have been used to pay for specific, high-cost projects (freeways, bridges, or tunnels), and are additional to existing charges. They inevitably create a sense of injustice: "I've paid once; why should I pay again?" The Group agreed, and, except for congestion charging (which has a different purpose), did not recommend tolls in addition to other charges. Eventually, when all present charges are abolished, users would pay one fee alone for using a particular road at a particular time. There would not be several charges, all dipping into the same pocket, with users paying twice for the same road.

Congestion Charges

The old solution to traffic congestion was to build more roads, but that is often now unacceptable and usually offers only temporary relief. Increased spending under old, unreformed structures only encourages urban sprawl and further traffic growth. Congestion is not solved simply by spending more money, even when it is available. Better outcomes will be achieved under new structures that facilitate use of congestion pricing. "It is," says one commentator "sheer folly simply to go on constructing roads to meet demand which is not properly priced."[30]

What is the difference between congestion charges and tolls? Tolls fund specific projects. Congestion charges shift traffic from peak times and congested roads, reducing the need for new roads or, if that need is unavoidable, providing funds for new investment. However, cash flows (and the final use of this money) may be similar in both cases.

Environmental and Safety Issues

Some critics expressed concern that commercially motivated companies would build more roads, ignoring environmental consequences. RAG recommended that companies not only be required to comply with relevant environmental legislation but also be clearly accountable for water, land, and air impacts (presently, they are only very generally accountable for the first two).

Companies would also have to manage traffic flows to control emissions from vehicles idling in congestion, and would be liable for pollution from stormwater run-off. The Group wanted to see an end to untreated water (with oil, rubber, heavy metals, and other contaminants) spilling from roads directly into waterways.

Similarly, all roads would be subject to a common safety regime. Drivers and cars are subject to stringent safety requirements, but presently only State Highways operate under formal safety rules. Local roads are not similarly regulated. That too should change.

Overall, the Group was concerned at the adverse impact of congestion, water run-offs, and other aspects of unregulated road management. Although, in saying that it had to rely largely on historical evidence, its concerns were confirmed several years later with the release of a report[31] concluding that New Zealand's "invisible road toll" of premature deaths caused by road vehicle pollution (including congestion and vehicle emissions) is worse than the "visible toll" resulting from traffic accidents.

Road projects often attract community opposition. This will be as true under the new structure as the old. The Group accepted that applying all environmental laws to roads might further encourage environmentally based objections. However, better environmental outcomes should result.

Moreover, project financing (with the project supported only from its revenues) would mean that roads are only built when there are accurate, credible traffic and revenue projections supporting the project. That too should also deliver better environmental and community outcomes.

Public Transport

Public transport was outside the Group's terms of reference. However, proper road pricing would make public transport faster, more efficient, comparatively less costly, and thus more attractive. Experience from London's road pricing scheme suggests that the imposition of market pricing would make travelers evaluate their vehicle use more carefully and consider public transport.

Auckland is trying to solve its congestion problems by new public transport investment. However, two American experts have suggested that this expenditure would be better applied to roads, arguing that, having grown up with freeways, "younger cities" (in North America and elsewhere) have different layouts.[32] Therefore, public transport feeds into central business districts while other centers (often with larger workforces) remain poorly served.

Even public transport advocates must accept that the parlous state of public transport worldwide isn't evidence of some natural law. It is—ironically—the predictable consequence of getting road prices wrong. In some cities, subsidies for fixed-track public transit benefit few users, with most commuters continuing to use cars. Only better road pricing will achieve any transport balance. Road users would then compare the true cost of journeys over crowded roads against public transport alternatives. Until that happens, public transport will not have a viable future beyond the subsidy begging bowl, and future generations will continue subsidizing public transport that is used by fewer people.

Earning "Profits" from Roads

In effect, RAG recommended that, through the new companies, local and central government owners should earn "profits" from roads. Why should this be?; and how can it be justified?

Despite impressions to the contrary, publicly invested capital is not a "free good." There is an opportunity cost associated with such investments. New Zealand's unique "balance sheet" approach to public sector accounting requires managers to account for the cost of capital employed, thus forcing proper management of assets.[33] There should be no exception with roads. All other transport sectors operate under commercial structures, earning returns for their owners. The lack of an explicit financial return from roads[34] means that, relative to other modes, road use is under-priced.

It is, therefore, appropriate that returns be earned on roads. Central and local government stockholders could, if they wish, use this income to fund additional road investment, but would not be *obliged* to do so. Indeed, the owners could use surpluses to enhance general revenues, and could even use dividends to fund public transport. That would, however, be their decision for which they would be accountable.

Private Sector Capital Markets and Project Sponsors

The Group sought better funding mechanisms, including an end to today's users and taxpayers funding roads that will be largely traveled by tomorrow's drivers. Although privatization of the total road network was expressly excluded from the Group's terms of reference it was allowed to consider the possibility of using private sector capital markets to accelerate the provision of new roads. Even without privatization, private sector capital markets and project sponsors would be able to provide additional funding—both debt and equity—for roads through mechanisms such as build, own, operate, transfer (BOOT) projects. This would enable additional investment and accelerate projects that might otherwise be delayed, and would be facilitated by direct charging for every road.

Most countries lack sufficient public funds to meet all road requirements, compounded in New Zealand by the fact that debt is not generally used to fund roads. Successful road financings in other countries have introduced additional equity and debt while at the same time securing long-term public ownership. Commercializing roads allows more innovative financing and delivers more efficient and cost-effective outcomes that benefit road users. If projects stack up, they can support debt, servicing it from future income. Debt has a "back-ended" repayment profile, with future users making their share of the repayments.

The benefits of using private sector capital markets to fund roads are well-known internationally; with particularly useful experience being offered by New Zealand's near-neighbor, Australia, where projects (particularly Sydney's M2, M4, M5, and Eastern Distributor, and Melbourne CityLink) were "banked" without government financial support or revenue guarantees.[35] Ultimate ownership of the road vests in the government.

Private sector proposals for Sydney's M2 and Eastern Distributor were sought on a "negative tender" basis. The state government believed they were not commercially viable and sought tenders for the required one-off subsidies. Both winning tenders bid zero-subsidies[36] as against government assessments that subsidies exceeding $60 million would be required. Increasingly, rather than seeking subsidies, bidders are now offering payments *to* governments, sometimes triggered once equity benchmarks are achieved.

Funding of Australian toll roads went through three distinct phases. Between 1983 and 1987, for projects such as Sydney Harbour Tunnel, governments guaranteed the financings and the revenues. From 1988 to 1990, they gave no revenue guarantees; projects (such as M4 and M5) were financed with substantial bank debt. In the third phase, sponsors made full use of private sector capital markets, with project financing and publicly raised equity through initial public offerings (IPOs).

As deals became more sophisticated and parties more confident about the risks, equity returns and debt margins have halved.[37] The risk profile has significantly changed; toll roads are now regarded as less risky. The evolution of risk assumption has been significant: On Sydney Harbour Tunnel, sponsors took no traffic risk; on M4 and M5, they assumed traffic risk but with government support; by the time M2 and Eastern Distributor were developed, sponsors were actually making payments *to* the government! Australia has progressed from government-guaranteed financing to full use of private sector capital markets, with private sector sponsors and investors and their bankers assuming risks previously taken by governments. These are excellent outcomes for governments and road users.

What has Happened Since?

The Roading Advisory Group embarked on its task with much goodwill. Reform was actively sought by local councils. The minister of Transport, Jenny Shipley, declared that the government supported "a more commercial approach to the management and funding of . . . roads." Within six months, Shipley had become prime minister and her successor as minister took up her theme, saying, "it is not a question of whether we do anything, it is a question of what we do."

Government action on the Group's Report was, however, slow and methodical. For twelve months ministers and advisers worked on a response. Meanwhile, those opposing reform gathered force. Local Government NZ, representing local councils, had pressed for change: "New Zealand cannot continue to manage and fund roads as it has in the past," it said. Now, however, it hedged its bets; it still supported reform, but not *this* reform. Having lived with the issue for years, the Ministry of Transport remained supportive, but some government agencies were more ambivalent. The Treasury objected to the government holding minority stakes in road companies, even though its representatives on the Group had supported the idea. Many lobbyists, however, supported reform, including business, farming, forestry, road transport, and rail groups. The proposals also attracted international interest.

Finally, in December 1998, the government published its response,[38] in which it pointed out—yet again—that the system was under pressure, with serious congestion in larger cities. Farming, forestry, and tourism developments were imposing pressure on rural roads. Roads were not as safe as they could be, said the paper. Environmental costs were too high. There were too many road managers. A system was needed "where people are given a clear understanding of the costs of their road use, and that is smarter at deciding where new investment should go."

The document then proposed a commercially focused system that would encourage innovation and efficiency, but with safeguards to protect the public interest. Between five and nine companies, separately owned by the government or local councils,[39] would manage roads. They would be directly responsive to users' needs. Property taxes would no longer fund roads. Users could choose how they paid for roads and could join together to negotiate better deals. Roads would not be privatized; access rights would remain; charges would be "sensibly constrained." Decisions would reflect environmental costs, and there would be a new national safety regime.

To RAG, none of this was new. While some detail had changed, its basic recommendations had survived a challenging review. Significantly, this new document's supporting papers included draft legislation implementing the proposals. That augured well for the "revolution in roading."

However, because of the importance of the issues, the government embarked on another round of consultation. Local Government NZ remained unconvinced, saying it was "still concerned about the need for more incentives for passenger transport, and the environmental impacts and effects on rural communities" (this despite strong support for the proposals from the country's largest rural lobby).

And an election loomed in November 1999. The opposition Labour Party had undertaken dramatic reforms in the 1980s,[40] but now had returned to its center-left roots and was unhappy with the proposals. Its likely coalition partners—even further to the left—were outright opposed. But Labour understood the problems. It would still consider reform, but on its own terms. In August 1999, Labour's leader, Helen Clark, said Labour might "speed up" investment by "allowing [roads] to be built by developers on a build, operate, toll, and transfer basis." While rejecting "commercialization," Labour apparently backed BOOT projects. Clark favored leaving accountability for roads with local councils, "which themselves are accountable to local communities"; but expressed interest in regional clustering of road responsibilities. The door to reform—maybe less "revolutionary" reform—appeared to remain open.

Hurry up and Wait

After the 1999 election, Labour became the senior partner in a center-left coalition government. In its briefing for the new government, the Ministry of Transport continued its reform advocacy:

> . . . the roading system is under strain. . . . These issues are systemic, nationwide, and can be traced to a road system where users do not face the real cost that their road use imposes on the road network and on society.

Things became less clear, however, when the government quickly said it would "not proceed with the previous government's proposals to commercialize roading." Nonetheless, providing policy advice on "efficient road pricing" remained one of the formal "results" sought by the government from the Ministry. Identifying, yet again, all the usual problems, the new minister spoke of the "need to fix them." "Our roads," he said, "daily demonstrate that they are becoming inadequate for the task." More important, he acknowledged that "charging systems are reaching their limits . . . new automotive technologies will make the current petrol tax system an increasingly unreliable and unfair way of paying for road use." He has said that "we also need to think about whether our present management structures can be improved"; and has even foreshadowed use of new technology for collecting Road User Charges.

The government issued a further discussion paper on possible tolling,[41] noting that, while taxation sources remain limited, road demand continued to grow, and that tolls could expedite new projects and give users better signals of the true costs of road use (including environmental and safety costs) and could facilitate efficient management of key urban corridors. The paper noted that "overseas experience indicates that direct charges can only be imposed where there are alternatives available and the funds raised are used in a transparent manner that benefits those paying." It also discussed the benefits of private sector BOOT and DBFO (Design, Build, Finance, Operate) projects; speculated that legislation might allow new charging technologies; and discussed shadow tolling (as used in the UK). All this suggested a government willing to embrace new approaches to road funding and management.

Nonetheless, despite acknowledging the problems and rejecting its predecessor's plans, the government still did not offer its own solutions.

It did, however, increase public transport spending, undertake safety initiatives and foreshadow new vehicle emission standards and suggest that emission rules should apply to roads, and foreshadowed action on water runoff and noise impacts.

"All We Want to See is a Good Road"

Despite all these delays, one thing had become clear: The development of new ideas and attitudes about road provision was now an ongoing process, supported by significant changes of view among key players. While RAG's report may have been ahead of its time and was not immediately implemented, it triggered a substantial re-think about the future, and aspects are appearing in the policies of the majority of political parties (and in other countries). Whatever opponents of reform said at the time about RAG's suggested solutions, no one now seriously questions the Group's detailed analysis of the problem.

While successive governments deliberated, the Auckland region produced a *Growth Strategy* acknowledging that a new approach to road pricing was inevitable, and Local Government NZ now supports that view. A new Auckland Mayor[42] supported Public-Private Partnerships—and toll roads—to address the region's urgent road requirements, but his enthusiasm for an unpopular road project saw his defeat after just one term (a reminder that, under any system, such projects can be controversial). A small, rural council decided that operating roads was too expensive and no longer part of its "core business," and transferred all road operations to Transit, with a minimum 10 percent cost saving. Other councils are also considering that approach, or evaluating larger groupings that could be the basis for future regional road companies.

And Transit now uses "Performance Specified Maintenance Contracts" with private contractors for parts of its State Highway network. Contractors must deliver specified, measurable outcomes for a lump, fixed sum price. Positive outcomes include: use of higher quality pavement treatments and construction practices based on international best practice; pavement modeling to predict the need and timing of upgrades to ensure service requirements are met; and improved pavement quality assurance, driven by the need to avoid subsequent rework.

The Automobile Association now supports tolls on new roads. It may even consider lane pricing on existing roads and a survey of its Auckland members showed "overwhelming support" to the using tolls to pay for more for roads, provided they could see "positive outcomes in terms of alleviating congestion and improved safety."[43]

Likely use of electronic Road User Charge systems became largely accepted. The dairy industry, for example, already has GPS installations on all trucks collecting milk from farms, and could quickly move to electronic charging. Arguments about detail continued, but the circle of those who now accept the inevitability of change was steadily widening.

And the same lessons are being learned in other countries. In February 2002, a report[44] from Britain's Commission for Integrated Transport (established "to provide independent advice [to the government] . . . on the . . . integrated transport policy, [and] to monitor developments across transport, environment, health and other sectors"), offered thinking almost identical to RAG. It identified the problems (congestion, unfair taxation, pollution, economic downsides, and unfair competition with public transport), and concluded that "doing nothing was not an option," and that "current motoring taxation is a very blunt instrument which often penalizes those who can least afford it" (it had "not changed fundamentally since the early days of the car when it was the preserve of the few"). Noting that, on planes, trains and ferries . . . passengers . . . pay according to when and how they want to travel," it asked, "Why should roads be different?"

The Commission proposed a nationwide GPS-based system using smart-card units on every vehicle. Most roads would have no charges (the only significant difference from RAG's proposals), with others having fees based on their levels of congestion. Independent economic modeling of the proposals suggested that congestion could be cut by a staggering 44 percent, but with traffic levels falling by only 5 percent and allowing for speed increases of about 3 percent, and with real benefits to the economy, transport industry, public transport, rural motorists, and those with low annual mileages (such as pensioners).

Action at Last?

In February 2002, the government announced a number of policy decisions to be followed by legislation. These gave expected emphasis to initiatives such as a "widened policy focus on land transport rather than roads," "funding of alternatives to roads where these give better value," and "initiatives to fund cycling and pedestrian facilities"; and also to increased expenditure in a number of areas and to moves to a "level playing field" between road and rail; and to allow regional councils to own passenger transport infrastructure (since delayed, except for the Auckland region). Transfund was renamed as Land Transport New Zealand but remained a stand-alone agency, making independent funding decisions; the National Roads Fund, renamed as the National Land Transport Fund, continued as a separate fund with its own income source.

Moreover, and most significant for RAG and its proponents: Tolls and Public-Private Partnerships (PPPs) would be allowed to fund some future roads and public transport, and Road User Charges would be redeveloped into an electronic system (e-RUC), possibly using GPS (initially this would be voluntary, but the long-term plan is to move all diesel vehicles onto e-RUC). Further work was commissioned on use of congestion pricing to relieve congestion and provide environmental benefits, and Transit and local councils would be allowed to make "clustering" management arrangements to achieve operational economies of scale.

This was still not the commercially operated road system contemplated by RAG, but is certainly a step in the direction it had proposed four years earlier.

However, although the resulting legislation promised much, regrettably, it delivered less, partly because of the influence of the far-left Green Party. PPPs became less likely because of constraints such as a thirty-five-year maximum concession (or franchise) period (too short for the major roads that might require such project delivery), a multi-layered consultation process, and the possibility that ministerial approval might be withheld after significant project development and bid costs have been incurred. Moreover, the legislation is structured so that PPP projects can really only be sponsored by the present road authorities (the largest being Transit). Although there are projects ideally suited to this delivery model, and despite publicly stated support and interest from private sector providers, so far the authorities have shown no appetite for this, nor have they received any government "guidance" to "encourage" them in that respect.

The latest minister of Transport (the fifth in eight years, a turnover rate that also hasn't helped progress) has lamented that, while the government is "open for business" on road PPPs, "there were no firm proposals yet." He need look no further than his own legislation and agencies to find the answer.

Meanwhile, Transit has received government approval to toll a new highway, but using a system that is costly and inefficient and preempts any better system being used elsewhere.

For those committed to reform—and for the long suffering road user—it's been a roller coaster ride: Eight years after being described as "a world leader in its thinking about roading," New Zealand is, regrettably, still only "thinking" and not "doing."

Its task completed, the Roading Advisory Group was disbanded in 1997. Its members now watch developments from a distance and can see the glacial progress towards their goal of a fairer, more efficient system that responds to a challenge put to it by someone from a remote, economically disadvantaged part of New Zealand: "All we want to see is a good road."

Three words that sum up the whole rationale for reform: "A good road." That should certainly be enough motivation to find better ways to fund and manage roads.

Notes

1. Report of Roading Advisory Group, "Road Reform—The Way Forward," delivered to the New Zealand government in November 1997 and publicly released on December 11, 1997.
2. As of May 2, 2005, New Zealand's population was 4,094,360 (source, Statistics New Zealand).
3. As of June 30, 2003, Auckland's estimated population was 1,290,800, which means that nearly one third (31.5 percent) of all New Zealanders live in Auckland (source, Statistics New Zealand).
4. To facilitate understanding by a wider readership, common "international" terms have been used wherever possible. Therefore, motorways become freeways, kilometers become miles, shares become stocks, etc. Although they have official names ("City Council" or "District Council"), the term "council" or "local council" is used. The word "roading"—which appears to be used only in New Zealand—is wherever possible replaced with "road." All monetary amounts are shown in U.S. dollars.
5. Jack H. Nagel, *Social Choice in a Pluralization Democracy: The Politics of Market Liberalization in New Zealand* (Cambridge University Press, 1998).
6. Editorial, "The New Zealand Experiment," *Wall Street Journal*, July 12, 1994, p. A12.
7. In 2004, when the renamed TranzRail encountered financial and commercial difficulties and was taken over, the government reacquired the rail network, although the commercial operations remained in private hands.

8. Following a crisis in 2001, the government reacquired a controlling stake in the airline, although it remains publicly listed.
9. According to Paul Proctor in *Aviation Week & Space Technology* (April 27, 1992), "New Zealand's air traffic control system is showing substantial cost savings and increased efficiency four years after the government placed it on a corporate, for-profit footing. The success could fuel the commercialization of more ATC services worldwide as governments seek ways to cut deficits and free up tax dollars for other purposes. Airways Corp. of New Zealand now recovers full costs, pays taxes and has generated a total of $30 million in dividends to its sole shareholder—the government. . . Safety also has been enhanced. . . ."
10. Ralph Norris, chairman of the New Zealand Business Roundtable, from his speech, "Removing Lead from the Saddlebags," delivered at the Case for Roads conference, Auckland, March 8, 2001.
11. The Minister of Transport can give strategic directions to Land Transport NZ (for example, to focus on congestion problems in Auckland) but has no detailed project-by-project control.
12. LTNZ's 2004/05 National Land Transport Programme forecasts 72 percent of the NLTF to be spent on roads, 12 percent to part-fund public transport, walking, and cycling, 15 percent to safety administration, and 8 percent to meeting the costs of collection and administration.
13. This ratio varied throughout the 1990s. For a time it was as high as BC 5. The current target figure, over time, is BC 4, although, during 2000–2001, projects were funded at BC 3.
14. This "raiding" of road taxes for general revenue purposes is as controversial in New Zealand as elsewhere.
15. These charges are based on weight carried, distance traveled, and axle configuration for all vehicles over 3.5 tonnes gross, and all diesel vehicles.
16. Four percent of the income comes from "other sources," 2 percent of which includes specific allocation of Crown funds to Auckland primarily targeted at developing alternatives to roading.
17. Local councils can also—and often do—fund the full cost of local roads they consider desirable but that do not meet the current BC requirement. They do this, of course, entirely from their local tax income.
18. By law, Transit cannot borrow without the consent of the Ministers of Transport and Finance (Crown Entities Act 2004); so far, that consent has not been given and probably will not be forthcoming under present structures.
19. *AA Directions* (Winter 2001).
20. Norris, "Removing Lead from the Saddlebags."
21. "Jam Today, Road Pricing Tomorrow," *Economist*, December 6, 1997.
22. Martin Wolf, "The Road More Travelled Needs Expanding," *Financial Times*, November 15, 1999.
23. Revenue increases have been achieved by increasing the dollar amount of the excise.
24. "Hybrid" cars already offer fuel savings up to 50 percent. Within the next decade, more sophisticated systems will likely be even more cost-effective. This might be great for the environment but it is seriously bad news for any charging system based on fuel taxes.
25. The report *Options for the Future: Land Transport Pricing Study* was prepared by the Ministry of Transport and published in May 1997. It set out five possible

options for reform. The first two were versions of the status quo; the third, described as a "business option," proposed a commercial structure; and the fourth and fifth proposed formal corporatization.

26. This Treaty is not dissimilar to the treaties the United States has with some Native American nations.

27. While not strictly relevant to this chapter, these included issues associated with the need to establish legal title to many roads, and those arising from the Treaty of Waitangi.

28. Many of RAG's findings have been confirmed by subsequent studies. For example, the 2005 Surface Transport Costs and Charges concluded that charges paid by road and rail users do not cover the cost of those networks (and that some costs, especially environmental, are not paid by anyone); that rail users pay a higher proportion of their costs than do road users; and that users of urban local roads pay a lower proportion of costs than users of either rural roads or state highways.

29. Section 36, Commerce Act 1986.

30. Roger Kerr, executive director of the New Zealand Business Roundtable, from his speech, "Cars are a Good Thing," delivered at the New Zealand Automobile Association Annual Conference, Wellington, March 30, 2001.

31. Released March 20, 2002 (full text at www.transport.govt.nz/publications/niwa_report/index.shtml) commissioned by Ministry of Transport and undertaken by National Institute of Water and Atmospheric Research (NIWA) working with a number of eminent New Zealand air quality and public health researchers.

32. Wendell Cox (consultant demographer and transport analyst, Illinois) and Professor Randal O'Toole (environmental economist and lecturer at Utah State University), Case for Roads Seminar, Auckland, March 11, 2001.

33. The New Zealand approach to government sector accounting was succinctly summarized by Dr Graham Scott in *Public Management in New Zealand* (New Zealand Business Roundtable, 2001): "The use of generally accepted accounting principles, the liability for goods and services tax [a value-added tax] and the imposition of a capital charge on [government] departments ensures that the costs of outputs can be measured in a manner directly comparable amongst public agencies and between public and private sectors."

34. There is an exception to this. The extra excise duty on petrol (which goes to the government for general revenue purposes) represents an effective "return on capital" to the government.

35. The writer is executive chairman of Macquarie New Zealand Limited, a wholly owned subsidiary of Macquarie Bank Limited, Australia's largest investment bank. Macquarie is the major infrastructure project adviser in Australia, and its Macquarie Infrastructure Group is one of the largest owners of toll roads in the world.

36. These figures have since been adjusted by interest rate movements.

37. Reducing inflation and interest rates also had an impact on this trend.

38. *Better Transport Better Roads*. The full text of this paper and the earlier *Land Transport Pricing Study* can be found at the Ministry of Transport's website, http://www.transport.govt.nz.

39. If implemented, this change would have been significant. No longer would State Highways and local roads in a particular region be run separately; they would, instead, be operated by a single, homogeneous commercial entity.

40. Labour held office from 1984 to 1990. Particularly up to the end of 1988, under Finance Minister Roger Douglas, it implemented some of the most dramatic

reforms. From 1990, these reforms were continued by the center-right National Party.

41. *Land Transport Policy Development: Charging and Financing New Roads*, Ministry of Transport, September 2000.
42. Elected in October 2001.
43. *AA Directions*, Winter 2001.
44. This report can be found at http://www.cfit.gov.uk/reports/pfru/index.htm.

17

Development of Highway Concessions on Trunk Roads in the United Kingdom

Neil Roden

Abbreviations

BOT: Build, Operate, and Transfer
BOOT: Build, Own, Operate, and Transfer
DBFO: Design, Build, Finance, and Operate
NPV: Net Present Value
PFI: Private Finance Initiative

Introduction

In today's world, an effective transport system is not an optional extra—it is a prerequisite of modern life. Many essential public services depend upon it, as does the success of industry and commerce. This chapter describes the UK experience of commercializing the delivery, operation, and maintenance of the strategic highway infrastructure.

In the United Kingdom, the Private Finance Initiative (PFI) has become established as the procurement method of choice for many projects and services in central and local government. It is a natural development of other changes in government administration that were introduced in the 1980s and the early 1990s. Projects delivered in this way enable government to become a buyer of services on behalf of the public rather than a direct provider of those services to the public, taking advantage of private sector management skills and resources in their delivery. The PFI has demonstrated its ability to deliver value-for-money solutions in projects across a range of capital-intensive public services, but the greatest success in delivering projects has been in the transport sector.

Thus, the government need no longer construct roads, but may purchase miles of properly maintained and operated highway. It need no longer build prisons, but may buy custodial services. Neither does it always buy computers and software, preferring to pay for managed IT services.

In line with this thinking the British government's Highways Agency restructured and commercialized the management and maintenance of the English strategic road network for which it is responsible. The Highways Agency has been at the forefront of developing successful privately financed projects. This chapter explains the Agency's particular version of Design, Build, Finance, and Operate (DBFO) projects. These projects are delivering new and improved road construction and maintenance, providing better services to users of the country's strategic road network and achieving significant value-for money savings for taxpayers.

Background to the Commercialization of Transport in the United Kingdom

The challenge facing governments throughout the world is to deliver their objectives in a way that makes best use of all the resources at their disposal, both public and private. The public has a right to expect quality services delivered cost effectively, the means by which this is achieved being less important than the result. The private sector has strengths and skills that are not found in the public sector and, by harnessing those skills, services can be delivered more effectively and efficiently. For example, the private sector knows how to act commercially because it understands the marketplace and the need for competitiveness. It knows that, to be successful, it must not only respond to the needs of its customers, but strive constantly to improve its services. The private sector is also often better placed to manage many of the risks traditionally borne by government and it has access to new and more flexible sources of capital.

In line with this philosophy, the role of the state in the UK economy was redefined under the Conservative administrations of the 1980s and early 1990s, changing from that of a direct provider of services to one of enabler and regulator for the private sector provision of services. This was a key area of government policy that led to significant changes in the UK transport and utilities markets. It is well illustrated in the extensive measures that were taken to liberalize transport, remove barriers to entry, and reduce regulation. Public services delivered by government and for which the user paid directly, such as energy and telecommunications utilities, were privatized. Similarly, airports and airlines, many ports and, finally, railways, were privatized.

Box 17.1
The UK "Black Country" Proposal for Shadow Tolls

In the early 1980s, UK government funding for roads was cut back and much of its road construction industry idled. One consequence of this was an intense interest in private road financing, which resulted in a novel proposal for financing the Black Country route, a seven-mile road in the West Midlands. The proposal was submitted to the Department of Transport in July 1983 by the West Midlands County Council (WMCC), which prepared it in conjunction with TNS, a consortium consisting of Tarmac Construction Ltd., National Westminster Bank PLC, and Saturn Management Ltd.

The essence of the proposal was that TNS would provide a road to the design and specifications of the WMCC, which would pay the consortium an agreed amount for each vehicle-mile traveled on the new road and another amount for each square foot of new development in the vicinity of the new road. The payments were to start as soon as the road was open to traffic and to cease twenty-five years later.

The main advantage to the WMCC from the proposal would have been the earlier completion of the road, and the advantage to the Department of Transport that the risk of insufficient traffic to justify the road would have been taken by the private sector. The financing to the WMCC would have been at a higher interest rate than available from government funds, but TNS claimed that this disadvantage would have been offset by lower costs and quicker completion.

In the event, this type of financing was not then tried in Britain because the Secretary of State for Transport, David Howell (now Lord Howell of Guildford), who was interested to try it, left the Department. His successor, who was less interested, enabled the WMCC to get conventional financing for the Black Country route.

However, in 1994, following submissions from the Automobile Association (an organization representing British road users), and the 1994 report *Tolls and Shadow Tolls* by Stephen Glaister and Tony Travers (Automobile Association, England, April 1994), the Department of Transport announced that private consortia were to be invited to bid for contracts to design, finance, build, and operate four new road projects in England, and that the successful contractors would be paid by "shadow tolls." A major driving force behind the new policy was John MacGregor (now Baron MacGregor of Pulham Market), Secretary of State at the Department of Transport from 1992 to 1994.

In summary, whether through privatization, contracting out, or the provision of services and infrastructure that remained within the public sector, Britain's Conservative administrations believed that the greater involvement of the private sector provided opportunities to ensure improved quality, faster results, and better value for money for the taxpayer.

The election of a Labour government in 1997 saw many of the significant structural changes in the public sector over the life of the previous administrations consolidated and developed rather than overturned. This is particularly so in the case of the Private Finance Initiative (PFI) where the newly elected Labour government took steps to review and invigorate the initiative. In announcing the review, the then paymaster general, Geoffrey Robinson, MP, explained that, *"the success of the PFI is vital for Britain . . . in an age of tight public spending, value for money public/private partnerships will be at the heart of a much needed renewal of our public services."*

Creating the Highways Agency

For the last sixty years government ministers (currently the Secretary of State for Transport) have been directly responsible for the policies applying to trunk roads, which, since 1959, have also included motorways. They are also responsible for determining the resources to be spent on the network and the priorities to be given to spending and major new highway schemes. Initially, the funding for road improvements and maintenance was provided by the revenue obtained from vehicle license fees but, by the 1940s, this revenue was subsumed within general taxation. Unlike other countries, such as the United States and New Zealand, that have dedicated road funds, all revenue from UK motorists (amounting to some £30 billion per year), either in the form of vehicle license fees, driver license fees, or fuel duty, is treated as general taxation and the annual expenditure on trunk roads is decided as part of the overall spending decisions of the government.

Prior to 1994, the motorway and trunk road network had been managed directly by the Road and Vehicle Safety Command of the former Department of Transport. This part of the Department was also responsible for road and vehicle safety issues, and for wider policy, regulatory, advisory, and grant allocation functions relating to the whole road network, including that part of the network managed by local highway authorities.

However, as outlined above, since 1988 government departments have largely been reorganized in a way that focuses on the job to be done to enhance the effective delivery of policies and services. Under this initiative, known as "The Next Steps Programme," each of the executive functions of central government was examined to consider how it should be provided in the future

Figure 17.1
Trunk Road Network

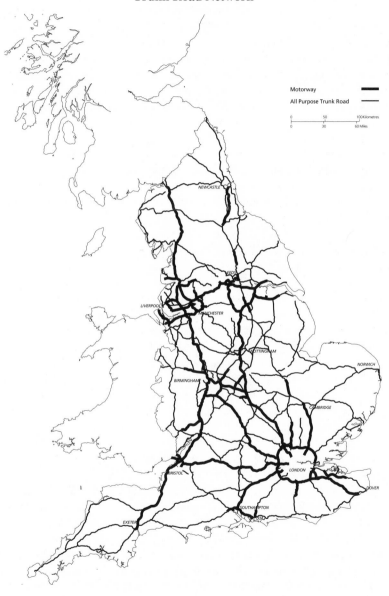

and, if it were to remain within government, the best framework for its management. This has resulted in responsibility for the delivery of many government services being transferred to executive agencies operating with a certain amount of autonomy and greater management freedom.[1]

An organizational review of the former Department of Transport's Road and Vehicle Safety Command in 1992 concluded that the main opportunities for transferring functions to an agency or agencies lay with the management of the motorway and trunk road network. That area of work represented a discrete business and within the business, the client side functions of strategic planning and control that needed to stay within the central department were already reasonably well separated from the delivery of the agreed work programs. As a result, the Highways Agency was established on April 1, 1994.

The Agency is responsible for maintaining, operating and improving the English motorway and trunk road network in support of the government's integrated transport and land use planning policies. Its core functions are to maintain the network, to operate the network making best use of the existing infrastructure and facilitating integration with other transport modes, and to deliver improvements to the network within the strategic policy framework and the financial resources set by government ministers.

Trunk Road Agency Management Arrangements

When the Highways Agency was established in 1994, much of the day-to-day work of managing and maintaining the 6,500-mile (10,400 km) motorway and trunk road network was undertaken by agents acting on behalf of the Highways Agency. Of the ninety-one of these agency agreements, eighty-five were with local highway authorities and the remainder with private sector consultants. These agency agreements covered the management of routine winter and capital maintenance, and a wide variety of other duties ranging from inspections of the network to accident investigation and data provision. They also covered identification, design, and supervision of capital maintenance works and minor road improvement schemes.

These standard agency agreements were first introduced in the 1940s and, at the time of the Highways Agency's launch, ministers set the Agency the task of keeping the arrangements with its managing and maintaining agents under review with a view to increasing opportunities for the private sector to participate in the work. This is not to say that the Agency or government ministers were dissatisfied with the existing service provided by the local highway authority agents. Rather, there was a desire to benefit from the opportunities that competition might bring and to encourage a market of potential suppliers for managing and maintaining the network encompassing both the public and private sectors. The motorway and trunk road network had to handle greater traffic volumes than ever before. It therefore made sense to maximize the Agency's options for ensuring that the network was maintained to an appropriate standard and for achieving a more consistent approach on a route basis.

The Private Finance Initiative

Although the Private Finance Initiative (PFI) was not announced until 1992, since the 1980s, the British government looked to partnerships with the private sector to deliver public sector projects and services of a higher quality more cost effectively.

The main focus of PFI activity to date has been in the area of services sold to the public sector and, in particular, projects where the public sector purchases services from the private sector, which is responsible for the "up-front" investment in the capital assets to support those services. The public sector client pays only on delivery of the services to the specified quality standards. Typically, the private sector, often acting in consortia, aims to reap synergies across design, build, finance, and operation. This restructuring of procurement is mutually beneficial for users of public services, taxpayers, and companies seeking profitable new business opportunities. Despite the additional private sector borrowing costs and the necessity for the private sector service provider to make a profit, combining the private sector's innovation and management skills generates significant performance improvements and efficiency savings. DBFO road projects are an example of the successful application of these principles in the delivery of road services, the first eight projects having delivered savings of between £230 million and £315 million (335 million USD to 460 million USD).

There are also a number of "pure" private sector projects in the UK. In these projects the private sector supplier designs, builds, finances, and operates an asset, recovering the costs entirely through user charges rather than through payments from the public sector. The concept of these Build, Operate, and Transfer (BOT) or Build, Own, Operate, and Transfer (BOOT) projects is well known and understood. The public sector's involvement is limited largely to enabling the project to proceed through assistance with planning and other statutory procedures. Apart from this, there is no public sector contribution or acceptance of risk. The primary examples of this type of project in the UK are in the transport sector where the Dartford Crossing of the Thames to the east of London and the Second Severn Crossing between England and Wales have been provided in this way. In addition, the M6 Toll Road in the West Midlands, which is the first overland tolled motorway in the UK, was also delivered by the private sector as a financially free-standing project.

The Development of Design, Build, Finance, and Operate (DBFO) Contracts in the United Kingdom

The Highways Agency's business is to manage and maintain the motorway and trunk road network and deliver the government's program of trunk road improvement schemes within the policy and resources framework set by government ministers. The 5,800-mile network (9,400 km) for which the Agency is responsible accounts for less than 4 percent of the total mileage of roads in England. However, the network is the backbone of the country's transport system and is used for about a third of all road journeys and about half of all lorry journeys.

It is also a network that is under pressure. While the government wishes to reduce the need to travel and influence the rate of traffic growth, demand could still rise by more than 50 percent over the next twenty years. Business users, private motorists, and others who use the strategic road network want a better, safer, and more reliable service. Yet concern about the environmental effect of traffic and of road building is growing. All the Agency's activities have to strike a balance between the environmental consequences and the economic, environmental, and safety benefits of improving traffic flows and removing through traffic from unsuitable roads in towns and villages. Achieving this balance to meet the needs of road users has to take account of the finite public funds for roads. While the government's Private Finance Initiative (PFI) cannot meet all future investment needs, it is a vital part of the Agency's strategy to provide the best possible service to road users.

The PFI was launched in November 1992 and while the label was new, the concept—certainly for the Highways Agency—was not. The first major British project to be developed in accordance with the principles of the initiative was the third crossing of the River Thames at Dartford to the east of London. This was a conventional BOT project where a concession was awarded to a private consortium to design, build, finance, and operate a new crossing (the Queen Elizabeth II Bridge) and the existing tunnels, and to recover the cost by levying user-paid tolls. Contracts were signed in 1987 and the new bridge opened in 1991, doubling the capacity provided by the existing tunnels under the river and delivering much needed relief for traffic on the M25 London Orbital Motorway.

The only public sector contribution to this project was the cost of the approach roads and the transfer of the revenue from the existing tunnels to the concessionaire. The concessionaire competed for the right to design, build, and operate the crossing, and to make a return on the investment by charging tolls. The concession was for a maximum period of twenty years. Toll rates, however, are regulated because of the near monopoly nature of the concession. This model was adopted again to provide a second crossing of the River Severn between England and Wales, which opened to traffic in June 1996.

With the exception of a small number of tolled river crossings on strategic routes, there is no recent tradition in the UK of charging users of roads at the point of use through direct tolls. Neither is there legislation in place that would enable user-paid tolls to be introduced on extensive parts of the existing motorway or trunk road network, although there are powers for new tolled motorways to be built and operated by the private sector. The M6 Toll Road was built and is being operated as a financially freestanding BOT project in this way. One of the previous government's policy objectives in deciding to proceed with DBFO projects was to encourage the development of a private sector road operating business in the UK prior to the possible introduction of user-paid tolls across the motorway network. Under the Labour administration, the introduction of the Transport Act 2000 enables road user charges to be introduced on the motorway, trunk road, and local authority road networks under limited circumstances. For motorways and trunk roads, for example, charging schemes may only be introduced if the road is carried by a bridge, or passes through a tunnel, of at least 600 meters in length. In addition, the Labour government has commissioned technical trials of electronic tolling systems.

Prior to the introduction of the PFI, the traditional approach to procuring road improvement schemes on overland routes was to contract with private contractors following a competitive bidding process. The contractor was paid by the Agency from public funds on achievement of agreed milestones reflecting the work carried out, which might involve building according to an Agency design or could also include some design elements. But, in both cases, the operational and maintenance responsibilities for the capital asset rested with the Agency and the public sector. A further disadvantage of these traditional forms of contracting was that the relationship between the Agency and the contractor tended to be adversarial. Once a contract was let, the contractor would claim for additional costs incurred on the basis that the assumptions on which the price was set were incorrect. For example, claims would be made if ground conditions were not as specified or if work could not be completed to timetable because of bad weather. This often resulted in time overruns and additional unbudgeted costs for the Agency.

The Highways Agency's Objectives for Design, Build, Finance, and Operate Projects

The Agency launched its use of the PFI to procure a road service in August 1994 having previously undertaken a market sounding exercise and consulted likely private sector participants. The Agency's objectives for each DBFO project were to:

- minimize the contribution required from, and to optimize the extent of the risk borne by, the public sector;
- ensure that the project roads were designed, maintained, and operated safely and satisfactorily so as to minimize any adverse impact on the environment and maximize benefits to road users;
- promote innovation, not only in technical and operational matters, but also in financial and commercial arrangements; and
- meet the former government's policy objective of fostering the development of a private sector road operating industry in the UK.

The DBFO concept of a road service includes assuming responsibility for the operation and maintenance of lengths of existing road and ensuring that specified new construction works along the length of road are built and made available for road users.

The main benefit of this arrangement is that, by transferring responsibility to the private sector for designing, constructing, financing, and operating roads, and increasing payment levels when road construction works are completed, the private sector starts to look at its obligations as a whole, over the thirty-year life of the contract, taking full account of the risks inherent at each stage of the project. There is a significant relationship, for example, between the way a new road scheme is designed and constructed and its operating costs. Under the earlier system, in which private contractors built the road that the Agency maintained, the private contractors had an incentive to reduce building costs even if this was at the expense of far greater operating costs. Under the new system these externalities are better internalized. The private sector has to make decisions about how it will provide the service to the level specified by the Agency. Allocating to the private sector those project risks that it is capable of managing results in a lower whole life cost for the Agency, and an improved and more efficient service for the road user.

The DBFO contract fixes the design of the new works elements that the winning bidder has proposed. It specifies the core requirements with which those works must comply, and the operational service requirements for the improved length of road and any existing roads included in the project. In return, the DBFO company receives regular payments from the Agency throughout the life of the contract, which, in the case of the first eight contracts, was based primarily on the number and type of vehicles using the project road.

The first eight DBFO contracts awarded are for thirty years. That period was selected partly because the construction costs of a project were likely to be financed predominantly by third party debt, a view confirmed by market research amongst potential bidders. Finance for this type of project in the mid 1990s generally had a maximum repayment period of less than twenty years and the payment mechanism had to be structured to allow repayment of debt over a similar timescale. The development of the market now means that repayment periods of forty years or more are available.

Payment Mechanisms and Incentives

The DBFO company receives payments for providing the road service based on road usage and performance over the lifetime of the contract. For the first eight contracts awarded the payments are based primarily on traffic levels and with different "shadow tolls" payable according to the number and type of vehicles using the road. There is a ceiling on the amount of shadow tolls payable to ensure that the Agency's maximum liability is capped. However, the DBFO contract is structured so that DBFO operators can also earn performance bonuses or incur deductions from the shadow toll payments if the road is not available to users or its use is restricted.

To expand on the payment structure, different payments are payable for traffic within different traffic bands and depending on the length of vehicle. Bidders were asked to bid the parameters of traffic levels for a maximum of four bands, with the proviso that the top band must have toll levels set at zero, so limiting the Agency's liabilities to DBFO companies and assisting with internal budgeting. Within each traffic band the bidders specified a toll for two categories of vehicle—vehicles over 5.2 meters long (which includes heavy goods vehicles) and those less than 5.2 meters. Bidders set the bands and tolls from their own assessment of traffic levels. Most bidders opted for four bands with the lower band representing existing traffic and with tolls in the lower band set at a level that would cover debt service requirements (but would not provide a return on equity). The result was that the lower band gave funders an adequate payment stream if traffic volumes were not to increase above existing levels.

The PFI concept of an availability payment applies where the project road consists of an existing stretch of road with one or more new construction schemes along its length. In that situation, shadow toll payments are made at a reduced level representing the availability of the existing road. These payments are set at a level that approximates to the operation and maintenance costs of the existing road. In the case of DBFO projects that have no lengths of existing road and the contract is concerned entirely with new con-

Figure 17.2
DBFO Projects Map

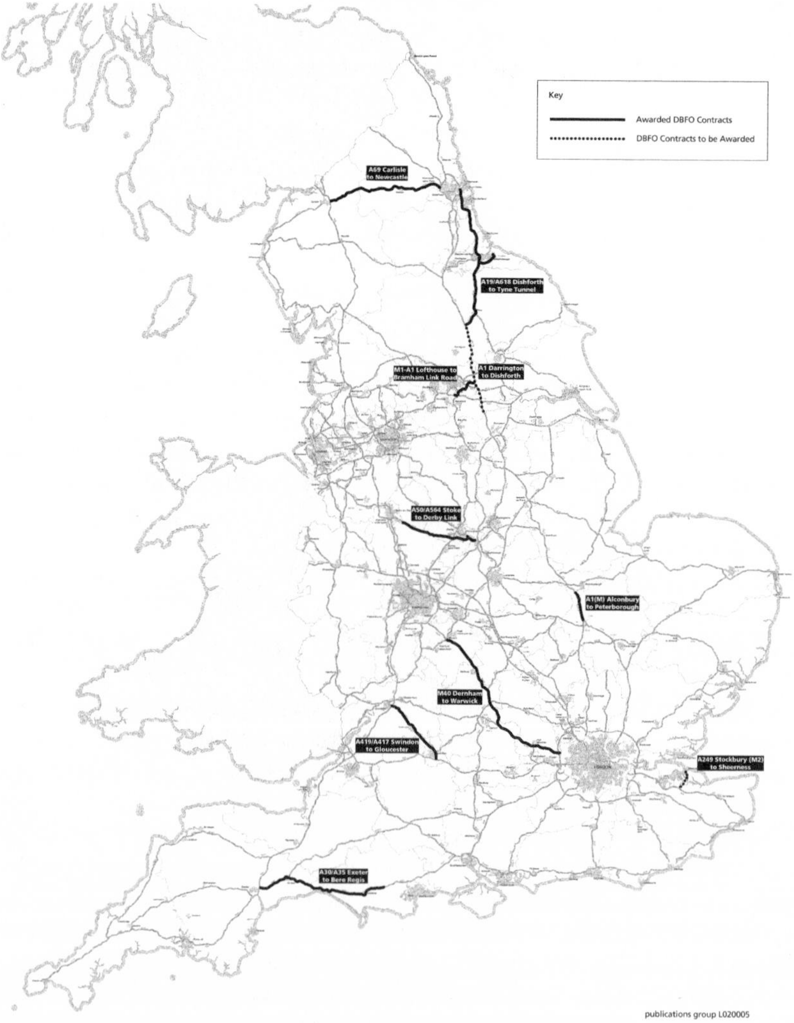

Key

——————— Awarded DBFO Contracts

•••••••••••••••••••• DBFO Contracts to be Awarded

A69 Carlisle to Newcastle

A19/A618 Dishforth to Tyne Tunnel

M1-A1 Lofthouse to Bramham Link Road

A1 Darrington to Dishforth

A50/A564 Stoke to Derby Link

A1(M) Alconbury to Peterborough

M40 Denham to Warwick

A419/A417 Swindon to Gloucester

A249 Stockbury (M2) to Sheerness

A30/A35 Exeter to Bere Regis

publications group L020005

struction, no payment is made until the Permit to Use is issued and the road opened to traffic.

Each construction scheme has a shadow toll profile attached to it. Once the Permit to Use is issued for a construction scheme, the DBFO Company receives 80 percent of that profile. Usually, there are minor ancillary works to

Table 17.1
Traffic Growth Scenario

	Low Growth	Best Estimate	High Growth
(A) Annual Average Daily Traffic	8,000	12,000	20,000
(B) Road Length	100	100	100
(C) Total average daily vehicle kilometres (A × B)	800,000	1.2 million	2 million
(D) Total annual vehicle kilometres (C × 365)	292 million	438 million	730 million

be completed after a new construction scheme has been opened to traffic and the DBFO company does not therefore, receive 100 percent of the shadow toll profile until the final Completion Certificate is issued.

There are also performance payments and penalties within the DBFO contract. One of the Agency's key objectives is to reduce accident rates on the

Figure 17.3
Typical banding structure proposed by bidders

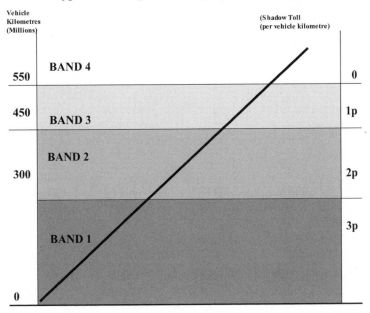

Table 17.2
Annual Traffic Flow and Shadow Toll Payments
under the Three Traffic Growth Scenarios

Traffic Band	Band Size (Million vehicle kilometres per year)	Best Toll (per vehicle kilometre)	SHADOW ESTIMATE GROWTH		LOW GROWTH		HIGH GROWTH	
			Vkm	£m	Vkm	£m	Vkm	£m
Band 4	Over 550	0p	0	0	0	0	180	0
Band 3	450–550	1p	0	0	0	0	100	1.0
Band 2	300–450	2p	0	0	138	2.76	150	3.0
Band 1	0–300	3p	292	8.76	300	9.0	300	9.0
Total Annual Traffic (millions of vehicle kilometres)			292		438		730	
Total Annual Payments (£ millions)				8.76		11.76		13.0

trunk road network and operators are encouraged to propose safety improvements that, if adopted, enable them to earn bonuses. The DBFO company builds and pays for the safety scheme and is compensated by receiving 25 percent of the economic cost of each personal injury avoided in the following five-year period. Injuries avoided are determined by comparing the actual statistics with data over the previous three years.

Disturbance and delays caused by lane closures are a major concern to road users and operators incur financial penalties if the use of the road is restricted. A deduction is made from the shadow toll payment, the size of which is dependent on the number of lanes closed and the time of the closure. This financial incentive ensures that operators consider the needs of road users and that users are inconvenienced as little as possible by roadworks.

For the first eight contracts one of the main reasons for using shadow tolls as the primary method for remunerating DBFO companies was to acclimatize the private sector to the concept of payment per vehicle as a steppingstone to the possible introduction of real toll roads. There are good reasons for paying by usage and it is not inconsistent with the wider aims of the government to reduce the need to travel, optimize the use of the existing network, and encourage greater use of alternative modes of transport. However, the Agency has moved away from a revenue stream predominantly determined by usage and developed alternative mechanisms that focus on the performance of the road and incentivizes DBFO companies to achieve the Agency's performance objectives while continuing to deliver value for money.

The lane availability charges and safety bonuses in the first eight contracts are two areas of operational importance that have payments (or deductions) linked to them. The Agency developed this concept in the A13 Thames Gateway DBFO project, which provides the vital transport infrastructure to support the regeneration of East London and Docklands. This was the first urban DBFO project and the first project to reflect the current government's integrated approach to transport by incentivizing the private sector to deliver a service in tune with the five fundamental criteria of integration, accessibility, safety, economy, and environmental impact. This is being achieved primarily through a payment mechanism that focuses on the availability of traffic lanes, incentivizing the DBFO company to manage their operations and maintenance in a way that is least disruptive to road users. There are also separate availability payments for footways and cycleways, encouraging the company to consider fully the needs of the non-motorized users of the road. Shadow toll payments based on usage still form part of the payment mechanism, but these are only payable in respect of public transport and goods vehicles rather than cars so that the DBFO company concentrates on managing the road for these vehicles and has no incentive to increase car commuting on this important radial route into the capital.

For the latest DBFO contracts the Highways Agency has developed the mechanism further. The Active Management Payment Mechanism comprises a congestion management payment and a safety performance adjustment. The mechanism encourages the DBFO company to actively manage the project road to reduce congestion and increase the reliability of journey times. This is achieved by reducing payments for times when congestion is experienced on the project road. This payment mechanism works in tandem with a safety performance adjustment similar to that adopted for the A13 Thames gateway DBFO.

Service Specification

For the first DBFO projects the scope for the bidders to innovate and achieve cost savings was limited to the detailed design of the new construction elements of the projects, because all the road schemes had completed the statutory approval process. It was a core requirement of these initial contracts that the bidders comply with the undertakings given by the Agency at public inquiries, and that the final design accord with the approved statutory orders. Following the Agency's design manuals and standards represented one option for meeting the core requirements, but these and the Agency's own proposals for junction layout and design of structures were illustrative requirements only. The bidders were not obliged to use these designs or standards but where bidders proposed to depart from the established standards, they had to demonstrate that their proposals would deliver a product of equivalent quality.

DBFO Procurement Process

These (DBFO) contracts are procured under the EU "negotiated procedure." Four tenderers are selected on merit from applicants that have responded to a notice in the EU Official Journal inviting candidates to prequalify for a competition. Applicants are assessed on the basis of responses made to a prequalification brochure published by the government; the objective is to select those tendering groups that are best qualified to undertake the project advertised— this includes assessing the groups' ability to raise capital efficiently. The competition itself is primarily concerned with two main issues: the achievement of a required level of technical quality, essentially a pass/fail test; and the assessed cost to the government over the life of the project. The cost of payments is calculated on an estimated net present value (ENPV) basis using the government's traffic forecasts and tenderers' stated rates per vehicle kilometer. The lowest ENPV of payments wins the competition.

Expiry of the Contract

Throughout the life of the DBFO contract, the Secretary of State for Transport retains ownership of the road and underlying land with the DBFO company occupying the road and land under a license. At the end of the term, the project road and all fixed facilities on it must be handed back to the Agency in a satisfactory condition, that is, the project road must have at least a ten-year life expectancy on hand-back.

Towards the end of the term, there is a mechanism for inspection and agreement about the action needed to ensure that the hand-back criteria are met. If necessary, the Agency can withhold shadow toll service payments to the DBFO company to ensure that if the road is handed back in a substandard condition, the cost of rectifying faults is not borne by the taxpayer.

The Public Sector Comparator

To ensure that bids satisfy the twin tests of delivering value for money and optimizing risk allocation, the Agency prepares a public sector comparator before inviting bids for the projects. The public sector comparator is calculated by costing what the public sector would have had to pay to procure the same underlying asset by traditional means, and the cost to the Agency of operating and maintaining the road over thirty years. A value is also added to represent the cost of the risks adopted by the private sector and priced for in their bids. Unless there are special circumstances, the DBFO contract is only let if the net present value (NPV) of the expected payment to the DBFO company is lower than the risk adjusted public sector comparator.

The public sector comparator has shown that, by using DBFO arrangements to deliver new road schemes and the ongoing operation and maintenance of the motorway and trunk road network, the Highways Agency is obtaining value for money savings averaging 15 percent. A study by the National Audit Office into the first four DBFO contracts concluded that DBFO procurement offered substantial savings in comparison with conventional procurement and that the savings on the first four projects totaled at least £100 million (13 percent—146 million USD).

The results of this comparison between the public sector comparator and the winning DBFO bid were calculated using an 8 percent real discount rate which was the Treasury's recommended rate for assessing road projects when these contracts were awarded in 1996. The Highways Agency undertook sensitivity tests to assess the impact of different discount rates. The effect of using a 6 percent real discount rate (which is now the recommended rate for assessing road projects) reduces the total savings to about £229 million (14.4 percent, 334 million USD).

Table 17.3
Value for Money Savings from the First Eight DBFO Projects

Project	Public Sector Comparator (£m)	Winning DBFO Bid (£m)	Value for Money (£m/USD)	Percentage Saving
M1–A1	344	232	112/164	32.6%
A1(M)	204	154	50/73	24.5%
A419/A417	123	112	11/16	8.9%
A69	57	62	(−5)/(−7.3)	−8.7%
M40	276	182	94/138	34.1%
A19	177	136	41/60	23.2%
A50/A564	77	67	10/15	13.0%
A30/A35	149	148	1/1.5	0.7%
Total	1,407	1,093	314/459	22.3%

Risk Allocation

Project risks should only be transferred to the private sector if, and to the extent that, the private sector is capable of bearing such risk. DBFO contracts transfer to the private sector a substantial degree of responsibility for constructing, operating, and maintaining the project road and for financing the relevant costs. Transfer of responsibility increases the scope for innovation by the private sector. The risks associated with those obligations are, in most cases, transferred to the private sector so that if the specified service is not provided, the Agency pays no more than agreed at the outset.

The Agency carried out an analysis of the risks attaching to each project by drawing up a risk register that set out in detail the risks relevant to each stage of the project, the likelihood of those risks occurring, and an estimate of the financial impact of occurrence. This analysis helped the Agency to establish the type and the quantum of risk they should ask the private sector to take. The DBFO contract is drafted so that the DBFO company bears all risks associated with an area of delivery, such as operation, unless the Agency is specified to take a risk, either through the payment mechanism, change mechanism, or termination events. Therefore, any unanticipated risk is borne by the private sector. This underlines the importance, for both the public and private sectors, of undertaking a detailed risk analysis for each project.

The concept of the PFI is that the private sector will generally be asked to take the risk of increased construction and operation cost overruns, the risk of delay to delivery of the service, the risk that the design of the underlying asset will not deliver the required service, and the change of law risk (other than any change of law that specifically discriminates against PFI companies). DBFO contracts are structured in this way. The allocation of highway specific risks such as traffic risk, protester risk, and latent defect risk is covered in greater detail below.

Traffic Risk. This is a key area of risk transfer in DBFO projects because traffic risk is very closely allied to revenue risk. The number of vehicles using the road affects the cost of constructing it with a reasonable life expectancy and of maintaining it to the required standard. The Agency has its own updated traffic projections for each project road that are based on the initial investment decision for road schemes within the DBFO project. These forecasts are kept confidential because of the objective of fostering the development of a private sector road operating industry with the skill base necessary to take strategic decisions on road design, construction, operation, and maintenance. A key skill is the ability to forecast road usage in the future. The Agency also uses its confidential forecasts during the evaluation of DBFO bids to calculate how much

Table 17.4
Allocation of Risks in DBFO Projects

Type of Risk	Public Sector	Private Sector	Shared
Design and Construction		Mostly with DBFO company, but provision for compensation in the event of Highways Agency changes. Detailed design undertaken by DBFO company, but government had already borne cost of initial route design.	
Latent/Inherent Defects		Defects, including those on existing routes and structures, which arise during the thirty-year contact period lie with the DBFO company.	
Delivery/Timing		Delay risks lie with the DBFO company and have an impact on revenue as shadow tolls are dependent on service delivery except in the case of delays due to government changes, in which case, compensation maybe payable.	
Planning	All projects to date have been taken through the statutory planning stages by Highways Agency.		
Traffic/Volume			Downside risk with private sector; upside risk with Highways Agency. However, structure of shadow tolls reduces upside risk by application of cap to maximum traffic flows on which shadow tolls are payable.

(Continued)

Table 17.4 (*continued*)

Type of Risk	Public Sector	Private Sector	Shared
Operation and Maintenance		DBFO company responsible for maintaining road to provide the service specified in the contract. Failure to do so can result in the award of penalty points. Closure of lanes can result in reduced payment to the DBFO company.	
Protestor Action			Varies between projects. On some projects it is entirely borne by the DBFO company, on others it is shared with the Highways Agency.
Force Majeure			Most force majeure risks lie with the government but the contract definition is very limited (for example, it excludes extreme weather), and the risk is shared because equity holders are not compensated if termination occurs as a result of the force majeure event.
Indemnity/ Insurance		Insurance and indemnity risk lie with the DBFO company, which indemnifies the Highways Agency against all claims from third parties arising from the design, maintenance, and operation of the road.	
Legislative		Risk of legislative changes is with the DBFO company except where the law is discriminatory against DBFO companies or roads. No compensation for lower revenues due to non-discriminatory laws, which have effect of suppressing traffic.	

risk each bidder's payment structure would place on its revenue stream at the Agency's "most likely" traffic forecast.

If bidders' traffic forecasts underestimate traffic, they will weight most of their return in the lower bands and therefore, their payment stream will be largely guaranteed and have little risk attached resulting in poor value for money. If, however, the bidder overestimates traffic growth and the return is weighted in the higher bands, their payment stream will have more risk, reducing that to the taxpayer and providing better value for money. But, there may be a point at which a bidder's assumptions on traffic growth are so optimistic that, in the Agency's view, the bidder's proposed structure is financially weak.

Protestor Risk. In the UK, a growing awareness of environmental issues has resulted in a vociferous anti-roads lobby, sections of which resort increasingly to direct action in attempts to frustrate and delay the construction of new or improved roads. This has given rise to significant extra costs for the Agency. There is a possibility of disruptive protestor action on some DBFO projects and the Agency recognized that value for money could be damaged if the bidders were asked to bear all the costs. However, DBFO companies would be in control of the works and, therefore, in the best position to determine the strategy to deal with problems. For this reason, bidders were asked to price options ranging from accepting 100 percent of the risk to none of it. The end result of negotiations was generally a project specific, risk sharing arrangement between the Agency and DBFO company providing encouraging evidence of bidders' willingness to accept new types of risk.

Latent Defect Risk. Where a DBFO project involves the DBFO company taking over responsibility for operating an existing length of road, bidders have had to take a view on the state of the road and any structures on the road. Their technical advisers have carried out investigations but there may be problems that cannot be detected or "latent defects" such as spalling of concrete or a structure component not meeting the expected design life. As with protestor risk, bidders were asked to bid on options ranging from 100 percent acceptance of risk to zero. The outcome of negotiations in all cases was that the preferred bidder accepted 100 percent of the latent defect risk. In later DBFO contracts, the allocation of risk for latent defects is not a biddable option—bidders are required to bid on the basis that they accept 100 percent of the risk.

Conclusions

The Highways Agency has been at the forefront of delivering innovative PFI projects through its DBFO program. For many major projects, the traditional method of contracting with private sector contractors building a length of road to the Agency's design and then passing responsibility for operating and maintaining it back to the public sector has been overtaken by DBFO arrangements in the last few years. The Agency is no longer buying a capital asset but buying the provision of a road service for thirty years on behalf of the road user. By transferring construction and operational risks to the private sector and by harnessing the private sector's entrepreneurial skills, the Agency has also achieved significantly better value for money for the taxpayer than if the projects had been procured conventionally.

Excluding the A13 DBFO, responsibility for which now rests with Transport for London, the Highways Agency has awarded ten DBFO projects. They involved the delivery of new road improvement schemes with a capital value of over £900 million (729 million USD (update)), enabling much needed road schemes to start earlier than if they had been dependent on conventional public sector funding arrangements. They also provide for the operation and maintenance of over 400 miles (650km) of existing road. The government's Transport Plan envisages that 25 percent of the funding for new road improvement schemes will come from the private sector through DBFO and other partnership arrangements.

The success of DBFO contracting arrangements in England has led to the model introduced by the Highways Agency being used in Wales and by local highway authorities. Scotland and a number of other European countries, such as Finland, Spain, and Portugal, have also adapted the concept.

Making the most efficient use of the motorway and trunk road network, and providing the best possible service to users of that network, is an immense challenge. The Agency's DBFO program and other public/private partnerships will not meet all the future investment needs. But, pursuing private finance opportunities and harnessing the skills and expertise of the private sector is likely to remain a vital part of the Highways Agency's strategy to deliver the best possible service to users of England's strategic road network.

Note

1. Despite the range and diversity of their functions, executive agencies share common features. Each agency has a clearly defined task, or range of tasks, that are set out in its published framework document, with key performance targets covering financial performance, efficiency, and service to the customer set by ministers and announced in Parliament. Most targets have become progressively more demanding year on year, reflecting the need to ensure that limited public resources are used in the most efficient way.

   Each agency has a chief executive who is directly accountable to ministers and with personal responsibility for the success of the agency in meeting its targets. The majority of chief executives have been appointed through open competition and more than half of those who have been appointed in this way have come from outside the civil service. Staff in executive agencies remain civil servants, accountable to ministers and governed by the same strict rules of conduct as those working in departmental headquarters.

References

Department of the Environment, Transport and the Regions. 1998. "A New Deal for Transport: Better for Everyone."

Department of the Environment, Transport and the Regions. 1998. "A New Deal for Trunk Roads in England."

Highways Agency. 1997. "DBFO Value in Roads: A Case Study on the First Eight DBFO Road Contracts and their Development."

H. M. Treasury. 2000. "Public Private Partnerships: The Government's Approach."

National Audit Office. 1998. "The Private Finance Initiative: The First Four Design, Build, Finance and Operate Roads Contracts."

Public Accounts Committee. 1998. "The Private Finance Initiative: The First Four Design, Build, Finance and Operate Roads Contracts."

Roden, N. W. 1997. "Delivering BOT Projects." *Routes/Roads* 295: 21–32.

Roden, N. W. 1985. "The UK Experience of Design, Build, Finance and Operate Highway Projects," in *Operation and Maintenance of Large Infrastructure Projects: Proceedings of the International Symposium, Copenhagen, Denmark, 10–13 May 1998*, edited by L. J. Vincentzen and J. S. Jensen. Leiden, The Netherlands: Aa Balkema, 1998, pp. 189–198.

Treasury Taskforce. 1997. "Partnerships for Prosperity: The Private Finance Initiative."

18

Commercializing the Management and Financing of Roads

Ian G. Heggie

Introduction

This chapter describes how countries have been reforming the management and financing of their road networks during the past twenty years. When the process of reinventing government started in the early 1980s, it started with the "easiest" infrastructure sectors—telecommunications, power, and water. Roads were considered more difficult. They were thought of as public goods, were administered within each country by a large number of road authorities, and it was unclear how a public enterprise style road organization could find a practical way of "charging" for roads. The pace of reform was therefore slow, as governments struggled to develop new institutional structures to manage and finance their road networks. However, since 1990 the road sector has been in the middle of an unprecedented period of restructuring, comparable to what happened to the other infrastructure sectors during the 1980s and early 1990s.

The reforms are being driven by four main factors: (i) the rapid growth in motorization; (ii) the corresponding growth of road networks; (iii) the large demands these road networks impose on the government's budget; and (iv) the acute shortage of fiscal revenues worldwide. Motorization has grown rapidly since the Second World War, with the result that road transport is now the dominant form of transport in most countries. It typically carries 60 to 80 percent of all inland passenger and freight transport and provides the only form of access to most rural communities. Countries have come to rely on an efficient and effective road network to support ongoing economic development. Traffic likewise continues to grow, usually faster than GDP. To accommodate this traffic, and to reduce congestion and road accidents, countries have expanded their road networks considerably. Growth of public road networks has been especially fast in Asia. In 1998, it was estimated that there were nearly 2.6 million km of roads in Asia (excluding China and India), 1.5 million km in Africa, 3 million km in Central and South America, just under 1 million km in the former Soviet Union, and 0.5 million km in the Middle East (Heggie and Vickers 1998). Large sums of money were invested to build these roads and significant sums continue to be spent on maintaining and improving them.

The rapid growth in the world's road networks is the second factor driving the reforms. There is growing recognition that the large sums of money invested in the road network have created large and valuable assets—road agencies have become "big businesses." For example, the Japan Highway Public Corporation manages assets about the same size as General Motors, while the UK Highways Agency, which is a relatively small road authority responsible for just over 10,000 km of national roads, manages assets the same size as IBM and AT&T. If these road agencies were publicly listed companies, they would feature in Fortune Magazine's list of the world's 500 largest companies. Likewise, in countries as diverse as Chile, Ghana, Hungary, and Indonesia, the asset value of the national and provincial road networks exceeds that of the railways and national airlines combined (Heggie and Vickers 1998). It is this recognition that has encouraged countries to argue that, if roads are big business, they need to be managed like a business.

The third factor driving the reforms also has to do with size. The road sector now places large demands on the government's budget and there is growing concern to ensure that road spending produces value-for-money. Although numerous countries have introduced private road concessions, most road financing still comes from the government's budget. The scale of this spending has caused many countries to raise questions about its effectiveness. Does it produce value for money? Ministries of Finance generally say no. They view road agencies (particularly the national road agency under the Ministry of Works) as a big spending department that wastes resources. They employ inefficient work methods (doing too much work in-house), responsibility for different parts of the road network is often unclear, priorities are often politicized, politicians and senior officials regularly interfere in day-to-day management decisions, and there is a lack of customer focus. Added to that, inflexible civil service terms and conditions of employment make it difficult to recruit and retain technically qualified staff.

The fourth and final driving force behind the reforms has been shortage of finance. Part of the reason for this is political. Roads have to compete for funds against other more visible (and popular) sectors like health, education, and law and order. When that is combined with the view that road agencies are large and inefficient spending departments, it places them at a considerable dis-

interest that weakens financial discipline and compromises efforts to control costs and maintain quality. Second, road agencies are usually public monopolies and are not subject to market discipline. As a result, the costs of road works are typically 20 to 30 percent higher than work subjected to competition.

Countries have tackled this problem in three main ways. Some road agencies have maintained their integrated structure, but assigned the planning and management of roads to one department and assigned the implementation of civil works to a separate department within the same road agency (as in Norway). Others have divided the road agency up into two separate organizations. One deals with planning and management of roads while the other handles implementation of works (as in Finland, Sweden, and New Zealand). Finally, some have kept the planning and management of roads within the road agency and have contracted out implementation to the private sector (as in South Africa and UK). Although New Zealand assigned planning and management of roads to Transit New Zealand in 1989, it kept the implementation of civil works with the Ministry of Works until 1991 when it was corporatized (i.e., design and civil works were made into separate subsidiary companies) and the corporatized entities were subsequently privatized.

The above reforms have produced spectacular results. Some of the most startling evidence comes from New South Wales in Australia. In 1991 their Roads and Traffic Authority decided to start contracting work out to the private sector and to expose their own in-house work to more outside competition. Four years later the costs of in-house work had fallen by approximately 25 percent, while the costs of work done by contractors had fallen by approximately 37 percent (Frost and Lithgow 1996). Sweden likewise has subjected an increasing share of in-house maintenance work to competition from the private sector and this has increased productivity by about 25 percent. The general message seems to be that exposing in-house staff to competition from the private sector can reduce costs by about 20 percent, whilst contracting the work out to the private sector can reduce them by a further 5 percent.

One of the major constraints hampering contracting out—even for relatively simple road works—is the underdeveloped nature of the local consulting and construction industries in many countries. The road agency cannot invite competitive bids unless the country already has consultants and contractors with road work experience. Furthermore, the road agency cannot be expected to prepare bid documents, award contracts, and supervise implementation of civil works using staff accustomed only to doing work in-house. Staff in the road agency must know something about the preparation of bid documents, contracting procedures, contract law, and arbitration procedures before the road agency can effectively contract road works out to private firms and hire consultants to design and supervise implementation. Most efforts to contract work out to the private sector are therefore accompanied by parallel efforts to develop the local consulting and construction industries.

More Autonomy

More autonomy is one of the cornerstones of a more commercial approach to road management. Road agency managers cannot behave commercially until they are able to operate without interference in day-to-day management. The first step to achieve this is usually to amend the road sector legislation to enable the road agency to operate at arm's length from government. Typically, they are established as a wholly-owned government corporation (as in New Zealand),[3] or as a semi-autonomous agency (like the Ghana Highway Authority, INVIAS in Colombia, and the UK Highways Agency), but are sometimes incorporated under the Companies Act with all shares held in the name of the minister (as in South Africa), or formed into non-profit joint stock companies (as in Latvia). Sweden has turned its road authority into a holding company with subsidiaries that deal with training, traffic data, ferries, etc. Each subsidiary has a director, advisory board, and a target return on equity. The subsidiaries are being progressively privatized.

The new road authorities are mainly managed by a representative board under an independent chairperson of standing. Although some of these boards remain weak, others have turned out to be examples of emerging good practice. The best have non-executive powers, a broad-based, representative membership defined in terms of clearly defined constituencies (e.g., key ministries, Chamber of Commerce, road transport associations, the professions, farmers, etc.). Typically, members are nominated by the constituencies they represented (i.e., they are not simply appointed by the minister or senior officials, as happens with so many other public enterprise boards) and the private sector members are usually in the majority. In the SATCC region, half the boards already have a majority of private sector members and the remainder are expected to follow shortly (Pinard and Kaombwe 2000). An added feature is that the chairperson is usually independent. Sometimes they are elected by the board (as in Zambia), appointed by the minister from the existing members of the board (as in New Zealand and Malawi), or appointed by the president or minister (hopefully) after consultation with the board (as in Namibia and Ghana). The board generally appoints the chief executive officer (CEO), under terms and conditions determined by the board, and delegates day-to-day management of the road network to the CEO.

These Roads Boards have had several impacts on the way the road agency is managed. First, they protect the road agency from unwelcome interference in day-to-day management matters by ministers and senior government officials. However, the boards cannot simply ignore the wishes of politicians. As one chairman put it, "we had to find ways of turning political interference into political input which could be weighed alongside the other technical considerations." Second, the non-governmental members on the board enable the road agency to draw on a wider range of skills and contacts. For example, the South African National Roads Authority attributes its highly successful toll road program to the important contribution made by its oversight board. Finally, the private sector members on the board help the road agency to recognize that it is in the business of delivering services to clearly defined customers and that they need to pay attention to the needs of these customers. This is particularly important when the road agency is trying to seek public support for more road spending.

Contract Plans

The third reform recognizes that, once responsibility for managing the road network is delegated to a Roads Board, there needs to be a formal way for the minister, as *de facto* owner and shareholder of the road business, to define the Board's objectives and performance targets. This is typically spelled out in the form of a contract plan (or equivalent). The normal procedure is for the road authority to prepare a multiyear rolling Business Plan that is then used as the basis for negotiating an annual performance agreement with the parent ministry.

The objectives often take the form of a vision statement from which the agency can derive its principal or statutory objectives. For example, Transit New Zealand's mission is, "To operate a safe and efficient state highway system." Within the context of this vision statement, the minister then sets a series of clearly specified performance targets that the Board is expected to meet. They cover issues like the number of road accidents, level of service provided to road users, condition of the road network, administrative efficiency of the road agency, level of administrative costs, and, increasingly, financial return on investment. These performance targets, together with the annual road program, are usually spelled out in an Annual Performance Agreement signed with the minister.

Commercialized Staffing Structure

There is no point in creating an autonomous road agency with commercial management, unless it is supported by an organization that can respond to market discipline. That primarily means having stable staff, selected on a competitive basis and paid market-based wages. The UK procedure under which staff who are senior civil servants can be moved anywhere across government within the Senior Civil Service is incompatible with a commercially managed organization. Likewise, staff need to be paid market-based wages. After all, they are employing and supervising the work of consultants and contractors and, if you pay them significantly less than the going market wage, you are asking for trouble.

Low salaries have created major problems for many road agencies. The difficulty is that it is generally not possible to pay market-based wages within the usual civil service structure. Even the Finnish Road Administration and the UK Highways Agency, though partly autonomous, are still classified as government departments and have to employ staff under civil service rules, although with more flexibility within salary ranges. Some road agencies have nevertheless managed to become sufficiently autonomous to enable them to operate outside the civil service rules. This has enabled road agencies in countries like South Africa, Ghana, Namibia, and Latvia to greatly improve their terms and conditions of employment. Prior to the civil war, the reforms in Sierra Leone even enabled the Sierra Leone Road Authority to attract back qualified highway engineers who had left to work in Europe.

Commercializing Road Financing

Many countries responded to the growing shortage of finance by attempting to earmark selected road related taxes and charges and depositing them into a special off-budget account, or road fund, to support spending on roads. These road funds unfortunately encountered numerous problems and, as time went by, countries increasingly adopted other financing strategies. The first was to commercialize road management (see previous section) to encourage better use of resources and, in the process, to "stretch" the existing budget. If actual allocations for roads were 20 percent below requirements, why not raise efficiency by 20 percent so that the existing budget could be stretched to cover all costs? However, although this led to significant productivity gains in countries like Finland, Sweden and UK, the gains tended to be eroded by further budget cuts and countries usually ended up back where they started from.

The second strategy was to introduce tolling. Numerous countries have introduced tolls, either in the form of public toll roads or private sector concessions, to cover operation and maintenance of selected parts of the road network and, where traffic volumes are high enough, to cover investment costs as well. Finally, based on the lessons learned from the earlier experiences with earmarking, several countries have introduced a new type of off-budget financing mechanism that is generally referred to as the "second generation" road fund.

The following sections review: (i) experience with earmarking and why it lost favor with both financing institutions and road users; (ii) experience with tolling; and (iii) the principles and practice underlying second generation road funds.

Earmarking

Earmarking is not a new idea and several earmarked road funds were set up between 1910 and the late 1930s, including the road funds in UK and South Africa (the latter was set up in 1935). The rationale behind these early road funds was to provide "machinery by which the owners of motor vehicles in combination and under State guidance [were] enabled to spend money on roads for their mutual benefit" (Jeffreys 1949). In the UK, there was a Road Improvement Fund from 1910 to 1920 and then a fully-fledged Road Fund from 1920 onwards. However, in 1937 the earmarking was suspended and the fund ceased to function as an independent financing mechanism.

These early road funds included a number of novel features. The UK Road Improvement Fund was administered by a board that was not directly responsible to Parliament. It had five members and the chairman was appointed from among the existing members of the board. Revenues came from: (i) the proceeds of an *increase* in taxes on motor vehicles; and (ii) a *new* petrol tax. In other words, the financing of roads was to be paid for from *extra* taxes paid by road users. The earmarking mechanism was thus explicitly designed to ensure that it did not assign more revenues to the road sector at the expense of other sectors. The funds were managed by a small secretariat that was advised on technical matters by a six-member Advisory Engineering Committee, primarily made up of local government engineers.

Although well designed in principle, the roads board declined in importance and eventually passed out of existence, as did the earlier Road Improvement Fund which had been closed in 1920 (Jeffreys 1949). There were several reasons for its failure. All board members, together with the chairman, were appointed by the Treasury and served only "during its pleasure." The criteria for selecting board members were unclear. They included someone from the railways as chairman, someone from the shipping industry, and people involved in banking, finance, and law. The board was dominated by the chairman, who rendered most decisions without consulting the board. The board did not develop a satisfactory relationship with Parliament, the Treasury exerted undue control, it made little effort to win public support, and it also built up a large cash surplus. With the onset of war in 1914, it was not surprising that the Treasury raided the Road Improvement Fund in 1915. The new Road Fund set up in 1920 was likewise raided in 1929, 1935, and 1937. The reasons for this were simple. First, with a railway magnate as chairman, there was little pressure to build a competing road network. Second, the revenues were collected under the government's tax-making powers and the Finance Act required the proceeds to be deposited into the consolidated fund. This made it easy for the Treasury to withhold funds whenever they were short of cash.

In spite of the failure of the Road Improvement Fund, many people continued to support the principle of earmarking funds for roads. They argued that it: (i) applied the benefit principle of taxation (i.e., those who benefited from the roads paid for them); (ii) assured a minimum level of expenditure for desirable or essential expenditures (e.g., maintenance); (iii) reduced the costs of civil works by assuring prompt and continuous funding; and (iv) helped to reduce the resistance of the public to new road taxes, or increases in them. All are valid points. The critics, on the other hand, argued that it: (i) hampered effective budgetary control; (ii) could lead to a misallocation of resources, with too much revenue going to the road network at the expense of other sectors; (iii) introduced inflexibility into overall budget management; (iv) weakened the powers of the executive and legislative branches of government; and (v) often resulted in the earmarking provisions remaining in force long after they were needed (Teja and Bracewell-Milnes 1991; McCleary 1991). However, many of the arguments against earmarking were based on a utopian view of how budgets were allocated by government. According to economic theory, funds are allocated among sectors until the benefits at the margin are equalized across sectors. This view has been challenged as being weak or invalid, since it assumes a system of public finance and democratic decision-making that bears little relation to reality (Teja and Bracewell-Milnes 1991).

Be that as it may, there was renewed interest in earmarking during the early 1950s when New Zealand, Japan, and the United States (at the federal level) set up their road funds. Both Japan and the United States accepted that their road programs—building a modern road system in Japan and an interstate defense network in the United States—could not be financed through regular budgetary allocations. Although the authors of these road funds appeared to accept that earmarking generally hampered effective budget management, they argued that road funds represented "benign" earmarking. Provided the taxes chosen were levied only on those people who benefited from the expenditures, they would act as surrogate prices and actually improve allocative efficiency. As the Japan road improvement special account put it, the road fund was "based on the concept that road users who enjoy the benefits of improved roads should bear the burden for their improvement." The United States likewise argued that the concept involved two elements: first the user pays, and, second, the government credits the user fees directly to a highway special account to avoid confusing them with other government revenues. These principles, which did not differ significantly from those underlying the earlier UK Road Improvement Fund, became known as the "user pay" concept (Heggie and Vickers 1998, Annex 4).

Many developing countries were attracted by these arguments and they went ahead and set up their own earmarked road funds in the 1970s and 1980s, while most Eastern and Central European countries did the same during the early 1990s. Apart from New Zealand (which restructured several times, most recently in 1996), the U.S. Federal Highway Trust Fund (which also restructured several times), and Japan (which is a special case), most of these road funds failed to deliver a secure and stable flow of funds for roads. At best, the road funds diverted revenues away from other sectors and undermined strict budget discipline while, at worst, they became nothing less than a den of thieves (Heggie 2000). The surprising thing was that they suffered from almost exactly the same problems as the UK Road Improvement Fund. No one appeared to have learned any lessons from this earlier experience.

The most important adverse side effects associated with the earmarked road funds set up after 1970 were:

i. the earmarking procedure allocated a larger proportion of the government's overall budget envelope to the road sector by clawing revenues back from other sectors[4];

ii. the road fund rarely received all the revenues it was entitled to—the Ministry of Finance often withheld funds (due to the weak legal basis of the road fund) and the staff managing the road fund were often engineers without any formal financial training[5];

iii. with little or weak oversight, funds were regularly used to pay for unauthorized items (e.g., hotel bills, refurbishment of houses/offices, etc.), or items that were never delivered to the road agencies (e.g., for vehicles that ended up registered in the names of private individuals);

iv. record keeping was poor and so was financial management—the staff (if any) managing the road fund usually did not know how to keep proper accounts and this meant that several road funds could not even be audited;

v. the road funds were regularly "raided," usually to finance roads in marginal constituencies just before election time, but sometimes simply to pay for "shopping trips" by officials to neighboring countries.

It was reminiscent of the problems that affected the UK Road Improvement Fund and its oversight board in the early 1900s. There was something fundamentally wrong with the incentive structure. No one was pressing the road agencies to produce better roads and the road fund was all too often viewed simply as a convenient slush fund that, being off-budget, was subject to less budget discipline. No wonder that Ministries of Finance and the International Monetary Fund (IMF) strongly opposed attempts to set up any further earmarked road funds.

Tolling

In the absence of an earmarked road fund, many countries turned to tolling to generate additional revenues for roads. However, tolls can only be economically collected on roads carrying relatively high volumes of traffic. The broad rule of thumb is that, with a twenty-year cost-recovery period and a toll of $0.03 to $0.06 per vehicle km for light vehicles, you need at least 10,000 to 15,000 vehicles per day (vpd) to cover all costs (International Road Federation 1996). You can often cover rehabilitation, operation, and maintenance costs only with 6,500 vpd, maintenance costs only with 3,500 vpd, and toll collection costs only with 1,500 vpd (see Box 18.2). Since the volumes required to cover all costs only occur on limited parts of the road network—typically on no more than 5 to 10 percent of the national road network and 1 to 2 percent of the total road network—this means that tolling can only meet a small part of the road sector's overall financing needs. However, since expressways are the busiest and most expensive sections of road to build and maintain, tolling can make a valuable contribution to the financing of the main trunk road network.

A recent innovation has been the public-private partnership, where the (tolled) road is operated under a concession agreement. The concessionaire collects as much revenue as possible from users, while the balance of the revenues comes from government, either in the form of an up-front payment, or as a recurrent shadow toll. Many of these concessions apply to existing roads where the toll revenue only has to cover the costs of operation and maintenance. This

---

Box 18.2
Volumes of Traffic Needed to Cover Costs on Toll Roads

Costs of construction	$ 4.0 million
Loans	20 years @ 10 percent
Toll rates	$0.065 per km

Volumes of traffic required to:
- Cover all costs   15,000 to 25,000 vpd
- Cover costs of operation   3,500 vpd
- Cover toll collection only   1,500 vpd

Source: Fayard, 1993.

has enabled many more roads to be tolled and hence more revenues to be collected directly from users. Argentina has taken this concept about as far as it can go and now has about 10,000 km of national roads operated under private sector concession agreements. These roads account for nearly one quarter of the national road network, but this still accounts for less than 5 percent of the overall road network. Several other countries in Latin America, including Chile, Uruguay, and Venezuela, operate similar road concessions.

When the volume of traffic, combined with the agreed (often regulated) toll, do not generate sufficient revenues to cover all costs, governments have to realistically accept shared costs. The South African Roads Board developed a fairly innovative way of dealing with their early toll roads. Many of them did not carry sufficient traffic to make them financially viable. So they developed the "loans supportable by revenue" (LSR) approach to toll road financing. The LSR approach involved taking the proposed toll level, combining it with the expected traffic volume, and calculating the net revenue the road would generate (net of operation and maintenance costs). The net revenues were then used to float revenue bonds on the domestic capital market. The difference, if any, between the initial capital costs of the toll road and the value of these revenue bonds, was then provided by government in the form of a grant, or soft loan (i.e., as a low, or zero, interest rate loan repayable only after all revenue bonds had been serviced and repaid).

Second Generation Road Funds

During the 1980s, people also started asking why roads continued to be managed through a government department and financed through general budget allocations—the same way that governments manage the health and education sectors (Heggie and Vickers 1998, Foreword). Why were they not managed like other commercially operated publicly owned enterprises? Furthermore, why not charge road users for usage of roads in the same way that the power, telecommunications, and water sectors charge for their services? More fundamentally, why not move roads closer to the boundary between the public and private sectors and subject them to the normal discipline of the marketplace where they would be forced to produce only what people wanted at a price they could afford?

This change of philosophy—away from earmarking and towards a market based, incentive driven management paradigm—was also informed by the studies carried out on existing road funds, including those in New Zealand, Japan, and the United States (de Richecour and Heggie 1995; Heggie and Vickers 1998; Talvitie and Sikow 1998).[6] These studies sought to find out why so many earmarked road funds had failed and what might be done to design a road fund that worked. The main review (de Richecour and Heggie 1995) ended up setting down five key design elements for an effective road fund:

i. The basic expenditures to be financed through the road fund should be fully funded by road users and not by any transfers from the government's general tax revenues (i.e., the road fund should aim to be financially independent).

ii. The road fund should be managed by an independent board that includes road users nominated by the organizations they represent. This would fundamentally change the incentive system by recasting road users as customers, rather than simply as taxpayers. The chairman should be a person of standing and the board should be supported by a small secretariat headed by a manager appointed by the board.

iii. The board should recommend the level of the road user charging system (the road tariff) and it should be regularly adjusted. The recommended tariff should initially be approved by the Ministry of Finance (while the road fund remained subject to the Finance Act), but the board should eventually have legislated powers to set its own tariff within guidelines laid down by the Ministry of Finance.

iv. The fuel levy should be collected under contract by the fuel companies and deposited directly into the road fund account. Where feasible, all other charges should be collected under contract and deposited directly into the road fund account. This would prevent diversion of funds.

v. The road fund should be managed according to sound commercial principles. It should have clear disbursement procedures and funds disbursed should be subject to an independent financial audit and a selective technical audit.

These are the guiding principles that became the basis of the so-called "second-generation" road funds.

Most of the road funds set up after 1990 attempted to apply these principles. The objective was to change the incentive system by creating some form of market discipline. The road funds borrowed many of their features from the road funds in New Zealand (the star performer whose key features are summarized in Box 18.3), the United States, and Japan. However, they also "invented" many of their features *de novo*. The new road funds were exclusively in developing and transition countries where their establishment was facilitated by the donor supported programs that were attempting more generally to reform management and financing of roads (Zietlow and Bull 2001; Heggie 1995; Schliessler and Bull 1993). Surprisingly, these second generation road funds tended to be strongly supported by Ministries of Finance, since they offered greater transparency (i.e., better governance), better financial management and tighter financial controls (see Box 18.4). Road agencies tended to be less enthusiastic for the same reasons—the road fund forced them to justify their programs and held them accountable for results.

The key features of these second generation road funds are as follows:

i. The road fund is managed through a separate road fund administration that channels funds to *all* parts of the road network.

ii. Oversight is provided by way of a public-private board under an independent chairman of standing.

iii. Revenues come only from charges related to road use (i.e., a road tariff, generally consisting of vehicle license fees and a levy added to the price of fuel) and the tariff is designed to ensure that the road fund does not abstract revenues away from other sectors. It is expected that these charging instruments will eventually be replaced by electronic charging.

iv. Day-to-day management is by a small secretariat that manages the road fund along commercial lines.

v. Once the fuel levy reaches about $0.03-0.05 per liter, procedures are generally introduced to ensure non-road users do not have to pay the fuel levy.

vi. Funds are disbursed to road agencies in ways that strengthen financial discipline.

vii. The road fund is supported by sound legislation and published financial rules and regulations.

Several of these road funds are starting to produce noteworthy examples of emerging good practice. A few examples, related to the above seven key features, are summarized below.[7]

Separate road fund administration. It quickly became apparent that second generation road funds had to channel some funds to all parts of the road network. The theoretical case rested on the fact that all road users were paying into the road fund via the fuel levy and hence all roads should be entitled to get something back from the road fund. However, there were also practical considerations. First, the road fund boards were not interested in political jurisdictions. Their constituents used all parts of the road network and they felt obliged to make sure that all roads were maintained to an acceptable standard. Second, there were the legislators. The new road funds rested on a sound legal

---

Box 18.3
Transfund New Zealand: Road Fund Good Practice

The original road fund was established in 1953. In 1989 it was renamed the Land Transport Fund and the management of the Fund was transferred to Transit New Zealand. However, since the road fund was used to finance Transit New Zealand's road program, as well as those of the Regional Councils and District Councils, there was thought to be a conflict of interest. On July 1, 1996 the Transit New Zealand Amendment Act therefore came into effect creating an independent Crown entity known as Transfund. The new institution:

- was set up as an independent road fund administration;
- has a five-person oversight board that is nominated by the responsible minister following consultation with people from the land transport industry;
- one of the existing members of the board is appointed as chairman;
- revenues come from motor vehicle registration fees, a gasoline levy, and weight-distance charges that are graduated according to axle weight;
- all revenues are collected under contract;
- off-road usage of gasoline is exempted (the system uses rebates);
- Transit New Zealand and local authorities apply for funds on the basis of cost-benefit analysis and the outcome of a Road Maintenance Management System (RAMMS);
- there are cost share arrangements with local authorities based on ability to pay;
- technical, financial, and procedural audits are carried out on a regular basis and, if funds are used improperly, the road agency has to repay them to Transfund;
- the road fund is supported by sound basic legislation (in the form of the Transit New Zealand Amendment Act 1995).

Other attractive features are that the road fund finances traffic enforcement by the police and the work of the Land Transport Safety Authority, and provides support for passenger transport. Under a recently introduced provision, it also supports "alternatives to roading" (typically, inland waterways and the like). The only weak point is that the Treasury still controls the flow of funds into the road fund. They have been unwilling to delegate responsibility for charging policy to the board.

Box 18.4
Commercialization of Roads:
The View of Jordan's Minister of Finance

"To start with, we need to think of road funds which reflect a desire to pursue an Agency Model of service delivery for roads under which the management of roads is commercialized with expenditure on roads being financed from user charges which should reflect the view that 'roads should be managed like a business, not like a bureaucracy.' My Ministry has no objection to the above 'user-pay' or 'fee-for-service' principle, but this involves not only the establishment of a road fund, but a rethinking of our whole approach to the road sector which often leads us to conclude that we need to establish a road fund. Let me mention in some detail the main concerns of my Ministry regarding the establishment of a road fund.

- First, we want assurance that the establishment of the road fund is part of a longer term strategy to commercialize the road sector, and that it is not simply a means of avoiding strict budget discipline.

- Second, we expect the road fund to be dedicated to maintenance. We must make sure that we maintain what we have, before starting to build anything new.

- Third, we expect to see the road fund as a purchaser, not a provider of services. It should be a separate agency with a clear mission statement, transparent objectives, physical output indicators and it should ideally work within an envelope of total input costs.

- Fourth, we expect the road fund revenues to come only from road-user charges, not from any earmarked taxes. That would not prevent the government from topping up the road fund from the consolidated budget, but topping up would only be done on a discretionary basis.

- Fifth, the most fundamental requirement of all. The user charges going into the road fund must not take revenues away from other sectors. We would like to see a clean break between the tax revenues which belong to the consolidated budget, and the user charges which belong to the road fund. The only existing revenues which should go into the road fund, must be confined to what is already allocated for roads through the annual budgeting process.

- Sixth, we expect to see the road fund managed by a strong and independent management board which should include private sector interests—both road users and the business community—and should be genuinely free from any vested interest groups.

- Seventh, we expect the management of the road fund to be handled by a secretariat and to employ commercial accounting systems and to have annual performance targets.

- Eighth, we want to see a fair degree of cost recovery through the user charges. We look in the long-term for a road public utility which does not receive any government subsidy.

- Ninth, we cannot escape from the fact that fuel is a convenient tax handle from the point of view of fiscal policy. That will inevitably put a burden on the road fund administration to explain to the public why all fuel price increases are not equal.

In brief, we are perfectly willing not only to consider establishing a road fund, but even to actively help to get it established. However, you have to assure us that what we are establishing is the right kind of road fund and that it will be based on sound fiscal principles."

Source: Text of speech given by His Excellency Suleiman Hafez, Minister of Finance, June 3, 1997.

---

base and this meant they had to be approved by the legislators and few legislators appeared willing to approve a road fund that only financed part of the road network (e.g., national roads only). Not only that, there was growing pressure to ensure that the road fund was managed independently of the national roads agency. The New Zealand road fund used to be managed by Transit New Zealand, which was also responsible for managing the national road network. This created a conflict of interest and, under pressure from local governments, the road fund was transformed in 1996 into an independent road fund administration. The Ministry of Works in Jordan did not understand this principle and refused to let go. As a result, their road fund, which had a promising start, was soon closed down by the Ministry of Finance.

Oversight arrangements. Oversight is typically provided through a public-private board made up of persons with a strong vested interest in well-managed roads—people whose livelihoods depend on having a well managed and adequately financed road network. There are several examples of effective oversight boards. The most notable is probably the Zambia National Roads Board

(NRB), which was one of six individuals and organizations nominated by the World Bank's roads staff in 1999 for the International Road Federation Man of the Year award. The miracle of the NRB is that it functions well, in spite of being set up under flimsy legal procedures that could be changed at any moment. It has eleven members—seven represent constituencies like the Chamber of Commerce, road transport industry, farmers, and Chartered Institute of Transport, while four represent concerned government departments. The board elects its own chairman (this also happens in Cameroon) and only the non-governmental members have the right to vote at board meetings (an important disadvantage, since it creates two classes of board members—the chairman has to work hard to achieve consensus and avoid votes). The board has won widespread public support for its work and even runs a weekly radio program, called "Our Roads," to keep the public informed about the annual road program and its financing. The NRB has now been replaced by a new board set up under basic legislation. In general, boards with independent chairmen perform better than those where the minister is chairman. They mobilize better public relations programs (i.e., they are better able to "sell" the road program to the public) and they are also able to raise more revenues.

The road tariff. The intention is to treat roads like any other commercially operated publicly owned enterprise. Road users must therefore pay for roads and they must know that they are paying to ensure that they demand value for money. In most second generation road funds, payment is made via a two-part tariff consisting of vehicle license fees (sometimes also a heavy vehicle surcharge) and a levy added to the price of fuel. The Ministry of Finance often pays the existing (budgetary) allocation for roads into the road fund in the form of an equivalent fuel levy and then all additional revenues come from extra payments made by road users. This ensures that the road fund remains budget neutral and does not abstract revenues away from other spending programs. The level of the tariff is adjusted from time to time, usually through the regular budgetary process. The board recommends changes in the tariff to the Ministry of Finance, nearly always after extensive consultations with road user groups, and the Ministry considers these changes alongside other tax changes and includes them in the annual budget. The ensuing revenues may be collected by the Ministry of Finance, by the road fund administration itself, or they may be collected under contract by a third party (e.g., in New Zealand, all road fund revenues are collected under contract). The proceeds are furthermore increasingly being deposited directly into the road fund administration's commercial bank accounts (this does not happen in New Zealand where the revenues are instead deposited into a separate interest bearing Treasury account).

Namibia is so far the only country that has set up its road fund administration as a *de facto* commercially operated publicly owned enterprise (see Box 18.5). Under the Namibia legislation, the board has powers to set its own road tariff, following consultation with the concerned minister (i.e., the minister does not "approve" the tariff, but simply issues a "no objection"). This means that the revenues are not earmarked. They are no longer collected under the government's tax-making powers and do not have to be deposited into the government's budget. The legislation defines the road user charges as a tariff that is paid in return for services rendered, in the same way that customers pay for rail services and water supplies. It is still too early to say how well this procedure will work. However, although there is only one functioning commercially operated publicly owned enterprise, the legislation passed on new road funds is getting increasingly flexible with more powers being delegated to the board. For example, the Malawi National Road Authority Act, 1997, gives the board powers to raise, "such road user charges as the Minister may, from time to time, on the recommendation of the Board and in consultation with the Minister responsible for finance, determine by order published in the *Gazette*." Sadly, the government has not yet implemented these provisions.

Day-to-day management. Most of the second generation road funds are managed by a small secretariat with a head (executive secretary), appointed by the board. The head then recruits and appoints the rest of the staff, subject to board approval. It doesn't take many staff to manage a road fund. Transfund employs about forty staff to manage a turnover of around $500 million, while Ghana has about three to five staff to manage a turnover of around $60 million. The staff collate the road programs prepared by the various road agencies, consolidate them into the "approved" national roads program, define the financial procedures to be followed by the various road agencies entitled to receive money from the road fund, allocate funds to support the approved programs, disburse funds to the road agencies, and then audit the results *ex post*. The outcome of the technical and financial audits is typically tabled before Parliament and often published in the press. The staff tend to be accountants, planners, and engineers and, since they are handling large sums of money, it is important to ensure that they are paid market-based wages. This creates problems in countries where civil service salaries are well below the market wage. Some road funds have therefore dealt with this by employing the required staff as consultants, while at least one has subcontracted the day-to-day management of the road fund to another organization. The Polish road fund is managed by their Development Bank under a contract with the Ministry of Infrastructure.

Box 18.5
Excerpts From the Namibia Road Fund Administration Act, 1999

18. (1) Subject to section 19 [this section deals with the annual expenditure program], the Administration may from time to time after consultation with the Minister and such parties as the Minister may direct, by notice in the *Gazette*, and in accordance with such principles as may be prescribed, impose any one or more of the following road user charges for the achievement of the objects of this Act, namely:

(a) A charge on any motor vehicle, whether registered in Namibia or not, in respect of the travelling distance in the course of on-road use, and which may be based on the mass, length, width or height of the vehicle or its loading, or the number of axles of such vehicle, or any combination of such factors;

(b) an entry fee in respect of motor vehicles not registered in Namibia that temporarily enter Namibia;

(c) registration and annual license fees in respect of motor vehicles registered in Namibia; or

(d) subject to subsection (4)(f) [this subsection deals with exemptions], a levy on every litre of petrol and every litre of diesel sold by any undertaking at any point in Namibia and which is to be included in any determination of the selling price of petrol or diesel, as the case may be, under any law relating to petroleum products.

Exemption systems. These apply mainly to off-road usage of diesel. A third or more of diesel fuel is typically used outside the transport sector for power generation and to operate heavy equipment in the construction, mining, and agriculture sectors. To avoid penalizing off-road usage of diesel—and to avoid widespread opposition to the introduction of a fuel levy—most countries with road funds therefore try to find ways of exempting off-road usage of diesel. Some countries operate rebate schemes or color un-taxed diesel, but both are difficult to administer. As a result, emerging good practice tends to focus on *ex post* compensation systems. Latvia, where their road fund was recently closed down, probably had the best developed system. In the case of farmers (use of diesel by farmers is one of the most difficult issues to deal with), Latvia required them to register their land holdings with the municipality, and the farmer could then claim back the levy paid on 100 liters of diesel fuel for each hectare of land under cultivation. China considered adopting a similar exemption system for their proposed Central Fuel Tax Fund. Mozambique uses an even simpler system. Twenty percent of the diesel levy is paid into a special fund that provides financial support for agriculture. Finally, there is the Zambian example. They offer no exemptions, but have agreed—at least at the current fuel levy of about $0.035 per liter—to keep farmers happy by nominally allocating slightly more funds for rural roads than would otherwise be the case (i.e., 40 percent of road fund revenues, rather than the usual 30-35 percent allocated by most other road funds).

Disbursing funds. Since most road agencies have little working capital (and a poor credit rating), there are two main methods of paying for approved road works. In countries with weak governance, the preference is for paying the contractors directly after work has been certified as done according to specification. This method is used in Zambia and Mozambique. Where governance is acceptable or improving, the preference is for a revolving fund. The road agency submits its annual program and, once it has been amended and approved, funds are disbursed on a regular basis. Replenishment of the revolving fund is dependent on submission of satisfactory evidence that all payments made were for work forming part of the approved expenditure program, the work has been certified, and contractors have actually been paid. In addition, all work financed from the road fund is subject to independent technical and financial auditing. This system is used in New Zealand and Ghana.

Legislation. Weak, or nonexistent legislation, was responsible for many of the failures of the first generation road funds (see Box 18.6). The preference with second generation road funds is thus to have legislation that is short and enabling, accompanied by published financial rules and regulations specifying how the road fund is to be managed. This provides more flexibility, since it enables the regulations to be revised from time to time without the need for further legislation. The best examples of emerging good practice for basic legislation are Malawi, Ghana, and Namibia. Lesotho has the best financial rules and regulations supporting a road fund set up under the Finance Act. Both the Malawi legislation and the Lesotho financial regulations have been turned into templates and several countries have based their legislation on these templates (e.g., Nepal, Pakistan, and Laos). In many respects, the legislation in some of these countries is one step ahead of New Zealand. The most innovative draft legislation—unfortunately not passed by Parliament—comes from Nigeria. The draft legislation proposed to effectively set up the road fund administration as if it was a limited liability company with all shares held by the public. Each

Box 18.6
The Need for Sound Legislation

Most first generation road funds were set up under the Finance Act—which often provides for the government to open a special account for a designated purpose—or under a Ministerial or Cabinet Decree. In one case, the road fund was simply set up on the basis of a telephone call between the president and the head of the Central Bank. These legal instruments provide a relatively weak basis for the road fund.

Weak legal instruments invariably lead to challenges. There are three main challenges. First, the Ministry of Finance often collects the earmarked funds, but refuses to deposit them into the road fund. Without a firm legal basis, the road fund (or road ministry) cannot do much about this. Second, weak legal instruments are nearly always accompanied by lack of clear financial rules and regulations governing management of the road fund. As a result, the road fund often deteriorates into a "slush fund." Money gets spent on hotel bills, purchase of computers and fax machines, vehicles, etc. In one case, the entire allocation to a district council was spent on entertaining friends at the main hotel in the capital city. Third, the road funds frequently get raided. Government—and officials—simply use the road fund as a contingency and regularly draw on it to finance other urgent programs.

On the other hand, sound legislation does not solve all the problems. You still need to have a strong oversight board. Furthermore, as the Zambia National Roads Board has shown, a strong board can work effectively without sound legislation, although lack of consistent legislation makes life much more difficult.

Source: PricewaterhouseCoopers 2000.

year, the board was required to call an open public meeting at which they had to explain to the public—as shareholders—what they had done with their money.

Ownership of the Road Network

Where does this leave the issue of potential private sector ownership of the road network? The above agenda calls for public roads to be commercialized and for road management to be subjected to the discipline of the marketplace.

It does not necessarily call for all public roads to be privatized (i.e., for ownership of the road assets to be transferred from the public to the private sector). Although there are numerous private roads in most countries, including roads in forestry areas, game parks, farming estates, etc., the issue here is whether roads that are publicly owned could be transferred from the public to the private sector. There are three broad cases to be considered: (i) high volume roads that can be tolled; (ii) low volume roads that primarily serve the needs of local communities (e.g., roads in farming areas, on housing estates, etc.); and (iii) those roads that lie in between—they primarily serve the needs of traffic and cannot be economically tolled.

High volume roads may account for a reasonable proportion of the national road network, but rarely account for more than about 1 to 2 percent of the total road network. Few of these roads are privately owned. The 745 km network owned by Cofiroute in France is one of the rare exceptions. However, a number of high volume roads are operated under concession agreements where temporary ownership of the road is assigned to a private sector concessionaire for a specified period of time (Fishbein and Babbar 1996).[8] They are typically free standing toll roads with concession periods of fifteen to thirty-five years, typically carrying at least 10,000 vehicles per day (vpd), with a toll rate for cars of $0.03 to $0.10 per vehicle km. The concession concept is likewise being applied increasingly to maintenance, with or without rehabilitation and upgrading. This enables governments to assign temporary ownership of the road to a private sector concessionaire on roads carrying much lower volumes of traffic. Typical contract periods for such concessions are seven to ten years on roads carrying at least 6,500 vpd.

At the other end of the spectrum are the low volume roads where efforts are being made to adopt the Scandinavian model of the private road association. The prime example being followed here comes from Sweden where roughly two thirds of the total road network, carrying about 4 percent of the total traffic, is owned and managed by private road associations. Other countries with similar arrangements include Finland, Norway, some U.S. states, and some Canadian provinces. The roads usually provide access to farms or summer residences, although there are some small municipalities that manage their road networks in this way. The association consists of the adjoining landowners, or people living alongside the road. Membership is compulsory for property owners who use the road. The members appoint their own chairman, secretary, trustee, and other office holders who organize the business of the association with advice, as needed, from the national road authority. Costs are shared between central government, the association, and (sometimes) local authorities. This model is being actively promoted in countries like Zambia and Estonia. It is likewise being looked at in Lithuania, Kenya, and Tanzania. Lesotho—

through its Village Development Councils—operates a similar system of village-owned tracks and trails.

The third group of roads are the ones in between. Thus far, no attempt has been made to transfer temporary or permanent ownership of these roads to the private sector, based on the concern that current charging mechanisms require a great deal of averaging (and hence extensive cross subsidies) and that the roads have considerable monopoly power. New Zealand is the only country that has been seriously considering a different form of ownership. They are considering dividing the overall road network up into four or five road operating companies that—at least initially—would be owned by central and local governments who would be permitted to sell shares to each other, but prohibited from selling them to third parties. Each company would operate commercially and would have full control of its revenues, which are expected to eventually include congestion charges. The proposals have not gone ahead, but nevertheless point to a possible next step in the process of reforming road ownership.

Conclusions

Countries have made considerable progress during the past ten years in reforming the way they manage and finance their road networks. However, the restructuring of road management is still at a very early stage and there are only a limited number of examples of emerging "good practice." The leading candidates are probably the National Roads Authority in South Africa, Transit New Zealand, the Swedish National Road Authority, the Finnish Road Authority, and VicRoads in Australia.

Namibia has also made great progress, but the reforms are more recent and the outcome still uncertain. Ghana has made similar progress since the Ghana Highway Authority was restructured in 1996, but it still has some distance to go. The Sierra Leone Road Authority was one of Africa's shining examples of road sector reform before it became engulfed in the civil war. It had a strong and independent management board, staff were paid market-based wages, it had an impressive road management system backed up by a detailed cost accounting system, and produced full commercial accounts.

Many other countries have followed the above examples and started to restructure the way they manage their roads. They include India, Malawi, Nepal, Pakistan, Tanzania, Uganda, Zambia, and Zimbabwe. However, major policy reforms take time and it will still be some years before the above reforms start to show positive results.

In the case of road financing, progress has been less balanced, but more impressive. Most progress has been made in developing and transition countries, which have moved ahead faster than industrialized countries. There are now notable examples of emerging second generation road funds in several developing countries, including Cameroon, Ghana, Guatemala, Honduras, Malawi, Namibia, Nepal, and Zambia. Brazil also has three state level road funds, of which the one in Parana State is probably the best example. None are perfect, but many contain features that qualify as examples of emerging "good practice." Indeed, in many respects, it is the developing countries that invented the concept of financing the road sector as if it was a commercially operated publicly owned enterprise. The idea of giving the board of the road fund administration the power to set its own tariff level, subject only to a ministerial "no objection," was pioneered in the Malawi legislation (though not fully implemented) and the idea was carried through into the legislation for Namibia. Several other countries are now proposing to follow suit.

Finally, though the second generation road funds do not involve privatization, since there is no transfer of ownership, they carry private sector involvement in the road sector well beyond all previous public-private boundaries. In essence, the private sector has taken over from government the overall responsibility for financing the road network. It is as if they were holding the road network "in trust." They are mobilizing the required revenues (by persuading the public of the need for more funding), managing the proceeds, allocating it in a way that ensures better value for money, and are transparently accounting for the way the funds are spent. Although the road network continues to be owned by government, its financing and (increasingly) its management are carried out as if the road network was owned by a coalition of private sector shareholders representing the people who use the roads, or benefit directly from them. Maybe the second generation road funds should therefore be viewed as an important step on the road to full commercialization. In the longer term, they may even lead to full privatization of the road network.

Notes

1. Sponsored by UN ESCAP and the World Bank, with support from the Swiss Agency for Development and Cooperation and the German Agency for Technical Assistance.
2. Sponsored by the World Bank with support from the Swiss Agency for Development and Cooperation.
3. Transit New Zealand is owned by government, there are no shares, and its management reports directly to an independent board that operates much like a company board. The board is appointed by the government and directs both overall policy and funding allocations.
4. Since the government's overall budget envelope is typically fixed—at least in the short term—any additional funds allocated to the road sector have to be taken away from the other sectors to which they were previously allocated.

5. The original Ghana road fund was simply a bank account and no one even took the trouble to check that all the revenues attributable to it had been collected and deposited into the road fund account.
6. The reviews were carried out on road funds in Japan, New Zealand, the United States (Federal Highway Trust Fund), Argentina, Benin, Colombia, Central African Republic, Chad, Ghana, Mozambique, Rwanda, Sierra Leone, South Africa, Tanzania, and Zambia. Later, this was supplemented by information on road funds in Hungary, Romania, Russia, and Ukraine.
7. The experience is based on information collected about existing, or proposed, road funds in Benin, Cameroon, Ghana, Guatemala, Honduras, Japan, Jordan, Kenya, Laos, Lesotho, Malawi, Mozambique, Namibia, Nepal, New Zealand, Nigeria, Pakistan, Poland, South Africa, the United States (Federal Highway Trust Fund), Yemen, and Zambia.
8. Fishbein and Babbar 1996 reviews eight concession projects in Chile, Colombia, Mexico, China, Malaysia, Hungary, UK, and the United States.

References

de Richecour, Anne B., and Ian G. Heggie. 1995. "African Road Funds: What Works and Why?" SSATP Working Paper 14, World Bank. Africa Technical Department. Washington, D.C.

Fayard, A. 1993. "Toll Financing, Risk Financing: How to Fit the Needs Without Dogmas." East-West European Road Conference, Varsovic, September.

Fishbein, G., and S. Babbar. 1996. "Private Financing of Toll Roads." RMC Discussion Paper 117, World Bank. Washington, D.C.

Frost, M., and C. Lithgow. 1996. "Improving Quality and Cutting Costs Through Performance Contracts." Paper presented at a road management seminar, World Bank. Washington, D.C.

Heggie, Ian G. 1995. "Management and Financing of Roads: An Agenda for Reform." Technical Paper 275, World Bank. Washington, D.C.

Heggie, Ian G. 2000. "Road Funds: What Went Wrong." *World Highways* (September): 35–37.

Heggie, Ian G., and P. Vickers. 1998. "Commercial Management and Financing of Roads." Technical Paper 409, World Bank. Washington, D.C.

International Road Federation. 1996. "Paying for Roads—World Trends in Road Network Financing: Private Sector Takes the Lead." *World Highways* (November/December): 25–26.

Jeffreys, Rees. 1949. *The King's Highway: An Historical and Autobiographical Record of the Developments of the Past Sixty Years*. London, UK: The Batchworth Press.

McCleary, W. 1991. "The Earmarking of Government Revenue: A Review of Some World Bank Experience." *The World Bank Research Observer* 6 (1): 81–104.

Pinard, M., and S. Kaombwe. 2000. "Restructuring the Management and Financing of Roads in the SADC Region." Proceedings of the REAAA Conference. Tokyo.

PricewaterhouseCoopers. 2000. *Sourcebook on Institutional Development for Utilities and Infrastructure*. Consultant Report prepared for UK Department for International Development (DfID). London.

Schliessler, A., and A. Bull. 1993. *Roads: A New Approach for Road Network Management and Conservation*. Santiago: United Nations Economic Commission for Latin America (ECLAC).

Talvitie, A., and C. Sikow. 1998. "Review of Road Funds in Latin America." Paper presented at a road management seminar, World Bank, Washington, D.C.

Teja, R., and B. Bracewell-Milnes. 1991. *The Case for Earmarked Taxes: Government Spending and Public Choice*. London, UK: Institute of Economic Affairs.

Zietlow, G., and A. Bull. 2001. *Reform of Financing and Management of Road Maintenance in Latin America*. Paris: International Road Federation (IRF) World Road Congress.

19

HOT Networks:
A New Plan for Congestion Relief
and Better Transit

Robert W. Poole, Jr. and C. Kenneth Orski

Introduction

Urban traffic congestion remains one of America's biggest problems, despite decades of efforts by federal, state, and local governments to address it. In 2001, according to the most recent annual Urban Mobility Report from the Texas Transportation Institute, American motorists in the largest seventy-five urban areas lost $69.5 billion in wasted time (3.5 billion hours of delay) and fuel (5.7 billion extra gallons) due to traffic congestion.[1] This was an all-time high for the nearly two decades during which TTI has been measuring the extent of congestion. The average annual amount of time an urban motorist lost to congestion during peak hours grew from seven hours in 1982 to twenty-six hours in 2001.

One reason for the increase in congestion is that driving increased far more than road capacity over the past three decades. TTI found a strong relationship between the extent to which congestion was kept more-or-less under control and the extent of capacity growth. As the TTI report explains,

> [T]he more that travel growth outpaced roadway expansion, the more the overall mobility level declined. The five urban areas with a demand-supply growth balance had their congestion levels increase at a much lower rate than those areas where travel increased at a much higher rate than capacity expansion.[2]

However, the high cost and political difficulty of adding significant highway capacity in congested urban areas was also noted by TTI's researchers. Only

451

five of the seventy-five urban areas were able to keep highway capacity growth within 10 percent of traffic growth. The vast majority that could not do so suffered considerably greater reductions in mobility due to congestion.

Federal, state, and metro-area governments have focused considerable efforts and funding over the past two decades on providing commuters with alternatives to driving alone. The two principal thrusts were to invest significant sums on (1) adding High-Occupancy Vehicle (HOV) lanes to urban freeways, and (2) expanding transit systems, especially by adding new rail systems. During the past twenty years or so, American taxpayers paid for the creation of 2,119 lane-miles of HOV lanes, according to the Federal Highway Administration.[3] At an estimated $4 million per lane-mile, that represents an $8.5 billion investment. American taxpayers also spent over $70 billion on transit capital investment during the past decade.[4]

Data from the 2000 Census provide a measure of how effective this two-part strategy has been in reducing congestion. Unfortunately, the conclusion is: not very effective. Nationwide, despite the major expenditure on HOV lane additions, carpooling to work declined from 13.4 percent in 1990 to 11.2 percent in 2000—a drop of 16 percent. Carpooling's mode share decreased in thirty-six of the forty largest metro areas. Transit's commuting mode share declined from 5.27 percent in 1990 to 4.73 percent in 2000—a decline of 10.3 percent (although transit mode share did increase in twelve of the forty largest metro areas). Meanwhile, driving alone actually increased nationwide, rising from 72.7 percent of all work trips in 1990 to 75.7 percent in 2000. And driving alone's share increased in thirty-six of the forty largest metro areas.

For purposes of this chapter, we will focus primarily on the ten most congested urban areas, as measured by TTI's latest report. While TTI provides several different measures of the extent of congestion, we have chosen annual hours of delay per peak road traveler as the best measure of the comparative severity of congestion. Table 19.1 lists the resulting ten metro areas, in rank order, along with their drive-alone, HOV, and transit mode shares in 1990 and 2000.

As can be seen, even in these highly congested metro areas, driving alone increased its mode share in seven out of ten of them. Correspondingly, carpooling lost market share over the past decade in seven of the ten. Transit lost commuting market share in half of these most heavily congested areas. These results came about despite large-scale efforts to expand HOV and transit capacity and to promote both carpooling and transit use.

Thus, the stage is set for the question to be explored in this chapter. As a nation, we have continued to lose ground against urban traffic congestion for several decades. To make meaningful progress, we need to try new approaches.

Table 19.1
Changes in Commuter Mode Choice in
the Most Congested Metro Areas

Name	Person-hrs delay per peak traveler*	Rank*	Drive alone %**		HOV %**		Transit%**	
			1990	2000	1990	2000	1990	2000
Los Angeles-Orange County	136	1	72.3	72.4	15.5	15.2	4.6	4.7
San Francisco-Oakland	92	2	68.3	68.1	13.0	12.9	9.3	9.5
Washington D.C.-MD-VA	84	3	66.1	70.4	15.5	12.8	11.0	9.4
Seattle-Everett	82	4	73.1	71.6	12.1	12.8	6.1	6.8
Houston	75	5	76.1	77.0	14.6	14.2	3.8	3.3
Dallas-Ft. Worth	74	6	78.6	78.8	13.9	14.0	2.3	1.8
San Jose	74	6	68.3	68.1	13.0	12.9	9.3	9.5
New York-Northeast NJ	73	8	55.4	56.3	10.4	9.4	24.8	24.9
Atlanta	70	9	77.9	77.0	13.0	13.6	4.5	3.7
Miami-Hialeah	69	10	75.3	76.6	14.5	13.4	4.4	3.9

* *Source*: TTI, *2002 Urban Mobility Report*, Exhibit A-2, 2000 Urban Mobility Conditions.

** *Source*: U.S. Census Bureau, "Journey-to-Work Trends for Selected Metropolitan Areas," available at www.census.gov. Note that the Census figures are based on the MSA, a larger geographic unit than used by TTI. Thus, for example, the Census defines a single MSA encompassing the entire San Francisco Bay Area, while TTI uses a separate urbanized area for San Francisco-Oakland and San Jose.

Can we make better use of the nation's investment in HOV capacity, and can we make transit more effective, while at the same time acknowledging the reality that for a complex set of reasons, driving (including driving alone) will continue to be the majority's mode of choice?

Origins of the Concept

The premise of this chapter is that HOV lanes can be transformed into a more effective component of our urban mobility system. By changing the access requirement from vehicle occupancy to willingness to pay a market price (for cars) but allowing super high-occupancy vehicles (buses and van-pools) to use the lanes at no charge, we can accomplish three important goals:

1. Generate significant new revenue to pay for building out today's frag-mented HOV lanes into a seamless network;
2. Provide a congestion-free alternative for motorists on every congested freeway in the metro area; and
3. Provide a congestion-free guideway for Bus Rapid Transit service that can make this form of transit significantly more competitive with driving.

Two key transportation innovations need to be combined to create these pro-posed HOT Networks: High-Occupancy Toll (HOT) lanes and Bus Rapid Transit (BRT). In this section, we provide an overview of both innovations. We also summarize several precursor proposals, which have not been implemented but suggest parallel thinking among others in the transportation community.

HOT Lanes

HOT lanes are defined as specialized lanes open to both qualifying high-occupancy vehicles (carpools and transit) and paying customers (typically solo drivers). The term and concept of High-Occupancy toll (HOT) lanes was first set forth in a 1993 policy study by the Reason Foundation,[5] and subsequently endorsed by the Federal Highway Administration, under its Value Pricing Pilot Program. HOT lanes are being embraced by transportation planners for sev-eral reasons[6]:

- First, by adding a controlled number of (paying) vehicles to underutilized carpool lanes, the HOT lane concept keeps HOV lanes at their optimum utilization and relieves political pressures to decommission them (i.e., convert them back to general-purpose lanes).
- Second, by diverting some solo drivers from the adjoining general-purpose lanes, HOT lanes help to reduce congestion in the general-purpose lanes.
- Third, HOT lanes generate increased revenues for transportation corridor improvements, both highway and transit.
- Fourth, HOT lanes provide a premium travel option for single occupant vehicle (SOV) drivers who have a special need to reach their destination on time and are willing to pay for better service.

In short, all user groups would benefit from HOT lanes. There should be no "losers" in the implementation of HOT lanes on a congested freeway.

The Federal Highway Administration (FHWA) fully supports HOT lanes. The 1991 Intermodal Surface Transportation Efficiency Act (ISTEA) created a Congestion Pricing Pilot Program, offering modest federal grant support to metropolitan planning organizations (MPOs) willing to experiment with the use of pricing mechanisms to improve highway operations. Projects to convert underused HOV lanes to HOT lanes were embraced by FHWA beginning in 1995, and the agency has provided funding to assist with feasibility studies, implementation projects, and evaluations of operational projects.

In 1998 the federal transportation program was reauthorized as TEA-21. Under Section 1216(a) of TEA-21, the Congestion Pricing Pilot Program was broadened and renamed the Value Pricing Pilot Program (VPPP). Pricing of lanes otherwise reserved for high-occupancy vehicles is explicitly authorized. However, in order to protect the integrity of HOV programs, priority will be given by FHWA to "those HOT lane proposals where it is clear that an HOV lane is under-utilized."

HOT Lane Implementation

Thus far, HOT lanes have been in operation for a number of years in three metro areas in two states, California and Texas. There is sufficient operational experience to be able to draw some preliminary conclusions about the lanes' performance and acceptability. Houston has converted two HOV-3 facilities to a limited form of HOT lane in which HOV-2 vehicles can purchase access during peak periods, but solo drivers are not allowed. In San Diego, an under-utilized reversible HOV facility on I-15 was opened to solo drivers willing to pay a price that varies every six minutes (based on the volume of traffic in the HOV/HOT lanes). And in Orange County, California, a private developer financed, built, and operated new HOT lanes in the median of a congested commuter freeway, managing traffic flow via a price schedule that charges different prices at different hours of the day.

Houston's QuickRide program began on the I-10 West (Katy) Freeway in 1998. The increase in HOV requirement from HOV-2 to HOV-3 had solved the previous congestion problem in the HOV lanes, but had led to significant underutilization. Permitting HOV-2s to purchase access for a $2.00 toll, paid via transponder, did reduce the extent of underutilization. The program was extended to a similar HOV facility on the Northwest Freeway (U.S. 290) in 2000. Unfortunately, the market for paying HOV-2 customers has been modest. Despite the sale of over 1,500 transponders, the average daily number of paid transactions on the two facilities is only 160, of which ninety are on the Katy and seventy on U.S. 290.[7]

San Diego converted the grade-separated, reversible HOV-2 lanes on I-15 to HOT lanes in two steps, first offering access to solo drivers who purchased a monthly permit in 1996. The plan shifted to per-trip charging, via transponder, in 1997. Introduced at that time was dynamic variable pricing, under which the price charged is varied every six minutes based on observed traffic levels in the lanes. The program is required to maintain level of service (LOS) C[8] or better, and variable pricing is the tool used for this purpose. Under normal conditions, the toll for the eight-mile drive ranges from 50 cents to $4.00. Although carpools still make up the majority of vehicles, the I-15 Express Lanes have been very successful in attracting paying solo drivers, who as of 2002 constitute 25 percent of all vehicles in the lanes.[9]

Orange County's 91 Express Lanes project represents a distinctly different application of HOT lanes, since this project involved the addition of two such lanes in each direction in the median of a heavily congested commuter freeway, SR 91. Furthermore, a basic rationale for the project was to use toll revenue to recover the costs of construction and operation, via a public-private partnership. Based on the strength of traffic and revenue projections, the company was able to finance the $135 million project via long-term toll revenue bonds. Traffic demand has been close to original projections, and the project is generating sufficient revenue to cover the debt service on the bonds, as well as all operations and maintenance costs. The variable toll structure has been adjusted upwards more than once a year since the lanes opened in December 1995, so as to limit the number of vehicles using the lanes and maintain free-flow conditions at 65 mph even during the busiest peak hours. (As of late-2004, tolls ranged from $1.05 to $7.00 for the 10-mile facility.) HOV-3s use the lanes at half-price, while HOV-2s pay the regular rate. HOV-3s constituted about 13 percent of vehicles in the Express Lanes, as of 1999, the last year for which detailed data were available.[10]

Proposed and Planned HOT Lanes

Although HOT lanes are currently operational in only three urban areas, serious efforts are under way on HOT lane projects in quite a few other localities with serious congestion problems. Here is a brief overview.

Atlanta. The Atlanta Value Pricing Task Force in August 2003 endorsed a HOT lanes strategy and suggested initial projects for the GA-400 and GA-316. Georgia DOT and the State Road & Tollway Authority are studying the feasibility of a network of HOT lanes.

Dallas. In addition to plans to add HOT lanes to the most congested 18.5-mile section of the LBJ Freeway (I-635), Dallas in 2003 launched a value pricing study that is considering adding value-priced toll lanes to all congested freeways.

Denver. Colorado DOT is proceeding with conversion of the underused 8-mile HOV lane on I-25N to a HOT lane. It is also reviewing proposals from private firms to add HOT lanes to I-70 between Denver International Airport and downtown and to the C-470 beltway. The new Colorado Toll Enterprise is studying the feasibility of a network of express toll lanes.

Houston. The local tollway authority is moving forward with the addition of HOT lanes on an 11-mile section of the Katy Freeway (I-10), as part of a major expansion. In addition, a study is under way on the possibility of converting all HOV lanes in the metro area to HOT lanes.

Los Angeles. The Southern California Association of Governments is carrying out feasibility studies on the addition of a system of truck toll lanes (essentially, HOT lanes for trucks) on three freeways heavily affected by truck traffic to and from the ports of Long Beach and Los Angeles: 20 miles of the Long Beach Freeway (I-710), 37 miles of the Pomona Freeway (SR-60), and 85 miles of I-15, all the way to Barstow. It has also proposed HOT lanes on U.S. 101 across the San Fernando Valley.

Miami. Florida DOT is doing an investment-grade traffic and revenue study of converting the HOV lanes on I-95 in Miami-Dade County to a variable-priced HOT lane facility. Studies are under way by the Miami-Dade Expressway Authority on adding tolled express lanes to SR 836 and SR 874. And value-priced express lanes are also being studied for the Homestead Extension of Florida's Turnpike (SR 821).

Minneapolis. The Twin Cities have begun the conversion of the HOV lanes on I-394 to HOT lanes. A feasibility study is under way on possible networks of HOT or express toll lanes.

Phoenix. The Maricopa Association of Governments has recently completed a feasibility study on adding a system of interconnected HOT lanes to the Maricopa County freeway system.

San Diego. The San Diego Association of Governments (SANDAG) and Caltrans are beginning a major expansion of the existing I-15 HOT lanes, adding two additional lanes and lengthening the 8-mile facility by another 12 miles. And SANDAG now plans to add HOT lanes to three other freeways: I-5 and I-805 and SR 52.

San Francisco Bay Area. The Metropolitan Transportation Commission has included a $3 billion HOT Network in its draft 2030 long-range transportation plan. Alameda County is moving forward to implement a HOT lane on the Sunol grade of I-680, and Santa Clara County is studying the feasibility of HOT lanes on U.S. 101 and several other freeways.

Seattle. Washington State DOT has identified SR-167 as the best candidate for a pilot project to convert underutilized HOV lanes to HOT lanes. HOT lanes are also being considered as part of the planned expansion of I-405.

Washington, D.C. In summer 2002 a private consortium proposed adding two HOT lanes in each direction on 14 miles of the Washington Beltway in Virginia, from the Springfield interchange to the Dulles Toll Road. The project has received numerous endorsements from local governments and chambers of commerce. VDOT in 2003 received another unsolicited proposal, to add HOT lanes to a section of I-95 south of the Beltway. Nearby Maryland's DOT is looking into possible HOT lanes for I-270, I-495, I-95, and U.S. 50.

HOT Lanes' Potential

A recent presentation about Orange County's 91 Express Lanes provided some powerful evidence about their potential for managing traffic flow.[11] During the busiest peak hours, which are Wednesday through Friday afternoons, the two peak-direction HOT lanes carry more than 40 percent of the total SR 91 traffic, even though they constitute only 33 percent of the freeway's capacity (two lanes out of six). In other words, their throughput (vehicles/hour) is greater at 65 mph than that of the congested regular lanes, which operate in stop-and-go conditions averaging 10–20 mph. These results suggest that HOT lanes may be significantly more effective than HOV lanes at relieving freeway congestion.

That empirical finding gets analytical support from a recent UCLA Ph.D. dissertation.[12] Eugene Kim used a travel-demand model to estimate the comparative travel times that would come about by converting an existing HOV lane on a congested freeway to either (a) a general-purpose (GP) lane, (b) a HOT lane, or (c) a toll lane. He also estimated long-term (twenty-year) costs and benefits of each alternative, as well as environmental impact. In almost all cases, HOT or toll lanes provided a greater degree of fiscal benefits, consumer welfare, and environmental benefits than any other expressway investments. In most cases, Kim concludes, society would be better off if the lanes were converted. Converting to GP lanes is most defensible when HOV use is less than 7 percent of all corridor trips, and there are under 700 vehicles/hour in the HOV lane. But in almost all cases, converting to a toll lane produces greater bene-fits, primarily because doing so can preserve free-flow conditions as traffic con-tinues to grow and freeway congestion worsens. Another benefit is that toll lanes generate substantial revenues for the transportation system.

Whether to convert only to HOT (carpools still go for free) or go all the way to toll receives detailed attention in Kim's work. Intuitively, one might expect that conversion to toll would produce less delay-reduction than conversion to HOT, because fewer people will continue to carpool if those vehicles have to pay. But the modeling shows that conversion to toll produces large delay-reduction benefits "regardless of whether the conversion . . . results in a significant increase or decrease in the initial proportion of HOVs." As Kim points out, tolling indirectly preserves economic incentives to ride-share, by (1) spreading the toll over more than one person, and (2) by providing insurance against travel time uncertainty in the event that a carpool participant unexpectedly cancels—an effect already observed on the I-15 HOT lanes. Toll lanes would continue to serve large numbers of people in high-occupancy vehicles if express buses are allowed to use the toll lanes at no charge—as in our HOT Networks concept.

Bus Rapid Transit (BRT)

As its name implies, Bus Rapid Transit (BRT) is intended to mimic rail tran-sit. BRT service typically involves high-capacity buses operating on special-ized rights of way, offering frequent service. In its ultimate form, BRT makes use of enclosed stations equipped with high platforms to facilitate rapid load-ing and unloading of passengers. Fares are collected upon entering the station, not on entering the bus, in order to speed up boarding and reduce time spent at stations. The overall intent is to give bus service some of the qualities it fre-quently lacks: faster operating speeds, greater service reliability, and increased comfort and convenience, matching the quality of rail transit service—but at lower cost.

BRT guideways can be either totally separated *busways*, that is, roadways reserved exclusively for bus operation, or *managed lanes* where free-flowing traffic is maintained at all times by controlling and constraining the volume of traffic—and hence the level of congestion. The control is maintained by apply-ing eligibility criteria (as in HOV lanes, reserved for "high-occupancy vehi-cles") or through pricing (as in HOT lanes). The best examples of large-scale high-capacity BRT systems are those of Curitiba (Brazil), Bogota (Colombia), Lima (Peru), Ottawa (Canada), and Paris (France). All five systems employ separate busways reserved exclusively for express buses.

In the United States, the BRT concept, as currently interpreted by the Fed-eral Transit Administration (FTA), includes (in addition to busways) express buses operating in dedicated bus lanes on arterial streets and freeways, and buses operating in dedicated lanes on city streets, using traffic signal preemption. Exclusive busways currently exist in Pittsburgh and Miami. Buses on HOV lanes operate in Dallas, Denver, Houston, Los Angeles, the San Francisco Bay Area, Seattle, Northern New Jersey, and Northern Virginia. A ten-city Bus Rapid Transit Demonstration Program was launched by the FTA in December 1998. Demonstrations are currently under way in Boston, Charlotte, Cleveland, Eugene, Hartford, Honolulu, Miami, San Jose, and San Juan. The demonstration program does not provide funding for construction but rather focuses on obtaining and sharing information on projects being pursued by local transit agencies. A 2001 General Accounting Office (GAO) review of Bus Rapid Transit systems found at least seventeen U.S. cities planning to implement some form of BRT.[13]

Bus Rapid Transit Economics

The FTA has begun to actively promote BRT as a lower-cost alternative to building light rail systems. Carving out a bigger role for BRT is seen by the FTA as potentially improving the return on federal investment in transit. Recent studies by the GAO have found that, on a capital cost per mile basis, BRT systems average from 26 to 39 percent less than light rail systems. Specifically, the GAO has found that capital costs averaged $13.5 million per mile for busways and $9.0 million per mile for buses on HOV lanes, while light rail capital costs ranged from $12.4 million to $118.8 million per mile (all figures adjusted to 2000 dollars).[14] Figure 19.1 graphically illustrates the difference.

According to the GAO, the higher per-mile capital costs for light rail systems are attributable to several factors. First, the light rail systems contain elements not required in the BRT systems, such as track bed, signalization, communications, and an overhead electrical power distribution system. Light rail vehicles, while having higher carrying capacity than most buses, also cost more— about $2.5 million each. In contrast, bus vehicles range from $280,000 for a typical 40-foot transit bus to $420,000 for a high-capacity bus.

GAO's findings on operating costs were mixed. On the one hand, it found lower BRT operating costs per vehicle revenue hour and per revenue mile. Operating cost per passenger trip was lower on four BRT systems and higher on two others, leading to no clear conclusion on that point.

BRT Performance

Bus Rapid Transit may also include certain features that further improve its performance and service quality. For example, many BRT systems have

Figure 19.1
Capital Costs of Light Rail and Bus Rapid Transit

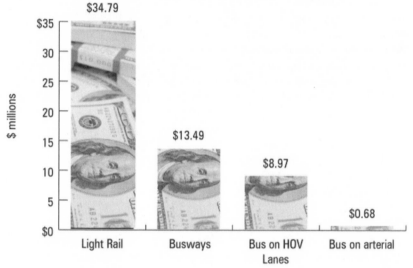

Notes: Cost escalated to fiscal year 2000 dollars.

Average Light Rail capital costs are for thirteen cities that built eighteen Light Rail lines since 1980. Busway capital costs are for nine busways built in four cities; in two cities these facilities were subsequently opened to private vehicles as HOV lanes. Capital costs for buses using HOV lanes are eight HOV facilities in five cities. Capital costs for buses on arterial streets are for three lines in two cities.

Source: "Mass Transit: Bus Rapid Transit Shows Promise," Washington, D.C.: General Accounting Office, GAO-01-984, September 2001.

enclosed bus stations where passengers pay prior to boarding the bus, thus speeding up the boarding process. Extra- wide doors facilitate prompt boarding and disembarking of riders. Intelligent transportation system (ITS) technologies maintain more consistent headways between buses and inform passengers when the next bus is coming.

The operating performance and level of service provided by BRT can thus be comparable to that of light rail transit. Indeed, in the six cities reviewed by the GAO that had both types of service (Dallas, Denver, Los Angeles, Pittsburgh, San Diego, and San Jose), BRT generally operated at higher speeds. In addition, light rail was found not to have a capacity advantage over BRT. The highest ridership on a light rail line was found on the Los Angeles Blue Line, with 57,000 riders per day, while the highest BRT ridership, also in Los Angeles, was on the Wilshire-Whittier Metro Rapid line with 56,000 riders per day. Most light rail lines in the United States carry less than half the Los Angeles Blue Line's ridership.[15]

BRT and light rail each have their merits and drawbacks. BRT generally has the advantage of greater operational flexibility than light rail. BRT's flexibility may be a potentially valuable feature for many communities with sprawling patterns of development. Light rail has the potential capability of stimulating joint development around transit stations and improving community image. Transit users also may prefer light rail service because they perceive it as faster, quieter, and less polluting. Proponents of BRT maintain that BRT can overcome this image by offering a high service quality that competes with private autos for discretionary riders.

Federal Support of BRT

Bus Rapid Transit is a relatively new concept. As of March 2002, only one of the Federal Transit Administration's twenty-nine New Starts projects with "existing, pending or proposed" grant agreements is a BRT project. Of the five New Starts projects nearing approval, again only one involves Bus Rapid Transit. Some BRT projects do not fit the exclusive right-of-way requirements of the federal New Starts Program and thus are not eligible for funding under the present federal guidelines. The BRT Demonstration Program, which involves the eleven projects noted above, does not provide funding for construction but rather focuses on obtaining and sharing information on projects being pursued by local transit agencies.

BRT is picking up substantial support within the transit community. Transit officials realize that the federal New Starts program can only fund a small fraction of the rail candidate projects currently in the pipeline. They see BRT as offering a new generation of less costly transit systems that would extend the benefits of rapid transit to a larger number of communities. The FTA expects to enter the period covered by the next reauthorization (fiscal years 2004 through 2009) with over $3 billion in outstanding New Starts grant commitments. In addition, FTA has identified five projects estimated to cost $2.8 billion that will likely be ready for grant agreements in the next two years. Even assuming that the total authorization for New Starts in the next program is higher than the current TEA-21 level ($6 billion), most of the New Starts funds will be committed early in the reauthorization period. The remaining funds would go further supporting BRT projects than costly rail projects, some of which are anticipated to require multi-billion dollar federal grants.[16]

HOT Network Specifics

For purposes of this chapter, we are defining a HOT Network as an interconnected set of limited-access lanes on an urban freeway system. These lanes may be used by buses and vanpools at no charge and by automobiles and light trucks (SUVs, pickups, etc.) upon payment of a variable toll. The prices would be varied so as to limit the number of vehicles per lane per hour to the maximum consistent with free-flow conditions. Tolling would be all-electronic, using dashboard-mounted transponders to debit prepaid toll accounts. Enforcement would be via video camera imaging of the license plates of vehicles either lacking a transponder, having an insufficient account balance, or whose accounts had expired.

Like HOV lanes, HOT Networks would be designed for relatively long-haul travel. Thus, they would have far fewer ingress and egress points than the freeways themselves. In most cases, the HOT Network would be composed of existing freeway HOV lanes (converted to operate as HOT lanes) linked with additional lanes planned as HOV but now built as HOT instead. Most of these lanes would be at-grade, like the freeway of which they are a part. But in some core portions of metro areas where right of way is very expensive (and where land takings would be politically difficult) those portions requiring lane additions would be built as elevated sections. The majority of initial HOT Networks would be configured as a single lane in each direction, separated from each other by a concrete Jersey barrier (and from adjacent general-purpose lanes by plastic pylons, as used on the 91 Express Lanes). But some portions would include two lanes in each direction and other portions—where commuting is heavily directional—would use reversible lanes.

Key to the definition of a HOT Network is its being a *network*. Unlike most of today's freeway HOV lanes, which do not make the transition from one freeway to another, our approach would provide for seamless connections at interchanges. Only a handful of transportation agencies (e.g., Orange County, California) have given priority to HOV-to-HOV connectors, because these elevated flyovers are very costly to build. But it is only these connectors that make a true network possible.

We expect that HOT Networks will attract more patronage than HOV lanes, for several reasons. First, precisely because they will be (1) uncongested and (2) networks, they will provide much greater time-saving (congestion-avoidance) benefits than today's mostly fragmentary HOV lanes. Second, they will be open to all motorists (except heavy trucks), not just to those who can arrange their lives so that they can carpool. Third, if implemented as we recommend, with strong participation by the Federal Transit Administration, they will bring about greatly increased use of such lanes by local transit agencies for express bus service. That will dramatically increase their overall person throughput compared with typical HOV lanes today.

A quantitative example will illustrate this point. Table 19.2 provides numbers illustrating the performance of what we might call typical HOV lanes in large metro areas. These are compared with an idealized high-performing HOV lane and our hypothetical HOT Network. First note the relatively good performance of the "typical" large-metro-area HOV-2 facility: 950 vehicles per hour but a person throughput of 2,275 per lane per hour (compared with perhaps 1,800–1,900 persons/lane/hour in a general-purpose lane). But note two other things about this typical case. First, there is still considerable unused vehicular capacity in this lane, of perhaps 750 vehicles/hour. This underutilization—even for what are considered well-performing HOV lanes—is a source of political opposition to HOV lanes, and is a genuine waste of capacity. Second, note the low use of the lane by express buses. In most metro areas (except Houston), it has not been a high transit-agency priority to run express buses on these lanes.

The second case is a "typical" HOV lane whose requirement has been increased to three or more persons/vehicle. Because assembling three people to carpool together on a regular basis is difficult for most people, most HOV-3 lanes are greatly underutilized. One of the handful of exceptions is the El Monte Busway on I-10 in Los Angeles County, the inspiration for the "ideal HOV-3" shown in the third column. Congestion is so bad in this corridor that a relatively large number of 3+ carpools can be maintained. But what really makes the difference in throughput in this case is the large number of express buses operated by Los Angeles County MTA and Foothill Transit using this facility.

Table 19.2
Comparative Throughput of HOV Lanes and HOT Network

	Typ. HOV-2	Typ. HOV-3	Ideal HOV-3	HOT Network
SOVs (avg.1.1 person/veh.)	0	0	0	1100
HOV-2s (avg. 2.1 person/veh.)	788	0	0	300
HOV-3s (avg. 3.2 person/veh.)	150	350	1200	200
Vanpool (avg. 7.0 person/veh.)	10	20	20	60
Express bus (avg. 35 persons/veh.)	2	3	40	40
Vehicles/hour	950	373	1260	1700
Persons/hour	2275	1365	5380	4300

The last column shows that nearly as great throughput can be achieved by the proposed HOT Network in high-demand corridors. With a comparable commitment of express bus service, the cost-sharing among carpoolers to split the toll, and active patronage by single-occupant vehicles, a full 1,700 vehicles/lane/hour can be accommodated, with passenger throughput 80 percent as high as the ideal HOV-3 case.

At this point, the question may be asked: Wouldn't it be better to seek to replicate the ideal HOV-3 case rather than shifting to the HOT Network model? The first rejoinder is that the latter model brings with it the huge benefit of toll revenue, which can help pay for the costly build-out of the system into a seamless network. Even if the ideal HOV-3 were better in principle, since it is unaffordable during the next two decades, when our metro areas are going to be choked with traffic congestion, it is of more theoretical than practical interest. Furthermore, HOV-3s are becoming a rarity. According to *Commuting in America II*, "Carpooling in America is now, fundamentally, a two-person phenomenon."[17]

Another point in favor of the HOT model is that very few transit agencies have made good use of existing HOV lanes for bus service, and there is little sign of this changing. But if Congress were to embrace the HOT Network model as an important step forward for urban transit, then the use of such networks for region-wide express bus service would be more than just a nice-sounding idea; it could well become the reality within a decade.

Another very practical advantage of the HOT Network as we have defined it is ease of enforceability. The first generation of HOT lanes in California, which lets carpools use the lanes at no charge (I-15) or at a reduced rate (91-Express) must combine electronic enforcement (transponders and video license-plate imaging) with visual inspection and deterrence by the highway patrol, as is done for HOV lanes. Enforcing one or the other is relatively straightforward, but enforcing both simultaneously is far more complicated. Patrol officers must distinguish between single-occupant vehicles legally in the restricted lanes (those with valid transponders) and those who are HOV violators. If the rules of the game are that only buses and vanpools go free—and that those vehicles, too, must have transponders—then enforcement can be almost entirely electronic, reducing both cost and operational problems (e.g., pulling over violators on what is supposed to be a high-speed express lane).

Acceptability of HOT Networks

The HOT Networks concept represents something of a departure from the past twenty years' focus on HOV lanes. HOT lanes themselves are still a relatively new idea, but those lanes still give special standing to carpools. Can this somewhat different approach to managed lanes gain enough acceptance to be implemented? We believe it can, for several reasons.

1. The public already supports HOT lanes. Commuters in the congested I-15 corridor in San Diego have had over seven years to experience or observe a HOT lane in the peak direction on that route. The project's sponsor, SANDAG, and the California DOT (Caltrans) plan to expand this project, quintupling its size from two lanes and eight miles (16 lane-miles) to four lanes and twenty miles (80 lane-miles). As part of the planning process, they carried out a major public-opinion effort, including focus groups, stakeholder interviews, intercept surveys (at bus and carpool locations), and household telephone surveys. What they found was overwhelming support, both for the existing HOT lanes and for expanding the project as the best way of dealing with congestion in the corridor. Over 88 percent of current paying customers support the existing project, as do two-thirds of other I-15 users. And majorities nearly that large support the proposed expansion.[18] This support extends, with only minor variations, across all income levels, ethnic groups, and age groups.

Strong user support has also been measured for the 91 Express Lanes.[19] In its early years, when the new capacity provided by that project led to reduced congestion in the adjacent general-purpose lanes, support among paying customers exceeded 80 percent, and general-purpose lane user support was nearly 70 percent. By 1999, after congestion had returned to the general-purpose lanes, support among non-customers in the corridor declined to 49 percent, but 72 percent of paying customers continued to express strong support.

These examples suggest that commuters understand and appreciate having the option of shifting from congested lanes to express lanes for those trips when their value of time is especially high. This support is often seen in stated-preference surveys about hypothetical HOT or express-toll lanes, generally in the 55–60 percent range.[20] But the acid test is not what people say they might do when presented with a hypothetical, but what they actually do when that possibility becomes a reality. By that standard, the two California HOT lanes have demonstrated strong public support.

2. HOT Networks will provide a significant increase in high-quality transit service at modest cost. We previously summarized GAO and FTA findings that Bus Rapid Transit on uncongested guideways can provide transit service of a quality comparable to that of light rail. And BRT is inherently less costly than light rail, according to these studies.[21] The beauty of the HOT Networks approach is that the uncongested guideway can be provided at little or no cost to the transit agency, because paying auto customers will provide the toll revenue stream needed to pay off the revenue bonds for building the network. Instead of devoting hundreds of millions of dollars to exclusive light-rail infrastructure, the transit agency can spend capital funds on a much larger fleet of express buses and related facilities. Furthermore, since the HOT Network will be built along existing freeway right of way, major controversies over land acquisition for rail right of way can be avoided. And large-scale capital investment in the HOT Network can be carried out over the span of a decade or so, rather than the twenty to thirty years needed to build out either HOV systems or rail systems under conventional, fiscally constrained long-range transportation plans. Thus, HOT Networks promise significantly more transit, much sooner, for far less transit capital expenditure.

3. Equity concerns are not justified; nearly everyone stands to gain from HOT Networks. To many people, a troubling aspect of HOT lanes or HOT Networks is the idea that they are elitist (Lexus Lanes is a common epithet). Careful thought, as well as data from the California HOT lanes, presents a rather different picture.

First, consider that all people—not just those at upper income levels—may place a higher value on their travel time under some circumstances than others. For example, a single mother with a child in daycare may consider it worth paying a $5 toll on a day she is running late after work, to avoid paying a $10 late fee. A plumber trying to get in one last appointment on a busy day may be quite happy to pay a toll to bypass congestion so as to get there in time to do the work. A family running late to catch a plane may also prefer to pay the toll rather than risk missing their flight. To presume that only the wealthy could value their time enough to pay to use a HOT Network is disrespectful of individuals' ability to make such tradeoffs for themselves. The denial of choice in transportation is discriminatory and regressive with respect to lower-income people. Those with the lowest income are the most severely harmed when they are denied such choice. The consequences of late fees or lost work are more severe for those with the lowest income.

Second, from the standpoint of social policy, consider the alternative to paying for large-scale HOV expansions via tolls. Such projects today are paid for primarily via gasoline taxes, and to an increasing degree (especially in California) by special sales taxes devoted to transportation. Both, especially the latter, are regressive taxes. By contrast, market-based tolls are a prime example of user pays. Only those who value time savings highly will voluntarily choose to pay this price. And yet in the HOT Network context, it is these people who will disproportionately be paying for the extensive new guideway for Bus Rapid Transit. To the extent that higher-income people make greater use of HOT Networks than lower-income people, this is a win-win public policy solution. In what other area of public infrastructure do we find a small fraction of the population willingly paying extra to provide a greatly improved public service?

Third, let's look at the actual data from the California HOT lanes. Evaluations of usage patterns on both the I-15 and 91 Express Lanes do show that propensity to use the lanes is roughly proportional to income quartile.[22] But the university-based evaluators in both cases noted that significant numbers of paying customers were found in every income quartile, supporting the first point noted above. Moreover, survey research data in both cases finds strong support for the idea that being able to choose, voluntarily, to pay more to bypass congestion when you decide it's worth it, is "fair." In the San Diego case, 78 percent of the lowest-income commuters in the corridor agree that "SOV drivers should be allowed to use the Managed Lanes for a fee," and 82 percent of this group favor the proposed extension of the I-15 lanes.[23]

Finally, it should be noted that while not all HOT *lanes* ensure bus service as part of the package, the HOT *Networks* concept features express bus (BRT) service as an integral part. Thus, the concern about those who cannot afford to pay the market-priced toll is misplaced. In the first place, they will still have just as many general-purpose lanes to use as before, since our proposal takes away none of these lanes. But more important, they will gain a whole new option in most metro areas—BRT on a high-speed, uncongested managed lane.

4. HOT Networks are the only urban transportation improvement that can be largely self-supporting. While the cost and revenue estimates that we develop later are very preliminary, we believe our calculations have been made conservatively; they are certainly in the right ballpark. And those calculations suggest that HOT Networks can be self-supporting to a significant degree. We know of no other large-scale planned or proposed urban transportation improvement that can make this claim. At a time when every reputable study suggests that the need for transportation capital investment greatly exceeds existing, traditional sources of funding, this is certainly good news. It means that America's largest and most congested metro areas have a new option available that offers both meaningful congestion relief and significantly improved transit service—and without the need for major new tax revenues. The funding will be largely volunteered by a subset of auto users, willing to pay for a higher quality of transportation than is now available to them.

But the financial viability of the HOT Networks approach depends critically on a majority of the vehicles being paying customers. Of the two successful HOT lanes in California, the I-15 is able to focus primarily on HOVs because it did not have to pay for its construction costs out of toll revenues. The grade-separated lanes were built using conventional fuel-tax funds and only later converted to HOT operation. Thus, they can afford to have 75 percent HOV users and 25 percent paying customers. By contrast, the 91 Express Lanes had to be built from scratch using toll revenues. In order to cover those costs, it's no surprise that the operating policy charges regular tolls to HOV-2s and half-price tolls to HOV-3s. And only 13 percent of its vehicles are HOV-3s.

These two contrasting cases illustrate the choice facing transportation policymakers. If we want to implement seamless networks of premium lanes on our major urban freeway systems—not "maybe someday, somehow" but realistically, within the current transportation improvement plan—billions of dollars in new transportation revenues must be found and dedicated to this purpose. The HOT Networks approach is the only way we can imagine of actually achieving that result.

Applying HOT Networks

In this section we illustrate the application of the HOT Networks concept in a number of America's most congested urban areas. For this purpose, we have relied on the rank-ordering presented previously in Table 19.1 of the ten most-congested metro areas as measured by TTI, using annual person-hours of delay per peak traveler as our metric. For this exercise, we have elected to omit the New York/Northeastern New Jersey metro area, because its greater population density and very high transit usage make it unique among U.S. urban areas. We have also chosen to combine the two urbanized areas in the San Francisco Bay Area (San Francisco/Oakland and San Jose) into one, since its freeway system is better thought of as a single, integrated system. Thus, we will apply the HOT Networks concept to the following eight metro areas: Los Angeles, San Francisco, Washington, Seattle, Houston, Dallas/Fort Worth, Atlanta, and Miami.

In each case, we describe the current extent of freeway HOV lanes and HOV-HOV connectors at freeway interchanges, and planned additions to the HOV system, whether funded or unfunded. Where possible, we also identify any other additions needed to link these components together into a seamless network over the principal freeways in the system. After sketching out the proposed HOT Network in this section, we will use this definition of each system to estimate its capital costs and revenue potential in the next.

Miami

Miami-Dade County has only one HOV facility in service, approximately 10 miles of concurrent-flow (one lane each direction) striped-off HOV lanes on

I-95, the area's busiest north-south artery. FDOT has a feasibility study under way on the possible conversion of these lanes to HOT lanes, including their extension southward to I-395.

Planned or potential HOV/HOT lane projects include the HOV lanes on the Palmetto Expressway (SR 826) planned by the Florida DOT. The Miami-Dade Expressway Authority has in its Five Year Work Program the planning and design of express toll lanes for its Don Shula Expressway (SR 874) and Dolphin Expressway (SR 836). These new lanes are being planned to include BRT service that will link the western part of the metro area with Miami International Airport. These lanes will connect with the proposed HOT or tolled express lanes on the Homestead Extension of Florida's Turnpike (SR 821) and a possible new north-south, all-electronic toll road—the Central Parkway from SR 112 to SR 924. With the addition of some connector links, especially at key interchanges, Miami-Dade could have a seamless HOT Network depicted in Figure 19.2.

Atlanta

The Atlanta metro area currently has 128 lane-miles of HOV facilities including sections of I-20, I-75, I-85, and the I-75/I-85 central section. The approved 2025 Regional Transportation Plan (RTP) for the Atlanta Metro Area includes approximately 262 miles of additional HOV lanes and fifty-five HOV ramps and connectors, adding additional HOV lanes on I-20, I-285, I-575, I-75, I-85, SR 316, SR 400, and U.S. 78. The development of the HOV system is currently the subject of a major study by the Parsons Transportation Group. Total cost at build-out is estimated at $3.4 billion. To this we have added 96 lane-miles worth of missing links, indicated by the dotted lines. As depicted in Figure 19.3, these additions would produce a reasonably complete HOT Network for the greater Atlanta area.

Dallas/Fort Worth

The current extent of Dallas HOV facilities totals just under 80 lane-miles. It includes the Southwest Texas Medical Center Busway, plus HOV lanes on the Love Freeway (I-35E and US 67), Stemmons Fwy (I-35E), LBJ Freeway (I-635), and I-30. The Dallas Metropolitan Transportation Plan, *Mobility 2025*, outlines a major expansion of HOV facilities for the Metroplex. The Plan identifies 397 lane-miles of new HOV lanes. Many of these HOV facilities are reversible. In several corridors, such as Interstate 635 (LBJ) and Interstate 35E (Stemmons), traffic flow is sufficiently strong in both directions to warrant two-

Figure 19.2
Miami HOT Network

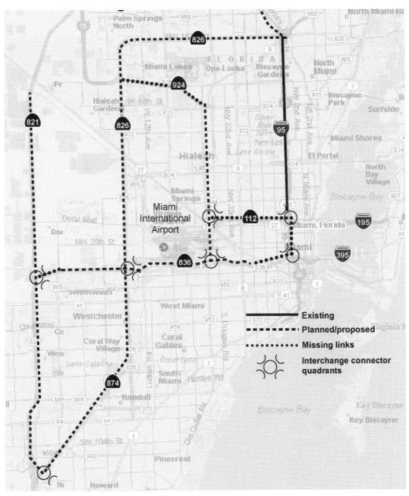

way HOV lanes. In addition to dedicated HOV lanes, the Plan also identifies future corridors likely to be built as toll roads where HOV lanes are also needed. In these corridors, the plan calls for HOV users to travel on the toll roads free or at discounted rates. *Mobility 2025* also recommends multi-lane peak-HOV lanes with off-peak express service. These facilities will be reversible in most corridors and designed to serve as express lanes for all traf-

Figure 19.3
Atlanta HOT Network

Figure 3: Atlanta
HOT Network

fic in the off-peak travel periods. The Plan includes recommendations from the recently completed I-635 (LBJ Freeway) Major Investment Study, which calls for a combination of HOV, toll, and express lanes in the corridor. Other detailed HOV recommendations are pending on-going and future major investment studies.

For purposes of this study, we have added missing links on US 75 and US 45 and on I-30, as well as a number of interchange connectors. The resulting HOT Network is shown in Figure 19.4.

Houston

Houston's current HOV facilities comprise 133 lane-miles of barrier-separated HOV lanes. Major facilities are on the Katy Freeway (I-10), Gulf Freeway (I-45), Northwest Freeway (US 290), North Freeway (I-45), and the Eastex/Southwest Freeways (US 59). The 2022 Metropolitan Transportation

Figure 19.4
Dallas HOT Network

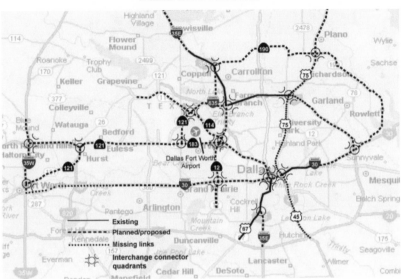

Plan/2002 Regional Mobility Update for the Houston metro area calls for an expansion of this system by 226 lane-miles, to 359 lane-miles. Major additions include extensions to the I-45, US 59 and US 290 HOV lanes and gap closures and extension on US 59. To this we have added missing links on the I-610 loop, the Katy (I-10) through downtown, and US 59 and I-45 through downtown. The downtown additions would be elevated. The resulting network is depicted in Figure 19.5.

Seattle

The Puget Sound region has an extensive core HOV system in place, with some 205 lane-miles on the region's most congested freeways including I-5, I-405, I-90, and SR 520 and SR 167.

Destination 2030 is the region's long-range transportation plan. It calls for adding additional HOV capacity to bring the total lane-miles to 329 by 2010 and to 505 by 2030. Included would be important missing links, including the SR 520 bridge, and major extensions into the Tacoma area to the south and Everett on the north. We have added a few more missing links and interchange connectors. For the additional lanes to be added to I-405, we have assumed

Figure 19.5
Houston HOT Network

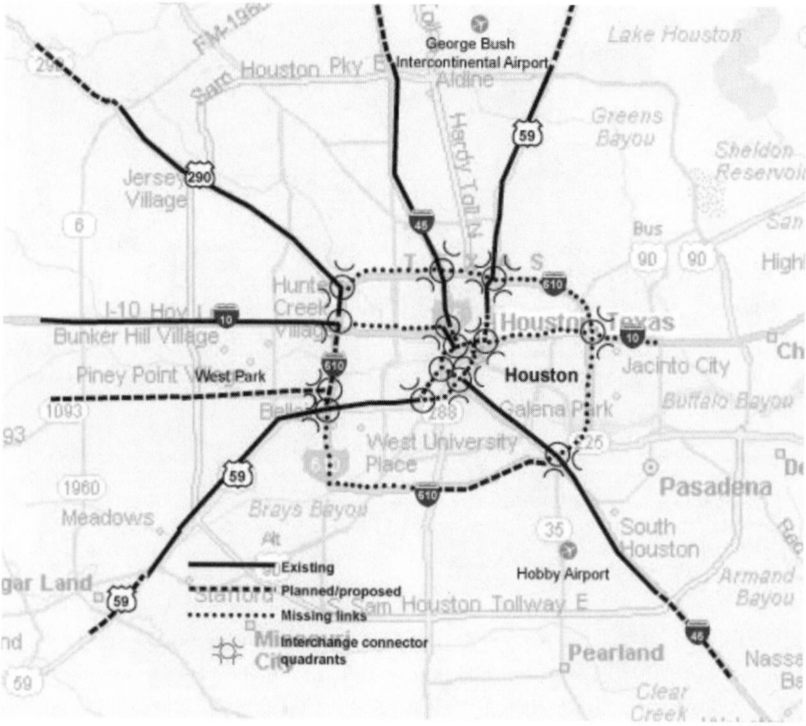

costs equivalent to adding these lanes as elevated rather than at-grade. The resulting system is depicted in Figure 19.6.

Washington, D.C.

The Washington metropolitan area's current HOV facilities comprise a total of 170 lane-miles, 134 of which are in Northern Virginia and 36 miles in Maryland. The HOV lanes are in four radial commuter corridors. They include Northern Virginia's I-95, I-66, and the Dulles Toll Road, plus Montgomery County's I-270 and US 50 in Prince George's County. The I-95 HOV facility is one of the oldest in the nation, having originally been built as a busway in the late 1960s.

The current Constrained Long Range Plan for the Washington metropolitan region includes 66 additional HOV lane-miles in Northern Virginia and 40 more

Figure 19.6
Seattle HOT Network

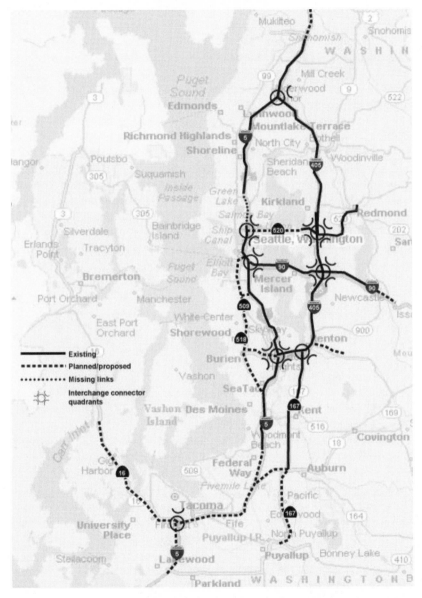

lane-miles in Maryland. Major projects in Northern Virginia include widening the existing I-95 HOV lanes (27 miles) from two to three lanes, extensions to the I-95 and I-66 lanes and HOV lanes on the Beltway (I-495), from I-95 to the Dulles Toll Road. In Maryland, major HOV projects include HOV lanes on MD 210. We have added additional lane-miles to fill in missing links in this system, which includes HOT lanes on the entire Beltway (two each way) and on I-95 all the way to Columbia, Maryland. (For the Beltway lanes, we used costs equivalent to elevated construction.) And given renewed expressions of support for the proposed Intercounty Connector in Maryland (including the new governor and county executive), we have included this facility as part of the network. Following the lead of former Governor Glendening's Transportation Solutions Group, we have assumed the entire roadway to be operated as a tolled facility.

The proposed HOT lanes on the Beltway have been the subject of a recent proposal by Fluor Daniel, one of the world's largest engineering and construction companies. The company has proposed to widen the Beltway between the Springfield Interchange (I-95) and the Dulles Toll Road with four HOT lanes, two in each direction. The project would be financed primarily with bonds underwritten by HOT lane revenue. Local and state officials have responded enthusiastically according to press reports.

Figure 19.7 depicts the potential HOT Network for the Washington, D.C. metro area.

San Francisco Bay Area

The San Francisco Bay Area has 285 freeway lane-miles of HOV facilities in service at present (plus another 50 lane-miles of expressway HOV lanes in Santa Clara County, which are not included in our calculations). The 2001 Regional Transportation Plan calls for adding 140 more lane-miles, and the 2003 Transportation Improvement Plan adds another 100 lane-miles of HOV.

This set of plans still leaves some key links without HOV facilities. We have filled these in, including 58 lane-miles of elevated capacity in such inner corridors as US 101 in San Mateo County and I-880 in Oakland. Because several major bridges (Golden Gate, San Francisco-Oakland Bay Bridge, San Mateo Bridge, etc.) constitute critical links in the freeway system and the proposed BRT network, we have also designated 47.4 lane-miles of existing bridge lanes as part of the HOT Network. Figure 19.8 depicts the completed network. That system would total 630 lane-miles.

The Bay Area's Metropolitan Transportation Commission is committed to making use of the expanded HOV network for BRT service. The $177 million initial implementation phase of the BRT system focuses on East Bay rapid bus connections to BART in the I-580 and SR 4 corridors. The initial BRT

Figure 19.7
Washington, D.C. HOT Network

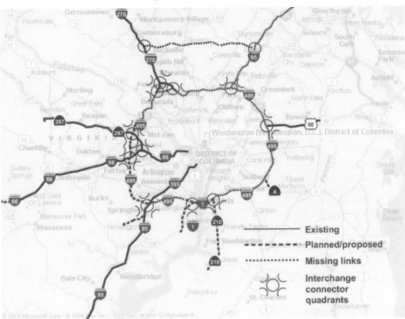

phase also includes North and East Bay routes using US 101 in Sonoma and Marin Counties, I-680 from the Benicia Bridge in the north to San Jose in the south, I-80 from Solano County to the East Bay and San Francisco, I-880 from San Leandro to San Jose, area-wide services in Santa Clara County along its freeway network, the I-280 corridor in San Mateo, and upgraded express services across most of the region's bridges. Needless to say, the much larger HOT Network proposed in Figure 19.8 would facilitate a much larger and more comprehensive BRT service than currently planned.

Greater Los Angeles

With the greatest amount and intensity of traffic congestion, as measured by TTI, Los Angeles (defined as Los Angeles and Orange Counties) also has the most extensive set of HOV facilities in the nation. The existing set of HOV facilities suggests the beginnings of a real network, especially in the Orange County portion of the region. The current long-range transportation plan's con-

Figure 19.8
San Francisco Bay Area HOT Network

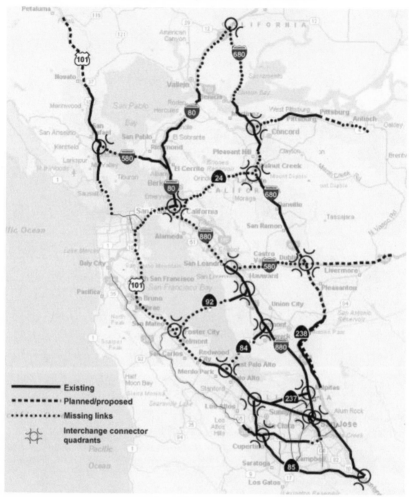

strained version would fill in a small portion of the system's missing links, focusing primarily on the addition of interchange connectors in Orange County. The unconstrained LRTP adds many more missing links and connectors, but even that plan still leaves a number of freeways without HOV lanes and over a dozen connectors unbuilt. Figure 19.9 includes all planned (constrained plus unconstrained) additions, as well as the additional links needed to complete the system as a seamless network on all but a few outlying freeways. The com-

Figure 19.9
Los Angeles HOT Network

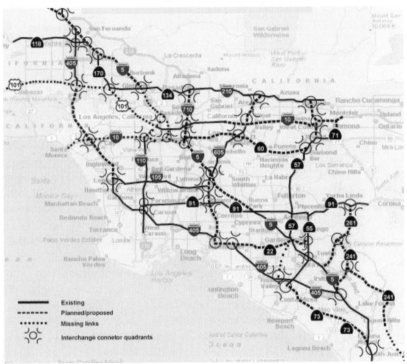

pleted system would include 1,009 lane-miles and ninety-three interchange connector quadrants.

Costs and Revenues for Proposed HOT Networks

HOT Network Capital Costs

What would a complete HOT Network cost? In this section we make order-of-magnitude estimates of the additional capital cost of building out the existing HOV facilities into the complete network shown for each of the eight metro areas. Our cost model contains four elements:

- New lanes added, at grade;
- New lanes added, elevated;

- New HOV-HOV connectors at interchanges;
- Conversion of entire system from HOV to HOT.

We first derive generic cost figures for each of these. Please note that we have not attempted to estimate capital costs for BRT components such as express buses or stations. The cost figures below are solely for the HOT Network guideway.

New, At-grade HOV/HOT Lanes

Generally, MPOs and state DOTs have tended to build the easier HOV projects first. When resources are scarce (as they generally are), an agency can have a greater sense of accomplishment if it can get a number of facilities up and running, rather than waiting many years to accumulate enough funds and overcome whatever obstacles there may be for more costly and difficult projects. For this reason, we were advised by several experts to ignore historic HOV lane costs, which have often been in the vicinity of $2–3 million per lane-mile. Three highway transportation experts we consulted—at a federal agency, a nonprofit research institute, and a major engineering/consulting firm—provided going-forward estimates of $10 million, $7.5 million, and $10 million per lane-mile, respectively. (These figures include the cost of right of way acquisition.) From the long-range transportation plans of the eight metro areas, enough projects carried cost estimates that it was possible to derive average costs per lane-mile for HOV projects planned for near-term implementation. These metro-area averages ranged from a low of $2.1 million (Houston) to a high of $10.1 million (Washington, DC). Averaging all ten of these figures (three expert and seven metro area), our overall average for new, at-grade HOV projects was $7.37 million per lane-mile, which we rounded off to $7.4 million. It should be remembered that the costs of individual projects may vary considerably, both above and below this average.

A typical at-grade stretch of a HOT Network is shown in Figure 19.10, taken from a Parsons Brinckerhoff feasibility study of adding HOT lanes to US 101 in Sonoma County, California.

New, Elevated (or Tunneled) HOV/HOT Lanes

In some corridors, there is simply no room to add additional lanes, without condemning significant high-value land alongside the existing right of way. In some of these cases, the more viable alternative is to build elevated (or tunneled) HOV lanes above (or below) the median, with limited ingress and

Figure 19.10
Typical AT-Grade HOT Network Lanes

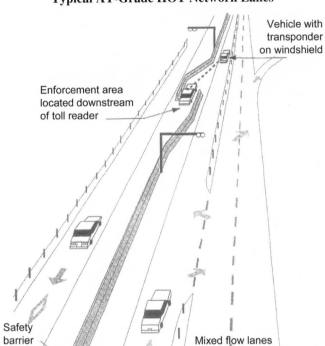

Source: Parsons Brinckerhoff, 1998.

egress, consistent with the usual HOV design concept. One example of such lanes is the Harbor Transitway in Los Angeles, added to the Harbor Freeway (I-110) during the 1990s.

Only very limited examples of actual or proposed elevated lanes were available. From these cases, we estimate a cost of $25 million per lane-mile. That would make an elevated two-lane project (one lane per direction) $50 million per mile, while an elevated four-lane project would be $100 million per mile.

These two variants of elevated HOT Network structures are illustrated in Figure 19.11.

Figure 19.11
Typical Elevated HOT Network Sections

A) One lane each direction

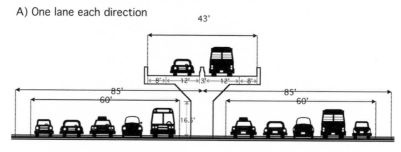

B) Two lanes each direction

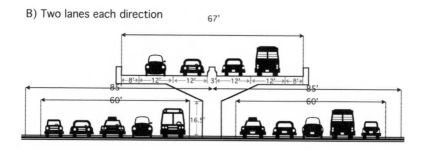

Interchange Connectors

HOT-to-HOT interchange connectors are commonly referred to as "fly-overs." They are elevated ramps that make connections from the HOT lanes of one freeway to those of another. Depending on the configuration of the interchange and the directionality of traffic flow, anywhere from one quadrant (e.g., north to east and east to north) to all four quadrants may be required. Our data from the eight metro areas showed a considerable range of estimated costs, ranging from a low of $14.6 million for one quadrant to as much as $164 million for four quadrants. We settled on $40 million per quadrant as a conservative figure for planning purposes.

HOV to HOT Conversion

Only a handful of HOV lanes have been converted to HOT lanes, but the cost elements are fairly straightforward. The difference between the two is primarily in signage and electronic toll collection equipment. Assuming (as we do) the use of variable pricing, the HOT lane will require changeable message signs to inform potential users of the price in effect at the point of use (or rather, at each decision point about use). It will also require overhead gantries with radio-frequency transceivers and video-enforcement equipment, as well as computers and fiber-optic lines linking the various elements together. For estimating purposes, we draw on a feasibility study of converting a conventional 25-mile (50-lane-mile) continuous HOV lane in Sonoma County, California into a HOT lane.[24] The added cost of doing this project as HOT instead of HOV was in the $5–7 million range. Using $6 million and dividing by 50 lane-miles gives us $.12 million per lane-mile. It should be noted that this estimate assumes the use of plastic pylon lane-separation treatment (as in Figure 19.10), rather than a concrete Jersey barrier. It is also not strictly accurate to estimate HOV-HOT conversion costs on a per-mile basis, because there are significant fixed costs, such as the computer systems and other back-office costs. However, for the large HOT lane networks we are talking about here, a per-mile figure derived from a small system should be conservative.

Estimated System Costs

Table 19.3 pulls all of these cost elements together for our eight metro areas. In each case, we use the totals from the analysis underlying Figures 19.2 through 19.9 for existing, new at-grade, and new elevated lane-miles, plus the number of connector quadrants involved. Using the average cost factors discussed above, we then calculate the cost of each proposed HOT Network. As can be seen, these costs range from a low of $2.7 billion in Miami to $10.7 billion in Los Angeles. While these numbers are large, they are in the same size range as actual or proposed rail transit networks in these and other metro areas. An important difference from those projects is that HOT Networks can generate significantly more of their own revenues.

HOT Network Revenues

Estimating the revenues from a HOT Network is challenging. In conventional toll traffic and revenue studies, the problem to be addressed is how much traffic can be attracted to the facility, given that it will be charging a toll. By contrast, in the highly congested freeway systems of interest here, there appears to be a very large unrealized demand for time savings. In the eight metro areas we are concerned with, TTI estimates the value of lost time and wasted fuel to be $30.7 billion per year. While not every rush-hour driver will be willing to pay a large toll to avoid congestion, a fraction will be.

Table 19.3

Estimated Capital Costs of Proposed HOT Networks ($Millions)

	Miami	Atlanta	Dallas/Ft. Worth	Houston	Seattle	Washington	San Francisco	Los Angeles
Existing Lane-Miles	20	128	80	133	205	170	332	624
New Lane-Miles, At-Grade	183	358	416	307	231	230	240	154
New Lane-Miles, Elevated	34	—	4	7	69	210	58	231
Total Lane-Miles	237	486	500	447	505	610	630	1009
New Connector Quadrants	11	55	40	27	19	26	32	93
HOV-HOT Conversion	$28	$58	$60	$54	$61	$73	$76	$121
At-Grade Construction	$1,354	$2,649	$3,078	$2,272	$1,709	$1,702	$1,776	$1,140
Elevated Construction	$850	$0	$100	$175	$1,725	$5,250	$1,450	$5,775
Connector Construction	$440	$2,200	$1,600	$1,080	$760	$1,040	$1,280	$3,720
Total Cost	$2,673	$4,908	$4,838	$3,580	$4,255	$8,065	$4,582	$10,756

On the 91 Express Lanes at the busiest peak times (eastbound on Friday afternoons), the two peak-direction HOT lanes attract more than 40 percent of the vehicles, despite having only 33 percent of the lane capacity (two out of six total peak-direction lanes).[25] And those paying customers are able to travel at 65 mph, while the adjacent lanes are operating under typical stop-and-go conditions. The HOT lanes operate under free-flow conditions, handling 1,700 to 1,800 vehicles per lane per hour.

Thus, we will assume that the problem for our proposed HOT Networks is to set the toll high enough that it will limit peak-hour usage to no more than 1,700 vehicles/lane/hour.[26] And because we want to ensure ample capacity for express buses and other super-HOV vehicles, we will assume a maximum of 1,600 paying vehicles/lane/hour in the peak direction during peak hours. On average, we will also assume that tolls in the non-peak direction will be low enough to attract 1,100 vehicles/lane/hour in the non-peak direction during peak hours. Thus, our average (both-direction) peak-period volume of paying customers is 1,350 vehicles/lane/hour.

The next question is what peak-hour/peak-direction toll can be charged. In a recent *Transportation Quarterly* paper, the head of the Value Pricing Pilot Program at FHWA modeled the addition of HOT lanes to a congested freeway, using peak-hour tolls of 49 cents per mile.[27] This number is at the upper end of our limited experience with HOT lanes. The highest rate on the 91 Express Lanes (peak-hour, peak-direction) at the time of our analysis was $4.75 for this 10-mile facility (47.5 cents/mile), while the maximum peak-hour, peak-direction toll on the I-15 HOT lanes was 50 cents/mile (but the average was 33 cents/mile).[28]

For purposes of revenue estimation, however, we must take into account not the highest (variable) rate charged during peak hours, but the average across all the hours defined as peak hours. And as noted above, we must also take into account that most urban freeways are at least somewhat "tidal" in nature, with much heavier traffic in one direction than the other during morning and afternoon rush hours. On 91 Express, the non-peak-direction toll during peak hours tends to be about half the peak-direction toll during those hours. Our analysis of 91 Express's toll schedule indicates that the average peak-hour, peak-direction toll was about 40 cents/mile. A recent study of proposed HOT lanes on Miami's SR 836 East-West Expressway proposed peak-period, peak-direction tolls averaging 35.2 cents/mile.[29]

It is reasonable to expect that willingness to pay a HOT-lane toll to avoid congestion would vary in proportion to the intensity of that congestion. We have used TTI's measure of delay-hours per commuter as our measure of congestion intensity. We have actual or proposed average peak-period, peak-direction tolls for HOT lanes in three metro areas: Los Angeles (Orange County), San Diego, and Miami. If we use those as markers for the upper and lower ends of the range of peak tolls for our eight metro areas, we can fill in intermediate values for the remaining metro areas, proportional to the intensity of congestion, as is done in Table 19.4. Note that we have also assumed, conservatively, that the average toll charged during peak hours in the non-peak direction is 50 percent of the rate charged in the peak direction in the two most congested cities, 40 percent as high in the next two cities, and 30 percent as high in the remaining cities. Since some of the freeways in our eight metro areas are congested in both directions during peak hours, our assumptions will tend to understate actual revenue.

Using the number of peak hours per weekday, the average peak period toll that applies across those hours, and the number of lane-miles in the HOT Network, we can compute the revenues generated during peak hours on weekdays for each of the HOT Networks. This is done in Table 19.5. Multiplying by 250 weekdays per year gives us annual revenue from peak operations. Like 91 Express, our proposed HOT Networks would also operate at non-peak times, charging much lower rates but offering a perceived higher quality of service for longer-distance trips. The 91 Express lanes generate between 20 and 25 percent of their revenue from non-peak period trips, on weekdays plus weekends and

Table 19.4
Proposed HOT Lane Peak-Period Tolls

Metro Area	Annual Delay-hours per Commuter	Number of Peak Hours per Weekday	Peak Direction Peak Toll per Mile	Non-Peak Direction Peak Toll per Mile	Average Peak Period Toll per Mile
Los Angeles	136	7	$.40	$.20	$.30
San Francisco	92	6	$.38	$.19	$.285
Washington	84	6	$.37	$.148	$.259
Seattle	82	6	$.37	$.148	$.259
Houston	75	5	$.36	$.11	$.235
Dallas	74	5	$.36	$.11	$.235
San Jose	74	5	$.36	$.11	$.235
Atlanta	70	5	$.35	$.10	$.225
Miami	69	5	$.35	$.10	$.225
San Diego	51	5	$.33	$.10	$.215

holidays.[30] Using 22.5 percent for non-peak revenue, we can then derive the total annual revenue for each network.

The revenue number for each system is the *baseline* annual revenue. This is the annual revenue several years after the complete network is opened and the initial user-familiarization period has transpired (sometimes called the "ramp-up" period for a new toll facility). Since we are proposing prices that will vary in accordance with demand, so as to manage the flow of traffic in these lanes, as overall traffic on the metro area's freeway system continues to grow, the prices on the HOT Network would increase, accordingly. The increased revenues would provide a source of funding for *operating costs* and ongoing maintenance, to the extent that they are more than needed to service the debt on toll revenue bonds issued to pay for build-out of the network.

As a very rough rule of thumb, based on observation of toll revenue bond issuance on other projects, it seems safe to estimate that a baseline annual toll revenue stream can support a toll revenue bond issue of approximately 10 times the amount of that baseline annual toll revenue. We have used that rule of thumb in Table 19.5. Comparing the size of the bond issue with the estimated cost of each system (from Table 19.3), we see that they generally could not be fully supported by toll revenue bonds. The San Francisco and Los Angeles networks come the closest to being self-supporting. At the low end of self-support, both Miami and Atlanta still have to build the large majority of their systems,

Table 19.5
Estimated Revenues of Proposed HOT Networks

	Miami	Atlanta	Dallas/Ft. Worth	Houston	Seattle	Washington	San Francisco	Los Angeles
Vehicles/lane/Hour	1350	1350	1350	1350	1350	1350	1350	1350
Average peak toll	$0.2250	$0.2250	$0.2350	$0.2350	$0.2590	$0.2590	$0.2600	$0.3000
Peak hours/day	5	5	5	5	6	6	6	7
Lane miles	237	486	500	447	505	610	630	1009
Peak revenue/day	$359,944	$738,113	$793,125	$709,054	$1,059,440	$1,279,719	$1,326,780	$2,860,515
Peak revenue/year	$89,985,937.50	$184,528,125	$198,281,250	$177,263,438	$264,859,875	$319,929,750	$331,695,000	$715,128,750
Off-peak revenue	$26,095,922	$53,513,156	$57,501,563	$51,406,397	$76,809,364	$92,779,628	$96,191,550	$207,387,338
Total revenue/year	$116,081,859	$238,041,281	$255,782,813	$228,669,834	$341,669,239	$412,709,378	$427,886,550	$922,516,088
Size of bond issue	$1,160,818,594	$2,380,412,813	$2,557,828,125	$2,286,698,344	$3,416,692,388	$4,127,093,775	$4,278,865,500	$9,225,160,875
Cost of Network	$2,673,000,000	$4,908,000,000	$4,838,000,000	$3,580,000,000	$4,255,000,000	$8,065,000,000	$4,582,000,000	$10,756,000,000
Percent Covered by Revenue Bonds	43%	49%	53%	64%	80%	51%	93%	86%

Summary Data:

Total Annual Revenues	$2,943,357,041
Total Bonds	$29,433,570,413
Total Cost	$43,657,000,000
Percent Covered	67.42%

and their smaller populations mean less toll-paying traffic. Overall, the fraction that we estimate could be paid for via toll revenue bonds ranges from a low of 43 percent (Miami) to a high of 93 percent (San Francisco). Over the eight metro areas combined, we estimate that toll revenue bonds could pay for about 67 percent of the cost of creating the networks.

In actual practice, each metro area's HOT Network would be unlikely to come about as a single huge project. Rather, individual projects would be developed, each with its own capital costs and potential toll revenues (even though the whole network would operate as an integrated system, once completed). Hence, even in those metro areas where the overall network could ultimately be self-supporting from toll revenues, a very meaningful role could be played by start-up and supplemental funding (and credit support) from the federal highway and transit agencies, as discussed below.

Policy Changes Needed

The approach recommended in this chapter is to combine two innovative concepts—High-Occupancy Toll (HOT) lanes and Bus Rapid Transit (BRT)—to create seamless metropolitan-wide networks of HOT lanes. They would serve as guideways for Bus Rapid Transit and provide a faster congestion-free travel option to toll-paying motorists. To implement this vision, we recommend that Congress authorize a multiyear program of HOT Network development to be jointly implemented by the Federal Highway Administration and the Federal Transit Administration. Specifically, the aim of the program would be to encourage states and metropolitan jurisdictions to:

1. Incrementally create networks of premium toll lanes (HOT Networks) by extending, linking, interconnecting, and filling in gaps in existing metropolitan HOV systems;

2. Implement Bus Rapid Transit services on the completed parts of the HOT Networks as soon as practicable; and

3. Develop innovative public-private financing arrangements involving tax-exempt toll revenue bonds, to help fund a significant portion of the capital cost of these projects.

Funds to support the federal portion of the program would come from special allocations from the FHWA's National Highway System (NHS) program (or, alternatively from the Surface Transportation Program), and from the FTA's Section 5309 New Starts program. The proportion of funds to be contributed by each agency would be determined by congressional action in the authorizing legislation. Eligible expenses under this program would include right-of-way acquisition (where needed); planning, design, and construction of premium toll lane facilities and ancillary bus stations; and acquisition of BRT rolling stock. The Section 5309 funds could only be used for transit-related expenses (such as BRT stations and rolling stock). The federal grant support could be supplemented, as needed, by long-term Transportation Infrastructure Finance and Innovation Act (TIFIA) loans.

Up to eight candidate metropolitan areas would be selected from among applicants for participation in the program. Candidates would be chosen according to a set of criteria established jointly by FHWA and FTA. The criteria would include the level of congestion (as measured by the TTI index), the ability to develop a meaningful area-wide network of premium toll lanes, the existence of a sound financial plan, and local political consensus.

Full Funding Grant Agreements (FFGA), modeled after those used in the FTA's New Starts Program, would be negotiated with each successful candidate jurisdiction. A Full Funding agreement would represent the federal government's commitment to participate financially in a HOT Network project up to an agreed dollar amount. The federal commitment would be subject to annual congressional appropriations. Each grant agreement would establish the terms and conditions of federal financial participation in the project including the maximum level of federal financial assistance and the minimum level of service (LOS) to be maintained in the premium lanes. (The setting of toll rates would thus be governed by the requirement to maintain the specified LOS). The grant agreement would also define the project's scope, its schedule, timetable for completion, costs, and disposition of any excess toll revenues. Since the Full Funding Grant Agreement limits the maximum federal funding for a project, the grantee would be responsible for any project increases that might occur after the agreement is signed, unless the agreement was amended.

State/Local Implementation Issues

States and metro areas may not be in a position to take advantage of a federal HOT Networks program if their current laws are not conducive to this new kind of transportation infrastructure. At least three areas need to be reviewed to be sure that such projects can be carried out.

First is the ability to charge tolls that can be used as a revenue stream to pay off toll revenue bonds issued to build the network. In many states (e.g., California) there is no current legal authority to charge a toll to use any portion of the state highway system. The two existing HOT lane projects in California each came about via special project-specific legislation. What some states (e.g., Florida, Minnesota, Texas) have done is to enact general enabling statutes that permit tolls to be charged, either in general or specifically for the purpose of HOT lane projects.

The second requirement may be enabling legislation (possibly combined with the toll-charging authority) that permits the conversion of existing HOV lanes to HOT lanes. In some states the definition of HOV lanes may be embodied in a statute spelling out occupancy requirements and permitting, for example, only car-pools of two or more people (plus transit and emergency vehicles) to use such lanes. It would be advisable to amend such legislation to convert the concept from HOV lanes to "managed lanes," a term introduced several years ago by the Texas Transportation Institute.[31] As TTI uses the term, a managed lane is distinguished from a general-purpose lane by the fact that it is limited to certain categories of vehicle and employs various operating strategies to move traffic more efficiently. Enabling legislation should give regional and local authorities the option of choosing the types of managed lane approaches that best meet their needs—which could include HOV lanes with various occupancy requirements, HOT lanes with various occupancy requirements (including the super-HOV requirement we propose in this chapter), toll express lanes, truck/bus-only lanes, etc.

The third type of legislation is a general enabling statute for public-private partnerships. While HOT lanes and HOT Networks can be developed and operated by existing transportation or toll agencies, they are also prime candidates for public-private partnerships (PPPs). The private sector is skilled at marketing services to various market segments, a prime requirement with HOT lanes and HOT Networks. The private sector is good at making use of advanced technology, such as electronic tolling that varies in real time. It is also very good at fast-track project delivery, using techniques such as design-build that are still uncommon in much of the public sector. And with the ability to finance at least the majority of the capital costs via toll revenue bonds, HOT Network projects lend themselves very well to tapping the private capital markets.

Over the past decade or so, nearly two dozen states have enacted PPP laws for transportation infrastructure. A few, like California's AB 680, were for pilot projects only. Several others, like Florida's (prior to a 2004 revision), were never used because of onerous provisions (in Florida's case, the requirement that each project be approved by a bill to be enacted [or not] by the state legislature). Far more successful have been the PPP laws in Texas and Virginia, which provide a welcome degree of flexibility. In addition to being general enabling laws, they include such key features as:

- Permitting projects to be approved by either the state DOT or any city, county, or other level of government with transportation responsibilities;

- Allowing for both government-initiated projects (via the issuance of an RFP) and private sector-initiated projects (via procedures for accepting unsolicited proposals);
- Allowing for a mix of public and private funding (as would be required for the HOT Network proposals outlined in this chapter).

PPP enabling statutes allow the responsible unit of government to select, via a competitive process, a private-sector team to finance, design, build, and operate the project over a long enough term to recover its investment with a reasonable rate of return. Globally, such franchises typically run for between twenty and fifty years, depending on the project. The franchise agreement deals with limits on either toll rates or the rate of return to the investors; the latter approach is relevant for HOT lane projects, since pricing must remain unconstrained in order to perform its traffic management function.

Potential HOT Networks Coalition

New policy ideas may look good on paper, but they can only become reality if sufficient support exists to constitute a critical mass. In this section, we look at the potential for a political coalition in favor of HOT Networks.

Mass Transit Supporters

The emergence of Bus Rapid Transit (BRT) as a new form of transit is one of the most important developments in decades. It represents a realization, by the FTA as well as by many transit supporters, that in many situations the creation of new rail systems (mostly light rail) is simply too costly to be feasible. We noted earlier that the FTA is currently confronting a situation in which it has far more light rail New Start requests than it can possibly fund. Yet BRT offers the potential of providing service of comparable quality to light rail at a fraction of the capital cost.

In order to provide high-quality BRT service, it must operate for as much of each trip as possible either on exclusive right of way (e.g., busways on arterials) or on a freeway lane that is managed so as to remain uncongested. The latter is what HOT Networks offer to a well-planned BRT express-bus system. And HOT Networks provide the freeway portion of this uncongested guideway at modest cost to the metro transit system because auto drivers willing to pay market-priced tolls will cover the majority of the capital costs.

Traditional HOV lanes have always received equivocal support from some in the mass transit community. Some segments of this community recall that a number of today's HOV lanes began as exclusive busways, and were only opened up to carpools due to political pressure caused by the large amount of unused capacity on these busways.[32] That was true even of America's most successful combined transit/HOV facilities, the El Monte Busway on I-10 in Los Angeles and the Shirley Busway on I-95 in Northern Virginia. In one sense, our proposal calls for a return to the earlier concept, in which the HOT Networks have as a major purpose the provision of uncongested guideways for extensive BRT service. But instead of using the remaining capacity for non-paying (carpool) vehicles, our proposal instead calls for charging all cars and light trucks that opt to use these premium lanes. That is necessary both to generate the funds needed to pay for the network and to manage traffic flow to preserve the time-saving advantage necessary for high-quality express bus service. This is a new way of thinking about transit and automobiles, but we believe the benefits are large enough that many members of the transit community will embrace it.

Smart Growth Advocates

Although HOT lanes have sometimes been opposed on smart-growth grounds (e.g., by former Maryland governor Parris Glendening), that should not be taken as a definitive verdict on HOT Networks by those concerned with transportation, land use, growth, and social justice issues. A countervailing example is the Bay Area Transportation and Land Use Coalition, which includes nearly ninety such organizations in the San Francisco metro area. In its major report, *World Class Transit for the Bay Area*, the Coalition endorsed a regional express bus system that relied on HOV lanes, but with the potential for tolls where it would increase efficiency on the road.[33]

Reviewing ongoing plans and proposals from the Metropolitan Planning Commission and various agencies, the authors noted the very high cost of additional heavy and light rail projects, stating that "express buses would be faster, less expensive, available sooner, and could carry many more people than new rail extensions." Such express bus service "will bypass traffic by using the Bay Area's growing High-Occupancy Vehicle (bus/carpool) lane system." Of particular significance, the authors note the importance of keeping those lanes free flowing by limiting the number of vehicles, while conversely avoiding the waste of highway space inherent in a lot of unused capacity:

> One way to avoid this [too much or too little traffic in these lanes] is to allow single occupancy vehicles to use the bus/carpool lanes for a fee, as has successfully been done in southern California. Tolls would rise as congestion in mixed-flow lanes increased to keep traffic flowing smoothly on the bus/carpool lane. Electronic signs would indicate the current toll, allowing solo drivers to decide if they wanted to enter the bus/carpool lane. Fares would be collected automatically and electronically so that cars would not have to stop.[34]

To be sure, this is just one report of one organization. Its proposal would still permit carpools to use the lanes at no charge, as in traditional HOV lanes. And where there are already four lanes in each direction on a freeway, the Coalition called for conversion of a general-purpose lane to HOV or HOT, rather than construction of a new lane. Yet the trade-off here is straightforward. The enormous cost of adding missing links to the existing HOV system, especially the freeway-to-freeway connectors needed for seamless express bus service, is so large that development of such a network via traditional means would take two to three more decades (as indicated in the regional transportation plans we reviewed above). But with the peak-period toll revenues available by charging all but super-HOVs to use the lanes, enough capital could be raised to complete the network within a decade.

Environmental Groups

Creating a HOT Network inherently involves adding lane-miles and interchange connectors to a metro area's freeway system. For that reason, despite its benefits for transit and mobility, some environmental groups will be unable to support the idea. But that is not the end of the story.

Several environmental groups have actively supported HOT lanes, even where implementation involved the addition of highway capacity. One case in point is Environmental Defense (ED). That organization supported the development of the 91 Express Lanes, which involved the addition of over 40 lane-miles of new capacity in the congested SR 91 corridor in Orange County, as well as the introduction of HOT lanes on US 50 in Maryland. The organization's support stemmed from its underlying goal of moving toward a system in which drivers pay directly for road use by means of pricing that reflects the cost of providing peak-period capacity. ED has also supported the I-15 HOT lanes project in San Diego, and it has proposed several HOT lanes projects in the San Francisco Bay Area. In the Washington, D.C. metro area, ED has consistently supported HOT lane proposals made by citizen groups and various advisory committees, and it has testified in their favor on Capitol Hill. ED has also stressed the importance of having adequate transit service in place where such pricing is used.

Several other environmental groups have endorsed "congestion pricing" in general, for similar reasons. Their support should not be ruled out for HOT Networks, given the concept's large benefits for transit and potentially positive impact on emissions.

The emissions question was studied by UCLA transportation researcher Eugene Kim. In his Ph.D. dissertation on HOT lanes, Kim modeled the potential conversion of an HOV lane on a congested freeway to either a general purpose lane, a HOT lane, or a tolled express lane, using a deterministic travel-demand model to estimate comparative travel times.[35] For his emissions analysis, he then used a model widely employed in California[36] to compare emissions of ROG, NOx and CO for each case. Kim's conclusion was that the tolled express lane (which is what our HOT Network proposal involves) would produce greater environmental benefits than continuing the lane as HOV:

> In terms of emissions, the baseline "no action" HOVL case produces a greater output of ROG, NOx, and CO than converting to either GPL [general purpose lane] or toll lane. Of the two competing investment alternatives, converting to toll lane will provide greater reduction [in emissions] than converting to general purpose use. (p. 245)

> A toll lane provides the largest emission reductions because it eliminates some vehicle trips (like an HOVL) while reducing congested conditions more effectively than a GPL, and partially addresses the effects of latent demand. (p. 249)

Business Leadership

Traffic congestion of the magnitude encountered in America's large metro areas puts those areas at a competitive disadvantage. In such locations, employers often must offer higher compensation to offset the poor quality of the commuting experience (and the transportation system, more generally). TTI estimates the annual cost of congestion—just in wasted fuel and people's time—at from $1.3 billion in Miami to $14.6 billion in greater Los Angeles. Projections of future congestion in these regions suggest that lost time may increase at a greater rate than personal income over the next several decades. Such considerations may well lead the business community to support the kind of large-scale efforts to improve metro-area transportation that HOT Networks represent. Previous major transportation investments—urban freeways in the 1960s and urban rail transit in the 1980s and 1990s—depended critically on support from business leadership in the metro areas in question. Business leaders may come to see HOT Networks as the next logical step in improving their region's competitiveness.

Auto Clubs

The record of automobile clubs on HOT lanes is mixed. Traditionally, auto clubs have been opposed to greater use of tolls on grounds of double taxation (i.e., paying both a toll and a fuel tax to use the same stretch of highway). And when HOT lanes were being debated in Maryland in 2001, one of the most outspoken opponents was the American Automobile Association's Mid-Atlantic region. However, in 2002, when HOT lanes were proposed for a section of the Washington Beltway in Virginia, that same spokesperson had a far more moderate reaction, telling the *Washington Post* that, "[T]he book is still open as to whether pricing these things really works." And he added that Triple A realizes the need for improved roads and new ways of paying for them, acknowledging that, "The time is probably here when the piper has to be paid."[37]

In Los Angeles, the Auto Club of Southern California has been guardedly supportive of HOT lanes. That organization was one of over sixty participants in a task force, funded by the Federal Highway Administration, to explore the possibilities for using pricing mechanisms to deal with congestion and emissions on the Los Angeles freeway system. That task force's main recommendation was that congestion pricing should be introduced via HOT lanes on the most congested freeways. The Auto Club supported that recommendation, clarifying its understanding that existing general-purpose lanes would not be converted to HOT lanes; rather, the HOT lanes would be developed via some combination of converting existing HOV lanes and adding new purpose-built HOT lanes.[38] More recently, this group has supported "further research and demonstration projects of direct road-use pricing."[39]

A more broadly based coalition of highway users, the American Highway Users Alliance, though it has not taken a formal position on HOT lanes, has indicated support for the concept of HOT Networks.[40]

Transportation Builders

An obvious member of a pro-HOT Networks coalition would be organizations representing public works construction firms, such as the American Road & Transportation Builders Association. While such groups already support more investment in highway and transit projects, a program of completing HOT Networks in major metro areas would mean that significantly more projects would be available for their members to build over the next decade, thanks to the availability of a new funding source, the toll revenues.

Pricing Advocates

There is a small but well-connected network of transportation planners and researchers who believe that direct pricing of road use at the time and place of use is a better long-term approach than continued reliance on fuel taxes. Their numbers include consultants at engineering and research firms, academic transportation economists, researchers at the Transportation Research Board and various think tanks, and transportation planners at MPOs, state DOTs, and the Federal Highway Administration and Federal Transit Administration. While not possessing much lobbying clout, this informal network of pricing supporters seems likely to respond favorably to the HOT Networks concept as a politically feasible way forward for urban road pricing. Their support could be very helpful in gaining respectability for the idea among opinion leaders.

Conclusions and Recommendations

Today's HOV lanes represent a valiant but thus-far unsuccessful effort to address traffic congestion in America's large metro areas. Despite many billions worth of capital investment, HOV lanes have failed to increase the fraction of commute trips made by carpool, even in places like Los Angeles where many HOV lanes are well utilized. Nor has their potential been used to provide extensive express bus service (with a few notable exceptions). And transit's commuter mode share has also continued to decline in most metro areas (again, with some notable exceptions).

This report suggests a new approach. The two California HOT lane projects have demonstrated the power of variable pricing to manage traffic flow under peak-demand conditions. They have also demonstrated that significant monetary demand exists for faster rush-hour trips, with the potential to produce large annual revenue streams. Those revenue streams could be the basis for issuing toll revenue bonds to finance the build-out of today's fragmented HOV facilities into seamless networks of premium lanes. Managing those lanes via market pricing would ensure that they operate uncongested, at high throughput, over the long term. The resulting network would provide a high-speed guideway for extensive express Bus Rapid Transit (BRT) service.

Our quantitative analysis suggests that a HOT Network approach along these lines could produce the extensive, seamless network of limited-access lanes only dreamed of in the "unconstrained" thirty-year plans of MPOs. These hugely beneficial networks could be in place in ten years, rather than thirty or more. And they could be largely paid for not with scarce federal, state, and local transportation funds but with monies willingly provided by those whose time makes it worth their while to pay for premium service during rush hours. Greatly benefiting from their largesse would be millions of transit riders, who would gain an extensive new BRT service spanning the whole metro area.

The tradeoff for achieving these good things is to change the operating concept of these systems of limited-access lanes. Carpools (which, in fact, are mostly "fam-pools") can no longer be allowed to use this premium capacity without paying for it. Only super-high-occupancy vehicles will get a free ride on the HOT Network. That will ensure enough saleable capacity to produce the needed toll revenue streams to cover the lion's share of the system's cost. In other words, this means adopting the business model of the 91 Express Lanes rather than that of the I-15 Express Lanes. The former is a set of toll lanes on which certain HOV users can drive at a discount; the latter is an HOV facility on which certain paying customers can drive for a fee.

To some this may seem to be a difficult trade-off, but our assessment is that the gains far outweigh the losses. Those gains include major investment in much-needed urban transportation infrastructure without drawing heavily on existing public-sector funding sources, a major expansion of high-quality transit service, and the availability of real congestion relief, when it really matters, to every driver in the metro area in question.

In summer 2005, Congress passed SAFETEA-LU, reauthorizing the federal Surface Transportation Program. Although the measure expands opportunities for HOT lane and HOT Network projects by further relaxing federal limits on tolling and on converting HOV lanes, it failed to create a joint FHWA/FTA program to foster the creation of HOT Networks, as recommended in this chapter. Despite this failure, transportation planners in congested metro areas may move forward on their own, as Houston is doing by adding such a project to the Katy Freeway.

Notes

1. David Schrank and Tim Lomax, *2003 Urban Mobility Report* (College Station: Texas Transportation Institute, Texas A&M University, September 2003).
2. Ibid, p. 33.
3. "Operational Characteristics of Selected Freeway/Expressway HOV Facilities," available at www.fhwa.dot.gov. This number does not include exclusive busways.
4. Table 14, "Capital Expense by Mode, Millions of Dollars," available at www.apta.org.
5. Gordon J. Fielding and Daniel B. Klein, *High Occupancy/Toll Lanes*, Policy Study No. 170 (Los Angeles: Reason Foundation, November 1993).
6. Robert W. Poole, Jr. and C. Kenneth Orski, *Building a Case for HOT Lanes*, Policy Study No. 257 (Los Angeles: Reason Public Policy Institute, April 1999).
7. Benjamin G. Perez and Gian-Claudia Sciara, *A Guide for HOT Lane Development* [Peer Review Draft], Parsons Brinckerhoff, Inc. (Washington, D.C.: Federal Highway Administration, July 2002), p. 80.
8. Highway engineers have defined five "levels of service" for traffic flow on freeways, ranging from A (completely free flow at low traffic volumes) to F (severe congestion with stop-and-go conditions).
9. R. J. Zuelsdorf, E. J. Regan et al., "I-15 Managed Lanes Project, San Diego, California, USA," Wilbur Smith Associates, paper presented at IRF Asia Pacific Roads Conference, Sydney, September 2002.
10. Edward Sullivan, *Continuation Study to Evaluate the Impacts of SR 91 Value-Priced Express Lanes, Final Report*, prepared for California Department of Transportation (San Luis Obispo: Cal Poly State University, December 2000).
11. Greg Hulsizer, "91 Express Lanes Update," presentation at Value Pricing Partners Workshop, sponsored by Federal Highway Administration, July 9–10, 2002.
12. Eugene Kim, "HOT Lanes: A Comparative Evaluation of Costs, Benefits, and Performance" (Los Angeles: University of California, 2000) (available online at www.uctc.net).

13. General Accounting Office, "Bus Rapid Transit Shows Promise," Washington, D.C.: GAO Report 01-984, September 2001.
14. Testimony of John H. Anderson, Jr., director, Physical Infrastructure, GAO, before the Subcommittee on Highways and Transit, House Transportation and Infrastructure Committee, June 20, 2002, GAO Report 02-840T.
15. GAO-02-840T, op. cit.
16. General Accounting Office, "FTA's New Starts Commitments for FY 2003," Washington, D.C.: GAO-02-603, April 2002.
17. Alan Pisarski, *Commuting in America II* (Washington, D.C.: Eno Transportation Foundation, 1996), p. 61.
18. Zuelsdorf, Regan, et al., op. cit.
19. Edward Sullivan, op. cit.
20. Thomas J. Higgins, "Congestion Pricing: Public Polling Perspective," *Transportation Quarterly* 51, 2, Spring 1997.
21. See pp. 16-24 of GAO-01-984, op. cit., for a discussion of the comparative capital and operating costs of BRT and light rail.
22. Edward Sullivan, op. cit., and Janusz Supernak et al., *I-15 Congestion Pricing Project, Monitoring and Evaluation Services: Task 13, Phase II Year Three Overall Report* (San Diego: Department of Civil and Environmental Engineering, San Diego State University Foundation), prepared for San Diego Association of Governments (SANDAG), Sept. 24, 2001.
23. Zuelsdorf et al., op. cit.
24. Parsons Brinckerhoff Quade and Douglas, Inc., "Final Report: Sonoma County U.S. 101 Variable Pricing Study," Oakland: Metropolitan Transportation Commission, June 6, 1998.
25. Greg Hulsizer, op. cit.
26. This is the maximum flow consistent with free-flow operations in a single lane, which would be the case for many of the HOT lanes making up the initial networks. Somewhat greater flows can be handled with two-lane facilities, but our calculations are all based on a maximum of 1,700/hour.
27. Patrick DeCorla-Souza, "The Long-Term Value of Value Pricing in Metropolitan Areas," *Transportation Quarterly* 56, 3, Summer 2002.
28. Zuelsdorf, Regan, et al., op. cit.
29. Wilbur Smith Associates, "MDX Systemwide Traffic and Revenue Update Study," Miami: Miami-Dade Expressway Authority, March 2001.
30. Email from 91 Express Lanes General Manager Greg Hulsizer to Robert Poole, September 30, 2002.
31. Tina Collier and Ginger Daniels Goodin, "Developing a Managed Lanes Position Paper for a Policy-Maker Audience," Project Bulletin 4160-5B, College Station, TX: Texas Transportation Institute, September 2002.
32. See, for example, Vukan Vuchic et al., "The Bus Transit System: Its Underutilized Potential," Washington, D.C.: Federal Transit Administration, May 1994.
33. Stuart Cohen (ed.), *World Class Transit for the Bay Are* (Oakland, CA: Bay Area Transportation and Land Use Coalition, January 13, 2000).
34. Ibid, p. 20.
35. Eugene J. Kim, "HOT Lanes: A Comparative Evaluation of Costs, Benefits, and Performance" (Ph.D. diss., University of California, Los Angeles, 2000).
36. EMFAC 2000.

37. Michael D. Shear, "Toll Plan Proposed to Widen Beltway," *Washington Post*, July 13, 2001.

38. REACH Task Force, "Final Report & Recommendations for Regional Market-Based Transportation Pricing," Los Angeles: Southern California Association of Governments, January 22, 1997.

39. Automobile Club of Southern California, *The Quiet Crisis* (Los Angeles: Automobile Club of Southern California, 2002), p. 44.

40. Personal communication from AHUA president William Fay to Robert Poole.

20

The Way Forward to the Private Provision of Public Roads

Peter Samuel

Introduction

Roads have become the western analog of the dysfunctional Russian super-markets of the Soviet era. Empty store shelves, the hoarding and queues that formed on rumors of new shipments, the surly store clerks . . . they were all the inevitable byproducts of non-functioning markets. So with roads. The shortage of road space for cars, and the resulting stop-and-go traffic throughout the world are similarly a predictable byproduct of market-defying government monopolies. Like the price of bread in Soviet Russia, the charges for the use of state roads depend on politics more than on economics or finance. Politicians benefit by being in charge of how highway funds are spent, but they don't want to be blamed for inflating road charges. So they tend to price roads in a way that best conceals their costs—with gasoline taxes, license fees, sales taxes, and the like.

Such charges provide no way of rationing scarce peak-hour capacity. They provide no feedback to the service providers as to what combinations of service and price customers want. As a result, road service is a one-size-fits-all affair and any suggestion of a differentiated offering provokes outbursts of egalitarian rhetoric and posturing about "equity." Moreover, being monopolists, the road service providers have little incentive to manage their assets efficiently. Indeed, as shown by John Semmens in chapter 2, perverse incentives are often at work. The worse the congestion on the roads the more likely are their political masters to bite the fiscal bullet and provide their highway departments with larger budgets. In order to assuage public anger, some governmental transportation departments—in the UK, for example—now discourage new road construction, saying it will only "encourage more traffic." Many have given up

501

on new construction and concentrate on management and tweaking the system they inherited.

However, this lackluster government ownership and operation of roads is not preordained. Governments have always been involved in roads, but the extent of their involvement has varied greatly. The Romans built them basically for military purposes, so they could move their legions around the empire efficiently. But in the age of animal power it was difficult to raise tax money to support roads. Tax the fuel? Rather tough in the days when the fuel was hay, water, and whatever else the horses, mules, and bullocks ate. Traditionally, adjacent property owners and local people were expected to maintain nearby roads. Many roads were maintained by compulsory labor. The local court in the township or village would post a notice requiring all able-bodied males between certain ages to appear to work on roads on several assigned days. It was often called the corvée, from the French. Citizens whose labor was requisitioned could hire someone to work on their behalf or make payment to the city in lieu.

But, as shown by Bruce Benson in chapter 11 on the history of UK non-government roads, toll roads originated from local people's observation that much of their hard road work was soon undone by the carts of merchants passing through the area. It is one thing to work for yourself and your immediate neighbors but people drew the line at maintaining roads for strangers from afar. So toll roads were instituted to finance the road work occasioned by the burgeoning freight. Some of the joint stock companies in the eighteenth and nineteenth centuries were toll road companies. They transformed surface transportation in the United States, Britain, Canada, and other countries. Many folded after railroads came in. Until the pneumatic tire and asphalt were devised at the end of the nineteenth century, road transport was not able to compete for more than very short trips with the steam-powered locomotive using the flanged steel wheels on rails. In the UK—the technological leader at the time—competition by steam-powered road vehicles was stymied by draconian governmental restrictions imposed in 1820, probably at the behest of horse-carriage and railway interests.

Rail's predominance lasted less than a century. Asphalt and concrete helped make longer-lasting roads than the stones and planks of their predecessors, and there was intense competition to develop power plants that could replace animal power. Bicyclists and farmers were the major lobby for hard-surfaced roads in the nineteenth century. In the twentieth century roads became the dominant transport infrastructure in virtually all countries because they supported a wide range of mass-produced and specialized vehicles, and because of their ubiquity. They went everywhere. Other modes—rail, canals, sea, air—suffered from their limited number of terminals, which meant that almost every trip, whether of freight or personal transport, began on a road and ended on a road. For most movements it did not make sense to incur the expense and time of transferring from road to water, or to rail and then back again to road, because journeys by road could be accomplished in one vehicle. In the twenty-first century, 95 percent of personal trips and some 90 percent of freight by value are carried by road. For the foreseeable future, the predominance of the road is likely to increase. Flexible work schedules, just-in-time deliveries of goods, a dispersion of job places and residences, and higher incomes all favor private transport over collective, and door-to-door capability over complex, "intermodal" transfers necessitated by rail and water.

Steam and battery-powered electric vehicles were tried but, by early in the twentieth century, the internal combustion engine with its dependence on petroleum products became the dominant means of propulsion. It was a tax collector's dream because—unlike animal power—its fuel was produced in huge centralized facilities—oil refineries—whose output was metered, and then measured as it was sold by the gallon into tanker trucks. So, by the 1920s, after the competition of steam and electric vehicles had waned, some governments—for example, state governments in the United States—began instituting taxes on gasoline and diesel fuel as the major means of raising money for the support of roads.

So long as road improvement was a matter of incremental improvements of existing roads, fuel taxes worked quite well as a financing mechanism. With better roads seen as placing a layer of asphalt over an existing stone road, regularly filling potholes, widening a narrow bridge, sealing cracks, eliminating some sharp corners with a more sweeping alignment, and doing a cut and fill to reduce grades it was possible to do the work on a pay-as-you-go-basis. If revenue was low one year, then the roadwork budget would be trimmed a bit and users would just have to wait a bit longer for some of the improvements to be done. By and large, each expenditure brought some benefits.

But two innovations got in the way of tax financing. One was grand crossings—bridges and tunnels at major water bodies. These require a large up-front investment. The whole bridge has to be built before there is any benefit so it makes sense to raise the capital in one lump sum. So the grand crossings such as the Brooklyn Bridge, the George Washington Bridge, and the Holland Tunnel were all financed by raising capital on the prospect of future toll revenues. The imposition of tolls provided some assurance to investors that there would be a revenue stream to repay the money they loaned or invested. Most of the grand crossings have therefore been toll financed. These include most of the crossings in the archipelago that is New York City, crossings in San Francisco, Boston, Norfolk, San Diego, and Baltimore harbors, bridges over the tidal segment of the Delaware River from Philadelphia to southern New Jersey, crossings of the freshwater sections of the Mississippi, Columbia, Hudson, Delaware, Detroit, Niagara, and Rio Grande Rivers, Cross-Harbor tunnels in Hong Kong, crossings over and under the Thames and other UK rivers, Lion's Gate Bridge in Vancouver, Sydney Harbour Bridge and tunnel, Tokyo harbor bridge and tunnel, and others.

In many of these cases a state or national boundary follows the river so bi-jurisdictional issues would have made tax financing very problematic. Easier to make the user pay tolls to service capital raised on the prospect of a calculable revenue stream.

A second innovation was the idea of completely new highways, tailor-made for motor vehicles. Like major bridges and tunnels, these were a completely new facility, built from the ground up. They required major right-of-way acquisition, a large design effort, major earthmoving, many bridges, and intense construction activity. Being fenced and access controlled, they also lent themselves to toll collection.

Most of the toll roads of the twentieth century were built by government-created toll agencies or government transportation departments. The private sector in the United States was largely confined to building bridges like the Ambassador bridge linking Detroit (Michigan) with Windsor (Ontario) and some of the Mississippi and Hudson River crossings.

Political Obstacles to Reforming Governmental Road Systems

When road provision is in the hands of government, improvements can be held hostage to the whims of the political process. A recent governor of Maryland, for example, vetoed a demonstration project of "High-Occupancy or Toll" (HOT) lanes in the Washington D.C. area, which would have allowed single-occupancy vehicles, on payment of a toll, to use spare capacity on lanes dedicated to high-occupancy vehicles. In his veto message he wrote:

> In the end, the concept of HOT lanes was rejected for two reasons: It is fundamentally unfair to give wealthy people the opportunity to buy a faster commute, and it provides a short-term solution that has the potential to create even more congestion in the long term. Why should a lawyer or lobbyist commuting to Washington DC, get to work faster than an entry-level employee just starting out, simply because the lawyer or lobbyist can bill the extra $1,000 to $2,000 yearly cost to clients? An easy commute should not be linked to a person's ability to pay . . . HOT lanes are also clearly inconsistent with efforts to curb sprawl and our goal to reduce the number of cars on the road. We know from recent studies that adding road capacity actually generates more traffic—and more pollution. That same principle applies to HOT lanes. They will encourage more people to drive instead of using transit and will provide an incentive for people to move farther away from established communities. (*USA TODAY* June 23, 2001)

The first objection seems to have been misplaced egalitarianism. In free societies, rich people are always able to buy better services than poor people. That is what being rich is about. The rich already have all kinds of ways of avoiding a bad commute. They can afford a house closer to their work or better situated in respect of transport. They are usually able to negotiate better times to travel to and from work. They can afford a car that is better fitted out with comforts that makes the commute go more quickly. The lawyer or lobbyist is always going to get a break over the entry-level employee, so opposing toll lanes in the name of equal treatment is mere populist demagoguery. As a matter of fact, a toll lane may actually be of great service to an entry-level employee on occasions. Lower level workers are sometimes held to higher standards of punctuality than those above, and sometimes might value the opportunity to buy their way past congestion as a job-saver.

The governor's second objection was the congest-them-out-of-their-cars theme, which holds that rail and bus are superior modes of travel to automobiles, so government policy should be to avoid doing anything that eases the plight of the motorist. This profoundly authoritarian thinking (which also seems to have taken hold of the "New Labour" government in the UK) would have government run roughshod over people's demonstrated preference for the automobile for most of their trips. Had the governor followed the logic of his policy not to add to highway capacity, even by using an HOV lane more efficiently, then he should have had a program for closing highway lanes in pursuit of greater transit use.

Existing Privately-Owned Roads

Public Works Financing (pwf 2002)[1] lists 291 privately developed road projects, costing in total over $132 billion, for which financing had been arranged since 1985. The costs of individual projects ranged from the $2.8 billion Highway 407 toll road concession in Toronto, to the $7.4 million North Kelang Straits Urban Bypass in Malaysia. Not included were less well-known projects such as the 55 miles of road built in East Pakistan in the 1960s by the Dhaka bus company Momin Motors for its own buses, and the 12-mile village access road in Guangdong province financed and built by the peasant Yuan Hudang at a cost to him of 1.6 million Yuan (about $200,000).

The world's largest investor-owned road system is in Italy. Autostrade SpA[2] operates a 3,120km (1,950mi) network of about twenty toll motorways, including some of the busiest in the country, like the A1 between Naples, Rome, and Milan. Autostrade had toll and other revenues of $2 billion in the year 2001 for a net profit of $280m. The stock is traded in the stock exchanges. The investor-owned company was formed out of a state-owned company that built most of the toll roads, but was privatized in stages in the 1990s. A similar privatization occurred in Portugal with the conversion of Brisa, the country's major state toll agency to investor ownership. And in Spain ENA Infraestructuras was put up for bid and sold to a large construction conglomerate. But the world's largest toll authority privatization, by far, is occurring in 2005 with the four large Japanese state toll authorities being converted to seven joint stock companies to be traded on the stock exchange. This includes the world's largest authority by revenue, Japan Highways Public Corporation, which operates almost all the interurban expressways in the country. Also being privatized are the intraurban toll authorities of Tokyo and Osaka.

America's biggest privatization is the Chicago Skyway, which the city put up for bid in 2004. In January 2005, after $1,830 million had been wired into the city's bank account, this toll road in the southeast of the Chicago metro area was turned over to a Cintra (Spain)-Macquarie (Australia) joint venture, which will maintain and operate the six-lane facility in return for the right to collect tolls for ninety-nine years. Governors in Indiana, New York, and New Jersey are examining privatization of toll facilities following the Chicago Skyway deal. In California Governor Arnold Schwarzenegger has requested legislative authority for the state to sign toll road development agreements with both private and public entities.

Six major toll roads in Australia's two major cities, Sydney and Melbourne,[3] were built by investors without government support and several more are either under construction or planned. The third city, Brisbane, is getting in on road privatization too with major underground facilities being designed. The big automated H-407 ETR ("electronic toll route")[4] toll road in Toronto was built by a provincial government authority but privatized two years later at considerable profit to local taxpayers. One of France's major toll road companies, Cofiroute,[5] is investor-owned, and so are major toll roads in Portugal,[6] Spain, South America, and Asia.

In the United States, investor-owned toll facilities include:

- The Ambassador Bridge, a suspension bridge that links Detroit (Michigan) with Windsor (Ontario), a major border crossing, which opened 1929;
- The Detroit-Windsor Tunnel, which opened 1930;
- The Dulles Greenway,[7] a toll road between Dulles International Airport and Leesburg, Virginia, 22km (14 miles) in length, which opened 1995;
- The State Route 91 Express Lanes,[8] described in chapter 9: 16 km (10 miles) four-lane toll road set in the middle of an eight-lane freeway in the Los Angeles area, operating with differential tolls to reflect different travel time advantages, which opened in 1995;

- The Camino Colombia toll road in Laredo, Texas is a 35 km (21 miles) link between I-35 and the Colombia-Solidarity Bridge, built and operated by a group of ranchers across whose land it passes, which opened 2000 but failed financially and has since been acquired at about a quarter its cost by Texas Department of Transportation;
- In Montgomery (Alabama): Two private toll bridges built by United Toll Systems, a private company of entrepreneur Jim Allen, 1997 and 1998;
- In Tuscaloosa (Alabama): A bridge over the Black Warrior River, also built by Allen, which opened 1999;
- In the eastern part of the San Diego area State Route 125 South is under construction by investors under a toll concession with the state of California.

The potential for investor financing of roads can be illustrated by developments in Australia in the last decades of the twentieth century. In parts of the two major cities, Sydney (population 4.1m) and Melbourne (3.3m), urban traffic speeds fell to 10 miles/hour and governmental funding for road improvement was politically unacceptable. In Sydney, private investors financed the Harbor Tunnel, which added about 50 percent to the capacity provided by the famous "coathanger" arch bridge in connecting the two sides of the metro area. Different investor groups then built in succession the M4 Motorway out to the west, the M5 Motorway to the southwest, the M2 Hills Motorway in the northwest, and the Eastern Distributor motorway from the central business district south to the main airport. The last incorporates an interesting two-deck six-lane Tunnelway under pricey gentrified inner suburbs. A Cross City Tunnel, which opened in late August 2005, and a Western Orbital Tollway will link the M2 and M4. Bids are being sought for a connection of the M2 Hills Motorway to the Gore Hill Freeway north of Sydney. This is another underground project under construction known as the Lane Cove Tunnel. Studies are underway on a Hills Motorway connection to the north to link with the Sydney Newcastle Freeway, and a link between the M4 and the city, also certain to be underground.

But perhaps the most ambitious single investor-built toll project is in the second city, Melbourne. A fully automated inner area toll road system of six to eight lanes totaling 18km (11 miles) length. It has full open road electronic tolling with no onsite toll collection. It involved major tunneling, difficult riverside, elevated construction, and environmental mitigation. Called CityLink, the system links close to the central business district and port of Melbourne three previously unconnected radial freeways. One of the major tunnels in CityLink encountered serious construction difficulties but these were overcome at the expense of the private investors. The resulting highway network has transformed mobility in the whole metro area and is a major political and financial success. Almost no tax money was needed for any of these projects and investors have done well too.

The first Australian investor-built project—the Sydney Harbor Tunnel—required government guarantees of traffic levels, but the others were all built at investor risk. And Australian investors have not confined their activities to Australia—in September 2002 the Macquarie Infrastructure Group signed an agreement to develop the $650 million State Route 125 toll road project in San Diego, California.

Bringing More Roads into the Market Economy

With such perverse and authoritarian notions bubbling around in all countries at all government levels, better service to the public may lie in treating roads as a service (like electricity or telecommunications in the United States) that is best offered by private businesses trying to give people what they want at minimal cost. How can we introduce roads to the advantages and disciplines of the market economy? This would involve two major changes:

- First, pricing and investment would have to be made responsive to costs and demand;
- Second, public ownership would have to give way to private.

Reforming the Pricing and Financing of Roads

As mentioned in chapter 1, the introduction of new methods to pay for road use raises issues of two kinds:

- First, there is the problem of collecting payments, preferably without having to stop those who pay; and
- Second, how to ensure that the monies collected for road use bring about investment in roads that users choose to pay for.

New methods of collecting payments for road use. New technology, much of it electronic, has revolutionized the possibilities of paying for roads. Ed Sullivan (chapter 9) describes the application of new technology in Southern California, and Gopinath Menon (chapter 6) reviews developments in Singapore. But they do not exhaust the possibilities. Technology in the form of Global Positioning System (GPS) units in cars plus short range radio data exchange transponders now allow vehicles to be tracked anywhere. By means of such "telematic tolling" it is possible for systems to track the use of all roads and to charge by type of road, time of day, and load being carried. And Oregon, which pioneered the financing of roads in the United States by surcharges on fuel, has set up a task force to explore the possibilities of replacing its gasoline tax with a GPS-based charging system.

A number of road authorities are designing such systems. In Germany, heavy trucks are being tolled using such location-finding devices, and Britain is planning to introduce similar arrangements. Switzerland has been using a mix of technologies to toll trucks traveling across the country and at the beginning of 2004 Austria began operating an open road tolling system on the whole of its motorway system for trucks using short-range transponders like those in use on other European toll roads.

In the United States, similar electronic tolling systems, which use windshield-mounted transponders and short range data exchange by radio signals, have been deployed in traditional toll lanes in traditional toll plazas; in fifteen years they have become responsible for collecting close to two-thirds of the tolls taken each day—quite a spectacular uptake of a new technology. In the near future, a transponder on the windshield will become the normal way tolls are paid in the United States and will soon account for 75 percent or more of tolls taken.

New toll roads are now being built with no cash payment at all on the road, tolls being paid by radio or video identification, and electronic funds transfer. The established toll roads and their customers have benefited from the new technology retrofitted into old toll plazas with 10mph to 40mph passage. The throughput of the toll plazas has doubled, and toll collection costs greatly reduced. Motorists like not having to wind down their windows and fumble for change. The benefits of this technology have come in two stages. The first was to retrofit it into the old toll plazas designed for stop-to-pay. But the real benefits of this technological revolution are now realized in a second stage. The same equipment can be used for full highway speed tolling in an open road, as described by Gopinath Menon in chapter 6. The only physical manifestation of tolling is a gantry structure supporting the antennas and cameras for automated tolling. Drivers can concentrate on their driving. Such open road tolling, as it is called began on new toll roads in Singapore, Denver, and Oklahoma ten years ago, and has been standard on new toll roads in the United States since that time. Houston and Dallas were the first to rebuild their old toll plazas for open road tolling in the period 1997 to 2001. Now there is a wave of reconstruction of mainline toll plazas under way on the busiest toll roads in the country, notably the Garden State Parkway, and the Illinois tollways, The Port Authority of New York New Jersey, the New York State Thruway, Orlando's toll roads, Florida Turnpike, and the Delaware Turnpike are also among those making the transition. America's first major toll road without any cash collection at all opened in Houston in 2004—the Westpark Tollway. Shaping up as one of the world's single biggest open road tolling system is a network of four new toll roads in Santiago, Chile.

Many European and Asian countries have lagged in implementation of open road tolling, not because of any technological problems but because of inadequate legal support for pursuing and deterring toll violators. The United States has a long established system in which the different states and Canadian provinces collaborate to collect unpaid speeding and parking tickets by one another's residents, and this has been successfully used in tolling. U.S. courts have also been persuaded to accept camera based evidence of violations and have allowed relatively low cost collection of penalties. So far this has not occurred in Europe although the Central London Congestion Charge scheme and the truck toll systems of Germany, Austria, and Switzerland are examples of open road tolling successfully underpinned by the law.

All major makes of cars by model years 2006 or 2007 are expected to have built into them as standard equipment an in-vehicle computer and data storage, GPS, a mobile phone antenna and sideband for data, probably supplemented with a 5.9GHz (high frequency) transponder for wireless data transfers between the vehicle and fixed devices—for toll collection, in-vehicle display of signs beyond visual range, e-commerce transactions such as gasoline and food purchases, downloads of video for a backseat entertainment unit, vehicle records, and diagnostics for the garage mechanics. A consortium of about ten state departments of transport are supporting a project for telematic tolling that could make use of this standard equipment standard in new cars.[9] A project at the University of Iowa is looking at the issues involved in using telematic tolls to transition away from fuel taxes as the main source of money for roads. One concept is that motorists would, for some years at least, have the option to pay gas taxes at the pump, as now, or, when they arrive at the gas station the gas tax portion of their fuel bill would be rebated if they used their telematic toll system to download a toll payment. The toll payment would be an accumulation of different charges from different road providers, public or private, on whose roads they had traveled since the previous fueling. The charges could be a mix of flat-rate tolls per vehicle and they could be crafted by type of road, level of congestion, or time of day. Variable message signs, in-vehicle signs, email messages, and websites would inform motorists of the telematic tolls on different routes. The tolls would be set independently by the different road providers, which might be cities, counties, state departments of transport, or other varieties of road owner, such as investor-financed roads. The collection system would use electronic funds transfer to remit the motorist payments to the different road agencies used by the motorist as recorded in the in-vehicle computer.

The telematic toll project is premised on the belief of many officials that the days of fuel taxes as the major source of road revenues are passing. There is already strong public resistance to higher fuel tax rates because of politicians' records in siphoning them off for non-road purposes. In many places, general sales taxes are being proposed as a financing mechanism for new road projects (often with rail transit and a few schools thrown in for good measure), which takes us completely away from the "user pays" principle that underlies the idea that roads would be financed by road-use charges. Moreover, there are practical limits on sales taxes, beyond which they cannot be pushed before people do their shopping outside the jurisdiction. And there are equity issues with fuel taxes. It tends to be the poor who own the older, gas-guzzling vehicles, so fuel taxes are regressive.

Hybrid engine vehicles, compressed gas, ethanol subsidies, and fuel cells seem likely to make existing fuel taxes increasingly problematic as a source of roads revenue. And since it is the wealthy who tend to pioneer new propulsion systems the poor get left funding the roads unless the new technologies are applied to this objective.

There is no direct relationship between payments by road users and the costs they impose. Herbert Mohring in chapter 7, and Gabriel Roth and Olegario Villoria in chapter 8, have shown that vehicles in congested traffic impose substantial delays on one another. But the current way of financing roads from the proceeds of fuel taxes takes no account of these congestion costs. Logically, when road space is scarcest it should be priced highest, so that only those consumers for whom the trip is worth more than the cost will make the trip. Furthermore, the prices paid send important signals about what customers are willing to pay for using particular stretches of road, and so helps investors to assess the profitability of potential road improvement projects. The overloading of a road, which occurs on a daily basis when there is no price management, is especially inefficient, as traffic flows can actually decline when stop-and-go conditions kick in. That familiar concertina-like movement of the vehicles in the roadway is a woefully unproductive use of roads and vehicles, as well as frustrating to drivers.

Management of highway loading by means of variable tolls can result in more efficient, less polluting, and safer traffic flow, as is demonstrated every day on the priced Express Lane projects in Southern California described by Ed Sullivan in chapter 9. One of these is privately owned and operated; the second is run by the local association of governments—an indication that both private and public entities can improve the pricing of road space. But there may be fewer arguments over the equity of high and varying tolls when ownership is private. Citizens understand that business is driven by profit and that peak-period facilities require additional investment that has to be paid for. Governments, on the other hand, are seen as having responsibilities for distributing things according to some notion of equity—a perception that can greatly complicate pricing of publicly owned roads and other congested facilities such as airport runways.

Enabling road users to pay for the roads they want. In most countries—for instance, Argentina, China, India, and the UK—taxes paid for road use are collected as "general revenues" with no substantial proportion dedicated to road improvement. Under those conditions, road expenditures are strongly influenced by short-term political processes; road users are denied the opportunity to "buy" the road facilities they are prepared to pay for; and the public agencies responsible for roads have no predictable funding streams to maintain or expand the assets under their control. When funding is cut, it is often politically expedient to reduce expenditures on maintenance, which greatly increases road costs in the long run.

If roads were privately owned and managed these problems would disappear, as private owners have strong financial incentives to maintain their properties, and payments to road providers would come directly from road users.[10] However, even in the absence of private road ownership, much could be done now to steer road funding to the roads actually demanded by road users, and this without setting up toll gates at every street corner.

To remove road funding from the day-to-day political process (and for other reasons), Ian Heggie (chapter 18) and others have suggested that dedicated road funds be established, at least for road maintenance. They would be supported by charges on road users and the monies drawn upon for road works, by road agencies of government or by private sector road suppliers. Dedicated road funds, which work well in over thirty U.S. states, are generally better for road users than funding out of general revenues. However, the ease with which such road funds can be "raided" for other purposes by strong politicians (e.g., Winston Churchill in Britain in 1929) suggests that it would be preferable to move the responsibilities for road funding into the private sector rather than to dedicated road funds within government. However, even while roads are in governmental jurisdiction, the following actions could be taken to improve the chances of road users getting the roads they are prepared to pay for:

First, revenues from dedicated road funds should be distributed to all road providers, public or private, without discrimination. The simplest way to do this would be on the basis of traffic counts. Such arrangements would enable private providers to provide road links and to receive payment based on traffic levels without the need to charge tolls. Such payments to road concessionaires are already being made in the UK, as described by Neil Roden in chapter 17.

Second, governments could help all toll projects by rebating the fuel taxes and other user fees for the mileage traveled on toll roads. To the extent that those taxes are levied for the support of roads,[11] those who use toll roads are required to pay twice. Just as rebates of taxes are given to farmers or boat-owners using gasoline off-road, so toll road users should be exempt. These charges range up to a third of the cost of tolls.

Third, a level playing field in tax treatment seems important to allowing investor capital to be drawn upon in highway projects. The present favoritism for government and not-for-profit roads stacks the deck against private enterprise, which has to borrow at market rates and has no access to government-guaranteed funding. It also produces toll projects that are financed almost entirely by debt, which, in many countries, has tax advantages over financing by equity. Most are financed by bonds, and have almost zero true equity. This makes them highly vulnerable to default by lenders (bond-holders) if traffic and revenue forecasts do not pan out, or if a recession intervenes, because there is no cushion of investor-owned funding to cover losses.

Fourth, in the United States, states should be allowed to toll congested segments of the Interstate system. Federal highway legislation enacted in 1956 was deeply hostile to tolls and virtually ended toll road construction for almost two decades. Federal policy has been relaxed since but states still have to get federal approval of tolls on an interstate project. They should be free to act on their own. The tolling of congested Interstate segments could increase their economic output, and the revenues could encourage the private sector to provide additional facilities for which users choose to pay.

Private Ownership Roles

The previous chapters suggest that government should get right out of the day-by-day management and operation of roads, which can be operated as a commercial business. Operation of roads involves a host of mundane but important custodial functions such as removing debris promptly, trimming verges, maintaining lights, signs, barriers and fencing, attending to drainage, re-striping lane markings, and the like. Over time, assessments must be made of the need for repaving road pavement and re-decking bridges. In busy urban facilities there are variable message signs to be deployed to communicate with motorists, safe closures of lanes to be implemented, and so forth. All these are functions best performed by managers unencumbered by civil service regulations and most likely to be economically done by managers whose income derives from saving on costs while maximizing customer satisfaction.

Opportunities for further private sector roles in the provision of roads. There are a number of ways to bring additional roads into the market system:

- First, privatize existing toll facilities;
- Second, convert HOV lanes to HOT lanes;
- Third, contract for the private maintenance of roads;
- Fourth, assist property owners to own and manage local roads;

- Fifth, provide roads dedicated to trucks ("Truckways");
- Sixth, provide new all-purpose toll roads; and
- Seventh, upgrade existing highways.

PRIVATIZE EXISTING TOLL FACILITIES. First off, many government-owned toll facilities—such as bridge, roads, tunnels—could be privatized, as the City of Chicago has demonstrated. These are operating businesses—some already highly profitable; others potentially profitable with profit-oriented management. They have valuable infrastructure and an established clientele as seen in their daily traffic flows. Their profitability is generally predictable and their economic risk is low. (Political risk may be another matter!) No government that owns toll facilities should get away unchallenged with their complaint that there is "no money" in their budget. They can always raise large amounts of cash by privatization of the toll facilities they presently own. There could be a case for regulating toll levels where monopoly elements exist.

CONVERT HOV LANES TO HOT LANES. Second, there are opportunities to emulate the Southern California toll express lanes, described by Ed Sullivan in chapter 9. In the United States there are some 3,200 lane-km (2,000 lane-miles) of carpool or HOV (High-Occupancy Vehicles) lanes in operation. Approximately the same total (2,850km) is under construction or planned. So, in the United States alone, there are over 6,000 lane-km (3,730 lane-miles) of potential HOT lanes.[12] Much of this HOV network is underutilized. Allowing drivers ineligible on grounds of occupancy to use the HOV lanes on payment of a toll is a win-win-win proposition. It gives road users the choice of paying a toll to avoid congestion, and also takes vehicles out of crowded lanes, while generating revenue to support the facility.

Carpooling can occasionally be too successful. Houston has had a couple of HOV lanes that have got clogged with two-occupant (HOV2) vehicles, yet if eligibility were altered to require three occupants, the lane would become relatively empty rather than over-full. The answer to that dilemma is to allow HOV2s to continue to use the facility but only if they pay a toll. The toll rate can be varied, as in Southern California, to prevent overloading the express toll lanes.

Note that toll buy-in—or conversion of HOV lanes to HOT lanes—is something that can usually be done immediately. It is a relatively low-cost innovation that can be done with simple electronics and signage, but will give new opportunities for road users with an urgent need to be on time.

The first such conversions to occur were of single lane reversible facilities in Houston, Texas. They have worked well enough but without much spare capacity to sell they earn little revenue. Minnesota opened a much larger HOV-HOT lanes conversion in the summer of 2005—at modest cost: $12 million. Located on I-394 this has quite complex entry and exit arrangements and toll rates are varied dynamically to maintain free flow. In Virginia investors are negotiating with the state toll franchises on HOV lanes on I-95 and I-395 (Shirley Highway) assuming a commitment to add a third lane to a reversible two-lane facility. On the Washington Beltway in northern Virginia they are negotiating addition of four express toll lanes to the existing eight free lanes. Maryland is doing detailed design work on express toll lanes on the Washington Beltway, the Kennedy Highway (I-95), and on I-270. It is expected to solicit joint venture arrangements with investors.

CONTRACT WITH PRIVATE FIRMS TO MANAGE AND/OR MAINTAIN ROADS. Third, the management and maintenance of roads can be contracted out to the private sector using performance-based contracts, as described by Gunter Zietlow in chapter 15. Such contracts specify only the outcomes required (e.g., the degree of smoothness of a road), so that the private contractors have incentives to devise new methods to achieve the required standards at lower costs. The Road and Traffic Authority of New South Wales initiated such contracts in 1990. In 1996, Uruguay was the first country to implement them in Latin America, and was followed by Argentina, Brazil, Chile, Colombia, Guatemala, and Honduras. Also in 1996, the Virginia Department of Transportation awarded VMS Inc. a performance-based contract to maintain 250 miles of Interstate highways.

Private sector responsibility for maintenance can also be provided by means of a long-term warranty agreement, whereby the builder of the road is obligated to maintain it for an agreed period, typically twenty years. The first agreement of this kind in the United States was made in 1998 in respect of New Mexico's State Route 44, obligating the developer Mesa PDC, LLC to provide the 118-mile highway and be responsible for its maintenance over a twenty-year period. The warranty is estimated to save taxpayers $89 million in maintenance costs over the life of the road. Similar warranties have also been arranged by the UK Highways Agency.

ASSIST PROPERTY OWNERS TO OWN AND MANAGE LOCAL ROADS. In chapters 13 and 14 Fred Foldvary, and Christina Malmberg Calvo and Sven Ivarsson, demonstrate the extent to which local roads can be privately owned and managed by property owners, or by property-owners associations. Thus, they disprove the conventional wisdom that the private sector can provide only toll roads. Can the experience of Sweden's rural roads and of Manila's "gated communities" be replicated elsewhere? The difficulties are likely to be those of management and of money. Management can be provided by private consultants. Money can, in principle, be routed to road providers out of dedicated road funds or other established mechanisms for financing roads, such as those discussed above. It is hard to believe that what works in both socialist Sweden and capitalist California cannot be adapted to work in other countries.

ALLOW THE PRIVATE PROVISION OF ROADS DEDICATED TO TRUCKS ("TRUCK-WAYS"). Fifth, encourage the private sector to provide "Truckways"—special roads for trucks. Trucks offer special opportunities and challenges to toll roads. Some of the longer distance turnpikes depend for a third or more of their revenues on trucks. In order to attract this business they allow truckers to operate larger and longer rigs than are allowed on competing free routes. For example, the Florida Turnpike allows 63.5t (140,000 pound) double trailer combinations that provide 29.3 m (96 foot) of box length. Normal Florida highways only allow 36.3t (80,000 pound) and 16.2 m (53 foot) of box length. Since the major cost of trucking is the fixed cost of the same tractor with its driver the cost per ton of operating with turnpike size and weight allowances is 35 to 40 percent below the cost of operations on the untolled roads. Toll roads in New York, Massachusetts, Ohio, Indiana, Kansas, and Oklahoma also attract truckers through their more generous size and weight allowances, and through special truck stop-type facilities and staging areas.

Drivers of light automobiles are wary of larger trucks—understandably, as their cars always come off worse in any encounter! But if heavy trucks can be segregated on toll truckways that have segregating barriers, their own ramps at interchanges, and staging areas for transferring goods to normal tractor-semi-trailer combinations, these concerns can be met, and such roads can have wide popular support.[13]

In the United States, special "truckways" within the right of way of Interstate highways could often be viable toll facilities if designed to operate free of the very restrictive federal limits on so-called Longer Combination Vehicles. On separate facilities, such toll truckways running efficient road trains could be an important source of toll business, as well as a major contribution to improved productivity. The beginnings of such a network of truckways exists in the United States in the Midwest and mountains states, but it needs to be carried through "gap" states like Illinois, Pennsylvania, and Arkansas, on to the Atlantic and Pacific coasts, and into the south.

Virginia got two competing bids for financing truck lanes on 325 miles of I-81, one for adding a no-trucks lane in the center, and the other adding two trucks-only lanes in each direction in return for toll rights. The state chose the more ambitious scheme and is negotiating the details of a plan that will convert a crowded 2×2 lane highway into a 2×4 lane facility with the center four lanes for trucks only. The Southern California Association of Governments in the Los

Angeles area is actively pursuing truck toll lanes on I-710, SR-60, and I-15 to provide better truck movement out of the ports of Los Angeles and Long Beach.

PROVIDE NEW TOLL ROADS. Sixth, there are new toll road opportunities. Many of these, as illustrated by the experience in Australia, depend on there NOT being the political will or ability to find funds for a free highway from government sources. In these situations, the use of prospective toll revenues as security for sale of bonds and securing of equity will often be the only practical way of getting capital. It provides a better climate for a toll proposal if many of the users of the toll road are to be not the local citizens or taxpayers but road users from elsewhere—non-taxpayers. That is why tolls are so popular in smaller states like New Jersey and Delaware, and in states where the state government is devolving responsibility for major new transport initiatives to a lower level of government such as has occurred in California, Texas, and Florida. South Orange County (California) favored toll roads because the alternative was taxing its citizens for roads such as State Routes 91 or 241/261, which were heavily used by commuters from adjacent Riverside County. In these circumstances the options can be posed as: "A taxing road, or a toll road, or no road."

New toll roads are most likely to be needed:

- in rapidly growing metro areas such as Phoenix, Arizona, southern California, Texas, central and western Florida, Virginia, the Carolinas;
- on the fringes of existing metro areas, especially where the core is stagnant or contracting (Washington, D.C. area, Pittsburgh, Chicago, Boston, etc.), to cope with the evening out of densities . . . what the critics call sprawl;
- to cater to newly developing trade (NAFTA corridor Toronto, Detroit, Indianapolis, Mississippi Valley, Houston, Laredo, Monterey CHP corridor 18/20);
- to connect to rapidly developing major facilities, like ports and airports;
- to cater to special needs such as providing specialized routes for heavy trucks in presently truck-unfriendly environments such as Long Island, New York;
- to add redundancy to facilities that are attractive terrorist targets.

Following the successful opening of M6 Toll in Birmingham, England, an extension north to Manchester is being considered. And in Wales there is a private toll road being considered as relief for the M4 a bit east of Cardiff. Spain has several investor-built toll roads under construction. Greece had a flurry of private sector toll projects to improve transportation for the Olympic Games. Eastern European countries are all doing private toll roads, and Russia has announced an ambitious program. The world's largest toll road building program is currently in China. Some are purely private ventures but most are a mix of provincial government and investors. India is developing a national highway network using private concessions.

UPGRADE EXISTING HIGHWAYS. Seventh, and perhaps largest, is the potential for the private sector to undertake major upgrades and improvements of existing highways. Many of the world's expressways, freeways, and parkways were built in the 1950s and 1960s and their basic pavement and bridges are obsolete—physically and functionally. And often they need extra lanes and more modern interchanges. Many rebuilt and upgraded projects cost more than the originals. There is every reason to consider these as toll projects now that tolling can be performed on the fly with a windshield-mounted transponder.

An example is the £210 million toll river crossing of the Thames at Dartford, in London, which supplemented the earlier Dartford Toll tunnel.

Roles for Government

The tradition of government involvement in roads is deeply established, and governments would have important roles to play in the roads sector, even if all roads were privately provided. Government would, as in other sectors, be concerned with safety issues; with uniformity of signs and standards, for example determining whether traffic should run on the left or right of the road and not, as in some unfortunate countries, in the middle. Where there are monopolies, governments should be concerned with the regulation of prices and the promotion of competition. And there are some roles specific to roads:

Safety

There is evidence to suggest that private road operators would have better safety records than roads operated conventionally: Statistics compiled by the International Bridge, Tunnel and Turnpike Association (IBTTA) show the accident rate on roads operated by its members to be 0.6 deaths per 100 million vehicle-miles, compared to 0.9 deaths per 100 million vehicle-miles on the US Interstate System, one of the safest non-commercial road systems in the world. Can government actions make roads safer still? Despite some unfortunate governmental policies that increase risks to road users (e.g., U.S. policies that require automobile makers to make cars lighter, and hence less safe, in order to save fuel),[14] it is possible to envisage government activities that would promote safety even on privately operated roads. These could include the designation of uniform signs and standards (e.g., for STOP signs); enforcement of regulations requiring road users to be insured against claims against them; educational safety campaigns; and the mandating of lighting and other relevant road standards.

Public-Private Partnerships

One form of collaboration that became the vogue in the 1980s and 1990s was the "public-private partnership" (PPP). In countries as diverse as China, Portugal, and Spain, in some U.S. states (Texas, Florida, and North Carolina), and elsewhere, toll roads were developed on the basis of mixing public and private funds, in unconventional ways that are often lauded as "innovative finance." The argument used in favor of these projects is usually that they cannot be financed on toll prospects alone, but that the tolls "leverage" public funds, or that public funds "leverage" private investment.

When a project in a market economy, say a factory or power plant, will not pay its way, it is generally judged to be not worthy of the investment. But special arguments may apply in the case of a toll road having to compete against a free road nearby, which constitutes subsidized competition. Mixed public/private projects do carry risks. The two parties to PPPs have very different objectives and styles of operation. A partnership may sound good in speeches, but can be difficult in practice. One kind of risk is that sharp promoters may see the partnership as one where the public provides the investment and they take the profits. This happened in New York in the 1930s, and gave rise to the expression "selling the Brooklyn Bridge." The opposite risk is that the government side will renege on its side of the deal and that further investor projects will be jeopardized. This was seen in Bangkok in 1994, when the Government of Thailand changed the toll rates agreed with the consortium that built Bangkok's Second Stage Expressway, just days before this toll road was due to open. This repudiation destroyed the basis of the project's financing; forced the consortium to sell out at a fire-sale price to Thai investors; and severely damaged Thailand's credit standing, which plummeted thereafter. The expressway was subsequently operated by the state-owned Expressway and Rapid Transit Authority—at the toll rates originally agreed with the private consortium.

Non-Compete Clauses

Few toll projects, whether public or private, can be financed without a government pledge not to establish a competing free facility. If a free flowing non-tolled facility is located alongside a tolled one, few will pay tolls, and the project will be bound to crash. "Non-compete" contracts are essential, but they need to be publicized and explained at the outset. Too often they are quietly entered into to get the road built, and then after the toll road has been in operation a few years, some journalist or politician will reveal the non-compete clause as a "scandalous" indulgence of the investors at the expense of road-users who are legally prevented from getting improved "free" facilities. As governments have the powers to undermine any toll road by building a competing "freeway," such clauses are essential if private funds are to be attracted.

California's SR91 profitable Express Lanes was sold by its private sector owners to Orange County government in 2003 following several years of rancorous argument and litigation over a non-compete clause in its agreement with the state. Some lawyers say it is possible to write more flexible agreements for compensation for extra free capacity, but clearly something better is needed if investors are to be attracted but also local sentiment assuaged.

Payment for Environmental Assessment

There may also be a case for government to pay the costs of environmental impact assessment and other permitting since these costs derive from government. The successful Australian investor-owned toll roads have had the government perform environmental and other permitting clearances before they are put out to bid. By contrast the CA-125 South project in San Diego has been delayed almost eleven years by permitting and right of way problems. The Tacoma Narrows bridge also seems to be running into a permitting wall.

Summary of Recommendations

Road transport can benefit greatly by being brought into the marketplace where its provision will be subject to the disciplines and incentives of commercial operation with access to capital markets. As the previous chapters have shown, there are many different ways to involve private markets in road provision. The era of financing roads with taxes or charges levied on fuels, and licenses, is threatened by the diversity of new fuel sources and the recognition that directly charging for road space with differential prices is the best way to relieve traffic congestion. Electronic toll collection technologies, that do not require vehicles to stop to make payments, have transformed the potential of this classic way of funding roads, so more commercial pricing of roads should be part of our future. Once commercialized, roads can be run as private businesses in the right regulatory environment. If government-owned they can usefully be privatized in a number of ways, for example by accepting competitive bids. Roads, like other expensive capital assets, should be deployed to produce maximum social benefit. This is more likely to happen when they are in the hands of people whose income depends on satisfying customers, rather than helping politicians gain votes in the next election.

The practical application of some of these concepts is illustrated in the figures that follow, which are accompanied by suggested changes that could be implemented relatively quickly.

Washington, D.C. and Baltimore Metro Area

- Truck/transit bus connection between downtown Washington D.C. and I-95 at the Beltway (I-495), an approximate 15 km (9 mi) missing link in the area highway system, cancelled as a freeway due to a bulldozer approach on the part of the state road planners in the 1960s. This should be revived but as a tight urban toll road limited to high value trucks, delivery vehicles, buses, and vans. As 2×2 lanes it can be built within an electricity right-of-way, alongside the Metro Rail Red Line and through light industrial establishments, avoiding the neighborhood oppo-

Figure 20.1
Washington, D.C./Baltimore Metro Area

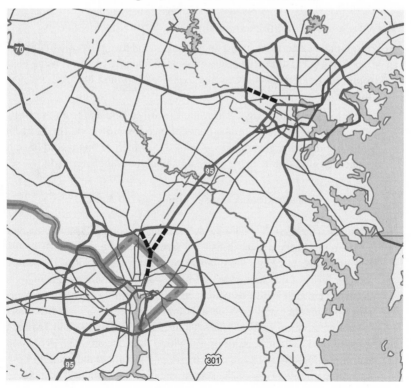

sition that originally thwarted these plans. Cars have the parallel Baltimore-Washington Parkway to travel on.

- Intercounty Connector, Gaithersburg to Laurel Maryland: Regarding this long-planned east-west link through the northern part of the metro area, 28 km (18 mi) in length, there is a longstanding roadway reservation for this road, so little demolition of buildings would be required. It would link the biotech and other businesses of the I-270 corridor directly with the major airport, Baltimore/Washington International, and the highway system to points northeast. At present all traffic has go a circuitous route via the overcrowded Washington Beltway.

- Potomac River Second Crossing: A westward extension of the ICC, this would link I-270 Maryland with the Dulles Airport area at VA-28/VA-7 with a 20 km (12 mi) toll road and bridge over the Potomac River.

- Upgrade of the Fairfax County Parkway, Virginia to full urban motorway standard including completion of the missing link at the southern end between VA-636 and I-95 near Lorton.

- Upgrades of US-1 in Alexandria including toll tunnelway to take through traffic out of the streets of Old Town Alexandria.

- Woodrow Wilson Bridge reconstructed as a toll bridge.

- Premium lanes network based on toll buy-in to HOV plus construction of extra lanes in existing area motorways as financially justified, using electronic tolling compatible with the existing Maryland M-TAG and Virginia Smart Tag systems.

- Urban tollway extending I-270 route inward (eastward) from the Baltimore Beltway (I-895) to make connections downtown via the Franklin Street Expressway and a connection to I-95. Much of this would have to be underground to minimize parkland and community impacts.

Chicago/Cook County Illinois Metro Area

- Southside Chicago toll truckway: A 2×1-lane specialized facility extending from the Indiana state line at the terminus of the Illinois Toll Road (I-90) northwesterly into the intermodal transfer yards and warehousing/trucking areas of the Southside by Midway Airport and north near Cicero Avenue. This area is riddled with aged and underutilized if not abandoned railroad lines that will provide a suitable corridor. This would enable longer combination vehicles such as long Turnpike Doubles and Triples to be assembled at their point of origin within the Chicago area, avoid congestion getting out of Chicago for trips east, and avoid the need for complex make-up operations at the staging areas on the Indiana Turnpike.

Figure 20.2
Chicago/Cook County Illinois Metro Area

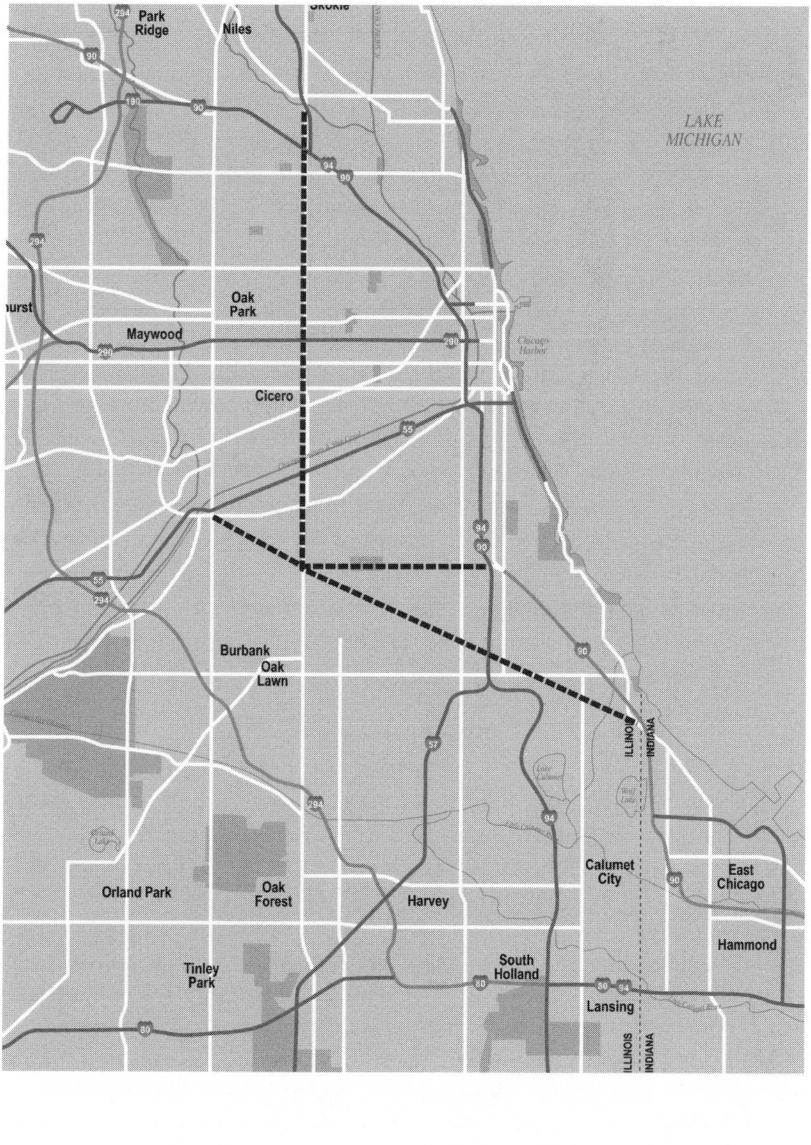

- Skyway West, an extension from the northern terminus of the Chicago Skyway at the Dan Ryan Expressway (I-94) west to Midway airport and I-55 at IL-171 to provide better links to the Southside, Midway Airport and points west and north, bypassing the congested Loop expressways.

- Il-50 Cicero Tunnelway to provide a new high quality north-south link. Parts might be done jointly with parts of the Toll Truckway.

- Extension of the North-South Tollway (I-355) southeasterly 24 km (15 mi) to I-80 and in a second stage 30 km (19 mi) to I-57. The state legislature has supported this project but the Illinois State Toll Highway Authority has been unable to accomplish it. It would provide major circumferential connections in the growing southwestern part of the metro area and support a planned new airport at Peotone.

- Northwest extensions of the North-South Tollway (IL-53) from its terminus in Palatine to the Wisconsin state line connecting to the US-12 Expressway in that state. This toll project would provide improved connectivity to the northwestern suburbs of the metro area as well as an alternate high quality road to Wisconsin and the Twin Cities area.

- Premium service toll lanes on the Dan Ryan (I-94), Kennedy (I-90), Stephenson (I-55), and Eisenhower (I-290) Expressways as financially feasible.

- Northbrook-Palatine Connector 13 km in length (8 mi) and possibly extending further west another 11 km (7 mi) to Barrington to improve east-west movement in the northern part of the metro area.

New York Area

The New York area is heavily organized for moving people by rail, at least to the central business district—generally described as Manhattan south of 59th Street. People will walk up to half a mile to and from a rail station, but cartons of food for the supermarket, office supplies, and doctors samples for the laboratory won't walk—except with a handcart over the sidewalk or via pallet-truck from the loading dock. They inevitably move on rubber tires taking advantage of the ubiquitous coverage of the pavement that constitutes the road system. Road connections remain crucial for goods distribution.

The inadequacies of road connections raise costs of doing business in New York unnecessarily. Surface streets are cluttered with trucks making pedestrian movement difficult. Ports and railheads for the whole of the northeast are heavily concentrated in northern New Jersey with warehousing along the New Jersey Turnpike and other New Jersey expressways. The CBD in Manhattan needs dedicated trucking connections to the New Jersey warehousing areas via a trucks-only tunnel under the Hudson River as part of the Holland Tunnel sys-

Figure 20.3
New York Area

tem. It would feed a north-south truckway spine along the west side of Manhattan, with short east-west spurs. Brooklyn is particularly badly served by trucks since it can only be reached via the congested Staten Island Expressway and Verrazano Narrows Bridge or via the George Washington Bridge. The direct route via the Hudson River tunnels and the East River bridges suffers from low tunnel ceilings that exclude modern 4.3 m (14 foot) trucks, and crowded Manhattan cross streets. Truck traffic is excluded from many motorway standard highways in the New York metro area by "no commercial vehicle" restrictions, forcing them to use slow signalized arterials. In the case of Brooklyn, truck-exclusion from the Shore/Belt Parkway forces trucks onto long circuitous routes via the Brooklyn-Queens Expressway, and Flatbush and Atlantic Avenues. Especially Brooklyn, but also Queens and the rest of Long Island (population 7.6 million), would benefit enormously from a Cross-Brooklyn Truckway. Built in the right-of-way of a largely abandoned Bay Ridge Extension of the Long Island Railroad, a truckway circling through the heart of Brooklyn could provide local truck service in this 2.5m population borough of

New York City but also support Queens, Suffolk, and Nassau counties on the "Island" by improving connections between the Jersey intermodal complex and the Long Island Expressway. A sput to the east could connect to the approaches to Kennedy Airport. The Cross-Truckway could take traffic right off the Verrazano bridge, or, better, be connected directly to New Jersey via a Cross-Bay Tunnel. This tunnel has been designed and permitted, but, unfortunately, for rail trains, for which it makes no sense whatever. Projected train traffic is tiny, mostly trash outward, and construction gravel inward, items better barged. Vast subsidies would be required for the tunnel as a rail facility, whereas a truck facility it would be heavily used and almost certainly profitable with tolls. Connections to the rest of New England and upstate New York and Canada would be greatly improved by extension of the reach of Longer Combination Vehicles into the Hunts Point yards and onto Long Island. Those vehicles run from the Pennsylvania line and from Boston Mass via the New York State Thruway to a staging area just outside New York City in Yonkers. A Thruway Truckway Extension in the Major Deagan Expressway/Metro North Corridor would provide greatly improved efficiency of operations into the Hunt Point area in the Bronx. It would provide further benefits if carried over the Hells Gate into Queens for linkage with the proposed Cross Brooklyn Truckway. From there it might also extend into Long Island via some special truck lanes on the Long Island Expressway.

Potential Private Sector Initiatives to Upgrade Road Travel in the Greater Los Angeles Area

1. Convert the various HOV lanes into a network of toll express lanes on all the major freeways. HOV lanes mostly redistribute traffic laterally, as well as create the need for more lane changing. Converted to toll express lanes, they would serve the useful social purpose of providing a premium service at a fee for those in need of a ride, due to congestion, and generate some revenue as well. They would also provide a high-speed, uncongested guideway for express bus service. Among the most critical missing links are to extend and link the El Monte Busway (along I-10) with the Harbor Transitway (on I-110) through downtown, adding elevated HOT lanes the length of the 101 Freeway from the western San Fernando Valley to downtown, and adding HOT lanes to the San Diego Freeway (I-405) from the Valley to Los Angeles International Airport.

2. Florence/Slauson Airport Tollway. This 14-mile investor-built toll road would link Los Angeles International Airport with I-110 south of downtown, providing a more direct link between downtown and the airport. This diagonal route would make use of little-used railroad right-of-way for nearly all of its length. This route would serve business travelers not only from downtown but

Figure 20.4
Potential Private Sector Initiatives to Upgrade Road Travel
in the Greater Los Angeles Area

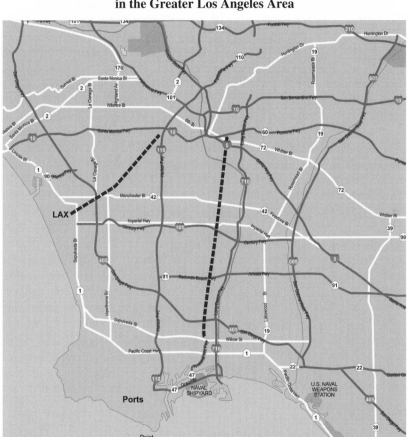

also from Pasadena, Hollywood, and other densely developed areas to its north. It would relieve traffic that presently takes circuitous routes via the I-10, I-110, and the highly congested I-405.

3. I-710 "missing link" in South Pasadena. South Pasadena is an upscale area that will never allow a surface freeway that is mostly of benefit to commuters from 20 miles away. Caltrans has failed for thirty years to get this freeway started, largely because it insists on property seizures and bulldozing, when this 5-mile route needs to be built largely underground. An investor group would be better placed to raise the funds for a toll tunnel and to do the deals needed to overcome local opposition.

4. Glendale Freeway extension. This freeway begins in Glendale and heads southward toward the area west of downtown Los Angeles. But it stops in the middle of a residential area, providing very poor connectivity on its southern end. The original Caltrans Freeway Master Plan had it extending southward to US 101, which would dramatically increase its usefulness. A further extension southwesterly would permit a connection to the Santa Monica Freeway (I-10), allowing traffic from the west side to head for Glendale and Pasadena without having to pass through highly congested downtown. Given the extensive built-up nature of the area, these extensions would probably be done as toll tunnels.

5. Glendale-Palmdale Toll Tunnel under the San Gabriel Mountains, extending the Glendale Freeway (SR 2) northward by 21 miles to provide a direct connection between the burgeoning Antelope Valley area to the rest of the Los Angeles area. Palmdale officials have said they want this tunnel and a preliminary study has already suggested it may be feasible. It is cheaper than a surface road because of the vast cuts and fills this would require. The area is a national forest, so a tunnel will arouse less environmental opposition.

6. Reseda Tollway/Tunnel. One of the main sources of traffic congestion in Los Angeles is the lack of high-capacity alternatives to just two freeway connections between the San Fernando Valley and the LA basin. The original Freeway Master Plan included three additional freeways across the intervening Santa Monica Mountains. Most needed is a modified version of the Reseda Freeway, which would head south from US 101 in the Valley at Reseda Blvd., tunnel beneath upscale Encino, emerge in the mountains just east of Topanga State Park, and head south to tunnel beneath Brentwood and Santa Monica to connect with the present terminus of the Santa Monica Freeway (I-10), already in a short tunnel.

7. Toll Truckways should be added to selected truck-heavy freeways to allow truck traffic to be concentrated in safer and more efficient combinations in barrier-separated lanes specifically engineered for heavy trucks. This would also enable heavy trucks to get past congested commuters on the freeways. A study sponsored by SCAG (Southern California Association of Governments) showed only a 40 percent cost coverage for a toll truckway on SR-60 (Pomona Freeway), but the proposal was limited to the present class of trucks on the freeways. Trucking firms would be willing to pay significantly higher tolls if they were allowed to haul considerably longer and heavier loads, such as those permitted on some eastern turnpikes. SCAG would like to add a network of toll truckways to the primary freeways serving the Ports of Los Angeles and Long Beach: the I-710 heading northbound, connecting to the I-5 northbound, and SR-60 eastbound, linking to I-15 northbound.

8. SR 57 Extension. This long-sought route would fill in a missing link in the Orange County freeway system by building above the concrete river channel of the normally dry Santa Ana River. At its southern end, this new tollway would connect with I-405, thereby creating a number of new circulation patterns.

9. SR 91 Express Lanes Extension. Significant traffic congestion occurs on SR 91 in Riverside County between I-15 and the Orange County line, where an underutilized HOV lane (one in each direction) transitions to the four-lane (two in each direction) 91 Express Lanes. The Express Lanes should be extended all the way to I-15. In addition, they need a direct connection to the SR 241 toll road, which heads south from the regular lanes of SR 91.

10. Riverside-Orange County Tunnel. Riverside County has become the bedroom community for job-rich Orange County, but the only freeway access route is the highly congested SR 91 in the north. A more southerly parallel route is badly needed to cope with present and future traffic demand, especially for commuters to and from the high-tech region in southern Orange County. Given that the mountainous area between the two counties is a national forest, the most environmentally acceptable solution is a straight-line, deep-bore tunnel of 10 to 12 miles. A likely route for the ROC tunnel is from west of the Cajalco exit of I-15 to east of the junction of the 241 and 133 toll roads. A private company has offered to provide and manage such a tunnel as a toll facility, at no charge to public funds (see www.TriTunnelExpress.com).

11. Foothill South Tollway. This extension of the successful SR 241 tollway would take it to the Orange County/San Diego County line adjacent to the Camp Pendleton Marine Corps base, linking into I-5 at that point.

Notes

1. Public Works Financing, pwfinance@aol.com, Westfield, New Jersey, August 2002.
2. See www.autostrade.it.
3. See www.macquarie.com.au.
4. See www.407etr.com.
5. See www.cofiroute.fr.
6. See www.brisa.pt/webnew/brisa_home.asp?Idioma=1.
7. See www.dullesgreenway.com.
8. See www.91expresslanes.com.
9. "Telematic Tolls," *Toll Roads Newsletter*, Number 53, January/February 2001, p. 16.
10. Including landowners desiring access to their properties.
11. It is not suggested that road users should be exempted from taxes not dedicated to the financing of roads.

12. HOV lane data are not collected by any government agency but only by a consummate professional engineer and the country's leading HOV designer, Chuck Fuhs of Parsons Brinckerhoff, fuhs@pbworld.com.
13. Toll truckways are the subject of longer discussion in a policy research paper by Peter Samuel, Robert Poole, and Jose Holguin Vargas for the Reason Public Policy Institute, June 2002, Policy Study 294. Available at www.rppi.org/ps294.pdf.
14. US CAFE (Corporate Average Fuel Economy) regulations were reported by the administrator of the U.S. Highway Traffic Safety Administration to have increased fatalities on U.S. roads by 2,000 a year. See Jerry Ralph Curry's testimony before the U.S. House of Representatives Subcommittee on Energy and Power, April 16, 1991.

About the Editor

Gabriel Roth, a research fellow at The Independent Institute, worked as a transportation economist for the World Bank for twenty years. He has authored studies for the governments of New Zealand and Sri Lanka, the U.S. Agency for International Development, the Inter-American Development Bank, and other organizations. His earlier books include *Parking Space for Cars: Assessing the Demand, Paying for Parking, A Self-Financing Road System, Paying for Roads: The Economics of Traffic Congestion, The Private Provision of Public Services in Developing Countries*, and *Roads in a Market Economy*.

About the Contributors

Bruce L. Benson, DeVoe Moore Distinguished Research Professor of Economics at Florida State University and senior fellow of the Independent Institute, has written extensively in the areas of law and economics, public choice, privatization, and spatial price theory. His many publications include *American Antitrust Laws in Theory and in Practice*, with M. L. Greenhut, *The Enterprise of Law: Justice Without the State, The Economic Anatomy of a Drug War: Criminal Justice in the Commons*, with D. W. Rasmussen, and *To Serve and Protect: Privatization and Community in Criminal Justice*.

Kenneth J. Button is professor of public policy and director of the Center for Transportation Policy, Operations and Logistics at George Mason University. He has published, or has in press, some eighty books and over 400 academic papers, in the fields of transport economics, environmental analysis, and industrial organization. He is visiting professor at the Universities of Bologna and Porto.

Christina Malmberg Calvo, a native of Sweden, is a lead economist in the World Bank's central transport unit. Over the last twenty years she has worked on rural infrastructure services and poverty reduction in Sub-Saharan Africa,

East Asia, and Latin America. She was declared IRF Woman of the Year 2005 for her lifetime's work on the development of rural roads and transport.

Fred E. Foldvary teaches economics at Santa Clara University, California. His books include *Soul of Liberty, Beyond Neoclassical Economics, Public Goods and Private Communities, Dictionary of Free-Market Economics*, and (co-edited) *The Half-Life of Policy Rationales*.

Ian G. Heggie is visiting professor at the University of Birmingham, and an independent transport consultant. Until 1999 he was a manager, and roads adviser, at the World Bank, where he coauthored the Bank's 1998 Technical Paper No. 409, "Commercial Management and Financing of Roads," and received the World Bank President's Award for Excellence. In 2001 he was selected as the International Road Federation's Man of the Year in "recognition of his many achievements as a reformer of road management and road finance practices in Africa and Asia during his tenure with the World Bank, and more recently in his important role as chairman of the Global Road Safety Partnership."

Sven Ivarsson served for forty-one years in the Swedish National Road Administration, the last twenty as chief engineer. In 2002 he took early retirement from the SNRA to become executive director of the National Federation of Private Road Associations, an NGO with a membership of over 8,000 road associations.

Daniel Klein is professor of economics at George Mason University in Virginia, and associate fellow of the Ratio Institute in Stockholm. He has published numerous original articles on the private toll-roads of nineteenth-century America, as well as books and articles on urban transit, modern toll roads, and remote sensing of auto emissions. He is the chief editor of *Econ Journal Watch*.

David Levinson is an assistant professor in the Department of Civil Engineering at the University of Minnesota. In 2005 he was awarded the CUTC/ARTBA New Faculty Award, presented by the Council of University Transportation Centers and the American Road and Transportation Builders Association. His books include *Financing Transportation Networks* (2002), *Assessing the Benefits and Costs of ITS* (2004), and *The Transportation Experience* (2005).

John Majewski is an associate professor in the History Department at the University of California, Santa Barbara. In addition to publishing numerous articles on transportation improvements in the nineteenth-century United States, he is author of *A House Dividing: Economic Development in Pennsylvania and Virginia Before the Civil War* (2000).

The Hon. J. K. (Jim) McLay was chairman of the Roading Advisory Group, which, in 1997, advised the New Zealand government on road reform. He is a former deputy prime minister, attorney general, and minister of justice, and is now executive chairman of *the* investment bank, Macquarie New Zealand Limited, managing director of JK McLay Limited, a consulting firm, chair of two publicly listed companies, and a director of a number of other companies.

Gopinath Menon teaches traffic engineering and management at Singapore's Nanyang Technological University. When serving in Singapore's Land Transport Authority he was closely involved with the development and implementation of the road pricing schemes introduced in 1975 and 1998.

Herbert Mohring is professor of economics emeritus at the University of Minnesota. He has long been interested in applying to transportation the pricing and investment principles that govern the activities of commercial firms in market economies. Some of his pioneering work appeared in 1962 in *Highway Benefits: An Analytical Framework*, coauthored with Mitchell Harwitz.

C. Kenneth Orski is editor and publisher of *Innovations Briefs*, a newsletter reporting on developments in the world of surface transportation. He also heads the Urban Mobility Corporation and directs the MIT International Mobility Observatory. A graduate of Harvard College and Harvard Law School, he served as associate administrator of the Urban Mass Transportation Administration in the Nixon and Ford administrations and as a member of President George W. Bush's transition team. He is former chairman of the Institute of Traffic Engineers Task Force on HOT Lanes.

Robert W. Poole, Jr. is director of Transportation Studies at the Reason Foundation in Los Angeles. He received B.S. and M.S. degrees in engineering from MIT. He has advised the U.S., California, and Florida Departments of Transportation, as well as the White House Office of Policy Development and/or National Economic Council in the Reagan, Bush, Clinton, and Bush administrations. He was a member of President George W. Bush's transition team. He serves on the board of the Public-Private Ventures division of the American Road & Transportation Builders Association and writes a monthly column on transportation infrastructure for *Public Works Financing*.

Neil Roden has a background in delivering major highway projects and was the Highways Agency's private finance manager responsible for developing the Agency's private finance strategy and for identifying and exploiting opportunities for partnerships between the Agency and the private sector. He is now head of Corporate Planning & Risk Management for the Agency.

Peter Samuel has specialized in writing on toll roads for the past ten years, first with the print *TOLL ROADS Newsletter*, now with the web-based TOLL-ROADSnews.com. He has also written reports for a number of think tanks, especially the Reason Public Policy Institute where he is an adjunct scholar. Of British birth, he grew up in Australia where he studied and taught economics. He settled in the United States in 1980 and lives in the Washington, D.C. area.

John Semmens, senior planner in the Arizona Department of Transportation, has nearly thirty years of experience in the field of transportation. He has authored over 400 reports, papers, and articles on transportation related topics. He can be reached at the Laissez Faire Institute, 828 North Poplar Court, Chandler, AZ 85226.

Edward C. Sullivan is a professor in the Civil and Environmental Engineering Department, California Polytechnic State University, San Luis Obispo, where he teaches traffic engineering, urban transportation planning, systems analysis, and introductory engineering design. Beyond his university activities, he has taught and consulted in transportation engineering and planning in this country and abroad, including China, South America, Africa, and India. He has authored many technical articles and reports on road pricing, transportation safety, transportation systems analysis, and modeling.

Dr. Olegario G. Villoria, Jr., senior project manager at Vanasse Hangen Brustlin, Inc., was associate professor and director of Graduate Studies at the School of Urban and Regional Planning, University of the Philippines (U.P.) Diliman, an affiliate faculty at the U.P. National Center for Transportation Studies, and senior lecturer at the U.P. College of Engineering. He served as assistant project manager in the 1996 Metro Manila Urban Transportation and Integration Study.

Gunter J. Zietlow has worked worldwide for more than thirty years as a transport economist for the German Agency for Technical Cooperation. He has authored numerous papers and articles and is a frequent speaker in the field of financing and management of highways and roads. In 2003 he was selected as the International Road Federation Man of the Year for pioneering activities and achievements in the realm of performance-based road management and maintenance contracts and road maintenance funds in Latin America. More details are on his home page, http://www.zietlow.com.

Index

NOTE: In this index there are italicized letters following some page numbers: f = figure, n = note, and t = table.
